CQ PRESS **GUIDE TO**

STATE POLITICS AND POLICY

For Shirley and Naniette

CQ PRESS **GUIDE TO**

STATE POLITICS AND POLICY

EDITED BY

RICHARD G. NIEMI
University of Rochester

JOSHUA J. DYCK
University of Massachusetts Lowell

Los Angeles | London | New Delhi
Singapore | Washington DC

Los Angeles | London | New Delhi
Singapore | Washington DC

FOR INFORMATION:

CQ Press
An Imprint of SAGE Publications, Inc.
2455 Teller Road
Thousand Oaks, California 91320
E-mail: order@sagepub.com

SAGE Publications Ltd.
1 Oliver's Yard
55 City Road
London EC1Y 1SP
United Kingdom

SAGE Publications India Pvt. Ltd.
B 1/I 1 Mohan Cooperative Industrial Area
Mathura Road, New Delhi 110 044
India

SAGE Publications Asia-Pacific Pte. Ltd.
3 Church Street
#10-04 Samsung Hub
Singapore 049483

Developmental Editor: Carole Maurer
Production Editor: David C. Felts
Copy Editor: Talia Greenberg
Typesetter: C&M Digitals (P) Ltd.
Proofreaders: Annie Lubinsky, Annette Van Deusen
Indexer: Joan Shapiro
Cover Designer: Michael Dubowe
Marketing Manager: Carmel Schrire

Printed in the United States of America

Library of Congress Cataloging-in-Publication Data

Guide to state politics and policy / edited by Richard G. Niemi, University of Rochester; Joshua J. Dyck, University of Massachusetts Lowell.

pages cm.
"CQ Press guide series."

ISBN 978-1-4522-1996-7

1. State governments—United States. I. Niemi, Richard G. II. Dyck, Joshua J.

JK2408.G875 2014
320.473—dc23 2013023413

This book is printed on acid-free paper.

13 14 15 16 17 10 9 8 7 6 5 4 3 2 1

★ SUMMARY TABLE OF CONTENTS

★ TABLE OF CONTENTS

★ ABOUT THE EDITORS

Richard G. Niemi is Don Alonzo Watson Professor of Political Science at the University of Rochester, where he has taught for forty-five years and has served as department chair, associate dean for graduate studies, and interim dean. He earned his PhD from the University of Michigan in 1967. Professor Niemi has been a Guggenheim fellow and a fellow at the Center for Advanced Study in the Behavioral Sciences. He has been a visiting professor at the University of Lund (Sweden) and at the University of Iowa. In 2007–2009 he was president of the American Political Science Association's Section on State Politics and Policy. He is a foreign member of the Finnish Academy of Science and Letters and a member of the American Academy of Arts and Sciences. He is the author, coauthor, or editor of numerous works on political socialization, civic education, voting behavior, and various aspects of state politics. He has an ongoing interest in the Native Americans of upstate New York and Wisconsin, from whom he can trace a portion of his ancestry.

Joshua J. Dyck is associate professor of political science and codirector of the Center for Public Opinion at the University of Massachusetts Lowell, where he has been on the faculty since 2012. Previously, he was associate professor of political science at the University at Buffalo, SUNY, where he was a faculty member for six years. He also spent a year at the Public Policy Institute of California during the 2005–2006 academic year as a predoctoral fellow. Professor Dyck received his master's degree and doctorate in government and politics from the University of Maryland and holds a bachelor's degree in economics and political science from Western Washington University. His research focuses on the intersection of social context and political institutions on political behavior in the mass public. Much of his research has examined the effects of direct legislation in the American states on public opinion and attitudes about democracy.

★ CONTRIBUTORS

James E. Alt
Harvard University

James Coleman Battista
University at Buffalo, SUNY

Lawrence Baum
The Ohio State University

Frederick J. Boehmke
University of Iowa

Cynthia Bowling
Auburn University

Ann O'M. Bowman
Texas A&M University

Paul Brace
Rice University

Laura Carlson
University of Arizona

Thomas M. Carsey
University of North Carolina at Chapel Hill

John Dinan
Wake Forest University

Joshua J. Dyck
University of Massachusetts Lowell

Margaret R. Ferguson
Indiana University–Purdue University Indianapolis

Richard C. Fording
University of Alabama

Joseph J. Foy
University of Wisconsin–Waukesha

Peter L. Francia
East Carolina University

James G. Gimpel
University of Maryland

Michael J. Hanmer
University of Maryland

Paul S. Herrnson
University of Connecticut

Laura S. Hussey
University of Maryland, Baltimore County

Martin Johnson
University of California, Riverside

Andrew Karch
University of Minnesota

David M. Konisky
Georgetown University

David Dreyer Lassen
University of Copenhagen

J. Celeste Lay
Tulane University

Tristany Leikem
University of Arizona James E. Rogers College of Law

Meghan E. Leonard
Illinois State University

Nicholas P. Lovrich
Washington State University

Nichole R. Lovrich
State of Montana, Office of the State Public Defender

Faith E. Lutze
Washington State University

Michael P. McDonald
George Mason University

Kenneth P. Miller
Claremont McKenna College

Monica Moore
University of North Carolina at Chapel Hill

Richard G. Niemi
University of Rochester

Laura Katz Olson
Lehigh University

Aditya Pai
Claremont McKenna College

Shanna Pearson-Merkowitz
University of Rhode Island

Justin Phillips
Columbia University

Soledad Artiz Prillaman
Harvard University

Beth Reingold
Emory University

Lilliard Richardson
Indiana University–Purdue University Indianapolis

Alan Rosenthal
Rutgers University

Peverill Squire
University of Missouri

Jeffrey A. Taylor
University of Maryland

Carol S. Weissert
Florida State University

Christopher Witko
University of South Carolina

★ ACKNOWLEDGMENTS

We would like to thank Doug Goldenberg-Hart, who while at CQ Press approached us with the idea of the book; Carole Maurer for dealing cheerfully and expeditiously with the myriad questions and concerns that came up during the presubmission stage and for reviewing and editing the chapters; David Felts for skillful oversight of the production process; Talia Greenberg for a superb job of copyediting; and especially the chapter authors, who contributed their expertise, doing so happily and in a timely manner, always in the face of heavy work schedules and sometimes despite personal situations that would have dissuaded less dedicated individuals from completing the task. We are grateful to you all.

The Past, Present, and Future of State Politics and Policy Research

Richard G. Niemi and Joshua J. Dyck

When the Constitution of the United States of America was ratified in 1789, the young nation was undertaking an experiment in representative government. Not only would citizens of all states become citizens of the United States, but they would retain their state citizenship, and states would have a considerable amount of governing autonomy. This experiment in federalism has now been in effect for more than two hundred years. At times, it has produced conflict, which has often centered on the relative autonomy of the federal government vis-à-vis the state governments. At other times, federalism has produced varied and creative institutions and forms of public policy. At all times, it has produced both elation and frustration with the task of studying fifty (or fifty-one, including the District of Columbia, or even more, including U.S. outlying areas) different governments and, in the past decade or more, increasing pleasure and lessening frustration due to greater availability of and access to data and to appropriate statistical models for dealing with multiple venues. Recent developments in data and methods have, in turn, led to an outpouring of research on the states—which is, of course, the reason for this guide.

For better or worse, states represent a major force in the politics and policymaking of citizens of the United States. States create institutions and make laws, often with greater flexibility than the federal government—institutions and laws that affect citizens differently according to where they happen to live. The *Guide to State Politics and Policy* is an attempt to bring together in a single volume the diverse and excellent research describing and evaluating the states. While we do not claim to have covered every piece of every topic, this thirty-three-chapter volume casts a wide net across what political scientists have learned about state governance and democratic governance generally. Each chapter is a highly approachable introduction to recent thinking about and research on the topic, while at the same time being comprehensive enough to bring up to date those who are familiar with the basics. For those who wish to explore further, the authors have provided a select set of scholarly references in the chapters' endnotes, as well as a number of suggested readings.

One thing this book is not is a historical account of each state; libraries are full of tomes of state histories. Rather, we are interested in the collective knowledge that has been acquired by the comparative empirical study of states. To accomplish this task, experts who write about each specific topic were recruited. While the *Guide to State Politics and Policy* can be read cover to cover, and includes cross-references to material that overlaps between chapters, the chapters are written to stand alone, so that an interested reader can be brought up to speed on major debates and findings in a specific research area by examining a single chapter.

THE REVOLUTION IN STUDIES OF THE STATES

Political scientist V. O. Key Jr. laid much of the groundwork for the scientific study of states in the 1940s and 1950s. Key used the variation present in states to attempt to draw inferences about citizen behavior, the organization and influence of political parties and interest groups, and the dynamics of the unique politics of the South, as well as to evaluate how well federalism was working. While Key's research was foundational, a relatively small number of trailblazers followed in his footsteps in the 1960s and 1970s.

Data about national politics had become more readily available thanks in large part to the American National Election Studies, which eventually became a discipline-wide resource funded by the National Science Foundation. Comprehensive aggregate election results, focusing primarily on the presidency and Congress though containing results for governors, were also published at this time (compiled initially by Richard Scammon). Legislative data became more accessible and digestible in the form of congressional roll call records and analysis by Congressional Quarterly. Nationwide public opinion surveys simultaneously expanded, though initially they went largely unused by scholars. While the singularity of the president, Congress, and the national electorate was a significant factor in the choice of research topics, to a certain extent high-quality empirical research simply followed the data. Information on the states lagged.

Studies of state voting behavior, specifically, suffered from both methodological and data-availability problems, and they were limited in terms of coverage and consistency. Many high-quality single-state and regional studies existed, but scholars lacked the ability to generalize across a large number of states, much less all of them. High-quality national surveys existed, but the sampling methods and small sample sizes even in the larger states made generalizing about state action from national surveys difficult. Likewise, little comprehensive data existed about roll call voting in state legislatures. At a theoretical level, scholars recognized the gains to be made from the variability of institutions, political processes, and policy outcomes across the states, but the difficulties of gathering systematic information from so many units meant that state-level research would take a back seat—not simply for a few years, but for several decades.[1]

In the past fifteen to twenty years, however, the comparative method outlined by Key has started to gain traction. A burgeoning community of scholars who belong to the American Political Science Association's Section on State Politics and Policy has generated untold new data sources, developed or borrowed empirical methods to better address questions of state effects, created its own journal,[2] and established an annual conference to present research on the states.[3] Changes of a similar magnitude have occurred in the extent to which states themselves, as well as organizations such as the National Conference of State Legislatures, the Pew Center on the States, the Council of State Governments, and numerous policy-related organizations, are willing and able to provide information about their operations and interests. Altogether, the amount of information available to state researchers has grown exponentially, creating the backdrop for the research that is summarized in this volume. In addition, we have included in the Guide to Information and Data about the States at the back of this volume citations to many common places that researchers access data and information on the U.S. states.

MAJOR THEMES OF THE BOOK

The task of this volume is to present a broad and thorough account of all corners of the state politics and policy subfield of American politics. However, in collecting the accounts from authors working in different literatures and on different research topics, a number of major themes have emerged.

Institutional Variation

The U.S. Constitution is difficult to amend. Since the passage of the Bill of the Rights, the U.S. Constitution has only been amended 17 times in over two hundred years. The Massachusetts Constitution, by contrast, has been amended 117 times; the Alabama Constitution, over 700 times. Amending state constitutions is a process considerably more fluid than amending the U.S. Constitution; in addition, almost every state refers constitutional changes to a popular vote of the public. Because this is so, states have been able to consider broad institutional changes that the federal government has either been unwilling or unable to attempt. Examples of these changes abound.

About half of all states have developed mechanisms that allow citizens to be both the agenda setters and legislators for proposed policies, circumventing the traditional legislative process that requires legislative and executive approval before a law is passed. Living with this institution, in many places for the better part of a century, has profoundly affected how citizens view democracy and their role within the system. It has also affected the types of policies adopted by the states and their electoral and campaign environments. Ballot initiatives and referendums expand the scope of policies under consideration and affect the participatory behavior of citizens who are exposed to these institutions.

States also are in charge of the conduct of both state and national elections. This being the case, states have found themselves at the center of controversy and subsequent innovation in election administration. States differ on a number of dimensions related to elections, including how far in advance voters must register to vote in order to participate in elections; whether in-person early voting or voting by mail are available; and, most recently, whether photo identification is required in order for an individual to vote. They also differ in the technology used to count ballots, an issue that came into focus after the presidential election recount debacle in Florida in 2000.

States are also in control of the process of drawing legislative districts both at the state and federal level. The process of redistricting, which occurs decennially, has become one of the most conflict-laden domains of partisan decision making in the United States, with both parties attempting to draw districts for their advantage. Redistricting also has become a hot topic for scholars of state politics as states adopt various reforms—including, most recently, reforms that involve average citizens in the redistricting process in an attempt to depoliticize the process.

One of the biggest points of variation among the states regards their levels of legislative professionalism and their adoption in the past two decades of "antiprofessionalism" reforms in the form of term limits. Some states mirror the national government in terms of the expectations set for state legislators, while others pay them a pittance, and the legislature is infrequently in session. This variation, as it turns out, is consequential for politics and policy. The anti-professionalism movement of the 1990s reflected an intense dissatisfaction with government. The subsequent decade saw some states reconsider term limits. This variation has given us a window into what significant government reform looks like and how government works.

At the national level, studies of the executive often focus on executive power. The U.S. president is curiously limited in formal power (especially in domestic affairs), yet exercises a good deal of power through informal means. In the case of state governors, there is a good deal of variation in both formal and informal powers. Some governors are endowed with formal powers like the line-item veto, while others are limited in their power through the diffusion of powers to other elected members of the executive. Likewise, there is a good deal of variation across the state legislatures, both in legislative and committee leadership.

The judiciary is another area where considerable institutional variation exists among states. Students familiar with U.S. politics are aware that federal judges are appointed to life terms in office. At the state level, however, selection processes for judges, including judges to the states' highest courts, vary considerably, and this too is consequential for institutional behavior. Many states have some form of electoral connection for state judges, including partisan elections, nonpartisan elections, or retention elections after appointment. In addition to selection mechanisms, the operations of the courts differ considerably from state to state, including the use of specialty courts in order to deal with the increasingly long dockets that state courts face.

The guarantee clause of the U.S. Constitution guarantees that each state will have a "republican" form of government. However, there is a considerable amount of variation in what this means in practice. The preceding discussion is by no means comprehensive, but it highlights just some of the institutional differences among the states. The institutions that states use differ considerably from one another and from the federal model, and these differences matter for the operation of democratic government, representation, responsiveness, and policy outcomes. Furthermore, the ability to amend state constitutions has fostered the ability of each state to chart its own institutional paths, adapting as it sees fit. Perhaps the most central theme that comes through in the *Guide to State Politics and Policy* is that institutions vary and change, and there is much to learn from studying this variation both cross-sectionally and over time.

State Populations, Behavior, and Diversity

It has frequently been observed that people are "different" in different states. Without giving much thought as to why, a casual observer will notice that customs and interactions are different in California than in Minnesota, or in Mississippi than in New York. Political scientists have often called the historical differences in religion, ethnicity, migration/immigration patterns, and shared experience "culture." To be sure, the concept of state political cultures has been subject to a great deal of debate as early studies of culture were decidedly impressionistic, making classification of states as well as changes in their cultures difficult to measure. Despite the challenges to measuring it, the differences in the people who live in the American states are interesting and consequential for American politics. Whether or not we term it "culture," however, is not as relevant as the fact that interesting variations exist in state populations both cross-sectionally and dynamically. States are different places, and they are places that change.

In their seminal book *Statehouse Democracy,* Robert S. Erikson, Gerald C. Wright, and John P. McIver attempted to measure the ideological and partisan predisposition of state electorates.[4] Their central finding was that they could reliably measure the opinion liberalism of states and that this measure is strongly associated with the liberalism of the policies that states adopt. They also found that errors in estimation are not uniform across states, and that states' shared identities affect the way they consider politics.

These findings have pushed research in two distinct directions. First, they indicate that political differences among states are identifiable and measurable, and that improvements in methods have allowed us to measure the relationship between opinions in states and the policies that are ultimately adopted. Yet these findings also suggest that state population diversity, apart from ideological and partisan leanings of citizens, is politically important. The implication here is that there are social and group differences in state populations that have politically meaningful effects.

Social and group differences are perhaps most noticeable when they involve racial and ethnic groups, as when a number of states, including nonborder states, have recently had to deal with increasing numbers of Latino and Asian immigrants. Yet they occur in other ways as well, as is apparent in the controversy over gun ownership and gun control, or in controversies over religious practices.

The politics of localities also plays an interesting role here, as metropolitan areas like Boston, New York, and Washington, DC, can span multiple states, thus creating both a shared identity for citizens across state borders, and also governance complications.

State populations also appear to have a different propensity and predisposition for political participation. Turnout in Massachusetts and Minnesota, for instance, is routinely higher than in Indiana, Mississippi, and West Virginia. Some of this differential can be explained by institutions, but it is also attributable in part to variations in the people who live in the states and their shared experiences.

By studying state populations, including their political predispositions, policy views, and propensity to participate in democratic government, much has been learned about the role of social forces in political behavior, as well as the interaction of individuals with various institutional structures.

Policy Innovation and Diffusion

The last of the themes we highlight in the study of the states is the nature of policy in a federal system. State government autonomy grants a high degree of flexibility to states to engage in policy experimentation. The study of any specific policy area in the states is inherently a study not only of the politics surrounding a certain policy domain, but also of the interactions among states, between states and the national government, and the process of learning that occurs over iterated interactions.

In some cases, like the 1996 welfare reform and the 2010 health care law, states acted as test cases for policies that were ultimately adopted at the federal level. In other cases, state policies have diffused across the states like smoking bans, lotteries, and term-limits laws. In still other cases, states have adopted major policy innovations, including assisted suicide and all-mail voting, without seeing much of any diffusion. Recently, states have experimented with legalization of marijuana, where the jury is still out on how much diffusion there will be.

Perhaps no policy's diffusion has gained greater attention in recent years than same-sex marriage. In the late 1970s, California was considering a ballot initiative that would have disqualified a person from being a school teacher if he or she were outed as a homosexual. The decade of the 2000s saw many states consider some form of a ban on gay marriage. Recently, however, an increasing number of states have seen their courts, legislatures, and voting public approve of same-sex marriage laws, while others passed laws defining marriage as between a man and a woman. In 2013, the Supreme Court issued two decisions on same-sex marriage, overturning part of the federal Defense of Marriage Act (1996), and refusing to grant standing to proponents of Proposition 8 in California, effectively leading to the legalization of same-sex marriage in the Golden State. However, the Court did not completely resolve the issue; its rulings for now leave the decision up to states as to the legality of same-sex marriages.

This kind of policy trajectory is a common one in the United States. Populations at the state level are more homogeneous than the U.S. population; along with more flexible constitutions and more direct ways of legislating, this creates an environment in which state electorates tend to lead on policy innovations. There is then an observable process by which laws may or may not diffuse to other states. However, the federal government often ultimately gets involved in state policy debates, either through congressional legislation or by decisions made by the U.S. Supreme Court. Thus state policymaking is often consequential not only for the state in which policies are passed, but for the future policy debate that occurs across the nation in other states, and in the nation as a whole.

These three themes weave a fascinating story of governance from the bottom up—from subnational governments to the federal level. States have diverse populations and interests, which lead to a diversity of interstate opinions on a host of policy issues. States exhibit variations in their institutional structures and their ability to experiment with institutional change. These population and institutional variations can lead to policy experimentation. The diverse policies that are adopted not only affect single-state populations, but they also set the agenda for discussion in other states and for national policy. Through rigorous empirical research, we have learned a great deal about the American states, our two hundred plus year-old experiment with federalism, and about representative government more generally. Our goal herein has been to make this vast literature accessible to a wide audience, including both students and those who may themselves be experts in one or another area of state politics and policy.

NOTES

1. The same dynamic was involved in comparative studies of elections and public opinion. Studies existed in multiple countries in the 1960s through the 1980s, but ones that were truly cross-national—such as *The Civic Culture* (Gabriel Almond and Sidney Verba, Princeton University Press, 1963) and *Political Action* (Samuel Barnes, Max Kasse et al., Sage, 1973)—were relatively rare.

2. *State Politics and Policy Quarterly,* founded in 2001 by Christopher Mooney, and now a Sage journal.

3. The State Politics and Policy conference, begun in 2001, is held in the spring of each year.

4. Robert S. Erikson, Gerald C. Wright, and John P. McIver, *Statehouse Democracy: Public Opinion and Policy in the American States* (Cambridge: Cambridge University Press, 1993).

PART I ★ FEDERALISM

Chapter 1

Federalism and Intergovernmental Relations

Carol S. Weissert

THE CONCEPT OF FEDERALISM is ubiquitous in high school civics classes, undergraduate American government texts, and law school cases. But familiarity does not breed respect. The eyes of students tend to glaze over at its mention, and anyone who raises it at a cocktail party or social event with adults might find themselves suddenly standing alone.[1] While federalism is an integral part of the fabric of the country, it is not generally viewed as engaging, relevant, or timely. But nothing could be further from the truth. Federalism is, in fact, dynamic and ever-changing. It is regularly defined and redefined by the Supreme Court, Congress, and the states. It affects how policies are made and implemented, how elections are held, and often how our civil liberties are protected.

Federalism and *intergovernmental relations* are terms that describe related but different relationships. Federalism is the relationship between federal (national) and state (or subnational) governments as set forth in a constitution that assigns responsibilities and autonomy to each. Federalism scholars typically focus on the institutional roles of these governments, such as constitutional responsibilities and differences in statutes and rules across governmental levels. Intergovernmental relations describes the interactions of federal, state, and local governmental officials (and nonprofits that contract with state and local government) and is often concerned with the effective delivery of public services. In short, federalism is primarily constitutional, legal, and jurisdictional, and deals with only the governments provided for in the U.S. Constitution (federal and state government). Intergovernmental relations is concerned with the behavior of all governments and nonprofit organizations, and is more likely to address administrative and behavioral issues.

This chapter begins with a historical reminder of what the Founders had in mind in putting in place this complex and often duplicative governance system. To be sure, federalism has evolved over time. In the early years of the country states were the dominant actors, but over time federal authority has expanded greatly. The chapter deals with the politics and policy of federalism and its advantages and disadvantages. It addresses how the federal government gets the states to act as it wishes, how states respond, and how states get what they want in federal policy. It highlights the theory and application of federalism and intergovernmental relations and how states and the federal governments cooperate, bargain, or conflict over policies and politics that often transcend jurisdictional boundaries.

FEDERALISM AT THE COUNTRY'S BEGINNING

Under the Articles of Confederation, the nation's first constitution, the states were strong and the national government was weak and ineffective. Each state had one vote and could veto major pieces of legislation. The national government relied on states for revenue and could not force them to implement its decisions. States competed with one another in trade wars and issued their own paper money. The Founders recognized that this system had to change—but they were also reluctant to adopt a unitary system like the one under which they had chafed for so many years. The solution was a federal system in which the states and the federal government share sovereignty. Federalism offers a "middle ground" between hypercentralizing unitary government and the chaos of a confederation.

The rationale for federalism is encapsulated in the *Federalist Papers,* written by James Madison, Alexander Hamilton, and John Jay to urge New Yorkers to adopt the U.S. Constitution. The authors emphasized the role of the states as an important check and balance for any overbearing national government and expressed the view that federalism promotes localism and undergirds representation. They recognized that both federal and state governments shared constituencies. *Federalist* No. 9 provides a visual interpretation as the states orbiting around the sun while retaining their separate status as planets.

In *Federalist* No. 46, Madison said, "Federal and state governments are in fact but different agents and trustees of the people instituted with different powers and designated for different purposes." It is these different purposes that have proven difficult to distinguish over the years. The allocation of authority to the two governments in the Constitution is generally vague and subject to interpretation. There is a short list of enumerated powers for the federal government including coining money, raising and supporting armies and a navy, punishing pirates, and regulating commerce with foreign nations, the several states, and Indian tribes. There is also what is called the necessary and proper clause, which says that Congress shall make all laws necessary and proper for carrying out the powers vested by the Constitution to the government of the United States. The supremacy clause states that where federal and state laws conflict, the federal law will prevail.

Importantly, the Tenth Amendment, the last component of the Bill of Rights, provides that "The powers not delegated to the United States by the Constitution, nor prohibited by it to the States, are reserved to the States respectively, or to the people." This provision, demanded by anti-Federalists who worried that the federal government might get too strong, was initially thought to give states considerable power because the *enumerated* powers were limited. But the 1819 Supreme Court decision in *McCulloch v. Maryland* (1819) expanded the notion of enumerated powers to include powers that might be "implied" from constitutional language, thus shoring up potential federal assignments of responsibility and leading to federal governmental involvement in most public policy areas.[2]

COOPERATION AND CONFLICT

The history of American federalism includes both cooperation and conflict. Daniel Elazar believes the pattern of coordination was set in 1790 when the national government settled the states' debts, thus ensuring that the federal government might furnish the money but states would spend it.[3] States administer federal elections, have joint authority over the militia, and participate in the process of amending the Constitution; state officials take an oath to defend the federal government.[4] Federal and state officials work daily on issues ranging from public health to education, from transportation to election standards.

However, intergovernmental conflict—where federal and state officials disagree on who should do what and even what should be done—has been part of the federalism *leitmotif* for generations. In 1994 a group of governors was so angered at what they thought was federal dominance that they proposed a constitutional amendment allowing three-fourths of the states to initiate constitutional amendments (thus bypassing Congress) and to repeal federal legislation or regulations that burden states or local governments (subject to a congressional override). In fact, the U.S. Constitution does provide that two-thirds of the states can call a constitutional convention, the product of which would go to the states for ratification by three-fourths of the states (effectively ignoring Congress). In the past few years, an Article V movement (from the location of the provision in Article V of the U.S. Constitution) has called for just such a constitutional convention to deal with what proponents see as a dysfunctional federal government. States are also ratifiers of U.S. constitutional amendments, which are first passed by two-thirds of the House and Senate and then sent to the states, where they must receive majority votes from three-fourths of the states (both their house and senate). But the process is cumbersome and difficult. Only twenty-seven constitutional amendments have been ratified since 1789, and ten of those comprise the Bill of Rights.

States were often described as being dominant in the early years of federalism until the 1930s, when the federal government grew in scope, size, and authority. However, the balance of power can shift between federal and state and back again over time and across different functions or responsibilities. The federal government makes a move to take on more state responsibilities, the states push back against the law, the Supreme Court may get involved if there is a question of constitutionality. In the 1990s, some scholars used the term *devolution revolution* to refer to what they viewed as a move toward giving more power to states. The term was associated primarily with a new welfare block grant, and only a few years later scholars had returned to concerns over centralization trends favoring the federal government.

THE EVOLUTION OF FEDERALISM

In the earliest years of the country, federalism was best described as dual in nature—with each government having functions for which it was responsible and little overlap or interaction among the levels. The size of government expanded tremendously during the New Deal in the 1930s. National government revenues were filtered to the states as a means of implementing a growing national domestic policy agenda. The idea of separate spheres of governance under dual federalism quickly dissipated. Under the New Deal, the federal government delved into areas previously provided by states, including housing, job creation, unemployment, and bank regulation. President Lyndon Johnson's Great Society further expanded the federal reach into health care, criminal justice, K–12 education, higher education, voting rights, clean air and water, and even school lunches. With the federal government involved in so many areas (along with states and localities), the term *cooperative federalism* came to describe the relationship between federal and state governments, where both governments were engaged in many functional areas working "cooperatively." As the "father" of cooperative federalism, Morton Grodzins, put it, "no important activity of government in the United States is the exclusive province of one of the levels."[5]

President Lyndon B. Johnson looking at portrait of President Franklin D. Roosevelt in the White House, February 10, 1965. Johnson's Great Society social programs resembled Roosevelt's New Deal in their scope but addressed different issues, notably civil rights, education, and health care.

SOURCE: LBJ Presidential Library, Austin, Texas; photo by Cecil Stoughton.

Dual federalism was commonly portrayed as a "layer cake" and cooperative federalism as a "marble cake." In the past few decades, scholars have abandoned the cake analogies, but there has been no recognized replacement. "Cooperative" seems to many scholars and practitioners as a misnomer for a relationship that is often competitive, contentious, and coercive. Erin Ryan argues that it is also atheoretical and cannot be used to answer the normative question of which government should do what.[6] Nevertheless, the call for a clearer sorting-out of responsibilities of federal and state governments seems rational. Alice Rivlin has argued that federal governmental responsibilities should be to control health care costs, ensure everyone has health insurance, and move toward a budget surplus.[7] In turn, she says, the states have responsibilities for providing education and training, social services, housing, community development, and public infrastructure. Others have urged a sorting-out based on whether the policies are redistributive, providing resources to those citizens who are unable to achieve a satisfactory level of resources on their own, or allocative, relating to the division of resources between public and private goods. The argument is that redistributive policies should be provided by the national government because states and localities are limited by the extent of their tax bases and the mobility of the poor across governmental levels. Allocative policies can be provided by both levels of government.

Apart from these normative views of what governmental level should do what, scholars have approached federalism in a more positive or empirical fashion. Some scholars have adopted the principal-agent model to understand federalism—with the states as agents of the federal principal. John Chubb finds that politics is the key component in understanding the principal-agent relationship between the national and state governments.[8] Craig Volden identifies credit-taking as a key to understanding why federal and state governments share program responsibilities.[9] Paul Peterson says the answer to the question, "Which government does what?" may be simple politics: it is what Congress wants it to be.[10] This notion of political federalism contrasts with the more rational model of functional federalism, whereby each level of government is focused on policy areas where it is the most competent that Peterson calls functional federalism.

An important component of legislative federalism is the multiplicity of venues available for interest groups. Groups can target a governmental venue that seems most politically amenable—regardless of governmental capacity. Indeed, businesses long encouraged state regulation as a means of better meeting their desired goals in a smaller and perhaps more persuadable venue—until states acted in ways they did not like (e.g., automobile emission standards). Businesses then preferred national legislation.

Why is there so much confusion? In part, it was intentional. With federalism, as with other areas of the Constitution, the Founders wanted to set parameters rather than a rigid framework. There are few clear lines to demarcate what is a federal and what is a state assignment. Thus it has fallen to the Supreme Court to draw these lines and serve as the arbiter of federalism.

SUPREME COURT AS ARBITER OF FEDERALISM

Over the country's history, the Supreme Court has determined whether state or federal law or activities overstep the boundaries set in the U.S. Constitution. These boundaries are fluid, so the resulting Court decisions are as well. Some Courts have been stridently supportive of the states; some have been similarly accused of bias toward the federal government. Even in one term, the Court sometimes rules in favor of the states and sometimes in favor of the federal government—establishing, revising, and occasionally overturning precedents of early years. Chief Justice John Roberts likes to say the Court is an umpire, calling the balls and strikes but not making the rules.[11] Nowhere is that more evident than in the two-hundred-plus-year history of federalism.

Every year there the Court decides a handful of federalism-related cases on issues relating to the commerce clause, necessary and proper clauses, Tenth Amendment, and the supremacy clause. The Court's decisions can affect the shifting power between federal and state governments. The commerce clause is a case in point. In *Hammer v. Dagenhart* (1918), the Court invalidated a federal law prohibiting interstate shipment of goods produced by child labor, thus limiting the federal economic reach; in *U.S. v. Darby Lumber Company* (1941), the Court reversed its earlier decision, saying that Congress should "to its utmost extent" use the powers reserved for it in the commerce clause.[12] A year later, in *Wickard v. Filburn* (1942), the Court took a seemingly extreme position of federal authority when it ruled that Congress could enforce a statute that prohibited a farmer from growing wheat on his own farm even if the wheat was used only for the farmer's personal consumption.[13] That expansive use of the commerce clause led to a long-standing enlargement of the scope of federal power.[14]

In 2012 the Court's decisions on federalism were the most important handed down that year and likely the most meaningful to the course of federalism in decades. One key case was brought by the federal government against Arizona's sweeping immigration reform. The Obama administration argued that Arizona was exceeding its authority because it was the federal government's exclusive prerogative to set immigration policy. The Court endorsed the federal government's argument for three of the provisions of the Arizona law but upheld one provision allowing state officials to ask for a suspect's immigration papers.

The most salient case that year was *National Federation of Independent Business v. Sebelius* (2012), in which Florida, joined by twenty-five other states, argued that certain provisions of the federal Patient Protection and Affordable Care Act (PPACA) were unconstitutional.[15] Most Court watchers had expected the case to be decided on the commerce clause. The federal government argued that health care was covered under the commerce clause, supported by a hefty mountain of case law articulating a broad definition of the commerce clause when the regulated activity is economic or commercial in nature. States argued that the provision in PPACA imposing an individual mandate requiring citizens to have health insurance or pay a fine was overreaching on the part of the federal government and beyond the scope of Congress's enumerated powers.

The Court's 5–4 majority upheld the federal law but did so using the rationale that the fee in question was a tax, and thus clearly constitutional. The Court dismissed the notion that the commerce clause applied, saying that upholding the individual mandate provision under the commerce clause would "justify a mandatory purchase to solve most any problem" and would change "the relation between a citizen and the federal government." This is an important distinction for the federal-state balance because it is a clear signal that the federal government

People protesting the implementation of Arizona's immigration law, SB 1070, gather along Washington Street in downtown Phoenix, Arizona, on July 29, 2010. Dozens were arrested during the protests. On June 25, 2012, the U.S. Supreme Court upheld the provision requiring state law enforcement officers to determine the immigration status of anyone they stop or arrest if there is reason to suspect that the individual might be in the country illegally. However, the Court also struck down other provisions of the law and affirmed the primary power of the federal government with respect to immigration policy.

SOURCE: Art Foxall/ART FOXALL/Newscom.

cannot assume that most policy issues fall under the commerce clause and thus are in the federal domain. In a sense, the Court was sending a message that there were real limits on the commerce clause.

In the second component of the ruling, a 7–2 majority overturned a provision in the federal health law asking states to expand their Medicaid program to more recipients (with federal dollars paying for most of the change). Medicaid is the mammoth federal-state health program for the poor. At issue was a provision in PPACA that if the states did not expand their eligibility, they would lose existing Medicaid dollars. The Court ruled that the threatened loss of funding was "economic-dragooning that leaves the states with no real option but to acquiesce in the Medicaid expansion." Chief Justice Roberts argued that Congress had put "a gun to the head" of the states with the provision and that states "must have a genuine choice." This finding seems to call into question the threat of loss of federal funds as a way the federal government obtains state acquiescence in policy change. This challenge to Medicaid as it has operated for nearly fifty years has the potential to reconfigure fiscal federalism in years to come.

THE POLITICS OF FEDERALISM

While the Court role is key in defining the allocation of responsibilities between federal and state government, the Court cannot implement those decisions. That role is primarily played by states, which put in place and operate federal programs ranging from highway repair to unemployment insurance, from Medicaid to restoring the Everglades. One example of such federal policy is the No Child Left Behind Act of 2001, the major educational program enacted under the George W. Bush administration. The federal government's role in education has traditionally been quite small (less than 10 percent of funding), with states and localities serving to set the policies as well as fund them. But in the 1990s there was much dissatisfaction with the quality of education and a fear that U.S. students were falling behind those in other countries. The No Child Left Behind Act, signed into law in 2002, put in place for the first time national standards and penalties for schools that did not meet those standards. But Washington could not implement these guidelines in the nearly one hundred thousand public schools in the country. Rather, it depended on the states to take leadership and make the project a success (see Chapter 29 for more on No Child Left Behind).

How the Federal Government Gets States to Act as It Wishes

Given the autonomy of states under our federal system, the national government cannot simply dictate to states what it would like them to do. So how can it persuade states to act? The most effective way is to provide money. There is an entire subfield called fiscal federalism that analyzes federal incentives—largely through federal grants to states and localities. In fiscal year 2012, some $600 billion went to states and localities in the form of federal aid. While federal grants can be traced to the Morrill Act of 1862, which made public lands available to states for support of agricultural and mechanical colleges, their use was quite modest until the 1930s, when as part of the New Deal federal grants were provided to states for such economic programs as free school lunches, emergency relief work, and emergency highway funds. In the 1960s and early 1970s, federal grants proliferated and provided funds to states for social programs with goals of alleviating poverty, equalizing education opportunities, cleaning the nation's air and water, and ensuring adequate health care for underserved populations. In 1965 alone some 150 federal grants were passed. Between 1965 and 1970 the dollars provided to federal grants doubled and then doubled again between 1970 and 1975.[16] In 2010–2011 federal grant funding increased thanks to the stimulus dollars designed to bolster state budgets through the worst of the recession—marking the most dramatic increase in federal aid to state and local governments since the 1970s.[17]

The federal grant tsunami of the 1960s and 1970s benefited the states in several ways. The grants provided services for which the states got political credit; they allowed states to hire state employees to run the programs, who then became experts in those areas; and they gave states the ability to negotiate and bargain with the federal government. Bargaining became the common way to describe federal-state relationships.

Most federal grants to states and localities are categorical grants—they provide money to these governments to implement a specific program in the manner desired by Washington. These moneys are allocated by a formula that reflects some type of need (number of school children, population, or poverty). But sometimes states compete with one another to receive the federal money in what is called project grants. The Obama administration's education program, Race to the Top, asked states to submit plans for how they would improve their state's education system in a number of ways, including developing a set of common academic standards that build toward college or career readiness, providing supporting data systems, and addressing struggling schools with innovative approaches. Only two states were funded in the first round and eleven in the second round of funding.

If grants can be viewed as the fiscal "carrots," there are also federal "sticks" that can be used against states without funding. These involve desired federal regulation that must be adopted by states or the states lose some federal funding (usually federal funding for highways), or the states see their regulatory authority replaced by federal authority.

The former is called cross-over sanctions; the latter partial preemption.

An example of crossover sanction was the federal desire to have a uniform drinking age in every state. The federal law said that if the states did not set the drinking age at twenty-one, those states would lose their highway trust fund dollars. South Dakota argued that Congress cannot bring about indirectly what it cannot do directly through enumerated powers, but the Supreme Court upheld this approach as a legitimate use of Congress's spending authority in *South Dakota v. Dole* (1987). This approach was so successful that the federal government "coerced" states to set a uniform speed limit of sixty-five miles per hour and ban unsightly billboards with the same threat of losing highway trust fund dollars. There are now well over a dozen financial penalties that involve losing highway trust fund dollars.

With partial preemption, the national government establishes rules and regulations calling for minimum national standards for a program. States can administer the program if they follow the standards; in states that fail—or do not wish—to do so, federal agencies will administer the program. Because many states would prefer to conduct these activities for their own citizens, they comply with this type of federal "blackmail." Partial preemption is often used in the environmental area in such laws as safe drinking water, surface mining, and clean air amendments. It also applies to state occupational health and safety. Half the states have chosen to administer that program; half have chosen not to do so. Another example was a federal law allowing states to settle issues of civil rights housing violations if the states passed laws setting forth desired federal components. More recently, PPACA had a provision asking states to set up their own health "exchanges," in which a variety of health plans would be provided and consumers given access to information and education about those plans. If states refused to do so, the federal government would set up and operate the exchanges in that state.

In a third type of "stick"—direct orders or mandates—the federal government orders lower governments to take certain types of action. Particularly troublesome for states is the tendency for Washington to mandate without federal financial assistance to pay for the newly required service. The Americans with Disabilities Act of 1990 and the Drug-Free Workplace Act of 1988 mandated state action without providing adequate funding. But the largest federal mandate is Medicaid: Congress has substantially broadened the scope and reach of the program over the past decade, arguing that the states could refuse the federal dollars. But in 2012 the U.S. Supreme Court found that the 2010 PPACA could not force states to expand Medicaid with the threat of a loss of funding for the existing program, thus for the first time defining when grant dollars can be too coercive.

Finally, the federal government can preempt state laws. More than 50 percent of all federal statutes preempting state and local authority enacted over the nation's two-hundred-year history were adopted during recent decades.[18] Transportation has a number of examples. In 1966 the federal government preempted state regulation of motor vehicle safety standards, and in 1982 federal law preempted state/local truck size and weight limitations on highways and roads. A preemption that was supported by many state officials was putting in place a national commercial motor vehicle operator license (the states supported this because some commercial drivers lost their licenses in one state but continued to drive in others).[19] In 2012 the federal government argued that its immigration laws preempted Arizona's immigration statutes, and the Supreme Court largely agreed.

The success of federal carrots and sticks led one scholar to discuss "permissive federalism," where a state's share of power rests on permission or permissiveness of the federal government.[20] But this seems a bit overstated because the states have their own fiscal resources, their own legal legitimacy, and their own preferences. Furthermore, sometimes the federal government's bark is worse than its bite. While Washington can cut off funding to a recalcitrant state, it is generally loath to do so because that would mean the program's recipients would not be served. Thus the threat of cutoff of funding is often empty—and the states know it.

But states also play an important role in implementing federal laws and grants. The federal government's reach does not include classroom teachers' competency or carbon monoxide levels in lakes: that belongs to states and localities. So when Congress passes a law, its implementation will be the responsibility of the respective state agency—for example, the California Department of Education or the Florida Department of Children and Families. State and local employees have the expertise and the knowledge at the ground level that will translate the federal law into reality.[21]

How Do States Respond?

Let's assume the federal government passes a law providing funding for an environmental program. The program is funded by formula, and the moneys coming to the states have to be spent on a program designed to ensure that inland waters provide a healthy home for native fish. States must issue regulations limiting pollution in inland lakes, and they have ten years to implement the law. Some states already have programs in place to protect their waters—probably more environmentally stringent than the federal law. Others have no water protection programs in place. Some states have strong state agencies to oversee inland waterways; others do not. Some have many environmentalists in their states; others do not. So from the beginning, there is a problem with implementation, given the varying resources of the states.

But apart from that, there are the preferences of the states' citizens. States whose citizens and elected officials are not supportive of the federal law might not wish to implement it in their states. What can they do? It turns out there are many options available to them.

First, states can refuse federal dollars. In 2009 Republican governors of Florida, Ohio, and Wisconsin refused federal dollars that would have funded high-speed rail projects in their states. Other Republican governors refused stimulus dollars tied to unemployment and education, fearing their states would be left with expanded programs when the stimulus dollars ended. Politics also played a role when states such as Florida demurred in spending federal grant dollars to set up health exchanges and otherwise implement PPACA provisions such as outreach programs and elder affairs counseling—costing the state millions of dollars.

Second, states can "stall." They can take the federal money and then slowly pursue the program. One example was the Low-Level Radioactive Waste Policy Act of 1980. Under this law, states were asked to form interstate compacts to deal with the low-level nuclear waste in their region. Instead, states dragged their feet, in part because of the uncertainty of potential new federal law, and there was little that could be done to speed up the process.[22] In a more recent example, in 2012 well over a dozen states were studying their options to create health exchanges under PPACA. These might well be viewed as stalling over two years after the law was signed.

Third, they can go to the courts in a type of legal pushback. In *Massachusetts v. EPA*, (2007), Massachusetts and twelve other states contended that the George W. Bush administration was not adequately implementing the 1990 Clean Air Act Amendments. In 2012, three states sued the federal government over the Defense of Marriage Act (DOMA), saying it unfairly discriminated against same-sex couples. The three states—Connecticut, New York, and Vermont—have enacted laws making same-sex marriage legal. One of the most active states in court is Texas, which in 2012 had seventeen lawsuits pending against the federal government challenging federal law or regulations on environmental standards, women's health, contraception in health benefits, voting rights, and redistricting. Texas's argument in these cases was that the Tenth Amendment grants state government more autonomy than many federal laws allow.[23]

Finally, states can refuse to implement the federal law, as they did in the Real ID law. This 2005 law was designed to set uniform standards on driver's licenses and establish a national database of driver's license information. It required states to issue their driver's licenses in compliance with federal standards; the punishment for noncompliance would be that their citizens would be unable to board airplanes or enter federal buildings. The states fought back; nearly two dozen states enacted laws specifically prohibiting compliance with the act. Ironically, Janet Napolitano, the head of the federal Department of Homeland Security—which is attempting to implement Read ID—signed a noncompliance law while she was governor of Arizona.

How the States Get What They Want

So the states as institutional actors have some recourse against unwanted federal law in a type of after-the-fact pushback. But what about a more proactive role, where the states can get what they want in federal law? How do they do this? The states do have some constitutional powers that give them leverage, such as the Electoral College (where states, not the people directly, elect presidents) and state control of both election administration (see Chapter 7) and redistricting (see Chapter 14). However, the states' primary paths of action are political. For example, in *Garcia v. San Antonio Metropolitan Transit Authority* (1985), the Supreme Court noted that if there were any limits on the federal government's power to interfere with state functions, they must be found in national political processes.

State interests are reflected in associations—such as the National Governors Association (NGA) and the National Association of Insurance Commissioners (NAIC)—that can be highly effective in Washington because of both their political prowess and policy-area expertise. John Nugent and Erin Ryan[24] provide examples in which state associations, particularly the NGA, were highly influential in crafting clean water amendments and welfare reform, drawing on both political credibility and their own experiences with the programs. Nugent describes the conditions under which governors are most likely to be successful in Congress, as articulated by then–Arkansas governor Bill Clinton. The problem must be one that involves a core American value on which both Republicans and Democrats can agree, and it must be a case in which the federal government cannot solve the problem without the heavy involvement from the states. The sticking point, of course, is the first component—bipartisan agreement. Even in 1994 it was difficult; in 2012 it was even more elusive.

There are regional and political associations of governors (the Republican Governors Association has been especially active in recent years) and issue-related offices (e.g., the Council of Great Lakes Governors). Individual states lobby Congress and the president in the form of "state" offices in Washington. Over half of the states have Washington offices; the others have state-federal contacts located in their state capitals.

The weakness of the intergovernmental lobby is that it is one of many voices trying to affect policy. The lobby might have been especially influential in an area like welfare reform, in which there were no strong business or professional interests at play. In other areas—health care reform, for example—state voices might be more easily ignored in favor of business interests.[25]

THE POLICY OF FEDERALISM

The policy rationale for federalism relates to the heterogeneity of the country and the desire for innovation. National policies affecting all 313 million U.S. citizens are broad indeed. National security, Social Security, and safe food and water are unquestionably important concerns to all citizens. But there are many policies in which support might differ by citizens' age, income, religion, or ideology. States are able to reflect these differences much more successfully than Congress. North Dakota is the only state without voter registration. Montana, Oregon, and Washington are the only states with legalized assisted suicide. Nine states issue marriage licenses to same-sex couples. In 2012, for the first time, voters in two states—Colorado and Washington—adopted provisions for the recreational use of marijuana for anyone aged twenty-one or older. And because of federalism, the citizens of Florida, Oregon, and Utah can implement policies that reflect their own citizens' preferences and needs. With a unitary or nonfederal system, these bonds of representation would not be possible.

A by-product of these different preferences is innovation. We are able to "try out" policies in states like Massachusetts, which has a highly successful health care system that served as a model for PPACA, and if they work (and other states want to adopt them), they will spread. Sometimes they remain in their original state. Sometimes the policies are so successful, they are adopted nationally. Supreme Court justice Louis Brandeis is credited with the term *laboratories of democracy,* applied to innovative states. This innovation often occurs in areas in which the federal government simply will not or cannot act. States then can step in to fill in the policy void. One example was in 1998, when forty-six state attorneys general took on the country's four largest tobacco companies. Arguing that the health costs of smoking were directly linked to Medicaid and other health programs, the state attorneys general successfully reached a $200 billion settlement (over twenty-five years), along with prohibitions against targeting of youth and against outdoor advertisements of cigarettes. The federal government was unable to reach its own agreement. Medical marijuana, same-sex marriage, and global warming laws are other examples in which states actions filled a policy void and in which there remains no federal law. (For more on this subject, see Chapter 25.)

One way the federal government takes advantage of states' expertise and varying preferences is through the availability of waivers. Waivers are a way that certain aspects of federal law can be "waived" or substituted in a manner agreed to by that state and the federal government. The waivers of longest standing are in Medicaid and the predecessor to the Temporary Assistance for Needy Families (TANF) program and its predecessor (Aid to Families with Dependent Children). No Child Left Behind allowed states to renegotiate the requirements set forth in the federal law that they find onerous and not implementable. In 2012 TANF waivers requested by a number of states became an issue in the presidential campaign. The Obama administration sent states a memo saying it would entertain proposals to test new ways to design programs "to improve employment outcomes for needy families." Republican campaign ads pounced—referring to the waivers as a plan to "gut welfare reform by dropping work requirements," even though Republican governors had sought these waivers.

THE COSTS OF FEDERALISM

While there are many upsides related to federalism, like policy experimentation and sorting, there are at least four downsides or problems associated with it. Specifically, federalism (1) promotes duplication, inefficiency, and a lack of clarity of responsibility; (2) leads to inequities among citizens in different states; (3) has contributed to

In areas hit hard by Hurricane Katrina, the Federal Emergency Management Agency (FEMA) set up posts where people affected by the storm could call for federal assistance. A call tent in Gulfport, Mississippi, is shown in this September 13, 2005, photo.

SOURCE: Dan Anderson/EPA/Newscom.

struggles over legalized and de facto racial discrimination; and (4) can encourage state and federal opportunism.

The ambiguities of the Constitution and the differing interpretations of the U.S. Supreme Court over time have exacerbated the mishmash that is the allocation of functions among governments. In recent years, the federal government has stepped up its role in education, criminal justice, and health care—all traditionally state and local responsibilities. But the truth is that there is no clear, bright line separating what is a federal responsibility from what is a state responsibility.[26] Most policies are in a gray area where both federal and state governments have a claim. These gray policies can lead to duplication and blame casting.

There is probably no better example of the dysfunction of federalism than the governmental response to Hurricane Katrina in 2005. There is ample blame to go around, but federalism with its shared governance may have exacerbated the problem. (See Hurricane Katrina and Federalism box.)

The second problem—what Paul Peterson calls the "price of federalism"—is inequity. A value of decentralization of responsibilities conflicts with a value of equity in which all citizens of the nation are treated the same. A poor person in Michigan is provided more services with

HURRICANE KATRINA AND FEDERALISM

Disaster relief provides one of the most visible examples of federalism and intergovernmental relations. Hurricanes, tornadoes, floods, fires, and terrorist attacks demand action across governmental levels, usually with private-sector assistance from groups like the Red Cross. The responsibility for dealing with such disasters is shared among federal, state, and local governments, which participate as partners.

The theory of disaster assistance is clear. The responsibility lies primarily with state and local governments; the federal government comes in only when needed to assist with local activities. Saundra Schneider calls it a "pull" system of intergovernmental relief, where local governments first respond until they exhaust their resources; then they "pull" in the state governments, which respond until they exhaust their resources; then they "pull" in the federal government.[1] Once brought in, a federal agency (the Federal Emergency Management Agency, or FEMA) coordinates with other federal offices to assist with housing, transportation, cash grants, and emergency medical care as needed. This "bottom-up" system has been in place for decades and generally works.

But it definitely did not work in the case of Hurricane Katrina in 2005, which caused the loss of more than 1,800 lives and over $100 billion in damages.

Two things happened that affected the Katrina case. First, after 9/11 FEMA was moved to a new Department of Homeland Security, whose focus was predominantly terrorism or man-made disasters. FEMA also had its staff and resources greatly reduced.[2] Also a new—and highly complicated—program was put in place in 2003 allowing the federal government to intercede when there are extraordinary catastrophic events (called Incidents of National Significance).

Shortly after Katrina hit, thousands of New Orleans residents fled to the convention center and Superdome, where there was no or inadequate preparation for food, water, sanitary facilities, and beds. Some citizens camped out on highway overpasses or were stranded on their rooftops. Looting was widespread, and no one seemed to be in charge. The reaction of all governmental officials was slow and often made without contact with their "partner" governments.

Power issues came to the fore when the governors of Mississippi and Louisiana refused to allow the president to put National Guard troops under federal control. The governor of Louisiana requested federal aid but failed to specify what assistance was needed; he also identified resources for relief but did not issue executive orders to move them into the stricken area. The federal government delayed its response—the first meeting of an interagency incident management team took place almost thirty-six hours after Katrina hit the Louisiana coast. There was much confusion about who was in charge at the federal level.

Sometimes intergovernmental collaboration did work. Martha Derthick notes that the evacuation of over one million people prior to the storm involved local and state cooperation and saved many lives.[3] The federal government also played a role, as the National Hurricane Center director placed personal phone calls to emergency directors and governors of Louisiana and Mississippi when his tracking of the storm indicated a hit on their coasts. Another success was search and rescue undertaken by federal, state, and local agencies.

The assessment of blame for the difficulties following Hurricane Katrina was shared by federal, state, and local governments. Some 37 percent of respondents in a national poll taken days after Katrina said the federal government was to blame for the "hundreds of thousands of people [who] were unable to evacuate the flooded city and they lacked food, water, and shelter." But 39 percent blamed state or local government.[4]

This case shows how reliant we are on intergovernmental roles and responsibilities in times of disaster. The relationships among governments and their officials are the glue of intergovernmental relations. Most of the time the glue holds; but when it doesn't, bad things can happen.

1. Saundra Schneider, "Who's to Blame? (Mis)perceptions of the Intergovernmental Response to Disasters," *Publius: The Journal of Federalism* 38 (2008): 715–738.
2. Thomas Birkland and Sarah Waterman, "Is Federalism the Reason for Policy Failure in Hurricane Katrina?" *Publius: The Journal of Federalism* 38 (2008): 692–714.
3. Martha Derthick, "Where Federalism Didn't Fail," *Public Administration Review* 67 (2007): 36–48.
4. Birkland and Waterman, "Is Federalism the Reason?"

higher incomes than a poor person in Texas. Indeed, different voting laws across states treat citizens differently: some states allow felons who have fulfilled their sentences to vote; others make it very difficult or prevent it altogether (see Chapter 7).

Third, federalism in the United States has contributed to a prolonged exclusion of civil and voting rights for African Americans. In the earliest years of the country, the Founders refused to deal with slavery at the national level, and states were able to continue slavery until the Civil War. Even after the Civil War, states were slow to allow full citizenship to African Americans. Beginning in the 1960s, strongly worded national laws emerged to ensure civil rights for all, but many states continued to lag in implementation. In the 2010s, some argue that another federalism legacy is the movement in dozens of states to require voter identification, limit early voting days, and curtail voting registration drives. In August 2012 a federal court blocked a new voter ID law in Texas that it argued would have a "regressive effect" on the ability of minority voters to cast ballots.[27]

A final problem relates to what Jenna Bednar and Tim Conlan call opportunism, where the states or federal government benefit from behavior that harms the collective. Federalism's decentralized structure creates incentives for opportunism.[28] Either the federal government or individual states can act opportunistically. The president and members of Congress can "encroach" on state areas such as education, voting, and even driver's licenses when it suits their political needs. Thomas Birkland and Sarah Waterman use opportunistic behavior to describe the move after 9/11 to change disaster policy to meet concerns over terrorism and ignoring state expertise and experience with how people and organizations behave in disasters.[29] States too will act in their own political interest even if that action is counter to the interests of the states as a whole. For example, in *Massachusetts v. EPA* (2007), in which thirteen states contended that the Bush administration was harming them by inadequately implementing the 1990 Clean Air Act Amendments, ten other states backed the Bush administration, including its claim that the states had no business being in court on the issue, largely on partisan grounds.[30] Most of the time, the events are relatively minor and do not adversely affect federalism. But Bednar and Conlan worry about the effectiveness of institutional arrangements such as the courts and the decentralized party system in curtailing opportunism.

CONCLUSION

Federalism is dynamic and adaptive; it is defined by its institutions and refined by behavior of federal and state officials. Politics and resources are key in understanding the impact of federalism. Federalism's U.S. lineage is pristine—going back to the Founders, who designed federalism as the "middle ground" between a unitary government and a confederation. Bednar argues that federalism is part of our culture and that our citizens don't try to "pit" one level of government against another.

Federalism is also adaptive to the needs and preferences of citizens of the time. As Woodrow Wilson put it in 1908: "The question of the relation of the states to the federal government is the cardinal question of our constitutional system. . . . It cannot, indeed, be settled by the opinion of any one generation because it is a question of growth, and every successive stage of our political and economic development gives it a new aspect." [31]

European and comparative scholarship has recently focused on multilevel governance, launched in large part by the attention on the European Union but also concerned with other countries where regions or states have become important in the governance process. Newly formed federations in Spain and Belgium and those that have been in existence far longer, such as in Canada and Germany, look very different from the United States in their institutional makeup. What they all have in common are the values of federalism, which have persisted in the United States over time. The most important values include checks and balances, accountability and participation, and innovation and competition. Other values include protection of private enterprise and markets (what has been called market-preserving federalism), military security, and state-federal problem-solving synergy.[32]

These values have played out as federal and state governments cooperate and compete, take credit and cast blame, and use politics to get their desired outcomes—all within our constitutional framework. Federalism continues to help provide balance and representation, much as the Founders envisioned.

NOTES

1. Alice M. Rivlin, "Federalism: A New Context for Domestic Policy?" *City Journal* (Winter 1993), www.city-journal.org/article01.php?aid=1142.
2. *McCulloch v. Maryland*, 17 U.S. 316 (1819).
3. Daniel Elazar, *The American Partnership: Intergovernmental Cooperation in Nineteenth Century United States* (Chicago: University of Chicago Press, 1962).
4. Robert Agranoff, "*Federalist* No. 44: What Is the Role of Intergovernmental Relations in Federalism?" *Public Administration Review* 71 (2011): S68–S76.

5. Morton Grodzins, *The American System: A New View of Government in the United States* (Chicago: Rand McNally, 1966).

6. Erin Ryan, *Federalism and the Tug of War Within* (New York: Oxford University Press, 2011).

7. Alice M. Rivlin, *Reviving the American Dream: The Economy, the State, and the Federal Government* (Washington, DC: Brookings, 1992); Alice M. Rivlin, "Rethinking Federalism for More Effective Governance," *Publius: The Journal of Federalism* 42 (2012): 387–400.

8. John Chubb, "Institutions, the Economy, and the Dynamics of State Elections," *American Political Science Review* 82 (1988): 133–154.

9. Craig Volden, "Intergovernmental Fiscal Competition in American Federalism," *American Journal of Political Science* 49 (2005): 325–42; Craig Volden, "Intergovernmental Grants: A Formal Model of Interrelated National and Subnational Political Decisions," *Publius: The Journal of Federalism* 37 (2007): 209–243.

10. Paul Peterson, *The Price of Federalism* (Washington, DC: Brookings, 1995).

11. Chief Justice Roberts used this metaphor in the opening statement of his testimony before confirmation hearings of the Senate Judiciary Committee on September 12, 2005.

12. *Hammer v. Dagenhart,* 247 U.S. 251 (1918); *U.S. v. Darby Lumber Company,* 312 U.S. 100 (1941).

13. *Wickard v. Filburn,* 317 U.S. 111 (1942).

14. Another example of the Court's actions affecting the balance of power is what is known as the incorporation decisions beginning in 1925 that applied the Bill of Rights to states as well as the federal government—see, for example, *Gitlow v. New York,* 268 U.S. 652 (1925). These decisions were especially important in validating a federal role in countering state actions in areas such as civil liberties and civil rights.

15. *National Federation of Independent Business v. Sebelius,* 567 U.S. __ (2012). The original case brought by the states was *Florida v. Department of Health and Human Services,* but the case decided by the Supreme Court consolidated the several cases into *National Federation of Independent Business v. Sebelius, Secretary of Health and Human Services.*

16. David B. Walker, *The Rebirth of Federalism: Slouching toward Washington,* 2nd ed. (Chatham, NJ: Chatham House, 2000).

17. Timothy J. Conlan and Paul L. Posner, "Inflection Point? Federalism and the Obama Administration," *Publius: The Journal of Federalism* 41 (2011): 421–446.

18. Joseph Zimmerman, "Congressional Preemption during the George W. Bush Administration," *Publius: The Journal of Federalism* 37 (2007): 432–452.

19. Lilliard Richardson and David J. Houston, "Federalism and Safety on America's Highways," *Publius: The Journal of Federalism* 39 (2009): 117–137.

20. Michael D. Reagan, *The New Federalism* (New York: Oxford University Press, 1972).

21. Implementation of these programs involves a variety of state officials. There are those who work at the state level and draft regulations and rules according to the federal and any related state laws, and there are those who actually work to deliver services. The latter group best fit Lipsky's notion of "street-level bureaucrats." Michael Lipsky, *Street-Level Bureaucracy: Dilemmas of the Individual in the Public Sector* (New York: Russell Sage Foundation, 1980).

22. Jeffrey Hill and Carol S. Weissert, "Implementation and the Irony of Delegation: The Politics of Low-Level Radioactive Waste Disposal," *Journal of Politics* 57 (1995): 344–369.

23. Becca Aaronson, Chris Chang, Ben Hasson, and Todd Wiseman, "Interactive: Texas vs. the Federal Government," *Texas Tribune,* August 30, 2012, www.texastribune.org/library/about/texas-versus-federal-government-lawsuits-interactive/#womens-health-program.

24. John D. Nugent, *Safeguarding Federalism: How States Protect Their Interests in National Policymaking* (Norman: University of Oklahoma Press, 2009); Ryan, *Federalism and the Tug of War Within.*

25. Keven Esterling, "Does the Federal Government Learn from the States? Medicaid and the Limits of Expertise in the Intergovernmental Lobby," *Publius: The Journal of Federalism* 39 (2009): 1–21.

26. Ryan, *Federalism and the Tug of War Within.*

27. Melanie Eversley, "Texas Voter ID Law Struck Down by Federal Judges," *USA Today,* August 30, 2012.

28. Jenna Bednar, *The Robust Federation: Principles of Design* (New York: Cambridge University Press, 2009); Timothy Conlan, "From Cooperative to Opportunistic Federalism: Reflections on the Half-Century Anniversary of the Commission on Intergovernmental Relations," *Public Administration Review* 66 (2006): 663–676.

29. Thomas Birkland and Sarah Waterman, "Is Federalism the Reason for Policy Failure in Hurricane Katrina?" *Publius: The Journal of Federalism* 38 (2008): 692–714.

30. *Massachusetts v. EPA,* 549 U.S. 29 (2007).

31. Woodrow Wilson, *Constitutional Government in the United States* (New York: Columbia University Press, 1908), 173.

32. Barry Weingast, "The Economic Role of Political Institutions: Market-Preserving Federalism and Economic Development," *Journal of Law, Economics, and Organization* 11 (1995): 1–31; Ryan, *Federalism and the Tug of War Within.*

SUGGESTED READING

Bednar, Jenna. *The Robust Federation: Principles of Design.* New York: Cambridge, 2009.

Elazar, Daniel. *Exploring Federalism.* Tuscaloosa: University of Alabama Press, 1987.

Feeley, Malcolm, and Edward L. Rubin. *Federalism: Political Identity and Tragic Compromise.* Ann Arbor: University of Michigan Press, 2008.

Joondeph, Bradley W. "Federalism and Health Care Reform: Understanding the States' Challenges to the Patient Protection and Affordable Care Act." *Publius: The Journal of Federalism* 41 (2011): 447–470.

Kincaid, John, ed. *Federalism.* Thousand Oaks, CA: Sage, 2011.

Manna, Paul. *School's In: Federalism and the National Education Agenda.* Washington, DC: Georgetown University Press, 2007.

Miller, Lisa L. *The Perils of Federalism: Race, Poverty, and the Politics of Crime Control.* New York: Oxford University Press, 2008.

Nugent, John D. *Safeguarding Federalism: How States Protect Their Interests in National Policymaking.* Norman: University of Oklahoma Press, 2009.

Peterson, Paul. *The Price of Federalism.* Washington, DC: Brookings, 1995.

Publius: The Journal of Federalism. Annual Review of American Federalism. Summer. Vols. 8–42 (1978–2012).

Riker, William. *The Development of American Federalism.* Boston: Kluwer, 1987.

———. *Federalism: Origin, Operation, and Significance.* Boston: Little Brown, 1964.

Ryan, Erin. *Federalism and the Tug of War Within.* New York: Oxford University Press, 2011.

Chapter 2

The Past, Present, and Future Role of State Constitutions

John Dinan

THE FIFTY STATE CONSTITUTIONS differ from the U.S. Constitution to an extent that it becomes possible to speak of a distinctive state constitutional tradition. State constitutions are generally revised and amended more frequently than the federal Constitution and are invariably longer and more detailed. Scholars have been concerned not only with explaining these enduring features of state constitutions but also with investigating variation among state constitutions. Some state constitutions are quite durable; but other states have operated under a sizable number of constitutions. Additionally, although some constitutions are only slightly longer than the federal Constitution, others are considerably longer.

Scholars have also been concerned with detailing various purposes served by state constitutional provisions and studying the effects of distinctive aspects of state constitutional design. Especially since the 1970s, state courts have relied on state constitutional provisions to provide expanded protection for individual rights beyond federal guarantees, even while state amendment processes have enabled opponents of these rulings to respond by overturning expansive state court rulings. Meanwhile, state constitutional provisions have long constrained policymaking, especially fiscal policy, and to a greater extent than is found at the federal level; but policy-constraining amendments of this sort have been enacted with particular frequency since the 1970s.

In part in response to the increasing length of state constitutions and adoption of various provisions constraining legislative discretion, efforts have been undertaken in recent decades to bring about wholesale reform of state constitutions. Although constitutional conventions were a regular vehicle for enacting such reforms in prior eras, legislators and citizens in the contemporary era have been more reluctant than their predecessors to support the calling of conventions. In fact, no full-scale conventions have been called in the last quarter-century. As a result, constitutional revision commissions and piecemeal amendments serve as the only viable options for adopting state constitutional reforms in the foreseeable future.

ENDURING FEATURES OF STATE CONSTITUTIONS

In explaining why state constitutions are changed more frequently and are longer and more detailed than the U.S. Constitution, scholars have identified the outlines of a state constitutional tradition that differs in important ways from the approach that characterizes federal constitution-making. But there is also wide variation among the fifty state constitutions in terms of how frequently they are revised and amended and regarding their length and level of detail, leading to consideration of factors that account for differences within the state constitutional tradition (see Table 2.1).

Frequency of Amendment and Revision

Federalist No. 49, in which James Madison argued in favor of constitutional durability and veneration, is the canonical text for understanding the federal approach to constitutional amendment and revision. Madison cautioned that because "every appeal to the people would carry an implication of some defect in the government, frequent appeals would, in great measure, deprive the government of the veneration which time bestows on everything, and without which perhaps the wisest and freest governments would not possess the requisite stability." He also counseled against "disturbing the public tranquility by interesting too strongly the public passions" as a result of frequently submitting constitutional questions to the people.[1] In keeping with Madison's expectation, the U.S. Constitution is the world's oldest current national constitution and has been amended twenty-seven times. Given that the ten amendments comprising the Bill of Rights were added shortly after ratification of the Constitution, only seventeen amendments have been approved in the last 220 years.

State constitution-makers, by contrast, have generally followed Thomas Jefferson's preference for generational constitutional revision as set out in a series of letters he exchanged with Madison in the founding era. Operating on

TABLE 2.1 **Basic Information about State Constitutions (as of January 2012)**

State	Number of constitutions	Date of current constitution	Word length of current constitution	Amendments to current constitution
Alabama	6	1901	376,006	855
Alaska	1	1959	13,479	29
Arizona	1	1912	47,306	147
Arkansas	5	1874	59,120	98
California	2	1879	67,048	525
Colorado	1	1876	66,140	155
Connecticut	2	1965	16,401	30
Delaware	4	1897	25,445	142
Florida	6	1969	56,705	118
Georgia	10	1983	41,684	71
Hawaii	1	1959	21,498	110
Idaho	1	1890	24,626	123
Illinois	4	1971	16,401	12
Indiana	2	1851	11,476	47
Iowa	2	1857	11,089	54
Kansas	1	1861	14,097	95
Kentucky	4	1891	27,234	41
Louisiana	11	1975	69,876	168
Maine	1	1820	16,313	172
Maryland	4	1867	43,198	225
Massachusetts	1	1780	45,283	120
Michigan	4	1964	31,164	30
Minnesota	1	1858	11,734	120
Mississippi	4	1890	26,229	125
Missouri	4	1945	69,394	114
Montana	2	1973	12,790	31
Nebraska	2	1875	34,934	228
Nevada	1	1864	37,418	136
New Hampshire	2	1784	13,060	145
New Jersey	3	1948	26,360	45
New Mexico	1	1912	33,198	160
New York	4	1895	44,397	220
North Carolina	3	1971	17,177	30
North Dakota	1	1889	18,746	150

State	Number of constitutions	Date of current constitution	Word length of current constitution	Amendments to current constitution
Ohio	2	1851	53,239	172
Oklahoma	1	1907	81,666	187
Oregon	1	1859	49,016	249
Pennsylvania	5	1968	26,078	30
Rhode Island	2	1986	11,407	10
South Carolina	7	1896	27,421	497
South Dakota	1	1889	27,774	215
Tennessee	3	1870	13,960	39
Texas	5	1876	86,936	474
Utah	1	1896	17,849	115
Vermont	3	1793	8565	54
Virginia	6	1971	21,899	46
Washington	1	1889	32,578	105
West Virginia	2	1872	33,324	71
Wisconsin	1	1848	15,102	145
Wyoming	1	1890	26,349	98

SOURCE: *Book of the States 2012* (Lexington, KY: Council of State Governments, 2012), 11.

the view that "the earth belongs always to the living generation," Jefferson argued that each generation, which lasted between nineteen and twenty years according to his actuarial calculations, should have the opportunity to reconsider the suitability of a constitution and take account of progress in the science of politics in the intervening years.[2] In accord with Jefferson's view, the fifty states have operated under 144 constitutions, for an average of nearly 3 constitutions per state.[3] As of January 2012 the current state constitutions have been amended 7,378 times, for an average of 147 amendments per state constitution (see Table 2.1).

Although state constitutions are generally revised and amended more frequently than the U.S. Constitution, there is wide variation within the state tradition (see Figures 2.1 and 2.2). A number of state constitutions have been relatively durable, to the extent that nineteen states continue to operate under their inaugural constitutions. This includes, as one might expect, all five states that entered the union in the twentieth century (Oklahoma, Arizona, New Mexico, Hawaii, and Alaska); but also two states that were admitted in the early half of the nineteenth century (Maine and Wisconsin) as well as the world's oldest constitution: the Massachusetts Constitution of 1780. Similarly, some state constitutions have been amended relatively infrequently. It is no surprise that some recently adopted state constitutions have fewer amendments than the U.S. Constitution, most notably the Illinois Constitution of 1971 (twelve amendments) and Rhode Island Constitution of 1986 (ten amendments). But even some long-standing constitutions have been amended relatively infrequently, including the Tennessee Constitution of 1870 (thirty-nine amendments) and the Kentucky Constitution of 1891 (forty-one amendments).

On the other end of the spectrum, some state constitutions are revised and amended at an especially rapid pace. Nine states have operated under five or more constitutions, topped by Louisiana (eleven constitutions) and Georgia (ten constitutions), and including South Carolina (seven constitutions), Alabama, Florida, and Virginia (six constitutions each), and Arkansas, Pennsylvania, and Texas (five constitutions each). Some state constitutions are also amended quite regularly. Twenty-nine current state constitutions have been amended more than one hundred times, topped by the Alabama Constitution of 1901 (855 amendments), along with the California Constitution of 1879 (525 amendments), South Carolina Constitution of 1896 (497 amendments), and Texas Constitution of 1876 (474 amendments).

FIGURE 2.1 **Number of Constitutions, by State (as of January 2012)**

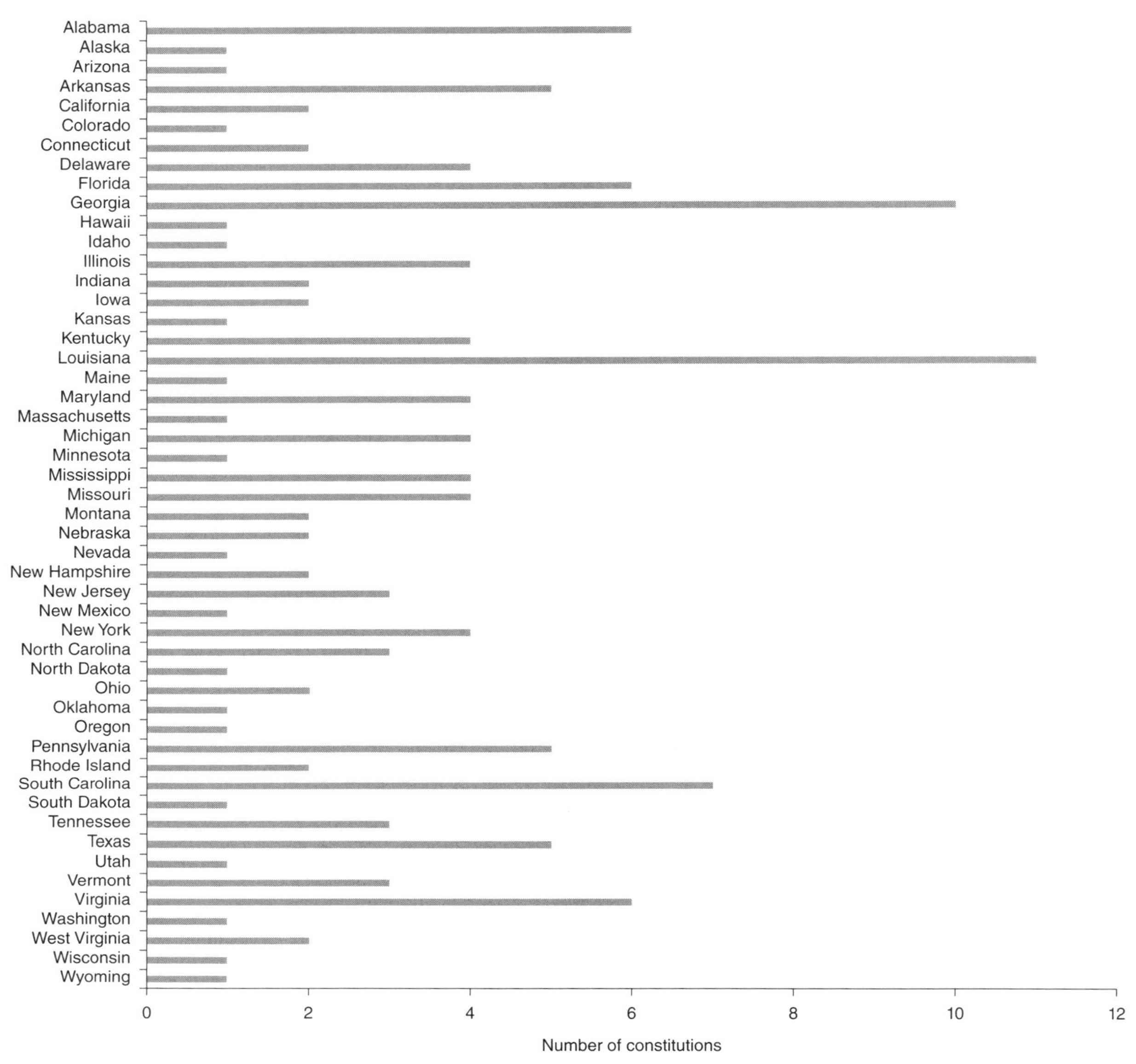

SOURCE: *Book of the States 2012* (Lexington, KY: Council of State Governments, 2012), 11.

The design of state constitutional amendment and revision procedures accounts in part for the relative durability of some state constitutions and exceptional malleability of other state constitutions. States vary especially in the flexibility of their legislature-initiated amendment procedures. Every state but Delaware requires that amendments be submitted for popular ratification, which in all but six states is achieved by securing a majority of votes cast on the amendment (several states require ratification by a popular supermajority or a majority of all voters participating in the *election*).[4] But states differ a great deal in how the legislature can place an amendment on the ballot. Some states permit the legislature to submit an amendment to the people by a bare legislative majority in a single session. But other states require approval by the legislature in two consecutive sessions. And still other states require amendments to be approved by a legislative supermajority, in some cases by a three-fifths vote and in other cases by a two-thirds vote. As Donald Lutz has shown, these differences in the percentage of legislators required to approve an amendment account for much of the variation in state amending rates.[5]

FIGURE 2.2 **Number of Amendments to State Constitutions, by State (as of January 2012)**

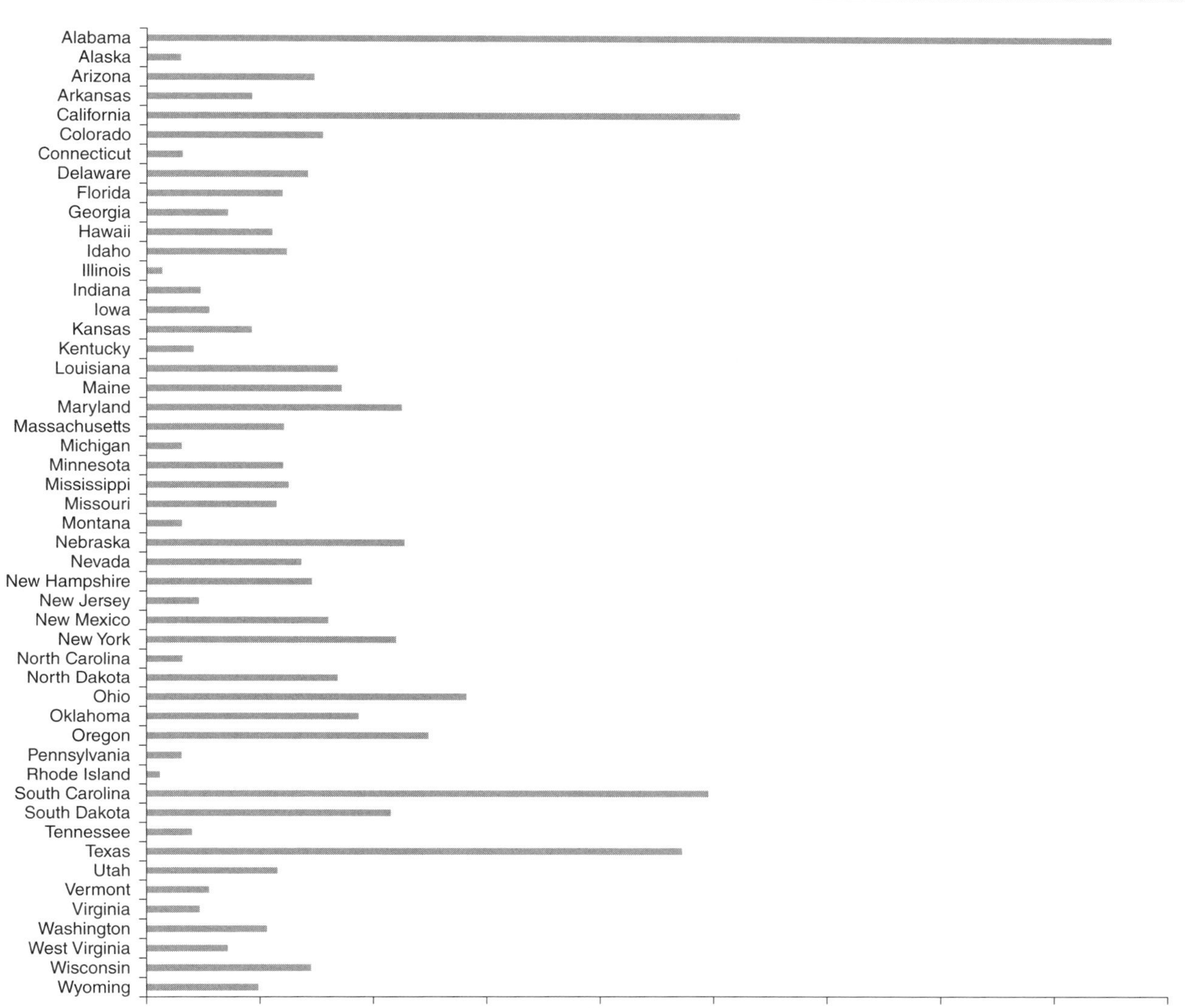

SOURCE: *Book of the States 2012* (Lexington, KY: Council of State Governments, 2012), 11.

Some states also allow citizens or revision commissions to place amendments on the ballot independent of the legislature. Eighteen states allow for citizen-initiated amendments, with all but two of these states (Massachusetts and Mississippi) providing for a direct initiative procedure in which voters can qualify amendments for the ballot without any role for the legislature. Meanwhile, Florida permits constitutional revision commissions to bypass the legislature and place amendments directly before voters.

Although all state constitutions have been understood as providing, whether explicitly or implicitly, for conventions that can consider amendments or revisions, states vary in how conventions are called. In most states, conventions can be called by the legislature, generally though not always upon a supermajority legislative vote, and in all but a handful of states upon approval in a popular referendum. However, four states (Florida, Montana, North Dakota, and South Dakota) also allow for conventions to be called through the initiative process. Fourteen states have been particularly drawn to Jefferson's call for generational constitutional revision, in that they also provide for the periodic submission to the people of a referendum on calling a convention. In seven of these states with periodic convention referendums the question

North Carolina's proposed state constitutional amendment to ban same-sex marriage, up for a referendum in May 2012, drew public opposition, such as this yard sign in Burlington, North Carolina. The referendum amending the state constitution to read "marriage between one man and one woman is the only domestic legal union that shall be valid or recognized in this State" passed 61 percent to 39 percent.

SOURCE: © Matt Maggio/Demotix/Corbis.

is automatically submitted to the people every twenty years. In several of these states a mandatory convention referendum is submitted as frequently as every ten years.

The relative flexibility or rigidity of amendment and revision procedures cannot account for all of the variation in state constitutional amendment and revision rates. Regional factors also play an important role, with southern states replacing their constitutions quite frequently on account of their secession from the Union and the ensuing Reconstruction. In many southern states secession was accompanied by drafting a new state constitution in 1861. Some of these states then replaced these constitutions in the mid-1860s as part of the presidential Reconstruction process, only to replace them once again in the late 1860s as part of the congressional Reconstruction process. Some states then adopted new constitutions once again in the period of Redemption in the 1870s and early 1880s as Bourbon Democrats regained power, and then yet again in the 1890s and early 1900s as federal influence over southern states receded completely. All told, 36 of the 144 state constitutions in effect throughout U.S. history were adopted in the eleven states of the Confederacy between 1861 and 1902.

It is also important to take account of differences in the constitutional culture of various states.[6] In some states, especially in New England, state constitutions have assumed a role somewhat similar to the U.S. Constitution, in that revision and amendment are not undertaken lightly. In fact, New England is home to the four oldest state constitutions: the Massachusetts Constitution of 1780, New Hampshire Constitution of 1784, Vermont Constitution of 1793, and Maine Constitution of 1820. By contrast, constitutional revision and amendment are viewed as a part of ordinary politics in some other states, and nowhere more than Louisiana, where constitutional revision "has been sufficiently continuous to justify including it with Mardi Gras, football, and corruption as one of the premier components of state culture."[7]

Length and Detail

The U.S. Constitution is a short and spare document comprised almost entirely of structural provisions. Chief Justice John Marshall provided the best explanation of the federal approach when he wrote in *McCulloch v. Maryland* (1819), while affirming the constitutionality of a national bank, that the nature of a constitution "requires, that only its great outlines should be marked, its important objects designated, and the minor ingredients which compose those objects be deduced from the nature of the objects themselves."[8] This understanding has guided federal constitution-making throughout U.S. history, with the lone exception of the Eighteenth Amendment regarding liquor prohibition, which was repealed just over a decade later by the Twenty-first Amendment.

Marshall's understanding has generally not prevailed at the state level, although there is significant variation within the state tradition, in that some state constitutions are only slightly longer than the 7,700-word U.S. Constitution, whereas others are dramatically longer (see Figure 2.3.). The 8,500-word Vermont Constitution is the shortest state constitution, and another nine state constitutions are between 10,000 and 15,000 words in length, including (from shortest to longest) the constitutions of Rhode Island, Minnesota, Indiana, Iowa, Montana, New Hampshire, Alaska, Tennessee, and Kansas. At the other end of the spectrum, the 376,000-word Alabama Constitution is the world's longest constitution and over four times as long as any other state constitution. Another nine state constitutions are between 50,000 and 100,000 words, including (from longest to shortest) the constitutions of Texas, Oklahoma, Louisiana, Missouri, California, Colorado, Arkansas, Florida, and Ohio.

Variation in the length of state constitutions can be explained in part by the concept of distinctive state constitutional cultures. In some states, especially in New

FIGURE 2.3 **Number of Words in State Constitutions, by State (as of January 2012)**

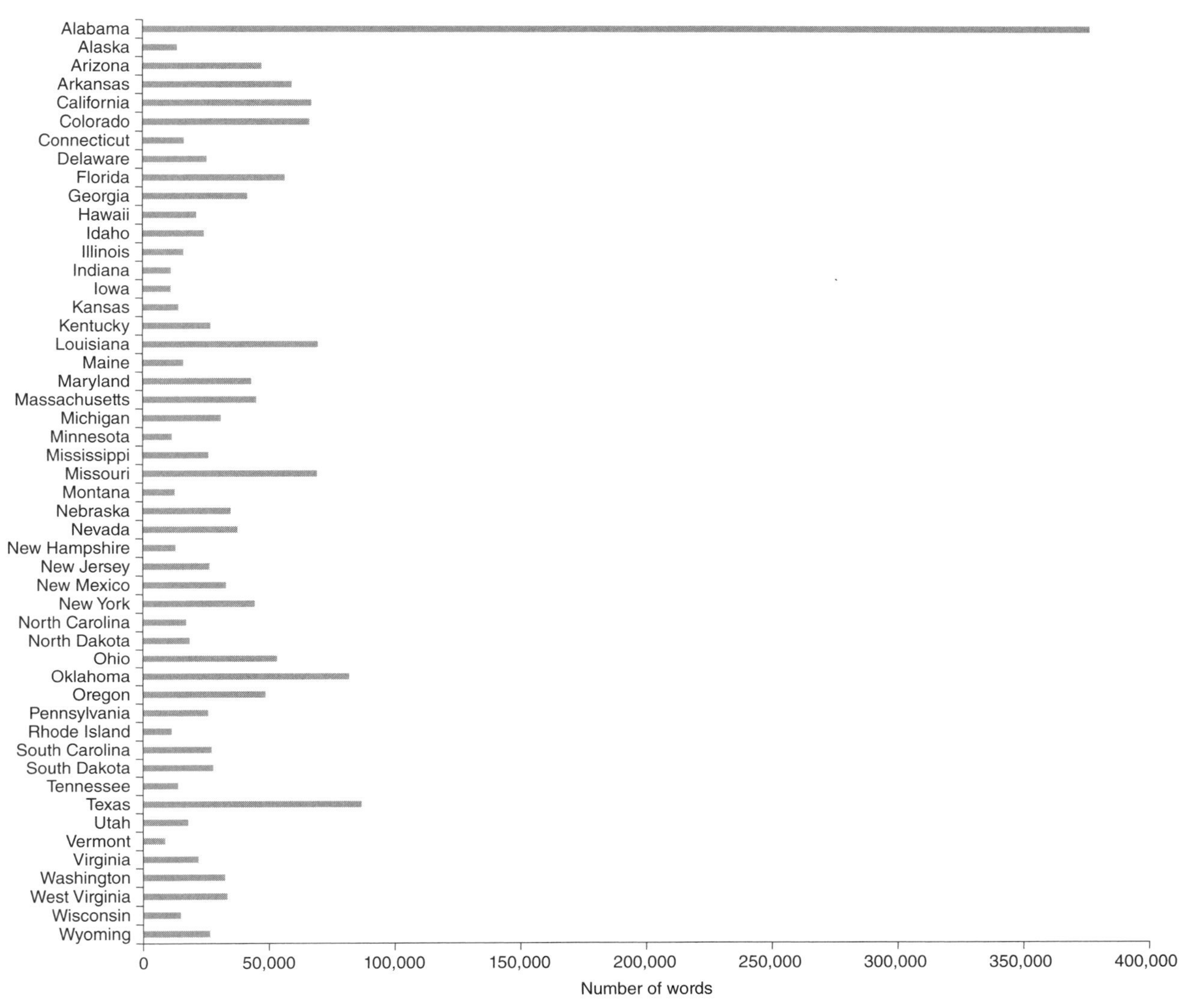

SOURCE: *Book of the States 2012* (Lexington, KY: Council of State Governments, 2012), 11.

England, constitution-makers generally follow the federal model of maintaining a relatively spare document and eschewing matters of policy and detail. On the other hand, in several states, especially in the South, citizens and public officials have come to expect that constitutional provisions will deal with public policy, and often in an exceptionally detailed fashion. This is carried to its fullest extent in Alabama, where alterations to local government structure and powers require adoption of constitutional provisions that must be approved in most cases by the statewide electorate. Most of the 855 amendments to the Alabama Constitution are local amendments of this sort.

The dominant understanding of what should be included in a state constitution has also changed throughout American history. Although state constitutions adopted in the late eighteenth century generally resembled the federal Constitution in their brevity, various nineteenth-century developments led constitution-makers to adopt detailed constitutional provisions for the purpose of constraining public officials. Then, during the twentieth century, a different understanding gained prominence, as exemplified by the National Municipal League's circulation of a Model State Constitution that sought to eliminate many of the detailed constitutional provisions adopted in earlier eras and exerted some influence on constitution-making in the late twentieth century.[9] As a result, and allowing for several exceptions, a number of state constitutions that have undergone wholesale revisions since 1970 are much shorter than their predecessors, including the Virginia Constitution of 1971, North Carolina Constitution of 1971, Illinois Constitution of 1971, Montana Constitution of 1973, and Rhode Island Constitution of 1986.

States that allow consideration of citizen-initiated amendments also tend to have longer constitutions, due to the reliance on the constitutional initiative process for addressing policy questions that are in other states resolved through the political process. Six states with constitutions of more than fifty thousand words have a constitutional initiative process: Missouri, California, Colorado, Arkansas, Florida, and Ohio. By contrast, only two states with constitutions of fewer than fifteen thousand words allow for citizen-initiated amendments: Montana and Alaska.

THE CONTEMPORARY ROLE OF STATE CONSTITUTIONS

Much like the U.S. Constitution, state constitutions play an important role in governance in establishing the structure of legislative, executive, and judicial institutions and the rules governing selection, tenure, and powers of officeholders. In a number of these respects, the fifty state constitutions resemble the federal Constitution. All state constitutions establish a presidential rather than a parliamentary system. Every state but Nebraska provides in its constitution for a bicameral legislature. All fifty state constitutions now provide for an executive veto. In other ways, though, state constitution-makers depart from the federal model in regard to the design of governing institutions. Most state constitutions provide for a plural executive, in that various executive branch officials are elected independently of the governor. Meanwhile, the vast majority of state constitutions require judges to stand for election of some sort, whether retention elections or partisan or nonpartisan competitive elections, and all but a few state constitutions stipulate that judges serve fixed terms.

State constitutions also guarantee rights that are at times similar to provisions in the federal Bill of Rights but are often phrased differently from comparable federal rights provisions or have no counterpart in the federal Constitution. Especially since the 1970s, in a movement dubbed the "new judicial federalism," state courts have interpreted state bills of rights as providing more protection than is guaranteed by the federal Bill of Rights, particularly with respect to rights of criminal defendants but also regarding free speech, religious liberty, privacy, and the death penalty. However, opponents have in some cases responded by securing adoption of constitutional provisions preventing state courts from exceeding federal guarantees. Much of the current importance of state constitutions revolves around their role in enabling and occasionally constraining independent state court protection of rights.

State constitutions also constrain policymaking, and to a much greater extent than the U.S. Constitution. It has been common since the mid-nineteenth century for state constitutions to contain detailed limits on law-making procedures. The nineteenth century also saw the enactment of various state constitutional provisions regulating the substance of lawmaking, by prohibiting legislatures from issuing debt without first securing approval from voters or barring operation of a state-run lottery or mandating prohibition of liquor. These sorts of policy provisions are a long-standing feature of state constitutions; but they were enacted with increasing frequency in the late twentieth century, most notably with passage of fiscal policy amendments.

Protection of Rights

Although state courts have had occasion to interpret state constitutional provisions throughout American history, it was not until the 1970s that they turned in a systematic fashion to engage in independent state constitutional interpretation to secure protection for rights beyond what the U.S. Supreme Court guarantees through interpretations of the federal Bill of Rights. Prior to this point, and particularly in the 1950s and 1960s under Chief Justice Earl Warren, the U.S. Supreme Court had been chiefly responsible for issuing expansive interpretations of individual rights, whether regarding school desegregation, free speech, religious liberty, or rights of criminal defendants. To some extent, this continued in the early 1970s, as the Supreme Court under Chief Justice Warren Burger issued rulings protecting abortion rights and imposing what amounted to a temporary moratorium on capital punishment. In other areas, though, the Burger Court was reluctant to continue expanding rights in the same fashion as the Warren Court, especially regarding rights of criminal defendants and on particular issues such as search and seizure. In this context, litigants seeking continued expansion of rights turned in the 1970s to press their case in state courts and grounded their arguments in state bills of rights.[10]

Several state supreme courts have been particularly active in undertaking independent interpretation of state bills of rights. The California Supreme Court issued a landmark ruling in 1972 invalidating the death penalty on the grounds that it was a *per se* violation of a state constitutional prohibition on "cruel or unusual" punishment,[11] even though the U.S. Supreme Court was not prepared to issue a similar interpretation of the Eighth Amendment ban on "cruel and unusual" punishment.[12] Meanwhile, after the U.S. Supreme Court in a 1973 case declined to read the Fourteenth Amendment's equal protection clause as guaranteeing a federal constitutional right to interdistrict equity regarding public school spending,[13] the New Jersey Supreme Court issued a ruling several weeks later invalidating the state's school funding system based on language in the state constitution committing the legislature to providing a "thorough and efficient system" of public schools.[14] These and other instances of independent state court interpretation of state bills of rights, which were particularly prevalent in Massachusetts, Oregon, Washington, and Wisconsin, among other states, were given a boost in 1977 by U.S. Supreme Court justice William Brennan, who penned an influential *Harvard Law Review* article encouraging independent state constitutional interpretation.[15]

Post-1970 state court interpretations of state bills of rights have frequently involved criminal procedure guarantees. State courts have been particularly active in holding that state search-and-seizure clauses require a more robust exclusionary rule than the U.S. Supreme Court has guaranteed based on its reading of the Fourth Amendment. When the U.S. Supreme Court announced a good-faith exception to the exclusionary rule, some state courts responded by interpreting state constitutional search-and-seizure clauses as setting a higher bar and disallowing introduction of any evidence obtained improperly, regardless of whether police understood they were proceeding properly. Meanwhile, a handful of state supreme courts followed the California Supreme Court in interpreting their state constitutions to ban capital punishment or prevent imposition of the death penalty for certain crimes.[16]

Most consequential for governance are a number of state supreme court decisions interpreting state education clauses or equal protection guarantees to require changes in how public schools are funded. During the 1970s and early 1980s, various state supreme courts relied on state constitutions to issue education "equity" decisions ordering state legislators to reduce disparities among school districts regarding per-pupil expenditures. Then, from the late 1980s onward, state courts issued education "adequacy" rulings focusing on overall funding levels and school performance. All told, equity or adequacy lawsuits had been filed in all but four states and have been successful in nearly half of the states, with significant consequences for school funding mechanisms in many of these instances.[17] In order to bring their school finance systems in compliance with state court rulings, some states have implemented new taxes or increased taxes to provide more funds for schools. In general, states have increased the state share of school funding and reduced reliance on local funding. In an effort to further target interdistrict disparities in per-pupil spending, some states have provided for the recapture of local funds from wealthier districts for transfer to poorer districts. In short, state constitutions have been the vehicle for state courts to bring about substantial changes in the way public schools are funded.

State courts have also relied on state constitutional provisions to guarantee rights of same-sex couples. Although the U.S. Supreme Court has not interpreted the federal Bill of Rights as guaranteeing a right to same-sex marriages, in the 1990s litigants pressed state courts to rely on state constitutions to recognize such a right. The Hawaii Supreme Court issued the first key ruling toward this end in 1993. Although the court stopped short of legalizing same-sex marriage, it held that denying marriage licenses to same-sex couples was suspect under the state equal protection clause and remanded the case to a lower court for a determination of whether the state could provide a sufficient justification for maintaining the policy.[18] In 1999 the Vermont Supreme Court became the first state supreme court to issue a final ruling that the denial of same-sex marriage violated the state constitution, although the court permitted the state legislature to satisfy this violation by recognizing same-sex civil unions.[19] The Massachusetts Supreme Court in 2003 became the first state supreme court to require legalization of same-sex marriage,[20] followed by similar state supreme court rulings in California (2008), Connecticut (2008), and Iowa (2009).[21]

Three couples who challenged the state of Vermont for the right to same-sex marriage celebrate at a news conference on Monday, December 20, 1999, in South Burlington, Vermont, after the state supreme court ruled that the right to same-sex marriage was protected under the state constitution. In response, the Vermont legislature passed a law authorizing same-sex civil unions the next year. From left rear, Stacey Jolles, Nina Beck, Peter Harrigan, and Stan Baker; at front, from left, Holly Puterbaugh and Lois Farnham.

SOURCE: AP Photo/Toby Talbot.

At the same time that distinctive state bills of rights clauses enable state courts to issue rulings exceeding federal guarantees, the flexibility of state amendment processes affords opponents an opportunity to overturn these decisions and prevent rights-expansive rulings. Court-overturning decisions are relatively rare at the federal level, due in part to the rigidity of the federal amendment process. Only four amendments to the U.S Constitution (the Eleventh, Fourteenth, Sixteenth, and Twenty-sixth) were enacted in response to U.S. Supreme Court rulings. But the relative ease of proposing and ratifying state constitutional amendments renders state court rulings more vulnerable to reversal.

At times, state constitutional amendments have declared that state courts may not interpret state bills of rights to provide more protection for rights than is guaranteed by U.S. Supreme Court interpretations of comparable federal guarantees. State constitutional amendments may not provide less protection for rights than is guaranteed by the federal Constitution. But state constitutional amendments can prevent state courts from exceeding federal guarantees. Toward this end, amendments were approved in Florida and California, among other states, in the 1980s and 1990s, stipulating that search-and-seizure guarantees and other criminal procedure clauses cannot be interpreted in a more expansive fashion than federal constitutional provisions.[22]

At other times, state constitutional amendments have explicitly overturned or preempted expansive state court rulings. Opponents of state court decisions barring use of the death penalty in California, Massachusetts, and Oregon secured passage of citizen-initiated amendments declaring that the death penalty shall not be deemed inconsistent with state constitutional provisions. Most important, thirty-one state constitutional amendments were approved between 1998 and 2012 for the purpose of preventing state courts from recognizing same-sex marriage. These same-sex marriage amendments differ in various ways. Hawaii's amendment, one of the first to be adopted in 1998, only prohibits state courts from legalizing same-sex marriage and reserves to the legislature the definition of marriage, whereas the other thirty amendments prohibit both state courts and state legislatures from legalizing same-sex marriage. State constitutional provisions also differ in whether they merely restrict recognition of same-sex marriage, as in eleven states, or go further and also limit recognition of same-sex civil unions and in some cases domestic partnerships, as in twenty states. Finally, all but one of the thirty-one state constitutional provisions is preemptive, in that the state's supreme court had not yet required recognition of same-sex marriage at the time the amendment was approved. But in California, the state supreme court had already legalized same-sex marriage in a May 2008 decision, and an amendment was approved in November 2008 for the purpose of overturning the court decision and halting further recognition of same-sex marriage. In a 2010 decision, however, a federal district judge invalidated this amendment, in a ruling that the U.S. Supreme Court effectively allowed to stand as a result of its ruling in *Hollingsworth v. Perry* (June 26, 2013).

Constraints on Governance

Although there is a long tradition of amending state constitutions to constrain public officials, this trend accelerated and took a somewhat different form in the 1970s. In the nineteenth century, state constitution-makers who were concerned with ensuring transparency in the legislative process adopted procedural requirements mandating that bills contain a single subject and an accurate title and receive three readings before they are approved. Late nineteenth-century state constitution-makers also adopted substantive limitations on lawmaking—such as prohibitions on passage of special or local legislation—to increase the likelihood that legislation conformed to the public interest. By the late twentieth century, however, state constitutional amendment activity was driven by additional concerns and led to adoption of provisions altering legislative design and powers, enacting policies disfavored by current officeholders, and constraining budgeting.

State constitutional amendments have occasionally been a vehicle in recent decades for enacting various changes in the design of governing institutions. Beginning in 1990 with adoption of citizen-initiated measures in California and Oklahoma, twenty-one states limited the number of terms state legislators can serve, generally through passage of state constitutional amendments. Over the next two decades, six of these state term limits measures were repealed by the legislature or invalidated by a state court; but legislative term limits are still in effect in fifteen states and are established by constitutional mandate in all but one of those states.[23] State constitutional amendments have also been approved in recent decades to regulate the redistricting process. At times, as with amendments adopted in California in 2008 and 2010, amendments take the redistricting responsibility away from the legislature and create an independent redistricting commission to perform this task.[24] In other cases, as in Florida in 2010, amendments establish criteria to guide legislators in drawing legislative and congressional district lines and try to prevent considerations of partisanship and incumbency.[25]

Recent decades have also seen the adoption of state constitutional amendments barring enactment or mandating adoption of various policies.[26] Five states that banned consideration of race or ethnicity in public hiring and contracting and college admissions in the 1990s and 2000s have done so through state constitutional amendment processes, beginning with passage of a citizen-initiated amendment in California in 1996. Two states that eliminated criminal penalties for medical marijuana in the 1990s and 2000s entrenched this policy in their state constitutions. Several states in the early 2000s enacted constitutional provisions regulating the state minimum wage, in some cases by setting a minimum wage higher than the current federal rate and in others by requiring automatic increases as necessary to keep pace with cost-of-living adjustments. Among other policy provisions added to state constitutions in recent years, voters in three states approved constitutional amendments between 2004 and 2006 supporting continuation of embryonic stem-cell research.

Supporters of enshrining policy commitments in state constitutions, rather than simply enacting them as legislative statutes or initiated statutes, have been motivated by various considerations. In some cases, such as affirmative action bans and medical marijuana legalization, policy goals were disfavored by public officials; in this context, advocates of these policy changes sought to entrench their gains against legislative interference by placing them on a constitutional footing. In other cases, policies were generally supported by one political party and opposed by another, as with stem-cell research and minimum-wage increases. By enacting these policies as constitutional provisions, supporters sought to limit the ability of the opposing political party to eliminate or revise these policies, as they could to do if the measures were framed as statutes.

Although in the post–1970s era state constitutional amendments have dealt with all sorts of policies, no policy area has been the target of more constitutional amendment activity than fiscal policy. State constitutions have for many years regulated the types of taxes that legislatures can impose; but beginning in the late 1970s the constitutional initiative process became a frequent vehicle for limiting tax increases. California voters' approval of Proposition 13 in 1978 has attracted the most scholarly attention, in light of its stringent limits on property taxes and a requirement that future tax increases be approved by a two-thirds legislative majority. But a number of other states passed tax-limitation amendments of this sort during the next three decades. Some provisions set detailed limits on tax rates, whether regarding property taxes or income taxes. Provisions in other states increase the hurdles that state or local governments must overcome in order to add new taxes or increase current taxes, generally requiring that they be approved by a legislative supermajority or in a popular referendum. Other state constitutional provisions limit spending increases. Colorado's 1992 Taxpayer Bill of Rights Amendment not only limits tax increases but also stipulates that expenditures can only increase according to a formula that takes account of population growth and inflation.

At the same time that constitutional amendments have been enacted to constrain legislators' taxing and spending authority, another set of amendments requires legislators to maintain certain levels of spending on specific programs, especially public education. California's 1978 constitutional limit on taxation coexists with a 1988 amendment that requires K–12 school funding to comprise a specified percentage of the state budget.[27] Meanwhile, Colorado's 1992 tax-and-expenditure-limitation amendment was followed by a 2000 amendment requiring school funding to increase by a certain percentage each year.[28] Other constitutional amendments impose other constraints on legislative discretion regarding school funding, most notably in Florida, where a 2002 amendment specifies the maximum class size for students in core-subject classes.[29] Still other amendments require that a specific portion of certain revenue sources be dedicated to certain projects such as road construction or wildlife preservation.

STATE CONSTITUTIONAL REFORM

In light of the continuing importance of state constitutions, it is no surprise that the contemporary era, no less than prior eras, has seen a number of state constitutional reform efforts dedicated to repealing constitutional provisions viewed as inhibiting effective governance. Contemporary reform efforts are motivated in part by a desire to eliminate outdated state constitutional language. For instance, some southern state constitutions contain assorted clauses that originated in the Jim Crow era and require maintenance of segregated schools. Meanwhile, some state constitutions contain voter age and residency requirements that were superseded by changes in federal law. These sorts of provisions were long ago rendered inoperative by U.S. Supreme Court rulings and have no current effect on governance. Nevertheless, efforts have been undertaken to eliminate them and remove these vestiges of earlier eras.

Other state constitutional reformers seek to eliminate provisions that constrain legislative discretion. Some constraining provisions, such as balanced budget requirements now found in thirty-six state constitutions (another thirteen states have statutory balanced budget rules), are so entrenched that they are unlikely to be eliminated.[30] But other provisions, including a number of fiscal policy provisions adopted from the 1970s onward, have been the frequent target of state constitutional reformers who have occasionally enjoyed some success in repealing them. Attention has focused in part on provisions requiring a supermajority vote in the legislature to enact a budget or raise taxes. Concerns have also been expressed about various constitutional provisions committing the legislature to provide a certain level of funding for particular programs, often for public schools but occasionally for other programs such as those regarding mental health.

Still other state constitutional reformers have focused on modifying constitutional initiative processes that have often been the vehicles through which constraining provisions have been adopted. That is, constitutional reformers who decry the effects of legislative term limits, tax-and-expenditure limitations, and education-spending requirements have at times tried to modify or repeal these constitutional provisions; but they have also targeted the constitutional initiative processes that were invariably responsible for their enactment. At times, reformers have worked to increase the number of signatures required to qualify constitutional initiatives for the ballot. At other times, reformers have pressed for more significant changes, such as replacing the direct constitutional initiative (currently in place in sixteen states) with an indirect constitutional initiative process of the sort found in Massachusetts and Mississippi, where the legislature can block or modify initiated measures.

State constitutional reformers have occasionally been successful in recent years in repealing or modifying provisions viewed as outdated or problematic. But these successes have been relatively infrequent and have been achieved almost entirely in piecemeal fashion through the amendment process. Voters in a number of states have approved legislature-referred amendments eliminating outdated or offensive language, such as older references to disfranchisement of "idiots" or "insane" persons that have been replaced by disqualification of persons of diminished mental capacity. Voters have also ratified legislature-referred amendments clearing away inoperative provisions, especially voter qualification provisions from earlier eras that have been superseded by congressional statutes, federal constitutional amendments, and U.S. Supreme Court decisions in recent decades liberalizing voter eligibility and preempting state constitutional requirements. On rare occasions, state constitutional reformers have secured passage of amendments eliminating fiscal constraints, as when California voters in 2010 repealed a requirement that two-thirds of the legislature must approve the state budget.

When it comes to wholesale reform of state constitutions, however, reformers have experienced little success in recent decades. State constitutional reformers have tried on various occasions to build support for calling conventions, especially in Alabama throughout the 2000s. Reformers sought in part to reduce the length of the world's longest constitution by eliminating outdated and inoperative provisions. They also pressed for revision of fiscal policy provisions that constrain taxing authority and earmark most revenue for specific programs, thereby significantly limiting legislative discretion over the budget. But they were unable to obtain the necessary votes in the state legislature to submit a convention referendum to voters.[31]

Alabama legislators' reluctance to submit a convention call to voters during the 2000s is illustrative of a general disinclination on the part of legislators and voters to support the calling of conventions, especially unlimited conventions. Although 233 state constitutional conventions have been held throughout American history, except for an unusual and ill-fated 1992 episode in Louisiana where legislators simply convened as a convention, no constitutional conventions have been called in the last quarter-century. The last full-scale conventions were held in New Hampshire in 1984 and Rhode Island in 1986 after voters approved automatically submitted convention referendums in those states.[32] In general, voters have been unwilling to approve convention referendums. In fact, voters defeated the last twenty-four automatic convention referendums in the fourteen states with such a procedure, including three submitted in 2008 and another four submitted in 2010.[33] Meanwhile, in states that lack an automatic convention referendum device, legislators have been unwilling even to submit convention calls for popular approval, due largely to fears that conventions would open a Pandora's box of issues and might not be limited to addressing a specific set of constitutional concerns.[34]

With constitutional conventions effectively foreclosed as a viable route to wholesale state constitutional reform, reformers have looked increasingly to constitutional revision commissions as an alternative. Florida is unique in providing in its constitution for the automatic establishment of constitutional revision commissions empowered to submit constitutional changes directly to voters. A Florida Constitutional Revision Commission is required to be created every twenty years, most recently in 1997–1998. A Taxation and Budget Reform Commission is also convened every twenty years, most recently in 2007–2008. These commissions have occasionally been successful in recommending significant constitutional reforms that were subsequently approved by voters.[35]

In other states, legislatures can establish constitutional revision commissions; but these commissions are invariably required to submit their recommendations for legislative approval before they can be sent to voters for ratification. Legislators are more favorably disposed to establishing commissions rather than conventions in part because they retain a good deal of control over their charge and staffing.[36] This route has been taken on various occasions, including in 2011 in Alabama and Ohio, where legislatures created revision commissions and charged them with undertaking a thorough reconsideration of the suitability of the state constitution (although the Alabama commission is prevented from examining the taxation article).[37] To the extent that state constitutional reformers are likely to be successful in eliminating constitutional provisions seen as inhibiting effective governance, revision commissions are the most promising route.

NOTES

1. Alexander Hamilton, James Madison, and John Jay, *The Federalist Papers,* ed. Clinton Rossiter (New York: Penguin, 1961), 314, 315.
2. Thomas Jefferson, "Letter to James Madison" (September 6, 1789), in *The Life and Selected Writings of Thomas Jefferson,* ed. Adrienne Koch and William Peden (New York: Modern Library, 1944), 491.
3. This and subsequent counts of the number of state constitutions and amendments are calculated from data presented in John Dinan, "State Constitutional Developments in 2011," *The Book of the States 2012,* vol. 44 (Lexington, KY: Council of State Governments, 2012), Table 1.1, 11.
4. This and subsequent information on state procedures for legislature-referred amendments, citizen-initiated amendments, and constitutional conventions are drawn from ibid., Table 1.2, Table 1.3, and Table 1.4, 13–17.
5. Donald S. Lutz, "Toward a Theory of Constitutional Amendment," *American Political Science Review* 88 (June 1994): 355, 361.
6. G. Alan Tarr, *Understanding State Constitutions* (Princeton, NJ: Princeton University Press, 1998), 31–34.
7. Mark T. Carleton, "Elitism Sustained: The Louisiana Constitution of 1974," *Tulane Law Review* 54 (April 1980): 560.
8. *McCulloch v. Maryland,* 17 U.S. 316 (1819), 407.
9. Tarr, *Understanding State Constitutions,* 153–157.
10. Ibid., 161–170.
11. *People v. Anderson,* 6 Cal.3d 628 (1972).
12. *Furman v. Georgia,* 408 U.S. 238 (1972).
13. *San Antonio Independent School District v. Rodriguez,* 411 U.S. 1 (1973).
14. *Robinson v. Cahill,* 62 N.J. 473 (1973).
15. William J. Brennan Jr., "State Constitutions and the Protection of Individual Rights," *Harvard Law Review* 90 (January 1977): 489–504.
16. Barry Latzer, *State Constitutions and Criminal Justice* (Westport, CT: Greenwood Press, 1991).
17. John Dinan, "School Finance Litigation: The Third Wave Recedes," in *From Schoolhouse to Courthouse: The Judiciary's Role in American Education,* ed. Joshua M. Dunn and Martin R. West (Washington, DC: Brookings, 2009), 96–98.
18. *Baehr v. Lewin,* 74 Haw. 530 (1993).
19. *Baker v. State,* 170 Vt. 194 (1999).
20. *Goodridge v. Department of Public Health,* 440 Mass. 309 (2003).
21. *In re Marriage Cases,* 43 Cal.4th 757 (2008); *Kerrigan v. Commissioner of Public Health,* 289 Conn. 135 (2008); *Varnum v. Brien,* 763 N.W.2d 862 (Iowa 2009).
22. These and subsequent court-constraining amendments are discussed in John Dinan, "Court-Constraining Amendments and the State Constitutional Tradition," *Rutgers Law Journal* 38 (Summer 2007): 983–1039.
23. National Conference of State Legislatures, "Legislative Term Limits: An Overview," www.ncsl.org/legislatures-elections/legisdata/legislative-term-limits-overview.aspx.
24. California Constitution, Article XXI.
25. Florida Constitution, Article III, Sections 20, 21.
26. John Dinan, "State Constitutional Amendment Processes and the Safeguards of American Federalism," *Penn State Law Review* 115 (2011): 1007–1034.
27. California Constitution, Article XIII (B)
28. Colorado Constitution, Article IX, Section 17.
29. Florida Constitution, Article IX, Section 1.
30. National Conference of State Legislatures, *NCSL Fiscal Brief: State Balanced Budget Provisions* (October 2010), www.ncsl.org/documents/fiscal/StateBalancedBudgetProvisions2010.pdf.
31. John Dinan, "Accounting for Success and Failure of Southern State Constitutional Reform, 1978–2008," *Charleston Law Review* 3 (Spring 2009): 483, 489–492.
32. John Dinan, "The Political Dynamics of Mandatory State Constitutional Convention Referendums: Lessons from the 2000s Regarding Obstacles and Pathways to their Passage," *Montana Law Review* 71 (Summer 2010): 395, 396–397.
33. Calculated from data presented in Dinan, "State Constitutional Developments in 2011," Table 1.4, 16.
34. Gerald Benjamin and Thomas Gais, "Constitutional Conventionphobia," *Hofstra Law and Policy Symposium* 1 (1996): 53–77.
35. Dinan, "Accounting for Success and Failure of Southern State Constitutional Reform," 497–501.
36. Robert F. Williams, "Are State Constitutional Conventions Things of the Past? The Increasing Role of the Constitutional Commission in State Constitutional Change," *Hofstra Law and Policy Symposium* 1 (1996): 1–26.
37. Dinan, "State Constitutional Developments in 2011," 4–5.

SUGGESTED READING

Adams, Willi Paul. *The First American Constitutions: Republican Ideology and the Making of the State Constitutions in the Revolutionary Era.* Chapel Hill: University of North Carolina Press, 1980.

Brennan, William J., Jr. "State Constitutions and the Protection of Individual Rights," *Harvard Law Review* 90 (1977): 489–504.

Connor, George E., and Christopher W. Hammons, eds. *The Constitutionalism of American States.* Columbia: University of Missouri Press, 2008.

Dinan, John J. *The American State Constitutional Tradition.* Lawrence: University Press of Kansas, 2006.

Elazar, Daniel J. "The Principles and Traditions Underlying State Constitutions." *Publius: The Journal of Federalism* 12 (1982): 11–25.

Friedman, Lawrence M. "State Constitutions in Historical Perspective." *Annals of the American Academy of Political and Social Science* 496 (1988): 33–42.

Fritz, Christian G. "Rethinking the American Constitutional Tradition: National Dimensions in the Formation of State Constitutions." *Rutgers Law Journal* 26 (Summer 1995): 969–992.

Gardner, James A. *Interpreting State Constitutions: A Jurisprudence of Function in a Federal System.* Chicago: University of Chicago Press, 2005.

Gardner, James A., and Jim Rossi, eds. *New Frontiers of State Constitutional Law: Dual Enforcement of Norms.* New York: Oxford University Press, 2011.

Hall, Kermit L. "The Irony of the Federal Constitution's Genius: State Constitutional Development." In *The Constitution and American Political Development: An Institutional Perspective,* ed. Peter F. Nardulli. Urbana: University of Illinois Press, 1992.

Kincaid, John. "State Constitutions in the Federal System." *Annals of the American Academy of Political and Social Science* 496 (1988): 12–22.

Levinson, Sanford. *Framed: American's 51 Constitutions and the Crisis of Governance.* New York: Oxford University Press, 2012.

Lutz, Donald S. "The Purposes of American State Constitutions." *Publius: The Journal of Federalism* 12 (1982): 27–44.

Sturm, Albert L. *Thirty Years of State Constitution-Making, 1938–1968.* New York: National Municipal League, 1970.

Tarr, G. Alan, ed. *Constitutional Politics in the States: Contemporary Controversies and Historical Patterns.* Westport, CT: Greenwood Press, 1996.

Tarr, G. Alan. *Understanding State Constitutions.* Princeton, NJ: Princeton University Press, 1998.

Tarr, G. Alan, and Robert F. Williams. "Foreword: Getting from Here to There: Twenty-first Century Mechanisms and Opportunities in State Constitutional Reform." *Rutgers Law Journal* 36 (2005): 1075–1124.

Tarr, G. Alan, Robert F. Williams, and Frank P. Grad, eds. *State Constitutions for the Twenty-first Century.* 3 vols. Albany: State University of New York Press, 2006.

Williams, Robert F. *The Law of American State Constitutions.* New York: Oxford University Press, 2009.

Chapter 3

Geography, Political Culture, and American Politics

James G. Gimpel

In July 2007, U.S. senator David Vitter, R-La., a self-identified conservative, was discovered to be a client of a Washington-area prostitution service. Under threat of being exposed by *Hustler* magazine, he first issued a statement and then organized a news conference where, appearing with his wife, he admitted to using the service, eventually acknowledging his commission of "serious sins." He refused to resign, and after just a few weeks Louisiana voters appeared quite ready to move on. In 2010, when he came up for reelection, he not only won the Republican primary, but won the general election comfortably, both against credible opponents. Charlie Melancon, a veteran House member and Vitter's Democratic opponent in the fall, had made honesty and integrity a cornerstone of his campaign.

In February 2008, just slightly over a year into his term, New York governor Elliott Spitzer was discovered to have regularly hired a New York–area prostitution service during his time as the state's attorney general and then as governor. Although a federal corruption investigation was underway, Spitzer was not found guilty of anything and no criminal charges were yet pending. Nevertheless, at a press conference on March 10, Spitzer also appeared with his wife, admitted to hiring prostitutes, apologized for his behavior, and insisted it was a "private matter." He announced his resignation from the governor's office two days later under the threat of impeachment by the New York General Assembly.

Although finer details of the cases are different, both posed a similar irony. Just as Vitter had spent a career trumpeting his commitment to family values conservatism, Spitzer had made headlines and furthered his career by rooting out corruption. The question is, Why did Spitzer face so much pressure to resign, while in Louisiana the public greeted the Vitter scandal with a wink? When news of the Spitzer resignation broke, some insisted that Vitter also do the honorable thing and resign. But in the end, the outcomes for the two politicians could hardly have been more different. Public indignation for hiring prostitutes is apparently a local matter shaped as much by political culture as by the political and institutional circumstances surrounding the two cases.

Differences in what people expect of government, and of politicians, cause very different public reactions to similar scandalous circumstances. Vitter and Spitzer are considered by many to inhabit very different political cultures. While it would be a stretch to say that Louisianans tolerate corruption in their politicians, the state does have a legacy of venality and political malfeasance among its elected officials that other states would be hard-pressed to match. Accordingly, the state's residents have been said to accept corruption as inevitable, and be faster to forgive it than citizens elsewhere.[1] Time after time, polling reveals that the residents of one locale can be exposed to the same circumstances and evidence as those in another, but the two groups will reach very different conclusions. The two groups' prior learning or acculturation is usually part of the explanation.

The study of politics and culture has not been as popular in research on American politics as in the study of comparative politics, probably because sensitivity to the subject is dampened by the focus on a single country. Cultural differences stand out more when studying multiple nations with very different histories. Social scientists developing cultural theories have not helped to advance the study of political culture by proliferating cloudy and inaccessible concepts of just what it is. Sometimes the term *culture* is not even defined, and readers are left to their own (variable) interpretations of what it means.[2] Sometimes culture is thought to mean simply explanations of political life that are "noneconomic," as in any explanation for behavior that is not economic must be cultural in origin. This is wrong if economic cognition and valuation are themselves subject to cultural forces.

As a field, political science has drawn increasingly from social-psychological understandings of culture. Following the classic example of Gabriel Almond and Sidney Verba, culture in research about U.S. politics is usually thought to be subject to investigation through the study of

In the photo on the left, New York governor Elliot Spitzer stands with his wife, Silda, while announcing his resignation at a press conference at his executive office in New York, New York, on March 12, 2008, following allegations that he was linked to a prostitution ring. In the photo on the right, U.S. senator David Vitter (R-LA) bows his head as he makes a statement with his wife, Wendy, during a news conference explaining his former involvement with prostitutes in Metairie, Louisiana, July 16, 2007. Despite similarities in the scandals, the political climate and culture surrounding each contributed to different outcomes: Spitzer resigned under threat of impeachment, whereas Vitter went back to work after apologizing for the scandal.

SOURCES: JUSTIN LANE/EPA/Newscom; REUTERS/Lee Celano.

attitudes and behavior. In this framework, a group's culture is its collection of behavioral norms and cognitions that are embraced within the group, but are not shared by other groups. A definition emerging out of the field of social psychology characterizes culture as "the collective programming of the mind, which distinguishes the members of one human group from another."[3] Cultural rules hold groups together, providing some minimum level of order that permits them to survive.

Cultures are not permanent, but they are entrenched by force of habit, intergenerationally transmitted through child-rearing and socialization, and endure for long periods. Social interaction is critical to the formation and maintenance of culture. Cultural conventions are taught by elders to offspring, old-timers to newcomers, sometimes explicitly and other times through unspoken means through observation and imitation of everyday practices.[4] Such instruction offers guidance and regulation to interpreting an otherwise disorganized experience, enables communication about that experience, and establishes continuity or tradition in meaning.

Throughout the previous research in the field of social psychology, several dimensions of culture are commonly identified.[5] While the precise terminology affixed to each one may differ, the key cultural attributes along which groups are thought to vary are these:

1. Individualism or collectivism—the extent to which the members belong to groups or are expected to take care of themselves without group support.
2. Assertiveness and advancement—the extent to which the members value competition, achievement, and performance over social solidarity and care for the disadvantaged.
3. Long-term orientation—the extent to which the members can delay gratification, save, persevere, and sacrifice in pursuit of a greater benefit to come at some indefinite future time.
4. Acceptance of hierarchy—the extent to which the members expect the decision-making power and influence in an organization or a political system to be unequal.
5. Uncertainty avoidance—the extent to which members require conformity to rules or are comfortable with new, surprising, or unusual situations. Openness to new experiences indicates a tolerance for uncertainty that adherence to tradition does not.

At least three of the five cultural dimensions described above have clear and direct relevance for politics: acceptance of hierarchy, rule-following to minimize uncertainty, and individualism. Two others, long-term orientation and assertiveness, certainly inform values that could be the source of variation in opinion about many contemporary policy issues. Individualism, as contrasted with collectivism, has received most of the attention in both psychology and political science, and is considered by many to be a dominant national trait in the United States, but there is probably considerable diversity across groups and individuals within the population on each of these cultural qualities.

POLITICAL CULTURE IN STATE POLITICS RESEARCH

Viewpoints about government's role in the economy, or as provider of a social safety net, are theorized to be derived from core cultural values, including basic religious and economic teachings that condition habits of mind with regard to work, merit, delayed gratification, self-efficacy, luck, risk tolerance, and self-reliance. Surely not all cultural teachings have implications for political life—which ones directly cause the variation in opinion and policy detected by research is certainly arguable. Probably in most cases the role of cultural beliefs on political preference is indirect, and not easily subject to experimental assessment.

Within the subfield of state politics research, Daniel J. Elazar's three-dimensional conception of political culture often comes to mind when the subject arises.[6] In this mainly history-based formulation, parts of the nation differ in the extent to which local populations adhere to individualist, moralist, or traditionalist conceptions of what government ought to do. Individualistic cultures desire government to focus on the basics: serving private concerns and enabling the marketplace, but otherwise not intervening. Moralistic cultures, on the other hand, believe the government has a positive role to play in resolving problems and creating a good society; politics is issue oriented, and involvement in politics is encouraged as an aspect of good citizenship. Traditionalistic cultures are accepting of hierarchy and consider government to have a role only within a well-defined sphere of activity; government is oriented not toward taking on new problems in response to citizen demands, but serves a custodial role aimed at preservation of existing institutional arrangements.

Although possessing an intuitive plausibility, the Elazar formulation and its variants have not met with lasting acceptance inside political science, much less outside the field.[7] Within political science, critics pointed out that that this framework was impressionistic, speculative, and not founded on any rigorous or clearly replicable statistical research. Others complained that it is erroneously used to characterize entire states even though most states are internally heterogeneous, and some do not seem to have a dominant culture. When attempting to capture cultural variation internal to states, the results often looked too much like guesswork, and the theoretical and empirical basis of categorization seemed entirely too extemporized. Sometimes the classification did not fit well with important criterion variables, such as religious group membership, which called into question its validity. The typology also failed to account for rapid population changes occurring in the late twentieth century in many parts of the southern and western United States that were likely to recast the culture of localities, regions, and even entire states. Relatedly, the Elazar typology did not take into account the cultures of nonwhite racial and non-European ancestry groups, both of which have become more important in shaping the politics of states and localities over the last forty years.[8]

Like culture concepts in other subfields of political science, and in other social sciences, the Elazar framework was critiqued as being naively circular, relying on observable characteristics to define culture but then suggesting that culture causes these characteristics. If the central claim is that culture explains attitudes and behavior, but then that variation in attitudes and behavior is used to define those same cultural differences, we have formulated a tautology by saying that something explains itself. Rather, the goal should be to extract some set of values emanating from culture (e.g., frugality, moral traditionalism) and use them to explain political opinions (e.g., views of the national debt, judgments about a politician's adultery), thereby tracing political views to their nonpolitical cultural roots.

Given the myriad problems with the Elazar scheme, by the 1990s, many scholars had turned away from the study of state political culture, though the Elazar typology is occasionally present in some recent studies. Scholars in the state politics and electoral studies subfields replaced the study of culture with studies of variation in state political ideology. With the development and increasing availability of a number of very large-scale surveys ($N \geq 30{,}000$) of the national electorate containing relevant instrumentation, it is now possible to develop a more comprehensive survey-based approach to understanding political culture. Of course, the difficult aspect is to define the "relevant instrumentation." Values that are commonly thought to be "core" or foundational to the opinions of citizens often turn out to be not present in anything like the uniformity one would expect to correspond to common conceptions of culture. Other times they might be present, but with so much qualification and nuance that they hardly seem like much of an attitude constraint, contrary to theoretical understandings of how culture is supposed to inform opinion.

Much of the challenge lies in the way in which accepted cultural concepts can run contrary to one another and in specific circumstances generate attitude conflict, which is then balanced-off in complex ways by individual citizens as they come to judgment. I may find a politician's behavior to be morally outrageous, but if I am acculturated to think of myself as politically inefficacious, or the functions of government as largely independent of citizen input, I may shrug off the offense, concluding, "That's just the way politicians are." This is how a predisposition like moral conservatism could exist alongside an accommodating reaction to a politician hiring a prostitute. A culture can possess both an element of traditional morality, resulting from the cultural impulse to avoid uncertainty, and an acceptance of hierarchy, downplaying citizen voice in public affairs. A passive reaction to something that is morally offensive can be the result of what citizens have come to believe about voice and government unresponsiveness. Such beliefs may be countered or changed, but that may require the departure from one cultural community and exposure to another, with an opportunity for resocialization—the learning of new values. New acculturation does happen, but often old cultural values persist to shape thinking even after they have supposedly been rejected.

POLITICAL CULTURE AND GEOGRAPHY

Social interaction is central to the establishment and maintenance of cultures. What this means is that geography plays an important role in any theoretical or empirical approach to cross-cultural research. Communication of norms and meanings is required, even if the communication is not always verbal. Social influence is also important, as some norms and meanings take precedence over others, leading to the emergence of dominant and widely held beliefs.

Communication and social influence, in turn, require spatial proximity. Individuals occupy predictable geographic spaces where they live out their lives. This stability of location ensures a regular pattern of social interaction with others living nearby. The diffusion of cultural norms is limited by distance because even in the Internet age social interaction is similarly limited. Culture therefore has a geography, and should be identifiable at the scale at which group-level regularities emerge.[9] Through repeated social interaction, dominant values arise on the basis of their persuasive power, resulting in a spatial clustering of shared viewpoints. This is why cultures can typically be mapped at some scale of observation, with smaller scales (city, neighborhood, workplace, household) usually displaying greater homogeneity. Social scientists can observe cultural variation across the national landscape within various social strata (ethnic, religious, economic). Of course, just because a location (country, state, city) might exhibit a greater tolerance for hierarchy than other places on the map does not mean that every individual at that location will express such tolerance. Cultural measures at the community or statewide level are often simply averages or general tendencies, and individuals living within them will exhibit variation.

While cultures can be said to have geographic contours, U.S. states are not considered to be the geographic scale at which political cultures form; nor are they the units at which opinion variation associated with culture is most evident. Even so, states are still sometimes described as having dominant political cultures that are the source of differences in public opinion, political organization, and policy output.[10]

Consider the fact that state boundaries define the groups and interests that must contend for power in the state capital. Adjusting a boundary might reconfigure those interests entirely, incorporating a large city that lies just outside existing lines, or excluding an area that presently serves as a major commercial or industrial powerhouse. Although a border is rarely noticed by the residents on both sides who traffic across it on a daily basis, residents still live different lives because of that border. On one side they may be subject to a state income tax, while on the other they might pay no income tax, but a higher sales tax. In one state, high school students may have the opportunity to attend a top-ten public university at very low tuition rates, while youth living across the border just a half-mile away have far less attractive options for college. Welfare benefits may vary across the two states, as well as the availability of branch banking and specific types of consumer credit. Living here as opposed to across the border may determine whether my state is battled for in a presidential election, or virtually ignored. Raised on one side of a border, one becomes familiar with a set of governing authorities, political names, and regular election practices that may be very different just a short distance away. State boundaries have the effect of unifying those living within the state's borders by a long list of legal traditions, policies, common experiences, and understandings—a development often described as state political culture.

POLITICAL CULTURE AND PERSONALITY

Recent developments in psychology have renewed interest in the linkage between cultural variation across the country and personality traits.[11] Culture is thought to be one of the environmental influences that shape personality, although the causal influence is thought to go both ways: from culture as a force that conditions the expression of personality traits, and from the expression of personality traits to the reinforcement of culture.

Some of the most intriguing research suggests an effect of personality orientations on the formation of politically and socially homogeneous communities. The central idea is that people with similar personalities often gravitate to the same locations to the extent that social and economic freedoms allow. Related research shows that people desire to create social and physical environments for themselves in which they can comfortably express themselves, without encountering regular conflict.[12] With time, such selectively migratory behavior produces pockets of shared values that both reflect and reproduce local cultures. Through socialization, particular personality traits are accentuated while others are muted, leading to an uneven geographic distribution of particular population characteristics and traits. Recent research finds support for the idea that people who share the personality trait of openness to diversity are found concentrated on parts of the West Coast where one can find the closely associated behaviors of reading books, attending art exhibits, going to the library, and expressing interest in other cultures. Other personality traits are dominant in other regions of the country: extraversion is especially high in the Midwest, for example.

Moreover, some personality traits have been associated with political preference: conscientiousness is associated with Republican voting, openness with Democratic voting.[13] Personality traits may also be associated with social capital—the high level of extraversion and lower level of conscientious in some areas seems associated with higher levels of social capital. Political psychologists have linked liberal and conservative political orientations to the personality traits of openness and conscientiousness.[14] Openness is associated with tolerant attitudes on same-sex marriage, marijuana use, and abortion. Conscientiousness, on the other hand, is related to religiosity and lower crime rates. Other studies have linked personality traits to interest in politics, political discussion, and political media consumption.[15] Personality seems to be an intervening variable positioned between culture and many political outcomes important to political scientists.

ECONOMIC RATIONALITY AND POLITICAL CULTURE

Economic or rational choice theories of political decision making are usually dismissive of cultural explanations, emphasizing the role of strategic calculation in opinion formation and behavior. Following rational choice theory, an assumption of much of political science is that the judgment and opinion processes political scientists study do not vary across space and time: individuals, wherever or whenever they are found, act freely and in their self-interest. By dismissing culture, however, such theories have a hard time accounting for aspects of politics that are undeniably important, such as the persistence of particular political orientations for long periods of time, well after the "self-interest-based" disputes and circumstances that originally shaped those beliefs have faded from the scene. Also problematic without some account of culture is explaining the frequent circumstances in politics in which both voters and political elites make choices directly contrary to their narrow self-interest.

Even in the realm of basic economic choice, acculturation seems to taint evaluations and behavior. Within income strata, and accounting for other clear-cut indicators of self-interest, some adults have bank accounts and others do not. Some save more for retirement and some risk more in the stock market. Many forms of expenditure for leisure, including gambling, seem to be the product of acculturation. Gambling is popular and encouraged by advertising within certain social contexts, discouraged and even punished within others. Attitudes toward borrowing and indebtedness are shaped by beliefs anchored in culture, and not by any universal definition of utility maximization. For some populations, borrowing has been found to be independent of straightforward economic considerations such as interest rates and related financing costs.[16] The use of money itself is shaped by normative and cultural constraints.[17] And we have already noted that attitudes toward welfare use and the welfare system are strongly acculturated.

The deployment of cultural concepts in political science research is not to deny that politics involves a measure of strategic choice, only that strategic calculations—such as the decision to resign from office or wait out the storm following a scandal—are informed by cultural considerations. For political scientists, this theoretical posture suggests that cultural and rational choice explanations can be complementary rather than mutually exclusive.[18]

POLITICALLY RELEVANT CULTURAL FORCES IN THE UNITED STATES

While not all cultural variation is relevant to political life in the United States, three traits would appear to be inarguably central to politics and public opinion: ethnic and racial diversity, religious observance, and variations in economic organization and consumption—including patterns of self-employment and views of thrift and debt. While these particular notions do not exhaust the various ways in which culture might find its way into politics, these are definable in sufficiently narrow terms to permit testable hypotheses about their impact on public opinion and other political outcomes.

Ethnic and racial diversity has been advanced as the main aspect of cultural variation across states, explaining many political and policy outcomes.[19] Scholars have theorized that white responses to black, Latino, and other ethnic populations are much of what defines politics in ethnically and racially mixed states. A more competitive type of pluralism emerges in heterogeneous locations compared with more homogeneous ones, perpetuating a more individualistic political culture in diverse states.

Dominant cultural traditions within ethnic and racial groups can have political implications.[20] For example, some immigrant groups from Asia and Latin America may be less participatory not just because many are new to the United States, but because they carry with them collectivist orientations to family and community that run contrary to a society that has long placed an emphasis on individual rights and self-assertion. Their political power lags well behind their population size, and this is not solely due to immigration status. Women in many traditional cultures have been disempowered politically and economically through patriarchal social systems. Groups with more recent immigrant histories may prove difficult to organize politically as a bloc or identity group because doing so might mean setting aside long-standing traditions and arrangements judged to be more important than any benefits of political action.

The institution of religion and exposure to religious teaching are important sources of political learning. Religion is a cultural resource that provides clear moral guidance and inculcates economic values such as hard work, frugality, and conservation. Religion has long been the major impetus for charitable work on behalf of the poor and needy. Political movements anchored in religious teaching are not just found on the right; religion has also been the guiding force behind the expansion of civil rights, opposition to the Vietnam War and more recent wars, the delivery of medical assistance to African countries facing the AIDs crisis, and ending genocide and ethnic cleansing in Sudan and other nations. To be sure, religious traditions, and denominations within them, do differ in the politically relevant doctrines they emphasize. Some churches are more politicized than others, but commonly the tendency for a church to be silent about politics is the consequence of a strong congregational preference to affirm conventional views.

With regular attendance at religious services declining steadily since the 1970s, and the percentage of those reporting that they "never attend" services on a corresponding rise, religious belief is not a force for cultural consensus the way it might have been in the past.[21] Religious diversity, along with the rise of secularism, has intensified disagreement over religion's role in political life. The greater variation in the extent of exposure to religious teaching across the population has contributed directly to the intensified political polarization of the polity. Recent research has shown that Evangelical Christians are apparently threatened by the presence of secular opposition within their communities, and are even more highly politicized in such settings.[22] Since religion remains an influence in the backgrounds of some, but has no influence at all in the personal history of a growing number of others, a gaping divide is now present on cultural issues such as abortion, women's rights, prayer in school, gay rights, and sex education.[23]

Finally, as noted above, within the economy there are alternative cultures of economic enterprise and consumption that shape partisanship and political choice. The country has always had conservationist, anticonsumption elements present in its culture. These arise from religious impulses hostile to materialism, greed, gluttony, and worldliness. Christian prudence, self-control, and modesty are anchored in Puritanism but remain a theme in many churches today, including some that sponsor ongoing financial education programs that discourage use of consumer credit and encourage saving. In more recent decades, the environmental movement has been a highly visible cultural force behind the value of thrift and opposition to conspicuous consumerism. Saving is a behavior that appears to depend on the culturally rooted desire to minimize uncertainty, but it also requires the capacity to delay gratification—another trait thought to be culturally transmitted. Indebtedness, once anathema to most citizens, seems to be related to the high debts of neighbors and accompanying calculations that credit is locally acceptable and routine, suggesting that cultures tolerant toward debt have taken firm root.

Cultural inheritance also produces attitudes toward borrowing, lending, and indebtedness that have only recently been observable, given a prolonged period of economic downturn. Comparative politics and cross-cultural research have long suggested that shared values are required for pro-business activities and sustained

Interfaith leaders held a press conference at the Colorado Capitol on March 20, 2003, asking that the Colorado legislature not pass HB-1128 that would put "In God We Trust" in public schools. Although school prayer can be a divisive political issue, Christian, Jewish, and Muslim religious leaders took part in this press conference. After the press conference then–House representative Alice Borodkin (D-Denver), left, who was also against HB-1128, spoke with Mohammed Jodeh (center) from the Colorado Muslim Society and Bradley A. Levin, chair of the Board of Directors, Anti-Defamation League–Mountain States Region (right). Representative Borodkin left the House floor every morning when the opening prayer was said in silent protest over the mixing of church and state.

SOURCE: Lyn Alweis/*The Denver Post* via Getty Images.

economic growth, trust being prominent among them. Trust is the basis for economic transactions, as many deals are struck simply with a handshake. Not surprisingly, trust is associated with higher levels of entrepreneurship.[24]

Certainly, one economic preference that has been studied in cultural terms is public opinion about social welfare spending and redistributive policy.[25] Very plausibly, locales that are more tolerant of inequality embrace individualistic attitudes about upward mobility and self-reliance, whereas those that demand redistribution adhere to a more collectivist and egalitarian outlook. Even locations with the same level of inequality may react disparately because of different value judgments they have come to accept. Notions of economic interest are themselves informed by what a group considers morally imperative. And within the institution of the economy, there are cultural guidelines for what counts as welfare.

A CONTEMPORARY GEOGRAPHY OF PARTISANSHIP AND POLITICAL CULTURE

To what extent do we find political preferences corresponding with these three aspects of culture: race and ethnicity, religion, and employment structure? To address this question from a political cultural standpoint, one might begin by examining the nation's geography, using counties as units of analysis.

First, a caveat: county-level data are not always optimal in scale for examining the nationwide distribution of culture or opinion. The examination of smaller units of analysis, such as precincts or zip codes, will exhibit different patterns than what the 3,140 U.S. counties reveal. But counties do prove to be convenient in the sense that many important data elements are reported at the county level. Although the average resident does not interact with the entire population of his or her county, usually this same resident's behavior is not confined to a single neighborhood or city within his or her county, either. Routine travel distance does vary by income, location, and age, but nationwide mean daily travel distances ranged from a low of nine to a high of thirty-three miles at various points along the age distribution, according to one household transportation survey.[26] For those of prime working age, between ages twenty-five and sixty-four, travel averaged about thirty-three miles per day, exposing most residents to social forces lying well outside their neighborhoods.

Partisan Support in Presidential Voting

Consider first the geographic distribution of partisanship as gauged by the average percentage of the Democratic vote for president in the 2000, 2004, and 2008 elections. A map of the county-level patterns is presented in Figure 3.1, showing lighter shading for Democratic counties and darker shades for Republican counties. Lighter shades cover many urban locations on the map, and are prominent throughout the Upper Midwest and Northeast. Republican percentages are more common in counties throughout the southern and Plains states, including many mid-sized cities, small towns, and rural areas. Without question, the partisan geography of the nation is chiefly an urban versus rural one, with greater variation within states than across states. These county maps do not display population size. The very darkest counties running from the Texas Panhandle to the Canadian border include some of the most rural in the nation, and many of them are depopulating. When viewing maps such as these, it is important to remember that a single urban county will contain as many voters as thirty or more red counties in Kansas and Oklahoma.

The locations in the intermediate gray-colored shading in Figure 3.1 are important because they are the most competitive counties—those where the vote for both parties has hovered between 45 and 55 percent since the 2000 election. The Upper Midwest, including Illinois, Iowa, Michigan, Minnesota, and Wisconsin, appear to have a lot of cities and towns that are about equally divided, but there are also some locations in the swing states of Florida, North Carolina, and Virginia that run about even.

Because standard maps that depict geographic variation along a variable of interest inevitably show where the land is better than they display where the population is concentrated, we have included the centrography of the actual distribution of Republican and Democratic voters (not percentages) in Figure 3.1 as well. Centrographic calculations offer pictures of two aspects of the geographic distribution of a variable: the mean center of the geographic distribution, shown as a point; and the one standard deviation dispersion contour, drawn as an ellipse around the mean center. As in elementary statistics, the standard deviation shows the typical dispersion of the population of interest, and most of that population will lie within the ellipse.

Figure 3.1 indicates that the Republican distribution of the presidential votes over the last three elections is slightly more western and southern than the Democratic distribution, but both lie to the east of the general population distribution (lighter black ellipse). The Democratic vote is pulled laterally more toward both coasts, reflecting the pull of California on the one hand, and the pull of New England on the other. The Republican vote lies more in the middle of the country, and is also more southern in its distribution. Neither of the major parties' grassroots support is as western as the population in general.

The three maps that follow in Figures 3.2 through 3.4 display indicators of several cultural influences with distinctive geographic distributions: ethnic/racial diversity, religion, and self-employment. The basic idea is to compare

FIGURE 3.1 **The Geography of the Presidential Vote, by County, 2000–2008**

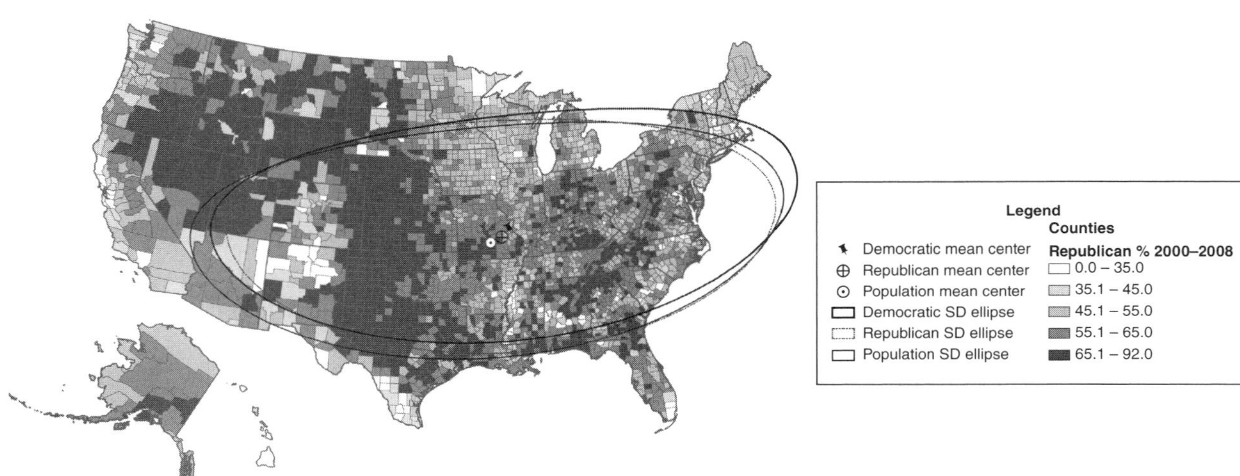

the mapped geography to evaluate the correspondence of the indicators of culture to those of presidential voting in Figure 3.1.

Latino and Black Population Distribution

According to the nationwide 2010 census count, African Americans constitute 13 percent of the population; Latinos, 16.7 percent; Asians, 5 percent; and Native Americans, 1.2 percent. Latino is not a racial classification, as 63 percent report that they are white, and there is some argument about how well they cohere as a political bloc. Latinos vary culturally by nation of ancestry, but working in favor of cultural coherence is a common language—Spanish—and a religious background in Catholicism.

Figure 3.2 displays with shading the percentage of the nonwhite population within the nation's counties. Notably, the nonwhite population is southern in terms of county concentrations. To be sure, there are large black and Latino populations in northern metro areas, which is why the centrographic images are important.

The mean center markers and ellipses in Figure 3.2 show that the two largest minority populations have markedly different geographic distributions from each other, and from the general population. Specifically, the black population is concentrated in the Southeast, and the mean center of its population is actually in Tennessee (near Nashville). The Latino population is geographically centered well to the west, in Oklahoma. When compared with that of African Americans, Latino geography is far more dispersed, but is also more southern, pulled downward toward the nation's southern border, and more western, influenced by the historically large Latino populations in Arizona, California, and New Mexico (see Figure 3.2).

Religious Population Distribution

Evangelical Christians are a politically active religious group that is often covered in the news. Consisting of churches whose biblically literal theology has mixed with a conservative brand of politics, members have come to be known as part of the Republican Party coalition, though there are important exceptions. While large Evangelical churches can be found in every state, they do have a particular geographic distribution, with especially high concentrations of parishioners in southern and Border South counties, as shown in Figure 3.3. The mean center of their presence nationally lies to the south of the general population distribution (approximately in northern Arkansas). Their dispersion across the country shows them to be a weaker presence in the western and northwestern states relative to the general population.

The comparison of the Evangelical distribution to the population of Mainline adherents is instructive. Mainliners (e.g., American Baptists, Episcopalians, Methodists, and United Presbyterians) are much more northern and even more eastern in their geographic distribution than Evangelicals. Their geographic center of concentration lies well to the east of the center of population for the entire nation (see Figure 3.3). Mainline churches have experienced a significant decline in membership over the course of the last fifty years, while Evangelicals have attracted a much larger share of the religious population. From the maps, it would appear that Evangelicals have also made far more gains in the western United States than Mainline denominations have.

FIGURE 3.2 **The Geography of the White and Nonwhite Population, by County, 2010**

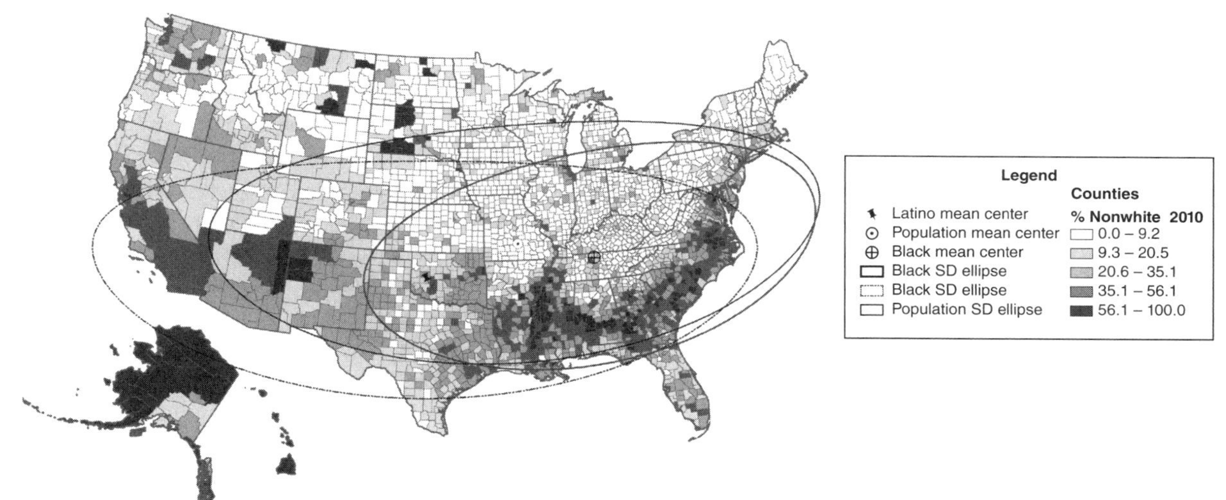

FIGURE 3.3 **The Geography of the Evangelical and Mainline Christian Population, by County, 2010**

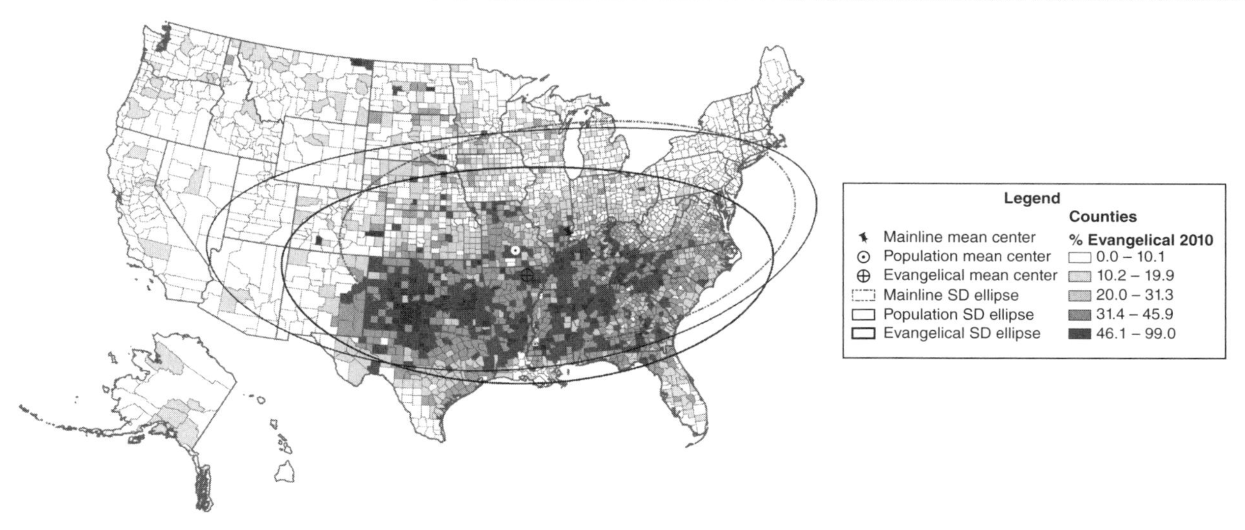

Variability in the Evangelical concentration across locations turns out to greatly influence their partisan leaning. Counties in the highest quintile (20 percent) in terms of their percentage of Evangelical adherents awarded an average of just 32 percent of their vote to Barack Obama in 2008, compared with 49 percent in the lowest quintile—a 17 percentage point gap. At the individual level, surveys suggest that the partisan gap between Evangelicals and others is even wider than these county data show.

Economic Culture: Self-Employment

Approximately 10 percent of the U.S. population is self-employed, in some kind of private business enterprise. Figure 3.4 exhibits the concentration and geographic distribution of this intriguing aspect of economic culture. Self-employment is most often associated with small-family farming, but only about 5 percent of self-employment is in agriculture. Owner operators are an important part of the occupational structure in small and mid-sized towns in myriad service businesses such as hotels, motels, restaurants, and dry-cleaners; automotive repair, plumbing, and other trades; accountants, attorneys, physicians, and dentists in private practice; and many "main street" enterprises engaged in retail and wholesale trade. Self-employment is to be contrasted with large corporate employers in vertically integrated sectors such as manufacturing or financial services, and also with government and military employment.

As Figure 3.4 reveals, the areas where self-employment is a dominant force in the local economy include locations dotting the Northern Plains and Mountain West. These are lightly populated cities and towns, generally distant from major metropolitan centers, commonly lying off interstate highways. Corporate culture and labor-management issues associated with manufacturing are less familiar. Notably, this region of high entrepreneurship does not correspond to the previous maps showing high concentrations of Evangelical adherence, or the regional foci of the Latino and black populations. Self-employed people who are also Evangelical, black, and Latino most certainly exist in large numbers, but in terms of their geographic concentration they occupy different areas of the country. The mean center of self-employment lies well to the north of the mean center of the population (see Figure 3.4). The dispersion of the distribution seems to rotate around a Northwest-Southeast axis, avoiding the old commercial center of the country—New England—but also the relatively new and fast-growing Southwest. Examining the distribution of nonagricultural self-employment proves to be very similar, although the distribution is not quite as stretched toward the rural reaches of the Northwest.

Self-employment by county has an undeniable impact on the vote for president, even if the agriculture portion of self-employment is removed. Counties in the highest quintile (20 percent) of nonagricultural self-employment cast an average of 39 percent of their votes for Obama in 2008, compared with 46 percent for those counties in the lowest quintile. These 7 percentage points of difference may seem modest, but they hold up well even after accounting for differences in income across locations. If the desire to be self-employed emanates from possessing the cultural trait of individualism, as many think it does, then individualism appears to steer political preference toward the Republican Party at the broad, regional level. Chances are good that if we examine these relationships at a scale below the county, they will be even stronger.

Other economic indicators one might map are highly related to self-employment, including indebtedness, and this shows that there is a close relationship between the geography of self-employment and related indicators of self-reliance, such as saving money and avoiding debt. In regional terms, self-reliance seems to be more closely related to the type of employment or chosen occupation than it does religion, though it also has roots in religious teaching, as discussed above. Even so, we still do not see a substantial intersection between Evangelical adherence and self-employment in the geography of the nation. The individualistic impulse toward self-reliance that informs contemporary Republican Party politics apparently has a different regional basis than the moralistic religious

FIGURE 3.4 **The Geography of Self-Employment, by County, 2010**

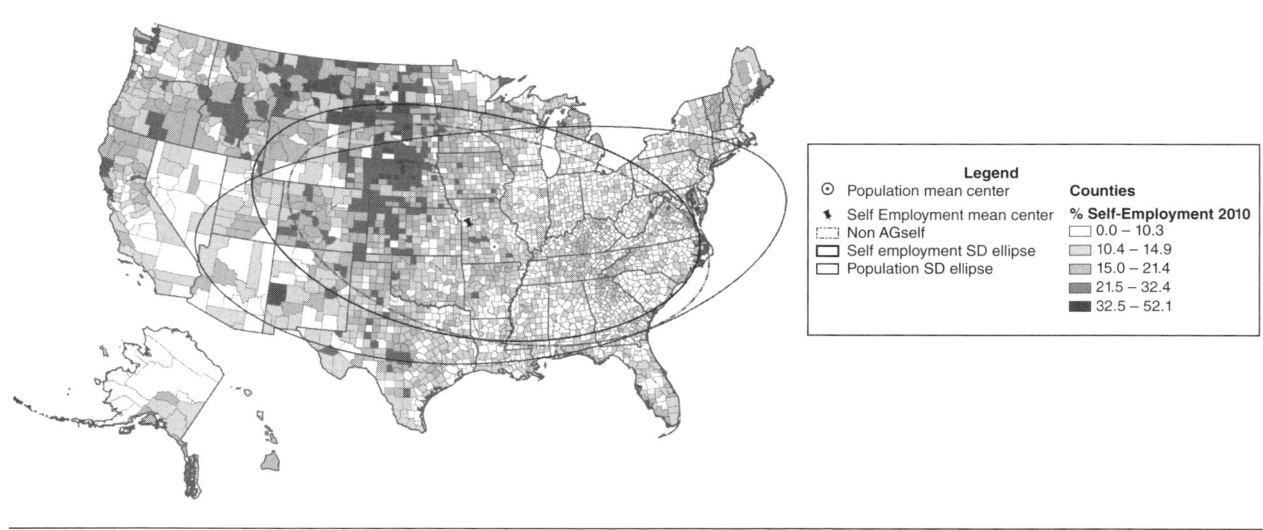

impulse springing forth predominantly from the southern and Border South states.

ADVICE FOR SCHOLARSHIP

Cultural measures are not relevant to every study in the subfield of state politics. But for those students who want to build cultural indicators into their empirical models of political and policy, outcomes need to start from a sound theoretical foundation. At the present time, that foundation is largely to be located outside the field, in the work of social psychologists who discuss the origin of values in culture. Eventually more of this research will be imported into political science, as it has always been a borrowing field. Given the long history of connection between psychology and political science, there should be no trepidation about going right to the primary sources. There is nothing inaccessible or mysterious about this body of work.

Fortunately, the availability of survey instrumentation and other data elements for measuring multifaceted constructs has increased immensely since the 1960s and 1970s, and it improves with every passing year. Perhaps not everything about political science research can be said to have improved over the decades, but data and measures certainly have. Singular, state-level indicators of cultural concepts only make sense if states are relatively homogeneous in their cultural traits. Most of the time, states are not homogeneous, in which case singular summary indicators are mostly misleading and likely to produce inaccurate statistical generalizations. Multiple indicators that more aptly capture local, internal variation in state cultures are more defensible. Statistical approaches aimed at teasing out latent variables or underlying structures will probably prove useful if samples are sufficiently large. These efforts may be anchored either in individual surveys or in nonsurvey data indicative of cultural elements such as religious belief, ethnicity, economic organization, and consumption habits.

CONCLUSION

Political cultural traits have a geographic distribution, and this chapter shows that mapping them can inform understandings of partisanship and American political behavior. Whether the point of analysis is to capture religious traditions, racial groups, or some fundamental aspect of economic activity, birds of a feather usually flock together, creating and sustaining local habits of thought and opinion that can last for generations. Cultures thereby inform local socialization patterns, having an impact on individuals quite independent of their narrowly conceived calculations of individual self-interest. Cultural traits also overlap, and sometimes compete for influence in the minds of individuals, creating attitudinal ambivalence that appears on the surface like contradiction, but rather suggests nuance.

Following pathways cut by the field of psychology, cultural orientations are increasingly measured at the individual level. Over the last twenty years, measures of cultural concepts have become sharper, and more survey data are available for evaluating the impact of cultural predispositions on political and economic behavior. Individualism and collectivism, achievement orientation, and acceptance of hierarchy are captured by questionnaire items that gauge the acceptance and expression of particular cultural traits. These measures can then be linked, perhaps causally, to other observed attitudes and behaviors of interest, showing that cultures push individuals in particular directions, in spite of individual differences, say, in income, occupation, or short-term self-interest.

An emerging body of scholarship is showing that personality and culture are linked in interesting and reciprocal ways, with shared personalities collecting in particular locations at which they find compatible social support. After all, people are usually not drawn (for very long) to cultural settings that prove to be alien or hostile. Social groups at these locations, in turn, reward compliant behavior, reinforcing the norms that drew them to the location in the first place. For instance, openness to new experiences is a personality trait that takes cultural form in bohemian neighborhoods in large cities throughout the United States, and particularly the West Coast.

Future work by political scientists studying American politics will carry us beyond research on the dominant cultural dimension of individualism and collectivism, to examine other sociopolitically relevant foundations of opinions and behavior. Study of political institutions is also called for, as particular legislative bodies, political offices, and bureaucracies have been said to operate with differing cultural norms in place. Organizational attributes such as decision-making hierarchy, participation, and collegiality are influenced by culture. First, however, many of the cultural theories currently extant in psychology must be adapted for these worthwhile purposes. This work is presently some distance off, but it promises a rewarding path of discovery for future scholars.

NOTES

1. Wayne Parent, *Inside the Carnival: Unmasking Louisiana Politics* (Baton Rouge: Louisiana State University Press, 2004); Michael L. Kurtz and Morgan D. Peoples, *Earl K. Long: The Saga of Uncle Earl and Louisiana Politics* (Baton Rouge: Louisiana State University Press, 1992).

2. Robert S. Erikson, Gerald C. Wright, and John P. McIver, *Statehouse Democracy: Public Opinion and Policy in the American States* (New York: Cambridge University Press, 1993).

3. Geert H. Hofstede, *Culture's Consequences: International Differences in Work-Related Values* (Beverly Hills, CA: Sage, 1980).

4. Daniel J. Elazar, *The American Mosaic: The Impact of Space, Time, and Culture on American Politics* (Boulder, CO: Westview, 1994).

5. I'm borrowing here largely from the work of Hofstede in Geert H. Hofstede, *Cultures and Organizations: Software of the Mind,* 3rd ed. (New York: McGraw-Hill, 2010). See also Hofstede, *Culture's Consequences,* and Harry C. Triandis, *Culture and Social Behavior* (New York: McGraw Hill, 1994); Harry C. Triandis, *Individualism and Collectivism* (Boulder, CO: Westview, 1995); Harry C. Triandis, Roy S. Malpass, and Andrew R. Davidson, "Psychology and Culture," *Annual Review of Psychology* 24 (1973): 355–378.

6. Daniel J. Elazar, *American Federalism: A View from the States,* 3rd ed. (New York: Harper and Row, 1984). See also Elazar, *The American Mosaic.*

7. There are many critics, and only a few will be noted here: Charles A. Johnson, "Political Culture in American States: Elazar's Formulation Examined," *American Journal of Political Science* 20 (1976): 491–509; Joel Lieske, "Regional Subcultures of the United States," *Journal of Politics* 55 (1993): 888–913; Joel Lieske, "American State Cultures: Testing a New Measure and Theory," *Publius: The Journal of Federalism* 42 (2011): 108–133; Peter Nardulli, "Political Subcultures in the American States: An Examination of Elazar's Formulation," *American Politics Quarterly* 18 (1990): 287–315.

8. Rodney E. Hero and Caroline J. Tolbert, "A Racial/Ethnic Diversity Interpretation of Politics and Policy in the States of the U.S.," *American Journal of Political Science* 40 (1996): 851–871.

9. Bibb Latané, "Dynamic Social Impact: The Creation of Culture by Communication," *Journal of Communication* 46 (1996): 13–25.

10. Jason Kaufman and Matthew Kaliner, "The Re-accomplishment of Place in Twentieth Century Vermont and New Hampshire: History Repeats Itself, Until It Doesn't," *Theory and Society* 40 (2011): 119–154; Tom W. Rice and Alexander F. Sumberg, "Civic Culture and Government Performance in the American States," *Publius: The Journal of Federalism* 27 (1997): 99–114; Erikson et al., *Statehouse Democracy.*

11. Peter J. Rentfrow, "Statewide Differences in Personality: Toward a Psychological Geography of the United States," *The American Psychologist* 65 (2010): 548–558; Peter J. Rentfrow, Sam Gosling, and Jeff Potter, "A Theory of the Emergence, Persistence, and Expression of Geographic Variation in Psychological Characteristics," *Perspectives on Psychological Science* 3 (2010): 339–369; Dana R. Carney, John T. Jost, Samuel D. Gosling, and Jeff Potter, "The Secret Lives of Liberals and Conservatives: Personality Profiles, Interaction Styles, and the Things They Leave Behind," *Political Psychology* 29 (2008): 807–840; Sam Gosling, *Snoop: What Your Stuff Says about You* (New York: Basic Books, 2008).

12. Rentfrow, "Statewide Differences in Personality." See also Harry C. Triandis and Eunkook M. Suh, "Cultural Influences on Personality," *Annual Review of Psychology* 53 (2002): 133–160.

13. Gosling, *Snoop,* 146–148. See also Alan S. Gerber, Gregory A. Huber, David Doherty, Conor M. Dowling, and Shang E. Ha, "Personality and Political Attitudes: Relationships across Issue Domains and Political Contexts," *American Political Science Review* 104 (2010): 111–133; Jeffrey J. Mondak, *Personality and the Foundations of Political Behavior* (Cambridge: Cambridge University Press, 2010); Jeffrey J. Mondak and Katherine D. Halperin, "A Framework for the Study of Personality and Political Behaviour," *British Journal of Political Science* 38 (2008): 335–362.

14. John T. Jost, Christopher M. Federico, and Jamie L Napier, "Political Ideology: Its Structure, Functions, and Elective Affinities," *Annual Review of Psychology* 60 (2009): 307–337.

15. Alan S. Gerber, Gregory A. Huber, David Doherty, and Conor M. Dowling, "Personality Traits and the Consumption of Political Information," *American Politics Research* 39 (2011): 32–84; Alan S. Gerber, Gregory A. Huber, David Doherty, and Conor M. Dowling, "Disagreement and the Avoidance of Political Discussion: Aggregate Relationships and Differences across Personality Traits," *American Journal of Political Science,* forthcoming.

16. Edward C. Lawrence and Gregory Elliehausen, "A Comparative Analysis of Payday Loan Customers," *Contemporary Economic Policy* 26 (2008): 299–316.

17. Simone Polillo, "Money, Moral Authority, and the Politics of Creditworthiness," *American Sociological Review* 76 (2011): 437–464.

18. James Johnson, "How Conceptual Problems Migrate: Rational Choice, Interpretation, and the Hazards of Pluralism," *Annual Review of Political Science* 5 (2002): 223–248.

19. Rodney E. Hero, *Faces of Inequality: Social Diversity in American Politics* (New York: Oxford University Press, 1998); Rodney E. Hero and Robert R. Preuhs, "Immigration and the Evolving American Welfare State: Examining Policies in the U.S. States," *American Journal of Political Science* 51 (2007): 498–517; Rodney E. Hero and Caroline Tolbert, "A Racial/Ethnic Diversity Interpretation of Politics and Policy in the States of the U.S.," *American Journal of Political Science* 40 (1996): 851–871.

20. Lieske, "American State Cultures."

21. Michael Hout and Claude S. Fischer, "Why More Americans Have No Religious Preference: Politics and Generations," *American Sociological Review* 67 (2002): 165–190.

22. David E. Campbell, "Religious 'Threat' in Contemporary Presidential Elections," *Journal of Politics* 68 (2006): 104–115.

23. Geoffrey C. Layman, *The Great Divide* (New York: Columbia University Press, 2001); Paul Dimaggio, John Evans, and Bethany Bryson, "Have Americans' Social Attitudes Become More Polarized?" in *Cultural Wars in American Politics,* ed. R. H. Williams (Chicago: University of Chicago Press, 1996); James Davison Hunter, *Culture Wars* (New York: Basic Books, 1991).

24. Luigi Guiso, Paola Sapienza, and Luigi Zingales, "Does Culture Affect Economic Outcomes?" *Journal of Economic Perspectives* 20 (2006): 23–48.

25. Lawrence M. Mead, "State Political Culture and Welfare Reform," *Policy Studies Journal* 32 (2004): 271–296; Erikson et al., *Statehouse Democracy;* Robert A. Jackson, "Effects of Public Opinion and Political System Characteristics on State Policy Outputs," *Publius: The Journal of Federalism* 22 (1992): 31–46; David R. Morgan and Sheilah S. Watson, "Political Culture, Political System Characteristics, and Public Policies among the American States," *Publius: The Journal of Federalism* 21 (1991): 31–48; Russell L. Hanson, "The 'Content' of Welfare Policy: The States and Aid to Families with Dependent Children," *Journal of Politics* 45 (1983): 771–785; Richard E. Dawson and James A. Robinson, "Inter-Party Competition, Economic Variables, and Welfare Policies in the American States," *Journal of Politics* 25 (1963): 265–289.

26. John Pucher and John L. Renne, "Socioeconomics of Urban Travel: Evidence from the 2001 NHTS," *Transportation Quarterly* 57 (2003): 49–77.

SUGGESTED READING

Carney, Dana R., John T. Jost, Samuel D. Gosling, and Jeff Potter. "The Secret Lives of Liberals and Conservatives: Personality Profiles, Interaction Styles, and the Things They Leave Behind." *Political Psychology* 29 (2008): 807–840.

Elazar, Daniel J. *The American Mosaic: The Impact of Space, Time, and Culture on American Politics.* Boulder, CO: Westview Press, 1994.

Erikson, Robert S., Gerald C. Wright, and John P. McIver. *Statehouse Democracy: Public Opinion and Policy in the American States.* New York: Cambridge University Press, 1993.

Feldman, Stanley, and John Zaller. "The Political Culture of Ambivalence: Ideological Responses to the Welfare State." *American Journal of Political Science* 36 (1992): 268–307.

Gerber, Alan S., Gregory A. Huber, David Doherty, and Conor M. Dowling. "Personality Traits and the Consumption of Political Information." *American Politics Research* 39 (2011): 32–84.

Guiso, Luigi, Paola Sapienza, and Luigi Zingales. "Does Culture Affect Economic Outcomes?" *Journal of Economic Perspectives* 20 (2006): 23–48.

Hero, Rodney. *Faces of Inequality: Social Diversity in American Politics.* New York: Oxford University Press, 1998.

Hout, Michael, and Claude S. Fischer. "Why More Americans Have No Religious Preference: Politics and Generations." *American Sociological Review* 67 (2002): 165–190.

Hunter, James Davison. *Culture Wars.* New York: Basic Books, 1991.

Layman, Geoffrey C. *The Great Divide.* New York: Columbia University Press, 2001.

Lieske, Joel. "American State Cultures: Testing a New Measure and Theory." *Publius: The Journal of Federalism* 42 (2011): 108–133.

Mondak, Jeffrey J. *Personality and the Foundations of Political Behavior.* Cambridge: Cambridge University Press, 2010.

Parent, Wayne. *Inside the Carnival: Unmasking Louisiana Politics.* Baton Rouge: Louisiana State University Press, 2004.

Rentfrow, Peter J. "Statewide Differences in Personality: Toward a Psychological Geography of the United States." *The American Psychologist* 65 (2010): 548–558.

Chapter 4

Interstate Interactions

Ann O'M. Bowman

IT IS COMMON TO THINK OF THE FEDERAL SYSTEM in terms of the relationship between the national government and the states, one that is characterized by divided power and shared rule. But there are two other sets of relationships that are essential in understanding the U.S. federal system: those among the states themselves and those between a state and its local governments. The first is a relationship among equals; the second is decidedly not. This chapter explores both of these relationships, beginning with that of the states with one another.

THE VALUE OF HORIZONTAL FEDERALISM

The relationship among states is important in maintaining the federal system. State governments in the United States interact with one another regularly, producing a complex network that links actors, institutions, and organizations across state boundaries. This web of interactions has become known as horizontal federalism. States cooperate with one another; after all, they often face similar problems or share certain perspectives. When they act as a unified entity, they are a force to be reckoned with. States also compete with one another, especially over appropriate levels of taxation and expenditures, conscious of the potentially mobile citizen or firm. Such competition over the price and performance of government contributes to stabilizing the federal system. Conflict can emerge among states as they pursue their self-interests, competing as they do for scarce resources. The design and practice of the federal system has, with one major exception, kept interstate conflict from becoming destructive.

THE CONSTITUTIONAL BASIS FOR INTERACTIONS AMONG STATES

The constitutional basis for interactions among states grew out of experiences during the Articles of Confederation period. The "firm league of friendship" that the Articles established was insufficient to bind the states into a workable whole. The ethos of state self-interest was strong, causing James Madison himself to warn of the "trespasses of the states on the rights of each other." And there was certainly reason to be wary. Several times during the Articles era, states erected trade barriers against goods produced in other states and levied fees on ships entering their harbors from other states, effectively interrupting interstate commerce. States insisted upon engaging in what Jenna Bednar has termed "individually beneficial but collectively counterproductive behavior."[1] As she explains it, one of the challenges of constitutional design was the creation of a system that would effectively ward off the tendency of states to engage in "burden-shifting"—that is, "imposing externalities on other states in the federation."[2] Inclusion of a set of rules to govern interstate relations was one of the ways the Framers of the U.S. Constitution dealt with the potential for state opportunism that had occurred under the Articles.

Legal Equality of States

States in the U.S. federal system possess de jure symmetry. That is, each state stands on equal legal footing with every other state, enjoying the same official relationship with the national government regardless of a state's location, its population size, the date it entered the union, and so on. De facto asymmetries exist among states, of course, whether it is the size of a state's economy, its degree of political power, or its supply of natural resources. Consequently, each state's relative influence within the U.S. federal system varies. As each state pursues its self-interest, the opportunity for conflict with other states, themselves bent on self-interest, is inevitable. The U.S. Constitution sets out some basic rules for state-to-state conduct in an effort to produce a functional federal system, one in which interstate issues can be accommodated and conflict can be minimized.

Four Provisions for Interstate Interaction

The U.S. Constitution fully anticipates the interactions of states. It sets out four provisions to facilitate and clarify the interactions. Although the purpose of these provisions varies, as a whole, they were intended to promote interstate harmony, something that was sorely lacking under the Articles of Confederation.[3]

Full Faith and Credit Clause

Article IV, Section 1, of the U.S. Constitution declares that "full faith and credit shall be given in each state to the public acts, records, and judicial proceedings of every other state." (Congress was given the power to clarify and supplement the clause.) This provision essentially creates reciprocity across states in civil matters such as marriages, divorces, adoptions, child custody and support, orders of protection, and contracts.

One problematic test of the full faith and credit clause involves the issue of same-sex marriage. As of 2013, thirteen states had sanctioned same-sex marriage while more than thirty-five states had enacted prohibitions, either through state constitutional amendments or statutes, of same-sex marriage, defining marriage as a legal union between one man and one woman. A federal Defense of Marriage Act, passed in 1996, which declared that states were not required to recognize same-sex marriages from other states, was ruled unconstitutional by the U.S. Supreme Court in *United States v. Windsor* (June 26, 2013). Time will tell whether the Court or Congress will determine that there is a federal right to marriage; whether states will harmonize their laws; or, more plausibly, whether states will agree to accept valid same-sex marriages from other states.

Interstate Rendition Clause

The interstate rendition clause is found in Article IV, Section 2: "A person charged in any state with treason, felony, or other crime, who shall flee from justice, and be found in another state, shall on demand of the executive authority of the state from which he fled, be delivered up, to be removed to the state having jurisdiction of the crime." This provision is intended to prevent persons charged with crimes from fleeing to another state to avoid prosecution. States have adopted additional statutes to deal with the details of a rendition request and delivery, and on occasion, a governor has balked at surrendering a fugitive.

Privileges and Immunities Clause

Article IV, Section 2, of the U.S. Constitution guarantees that "the citizens of each state shall be entitled to all privileges and immunities of citizens in the several states." In other words, citizens of other states cannot be discriminated against by a state; similarly, a state cannot favor its own citizens over citizens of other states. In practice, however, there are areas in which a legitimate state interest allows a state to differentiate between in-state and out-of-state citizens. For example, out-of-state citizens may be charged a higher tuition at a public university or pay a higher fee for a fishing license than in-state citizens.

Interstate Compact Clause

In Article I, Section 10, states are authorized to enter into compacts with one another. "No State shall, without the Consent of Congress . . . enter into any Agreement or Compact with another State. . . ." The goal of the compact clause was to give states an opportunity to address regional problems without the active intervention of Congress. Originally used to resolve boundary disputes between pairs of states, compacts have broadened in scope to become an important component of horizontal federalism.

These four constitutional provisions serve as the foundation for the development of interstate relationships that would serve to unify the fledging nation. Other constitutional provisions contributed to this objective, of course, notably the interstate commerce clause. Since then, statutes, court rulings, and practice have further clarified how states interact with one another.

THREE FORMS OF INTERSTATE INTERACTION

States interact with one another regularly, be it a pair of states that share a border, a group of states within a region, or a spatially scattered set of states with similar policy preferences. These interactions take three primary forms: cooperation, competition, and conflict. In the sections that follow, each of the interactive types is discussed and an illustrative case is highlighted. As will become apparent, even though these three forms are quite different, they are often intertwined.

Cooperation

Facing common problems or pursuing a similar agenda, states cast about for partners; they build alliances with and connections to other states. States cooperate in many ways: through the creation of interstate compacts, the pursuit of joint legal actions, the adoption of uniform state laws, and the promulgation of administrative agreements. Cooperating states expect this interaction, whatever its type, to be a "win-win" endeavor. It may grow out of recognition of a shared problem or the realization of a common objective, a "we're all in the same boat" ethos. It may emerge from interstate competition whereby rival states conclude that working together may yield a sufficiently satisfactory outcome, one preferable to the risk of losing to another state.

These four cooperative ventures can be differentiated according to the amount of engagement required of participating states. In most instances, an interstate compact develops from a series of repeated interactions among key actors in participating states. By joining the compact, a state is committing itself to continued engagement with other member states. State involvement in a multistate legal action, the second type of cooperation, typically occurs without a long-term administrative commitment. The attorney general's office in the initiating state (or small group of states) tends to assume most of the organizational effort, especially in the formative stages. A third type of formal cooperative action, the adoption of uniform state laws, establishes a common policy in each participating state. Conformance with a peer-established norm involves only a modicum of cooperation, typically information sharing. Individual states implement the law once it is enacted, thereby necessitating few interstate connections. Administrative agreements vary in their level of engagement. Some produce customary practice, in effect becoming self-executing. Others require extensive interaction among participants as circumstances demand.

Cooperation to Create and Maintain Interstate Compacts

An interstate compact is a formal agreement or contract between two or more states that allows states to address shared problems jointly. A compact does not become active until a second state joins the first participating state. Although Article I, Section 10, refers to the approval of Congress, in practice, congressional approval tends to be reserved for compacts that address areas of mutual federal-state concern. Of the 215 active interstate compacts, many are bilateral or regional with regard to focus and membership. However, 38 are national in scope, meaning that membership is open to each of the fifty states.

Clearly, compacts are no longer simply a mechanism through which two states can address a disputed border; increasingly, they include policy components and consequently, over time, compacts have become more important instruments of public policy. The substance of compacts has expanded to cover matters as diverse as criminal justice, education, natural resource conservation, and transportation, among others. Compacts have grown in another way: the average number of signatory states on a given compact has increased. Part of the explanation for this is the growing number of national compacts, compacts in which membership is open to any state. As both Joseph F. Zimmerman and Caroline N. Broun and her colleagues have shown in their separate analyses, not only the substantive but also the administrative, financial, and technical dimensions of compacts have expanded.

In some instances, compacts supplement extant state laws, but if there is a conflict between compact provisions and statutes, once a state joins the compact its conflicting state law must give way. In other words, states sacrifice some degree of sovereignty when they enter into a compact with other states. Once functional, these compacts create their own policies and rules, and often their own governance structures. And therein lies some of the criticism of compacts: that their rules, especially the reliance on a unanimity rule, and their lack of compliance mechanisms make them unwieldy and potentially ineffective in resolving conflicts. Studies by Edella Schlager and Tanya Heikkila on the operation of interstate water compacts have found otherwise, however.[4] Compacts have proven to be sufficiently flexible to revise rules and address zero-sum distributional conflicts.

The problem-solving nature of compacts—the opportunity to address shared problems and to produce collective goods—is fairly well established, but two other important aspects of compacts exist. When a state joins a compact that is already in place, it lowers the costs associated with policy design and experimentation for the late-joining state. Additionally, compacts provide a forum in which a group of states can promote a common agenda. This means that compacts have the potential to be used for political, even partisan or ideological, purposes. This potential became an active reality when groups of conservative state

In this April 30, 2012, photo, Rep. Mark Pody, R-Lebanon, debates his proposal for Tennessee to join an interstate health care compact during a house floor session in Nashville, Tennessee. The measure failed in the House on Tuesday, May 1, 2012, after falling five votes short of the fifty needed to pass the lower chamber.

SOURCE: AP Photo/Erik Schelzig.

legislators joined together in 2010 to promote the development of a compact that would dismantle federal health care reform. By 2012, health care compact legislation had been introduced in twenty-five states and enacted in seven states (Georgia, Indiana, Missouri, Oklahoma, South Carolina, Texas, and Utah). Except for Missouri, where the legislation became law without the Democratic governor's signature, unified Republican control of policy-making institutions prevails in these states. This is the first compact that attempts to shield states from a whole area of federal law, and congressional approval would be unlikely. Whether this signals additional commandeering of the compact mechanism for ideologically driven activity is an open question.

The Council of State Governments (CSG) assists states in developing interstate compacts and tracks their activity. Overall, Virginia participates in the most compacts, Hawaii in the fewest. When the focus narrows to the thirty-eight national compacts open to the participation of all states, states with the highest levels of compact participation include Colorado, Kansas, New Mexico, and Washington; those with the lowest are California, Louisiana, Massachusetts, and Mississippi. Researchers have shown that the explanations for compact joining are many, but prominent among them is a state's effort to enhance its policy-making capacity.[5]

Cooperation in Multistate Legal Actions

States cooperate when they enter into lawsuits with—not against—other states. From an individual state's perspective, this action represents an opportunity to demonstrate strength in numbers. A single state taking legal action against a firm (or the federal government) may not pose much of a threat, although it likely depends on which state it is and its relative importance to a firm. Still, a group of states acting collectively cannot be ignored. Witness the efforts of twelve mostly northeastern states that sued the U.S. Environmental Protection Agency in 2003 over the relaxation of rules related to pollution control equipment at coal-fired power plants. Another explanation for states banding together is more prosaic: these legal actions can be costly. Also, a professional association, the National Association of Attorneys General, has facilitated much multistate litigation.

The substantive focus of much of the litigation is consumer protection, primarily efforts to prosecute businesses for fraud, deceptive advertising, or antitrust violations. After a few high-profile cases in the 1980s (e.g., thirty-five states sued the Hertz Corporation for overcharging rental car customers for repairs), multistate lawsuits really came into their own in the 1990s. Both the number of lawsuits and the number of participating states increased. Colin Provost compiled data from this decade and found the highest levels of state participation in multistate litigation in California,

INTERACTIONS AMONG THE GREAT LAKES STATES

The Great Lakes states provide an interesting case of mostly cooperation, but not without occasional competition and conflict. The Great Lakes are major resources for the eight states that border one or more of them. Shared recognition of the value of the resource led to the creation of the Great Lakes Basin Compact in the mid-1950s. By 1965, all eight states had joined. The compact is administered by the Great Lakes Commission, and its intent is to develop a unified regional voice on water resource issues. Even with the compact in place, in 1983 the governors of six Great Lakes states, aware of the lakes' economic importance and distressed over their increasing pollution, concluded that another regional entity was needed—one with more political clout. The governors of Illinois, Indiana, Michigan, Minnesota, Ohio, and Wisconsin created the Council of Great Lakes Governors. New York and Pennsylvania joined six years later. (The premiers of two lake-bordering Canadian provinces, Ontario and Quebec, are associate members.) The primary purpose of the council is "to encourage and facilitate environmentally responsible economic growth through a cooperative effort between the public and private sectors."[1]

In its three decades of operation, the council has become an institutional force for cooperation in the region, forging several administrative agreements, and in 2008 hammering out the details of a new compact, the Great Lakes–St. Lawrence River Basin Water Resources Compact. This compact operates alongside the Basin Compact, although it has a separate administrative structure and a more explicit focus on water use, allocation, and diversion. Numerous other groups and alliances have emerged, such as Great Lakes USA, which promotes tourism in the region (in this instance, five states: Illinois, Michigan, Minnesota, Ohio, and Wisconsin; earlier members, Indiana and Pennsylvania, left the association).

Despite the many cooperative ventures, there remains a certain degree of competition among the Great Lakes states. One issue that has riven these states at times is economic development, illustrated by the incentives war conducted by Illinois and Ohio in 2011 to retain and attract, respectively, the Sears Holding Corporation. All of the states in the region have suffered economic disruption; all are seeking investment. Cooperation may be a smart regional strategy, but when it comes to economic development and tax bases, state self-interest tends to prevail. And there can be conflict within a seemingly cooperative venue. One issue that has split the states is the Asian carp, a nonnative fish so voracious that it has the potential to disrupt the lakes' ecosystem. The solution proposed by Michigan is opposed by Illinois and Indiana. The conflict led to a 2010 lawsuit by Michigan and four other Great Lakes states against the Chicago water authority.

1. "Overview: Mission," Council of Great Lakes Governors, accessed April 2, 3013, www.cglg.org/Overview/mission.asp.

Massachusetts, Minnesota, Missouri, New York, Texas, and Wisconsin.[6] States with the lowest aggregate participation rates were Alaska, Colorado, Hawaii, Montana, South Dakota, and Wyoming.

Analysis revealed that state-level characteristics such as a liberal populace, a more affluent citizenry, and the presence of more consumer protection groups helped explain why some states tended to join more of these lawsuits. But involvement in these lawsuits is not simply a matter of state characteristics. Another part of the explanation lies in the political ambition of the state attorney general. Often, state attorneys general who engage in more multistate lawsuits are positioning themselves to run for a higher political office, such as governor or U.S. senator.[7] Further analysis showed that the type of legal action matters as well. Cases that involve significant monetary damage to consumers and have high-dollar settlement value, such as antitrust cases and cases with a Fortune 500 company defendant, tend to attract more states.

Some of the awards to states have been quite significant, such as the successful effort to recover the Medicaid costs of treating tobacco-related diseases from four major U.S. tobacco companies. Five states—Florida, Massachusetts, Mississippi, Minnesota, and West Virginia—were among the first to band together to share information and design tactics in their lawsuits. They contended that the tobacco firms had engaged in a series of fraudulent and deceptive practices in promoting their products. Although a handful of states settled individually with the tobacco companies, forty-six states became part of the comprehensive settlement agreement in 1998 that committed the companies to a minimum of $206 billion in payments over a twenty-five-year period. In another case, two-thirds of the states joined together in a legal complaint against seven computer chip manufacturers, alleging that they engaged in illegal price-fixing. This action led the firms to settle out of court for $173 million.

Cooperation in the Adoption of Uniform State Laws

Congress often enacts a national statute as a remedy to the patchwork of state laws on the same subject. Congressional action will establish a common standard across the nation, regardless of the state. But there is another way for a single standard in all fifty states without encroaching on states: the adoption of uniform statutes by the states themselves. The establishment of the National Conference of Commissioners on Uniform State Laws in 1892, now called the Uniform Law Commission (ULC), formalized this process. This nonprofit, nonpartisan organization, composed of attorneys, judges, and legal experts from each state, engages in an iterative process of negotiating and drafting uniform laws and model acts. Each state has the option of enacting the law, thereby conforming its statute on a subject to the law of other enacting states. For example, the Anatomical Gift Act, finalized in 2006, had been enacted in forty-five states by 2012; the Conservation Easement Act (2007) had become law in twenty-one states by 2012.

It is the ULC's policy to draft acts that have a reasonable probability of being enacted into law by a substantial number of states. Another expectation is that ULC members will move to promote the act's consideration in their home states. Although some of the acts are adopted quickly by a large number of states, the adoption pace for others can be quite lengthy. And some uniform laws have not proven to be popular. For instance, as of 2012, the Model Victims of Crime Act (1997) had been enacted only in Montana; and only Maryland and Virginia had adopted the Computer Information Transactions Act (2002).

Legal researchers conducting cost-benefit analysis have shown that states sort among uniform law proposals and enact them in situations in which uniformity is most efficient.[8] Examining the decade of the 1990s reflects the larger trend. During that time period, the ULC finalized 22 new uniform laws. By the start of the next decade, states, on average, had enacted 7.7 of these laws, from a high of 14 in New Mexico to a low of 4 adoptions in Georgia, Massachusetts, New York, and Wisconsin. The explanation for the variation in the rate at which states enact uniform laws and model acts is not altogether clear. Initial research on this question focused on a state's political culture; later research has looked more to uniform state laws functioning as a substitute for state policy-making capacity. For example, a statistically significant inverse relationship exists between state institutional capability and rates of enactment of uniform laws.[9]

Although organizations other than the ULC propose model acts for legislative consideration (e.g., the National Association of Insurance Commissioners), one group has become quite active: the American Legislative Exchange Council, or ALEC. With its stated goal of advancing principles of limited government, free markets, and federalism, ALEC creates task forces to draft model legislation on a wide variety of topics. The organization's goal is not to establish uniformity across states, but rather to push the policy dialog in a conservative direction.

Cooperation on Administrative Agreements

Administrative agreements offer an alternative to interstate compacts. These agreements do not require legislative action and can be negotiated more quickly and adjusted more easily as circumstances evolve. Also, administrative agreements are less binding on states because they do not supersede state statutes. To some degree, they offer a way to fill in a gap, to address a problem that arises. Informal administrative agreements may produce less durable solutions to joint problems; however, in a rapidly changing environment, speed and flexibility may be more valuable than durability.

Administrative agreements have not been studied systematically by scholars, partly because no compendium of these agreements exists. But those who do write about them, such as Joseph Zimmerman, suggest that their numbers are quite substantial and on the rise.[10] They run the gamut of policy domains, literally from agriculture to water. This is not surprising because these agreements are facilitated by networks of regional associations of state agency heads. Some agreements are fairly simple, motivated by a specific problem such as a structurally unsound bridge spanning Lake Champlain. Transportation commissioners in New York and Vermont, the states that jointly own the bridge, signed an administrative agreement in 2009 to replace it. Some are quite lucrative, such as the agreement among thirty states to form the multistate Powerball lottery, or the agreement among the twelve states that participate in the Mega Millions lottery.

Other multistate administrative agreements are less about immediate problem solving and more about tackling long-term dilemmas. One example is the Western Climate Initiative (WCI) formed by Arizona, California, New Mexico, Oregon, and Washington in 2007 (and later joined by Montana, Utah, and four Canadian provinces) to develop a regional approach to reducing greenhouse gas emissions. Modeled after the Regional Greenhouse Gas Initiative in the Northeast, the WCI developed a cap-and-trade system for controlling emissions that was to be implemented in each member state by 2012. But administrative agreements, while easy to enter into, are easy to scuttle. By 2011, all states except California had defected from the WCI, citing concerns about the emissions plan's effect on state economic recovery. Thus, like the other kinds of cooperative ventures, state participation in administrative agreements is subject to the same calculus of state self-interest. But their potential to produce win-win outcomes makes them popular among state officials.

This March 10, 2008, file photo shows the Four Corners Power Plant near Fruitland, New Mexico. The Western Climate Initiative, a coalition of seven western states and four Canadian provinces, on Tuesday, July 27, 2010, issued an update to its strategy for a regional cap-and-trade market to reduce greenhouse gas emissions. It would focus first on power plants, then transition to other industries and transportation.

SOURCE: AP Photo/Paul Foy.

Competition

Interstate competition is inherent in a federal system. States compete among one another when they seek the same scarce objective. The outcome of some competitive interaction can be zero-sum, even as the outcome for the federal system as a whole may be efficient and optimal. Interstate competition can be differentiated in terms of mediation. Some competitions among the states are mediated by external actors. For example, government institutions determine winners and losers in the case of federal grant funding. Unmediated competition occurs in open-market situations—for example, states seeking tourists or firms, in which there is no government institution to select winners.

Consider the ubiquitous lists that rank the states from top to bottom, from number one to number fifty. Some of the comparisons of states reflect fundamental characteristics such as land area or population size. Others involve policies—the generosity of welfare benefits, the level of per pupil expenditures, the commitment to environmental protection—features that reflect a choice made by policymakers. Still others capture governmental performance with the high school graduation rate, the level of violent crime, the amount of substandard infrastructure, and so on. High-ranking states celebrate; low-ranking states commiserate. At least in theory, competition for highly desired outcomes should generate learning and emulation.

A behavior that typifies the competition inherent in interstate relations is the "race to the bottom" (RTB). Each state has an incentive to avoid an undesirable outcome—for example, becoming a so-called welfare magnet or losing investment to states with lax environmental laws. Therefore, assuming each state acts similarly, welfare benefits would become increasingly less generous and environmental regulations would become increasingly lenient. A downward spiral, a race to the bottom, would ensue. States will enact policies and pursue programmatic actions based on what other states do. The logic is compelling: to secure a competitive advantage, a state would lower its welfare benefit or relax its environmental regulatory standards. Research has not produced unequivocal evidence on this issue. Some argue that states are less generous due to interstate competition, but others have found a different pattern.[11] Harrell Rogers and his colleagues took up the RTB question in research on state welfare programs, trying to determine whether states adjusted their welfare benefits based on the actions of other states. Data analysis showed that states have remained relatively stable in their welfare and income support policies since the welfare reform of the mid-1990s. No race to the bottom was found.

In environmental protection policy, the results are similarly mixed.[12] For instance, in looking at the behavior of state surface-mining agencies, Neal Woods finds that state enforcement stringency is sensitive to the actions of neighboring states; David Konisky finds a similar pattern in data from surveys of senior environmental managers. Not only are state environmental officials familiar with the regulatory practices of other states, they indicate that, because of interstate economic competition, agency regulatory relaxation occurs as a consequence. However, other work by Konisky calls into question the assumption that interstate economic competition motivates state changes in enforcement behavior in three major pollution control programs (see Chapter 30). More work remains to determine the causal connections and assess the reality of a race to the bottom. Some observers have noticed an alternative state behavior, an apparent "race to the top" in some policy areas (see Chapter 25).

Competition for Economic Development

All states want healthy economies, and they have been taking actions intended to achieve that outcome. The first statewide program of industrial recruitment was created during the Great Depression when Mississippi, with its Balance Agriculture with Industry plan, made it possible for local governments to issue bonds to finance the construction or purchase of facilities for relocating industry. Other southern states followed suit, luring businesses from elsewhere with tax breaks, public subsidies, and low wages. Called smokestack chasing, aggressive industrial recruitment had spread throughout the country by the 1970s. The behavior continues to this day, although locational incentives aim beyond industrial recruitment to high-tech firms, biomedical businesses, start-up companies, and the like. States go to great lengths to make themselves attractive to footloose firms, just as they desire to retain and grow the firms already in the state.

The television business network CNBC is one of the entities that evaluate states annually on measures related to business competitiveness. CNBC weights and aggregates forty to fifty different measures to produce scores and rankings: items such as tax burden, training programs, wage rates, regulatory environment, venture capital availability, and quality of life, among others. Virginia was the top-scoring state in CNBC's 2011 survey; Rhode Island had the lowest score; in 2012, it was Texas at the top, while Rhode Island remained at the bottom.

A legitimate question is whether state government actions—providing tax breaks, relaxing regulations, investing in infrastructure, training workers, and the like—have any effect on firm locational decisions. The literature suggests that giveaways may attract a specific firm to a particular place, but in general, factors that are beyond state control play a major role in a firm's decision.[13] And the incentives offered often come at a high price, as Alabama learned when it outbid four other finalist states to attract German automaker Mercedes-Benz. Cognizant of this, most states feel as if they have to offer concessions simply because other states do so. A recent study by the Pew Center on the States found that only one-quarter of states have undertaken comprehensive reviews to assess the economic impact of their incentive programs.[14]

Competition over Tax Systems

States rely on different combinations of revenue sources to fund the operation of government. Regardless of the revenue sources, in the competitive world of horizontal federalism, where capital is mobile but government jurisdictions are not, no state can afford to be too out of line in terms of its relative tax burden. The Tax Foundation provides an estimate of the combined state-local tax burden of residents of each state measured by the percentage of income residents pay in state and local taxes.[15] The distribution is relatively tight, as would be expected in a competitive tax environment. For 2009, the range extended from New Jersey (12.2 percent), New York (12.1 percent), and Connecticut (12.0 percent) at the top to Alaska (6.3 percent), Nevada (7.5 percent), South Dakota (7.6 percent), and Tennessee (7.6 percent) at the bottom. (Any discussion of Alaska should note its reliance on revenue from taxes on oil extraction, a burden that falls mostly on residents of other states.)The fifty-state average was 9.8 percent; it was 9.9 percent in 2008, 9.8 percent in 2007. Of course, states try to export their tax burden to the degree possible by taxing extractive resources (oil, gas, coal, minerals), tourism (hotel rooms, rental cars) and nonresidents (higher property tax rates for nonresidents).

A recent dustup between the governors of Texas and Washington reflects the competitive behavior. In 2010 Washington placed a tax increase question on its ballot. During the run-up to the vote, Texas governor Rick Perry sent letters to ninety top businesses in Washington that read,

"As the State of Washington considers a multibillion-dollar tax increase for citizens and businesses, I invite you to consider your future in America's new land of opportunity: the State of Texas."[16] The governor of Washington, Christine Gregoire, responded vigorously, garnering headlines with the claim that her state's business climate had been better than that of Texas in recent years. Debate ensued regarding which rankings of state business climates were best. (On Election Day, Washington voters rejected the tax hike.)

Do states consciously design tax systems with other states in mind? The answer appears to be "yes." Some emulative behavior exists, with policymakers more likely to propose tax increases when neighboring states are doing the same. Also, there is evidence to suggest that voters look at the tax increases in neighboring states to gauge whether a proposed tax increase is justifiable. And where the incidence of cross-border shopping is high, allowing residents to escape certain types of taxes, states do tend to be responsive to levels of taxes in nearby states.

Conflict

The fact that conflict occurs even among the most cooperative of states should come as no surprise, given the legacy of the Articles of Confederation and the squabbling among states—especially the disputes between large states and small states over representation during the Constitutional Convention. The most destructive example of interstate conflict in the United States is, of course, the Civil War of the mid-nineteenth century when eleven Southern states seceded and unsuccessfully fought the Union, and in effect, the states that remained. Lest there be any future debate, a ruling by the U.S. Supreme Court in *Texas v. White* (1869) made it explicit that the United States is an indissoluble entity and that once joined, the union between one state and another is perpetual.[17] Contemporary conflict results from opportunistic behavior by states and is unlikely to lead to one state taking up arms against another, but it has certainly generated legal action. Facing a non–zero sum outcome, interstate alliances can disintegrate.

Conflict Related to Burden Shifting and Opportunistic Behavior by States

Even with constitutional mechanisms designed to facilitate interstate cooperation, the motivation to cooperate is frequently offset by an incentive to behave opportunistically. Wallace Oates sums it up succinctly: "Policymakers in one jurisdiction often have little incentive to worry about the costs that their actions impose on their neighbors."[18] Even if this pursuit of self-interest is an expected behavior, it can result in the suboptimal performance of the federal system as a whole. Similar to Oates, Bednar identifies the potential for interstate burden-shifting: "States do not automatically take into account the effect that their policy has on the citizens of another state. Policy effects spill across borders, sometimes harming and sometimes helping the people living in neighboring states."[19] Externalities and spillovers occur regularly. Consider, for example, the long-standing complaint of northeastern states regarding the pollution generated by coal-fired power plants in midwestern states that drifts into the region. The benefits of the power plant such as plentiful electricity for consumers and jobs for residents are enjoyed by states in one area; the costs of the power plant in terms of pollution are experienced by states in another area.

A state cannot be completely unperturbed about the effect of its actions on other states, if only because of the potential for retaliation. After all, just as encroachment by the federal government into a state's domain can provoke a reaction from states, so can the opportunistic behavior of a state toward its brethren. Among states, the prospect

VIRGINIA WINS THE COMPETITION FOR ROLLS-ROYCE

The competition among states for economic growth and development can be fierce. Eight states—Georgia, Indiana, Mississippi, North Carolina, Ohio, South Carolina, Texas, and Virginia—vied to become the location for a new $500 million jet engine facility being developed by British manufacturer Rolls-Royce. Each of the competing states set about identifying possible sites and assembling incentive packages in an effort to attract the company. With the exception of Ohio, each of the states is a right-to-work state, thus minimizing that issue as a deciding factor. After reviewing the proposals and promises, Rolls-Royce selected Virginia in 2007 as the site. Several factors worked in the state's favor, including the availability of a large (1,025 acres) site in an industrial zone and the presence of a skilled workforce. The value of the state's incentives to Rolls-Royce—land, infrastructure development, job training, and tax breaks—total $56.8 million over a multiyear period. Virginia was willing to provide these sweeteners because of the several hundred jobs involved and the likelihood that landing Rolls-Royce would have a ripple effect and attract other advanced manufacturing facilities to the state. Virginia felt compelled to offer a generous incentive package because its competitors were doing so. A Virginia official assessed the situation practically: "If you're going to play in the big leagues, you have to come to the field with more than your glove."[1] Economic development remains a competitive process, often pitting one state against another.

1. Jack Lyne, "Virginia Readies for Rolls," Site Selection, www.siteselection.com/ssinsider/bbdeal/bd071206.htm.

of mutual retaliation remains a powerful safeguard to interstate burden-shifting. And if the conflict were to intensify, the prospect of future interstate cooperation dims. Too much horizontal conflict complicates the coming together for collective action, and it weakens the federal system.

Conflict as State versus State Legal Action

The U.S. Supreme Court is the mediator of formal conflict among states. The potential for intervention and resolution by the Court serves as another safeguard against excessive interstate conflict. It functions as a last resort, an option that is utilized when states are unable to negotiate their way to a mutually satisfactory solution. Cases that end up before the Court often reflect long-standing disputes or significant issues. The substance of the legal disputes, according to Zimmerman who has studied the topic, tends to involve boundaries, taxation, or resources. The earliest cases, such as a 1799 dispute between New York and Connecticut and an 1838 battle between Massachusetts and Rhode Island, involved land grants of the colonial era. Boundary disputes that have arisen in contemporary times, as evidenced in lawsuits between Illinois and Kentucky, and between Georgia and South Carolina, tend to involve a river that has changed course. To deal with these situations in a less litigious manner, many states have entered into boundary compacts.

Interstate tax controversies that reach the level of litigation have involved taxation of estates and tax exportation, and represent an escalation of interstate tax competition. The estate tax conflict usually involves the issue of legal domicile, a problem that led the UCL to promulgate uniform state estate tax laws that a subset of states has adopted. The tax exportation conflict addresses the differential availability and use of tax credits by in-state and out-of-state residents.

Resources, particularly water, can be the impetus for interstate conflict. The issues revolve around water allocation, diversion, and pollution. In an effort to minimize conflict and avoid legal action, interstate compacts have been created to deal with many of these water issues. Ironically, some of the compacts themselves have produced additional conflict, especially over compliance issues. Some conflicts have been resolved via the compact commission itself; the more intransigent conflicts have led to legal action. In some cases, just the threat of legal action was sufficient to produce resolution. Studies of western water compacts have shown that the venue for resolution has a significant influence on the remedy.[20] Compliance costs are likely to be more equally shared when states use voluntary venues such as the compact commission or state-to-state negotiations for settling disputes. In compulsory venues such as the Court, upstream states tend to bear the costs.

Other conflict has emerged from interstate cooperation gone awry. Two cases involve low-level radioactive waste compacts, regional agreements to dispose of nuclear waste. Although member states want a site for waste disposal, no state actively desires to host the site. In 1987 the Midwest compact, with seven member states, selected Michigan (the state projected to produce the most waste) as its host site for a waste disposal facility. Michigan concluded that none of the possible locations within its borders was appropriate and refused. In retaliation, the other states revoked Michigan's membership in the compact, citing the state's failure to fulfill its obligation to them. (Unaffiliated with a compact, Michigan will have to construct its own facility for in-state, low-level waste.) Meanwhile, in 1988 Nebraska was selected as the host site for the five-state Central compact. Nebraska located its site on its northern edge, near South Dakota, and began a lengthy and costly review process. The compact commission imposed a deadline for Nebraska to act, and the state

Fisherman Gordon Haughey casts his line into Lake Superior near Marquette, Michigan, in this April 28, 2003, photo. It would be nearly impossible to divert large amounts of water from the Great Lakes to other areas of the country under the provisions of a sweeping amendment to an interstate and international compact aimed at protecting and improving the Great Lakes. In 2004 the Council of Great Lakes Governors proposed that the Great Lakes Basin Water Resources Compact allow only new or increased withdrawals on any of the five Great Lakes if they immediately return water taken out of the lakes and improve the condition of the lakes.

SOURCE: AP Photo/Brian Halbrook, file.

responded with a lawsuit over whether the commission had the power to do so. Having lost in court, Nebraska in 1998 refused to license the facility. The Central compact's response to Nebraska's refusal was a lawsuit against the state, which Nebraska eventually settled for $140 million. Like Michigan, Nebraska is going it alone.

STATES' RELATIONSHIPS WITH THEIR LOCAL GOVERNMENTS

The relationship among states is one of legal equals. This is not the case for the relationship of states to their local governments. Moreover, there is not a universal state-local relationship; there are fifty states, each with its own history, politics, and institutional arrangements. Local governments are not mentioned in the U.S. Constitution. The failure of the Constitutional Convention to address local governments and their standing in the newly created nation allowed states to assume primacy in the state-local relationship.[21]

Power and Authority

The basic explication of state-local relations is summed up this way: local governments are creatures of their states. In effect, within the U.S. federal system, the relationship between states and their local jurisdictions resembles a unitary system: the state holds all legal power. Iowa judge John F. Dillon first laid down what became known as Dillon's Rule in *The City of Clinton v. The Cedar Rapids and Missouri River Railroad Company* in 1868.[22] Dillon's Rule established that local governments may exercise only those powers explicitly granted to them by the state, those clearly implied by the explicit powers, and those absolutely essential to the declared objectives and purposes of the local government. Any doubt regarding the legality of any specific local government power is resolved in favor of the state. One operational outcome of such an approach was the ability of the state legislative delegation from a particular county to, in effect, run the county from the state capital through the passage of special legislation.

An opposing legal view, that of Michigan Supreme Court justice Thomas Cooley, emerged during the same period. In two rulings in the early 1870s, Justice Cooley declared that the state of Michigan could not require the city of Detroit to appoint public works commissioners handpicked by the legislature; nor could the state construct public parks within the city's limits at the expense of the city. Justice Cooley argued that local affairs should be managed by local authorities. To animate his argument, he looked to the self-rule enjoyed by township governments in colonial New England that predated the U.S. Constitution. Some state courts, among them Indiana and Texas, embraced the Cooley doctrine. However, when the U.S. Supreme Court upheld Dillon's Rule in a 1903 Kansas case and a 1923 New Jersey case, the Cooley perspective lost favor. But even as Dillon's Rule became accepted legal doctrine, the issue of local self-government remained on the agenda.

Dillon's Rule and Home Rule

Dillon's Rule runs counter to a more Jeffersonian concept that local governments are imbued with inherent rights. Still, as Dale Krane and his colleagues note, Dillon's Rule does not necessarily mean that a legislature must constrain

NEW JERSEY V. NEW YORK: ELLIS ISLAND

One of the most celebrated recent state-versus-state legal battles was between New Jersey and New York over Ellis Island—or, more specifically, state jurisdiction over twenty-four acres of landfill that had been added to the island over time. In 1993 the state of New Jersey filed a lawsuit claiming its jurisdiction over the acreage, assembling a team of experts, historical documents, and maps to support its case. New York countered with its own collection of experts, deeds, records, and maps. Although Ellis Island's distinctive contribution to U.S. history accorded it some intangible value, the commercial development potential of the landfilled portion of the island was a prime motivator of the 1993 lawsuit.

This was not the first time the states had battled over Ellis Island. In 1829 New Jersey filed suit and in 1834 was given control of the underwater portions of the western half of the harbor. New York was awarded Ellis Island—at that point, a three-acre site. (An interstate compact was used to set the boundary line.) Much of the subsequent landfilling has occurred on the western half of the harbor, hence New Jersey's claim that the land belongs to it. New York countered that the compact was silent on the issue of land enlargement and contended that the silence reflected the drafters' assumption that any filled-in portions would be under New York's jurisdiction. In 1998 the U.S. Supreme Court ruled that New Jersey did indeed have sovereign jurisdiction over the disputed landfilled sections of Ellis Island.[1]

Although the Ellis Island conflict has been settled, the two states continue to spar over many things such as the movement of some labor-intensive back-office operations from New York City to lower-cost facilities in New Jersey. And the jousting can take on humorous dimensions, such as the penchant of New Jersey governors to remind folks that the area's professional football teams, the New York Giants and the New York Jets, play their home games in a stadium in New Jersey.

1. *New Jersey v. New York*, 523 U.S. 767 (1998).

its local governments, but rather that the legislature can decide how much power to give them. This grant of power can be narrow or it can be broad. The latter is where the concept of home rule fits. Home rule provides some degree of self-government to a local jurisdiction. Although each state defines it somewhat differently, a grant of home rule allows local officials more discretion to design governance (e.g., structure, policies, finances) to fit their community. It is intended to diminish the amount of state legislative interference in local government. And it reinforces local democracy.

Some observers have concluded that the concepts of Dillon's Rule and home rule mask the complexity and variability of state-local relations.[23] After all, many Dillon's Rule states have adopted home rule provisions for their municipalities and counties. Therefore, the presence or absence of Dillon's Rule or home rule may not accurately convey the actual distribution of power in a state-local system.

Second-Order Devolution: Efficiency and Local Self-Government

Local self-government is a valued ideal. But the issue of how much power local governments should possess is not merely an abstract enterprise; it is also a matter of efficiency. How can the range of public services provided by state and local governments be delivered most efficiently? This question has vexed various waves of reformers intent upon identifying an efficient allocation of service responsibilities across the two levels of government.

According to U.S. Census Bureau figures, on average, state government provides approximately one-third of the general revenue available to local governments. This figure varies across states and within a state, across types of local governments, so it should be considered a rough estimate. But the point is that states are an important revenue source to their local jurisdictions. State governments have relied on mandates, essentially direct orders, to ensure that local governments perform vital activities and achieve desired goals. State mandates promote policy and program uniformity across jurisdictions, which can yield some economies of scale. Local governments, however, chafe under the weight of state mandates, especially those that are underfunded. To them, mandates represent an unnecessary intrusion into their operational sphere.

Second-order devolution is a shift in power from the state level to the local level. This devolution can be administrative in nature, providing more discretion in program administration; it can be substantive, shifting responsibility for policymaking with or without adequate fiscal capacity. If both administrative and substantive devolution were to occur, efficiencies in service delivery would be achieved and transparency and accountability would increase.

Fiscal stress may provide an impetus for states to reconsider their local government systems. In cash-strapped Ohio, where lawmakers cut state funds for local governments by 50 percent over a two-year period, a simultaneous effort was made to restore some of that funding through a new system of grants and loans to localities. The intent of the Local Government Innovation Fund, created in 2011, is to encourage local governments to devise new and better ways to provide services to their residents. The underlying thinking is that a financial incentive will inspire localities to innovate.

How would an optimal system of state-local relations be designed? If one were starting with a blank slate, the task would be substantially easier. But in an extant state-local government system, redesign is difficult. Consider the case of Michigan, a state with more than 2,500 units of local government, many of which are townships. In 2010 the Michigan ballot included a question on authorizing a state constitutional convention. Among the major topics for the convention's consideration was the redesign of the system of local governments, especially streamlining the layers of local government and reallocating functions. However, Michigan voters defeated the constitutional convention question by a margin of 67 percent to 33 percent, and with it the opportunity for fundamental redesign.

Variation across States

As noted, there is substantial variation across the states with regard to the empowerment of local governments. Ross Stephens developed an index of state centralization at various points in the twentieth century using measures of fiscal responsibility, service delivery, and public employment. He found a general trend toward increased centralization, with states providing more direct services, exercising greater control over public policy, and taking on increased financial responsibility.[24] In updating the Stephens index to 2008, researchers noted that states had continued to enlarge their financial and service responsibilities, albeit at a slower pace, but that employment remained fairly decentralized.[25] States that were most centralized were Alaska, Delaware, Hawaii, and Vermont; the most decentralized states included California, Florida, Illinois, and Nevada.

Other research has analyzed the state-local relationship by measuring the importance of localities, their level of discretion, and their capacity to act—quite a different set of factors than the Stephens index. Based on 2002 data, states that granted their localities the greatest autonomy were Kansas, New York, Ohio, and Tennessee; those allowing the least were Connecticut, Rhode Island, and Vermont, and West Virginia.[26] Harkening back to an earlier point, states with high levels of local government autonomy represent a mix of Dillon's Rule and non–Dillon's Rule states, as do states with low levels of local government autonomy.

MICHIGAN, LOCAL GOVERNMENTS, AND FINANCIAL MANAGERS

Michigan—not surprisingly, given the perspective of its former solon, Justice Thomas Cooley—provides its municipalities broad home rule powers. Still, the state is far from hands-off in its dealings with local governments. In a Michigan statute that could be considered Dillonesque, if the governor deems it necessary, he or she can appoint a financial manager to run a local government. The financial manager possesses the authority to hire and fire city employees, renegotiate contracts, and sell city property. The power of the elected city council and the mayor is diminished substantially. Laws granting this power—particularly Michigan's original Public Act 72, which established the state's authority to intervene in local jurisdictions on the brink of bankruptcy, and Public Act 4 of 2011, which allows the state to step into financially distressed cities earlier—are designed to help cities recover and establish a path to fiscal solvency. If a Michigan city on the financial edge declared bankruptcy, the state and its taxpayers would be responsible for the city's debt. Stripping a local government of much of its authority and granting it to an emergency manager strikes some state leaders as an effective way to make fiscally sound decisions that are not beholden to local interests.

As of 2012, four Michigan cities were operating under the control of a financial manager: Benton Harbor, Ecorse, Flint, and Pontiac; as were the school districts in Detroit, Highland Park, and Muskegon Heights. Clearly, the solvency of a city government or school district is a concern of the state. In these four cities, home rule has been replaced by state authority.

CONCLUSION

In the U.S. federal system, each state pursues its self-interest and, in doing so, collides with other states bent on their own self-interests. Sometimes these self-interests converge, and the result is an interstate compact or a multistate lawsuit. Other times the interests diverge, and states find themselves in competition with one another—or, less frequently, locked in conflict. As emphasized here, these horizontal relationships contribute to the maintenance of the U.S. federal system.

NOTES

1. Jenna Bednar, *The Robust Federation: Principles of Design* (New York: Cambridge University Press, 2009), 66.
2. Ibid., 9.
3. Joseph F. Zimmerman, *Horizontal Federalism: Interstate Relations* (Albany: State University of New York Press), 2011.
4. Edella Schlager and Tanya Heikkila, "Resolving Water Conflicts: A Comparative Analysis of Interstate River Compacts in the Western United States," *Policy Studies Journal* 37 (2009): 367–392; Edella Schlager, Tanya Heikkila, and Carl Case, "The Costs of Compliance with Interstate Agreements: Lessons from Water Compacts," *Publius: The Journal of Federalism* 42 (2012): 494–515.
5. Ann O'M. Bowman and Neal D. Woods, "Strength in Numbers: Why States Join Interstate Compacts," *State Politics and Policy Quarterly* 7 (2007): 347–369.
6. Colin Provost, "The Politics of Consumer Protection: Explaining State Attorney General Participation in Multi-State Lawsuits," *Political Research Quarterly* 59 (2006): 609–618.
7. Colin Provost, "When Is AG Short for Aspiring Governor? Ambition and Policy Making Dynamics in the Office of State Attorney General," *Publius: The Journal of Federalism* 42 (2010): 597–616; Colin Provost, "An Integrated Model of U.S. State Attorney General Behavior in Multi-State Litigation," *State Politics and Policy Quarterly* 10 (2010): 1–24.
8. Larry E. Ribstein and Bruce H. Kobayashi, "An Economic Analysis of Uniform State Laws," *Journal of Legal Studies* 25 (1996): 131–199.
9. Ann O'M. Bowman, "Horizontal Federalism: Exploring Interstate Interactions," *Journal of Public Administration Research and Theory* 14 (2004): 535–546.
10. Zimmerman, *Horizontal Federalism.*
11. See the discussion in Mark Carl Rom, "Social Welfare Policy," in *Oxford Handbook of State and Local Politics,* ed. Donald Haider-Markel (New York: Oxford University Press, 2012); Harrell R. Rodgers Jr., Glenn Beamer, and Lee Payne, "No Race in Any Direction: State Welfare and Income Regimes," *Policy Studies Journal* 36 (2008): 525–543.
12. See the discussion in Neal D. Woods, "Interstate Competition and Environmental Regulation: A Test of the Race-to-the-Bottom Thesis," *Social Science Quarterly* 87 (2006): 174–189; David M. Konisky, "Regulator Attitudes and the Environmental Race to the Bottom Argument," *Journal of Public Administration Research and Theory* 18 (2008): 321–344; David M. Konisky, "Assessing U.S. State Susceptibility to Environmental Regulatory Competition," *State Politics and Policy Quarterly* 9 (2009): 404–428.
13. Paul Brace, *State Government and Economic Performance* (Baltimore, MD: Johns Hopkins University Press, 1993).
14. Evidence Counts, Pew Center on the States, www.pewstates.org/uploadedFiles/PCS_Assets/2012/015_12_RI%20Tax%20Incentives%20Report_web.pdf.

15. Mark Robyn and Gerald Prante, "State-Local Tax Burdens Fall in 2009 as Tax Revenues Shrink Faster Than Income," Tax Foundation, http://taxfoundation.org/sites/taxfoundation.org/files/docs/sr189.pdf.

16. As quoted in "Washington State Gov. Chris Gregoire Says That Washington Has Consistently Ranked in the Top Five of Forbes' Best States for Business, Ahead of Texas," www.polifact.com.

17. *Texas v. White* 74 U.S. 700 (1869).

18. Wallace E. Oates, "A Reconsideration of Environmental Federalism," Resources for the Future, Discussion Paper 01-54 (2001): 10.

19. Bednar, *The Robust Federation,* 65.

20. Schlager and Heikkila, "Resolving Water Conflicts"; Schlager, Heikkila, and Case, "The Costs of Compliance."

21. Dale Krane, Platon N. Rigos, and Melvin B. Hill Jr., *Home Rule in American: A Fifty-State Handbook* (Washington, DC: CQ Press, 2001).

22. *The City of Clinton v. The Cedar Rapids and Missouri River Railroad Company,* 24 Iowa 455 (1868).

23. Jesse J. Richardson Jr., "Dillon's Rule Is from Mars, Home Rule Is from Venus: Local Government Autonomy and the Rules of Statutory Construction," *Publius: The Journal of Federalism* 41 (2011): 662–685.

24. G. Ross Stephens. "State Centralization and the Erosion of Local Autonomy," *Journal of Politics* 36 (1974): 44–76.

25. Ann O'M. Bowman and Richard C., Kearney. "Second-Order Devolution: Data and Doubt," *Publius: The Journal of Federalism* 41 (2011): 563–585.

26. Harold Wolman, Robert McManmon, Michael E. Bell, and David Brunori, "Comparing Local Government Autonomy across States," in *The Property Tax and Local Autonomy,* ed. Michael E. Bell, David Brunori, and Joan M. Youngman (Cambridge, MA: Lincoln Institute of Land Policy, 2010).

SUGGESTED READING

Bednar, Jenna. *The Robust Federation: Principles of Design.* New York: Cambridge University Press, 2009.

Broun, Caroline N., Michael L. Buenger, Michael H. McCabe, and Richard L. Masters. *The Evolving Use and the Changing Role of Interstate Compacts: A Practitioner's Guide.* Chicago: ABA Publishing, 2006.

Crain, W. Mark. *Volatile States: Institutions, Policy, and the Performance of American State Economies.* Ann Arbor, MI: University of Michigan Press, 2003.

Feiock, Richard C., and John T. Scholz, eds. *Self-Organizing Federalism: Collaborative Mechanisms to Mitigate Institutional Collective Action Dilemmas.* New York: Cambridge University Press, 2010.

Frug, Gerald E., and David J. Barron. *City Bound: How States Stifle Urban Innovation.* Ithaca, NY: Cornell University Press, 2008.

Kenyon, Daphne A., and John Kincaid, eds. *Competition among States and Local Governments: Efficiency and Equity in American Federalism.* Washington, DC: Urban Institute Press, 1991.

Zimmerman, Joseph F. *Horizontal Federalism: Interstate Relations.* Albany: State University of New York Press, 2011.

———. *Interstate Disputes: The Supreme Court's Original Jurisdiction.* Albany: State University of New York Press, 2006.

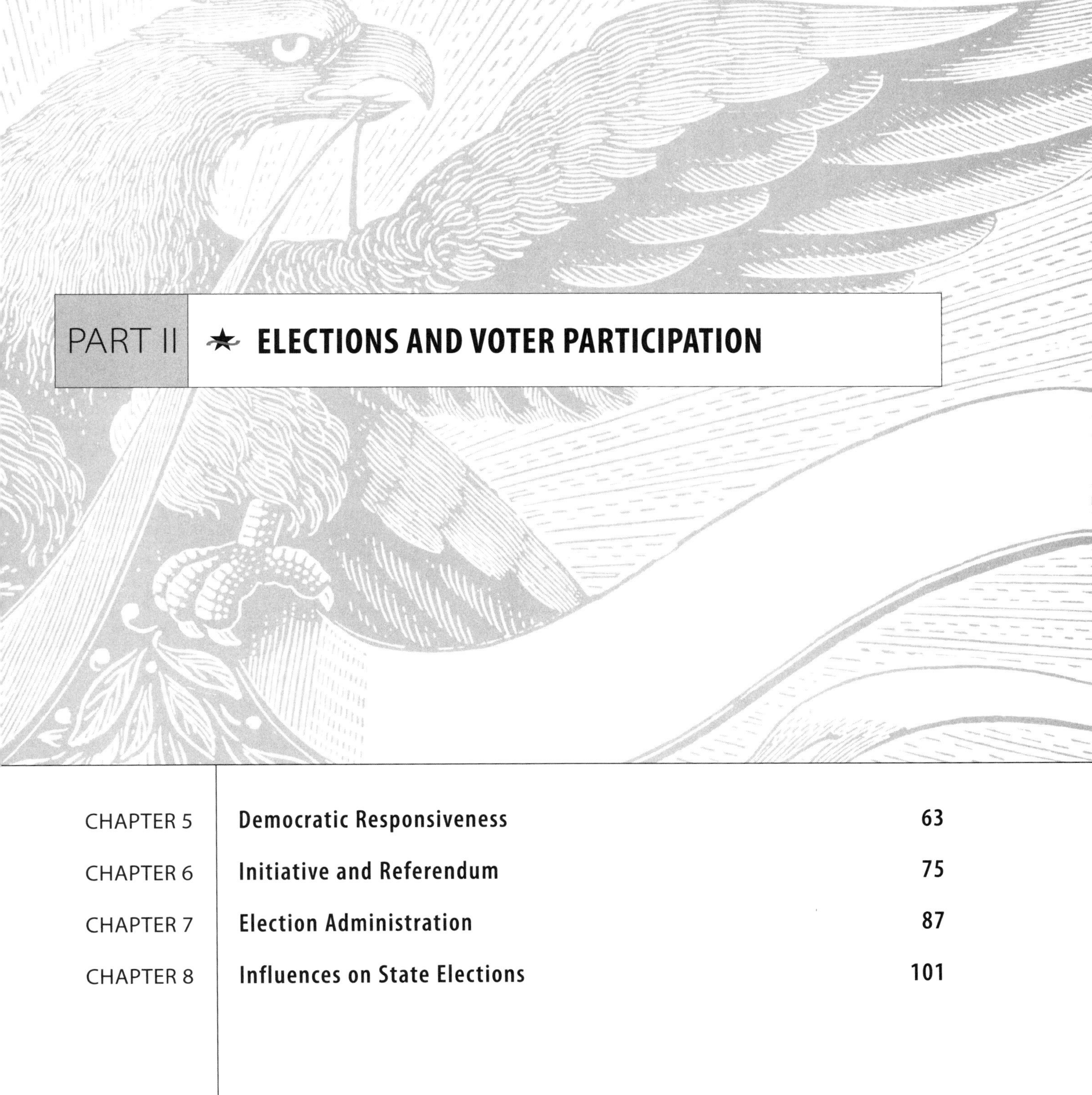

PART II ★ ELECTIONS AND VOTER PARTICIPATION

Chapter 5

Democratic Responsiveness

Justin Phillips

In normative accounts of representative democracy, the preferences and opinions of the public play a critical role in shaping government policy. While there is certainly disagreement over the extent to which elected officials should defer to public opinion, there is near-universal agreement that a functioning democracy requires some minimal matching of government action to citizen preferences. Indeed, the responsiveness of elected officials to the preferences of their constituents is one way that scholars can and do evaluate the quality of a democracy.

Unsurprisingly, then, investigations into the opinion-policy linkage have been a central area of inquiry in the study of state politics. State governments—through the actions of governors, legislators, bureaucrats, and judges—play a crucial role in shaping many of the nation's most important domestic policies, including those related to public education, criminal justice, health care, and minority rights. Because the policy decisions of state governments have far-reaching consequences, it is important that they be shaped, at least in part, by the opinions of voters.

Of course, studying the responsiveness of state governments does much more than tell us about the quality of state-level democracy. Because states vary widely in terms of their political and institutional environments, scholars can use the American states as a laboratory for evaluating factors that may either strengthen or weaken government responsiveness. Can the quality of democratic performance be improved through institutional design? Which features of political institutions do so? Does the interest group or political environment matter? Work on state public opinion allows scholars to address these questions in ways impossible at the national level simply.

This chapter presents an overview of the study of government responsiveness at the state level. It considers the challenges that exist to achieving a high level of responsiveness, the different types of preferences that scholars measure, and their techniques for doing so. It also presents the approaches scholars have taken to evaluate the strength of the opinion-policy linkage and the conclusions that they have reached. In discussing the findings of this research, a special emphasis is placed on insights scholars have generated about the conditions (institutional and otherwise) that strengthen or weaken the influence of public opinion on policymaking.

CHALLENGES TO REPRESENTATION

There are numerous paths by which opinion can shape policy, but the most obvious is the "electoral connection." Elections provide citizens with the opportunity to choose from a set of candidates with differing ideological and policy positions. This enables voters to select governors, legislators, and in some states even judges who share their preferences. Of course, there are obstacles to achieving high levels of government responsiveness. In general, people do not pay a great deal of attention to politics and policymaking, particularly at the state level. Surveys consistently find that only 25 to 30 percent of respondents are very interested in or very attentive to state politics. Indeed, many citizens are woefully uninformed about who represents them in the state capital and about government policies, even in highly salient issue areas. The complexities of American federalism also mean that some people are simply unaware of the functions and responsibilities of state governments. (See Citizen Knowledge of State Policy, Political Institutions, and Responsibilities box.)

Additionally, incumbent lawmakers enjoy resources that give them electoral advantages over most challengers, making them difficult to defeat even if they are unresponsive. Incumbents have higher name recognition, easier access to publicity, and easier access to the money needed to run a political campaign. This is especially true in states with professionalized legislatures. In these chambers, lawmakers have large staffs and travel budgets, which assist in creating name recognition and visibility.[1] The security of lawmakers is ultimately reflected in high rates of reelection—nearly 90 percent for state legislators in many years.

CITIZEN KNOWLEDGE OF STATE POLICY, POLITICAL INSTITUTIONS, AND RESPONSIBILITIES

How much do voters know about state politics and government? Existing survey data provide us with insight. First, large majorities know at least some pertinent information about high-profile state political figures such as governors and senators. These individuals are elected statewide and tend to be the focus of media coverage of state politics. In the month before the 2010 elections, for example, approximately eight out of every ten survey respondents could recognize the name and recall the partisanship of their governor. Not surprisingly, citizens know much less about lower-profile officials. Very few people can recognize the names of the individuals who represent them in the state legislature. Moreover, in a recent national survey, only half of all respondents could correctly identify the political party that controlled a majority of seats in the state legislature.

When it comes to knowledge of state policy and political institutions, the evidence is also mixed. Voters know a great deal about those policies that directly impact their lives. For example, 83 percent of survey respondents correctly answered a question about whether their state imposes a personal income tax. But when it comes to other policies—including some that are quite salient, such as same-sex marriage—the American public is significantly less knowledgeable. The same is true for a variety of political institutions, including many that have been the subject of a great deal of academic inquiry. For example, only 60 percent know that their state has a constitution of its own, while less than a majority know whether their state imposes term limits on legislators.

Not being able to recall these types of facts about state government may be less important than possessing an understanding of its powers and responsibilities. Again, however, the record is mixed. When it comes to immigration policy, large majorities understand that the federal government bears primary responsibility. However, in other policy areas, such as education, criminal justice, and Medicaid, the public appears less informed.

Item	**Response was:**		
To the best of your knowledge, does your state currently have the following:	Correct	Incorrect	Don't know
A personal income tax	83%	5%	12%
A constitution of its own	61	9	30
A ban on same-sex marriages	52	21	27
Term limits for state legislators	46	28	26
Which unit of government—federal or state—is **most responsible** for each of the following:			
Immigration	76%	11%	13%
Public education	63	25	12
Criminal justice	58	27	14
Who currently pays for the Medicaid program—the federal government, state governments, or both the federal and state governments?	56%	33%	11%

SOURCE: 2010 Cooperative Congressional Election Survey (common content and Columbia University module).

Additionally, to be responsive, elected officials need to know the preferences of their constituents. This is not always a straightforward task. State lawmakers and governors typically only have state polling data for a handful of very high-profile or particularly controversial topics. Such data are simply not available for most issues that governors and lawmakers will confront during the legislative session. Furthermore, those surveys that exist measure statewide opinion, potentially providing very little guidance to individual legislators whose districts are often quite different from the state as a whole.

An alternative to opinion surveys are the contacts that elected officials have with constituents and interest groups. Lawmakers regularly hear from voters via mail, e-mail, telephone calls, and grassroots lobbying efforts, and as they travel through their districts. In a large national survey, 7 percent of respondents reported contacting their state representative and 5 percent reported contacting their state senator over a twelve-month period. Of these, more than half said they were expressing an opinion on a specific bill or policy issue.[2] Lawmakers also hear from organized interest groups and paid lobbyists throughout the legislative session. These contacts from voters and interest groups, while unquestionably helpful, do not represent an unbiased sample of the public. Those who will be most affected by a bill are most likely to contact officials, and not all citizens are equally represented in America's interest group system. In particular, we know that groups working for business and well-to-do individuals have proliferated and often hire the most lobbyists and contribute the most money to political campaigns.

All of this being said, state elected officials report that public opinion is important to them. They are aware that mismatches between their behavior in office and the preferences of their constituents, if exploited by political opponents, can lead to electoral defeat. Indeed, studies of Congress show that lawmakers lose votes when they take extreme policy positions, and the same is likely true at the state level.[3] Of course, even if lawmakers are unaware of constituent opinion on a particular issue, they are very likely to know the general ideological leanings of their district or state. This can be an important guide when determining how to vote on a bill.

ALTERNATIVE MEASURES OF STATE PUBLIC OPINION

To evaluate government responsiveness, researchers first need to know something about what constituents want. While no single measure can be said to fully capture public opinion, researchers have several measures of state-level preferences at their disposal. Four are discussed here—ideology, partisanship, policy mood, and issue- or policy-specific opinion. Each of these measures captures a distinct aspect of public opinion and has been successfully employed to study responsiveness. Individually and collectively, they have also generated numerous insights about what voters want from government and the ways in which public preferences differ across states and over time. Each measure has its advantages and limitations. In deciding which to use, scholars consider the particular nature of their research question, the policies being studied, and data availability.

Mass Ideology

Researchers commonly employ state-level estimates of voter ideology. Ideology (like partisanship) is intended to capture the ways in which state voters view and understand politics. A voter's ideology summarizes his or her core political values and principles. Ideological labels are typically reduced to a left-right continuum, with "liberal" on one end and "conservative" on the other. The meanings of these labels evolve over time, often as the result of electoral coalition building and as new issues become politically salient. In contemporary American politics, liberal has come to imply support for a more robust public sector, including government intervention in the economy, more vigorous redistributive programs to help the poor and minorities, and increased environmental protection. Conservative, on the other hand, connotes general suspicion of government power and preference of private-sector solutions to economic problems. When it comes to social and cultural issues, liberals tend to be more permissive than conservatives, and usually support abortion rights and increased legal protections for gays and lesbians.

It can be hard to identify logical connections between the policy positions associated with liberals and conservatives, since these connections are often formed for political expedience. That being said, for researchers ideology is a useful classification that contains a considerable amount of information. For many people, particularly those who are politically knowledgeable, ideology structures their political behavior and opinions—it is very closely linked to the choices they make in the voting booth, their evaluation of political events, and the positions they hold across a variety of issues. Among less politically sophisticated individuals, however, ideology sometimes has little relevance to the ways in which they respond to the political world.

To measure ideology, scholars typically rely on survey questions that ask respondents something like the following: Generally, do you think of yourself as liberal, moderate, or conservative? The resulting data show that the plurality of Americans self-identify as ideological conservatives. While the specific results vary somewhat across surveys, polling indicates that about 40 percent of Americans call themselves conservative, another 20 to 25 percent identify as liberals, and the remaining indicate ideological moderation. Correspondingly, state electorates tend to be conservative, though the specific ideological balance varies. In all but a handful of states, the share of self-identified conservatives outnumbers liberals. The size of the conservative advantage is greatest in the South, where it averages over 25 percentage points, and smallest in New England, the only region of the country in which most (but not all) state electorates tilt in the liberal direction.[4]

Research suggests state-level ideology is quite stable, and that it has changed relatively little over the past three decades. The most liberal states in the 1970s and 1980s remain the most liberal states today. A recent analysis finds that the correlation between state ideology at the beginning and end of their time series (the administrations of Jimmy Carter though George W. Bush) is a very powerful 0.86.[5]

Mass Partisanship

Like ideology, partisanship is a widely used measure of global preferences. Partisanship captures the disposition of individuals toward the Democratic and Republican Parties. This is the attitude that most structures the political opinions of Americans and, unlike ideology, it is meaningful for individuals across nearly all levels of political sophistication and knowledge. Though ideology and partisanship are strongly correlated, they are not the same thing. Republicans are more likely to identify as conservative than are Democrats, but a substantial (though shrinking) number of Americans—liberal Republicans or conservative Democrats—do not fit neatly into this categorization.

To create measures of mass partisanship, scholars again rely on survey data. The questions used typically ask respondents: Generally speaking, do you consider yourself to be a Democrat, Republican, Independent, or what? From the 1930s to the 1970s, Democrats enjoyed a large numeric advantage over Republicans. Since the 1980s, however, something closer to parity was achieved, though more people still identify as Democrats. This means that despite being ideologically conservative, state electorates tend be more Democratic than Republican.

According to a recent analysis, self-identified Democrats outnumber Republicans in thirty-three states.[6] This advantage is largest in Massachusetts (25 percent) and smallest in Utah (−34 percent). The Democratic advantage persists even in some states that are quite ideologically conservative, such as Arkansas, Kentucky, and West Virginia. Meanwhile, neither political party reaches a majority in voter identification in any state, indicating that Independents are crucial for shaping the outcomes of elections.

State-level partisanship is less temporally stable than ideology. Since the 1970s the southern (and border) states have abandoned their traditional alliance to the Democratic Party and transitioned to more competitive two-party systems. Several southern electorates now have more self-identified Republicans than Democrats. This circumstance would have been very difficult to imagine four decades ago. Over this same period of time, states in the Northeast and Midwest have been more Democratic. Though partisanship is dynamic over time, changes do not occur rapidly.

An additional and equally noteworthy change is the growing correlation between state-level measures of partisanship and ideology. During the Carter administration state liberalism and Democratic identification were very weakly correlated at 0.06. Liberal states were, on average, no more likely to have Democratic electorates than were their more conservative counterparts. By the presidency of George W. Bush, this correlation had risen to 0.66.[7] Today, the most liberal states tend to be the most Democratic (with a few exceptions), and the most conservative states are the most Republican.

Evidence indicates that this change emerged because voters have been slowly shifting their partisan identification so that it is consistent with their ideology. Simply put, liberal Republicans and conservative Democrats are becoming less common. Today, ideology and partisanship reinforce one another in a way they did not thirty years ago. A consequence of this change is that state political parties are becoming more ideologically polarized. Furthermore, state ideology is now the dominant predictor of how states will vote in presidential elections, and its impact has grown monotonically since the 1972 election.

Public Mood

Public sentiment at the state level has also been measured using indicators of policy mood. Policy mood is a concept first introduced in studies of public opinion at the national level, and refers to the public's general disposition toward government, particularly its support for New Deal/social welfare–type policies. According to James Stimson, mood "connotes shared feelings that move over time and circumstance."[8] Unlike partisanship and ideology, policy mood is not a long-standing decision. Instead, it responds to the ever-changing context of politics.

In particular, mood reacts to the policy proposals and enactments of elected officials, fluctuating between preferences for more and less government. The overall policy orientation of the public (at least at the national level) is moderate, but when elected officials push policy too far to the right for the average voter, policy mood becomes more liberal; when officials push policy too far to the left, it becomes more conservative. Voters respond to changes in their mood by changing the identity of policymakers, often replacing incumbent officials with members of the opposition party.

Mood is typically measured using a multitude of survey questions that ask respondents about their policy preferences, such as their support for gun control, labor unions, government efforts to help minorities, and current levels of government spending. The results of these surveys are combined into a single measure using an algorithm developed by Stimson in his influential book, *Public Opinion in America*.[9] One team of researchers has developed a surrogate measure of state policy mood that does not rely on survey data.[10] Instead, the researchers use state election results and federal-level data on the liberalness of the roll call votes cast by members of Congress.[11] Even though this measure only indirectly captures voters' policy preferences, it compares favorably to survey-based measures.

There are important differences in policy mood across the states. First, states exhibit very different baseline

Protestors demand less government at a noon "Cut Spending Now Revolt" near the steps of the Capitol building in Washington, DC, on April 6, 2011, to urge lawmakers to reduce federal spending. The Tea Party–style rally was organized by Americans for Prosperity, a conservative, free-market group. Party leaders on Capitol Hill were racing to overcome an impasse in budget talks that threatened a partial shutdown of the United States government.

SOURCE: Jeff Malet Photography/Newscom.

or average policy orientations. Over each of the prior fifty years, for example, the policy mood in New York has been more liberal than that of Utah, though the mood in both states has experienced fairly significant cyclical fluctuations.[12] Second, though fluctuations in state policy mood are strongly correlated with events at the national level as well as changes in national mood, states do not always move in lockstep. This is not surprising, given that mood reacts to state (as well as federal) policymaking. Moreover, voters in different states may have divergent responses to events at the national level.

Issue-Specific Opinion

In addition to global measures of opinion such as partisanship, ideology, and policy mood, researchers are often interested in issue- or policy-specific opinion. Are voters pro-choice when it comes to abortion, or are they pro-life? Do a majority of state voters favor same-sex marriage, or are they opposed? Global preference measures do not necessarily reveal how state voters feel on specific issues like these. Indeed, pollsters find that many voters hold opinions that are inconsistent with their stated global preferences.

This does not mean that global measures cannot provide guidance to issue- or policy-specific opinion, but researchers must be careful. For example, attitudes on abortion, gay and lesbian rights, and government spending are all highly correlated to a person's self-identified ideology. However, opinions on a host of education policies and political reforms are not. Thus in some issue areas ideology may be a reasonable (if imperfect) substitute for specific opinion, but in others using ideology does not adequately represent voters' preferences. Interestingly, state partisanship tends to have fewer clear relationships to specific opinion than does ideology.[13]

Like ideology and partisanship, specific opinion varies across states. The amount of variation, though, is contingent upon the particular issue or policy under consideration. Legislative terms limits, for example, are popular everywhere, whereas same-sex marriage enjoys majority support in some states but has very little public support in others. Research also indicates that majorities of the voting-age population in all states (regardless of the state's overall partisan or ideological leanings) support some policies that are typically associated with liberals and some that are typically associated with conservatives. For instance, majorities in California and Massachusetts (both liberal states) support the death penalty, legislative term limits, and various abortion restrictions, while opinion majorities in Alabama and Arizona (both conservative states) support laws protecting gays and lesbians from employment discrimination and laws allowing for medical marijuana.[14] The particular set of liberal or conservative opinion majorities is not the same across states; nor is the balance between the two.

While specific opinion allows researchers to capture more nuance than do global measures of preferences, there are some cautions. Many Americans are not very knowledgeable about politics or public policy and therefore may not have strong or well-formed preferences across a wide range of policies. This is particularly likely for issues that are complex or that do not receive much media attention. The lack of an informed or considered opinion does not necessarily prevent respondents from answering survey questions. Furthermore, specific opinion often changes over time (much more so than ideology or partisanship) and can sometimes be manipulated through question wording and placement.

APPROACHES TO ESTIMATING STATE-LEVEL PUBLIC OPINION

Typically, political scientists measure and study public opinion using scientific polling. The beauty of a well-constructed and properly administered poll is that it will almost always provide a reasonably accurate snapshot of opinion. Unfortunately, systematic opinion surveys at the state level are rarely available, forcing researchers to rely upon other approaches to generate estimates of state preferences. This section discusses the extent of state-level polling as well as two of the alternative approaches employed by political scientists—disaggregation and simulation.

State-Level Polls

There is a rich and growing tradition of state-level polling. A recent effort to document and publicize state opinion surveys uncovered a handful of state polls that date back to the 1940s, including the nation's oldest ongoing opinion survey, the Iowa Poll, which was started by the *Des Moines Register* in 1943.[15] Today, there are fifty-four ongoing polls in thirty-five states, most of which are rigorous and ambitious in scope. As technological advances have made public opinion polling faster and cheaper, we have also witnessed an explosion in nonacademic state polling by local media, candidates for public office, political parties, and for-profit polling firms.

Despite the growing number of state opinion surveys, finding comparable polls across states can be daunting and in most cases impossible. Similar questions are almost never asked in surveys across all or even many states. When they are, differences in timing, question wording, survey techniques, and response categories can make comparisons difficult. Nonacademic polling is largely of the horse-race variety, focusing almost exclusively on races for state elected office. Data from these polls are proprietary and only rarely made available to academic researchers.

However, some researchers have been able to effectively use state polls, either for single-state studies or for cross-sectional analyses. One of the more impressive efforts is that of Thad Beyle, Richard G. Niemi, and Lee Sigelman, who compiled a dataset of gubernatorial approval ratings.[16] These data, though inconsistently available and missing for many governors (especially those from less populous states), have helped researchers better understand the causes and effects of the approval ratings of state officials. In general, however, state polls are not a dependable source of public opinion data, and their absence is a source of much frustration for researchers engaged in the comparative study of state politics.

National opinion polls, while much more common, are not designed to measure public opinion at the state level. These polls rarely sample enough respondents from each state to make meaningful cross-state comparisons possible. An average-sized national survey is likely to include just a few people from smaller-population states such as Delaware, North Dakota, and Vermont. Constructing a single poll with a representative sample from each of the fifty states is prohibitively expensive for all but the most specialized surveys. That being said, recent years have seen the development of a handful of large collaborative academic polling projects such as the Cooperative Congressional Election Study (CCES). These polls are very large (typically well over thirty thousand respondents) and aim to provide representative samples in all or most states. While these polls are a great new source of opinion data, they include only a limited number of questions about state politics and policy.

Disaggregation

One approach to dealing with the lack of systematic state-level opinion polling is disaggregation. This technique is fairly straightforward. Scholars pool (i.e., combine) national surveys until large enough state samples have been created. After pooling, one calculates mean opinion for each state. The only necessary data are the respondent's answer to the relevant survey question and his or her state of residence. No further statistical analysis is required.

Robert S. Erikson, Gerald C. Wright, and John P. McIver pioneered this approach in their seminal book *Statehouse Democracy*.[17] In this book, they generate estimates of the ideology and partisanship of state voters by pooling 122 national CBS/*New York Times* surveys conducted between 1976 and 1988. In total, these surveys provided over 150,000 respondents. By pooling the surveys, the authors were able to obtain a large sample of respondents in each state, all of whom were asked whether they were a Democrat, Republican, or Independent, and also whether they were liberal, conservative, or moderate. Because the CBS/*New York Times* polls were conducted using random-digit dialing, these pooled state samples were likely to be representative of the state population, almost as if a separate poll had been conducted in each state.

After the work of Erikson, Wright, and McIver, disaggregation became the standard approach for estimating public sentiment at the state level, and its reliability has been repeatedly confirmed. In addition to being used to estimate measures of global preferences like state partisanship and ideology, it has occasionally been employed to estimate issue- or policy-specific opinion.

Despite its popularity, disaggregation has important practical limitations. The principal disadvantage is that it requires a large number of national surveys—often over a decade or longer—in order to create a sufficient sample size within each state. Thus the technique can be used only for questions that consistently appear in surveys. Such questions are typically those that deal with core political attitudes such as ideology and partisanship. Questions about a timely policy debate, however, are likely to appear in just a few polls, soon to be replaced by the next newsworthy concern.

Furthermore, pooling surveys should be done only for opinions that are stable. Combining surveys over long periods of time obscures temporal dynamics within or across states. Although ideology and partisanship may be slow to change, other attitudes, such as voters' approval of the president or their support for same-sex marriage, can and do change over a short time span. Additionally, national surveys, while representative at that level, are often flawed in terms of representativeness or geographic coverage at the state level, due to clustering and other survey techniques utilized by polling firms.

Simulation

An alternative to pooling is simulating state opinion using national level surveys as well as demographic and geographic data. Simulation as a method for studying state public opinion originally gained popularity in the 1960s and 1970s. However, early efforts failed to properly account for geography (i.e., state and region) as a determinant of opinion. Furthermore, these efforts, due to limitations in computing power and in the available statistical tools, only focused on a fairly narrow set of voter types, thereby limiting the accuracy of estimates. These criticisms caused simulation to fall out of favor and led scholars to prefer the disaggregation approach.

Recently, a modern variant to simulation, known as multilevel regression and poststratification (MRP), has been developed and popularized.[18] MRP proceeds in two stages. In the first stage, individual survey responses and regression analysis are used to estimate the opinions of different types of people. (This is the "multilevel regression" part of MRP.) A respondent's opinions are treated as being, in part, a function of his or her demographic characteristics. Research has consistently demonstrated that demographic variables are crucial determinants of individuals' political opinions. The groups to which people belong structure their life experiences and possibly their future opportunities. Group memberships also shape the political attitudes and beliefs to which a person is exposed on an ongoing basis. The demographic variables that are typically employed include a respondent's age, education, gender, and race.

In addition to demography, survey responses are treated as a function of a respondent's state and region. Why are geographic predictors included? The state and region of the country in which people live are important predictors of their core political attitudes as well as their opinions on a variety of policy debates. Erikson, Wright, and McIver, for example, discovered that the effect of state residency on ideology can be as large as the effect of income.[19] Though it is not clear why geography is such an important predictor of opinion, researchers typically point to unique state and regional political cultures, which may owe their origins to the differing immigration patterns and social and economic histories of places. It is likely that exposure to the predominant political culture of their state sometimes influences citizens to hold political views that they otherwise would not.

The regression estimates from stage one of MRP tell researchers the probability that a type of person (for example, black females in New York of ages eighteen to twenty-nine with a college degree) will hold a particular opinion. Most applications of MRP estimate opinion for close to five thousand demographic-geographic types. This is many more than were utilized in early simulation approaches.

The second stage of MRP is referred to as post-stratification. Based on data from the U.S. Census, scholars know what proportion of a given state's population is comprised by each demographic-geographic type from stage one. (For example, the subset of New York residents mentioned above comprise approximately 0.2 percent of the state's total population.) Within each state, researchers simply take opinion across every demographic-geographic type and weight it by its frequency in the population. Finally, these weighted estimates are added up in each state to get a measure of overall state-level support for a nominee.

Simulation, if executed properly, requires many fewer surveys than disaggregation, allowing researchers to estimate state opinion on an issue without having that issue appear in several polls. These techniques have been validated by comparing the accuracy of opinion estimates generated via simulation to the results of actual state polls, to state voting in presidential elections, and to the estimates of public opinion obtained by pooling many national surveys. These comparisons demonstrate that simulation performs quite well and that it can be used to generate opinion estimates, sometimes employing as little as a single average-sized national poll.

Not surprisingly, MRP has resulted in a revival of simulation in studies of state opinion and has been used to estimate state-level measures of public preferences across a large number of issues. With a single poll, simulation can be used to provide a snapshot of opinion across the fifty states; using surveys conducted over many years, one can estimate more dynamic measures of opinion.

THE INFLUENCE OF PUBLIC OPINION ON POLICYMAKING

The development of techniques for estimating state-level measures of public opinion has spurred valuable new research into the influence of public preferences on policymaking. In doing so, researchers have considered two features of the opinion-policy linkage: responsiveness and congruence. Evaluations of responsiveness consider whether there is a positive correlation between opinion and policy. In a responsive political system, as support for a particular policy increases, so should the probability of policy adoption. Tests for congruence consider whether state policy matches majority opinion—that is, if a majority of voters want a state lottery, how likely is it that their state will adopt one? Although responsiveness and congruence are related concepts, they are not the same thing. It is possible for policy to be generally responsive but still remain incongruent with majority opinion in many states. In political systems in which there is a very strong opinion-policy linkage, one would expect high levels of both responsiveness and congruence.

The seminal work on the responsiveness of state governments is that of Erikson, Wright, and McIver. The authors compare a state-level measure of global preferences—voter ideology—to a measure of the ideological tone of state policy, which they refer to as a state's "policy liberalism." Erikson, Wright, and McIver find a very strong relationship between voter ideology and policy liberalism, concluding that "state political structures appear to do a good job of delivering more liberal policies to more liberal states and more conservative policies to more conservative states."[20] This study was the first to demonstrate a relationship between voter sentiment and government action at the state level, overturning the long-standing view that the public, due to its lack of knowledge and interest in state politics, had little influence over state policy.

While the work of Erikson, Wright, and McIver unquestionably altered our understanding of democracy at the state level, the use of ideology as a measure of public preferences can be problematic. Problems arise because researchers cannot know exactly how global preference measures ought to translate into policy. That is, policy and ideology (or policy mood, for that matter) lack a common metric. For example, how liberal should policy be in a state in which 30 percent of voters self-identify as liberal? Clearly, policy in a state with 35 percent liberals should be even more liberal, but how much more? A high correlation between ideology and policy reveals a strong relationship between the two, but without knowing the mapping of ideology to voter policy preferences, we cannot tell if policy is over- or under-responsive to preferences (i.e., are voters really getting what they want?).[21]

This dilemma has led scholars increasingly to rely on issue- or policy-specific measures of preferences (when possible). A number of recent studies have examined the relationship between specific opinion and state policymaking on that topic. These studies have focused on a wide range of issues, including abortion rights, capital punishment, environmental policy, gay and lesbian rights, and antismoking legislation.[22] Studies find that, like ideology, specific opinion matters, though its correlation with policy ranges from modest to very strong, depending on the policy area. One of the most comprehensive investigations examines the correlation between specific opinion and government action for thirty-nine policies in eight different issue areas.[23] This study finds that specific opinion is, on average, the strongest predictor of policy adoption, even after taking into account other potential influences, including the partisanship of elected officials. The authors find that policy is responsive to both global preference measures (voter ideology) and policy-specific opinion.

Although policy is generally responsive to public sentiment, a surprising amount of incongruence exists—that is, policy is often inconsistent with the preferences of the median constituent. Two recent studies find that state policies, at least when it comes to contested issues, match majority opinion only about half the time.[24] While no one would expect (or maybe even want) opinion majorities to prevail in all policy debates, a congruence rate of 50 percent is fairly low and could be achieved if policy were decided by tossing a coin. The frequent mismatch between majority opinion and policy can be thought of as a "democratic deficit."

The amount of incongruence as well as its ideological direction varies meaningfully across states. The states that do the best job matching policy to majority opinion are California and Louisiana, both of which do so 69 percent of the time. The states that score the poorest are New Hampshire, Pennsylvania, West Virginia, and Wyoming. In each of these, only 33 percent of the policies studied are consistent with majority opinion. The ideological direction of a state's incongruence is strongly correlated to the ideology of its voters. Elected officials in liberal states tend to go "too far" in adopting liberal policies, and elected officials in conservative states tend to go "too far" in adopting conservative policies. To put it simply, policy is polarized relative to specific opinion.[25]

ACCOUNTING FOR DIFFERENCES IN RESPONSIVENESS AND CONGRUENCE

After two decades of research on the opinion-policy linkage, few would argue (as they once did) that public opinion is not a crucial determinant of government action. Scholars are now training much of their effort on accounting for observed differences in responsiveness and congruence across issue areas and states. Why does public opinion matter more in some policy areas than others? Why is the opinion-policy linkage stronger in some states? Existing work has identified several key explanatory variables.

Issue or Policy Salience

The first of these is the salience of a particular issue or policy—as the salience increases, so does the opinion-policy linkage. Salient issues are those that are highly visible to the public, particularly in the mass media, or felt directly by constituents. For salient policies, the public is much more likely to hold strong opinions, to convey those opinions to their representatives, and to hold their representatives accountable. Thus the electoral incentives are clear: on one side, the legislators will have greater information about public opinion, and on the other side, the greater visibility of policy choice should decrease the ability to get away with skirting the public will.

When salience is low, officials may be unaware of their constituents' preferences. In this case, lawmakers who want to be responsive to public sentiment but are unaware of what their constituents want on the particular issue may rely on voter partisanship or ideology. In fact, research shows that when salience is low the impact of specific opinion declines and the effect of voter ideology on outcomes grows.[26]

Morality Policy

Policymakers are particularly responsive to public preferences and values on issues of morality.[27] Morality policies are defined by debates over basic values in which at least one side portrays the issue as involving morality or sin. These debates are fundamentally clashes over right and wrong and have their origins in differences in individuals' core values. Examples of morality policy include gay and lesbian rights, abortion, and the death penalty.

Three defining characteristics of morality policy explain why the opinion-policy linkage is so strong in this area. First, morality policy tends to be technically simple. Unlike debates over health care reform or environmental regulation, a potential voter does not need a lot of information to participate. Second, morality policy issues tend to be highly salient. These issues, when they are on the agenda, receive a great deal of media attention. Ongoing debates over same-sex marriage illustrate this point quite clearly. Third, morality politics is characterized by high levels of political participation. When a morality policy issue arises, those citizens whose basic values are being challenged have a strong incentive to mobilize. (For more on morality policy, see Chapter 27.)

Interest Groups

The state interest group environment has also been found to shape the opinion-policy linkage, doing so in a nuanced way. Interest groups are important actors in state politics, giving voice to citizen demands and helping citizens obtain access to elected officials. As a result, they can increase responsiveness by assisting opinion majorities in the potentially long and difficult process of translating their preferences into policy. On the other hand, powerful interest groups may use their resources to block popular policies, and elected officials may be pressured to satisfy such groups instead of the median voter (to garner campaign contributions or other types of support). There is empirical support for both propositions—interest groups do not consistently have a positive or negative effect on the opinion-policy linkage. Research shows that powerful interest groups enhance responsiveness when the policy objectives of these groups line up with majority opinion, but have a dampening effect when a powerful group is opposed to the majority opinion.[28] As a result, it is the balance of interest groups in a particular state that is key.

Of course, a state's interest group environment can be shaped by public opinion itself. In their study of the fiscal priorities of state governments, Saundra K. Schneider and William G. Jacoby found that opinion has its greatest impact through its effect on the composition of the state interest group population.[29] They discovered that state spending on collective goods is strongly correlated to the number of groups that support such expenditures and that the number of these groups is shaped by the ideology and partisanship of state voters. (For more on interest groups, see Chapter 10.)

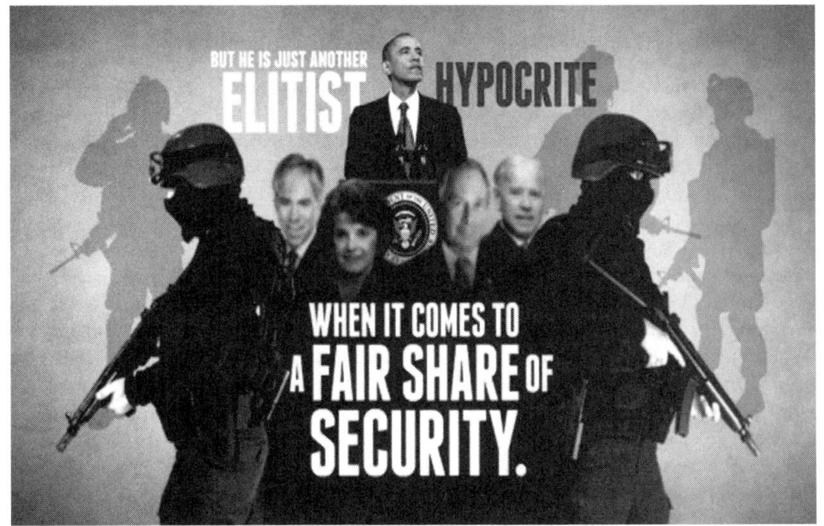

The National Rifle Association has successfully opposed both state and federal efforts to enact more restrictive legislation concerning the purchase of guns and "open carry" and "concealed carry" practices. This image shows a scene from a controversial video released by the National Rifle Association on January 16, 2013, that labels President Barack Obama an "elitist hypocrite" for allowing his daughters to be protected by armed Secret Service agents while not embracing armed guards for schools. "Are the president's kids more important than yours?" a male narrator asks in the video. "Then why is he skeptical of putting armed security in schools, when his kids are protected by armed guards in their school?"

SOURCE: AP Photo; image from National Rifle Association video.

Political Institutions

Numerous analyses have also considered the consequences of institutions on the opinion-policy relationship. In general, two features of institutions have been shown to condition this relationship. The first is an enhanced *capacity* to assess and respond to public opinion. Such institutions include professional legislatures.[30] Longer sessions allow lawmakers in these chambers to consider more issues, including those of relatively lower salience, and outside employment is less likely to constrain their attention to constituent interests. Seats in professional chambers are also more valuable, so there are greater incentives for lawmakers to be responsive.

The second feature of institutions that has been shown to matter is *majoritarianism*. It has long been hypothesized that institutions that empower electoral majorities increase the effect of public opinion on policy. Two such institutions are the election of judges (see Chapter 21) and access to the citizen initiative (see Chapter 6). Elected judges, because they can be held accountable to voters, may be less likely to overrule the popular actions of legislatures and less likely to issue unpopular decisions on contentious social issues such as gay and lesbian rights, the death penalty, and abortion. Access to the citizen initiative allows voters to circumvent unresponsive legislatures and set policies themselves, or at least threaten to do so as a means of spurring legislative action.

CONCLUSION

Thirty years ago, many scholars believed that the public had little influence over policymaking at the state level. Advances in measuring state public opinion have fundamentally altered this understanding. We can now safely conclude that public opinion matters, and that it does so across a wide range of issue areas. Indeed, studies consistently find that public opinion, when compared with other potential determinants of outcomes (including the partisan control of government), has the largest substantive impact on policymaking. That being said, the opinion-policy link is complicated. Newer research has uncovered evidence of a surprisingly large democratic deficit. On average, policy matches majority opinion only about half the time. Even though opinion matters, the democratic performance of state government remains imperfect.

NOTES

1. William Berry, Michael Berkman, and Stuart Schneiderman, "Legislative Professionalism and Incumbent Reelection: The Development of Institutional Boundaries," *American Political Science Review* 94 (2000): 859–874.

2. Richard G. Niemi and Lynda W. Powell, "United Citizenship? Knowing and Contacting Legislators after Term Limits," in *The Test of Time: Coping with Legislative Term Limits,* ed. Rick Farmer, John David Rausch Jr., and John C. Green (Lanham, MD: Lexington, 2001).

3. Robert S. Erikson and Gerald C. Wright, "Voters, Candidates, and Issues in Congressional Elections," in *Congress Reconsidered,* 9th ed., Lawrence C. Dodd and Bruce I. Oppenheimer, eds. (Washington, DC: CQ Press, 2009).

4. Justin H. Phillips, "Public Opinion and Morality," in *Politics in the American States: A Comparative Analysis,* 10th ed., Virginia Gray, Russell Hanson, and Thad Kousser, eds. (Washington, DC: CQ Press, 2012).

5. Robert S. Erikson, Gerald C. Wright, and John P. McIver, "Public Opinion in the States: A Quarter Century of Change and Stability," in *Public Opinion in State Politics,* ed. Jeffrey E. Cohen (Stanford, CA: Stanford University Press, 2006).

6. Phillips, "Public Opinion and Morality."

7. Erikson, Wright, and McIver, "Public Opinion in the States."

8. James Stimson, *Public Opinion in America: Moods, Cycles, and Swings* (Boulder, CO.: Westview, 1991), 20.

9. Ibid.

10. William D. Berry, Evan J. Ringquist, Richard C. Fording, and Russell L. Hanson. "Measuring Citizen and Government Ideology in the American States, 1960–93." American Journal of Political Science 42 (1998): 327–348.

11. The measure created by Berry et al. (1998) was originally proposed as an indicator of voter ideology and has been used as such in many empirical analyses in the state politics literature. However, subsequent work suggests that the measure better captures policy mood. See William Berry, Evan Ringquist, Richard Fording, and Russell Hanson, "The Measurement and Stability of State Citizen Ideology," *State Politics and Policy Quarterly* 7 (Summer 2007): 111–132; William Berry, Richard Fording, Evan Ringquist, Russell Hanson, and Carl Klarner, "Measuring Citizen and Government Ideology in the U.S. States: A Re-appraisal," *State Politics and Policy Quarterly* 10 (Summer 2010): 117–135. By using election results and interest group scores—data that are readily available—Berry et al. succeed in creating yearly estimates of policy mood for all fifty states.

12. Berry et al., "Measuring Citizen and Government Ideology in the American States, 1960–93"; Phillips, "Public Opinion and Morality."

13. Barbara Norrander, "Measuring State Public Opinion with the Senate National Election Study," *State Politics and Policy Quarterly* 1 (2001): 111–125.

14. Jeffrey Lax and Justin Phillips, "The Democratic Deficit in State Policymaking," *American Journal of Political Science* 56 (2012): 148–166.

15. Janine A. Parry, Brian Kisida, and Ronald E. Langley, "The State of State Polls: Old Challenges, New Opportunities," *State Politics and Policy Quarterly* 8 (2008): 198–216.

16. Thad Beyle, Richard G. Niemi, and Lee Sigelman, "Gubernatorial, Senatorial, and State-Level Presidential Job Approval: The U.S. Officials Job Approval Ratings (JAR) Collection," *State Politics and Policy Quarterly* 2 (2002): 215–229.

17. Robert S. Erikson, Gerald C. Wright, and John P. McIver, *Statehouse Democracy: Public Opinion and Policy in the American States* (Cambridge, UK: Cambridge University Press, 1993).

18. Andrew Gelman and Thomas C. Little, "Poststratification into Many Categories Using Hierarchical Logistic Regression," *Survey Methodology* 23 (1997): 127–135; David K. Park, Andrew

Gelman, and Joseph Bafumi, "State Level Opinions from National Surveys: Poststratification Using Multilevel Logistic Regression," in *Public Opinion in State Politics,* ed. Jeffrey E. Cohen (Stanford, CA: Stanford University Press, 1993); Jeffrey Lax and Justin Phillips, "How Should We Estimate Public Opinion in the States?" *American Journal of Political Science* 53 (2009): 107–121.

19. Erikson, Wright, and McIver, *Statehouse Democracy.*

20. Ibid., p. 65.

21. John G. Matsusaka, "Problems with a Methodology Used to Evaluate the Voter Initiative," *Journal of Politics* 63 (2001): 1250–1256.

22. Barbara Norrander and Clyde Wilcox, "Public Opinion and Policymaking in the States: The Case of Post-*Roe* Abortion Policy," *Policy Studies Journal* 27 (1999): 707–722; Christopher Z. Mooney and Mei-Hsein Lee, "The Influence of Values on Consensus and Contentious Morality Policy: U.S. Death Penalty Reform, 1956–1982," *Journal of Politics* 62 (2000): 223–239; Martin Johnson, Paul Brace, and Kevin Arceneaux, "Public Opinion and Dynamic Representation in the States: The Case of Environmental Attitudes," *Social Science Quarterly* 86 (2005): 87–108; Jeffrey Lax and Justin Phillips, "Public Opinion and Policy Responsiveness: Gay Rights in the States," *American Political Science Review* 103 (2009): 367–385; Julianna Pacheco, "The Social Contagion Model: Exploring the Role of Public Opinion on the Diffusion of Anti-Smoking Legislation across the American States," *Journal of Politics* 74 (2012): 187–202.

23. Lax and Phillips, "The Democratic Deficit in State Policymaking."

24. Ibid.; John G. Matsusaka, "Popular Control of Public Policy: A Quantitative Approach," *Quarterly Journal of Political Science* 5 (2010): 133–167.

25. Lax and Phillips, "The Democratic Deficit in State Policymaking."

26. Lax and Phillips, "Public Opinion and Policy Responsiveness: Gay Rights in the States"; Donald P. Haider-Markel and Kenneth J. Meier, "The Politics of Gay and Lesbian Rights: Expanding the Scope of the Conflict," *Journal of Politics* 58 (1996): 332–349.

27. Lax and Phillips, "The Democratic Deficit in State Policymaking"; Haider-Markel and Meier, "The Politics of Gay and Lesbian Rights."

28. Lax and Phillips, "The Democratic Deficit in State Policymaking."

29. Saundra K. Schneider and William G. Jacoby, "Citizen Influence on State Policy Priorities: The Interplay of Public Opinion and Interest Groups," in *Public Opinion in State Politics,* ed. Jeffrey E. Cohen (Stanford, CA: Stanford University Press, 2006).

30. Lax and Phillips, "The Democratic Deficit in State Policymaking"; Cherie Maestas, "Professional Legislatures and Ambitious Politicians: Policy Responsiveness of State Institutions," *Legislative Studies Quarterly* 25 (2000): 663–690.

SUGGESTED READING

Berry, William D., Evan J. Ringquist, Richard C. Fording, and Russell L. Hanson. "Measuring Citizen and Government Ideology in the American States, 1960–93." *American Journal of Political Science* 42 (1998): 327–348.

Brace, Paul, Kellie Sims-Butler, Kevin Arceneaux, and Martin Johnson. "Public Opinion in the American States: New Perspectives Using National Survey Data." *American Journal of Political Science* 46 (2002): 173–189.

Carsey, Thomas M., and Jeffrey Harden. "New Measures of Partisanship, Ideology, and Policy Mood in the American States." *State Politics and Policy Quarterly* 10 (2010): 136–156.

Cohen, Jeffrey E., ed. *Public Opinion in State Politics.* Stanford, CA: Stanford University Press, 2006.

Erikson, Robert S. and Kent L. Tedin. *American Public Opinion: Its Origins, Content, and Impact,* 8th ed. Boston: Longman, 2011.

Erikson, Robert S., Gerald C. Wright, and John P. McIver. "Public Opinion in the States: A Quarter Century of Change and Stability." In *Public Opinion in State Politics,* edited by Jeffrey E. Cohen. Stanford, CA: Stanford University Press, 2006.

———. *Statehouse Democracy: Public Opinion and Policy in the American States.* Cambridge: Cambridge University Press, 1993.

Gelman, Andrew, David Park, Boris Shor, Joseph Bafumi, and Jeronimo Cortina. *Red State, Blue State, Rich State, Poor State: Why Americans Vote the Way They Do.* Princeton, NJ: Princeton University Press, 2008.

Hogan, Robert E. "Policy Responsiveness and Incumbent Reelection in State Legislatures." *American Journal of Political Science* 42 (2008): 858–873.

Lax, Jeffrey, and Justin Philips. "The Democratic Deficit in State Policymaking." *American Journal of Political Science* 56 (2009a): 148–166.

———. "How Should We Estimate Public Opinion in the States?" *American Journal of Political Science* 53 (2009b): 107–121.

———. "Public Opinion and Policy Responsiveness: Gay Rights in the States." *American Political Science Review* 103 (2009c): 367–385.

Lupia, Arthur, Yanna Krupnikov, Adam Seth Levine, Spencer Piston, and Alexander Von Hagen-Jamar. "Why State Constitutions Differ in Their Treatment of Same-Sex Marriage." *Journal of Politics* 72 (2010): 1222–1235.

Mooney, Christopher Z., ed. *The Public Clash of Private Values: The Politics of Morality Policy.* New York: Chatham House, 2001.

Norrander, Barbara, and Clyde Wilcox. "Public Opinion and Policymaking in the States: The Case of Post-*Roe* Abortion Policy." *Policy Studies Journal* 27 (1999): 707–722.

Pacheco, Julianna. "Measuring State Public Opinion over Time Using National Surveys: A Guideline for Scholars." *State Politics and Policy Quarterly* 11 (2011): 415–439.

Parry, Janine A., Brian Kisida, and Ronald E. Langley. "The State of State Polls: Old Challenges, New Opportunities." *State Politics and Policy Quarterly* 8 (2008): 198–216.

Rigby, Elisabeth, and Gerald C. Wright. "Whose Statehouse Democracy? How State Policy Choices Align with the Preferences of the Poor, Middle-Income, and Wealthy Segments of the Electorate." In *Who Gets Represented,* ed. Peter Enns and Christopher Weleziew. New York: Russell Sage Foundation, 2010.

Warshaw, Christopher, and Jonathan Rodden. "How Should We Estimate District-Level Public Opinion on Individual Issues?" *Journal of Politics* 74 (2012): 203–219.

Chapter 6

Initiative and Referendum

Frederick J. Boehmke and Joshua J. Dyck

IN THE 1780S, ARGUMENTS FOR THE U.S. CONSTITUTION sought to distinguish between representative democracy—a republic—and direct forms of democracy that were founded on ideas of populism and majority rule. James Madison famously wrote in *Federalist* No. 10 that "democracies have ever been spectacles of turbulence and contention; have ever been found incompatible with personal security or the rights of property; and have in general been as short in their lives as they have been violent in their deaths." Equal to the fear of tyranny in the form of a single ruler was the fear of tyranny from the mob. Representation, separation of powers, checks and balances, and federalism became the defining parts of American constitutional democracy.

Yet a commitment to federalism and state autonomy has led to both policy and institutional experimentation at the state level. Much of U.S. history can be written and understood simply by understanding the sharing of power between the national and state governments (see Chapter 1). Perhaps no institutional reform in the history of the United States challenged the philosophical precepts of America's constitutional republic more than the direct democracy reforms proffered by reformers at the turn of the twentieth century.

This chapter focuses on the legacy of more than a century of experiential direct democracy in many of the American states in the form of the initiative and referendum. It first describes the history and development of the initiative process, then turns to the effect of ballot measures on policy, citizens, interest groups, and minority interests. The chapter ends with a discussion of the future of research on direct democracy in the American states.

HISTORY AND PROCESS

Every state presently allows legislatures to place measures on the ballot for a popular vote, and every state but Delaware requires constitutional changes to be approved by the voters in the state in a process commonly referred to as the *legislative referendum.* The ballot initiative and popular referendum, however, are different. These methods allow voters to write and pass new laws and veto and repeal laws passed by the legislature. Using the *initiative,* a citizen or group can write their own piece of legislation, collect a predetermined number of signatures from other citizens, and qualify the proposed law for an "up" or "down" popular vote by the state electorate. Some states use the *direct initiative,* allowing a proposed law that meets signature qualification to go directly to the ballot, while other states use the *indirect initiative,* allowing the legislature a full session to pass the bill before it is referred to a popular vote. In some cases initiatives can be used to change statutes, and in others they can be used to change constitutions. Fully twenty-four states have some form of the initiative process. In eighteen states, initiatives can be used to alter constitutions. The *popular referendum* (often referred to simply as the *referendum process*), by contrast, allows citizens to petition for a vote to repeal a bill passed by the legislature. A total of twenty-five states have a provision for the referendum; many are also states that have the initiative process. In practice, the initiative process has become far more important than the referendum process and is used much more frequently.

Initiatives and referendums were institutional innovations that came out of the reform movements of the early twentieth century. Progressive reformers argued that the stranglehold of party machines on government could only be broken if the public had some form of popular recourse. Direct legislation was never intended to replace representative government in the states, but rather to check it. The resulting system is what some scholars have called "hybrid democracy."[1] South Dakota was the first state to adopt the initiative, in 1898, although the state only used the process twice between 1898 and 1978. Other states rapidly followed suit, with a total of twenty states adopting the initiative in some form by 1918. Only Alaska (1956), Wyoming (1968), Illinois (1970), Florida (1972), and Mississippi (1992)[2] added the initiative process after 1918. Table 6.1 shows the year of adoption and average yearly usage of the initiative process.[3]

What explains why some states have adopted direct democracy and others have not? Interparty political competition at the time of adoption appears to have been critical to the adoption of direct democracy reforms. In addition, the presence of reform and third-party movements, including support for the Populist Party and the Socialist Party, were also important, as was the degree of homogeneity of the public.[4] It is somewhat curious that the diffusion of this institutional innovation essentially stalled at the end of the Progressive Era. The response of the overall political system to reforms posed by Progressives likely had much to do with this. However, in more recent years, the initiative has been viewed increasingly through a partisan political lens. By giving citizens the option of the initiative, the party that controls the legislature would essentially be voting to take away its own power. In New York State, for instance, the Republican-controlled state senate has regularly passed a

TABLE 6.1 **Initiative History and Usage, 1898–2010**

State	Year of adoption	Legislative domain	Total initiatives, 1898–2010	Average biennial initiatives
Alaska	1956	Statute only	47	1.7
Arizona	1911	Both	172	3.4
Arkansas	1910	Both	120	2.4
California	1911	Both	340	6.8
Colorado	1912	Both	215	4.3
Florida	1972	Constitutional only	32	1.6
Idaho	1912	Statute only	28	0.6
Illinois	1970	Constitutional only	1	0.0
Maine	1908	Statute only	52	1.0
Massachusetts	1918	Both	72	1.5
Michigan	1908	Both	72	1.4
Mississippi[a]	1992	Constitutional only	2	0.2
Missouri	1908	Both	81	1.6
Montana[b]	1904	Both	77	1.4
Nebraska	1912	Both	46	0.9
Nevada	1905	Both	54	1.0
North Dakota	1914	Both	179	3.7
Ohio	1912	Both	77	1.6
Oklahoma	1907	Both	85	1.6
Oregon	1902	Both	355	6.5
South Dakota	1898	Both	64	1.1
Utah[c]	1917	Statute only	20	0.4
Washington	1912	Statute only	163	3.3
Wyoming	1968	Statute only	6	0.3

NOTES:

a. Mississippi passed it in 1914, but it was ruled unconstitutional in 1922.

b. Montana added the constitutional initiative in 1972.

c. Utah voters approved of the ballot initiative in 1900, but the legislature balked at implementing the law until 1917.

SOURCE: Initiative and Referendum Institute at the University of Southern California, www.iandrinstitute.org.

bill to bring the initiative to the Empire State and the Democrats in the State Assembly continue to ignore it, creating a legislative impasse. Of course, much of the reason why Republicans in the Senate prefer the initiative is that Republicans are the minority party in New York. Thus it is hard to imagine a state adding the initiative process without a constitutional convention or a political movement that rivaled the success of the Progressives. As this impasse is likely to continue in New York and elsewhere into the foreseeable future, social scientists have been provided with a nice natural experiment that nearly maximizes variation—twenty-four states with the initiative and twenty-six without.

These twenty-four states have had far-ranging experiences with the initiative process over the last century. Some, such as Mississippi, Utah, and Wyoming, have seen only a handful of measures actually qualify for the ballot—less than one every five years. Others have seen a flood of ballot measures, with seven states having more than one per year, on average, and two—California and Oregon—with a total of more than three hundred in the last century. Some states have seen legislators and voters pass laws restricting the ability to qualify and pass measures, often by increasing the signature requirements or shortening the signature circulation period, while others have seen some liberalization through decreased signature requirements.

In combination with shifting political movements and eras, the importance and use of the initiative process has waxed and waned over the years. In the early days, Progressives and others used the process heavily as they continued to push for their desired reforms. These included governmental reforms to improve regulation of powerful industries such as the railroads, but also forays into social policy, such as the co-called Ham and Eggs initiatives in California in the late 1930s that would have created a public pension system. The frequency of initiatives dropped off after World War II and bottomed out in the late 1960s, but it began rising again in the 1970s.

The tax revolt of the late 1970s is largely credited with reigniting interest in the initiative process. The most famous of these measures is Proposition 13, a 1978 ballot initiative that sought to reduce property taxes in California and created supermajority requirements for the legislature when considering future tax increases. The measure passed overwhelmingly, with 63 percent of the vote, and led several other states to consider a wide variety of tax-cutting proposals.

Since the resurgence of initiative use following the tax revolt, the number of ballot measures per election has continued to increase. In 2000 alone, Oregon voters faced thirty-two ballot measures, eighteen of which were placed there by citizens, while California voters faced twenty-nine. As in the past, recent decades have continued to see a number of controversial policies put before the voters, including bans on same-sex marriage, physician-assisted suicide, decriminalization of marijuana, and term limits, as well as on affirmative action in state hiring and public universities. A number of less controversial topics also reached the ballot from time to time, including a California measure to ban exporting horse meat for the purpose of human consumption, a Florida measure to forbid keeping pregnant pigs in cages in which they could not turn around, and an Oklahoma measure to prohibit cockfighting.

FIGURE 6.1 **Number of Initiatives in U.S. States (bi-yearly), 1904–2012**

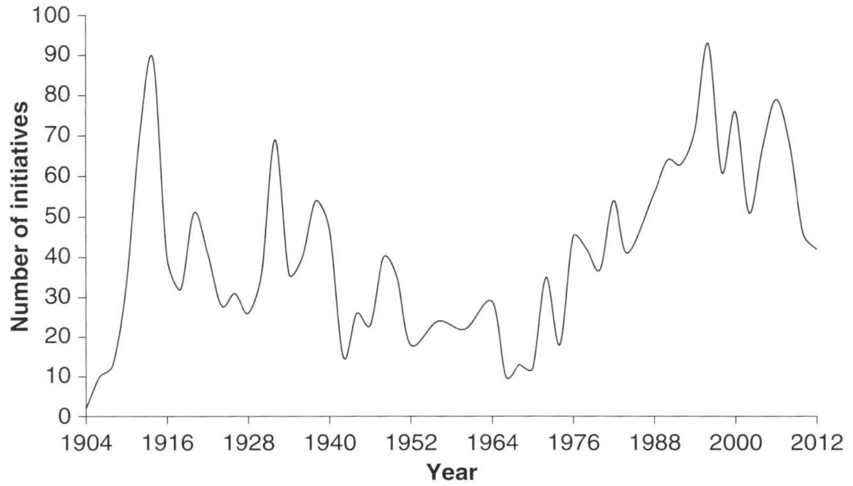

SOURCE: Initiative and Referendum Institute at the University of Southern California, www.iandrinstitute.org.

As an advocate for California's "Ham and Eggs" or "$30-Every-Thursday" plan, a Progressive Era, social-policy initiative aimed at securing old-age pension plans, Carl S. Kegley presents his view to the House of Representatives' Ways and Means Committee in Washington, DC, on February 7, 1939.

SOURCE: Library of Congress. Reproduction Number LC-DIG-hec-26013.

(To see how initiatives qualify to be on the ballot, see Initiative Entrepreneurs box.)

POLICY RESPONSIVENESS

Direct democracy primarily functions as a tool to shape public policy. Any evaluation of its possible merits must therefore begin with an understanding of its effect on state policy outcomes. A quick scan of proposed measures on state election ballots or concurrent news reports makes it abundantly clear that hundreds of policy changes have been enacted through the initiative or legislative referendum process and that even a few new policies passed by the government get undone by popular referendum. And since voters passed these policies, it should also be clear that they get policies that they prefer in the absence of initiatives.

Clearly, then, it would seem obvious that direct democracy influences policy and produces better outcomes. Surprisingly, though, evidence on this matter is mixed. To understand this conundrum, we must first realize that the question that needs to be answered is not whether policies get passed through the initiative, but whether successful initiatives lead to policies that the state would not have adopted otherwise, or would have adopted via the legislature in just another year or two. This proves tricky to demonstrate because we cannot observe what would have happened if a policy had not been enacted by initiative.

The situation becomes even more challenging when we realize that the initiative process can influence policy without an initiative even passing. Thus in addition to what researchers refer to as the direct effect of the initiative process, which occurs when measures pass and change the law, direct democracy can also have indirect effects. Such indirect effects occur when the legislature anticipates that some group will sponsor an initiative to change policy in a way that the legislature does not like. To prevent this from happening, the legislature can pass a more moderate or more limited policy that voters will look upon favorably, thereby discouraging advocates from spending the time and money to qualify and campaign for passage of a measure. The threat of an initiative proposal can therefore lead to policy change even without a measure appearing on the ballot.[5] Furthermore, because the legislature moves policy to preempt a ballot proposal that requires majority support, its new policy should be closer to what the majority wants compared with the status quo.

In this photo, taken on May 1, 1978, Los Angeles, California, homeowners wield signs protesting rising property taxes and supporting the Proposition 13 tax revolt. Proposition 13, a ballot initiative that sought to reduce property taxes in California and created supermajority requirements for the legislature when considering future tax increases, was approved by nearly 63 percent of voters.

SOURCE: Photo by Tony Korody//Time Life Pictures/Getty Images.

INITIATIVE ENTREPRENEURS

In order to have initiatives, someone has to take the initiative, so to speak, and work to qualify a measure for the ballot. Qualification rules vary considerably by state, but all states require some minimum threshold of signatures from voters. The initiative process has produced its fair share of entrepreneurs over the years. Ward Connerly became the face of California's successful 1996 anti–affirmative action initiative, Proposition 209, which forbade the use of race in making state decisions about hiring or university admissions. He then helped pass similar measures on the ballot in other states, including Washington's Initiative 200 in 1998. He subsequently fought unsuccessfully with the Florida Supreme Court to place a similar measure before Florida voters in 2000. This record of success with some failures continued, as a similar measure passed in Arizona in 2010, one failed in Colorado in 2008, and one in Oklahoma was withdrawn from the ballot in 2008 amid questions about the signature-gathering process.

But Connerly was not the only initiative entrepreneur involved in these measures. The 1998 measure in Washington was sponsored by Tim Eyman, a well-known initiative activist in that state. Since the late 1990s, Eyman has been involved with dozens of different ballot measures, many of which sought to lower taxes or fees either directly or by making it harder for the state legislature to raise them in the future. Most famously, he sponsored Initiative 695 in 2000, which lowered car registration fees to $35; since Washington State does not have an income tax, a series of high excise taxes had been put in place, including car tabs, which could run several hundred dollars for larger and newer vehicles. Along the way he has been involved in a number of controversies, including misuse of campaign funds and arguments with the secretary of state's office over whether some of his measures had obtained sufficient numbers of signatures to qualify for the ballot.

Some of his failures led to a public backlash against his tactics. In 2003, after a string of Eyman's initiatives were struck down by the courts for violating the state's single subject law, David Goldstein, a Seattle-area software developer, decided to offer the state's voters a chance to voice their opinion about Eyman by seeking to qualify his own measure, I-831.[1] The proposed measure would have declared that Eyman's "anti-tax initiatives are an irresponsible means of legislating tax policy, an abuse of the initiative process, and insult to our system of representative Democracy." More pointedly, it concluded by declaring that "Tim Eyman is a Horse's Ass" and would have required that "copies of this resolution be immediately transmitted to Tim Eyman, his wife, and his mother."[2] Voters would never get their chance, though, as a judge declared that the measure went too far because it was "not legislative in nature."[3]

1. Neil Modie, "A Joke Gone Too Far? I-831 Kicks Off," *Seattle Post-Intelligencer,* February 26, 2003, www.seattlepi.com/news/article/A-joke-gone-too-far-I-831-kicks-off-1108440.php.
2. See the full text of the proposed measure at Washington Secretary of State, www.secstate.wa.gov/elections/initiatives/text/i831.pdf.
3. "Voters Won't Be Able to Declare Eyman a 'Horse's Ass,'" KOMO News Radio, March 14, 2003, www.komonews.com/news/archive/4086966.html.

It can be difficult to detect whether such hard-to-observe indirect effects occur in the real world and if they occur systematically. Evaluating the effect of direct democracy on policy outcomes requires knowing what would have happened in the absence of an actual initiative as well as in the absence of the mere opportunity to propose an initiative. Researchers have generally taken two approaches to answering this question.

First, a series of studies examines whether direct democracy states enact new policies faster than states without direct democracy. These studies focus almost exclusively on the indirect effects, finding their evidence—especially when public opinion leans toward a policy—by exploring the timing of adoption of anti-abortion laws,[6] term limits,[7] or bans on same-sex marriage.[8] Yet not all studies find evidence that the initiative process leads to faster adoption. For example, Edward L. Lascher Jr., Michael G. Hagen, and Steven A. Rochlin study eight different policy areas and find no evidence that the initiative process enhances the relationship between what citizens prefer and the current policy in their state.[9]

Second, researchers also examine whether the cumulative effects of direct democracy lead to differences in realized policy outcomes in initiative states. These studies account for both the direct and indirect effects of ballot measures. For example, John Matsusaka focuses on the frequent use of the initiative process to change state taxation rates, as it did most famously with Proposition 13 in California. Comparing state tax revenue from 1970 to 2000, Matsusaka finds that initiative states tax and spend about 4 percent less than states without the initiative process.[10]

MAJORITY TYRANNY

While demonstrating policy responsiveness is more difficult than was perhaps first imagined, a related question is whether policy responsiveness is, in fact, desirable. If the ballot initiative process is "for the many," as Matsusaka has argued, what about minority interests? Majority rule can always potentially lead to majority tyranny. The Founders saw majority tyranny playing out along the lines of wealth and property. However, in political science literature and media accounts, concerns about majority tyranny have more frequently been raised regarding civil rights issues, particularly those involving racial and ethnic minorities, and more recently over issues of equal rights for GLBTQ (gay, lesbian, bisexual, transgender, and questioning) populations.

Empirical social science has struggled with how to define the term *tyranny.* Some early studies of civil rights and ballot initiatives found evidence of rampant tyranny, but suffered from the problem selection bias in that they did not provide a comprehensive catalog of all initiatives, nor all initiatives that might be classified as "majority tyranny."[11] Other research was quick to point out that most minority groups (and groups more generally) are on the winning side of initiatives more than they are on the losing side.[12] That is, most initiatives do not have anything to do with issues of civil rights, which authors took as evidence that fears of majority tyranny had been overstated. Both of these explanations, however, fail to account for an adequate definition of what tyranny is and is not. For instance, several states have passed ballot initiatives that prevent preferential treatment in state hiring and university admissions, effectively ending affirmative action in higher education. California has also seen a number of ballot measures targeted at immigrant populations. The most famous of these was Proposition 187 in 1994. California voters approved the measure, voting to deny social services to undocumented immigrants and their children (see Ballot Initiative Backlash box). Should all of these be regarded as examples of tyranny?

Two important pieces of information complicate the majority tyranny argument. First, policy disagreements about issues like affirmative action and illegal immigration often fall upon partisan and ideological lines, with both sides repeatedly making appeals to fairness. A social scientist, therefore, would have a hard time categorizing "tyranny" and "not tyranny." In a sense, any majority decision can be seen as tyranny of the majority. Second, the ballot initiative process still must contend with obstacles to implementation by legislatures and the bureaucracy, as well as legal challenges in the court system. Proposition 187, for instance, was quickly ruled unconstitutional by the California Supreme Court. (For more details, see Chapter 23.)

Some recent research, however, has placed renewed focus on majority tyranny and ballot initiatives. Direct democracy states, for instance, were more likely to support the diffusion of same-sex marriage bans throughout the U.S. states, and citizens who face consistent exposure to ballot measures in places with high levels of racial and ethnic diversity have seen waning social trust[13] (see Chapter 27).

BALLOT INITIATIVE BACKLASH

One of the headlines from the 2008 and 2012 elections was that Republicans have seen declining support among Latinos. Barack Obama won 71 percent of the Latino vote in 2012, compared with only 27 percent for Mitt Romney, whereas John Kerry only edged out George W. Bush among Latinos by a 53 percent to 44 percent margin.[1] Blame was put on the harsh rhetoric of the Right for turning off Latinos. Mitt Romney, for instance, took a very hard-line stance on illegal immigration in the 2012 primaries, supporting a policy of "self-deportation."

The Republican Party would have done well to learn a lesson from California that took place more than a decade earlier. Between 1994 and 1998, Republicans in California supported a series of ballot measures that were aimed at racial and ethnic minorities, particularly Latinos in California. In 1994 they supported Proposition 187, which would have denied social services to undocumented immigrants and their children. In 1996 they supported Proposition 209, which ended affirmative action in state government hiring and public university admissions. In 1998 they supported Proposition 227, which ended bilingual education programs. All of the measures passed muster with the voters, although Proposition 187 was quickly ruled unconstitutional by California's high court.

In 1991 Latinos in California were equally likely to identify as Republicans as they were Democrats. However, by 2002, Latinos became 20 percentage points more likely to identify as Democrats than Republicans. While Republicans were able to win their campaigns at the ballot box, several authors have suggested that their support for these measures created a sea change in party identification among Latinos in California. These changes have been a big part of the reason why a historically competitive state has become one of the solid Democrat strongholds in the country.[2]

There is clearly a lesson to be taken from California. Most certainly, ballot initiatives have consequences, but they are not always the consequences that their supporters intended. Short-term wins can turn into long-term losses.

1. CNN.com, www.cnn.com/election/2012/results/race/president; CNN.com, www.cnn.com/ELECTION/2004/pages/results/states/US/P/00/epolls.0.html.
2. Joshua J. Dyck, Gregg B. Johnson, and Jesse T. Wasson, "A Blue Tide in the Golden State: Ballot Propositions, Population Change, and Party Identification in California," *American Politics Research* 40 (2012): 450–475; Shaun Bowler, Stephen P. Nicholson, and Gary M. Segura, "Earthquakes and Aftershocks: Race, Direct Democracy, and Partisan Change," *American Journal of Political Science* 50 (2006): 146–159.

Pro, left, and con Proposition 187 activists are separated by police during a rally in Los Angeles in this photo taken August 10, 1996, during a time when 187 proponents worked to revive portions of the proposition after it was overturned by the U.S. Supreme Court. Shadowing the latest proposal to overhaul immigration law is a hard lesson Republicans learned in California in 1994—get-tough laws targeting undocumented immigrants can have lasting political consequences. Californians approved Proposition 187, but fierce Latino backlash against the initiative and its GOP backers helped ensure Democratic dominance in California.

SOURCE: AP Photo/Frank Wiese.

DIRECT DEMOCRACY AND THE DEMOCRATIC CITIZEN

Apart from the effects that ballot initiatives and referendums may have on matters of public policy, many scholars have grown increasingly interested in the secondary or spillover effects of ballot initiatives on citizens. Democratic theorists have often asserted that citizens will become more interested, engaged, and active in their democracy if they are given more meaningful avenues to participation. Progressive Era advocates of the initiative process also recognized the possibility of renewed interest and knowledge about politics among the population and touted them as among the many benefits of the initiative and referendum. Participation is a learned activity, and behaviors such as voting become a habit; some have posited that the process of voting on policy matters acts as a counterweight to widespread apathy, disengagement, and lack of information about politics.

The underlying dynamic of participatory theory is that the experience of voting on ballot measures and being exposed to ballot measure campaigns create a heightened sense of interest in politics. This interest manifests itself in greater belief in the democratic process, leading to higher levels of efficacy and trust. Engaged, interested, knowledgeable, efficacious, and trusting citizens thus take to the polls and get involved in politics. Most early studies of the effects of ballot initiatives on citizens showed widespread support for the participatory perspective. More recently, however, scholars have begun to cast serious doubt on this perspective. Despite some disagreements, we have learned a great deal about when, how, and why ballot measures may impact democratic citizens and their views on democracy and participation.

Turnout

The strongest empirical evidence of the possible spillover effects of ballot measures regards the propensity of individuals to turn out to vote. Numerous studies at the individual level demonstrate that voters are more likely to vote when issues are on the ballot. The strongest evidence of the ability of ballot measures to increase turnout is when initiatives are coupled with low-salience candidate elections. In line with this, the literature has consistently found that initiatives are more likely to spur participation in midterm elections, as presidential elections already draw on the pool of voters at the periphery of politics for whom the major decision of the election is whether or not they will turn out to vote, not for whom they will vote. Furthermore, we have also learned a great deal about *why* voters have higher propensities to turn out. Party-based mobilization, competitive elections, and salient social issue ballot measures tend to increase turnout.[14] However, there is also some evidence that ballot measures induce long-term turnout effects as voters are socialized into being more participatory over their lives.[15]

Knowledge, Efficacy, and Other Effects

Since turnout seems to be motivated by the right mix of low-salience candidate elections and salient and/or controversial content of ballot measures, it seems less clear that we would expect citizens who participate in direct democracy to gain other characteristics like greater knowledge, interest, efficacy, and/or political trust. While several studies have suggested that citizens gain knowledge, interest, and efficacy by participating in direct democracy elections, others have argued that these effects are underwhelming and more often than not fail to meet standard levels of statistical significance.[16] Furthermore, ballot initiatives also appear to drive a wedge between voters and their government, fostering greater distrust in government.[17] And while studies of Swiss cantons have argued that direct democracy leads to greater life happiness and satisfaction, studies of the American states suggest that the great heterogeneity of state populations abates the acquisition of interpersonal trust.

If we take all of these results together, it seems that the ballot initiative has the potential to intensify conflict in American democracy. Unlike the system of gridlock and compromise favored by the Founders, ballot initiatives provide a mechanism where the most contentious issues can be fought at the polls. Furthermore, ballot initiatives can also create instability in state constitutions, as they are frequently altered by simple majority rule (see Chapter 2). In addition, while this democratization has the potential to create more participation, perhaps its greatest impacts have been indirectly placed on citizens through the profound impact on the interest group system.

THE BALLOT INITIATIVE AND ORGANIZED INTERESTS

One of the primary motivations of Progressive reformers who advocated for the initiative and referendum process was its potential to undermine the influence of powerful organized interests that seemed to dictate legislative decisions around the turn of the twentieth century. Good government reformers wanted to break the apparent stranglehold of these huge interests, such as the railroads in California, on government policy and return some control back to the people. Their goals appear to have been met in some important respects, but almost certainly not to the degree that they had hoped.

In order to understand how the initiative process affects organized interests, we must first consider what groups desire and how direct democracy can help them achieve it. This requires some simplification, since the term *organized interests* encompasses a wide cast of characters: large, voluntary membership groups that represent a broad swath of the public; more narrowly defined—but still membership-based—interests based on occupational status or union membership; corporations, whether acting alone or through industry-based associations; nonprofit institutions such as schools and places of worship; or various government-related groups such as associations of county governments or school districts. What these various entities have in common is a desire to influence government decisions and some level of organization through which to achieve that goal. Note that taking action is critical to this definition: collections of individuals with a common interest or organizations that do not seek to influence government do not count as organized interests; rather, they remain latent or potential interests that may be activated at some later date.

The centrality of influencing government decisions in this definition immediately suggests possible interactions between direct democracy and organized interests. Groups typically lobby legislators directly through face-to-face meetings or testimony, or indirectly by attempting to raise an issue's importance among the public with the hope of motivating legislative action. The initiative process adds another point of access through which organized interests may seek to influence policy, either directly or indirectly, as we discussed in the section on policy consequences of direct democracy. The primary distinction from other forms of influence rests in the fact that direct initiatives and popular referendums can change policy without legislative involvement. This makes the initiative a powerful but potentially expensive form of influence.

Given its role as a potential pathway to policy influence, the effect of direct legislation on organized interests will depend first on their ability to successfully propose and pass ballot measures and second on the underlying causes of why they turn to this process. In an important study that seeks to address these factors, Elisabeth Gerber argues that in today's environment successful use of the initiative process requires two resources: money and people. Qualifying and campaigning for a ballot measure becomes more expensive every year, but money is generally not enough. Proponents need people to help gather signatures and spread the word about their cause. And while money can to some degree substitute for people, groups with access to both tend to have more success at the ballot box. And, because of their greater ability to impose the direct effect of the initiative process, these groups can also exert greater leverage through the indirect effect, making legislators more responsive to their more traditional direct and indirect lobbying efforts.

As to why organized groups turn to the initiative process, consider which groups may need to rely on this way of influencing government decisions. Groups with high levels of access to elected officials generally have little need to seek alternate paths to influence. Rather, organized interests that tend to have trouble gaining access or tend to be on the losing side in the legislature should find access to the initiative process to be of the greatest advantage. In combination, then, these two answers suggest that the initiative process will tend not to benefit wealthy institutional interests, but will instead provide an alternate form of influence for groups with members and money and that tend to have less success in the legislature. This description does not seem too far off from what Progressive reformers intended.

While groups that can benefit the most from direct democracy will use it to influence policy outcomes, direct democracy will also shape these groups in return. If groups need members to successfully utilize ballot measures, then they will seek to invest resources toward increasing their membership in order to create a greater chance of success, whether to pass initiatives or to scare the legislature by threatening to do so. Some of this may be intentional resource marshalling on the part of groups in order to better

In this December 8, 2011, photo taken at the Department of Motor Vehicles office in Littleton, Colorado, volunteers Emmett Reistroffer, second from left, and Justin Dreyer, second from right, collect signatures on a petition to legalize marijuana in Colorado. After collecting enough signatures, the question of legalizing marijuana for recreational purposes was made an initiative on the Colorado ballot in the fall of 2012 and was approved by voters, making Colorado one of the first states (Washington also passed a similar initiative in fall 2012) to end marijuana prohibition.

SOURCE: AP Photo/Ed Andrieski.

position themselves, but some of it may also be an unintended consequence of ballot measure campaigns. Initiatives often produce high-profile campaigns that may attract new members to join groups, which could also expand membership. The next two sections consider the evidence for these two types of effects.

The Initiative Process and the Ecology of Representation

To understand the effect of direct democracy on organized interests, we need a baseline against which to compare. Fortunately, Virginia Gray and David Lowery, along with various colleagues, have compiled a vast listing and categorization of organized interests in the American states over the past four decades. Their goal has been to demonstrate the many values of applying population ecology models of species density and diversity to populations of organized interests, which provides an excellent starting point from which to view the effect of direct democracy.[18]

In general, studies of representation among organized interests at the state and national levels indicate an abundance of business- and economic-related interests and a simultaneous dearth of broad-based, citizen interests.[19] This means that policymakers tend to hear more from one side of an issue and that groups with money rather than members appear to be better represented, just as the Progressives sensed over one hundred years ago. Given that direct legislation should benefit citizen interests over narrow economic interests, then, we can ask to what extent direct democracy has potentially ameliorated this imbalance.

A series of studies has found that access to direct democracy has the expected effect. Interest group populations in states with the direct initiative process consist of more groups than in the twenty-six states without it; and, importantly, the increase is disproportionately among citizen groups, whose numbers average about 45 percent greater in initiative states, compared with only 22 percent for economic groups. Thus the initiative process helps level the representational playing field a bit. Furthermore, based on a survey of groups in five states, organized interests in initiative states tend to have greater memberships and fewer financial resources than groups in noninitiative states.[20]

An interesting, and potentially unanticipated, consequence of the initiative process is an increase in the volatility of state interest group populations. Some of the latent groups that mobilize around ballot measure campaigns cannot sustain themselves after the election, while some remain—either to continue an unsuccessful fight or to monitor implementation of their new policy and potentially advocate new or related issues. This volatility can be separated into two components: entry and exit. A comparison of interest group populations in 1990 and 1997 shows that organized interests enter at a greater rate in states with the initiative process, with an effect of nearly 7 percent for membership groups.[21] Membership groups also exit at a greater rate of about 8 percent per year. The implications of this increased churning remain an open research question.

Ballot Measures and Participatory Behavior

So far, we have primarily examined the effect of the initiative process on organized interests themselves. But what about its effects on citizen involvement with such interests? If ballot measures can increase turnout under some conditions, what effect might they have on interest group membership? Campaigns create excitement about issues and may provide just the push that individuals need to finally take action and join a group. Because the initiative process favors groups with members and money, it also creates an incentive for interests to recruit more members. Finally, the presence of more citizen and membership groups in direct legislation states creates more options for citizens looking for a cause to support.

While we already noted that groups in initiative states have more members, we do not know if this means that more people are joining more groups or merely that the same people join more groups. Answering this question requires information on the behavior of people rather than of groups. While data on group membership by individuals may be hard to come by, the General Social Survey has routinely asked thousands of people this question every two years or so for the last forty years. This allows a comparison between the rate and number of interest group memberships reported by a random sample of citizens.

A study using these data confirms our intuitions: citizens living in states with the initiative process join groups at about a 2 percent greater rate than citizens living in noninitiative states.[22] The motivation appears to be driven largely by campaigns and the resulting public conflict between opposing sides, with only a small increase in initiative states with very few measures on the ballot and a larger increase upwards of 6 percent in states with high usage.

FUTURE DIRECTIONS

Research on direct democracy has in some ways reached a critical juncture. We know a fair bit about whether direct democracy influences state politics at the aggregate level through differences in public policy or interest group populations; we also have a great number of studies that examine the effect of direct democracy on individuals. To this point, however, the bulk of the work evaluating the effect of direct democracy has asked some form of the following question: Is some outcome of interest, whether state tax revenue or individual turnout rates, different because of the presence or use of direct democracy?

Answering this question was critical in order to develop a literature on direct democracy in the first place, and it seems the obvious place to start, particularly in light of the benefits of the initiative and referendum touted by Progressive Era reformers. On this front, the literature has largely been successful. Evidence of differences in individual behavior abounds through the influence of ballot measures on citizens' participation rates, political knowledge, or opinions about government. Furthermore, studies have shown important differences in outcomes for some policies in initiative states. Thus the answer seems to be quite simply that direct democracy institutions do matter and that they matter in a number of ways.

Yet, at the same time, a growing literature has emerged that questions these supposed effects of direct democracy. This literature suggests that the proper question to ask is no longer whether direct democracy matters. It does, but only sometimes. Understanding the conditions under which it matters should therefore be the next step in the evolution of our understanding of direct democracy and state politics.

We believe that progress can be made by focusing greater attention on the underlying process through which direct democracy influences politics and political behavior. By understanding this process, we can more clearly delineate the conditions under which we might expect direct democracy to affect outcomes. At the individual level, we need to know, for example, how direct democracy influences turnout and other forms of participation. At the aggregate level, we have very little understanding of how the initiative and referendum influence government outcomes other than policy decisions. We discuss each of these broad areas in turn.

Conditionality

Scholars have demonstrated a wide variety of secondary effects of the initiative process, including differences in turnout rates, trust in government, contributions to political action committees (PACs), and membership in organized interest groups. The theoretical arguments generally focus on both the immediate and longer-term, cumulative effects of the initiative process. In general, though, they have adopted a one-size-fits-all approach to understanding how ballot measures influence individuals. Yet it seems quite likely that the initiative will influence people in different ways.

For example, ballot measures may increase the chance that people turn out, but it is unlikely that it affects highly educated, politically aware individuals in the same way that it influences those with lower socioeconomic status. The first are quite likely to turn out already, whereas the latter may be much less likely to participate. Furthermore, the potential information effects will also differ between these two types of individuals. As we noted earlier, findings in the literature already suggest such conditional effects: ballot measures routinely increase turnout in midterm elections but not in presidential elections. Why? Differential effects may point the way, since increased turnout in presidential elections means that those who do not turn out may be harder to motivate than those just at the cusp of turning out for midterm elections.

Better arguments for how ballot measures influence citizens as well as the types of individuals most susceptible to such influences will help us develop a better understanding of the conditional nature of the influence of direct democracy. It certainly does not matter all the time. In fact, a growing strain of literature argues that educative effects have been overstated and misinterpreted. Both sides of the debate will prosper from more clearly delineating when and for whom direct democracy matters.

Cross-Institutional Influences

A similar prescription exists for aggregate-level studies, but with even more room to explore, given the relatively narrow focus of work in this area. The debate over policy effects of direct democracy could profit from a better understanding of when the initiative process should matter. Theoretical explanations do not suggest that it should always lead to different policy outcomes; rather, policy effects should occur only when the legislature does not pass legislation in line with what citizens want. There must be divergence in order for the initiative to produce convergence. But when does such divergence happen? Clearly, policies like term limits, on which legislators have clear preferences that diverge from what citizens want, offer a clear-cut case. But a more systematic identification of broad classes of policies with divergent outcomes would help.

The variation may not just be across policies, but also across states. For example, an understanding of whether certain legislative structures also lead to more divergent outcomes would help us understand the conditions in which initiatives can shape policy outcomes. An interesting question here that has not been explored much is whether direct democracy itself changes the legislature in a way that leads to different policy outcomes. In addition to term limits, voters have often imposed alternate rules for passing budgets or taxes in initiative states, which could have far-reaching effects on other legislative endeavors.

Going even one step further, political science has not thought much about the broader consequences of the initiative process on traditional state government institutions, including the legislature, the governor, and the executive branch more broadly. Yet if the initiative process helps determine campaigns, legislative rules, and policy outcomes, it seems likely that it could also influence who is elected as a result of those campaigns and how they behave once in office. This means a greater incorporation of direct democracy into traditional models of elections and legislator behavior in office.

NOTES

1. Elizabeth Garrett, "Hybrid Democracy," *George Washington Law Review* 73 (2004–2005), 1096.
2. Mississippi initially added the initiative in 1914, but the court ruled it unconstitutional in 1922 on a technicality. It was not until 1992 that the Mississippi legislature revisited the issue and approved a form of the indirect initiative.
3. Initiative and Referendum Institute at the University of Southern California, www.iandrinstitute.org.
4. Daniel A. Smith and Dustin Fridkin, "Delegating Direct Democracy: Interparty Legislative Adoption of the Initiative in the American States," *American Political Science Review* 102 (2008): 333–350; Eric Lawrence, Todd Donovan, and Shaun Bowler, "Adopting Direct Democracy: Testing Competing Explanations of Institutional Change," *American Politics Research* 37 (2009): 1024–1047.
5. Elisabeth R. Gerber, "Legislative Response to the Threat of Popular Initiatives," *American Journal of Political Science* 40 (1996): 99–128.
6. Elisabeth R. Gerber, *The Populist Paradox: Interest Group Influence and the Promise of Direct Legislation* (Princeton, NJ: Princeton University Press, 1999).
7. Caroline Tolbert, "Changing the Rules for State Legislatures: Direct Democracy and Governance Policy," in *Citizens as Legislators: Direct Democracy in the United States,* ed. Shaun Bowler, Todd Donovan, and Caroline J. Tolbert (Columbus: Ohio State University Press, 1998).
8. Arthur Lupia, Yanna Krupnikov, Adam Seth Levine, Spencer Piston, and Alexander Von Hagen-Jamar, "Why State Constitutions Differ in Their Treatment of Same-Sex Marriage," *Journal of Politics* 72 (2010): 1222–1235.
9. Edward L. Lascher Jr., Michael G. Hagen, and Steven A. Rochlin, "Gun behind the Door? Ballot Initiatives, State Policies, and Public Opinion," *Journal of Politics* 58 (1996): 760–765.
10. John G. Matsusaka, *For the Many or the Few: The Initiative Process, Public Policy, and American Democracy* (Chicago: University of Chicago Press, 2004).
11. Barbara S. Gamble, "Putting Civil Rights to a Popular Vote," *American Journal of Political Science* 41 (1997): 245–269.
12. Zoltan L. Hajnal, Elisabeth R. Gerber, and Hugh Louch, "Minorities and Direct Legislation: Evidence from California Ballot Proposition Elections," *Journal of Politics* 64 (2002): 154–177.
13. Daniel C. Lewis, "Bypassing the Representational Filter? Minority Rights Policies under Direct Democracy Institutions in the U.S. States," *State Politics and Policy Quarterly* 11 (2011): 198–222; Joshua J. Dyck, "Racial Threat, Direct Legislation, and Social Trust: Taking Tyranny Seriously in Studies of the Ballot Initiative," *Political Research Quarterly* 65 (2012): 615–628.
14. Matt Childers and Mike Binder, "Engaged by the Initiative? How the Use of Citizen Initiatives Increases Voter Turnout," *Political Research Quarterly* 65 (2012): 93–103; Daniel L. Biggers, "When Ballot Issues Matter: Social Issue Ballot Measures and Their Impact on Turnout," *Political Behavior* 33 (2011): 3–25; Joshua J. Dyck and Nicholas R. Seabrook, "Mobilized by Direct Democracy: Short-term versus Long-term Effects and the Geography of Turnout in Ballot Measure Elections," *Social Science Quarterly* 91 (2010): 188–208.
15. Daniel A. Smith and Caroline J. Tolbert, *Educated by Initiative: The Effects of Direct Democracy on Citizens and Political Organizations in the American States* (Ann Arbor: University of Michigan Press, 2004); Dyck and Seabrook, "Mobilized by Direct Democracy."
16. Smith and Tolbert, *Educated by Initiative;* Daniel Schlozman and Ian Yohai, "How Initiatives Don't Always Make Citizens: Ballot Initiatives in the American States, 1978–2004," *Political Behavior* 30 (2008): 469–489.
17. Joshua J. Dyck, "Initiated Distrust: Direct Democracy and Trust in Government," *American Politics Research* 37 (2009): 539–568.

18. Virginia Gray and David Lowery, *The Population Ecology of Interest Representation* (Ann Arbor: University of Michigan Press, 1996).

19. Kay Lehman Schlozman, "What Accent the Heavenly Chorus? Political Equality and the American Pressure System," *Journal of Politics* 46 (1984): 1006–1032; Virginia Gray and David Lowery, *The Population Ecology of Interest Representation* (Ann Arbor: University of Michigan Press, 1996).

20. Frederick J. Boehmke, *The Indirect Effect of Direct Legislation: How Institutions Shape Interest Group Systems* (Columbus: Ohio State University Press, 2005).

21. Frederick J. Boehmke, "The Initiative Process and the Dynamics of State Interest Group Populations," *State Politics and Policy Quarterly* 8 (2008): 362–383.

22. Frederick J. Boehmke and Daniel Bowen, "Direct Democracy and Individual Interest Group Membership," *Journal of Politics* 72 (2010): 659–671.

SUGGESTED READING

Boehmke, Frederick J. *The Indirect Effect of Direct Legislation: How Institutions Shape Interest Group Systems.* Columbus: Ohio State University Press, 2005.

Ellis, Richard J. *Democratic Delusions: The Initiative Process in America.* Lawrence: University Press of Kansas, 2002.

Gerber, Elisabeth R. *The Populist Paradox: Interest Group Influence and the Promise of Direct Legislation.* Princeton, NJ: Princeton University Press, 1999.

Lupia, Arthur. "Shortcuts versus Encyclopedias: Information and Voting Behavior in California Insurance Reform Elections." *American Political Science Review* 88 (1994): 63–76.

Magleby, David. *Direct Legislation: Voting on Ballot Propositions in the United States.* Baltimore: Johns Hopkins University Press, 1984.

Matsusaka, John G. *For the Many or the Few: The Initiative Process, Public Policy, and American Democracy.* Chicago: University of Chicago Press, 2004.

Schlozman, Daniel, and Ian Yohai. "How Initiatives Don't Always Make Citizens: Ballot Initiatives in the American States, 1978–2004." *Political Behavior* 30 (2008): 469–489.

Smith, Daniel A., and Caroline J. Tolbert. *Educated by Initiative: The Effects of Direct Democracy on Citizens and Political Organizations in the American States.* Ann Arbor: University of Michigan Press, 2004.

Chapter 7

Election Administration

Michael J. Hanmer and Richard G. Niemi

WHO CAN VOTE AND WHAT OFFICES Americans vote for have been the subjects of numerous actions on the part of the federal government, including amendments to the U.S. Constitution and major pieces of legislation.[1] Yet how we vote and who oversees the administration of voting processes have been largely left to states and localities. It was not until the 1990s that the federal government undertook a major action intended to change election practices; this was the so-called motor voter law, and it affected registration but not voting, per se. Only after the debacle of 2000 in Florida that left the presidential election hinging, in part, on what had been obscure matters of ballot design and administrative recordkeeping did Congress pass a law—the Help America Vote Act of 2002 (HAVA)—about the way we cast and count ballots, backing it up with a new federal commission and money to pay for new voting equipment.

Even with these recent changes, however, responsibility for carrying out elections has remained largely with the states and their subdivisions (usually counties). Writing in 2009, Alec Ewald recounts one action after another, indicating that "local administration of elections has proved far more durable than many reformers suspected."[2] Perhaps an even more telling indication of this reality is that the Federal Election Commission that was established in 2002 has since become dormant and faces an uncertain future.

Overlaid on the post-2000 specter of unfair elections and nightmarish outcomes was a concern over what appeared to be seriously eroding turnout. It was long known that turnout had declined after the introduction of personal registration and the waning of the strong party era in the late nineteenth century, but when turnout in presidential elections dropped into the low–50 percent range in 1988, with the prospect of even lower levels in the future, alarms were sounded and calls were made to do something to reverse the ominous trend. We now know, of course, that turnout of the eligible electorate did not decline as much as thought and that it rebounded in three straight elections after 1996.[3] Even now, however, turnout in the United States remains low by international standards, so increasing turnout remains a goal of many election reforms.

This chapter focuses on recent reforms made by the states. Most of the reforms are intended to increase citizen faith in the integrity of elections, bring about greater equality of access across diverse constituencies, modernize voting equipment, improve the overall administration of elections, and, often, increase turnout by making registration and turnout easier. Yet other laws, while nominally aimed at preventing voter fraud, are regarded by many as thinly disguised partisan efforts to dampen turnout among groups that are likely to vote for the opposing party. These laws, mostly involving voter identification (voter ID), are also noted.

Taking a longer view, there is a rich, colorful, sometimes disreputable history of election administration stretching back as far as the beginning of the country and beyond. Election Day has sometimes been a raucous affair, and stories of incompetence, discrimination, fraud, and the like are all too true.[4] Yet the end of overt, state-sanctioned racial discrimination in the 1960s and the adoption of supposedly better voting equipment (including now-abandoned punch-card systems) suggested that election administration was a routine, even dull matter of concern only to administrative specialists. The focus of this chapter is on what we have learned, and how the states have reacted, since 2000.

HOW, WHEN, AND WHERE WE REGISTER TO VOTE

Discussions of voting in the United States often start with consideration of the system of voter registration. Since the 1970s, there have been several significant developments related to this aspect of voter administration.

Election Day Registration

Election Day registration (EDR) allows eligible citizens to register and vote with a single trip to polling places on

Election Day. Statewide EDR policies for all elections were first implemented in the 1970s in Maine (1973), Minnesota (1973), and Wisconsin (1975).[5] Some localities in Maine had registration services at a central location but not at the polling places, a point that became important later on. Oregon also adopted EDR in 1975 but did not provide registration services in the actual polling places, and in 1985 it ended EDR. The latter action was prompted by a failed attempt by Bhagwan Shree Rajneesh and his followers to elect their slate of candidates in Wasco County by registering homeless people they bused and flew in from across the country.

EDR did not expand to other states until the early 1990s. While EDR was adopted in the first wave of states for the purpose of making registration easier, EDR was adopted in Wyoming (1993), Idaho (1994), and New Hampshire (1994) because it was viewed as a more tolerable alternative than the 1993 National Voter Registration Act (NVRA). That is, once it was clear the federal government was going to impose some change, these states opted for EDR over the NVRA, through the NVRA's nonapplicability clause, section 4(b).

Since the mid-1990s two additional states and the District of Columbia have adopted EDR. Montana was the first state to adopt in the third wave of EDR expansion, doing so in 2005. Iowa followed soon thereafter, adopting EDR in 2007. The District of Columbia, the most racially diverse jurisdiction to adopt EDR, did so in 2009.

Though attempts to eliminate EDR have come up from time to time, the first serious threat to EDR came in 2011, when the Maine legislature passed and the governor signed a bill that eliminated this practice in the state. A coalition of citizen organizations used the "people's veto," putting the issue of keeping EDR on the November 2011 ballot; EDR was reinstated when 60 percent of those who cast a vote on the issue voted to reject the section of the law that repealed EDR.

For the most part, recent scholarship has shown that EDR has a small positive effect on voter turnout, perhaps as high as 5 percentage points. One recent study that separates the early adopters from those that adopted EDR to avoid the NVRA suggests that while the early adopters saw gains in turnout after implementing EDR, the second wave of states did not see any boost in turnout. Thus EDR might not work to raise turnout in all contexts. To date, studies of the third wave of adopters have not been published.

National Voter Registration (Motor Voter) Act of 1993

A crucial part of any discussion of voter registration is the fact that the United States is unique in that the responsibility for registering to vote is placed on the individual, not the government. A major change in this approach came when Congress passed and President Bill Clinton signed into law the National Voter Registration Act of 1993 (NVRA), the first major federal action on voting since the Twenty-sixth Amendment was approved in 1971. The NVRA was intended to make registration easier by bringing registration services to the citizenry. It was put into effect across the United States on January 1, 1995. The key places where registration services were expanded were in motor vehicle offices and public service agencies. The NVRA also established provisions for registering by mail. Another core component was its rules for removing (a.k.a. purging) registrants from the voter rolls. The NVRA ended the practice of removing registrants from the rolls without notice simply because they did not vote in the last few elections.

It is important to note that the NVRA was not designed by the federal government; rather, it emerged from the states. Michigan, home of the U.S. automobile industry, established the practice of linking voter registration transactions to driver's license transactions in 1975, giving rise to "motor voter" as a nickname for the law. The policy spread to a number of other states and won the support of two scholar-activists, Francis Fox Piven and Richard Cloward, who steered the idea over a variety of bumps in the twisting road toward passage. The expectation that about 90 percent of eligible citizens would engage in driver's license transactions or be in contact with the expanded set of registration services at public service agencies—points of contact for many low-income people—led to high hopes that the NVRA would increase turnout, especially among those with low incomes.

Though the NVRA is a federal law, not all states are subject to its provisions. A clause in the early drafts of the legislation exempted states that either did not have a voter registration system or had EDR at the polls. This applied to North Dakota, which has not had a voter registration system since 1951, and Minnesota and Wisconsin, which had EDR since the 1970s.[6] As noted above, Wyoming, Idaho, and New Hampshire successfully leveraged this clause to bypass NVRA, with Wyoming passing EDR before the NVRA was passed and the other two states passing EDR retroactively.

Studies of the NVRA and its state-level predecessors generally conclude that though the laws serve to raise registration rates, the effects on turnout are minimal, amounting to a few percentage points. Moreover, motor voter seems to do little with respect to altering the composition of the electorate; lax implementation of the public agency requirements might well drive part of this result.[7] Citizen groups have been tracking agency registration in the states and through the legal process have improved compliance in a number of states.

Felon and Ex-Felon Voting

States have long prevented felons from voting. On the eve of the Civil War, as many as two dozen states had laws preventing those convicted of some classes of crimes, usually felonies or "infamous" crimes, from voting. By 1920, most states had such laws. In many cases the disfranchisement was permanent, thus preventing ex-felons from voting even when they had completed their sentences, including any period of parole or probation. Provisions were and are complicated, sometimes allowing for restoration of voting rights after varying waiting periods or upon completion of complicated paperwork and hearings. Even now, information is seldom clear and readily available, laws are sometimes contradictory, and handling of cases is often slow and shrouded in secrecy.[8]

The rationale for disfranchisement of felons and ex-felons has never been especially coherent, as suggested by the variety of crimes to which it applies and variations in the length of application and restoration processes. The enactment of many such laws in the post–Civil War period, along with targeting of crimes thought to be especially likely to be committed by blacks and occasional explicit statements of racial prejudice, all suggest a strong racial component to such laws, at least in southern states. Presently, arguments in support of felon and ex-felon disfranchisement are under fire, yet courts have by and large continued to uphold the right of states to establish the rules, and legislation limiting their right to disfranchise ex-felons in federal elections failed in Congress.

Beginning in the late 1950s and extending to the present, states have liberalized laws relating especially to ex-felons. Nonetheless, about a dozen states still deny the right to vote at least for some categories of offenders even after they have completed their sentences. Many more states disallow voting while felons are out of prison but on parole or probation. All but Maine and Vermont deny the right to vote to felons while incarcerated, and only thirteen more, plus the District of Columbia, restore voting rights immediately upon release from prison.

A major reason for contemporary arguments over felon disfranchisement is the unusually large number of persons incarcerated in the United States, especially since the increased trend toward harsher punishments and stricter enforcement of drug laws since the 1980s. And while laws preventing felons from voting are on their face race-neutral, their impact is clearly not. In 2010, for example, the rate of incarceration for black men was slightly over 3 percent, compared to about 1 percent for Latinos and less than .5 percent for whites.[9]

The issue of ex-felon disfranchisement remains contentious, both legally and politically. Though the tide of recent voting rights history is on the side of fewer restrictions, it is unlikely that the patchwork pattern of state prohibitions regarding felon or ex-felon voting will disappear in the near future.[10]

College Student Registration

College students, especially undergraduates living in cities or states different from where they grew up, are a small fraction of the adult population, yet they draw a considerable amount of attention, sometimes bordering on outright hostility, when it comes to the matter of where they should register and vote. Feelings are strongest, no doubt, in towns in which (noncommuter) students make up a large proportion of the overall population, but even in places where students are only a small part of the population, the feeling among many is that students "do not really live here" and therefore should vote "where they came from."

Of course, voting in one's hometown (where one graduated from high school) is a viable option for most college students, and perhaps two-thirds of them choose that option.[11] In some instances, however, students can no longer vote there (e.g., if their parents have moved), or they simply wish to vote in their college towns, possibly for the sake of convenience or because they develop an interest in their new location. In those cases, it is surprising, considering that eighteen- to twenty-year-olds were granted the right to vote in 1972, that legal issues surrounding student voters have been clarified only recently. And even now, significant

College of Charleston student Megan McCorry of Ashburn, Virginia, asks a question at a voter registration drive on campus in Charleston, South Carolina, Thursday, September 27, 2012. Voter registration drives such as this are often offered by student government associations and other political organizations to answer questions students may have about where and how to register to vote, and to encourage participation in elections.

SOURCE: Randall Hill/MCT.

differences across states, along with new laws aimed directly at them, make it difficult for students to know whether they can register and vote in their college towns and precisely what they must do in order to qualify.

Historically, some states, such as Iowa and Missouri, have allowed students to vote with no restrictions other than that they attend college in the state. Other states, such as Idaho and New Hampshire, strongly discourage students from registering in the state and make it difficult for them to do so. Such efforts are within the law if the state says only that students, like all citizens, must meet certain residency requirements before they are allowed to vote; this can mean, for example, that they have to acquire an in-state driver's license in order to be considered a state resident.

States can no longer prevent students from registering on the grounds that they do not intend to be permanent residents of the area.[12] Nonetheless, one still finds statements on a few state-sponsored websites suggesting that this is the case. An Idaho website, for example, contains a statement declaring, "A qualified elector shall not be considered to have gained a residence in any county or city of this state into which he comes for temporary purposes only, without the intention of making it his home but with the intention of leaving it when he has accomplished the purpose that brought him there."[13]

The battle over student voting is far from over. Most recently, fights over voter ID requirements have included the question of whether college IDs are a sufficient form of identification. A 2012 study in Pennsylvania found that more than 80 percent of the state's colleges and universities do not have IDs that meet state requirements (including an expiration date).[14] In Wisconsin, schools reacted to a new law by creating voter ID–compliant student IDs for those who asked for them.[15] Given the contentiousness of state and national politics, the awareness of at least some students that they can register strategically (at home or in their college towns, depending on the competitiveness of the state), and strong feelings about the appropriateness of students voting in their college towns, this battle is likely to continue for the foreseeable future.

WHEN, WHERE, AND HOW WE VOTE

Convenience Voting (No-Excuse Absentee Voting, Vote by Mail, Early Voting)[16]

No-excuse absentee voting (a.k.a. unrestricted absentee voting), voting by mail, and early in-person voting make up the set of reforms commonly referred to as convenience voting reforms. Though they are different from one another in important ways, they share two common features: (1) they were designed to make voting easier for those who are already registered; and (2) they extend the period of voting to the days and weeks prior to Election Day. The growth in the percentage of votes cast prior to Election Day, largely due to voters who take advantage of these policies, has been dramatic. Whereas estimates suggest that about 14 percent of the votes cast in the 2000 presidential election were cast prior to Election Day, in 2008 the percentage jumped to 30 percent.[17]

Prior to the Civil War, Oregon was the only state to allow absentee voting. Starting in 1857, Oregon allowed men who were out of town on Election Day to vote via absentee ballot.[18] During the Civil War, nineteen states adopted absentee voting laws that allowed Union soldiers to vote from their stations. Absentee voting for military personnel expanded to other states, followed by coverage for others who were away from their homes on Election Day because of duties related to their jobs, and then to a variety of other circumstances that prevent voters from voting in person on Election Day. It wasn't until the 1970s that states began to allow anyone to vote via absentee ballot without having an excuse for doing so. Washington, in 1974, and California, in 1978, were the first states to expand absentee voting to anyone who wanted to vote by mail before Election Day. Oregon followed suit in 1985. The adoption of no-excuse absentee voting took off in the 1990s, when another seventeen states enacted it. By 2011, twenty-seven states and the District of Columbia allowed no-excuse absentee voting.

Washington, in 1993, and California, in 2001, again led the way on developing a system of permanent absentee voting, a somewhat natural extension of no-excuse absentee voting. This policy allows registrants to declare that they wish to vote via absentee ballot in all future elections. As of 2013, seven states and the District of Columbia offer this to all of its registered voters, and another seven allow it for certain types of registrants.

Growing out of their experiences with absentee voting, Oregon and Washington now conduct all of their elections by mail. That is, all who are registered to vote receive their ballot in the mail and can cast it either by mailing it to the appropriate election official or taking it to an official drop site. In each state the process was a gradual one that began as options for local jurisdictions in smaller-scale elections. Oregon moved all of its elections to the vote-by-mail system via a ballot initiative that passed in 1998. Reflecting the high rate of absentee ballots cast (68 percent in 2004), in 2005 Washington allowed its counties to choose whether they wanted to implement all-mail elections. Through the 2008 elections, all but King and Pierce, the two most populous counties, chose all-mail elections, with King moving to mail elections in 2009. The state achieved uniformity when it passed legislation in 2011 that required all counties to conduct all of their elections by mail.

Early in-person voting is a policy that allows any registered voter to cast his or her ballot at polling places prior to Election Day, usually with the same voting machines, without having to provide an excuse for wanting to do so. Early voting was first adopted in 1987 in Texas. A steady stream of states adopted early voting in the 1990s and 2000s; by 2011, thirty-two states and the District of Columbia offered in-person early voting to its registered voters. The days and hours of operation vary state to state. The average number of days prior to the election during which early voting is available is nineteen, but it is as short as four and as long as forty-five. The ending day for early voting is most frequently the Monday before the election but can be as early as the Thursday before the election.[19] The number and types of locations also vary and include places as diverse as county offices and shopping centers.

Several states have created a new reform by combining early voting with voter registration. This practice, referred to as same-day registration, allows eligible citizens to register to vote during the early voting period at early voting polling places. North Carolina began this practice in 2007 and allows for voter registration at early voting sites even after the closing date for registration passed. However, North Carolina did not take the leap to EDR.

Election Day vote centers are another reform that might be more widely adopted in the coming years. Vote centers are used on Election Day and replace the more numerous traditional precincts that serve a localized residential area in which everyone uses the same ballot with more centrally located polling places that serve a wider range of voters, such as all those in the county. Voters can choose to vote at any vote center within the county, which might be on the way to work or at a popular shopping destination, and can access the ballot appropriate for their place of registration. Larimer County, Colorado, first utilized vote centers in 2003 and in the process reduced its precincts from over 143 to 22 vote centers.[20] Vote centers have also been used in other states, such as Indiana, but no state has moved to statewide implementation.

Reformers hoped that the set of convenience voting policies, by reducing the cost of voting, would increase turnout and increase the equality of turnout by raising the turnout rates of the resource poor, who tend to have low turnout rates. Though there is some disagreement, the consensus is that these reforms have failed to increase turnout and have actually increased rather than decreased the turnout gap between the resource rich and resource poor.[21] Rather than mobilizing new voters, these reforms work to retain existing voters by shifting their participation from Election Day to earlier. That is, it seems that the primary effect of these policies is to serve as a substitute for those who would have likely voted on Election Day if the convenience reforms were not available.

An interesting line of research that scholars have yet to embark upon would examine systematically the social and political factors behind the adoption of convenience reforms. Because they are designed to affect those who are already registered rather than to facilitate or impede future registrations, it is unlikely that partisan considerations play much of a role. However, there have been a few instances in which an effort has been made to roll back these reforms, suggesting partisan motivations.

Voter ID Requirements

Most of the election reforms enacted over the last several decades have aimed at making voting easier. That trend has been interrupted by a recent flurry of laws requesting or requiring that voters provide identification at the polls. Laws requesting or requiring photo identification have grabbed the headlines, but voter identification laws have a long history in the United States; and, as with most features of the U.S. electoral system, they vary widely across states.

Voter identification laws date as far back as 1950, when South Carolina passed a law requiring identification at the polls. The spread of identification laws over the next several decades was quite slow, with just four states adopting a law by the end of the 1970s, and another eight by 1999. But from 2000 to 2012, the number of states passing voter identification laws for the first time more than doubled (from thirteen to thirty-four). The policies on identification can be placed into three broad categories: (1) require identification in order to have one's vote counted; (2) request identification but allow one to vote by verifying identity in another way (such as verifying one's signature); and (3) neither request nor require any identification. Under the strictest set of rules (category 1), since HAVA, voters who do not have the required ID at the polls can still cast a ballot. However, they must do so using a provisional ballot that is kept separate from the regular ballots until election officials can verify the voter's eligibility; those who did not bring the requisite ID to the polls must then provide such ID within the required time frame in order to have the ballot counted. The types of documentation requested or required vary considerably, but in the least strict cases include a utility bill that includes one's name and address, and in the most strict cases require a government-issued photo ID, such as a driver's license.

Much of the ID legislation over the last few years has either expanded existing law to include a request or requirement of photo ID or has established such a law for the first time. Though relatively rare through 2004, photo ID legislation is not new. In 1970 Hawaii was the first state to request photo ID; by 1999 three other states (Florida, Louisiana, and Michigan) added photo ID request laws, and South Dakota enacted a photo ID request law in 2003. What is new is the stricter requirement that voters show a photo ID before their vote will be counted.[22] The first states to require registrants to present a photo ID in order for their vote to be counted were Georgia and Indiana, which passed their photo ID legislation in 2005. While Georgia built on existing law that requested voters show a nonphoto ID (passed in 1997), Indiana's photo ID requirement was its first law relating to voter ID. Challenges to the Indiana law made it to the U.S. Supreme Court, which in *Crawford vs. Marion County Election Board* (2008) upheld the law as constitutional.[23] By the summer of 2012, another seven states (Kansas, Mississippi, Pennsylvania, South Carolina, Tennessee, Texas, and Wisconsin) enacted a photo ID requirement, and two other states (New Hampshire and Rhode Island) added a photo ID request. Importantly, some of the laws were struck down in state court, some states delayed implementation, and Texas's law was not implemented because a federal district court ruled it to be discriminatory. The situation remains uncertain in a number of states as challengers to the laws continue to emerge and the states continue with the appeals process.

The most controversial of the laws are those that request or require a photo ID. Democrats and Republicans are clearly divided on the need for voter identification. Republican governors and legislatures have generally led the charge for the recent wave of voter identification laws, claiming that they improve the integrity of elections by reducing fraud. Proponents also argue that the burdens are minimal, comparing them to other activities that require identification such as getting a prescription or boarding an airplane. Democrats have largely opposed the laws, asserting that they are designed for Republicans to gain electoral advantage by suppressing turnout among the poor and minorities, who are less likely to have the appropriate identification.

Empirical research on voter identification laws is still in its infancy. One common finding from the literature is that those with low incomes, blacks, and Latinos are less likely to have a driver's license.[24] Whether this translates into lower turnout and/or less equal turnout remains an open question. The studies of the effect of the ID laws on turnout have posited that voter ID laws will reduce turnout because some will not have the appropriate ID or because confusion over what ID is necessary will deter some from voting in the first place. Thus far, the results have been mixed. But the most compelling research on the effects of the first wave of photo ID laws on turnout suggests that it is simply too early to tell what effect, if any, the laws have in practice.[25] It is clear that scholars have much more work to do; and with the recent expansion of photo ID laws, scholars have more opportunities and more leverage to study the effects.

Military and Overseas Voting

Unlike some countries, the United States allows its citizens to vote for federal offices regardless of their physical location. But for between four and six million U.S. citizens living or working in other countries, both near and far, in metropolitan areas and remote locations (on land, on water, and even submerged under water), voting can be a significant challenge.

The Uniformed and Overseas Citizens Absentee Voting Act (UOCAVA), federal legislation passed in 1986, requires that U.S. citizens abroad be allowed to vote via absentee ballot for federal offices. The act covers U.S. citizens who are active members of the uniformed Services and the merchant marine, plus their family members, and any U.S. citizens residing outside the United States.[26] Members of the uniformed services, the merchant marine, and their family members can vote for state and local offices as well in all of the states, but whether other citizens residing outside the United States can do so depends on state law.

Despite UOCAVA and widespread support for ensuring that members of the military can vote, state laws and practice made voting difficult and in some cases next to impossible. In 2009 the Pew Center on the States issued a report revealing that military voters from sixteen states and the District of Columbia did not have enough time to request, obtain, and submit an absentee ballot in time for it to be counted.[27] The report also showed that in a number of states military voters only had enough time to vote if they returned their voted ballots by fax or e-mail, thus

On Thursday, August 16, 2012, ninety-three-year-old Viviette Applewhite holds up the temporary photo ID she was able to obtain in Philadelphia, Pennsylvania. She wants to be able to vote in the next election and was able to overcome obstacles to meet the legal restrictions of the state's new voter identification law. "You just have to keep trying," Applewhite said. "Don't give up."

SOURCE: Michael Bryant/Philadelphia Inquirer/MCT.

giving up their privacy and raising concerns that the transmission could be intercepted.

Recognizing the problems citizens residing outside the United States face, in 2009 Congress passed and President Barack Obama signed the Military and Overseas Voter Empowerment (MOVE) Act. The key features of the act were a requirement that ballots be available to send to overseas citizens forty-five days prior to Election Day, the elimination of notary requirements, and the implementation of mechanisms for electronic transmission of blank absentee ballots. Most states came quickly into full compliance, but some had to file for waivers, as other aspects of their election administration system—such as primary dates—had to be revisited in order to comply. One quick sign of success was the remarkable increase in the number of states allowing electronic transfer of blank absentee ballots, which went from twenty states in 2008 to fifty (fifty-one including the District of Columbia) in 2010. Importantly, overseas voters who requested but did not receive their ballot can use the Federal Write-in Absentee Ballot (FWAB) to cast their votes for federal offices in all states, and in some states, other offices as well.

THE MECHANICS OF VOTING

Voting Equipment

Since the early days of the nation, voting methods and equipment have been selected by state and local jurisdictions. This resulted in an extreme amount of heterogeneity in voting systems that has continued to the present, though with more statewide systems in use today. In the first part of the nineteenth century, voting was done by various paper methods, voice voting, and unorthodox methods such as using beans or corn to designate one's vote. By the middle of the century, party-prepared ballots were the norm. Typically, parties prepared their own ballots, which were made distinguishable so they could be easily recognized by voters and by party workers. Voting was obviously not secret, and voting a split ticket was difficult to impossible.

Late in the nineteenth century, three major changes occurred: the Australian or secret ballot came into use; the ballot was prepared by the government, thus eliminating party-prepared ballots; and the ballot contained candidates from all parties. It was at this time, as well, that inventors began to think of mechanical methods for casting and counting votes. The resultant lever machine, though not uncontroversial, began to take hold, and by 1964, nearly two-thirds of all voters used it.[28] About that time, punch-card systems made their entry and gradually became widespread. Later in the twentieth century, computers were adapted for voting, and by 2000, some 12 percent of voters were using electronic systems.

The pace of change in the early twenty-first century was furious; two-thirds of voters saw changes in their voting between the presidential elections of 2000 and 2008. Initially, electronic systems (often referred to as DREs, or direct recording electronic systems) saw the biggest increases. Their portability and adaptability (e.g., they could be programmed with multiple languages; their font-size could be increased for voters with visual impairments; they could be coupled with speakers for voters with hearing impairments; they could be programmed to call attention to under-voting) made them attractive. Moreover, they could prevent over-voting and stray or "unacceptable" ballot markings that previously invalidated a large number of ballots nationwide. And at the end of the day, they provided instantaneous and presumably accurate vote counts. The pervasiveness of computers in other domains, especially in banking and other financial transactions, also seemed to make their adoption inevitable. Their use climbed about 38 percent by 2006.

Soon, however, multiple concerns were raised. After all, DREs are computers, and computers can malfunction or crash; and under some circumstances they can be hacked, with potentially catastrophic consequences. Some of these concerns were no doubt overblown; yet the biggest concern was genuine—that in the event of a real or perceived problem with the voting, there was nothing on which to fall back. That is, with a DRE, there is no paper trail that can be used to verify the votes; a recount can only mean rechecking the output of the (possibly flawed) computer. Thus, after the initial growth, the use of DREs declined, with optically scanned paper ballots picking up the slack. In 2012 they were used by two-thirds of voters.[29] It should be noted, of course, that the use of paper ballots (with or without counting by optical scan machines) has not made voting fool-proof (voters can mark them incorrectly) or fraud-proof (ballot-box stuffing is still possible).

Despite the overwhelming adoption of DREs or optical scan systems, changes in voting systems over the past decade have not entirely erased the heterogeneity of U.S. voting systems. In addition to having two broad types of equipment, multiple types of DREs are in use, some with quite distinctive features, and a variety of optical scan models are available. In the latter case, there is also a fundamental distinction between states that use only centralized optical scanning and those that have optical scan machines in every precinct. In addition, in response to HAVA, special electronic voting systems are now in use in most precincts to provide voters with disabilities a means of voting without the assistance of others (or the consequent loss of ballot secrecy).

Ballot Forms

As with voting equipment, ballot forms have changed considerably over time. The adoption of state-prepared ballots late in the nineteenth century meant that all candidates would appear on one ballot. Other than that, there was and is currently no assured uniformity across states. The effect of variations in ballot format is rarely as dramatic as occurred with the "butterfly" ballot used in Palm Beach County, Florida, in 2000, but effects are large enough for candidates and parties to pay close attention to their design.[30]

The most fundamental distinction between ballot types is whether the design emphasizes office or party (see Types of Ballots Used in the United States box).

TYPES OF BALLOTS USED IN THE UNITED STATES

The two basic types of ballots are the standard office bloc ballot and the party column (or row) ballot.

Office Bloc Ballot (partial view)

On this ballot all the candidates for a given office are grouped together in a bloc. It is the most common type of ballot used in the United States. Compared to the party column/row ballot, it is thought to deemphasize political parties in favor of an emphasis on each office and the candidates for that office, and hence to minimize straight-ticket voting.

INSTRUCTIONS TO VOTER

1. To vote, completely blacken the CIRCLE o to the LEFT of the candidate. Do not vote for more than the authorized number of candidates.
2. Use only the #2 pencil provided.
3. To vote for a person whose name is not on the ballot, write in the candidate's name on the Write-In line AND completely blacken the CIRCLE o to the LEFT of your choice.
4. If you make a mistake while voting, return the ballot to the election official for a new one. A vote that has been erased or changed will not be counted.

PARTISAN OFFICES

President & Vice-President of the United States
(Vote for ONE.)

- o Edward Z. Jones—President
Steve Kaiser—Vice-President
Democrat
- o Curtis G. Tucker—President
John Fisher—Vice-President
Republican
- o Nathan Davis—President
Phillip Knox—Vice-President
Libertarian

United States Senator
(Vote for ONE.)

- o Frank Searer
Democrat
- o Alan Slocum
Republican
- o Linda Fisher
Libertarian
- o ____________
Write-In

U. S. Representative District 28
(Vote for ONE.)

- o Larry Herman
Democrat
- o Rebecca Rehberg
Republican
- o William Petelos
Natural Law
- o ____________
Write-In

Governor & Lt. Governor
(Vote for ONE.)

- o Conrad Schweitzer—Gov.
James Milligan—Lt. Gov.
Democrat
- o Gov. Joyce McGrath—Gov.Ethan J. Edwards—Lt.
Republican
- o Write-In ____________

Secretary of State
(Vote for ONE.)

- o Matthew Prior
Democrat
- o ____________
Write-In

Attorney General

State Auditor
(Vote for ONE.)

- o Jose Rodriguez
Democrat
- o Roger Laird, Jr.
Republican
- o ____________
Write-In

State Senator District 5
(Vote for ONE.)

- o Bill Forbes
Democrat
- o Victoria Snyder
Republican
- o Joseph A. Jackson
Libertarian
- o ____________
Write-In

State Representative District 3
(Vote for no more than TWO.)

- o Cheryl Adams
Democrat
- o Jonathan Davic
Democrat
- o Leonard Arnold
Republican
- o Samantha Bolin
Republican
- o Jeffrey Jones
Libertarian
- o Michael R. McCloud
Libertarian
- o Helen Barclay
Natural Law
- o ____________
Write-In
- o ____________

An office bloc format contains a straight-party feature in about fifteen states, allowing a voter with one mark to vote for the candidate of one party in all partisan contests on the ballot. This creates a relative emphasis on parties within the office-bloc format.

Straight party voting
o Democratic Party
o Republican Party
o Green Party
o Libertarian Party

Party Column Ballot (partial view)

The party column (or row) format lists candidates for different offices from a single party underneath (alongside) one another—that is, in a single column (row). Modeled after the party strips used in the 1800s before the introduction of the consolidated ballot, it was designed to encourage voting for a single party (straight-party voting).

INSTRUCTIONS TO VOTER

1. To vote, completely blacken the OVAL (⬬) to the LEFT of the candidate. Do not vote for more than the authorized number of candidates.
2. Use only the #2 pencil provided.
3. To vote for a person whose name is not on the ballot, write in the candidate's name on the Write-In line AND completely blacken the OVAL (⬬) to the LEFT of your choice.
4. If you make a mistake while voting, return the ballot to the election official for a new one. A vote that has been erased or changed will not be counted.

PARTISAN OFFICES					
President & Vice-President of The United States (Vote for ONE.)					
⬭	Edward Z. Jones President Steve Kaiser Vice-President	⬭	Curtis G. Tucker President John Fisher Vice-President	⬭	Nathan Davis President Phillip Knox Vice-President
	Democrat		Republican		Libertarian
United States Senator (Vote for ONE.)					
⬭	Frank Searer	⬭	Alan Slocum	⬭	Linda Fisher
	Democrat		Republican		Libertarian
United States Representative District 28 (Vote for ONE.)					
⬭	Larry Herman	⬭	Rebecca Rehberg		
	Democrat		Republican		
Governor & Lt. Governor (Vote for ONE.)					
⬭	Conrad Schweitzer Governor James Milligan Lt. Governor	⬭	Joyce McGrath Governor Ethan J. Edwards Lt. Governor		
	Democrat		Republican		

A second major distinction also relates to the relative emphasis on party. Straight-party options allow voters, with one mark or click, to vote for all of a given party's candidates running in partisan offices on the ballot. It is currently used in about fifteen states. There are variations (such as allowing voters to cast a straight-party vote but then override it for individual offices), but the basic point is to make it easy for voters to vote for all of a party's candidates and therefore more likely that they will do so. Indeed, it is known that undervoting (failing to vote) for offices below the top of the ticket is reduced and straight-party voting is more frequent when a straight-party option is available.

In addition to these basic distinctions, ballots differ among states, and sometimes within states, in innumerable smaller ways (see U.S. Ballots: Variations on a Theme box). One might suppose that ballots are uniform at least for the election of the president and vice president. Such is not the case. Candidates are selected on a state-by-state basis, so it sometimes happens that a given party does not even nominate the same candidates in every state. This happened in 1948, when the Dixiecrats splintered the Democratic Party. As a consequence, the Democratic Party in Alabama, Louisiana, Mississippi, and South Carolina listed Strom Thurmond as its nominee; in Alabama, President Harry Truman was not even on the ballot. In 2000 the Arizona Libertarian Party refused to recognize Harry Browne (the nominee in other states) as its nominee and instead gave the ballot line to L. Neil Smith.

Ballots vary greatly in length (reflecting different numbers of offices and ballot propositions that are to be voted on); in whether they contain more than one language (or, sometimes, whether separate, non-English ballots are available); in whether candidate order is randomized; in how one indicates a preference (clicking or filling in an oval versus connecting parts of an arrow); in whether or not write-in candidates are permitted; and in a myriad of details such as size and type of print, readability of instructions, use (or not) of nicknames, use (or not) of party emblems, and so

U.S. BALLOTS: VARIATIONS ON A THEME

U.S. ballots vary in myriad ways.

Which Offices Are Elective

Voters in every state vote for the president, U.S. senators, U.S. House members, and a state governor. Most vote for a secretary of state and a state attorney general, and some judges (state supreme court, court of appeals, circuit, chancery). But voters in only some states vote for

- agriculture commissioner
- board of equalization (tax commission)
- environmental quality board
- insurance commissioner
- labor commissioner
- land commissioner/commissioner of public lands
- railroad commissioner
- superintendent of public instruction
- tax commissioner

County/local elected offices include

- coroners
- drain commissioner (MI)
- high bailiff (VT)
- rural landowner or occupier conservation district supervisor (SD)

What the Same Office Is Called in Different States

Office as listed	State	Office as listed	State
Representative in Congress	Michigan; multiple states	United States House of Representatives	Tennessee
Representative to Congress	Maine; Ohio	United States Congress	Arkansas
United States Representative/U.S. Representative	California; Oklahoma	Member of Congress	North Carolina*

*U.S. Senate is listed on a separate line, not as a "member of Congress."

Whether Presidential Electors Are Named on the Ballot

Most states use the so-called short ballot, which lists only the names of the presidential and vice presidential candidates. "A few states, however, feel it is necessary to list the electors' names. North and South Dakota, each with only three electors, and Arizona with eight electors, list them in small print next to or below the candidates' names. Louisiana, with nine electors, lists them in what can only be described as microscopic type. On the ballot provided to us, from a lever voting machine, electors for some of the parties occupy a column with no levers while electors for other parties occupy a space under three (presumably nonactivated) levers. Georgia lists its 13 electors using larger print than for the presidential and vice presidential candidates."[1]

What the Presidential Candidates Are Called

In 2000, the Democratic candidate for president was listed as

Al Gore	multiple states
Albert Gore	Hawaii
"Al" Gore	New Hampshire
Gore	Arizona, Kansas, North Dakota
Vice President Al Gore	Arkansas

The Republican candidate for vice president was listed as

Dick Cheney	multiple states
Richard B Cheney	Delaware
"Dick" Cheney	New Hampshire
Cheney	Kansas
Not listed	Arizona, North Dakota
Dick Chaney*	Arkansas

*Misspelling on the official ballot

How We Mark Our Ballots

TO VOTE: Completely darken the oval opposite each choice as shown:

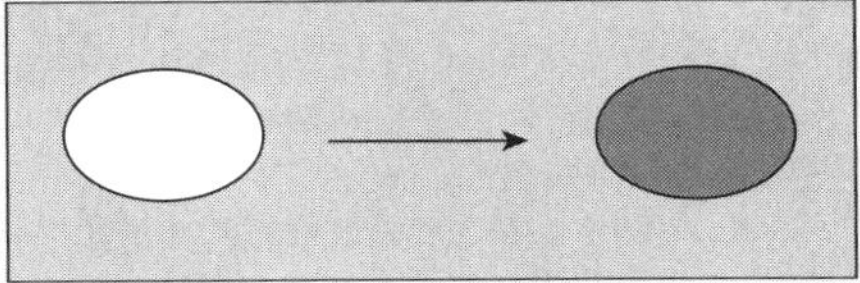

or, **TO VOTE:** Complete the arrow opposite each choice as shown:

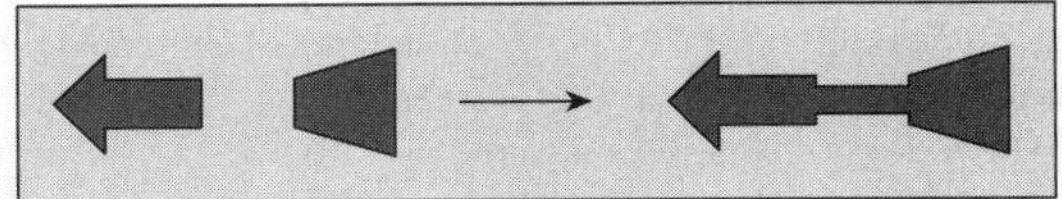

1. Niemi and Herrnson, "Beyond the Butterfly."

SOURCE: Richard G. Niemi and Paul S. Herrnson, "Beyond the Butterfly: The Complexity of U.S. Ballots," *Perspectives on Politics* 1 (2003): 317–326.

on. When voting is on DREs, ballots differ in another fundamental way as well—that is, in how many offices are shown on a single screen. They again differ in details—colors being added to all the ways in which paper ballots vary. Many of the smaller variations are perhaps inconsequential, but they add immeasurably to the heterogeneity of election administration in the United States.[31]

CONCLUSION

In the aftermath of the 2000 presidential election in Florida, and reflecting on the infamous butterfly ballot, more than one cartoon appeared picturing a ballot with a box for George W. Bush and a box for Al Gore with a caption: "How Hard Can It Be [to design a simple, unambiguous ballot]?" In fact, in a country the size of the United States, with a federal system, and in which we elect people to a large number of offices in elections held throughout the year, no aspect of voting administration is as simple as this sort of cartoon would have it.

Nor do we anticipate much simplification in the near future. Still, there is likely to be continuing evolution both in the way voters are registered and in the way they cast their ballots. As technology progresses, we may see more and improved use of electronics. Already, statewide voter registration databases have been developed, but they are still subject to considerable revision before they meet the standards required by HAVA (especially, coordination of the voter database with other state agency databases). With an expanded use of electronic files, a voter could also imagine being able to vote at any precinct in a state, with a "ballot-on-demand" being produced for the precise address at which he or she is registered. We also do not foresee quick adoption of Internet voting, chiefly because of security concerns but also because of possible problems such as being able to sell one's vote.

Whatever the pace of changes, we do not expect much of a reduction in heterogeneity across states. As we noted at the outset, voting administration has been in the hands of the states throughout the history of the country, and we can expect a great deal of resistance to any attempts at greater federalization of the process. Nor, finally, do we expect to see a reduction in controversies over registration and voting. In an era of heightened partisan polarization, *how* we vote is as contentious as who we vote for. Thus we can expect continuing controversy about how and where we register and vote, as individuals, groups, and states jockey for partisan advantage.

NOTES

1. Relevant constitutional amendments include the following: Fifteenth Amendment, race; Seventeenth Amendment, direct election of U.S. senators; Nineteenth Amendment, women; Twenty-third Amendment, District of Columbia; Twenty-fourth Amendment, poll tax; Twenty-sixth Amendment, eighteen-year-old vote. Legislative acts include an 1845 law establishing a uniform time for the election of presidential electors, the Voting Rights Act of 1965, the Voting Accessibility for the Elderly and Handicapped Act of 1984, and others.

2. Alec C. Ewald, *The Way We Vote: The Local Dimension of American Suffrage* (Nashville: Vanderbilt University Press, 2009), 7.

3. Michael P. McDonald and Samuel Popkin, "The Myth of the Vanishing Voter," *American Political Science Review* 95 (2001): 963–974.

4. See, for example, V. O. Key Jr., *Southern Politics in State and Nation* (New York: Knopf, 1949); Richard Franklin Bensel, *The American Ballot Box in the Mid-Nineteenth Century* (Cambridge: Cambridge University Press, 2004); Tracy Campbell, *Deliver the Vote: A History of Election Fraud, An American Political Tradition—1742–2004* (New York: Carroll and Graf, 2005); Alexander Keyssar, *The Right to Vote: The Contested History of Democracy in the United States*, rev. ed. (New York: Basic Books, 2009).

5. Prior to statewide implementation, EDR was available or effectively available in some jurisdictions within these states. Registration on Election Day was allowed in less populous jurisdictions in Maine as far back as the 1800s. In Wisconsin, until the Help America Vote Act of 2002 was implemented, jurisdictions with a population of less than five thousand did not need to have a registration system at all. Similarly, until 1984 registration was not required to vote in parts of Minnesota. Wyoming allowed EDR in primary elections dating back to 1951. In studies of voter turnout, North Dakota is often treated as having EDR, since it does not require registration. For information on the adoption and effects of EDR, see Michael J. Hanmer, *Discount Voting: Voter Registration Reforms and Their Effects* (New York: Cambridge University Press, 2009).

6. Maine was not exempt because EDR was not available at all polling places. The move to the NVRA was eased by the fact that it already had motor voter provisions.

7. See Benjamin Highton, "Voter Registration and Turnout in the United States," *Perspectives on Politics* 2 (2004): 507–515, on the composition of the electorate; and see Douglas R. Hess and Scott Novakowski, "Unequal Access: Neglecting the National Voter Registration Act 1995–2007," www.projectvote.org/images/publications/NVRA/Unequal_Access_Final.pdf, on NVRA implementation.

8. Two excellent, occasionally discrepant discussions of felon and ex-felon disfranchisement are Keyssar, *The Right to Vote;* and Jeff Manza and Christopher Uggen, *Locked Out: Felon Disenfranchisement and American Democracy* (Oxford: Oxford University Press, 2006).

9. Paul Guerino, Paige M. Harrison, and William J. Sabol, *Prisoners in 2010*, rev. ed. (Washington, DC: Bureau of Justice Statistics), 27.

10. Current information on felon disfranchisement is maintained by the Sentencing Project, sentencingproject.org, and other websites.

11. Richard G. Niemi and Michael J. Hanmer, "Voter Turnout among College Students: New Data and a Rethinking of Traditional Theories," *Social Science Quarterly* 91 (2010): 301–323.

12. Richard G. Niemi, Thomas H. Jackson, and Michael J. Hanmer, "Where Can College Students Vote? A Legal and Empirical Perspective," *Election Law Journal* 8 (2009): 327–348.

13. "Students and Voting Residency," Idaho Votes, www.idahovotes.gov/VoterReg/Students_Voting%20Residency.htm.

14. "Survey of Student IDs at Colleges and Universities in Pennsylvania," PennPIRG, http://pennpirg.org/sites/pirg/files/resources/PA%20Colleges%20Voter%20ID.pdf.

15. University of Wisconsin System, "Voter ID Compliant Student ID Cards," http://web.uwsa.edu/wisconsin/resources/vote-old-2012-10-29/documents/voter-id-compliant-student-id-cards/.

16. State law classifications are from the National Conference of State Legislatures, www.ncsl.org/legislatures-elections/elections/absentee-and-early-voting.aspx#no_excuse; Roger Larocca and John S. Klemanski, "Election Reform and Turnout in Presidential Elections," *State Politics and Policy Quarterly* 11 (2011): 76–101; and the authors' review of state statutes.

17. Paul Gronke, Eva Galanes-Rosenbaum, Peter A. Miller, and Daniel Toffey, "Convenience Voting," *Annual Review of Political Science* 11 (2008), 437–455. Since not all states have kept records on the number of votes cast before Election Day, it is difficult to assess the rates prior to 2000. Survey-based estimates suggest that less than 5 percent voted prior to Election Day in 1972 and that this rate did not break the 10 percent mark until 1996 (Michael P. McDonald, Figure 1 at http://elections.gmu.edu/early_vote_2010.html).

18. On absentee voting in the nineteenth century, see Keyssar, *The Right to Vote*.

19. National Conference of State Legislatures, www.ncsl.org/legislatures-elections/elections/absentee-and-early-voting.aspx#no_excuse.

20. Robert M. Stein and Greg Vonnahme, "Engaging the Unengaged Voter: Vote Centers and Voter Turnout," *Journal of Politics* 70 (2008): 487–497.

21. Adam J. Berinsky, "The Perverse Consequences of Electoral Reform in the United States," *American Politics Research* 33 (2005): 471–491.

22. As noted earlier, one can cast a provisional ballot but must ultimately provide the necessary ID by the end of the time frame set aside to review provisional ballots.

23. *Crawford vs. Marion County Election Board,* 553 U.S. 181 (2008).

24. See, for example, Matt A. Barreto, Stephen A. Nuño, and Gabriel R. Sanchez, "The Disproportionate Impact of Voter-ID Requirements on the Electorate—New Evidence from Indiana," *PS: Political Science and Politics* 42 (2009): 111–116.

25. Robert S. Erikson and Lorraine C. Minnite, "Modeling Problems in the Voter Identification–Voter Turnout Debate," *Election Law Journal* 8 (2009): 85–101.

26. U.S. Department of Justice, UOCVA statute, www.justice.gov/crt/military/uocava_statute.htm. The usual age and eligibility rules apply. UOCAVA defines the uniformed services as "Army, Navy, Air Force, Marine Corps, and Coast Guard, the commissioned corps of the Public Health Service, and the commissioned corps of the National Oceanic and Atmospheric Administration" (42 U.S.C. § 1973ff).

27. Pew Center on the States, "No Time to Vote: Challenges Facing America's Overseas Military Voters," 2009, www.pewtrusts.org/uploadedFiles/wwwpewtrustsorg/Reports/Election_reform/NTTV_Report_Web.pdf.

28. Roy G. Saltman, *The History and Politics of Voting Technology* (New York: Palgrave Macmillan, 2006), 157.

29. Verifiedvoting.org.

30. Jonathan N. Wand, Kenneth W. Shotts, Jasjeet S. Sekhon, Walter R. Mebane Jr., Michael C. Herron, and Henry E. Brady, "The Butterfly Did It: The Aberrant Vote for Buchanan in Palm Beach County, Florida," *American Political Science Review* 95 (2001): 793–810.

31. The number of offices on a DRE screen was a significant factor in a Sarasota County, Florida, congressional race. See Laurin Frisina, Michael C. Herron, James Honaker, and Jeffrey B. Lewis, "Ballot Formats, Touchscreens, and Undervotes: A Study of the 2006 Midterm Elections in Florida," *Election Law Journal* 7 (2008): 25–47.

SUGGESTED READING

Alvarez, R. Michael, and Thad E. Hall. *Electronic Elections: The Perils and Promises of Digital Democracy.* Princeton, NJ: Princeton University Press, 2008.

Alvarez, R. Michael, Thad E. Hall, and Susan D. Hyde, eds. *Election Fraud: Detecting and Deterring Electoral Manipulation.* Washington, DC: Brookings, 2008.

Bensel, Richard Franklin. *The American Ballot Box in the Mid-Nineteenth Century.* Cambridge: Cambridge University Press, 2004.

Campbell, Tracy. *Deliver the Vote: A History of Election Fraud, An American Political Tradition—1742–2004.* New York: Carroll and Graf, 2005.

Ewald, Alec C. *The Way We Vote: The Local Dimension of American Suffrage.* Nashville: Vanderbilt University Press, 2009.

Frisina, Lauren, Michael C. Herron, Manes Honaker, and Jeffrey B. Lewis. "Ballot Formats, Touchscreens, and Undervotes." *Election Law Journal* 7 (2008): 25–47.

Hanmer, Michael J. *Discount Voting: Voter Registration Reforms and Their Effects.* New York: Cambridge University Press, 2009.

Herrnson, Paul S., Richard G. Niemi, Michael J. Hanmer, Benjamin B. Bederson, Frederick C. Conrad, and Michael W. Traugott. *Voting Technology: The Not-So-Simple Act of Casting a Ballot.* Washington, DC: Brookings, 2008.

Keyssar, Alexander. *The Right to Vote: The Contested History of Democracy in the United States,* rev. ed. New York: Basic Books, 2009.

Kropf, Martha, and David C. Kimball. *Helping America Vote: The Limits of Election Reform.* New York: Routledge, 2012.

Lausen, Marcia. *Design for Democracy: Election Design.* Chicago: University of Chicago Press, 2007.

Manza, Jeff, and Christopher Uggen. *Locked Out: Felon Disenfranchisement and American Democracy.* New York: Oxford University Press, 2006.

Minnite, Lorraine C. *The Myth of Voter Fraud.* Ithaca: Cornell University Press, 2010.

Niemi, Richard G., Thomas H. Jackson, and Michael J. Hanmer. "Where Can College Students Vote? A Legal and Empirical Perspective." *Election Law Journal* 8 (2009): 327–348.

Piven, Frances Fox, Lorraine C. Minnite, and Margaret Groarke. *Keeping Down the Black Vote: Race and the Demobilization of American Voters.* New York: New Press, 2009.

Rusk, Jerrold G. "The Effect of the Australian Ballot Reform on Split Ticket Voting: 1876–1908." In Richard G. Niemi and Herbert F. Weisberg, eds., *Classics in Voting Behavior* (Washington, DC: CQ Press, 1993), 313–330.

Saltman, Roy G. *The History and Politics of Voting Technology.* New York: Palgrave Macmillan, 2006.

The Sentencing Project, www.sentencingproject.org. Click on Voting Rights, then Publications, then (under Key Publications) Felony Disenfranchisement Laws in the United States.

Chapter 8

Influences on State Elections

Thomas M. Carsey and Monica Moore

While national attention focuses every two and four years on presidential contests and/or a handful of congressional elections that might tip the balance of power in Washington, DC, citizens across the country are also electing fifty state governors, nearly 7,200 state legislators, and a large number of other state and local officials. Many of these elections unfold largely unnoticed, but most gubernatorial races are hotly contested, and even while most state legislative races are not close, control of the legislative chamber often hangs in the balance of a few close contests. Like all elections, state elections are dynamic events that unfold within their own environmental, institutional, and political contexts. Some of these features vary across the states, but others exist at the national level, making their influence felt across the states. This chapter explores both state-level and national-level factors that shape how state elections unfold. The focus is on contests for governor and for seats in the state legislature. Along the way, the chapter will explore every stage of the election process, from the emergence of candidates to winning on Election Day.

WHO RUNS FOR OFFICE?

Running for Governor

In order to understand how elections unfold, we must begin with understanding who runs for office and whether or not they face a hotly contested challenge or not. While nearly every gubernatorial contest features at least one candidate from each of the two major parties, there is some variance in how closely contested gubernatorial contests are. For example, an incumbent with a high level of approval among voters is less likely to be seriously opposed in the general election, and the incumbent is especially unlikely to be challenged in his or her own party's primary in states that have formal party endorsement of gubernatorial candidates. However, if an incumbent governor is opposed, a challenger will be better equipped and more likely to match the incumbent's level of campaign spending if he or she has significant political experience, is generally considered a higher-quality candidate, and/or is able to accept public funding as a way to ensure sufficient funding to run a campaign. Still, most states see viable candidates from both major parties emerging, and most states have elected governors from both parties at some point in recent decades. In short, gubernatorial elections are normally contested by plausible candidates from both parties. (For information on special elections and recall elections, see Special Elections box.)

Running for State Legislature

The same is not true for state legislative contests. It is not uncommon for 35 to 40 percent of state legislative elections to be uncontested, with nearly 75 percent of state legislative primaries going uncontested. Furthermore, many elections that are contested are not seriously contested. In recent years, only about 40 percent of state legislative contests are closely contested (winning margin of 20 percent or less), with often no more than 20 percent being closely contested (winning margin of 10 percent or less). In this regard, state legislative contests are quite similar to elections for the U.S. House of Representatives. What drives these patterns?

Scholars have defined three key sets of actors involved in determining who contests an election: potential serious candidates, potential nonserious candidates, and political parties.[1] The choices made by these actors are shaped by the probability of success and the value of the office being contested. In the U.S. context, that probability of success must be divided further into the probability of winning the general election should the candidate be nominated, multiplied by the probability of gaining the nomination should the candidate seek it. Potential serious candidates—individuals who define success as winning the race—are more likely to participate when the combination of the probability of success and the value of the seat is maximized. Nonserious candidates—those who define success as something other

SPECIAL ELECTIONS

One subject area within the realm of state elections that is lacking in extensive research is the special election. The recall election and other special elections, while relatively uncommon in their occurrence, provide interesting windows to examine the ways in which shocks to the political system can affect voters and other politicians. For example, California's 2003 recall election—held during the course of the state's legislative session—provided researchers with a way to investigate the impact of a strong electoral signal on how the legislature performed that was entirely isolated from all other political changes. For voters, the complexity and hurried nature of recall elections seem to create obstacles to becoming sufficiently informed about the candidates and the process, factors that can lower voter participation. The California recall election was characterized by broad precinct consolidations that greatly reduced the number of polling places, a lack of multilingual balloting, a faulty ballot design, and a suspected loss of a sizeable number of ballots.[1] These circumstances—which might be fairly typical for recall elections—lead to lingering questions about the legitimacy of special elections from the perspective of voters. For state politicians, a special election can provide an unscheduled electoral signal that can affect legislative behavior. In the case of California, after the recall results showed a surge of support for the Republican Party, Democratic state legislators in general responded by moderating their voting behavior toward the right to ideologically adapt to apparent constituent attitudes. In another study of special elections in California and Oregon that focused on ballot initiatives held in 2005, the authors found that high-stimulus special elections had their greatest mobilization impact on voters attached to one of the two major political parties.[2]

Special elections can also become the focus of national politics, as they generally do not compete for press attention with other elections. This was certainly true of the California recall election, but it was also a significant feature of a special election in Wisconsin held on June 5, 2012, that targeted Republican governor Scott Walker for recall. The race was closely contested, and was viewed by many observers as a potential indicator of how the presidential election would unfold later that November. As a result, the race received national attention, and more than $80 million was spent by the candidates, parties, and outside groups, with vast majorities of the funds on both sides coming from outside groups. As a result of this hotly contested and nationally visible campaign, nearly 58 percent of eligible voters in Wisconsin participated in this election—the highest turnout rate in a Wisconsin gubernatorial contest that did not also have a presidential contest on the ballot in Wisconsin history. In the end, Walker retained his office with a margin of about 7 percentage points, though President Barack Obama went on to win Wisconsin by about the same margin five months later.

1. R. Michael Alvarez, Melanie Goodrich, Thad E. Hall, D. Roderick Kiewiet, and Sarah M. Sled, "The Complexity of the California Recall Election," *PS: Political Science and Politics* 37 (2004): 23–26.

2. Joshua J. Dyck and Nicholas R. Seabrook, "Mobilized by Direct Democracy: Short-Term versus Long-Term Effects and the Geography of Turnout in Ballot Measure Elections," *Social Science Quarterly* 91 (2010): 189–208.

than winning—do not respond to these pressures in the same way. Nonserious candidates, whom scholars have labeled "sacrificial lambs," define success in terms of personal satisfaction, self-promotion, or helping the party by at least not leaving a race uncontested. Parties enter into the process by helping to recruit candidates, particularly sacrificial lambs.

At the district level, the single best predictor of a potential challenger's probability of winning a general election is the share of the vote the losing party received in the previous election. This measure is certainly influenced by the specific candidates who ran in the last election, but it also provides a strong signal to potential candidates and political parties in the state regarding the underlying support candidates from both parties can expect to receive. When the losing party's vote share is low, it is often the case that no candidate from that party will run in the next election. Furthermore, if a candidate from the losing party does emerge, he or she will likely be a sacrificial lamb. At the other extreme, if the losing party came very close to winning an election, it is almost certain that a strong serious candidate from that party will run again in the next election.

The second biggest predictor of whether a challenger emerges is the level of legislative professionalism in a state. Legislative professionalism serves as an indicator of the value of holding a legislative seat. A more professionalized legislature offers legislators better salaries, more staff resources, and more generally the opportunity to pursue politics as a full-time career. As a result, nearly every legislative seat is contested in the most professionalized state legislatures. However, the odds of seeing an uncontested race for a legislative seat go way up for the least professionalized state legislatures.

Another key predictor of whether a challenger emerges is whether the person currently serving in the legislature—the incumbent—runs again in the current race. However, the impact of incumbency on deterring challengers is smaller in magnitude than is the margin by which the losing party lost the last election. The chance that a legislative race is uncontested only changes by about 4 percentage points on average, depending on whether the incumbent is running or not.

Returning to legislative professionalism, scholars have found that it also impacts the sort of challenger that runs for state legislature. For example, more professional legislatures are associated with attracting high-quality, politically ambitious candidates. On a related point, it is also evident that the availability of public funding for campaigns encourages the emergence of high-quality candidates, particularly those who lack broad networks to raise high levels of private contributions. However, there is no evidence to suggest that underrepresented groups will take advantage of campaign subsidies to run for office.

The previous comment leads to another point regarding the study for scholars regarding the types of candidates that emerge: the opportunity to run for office is not distributed equally. While the rate at which female candidates emerge can vary based on the accepted sociopolitical norms within a state, it has been shown across the board that women who share the same personal characteristics and professional credentials as men express significantly lower levels of political ambition to hold elective office.[2] When women do run for political office, evidence suggests that they tend to run for offices with duties that are consistent with traditional stereotypical roles of women. Chapter 15 provides a more detailed discussion of diversity in state legislatures.

Finally, we note that many states have imposed term limits on their state legislators (fifteen states currently). The overall impact of term limits is beyond the scope of this chapter (for more, see Chapters 13 and 17), but there is evidence that they create somewhat more turnover in the composition of state legislatures. Term limits create new opportunities for candidates to run without an incumbent in the race, though it is quite common for legislators who are termed out of the lower chamber in their state to seek a seat in the upper chamber. Like legislative professionalism, term limits represent an institutional arrangement that (1) varies significantly across states, (2) impacts state legislative elections, and (3) is at least potentially subject to change or reform.[3]

POLITICAL PARTICIPATION IN STATE ELECTIONS

Who Is Allowed to Vote?

In the previous section, we considered factors that affect which candidates participate in elections. In this section, we consider the equally important question of factors that affect which voters participate. One determinant of a state's turnout is the set of laws that define the right to vote. As of 2000, nearly 10 percent of the persons of voting age living in the United States were ineligible to vote, and these ineligible persons are unevenly distributed among the states. This results in a key difference in the measurement of the Voting Age Population (VAP) and the Voting Eligible Population (VEP).[4] There are two primary causes of the differences between VAP and VEP. First, VAP includes noncitizens in its count of the population, but noncitizens are ineligible to vote. Second, VAP includes convicted felons and ex-felons, a class of citizens with voting rights that are restricted by law in many states. According to data collected by the Sentencing Project, nearly six million citizens are denied the right to vote based on felony disenfranchisement laws, with the most restrictive laws in states located in the Southeast and to a lesser extent though the central and southern plains.

Because the U.S. Constitution gives most of the responsibility for managing and conducting elections to the states, states differ in a range of other ways that affect voter participation. Some states require voters to register in advance of an upcoming election, while others do not. States differ in how long the polls are open on Election Day and how easy it is to vote early. In 1998 voters in Oregon approved a ballot initiative making it the first state to use vote by mail for all of its elections. These and other regulations that affect voter participation are discussed in more detail in Chapter 7.

There were also numerous legal struggles in more than a dozen states leading up to the 2012 election over attempts by state governments to curtail early voting, pass voter identification laws, and institute other reforms that opponents claimed would unfairly restrict access to voting in ways that would disproportionately affect some groups relative to others. The implementation of many of these laws was delayed by state courts, but we expect these issues to continue to draw the attention of state legislators leading up to the 2014 and 2016 elections, making this an area where more systematic research is needed.

The accurate determination of VEP relative to VAP has also proven critical for correctly understanding how other factors affect citizen participation in elections across the states. For one example, two scholars found that the size of a state's Latino population is negatively correlated with overall turnout in a state.[5] However, just how strong that correlation is depends on whether scholars are considering VEP or VAP, with the correlation based on VEP being much weaker. For another example, these same scholars found that voter turnout is higher where there are initiatives on the ballot. However, that positive correlation appears to be much stronger with VEP compared to VAP. Overall, these scholars argue that researchers would reach different conclusions about whether or not state per capita income, the average age of a state's population, the size of the Latino population in a state, and the number of initiatives on the ballot were significant predictors of state voter turnout or not based on whether they analyzed VEP or VAP.

In a photo from Thursday, November 1, 2012, David Herbeck prepares to give Katherine Davenport some campaign literature as he walks door-to-door in a Livonia, Michigan, suburb reminding voters to vote on Tuesday. Although the impact of this election strategy is not definitive, studies seems to show that door-to-door canvassing may indeed increase voter turnout.

SOURCE: AP Photo/Carlos Osorio.

What Predicts Participation?

At the individual level, the characteristic most strongly linked to likelihood of voting has historically been level of education. However, state contextual factors also interact with individual characteristics to determine who votes. Such contextual factors are campaign spending, the closeness of the electoral contests themselves, the extent of district partisanship, and the degree of party competition. Also, unsurprisingly, while midterm election turnout is generally lower than presidential election year turnout by about 20 percentage points, midterm years that include a gubernatorial race, a U.S. Senate race, or a controversial initiative on the ballot do tend to exhibit a measurable spike in turnout that reaches the level of recent presidential contests.

Turnout can also be influenced by the actions of political candidates and their campaigns, whether or not the campaign is actively attempting to "get out the vote." There is some evidence that particularly negative campaign tactics can depress voter turnout. While voters may report having a distaste for negative campaigns, scholars argue that negative campaigns provide voters with information that clearly differentiates the candidates, with information upon which voters may place more weight, and with information more likely to evoke an emotional response.[6]

More recently, candidates have turned to the Internet, social media, and online political news outlets as ways to spread information and stimulate turnout. Access to online political news and other sources of political information has been linked to a substantively significant increase in turnout in the election in 2000. These sources of information are also linked to increases in other forms of political participation, such as attending meetings or making financial contributions to candidates. Candidates for governor and state legislator have been moving aggressively to improve their online presences in order to capitalize on these trends.

Finally, political scientists have focused a good deal of attention recently on the mobilization efforts of both candidates and other organizations through the analysis of field experiments. In these studies, scholars use some mechanism to randomly assign some groups of voters to receive a stimulus designed to increase their likelihood of voting, while other voters are randomly assigned to a control group that does not receive this stimulus. This research design goes back almost one hundred years to early studies in which Harold F. Gosnell randomly sent postcards to some voters encouraging them to vote; however, it has reemerged in response to a number of publications by Alan Gerber, Donald Green, and their various coauthors.[7] The evidence is mixed on the impact of door-to-door canvassing efforts, though the bulk of the evidence suggests that such efforts do increase turnout at the margins. Scholars have also found that social pressures, radio advertisements, television advertisements, and phone calls all have some positive impact on voter turnout. While the effect of these efforts tends to be small—only a few percentage points or less—that can certainly be enough to impact the outcome of a close election. This research is critical for state-level candidates and the scholars who study them because many of the research projects focus on the types of tools local candidates can use to stimulate turnout when they do not have the resources to run large-scale television advertising campaigns.

WHICH CANDIDATES DO VOTERS SELECT?

Understanding what gets voters to the polls is critical, but we also need to understand how they will vote once they are there. The factors that influence voters' choices generally fall into those that operate at the individual level, those associated with state or local contextual factors, and those associated with national factors. This section explores each in turn.

The Importance of Party Identification

As with nearly every kind of election in the United States, the single strongest predictor of how citizens vote in a gubernatorial or state legislative election is their party identification. Voters use party identification as a lens through which they filter their political atmosphere. Partisanship also leads voters to link their voting behavior across different offices. For example, if the president is popular, voters become more likely to support candidates for governor and state legislature who share the president's party. Thus, while the focus of this section is on how state and national factors shape voting in state elections, readers should keep in mind the foundational role played by party identification.

The Impact of the Economy

Voters don't take their personal characteristics and pure policy preferences alone to the polls when they vote for their governor or state legislator. These microlevel factors interact with the setting that surrounds the election within the state. Each state's electoral environment is different and can influence voters' feelings toward those candidates who are running for the office in question. Most research in this area on gubernatorial elections focuses on how the state economic conditions, along with the incumbent governor's economic policy choices, affect voters' assessment of candidates and eventual vote decision.

The general consensus among past researchers is that voters engage in retrospective evaluation of their state's economy, and their evaluation of the state is a significant contributing factor to their voting behavior.[8] Indicators of unemployment are a particularly salient source of information for voters when evaluating the state economy. In general, an increased level of state unemployment is associated with a negative assessment of the incumbent governor. However, this effect is rarely symmetric: voters are much more likely to punish the incumbent for higher unemployment than they are to reward the incumbent for lower unemployment. This suggests that voters are generally risk-averse in that they prefer to emphasize minimizing bad outcomes over maximizing good outcomes.

Two other areas of economic policy within a state where voters look to assess the governor's performance are tax policy and job creation. Not surprisingly, increased state taxation yields a weak but consistently negative overall effect on the electoral chances for the governor in power and the party to whom he or she belongs. Scholars also note that the only type of tax increase that seems to exhibit this negative electoral effect in any consistent and significant way is the general sales tax. Less research exists on how voters might hold governors accountable for job creation, but there is some evidence that policies of "smoke-stack chasing," while exhibiting immediate job growth and per capita income increases, do not increase electoral support for the governor. If anything, there seems to be a slight negative impact on the vote total a governor receives in a given county in response to recruiting industrial firms or jobs to that county. This may be because those efforts create short-term displacements in those local areas or new competition for other local businesses. It might also be that recruiting new businesses to a county is symptomatic of a weak economy in that county, and that weak economy is what is costing the governor votes on Election Day. This is another area where more research is needed.

National Context

Voters consider their state's electoral environment when voting for governor, but they also receive information from the national context that can influence their voting preferences. The national political climate and perceptions of the national economy are the most studied and most relevant considerations on the minds of voters as they consider their choice for governor. Research has shown that voters use their approval of national-level officials to inform their approval of state-level officials. Voters base their evaluations of the incumbent governor at least in part on both the dominant ideological leaning of the national political system and how they evaluate national politicians. As we noted, this occurs in part because voters link state-level candidates to national politicians like the president through political party membership. Thus state-level candidates receive a boost if the president is from their party and has a high job approval rating.

Despite the general influence of presidential politics on state-level elections, many scholars have also found evidence that voters are able to separate state and national factors when holding state-level politicians accountable. Voters, in general, are thought to assign more responsibility for the national economy to U.S. congressional and presidential incumbents than to their subnational counterparts. This would mean that incumbent governors are generally not electorally punished for national economic conditions because they are not seen as having power over that area. At the same time, voters do hold candidates for governor accountable for the performance of their state's economy. This "issue-sorting" based on level of government also takes place in issue areas other than the national economy. In particular, policy areas such as education, the environment, and transportation are generally seen more as the responsibility of governors, while foreign policy and nationwide redistributive issues are viewed as falling much more under the jurisdiction of national officials such as U.S. senators. Findings such as these show that the organization provided by federalism can serve as a powerful frame for voters' perceptions of policy responsibility and can have a substantial impact on electoral evaluations of executive officials at the state level.[9]

GUBERNATORIAL CAMPAIGNS

The Impact on Voters

Campaigns play a major role in shaping the outcomes of gubernatorial contests. They create an essential opportunity for candidates to communicate with voters, and they provide a forum for candidates to stress the policy dimensions they want to serve as the focus of the election. The particular issues gubernatorial candidates stress during their campaigns systematically alter the influence of various issue preferences and demographic factors on citizens' voting behavior. This even extends to the impact of national politics on state-level elections; in states where the Republican Party stressed linking the Democratic gubernatorial candidate more closely to Bill Clinton in 1994, voters linked their approval/disapproval of Clinton more strongly to their vote choice for governor.[10]

The level to which candidates can employ their campaigns as tools to cast themselves in a positive light depends in part on the amount of money they are able to allocate to their campaign activities. Campaign spending by gubernatorial contestants dramatically influences the outcomes of these races, but it does not do so evenly across all types of candidates. Spending by incumbent governors has no independent impact on their vote share after controlling for the incumbent's own popularity level. Of course, this does not mean that incumbent spending does not matter at all. Rather, it is likely that this pattern emerges because the safest incumbents do not have to spend as much as do those incumbents who face a serious challenge. No one would argue that incumbents who face strong challengers would do just as well whether they spent a lot of money or not. Meanwhile, spending by challengers is effective in pulling votes away from the incumbent, even after controlling for the challenger's quality as a candidate. Challengers are incentivized to spend more on campaigns, and therefore are more likely to reach spending limits. Because out-party candidates are especially sensitive to spending limits, this raises a normative concern that limits on spending may be intended to insulate in-party candidates from viable competition.

Candidate Interaction during Campaigns

While most research on campaigns focuses on how voters respond (or not) to what the candidates do and say during their campaigns, there is a smaller literature on how state-level candidates respond to one another over the course of their campaigns. In one such study, scholars argue that candidates at least partially adopt a rational expectations perspective regarding the behavior of their opponents during a campaign.[11] Specifically, candidates appear to anticipate the campaign advertising behavior of their opponents and take action based on those expectations. In other words, candidates do not sit around and wait for their opponents to increase their ad buy or to ramp up their negative attacks, punching back only after they see what their opponents do. Rather, gubernatorial candidates at least partially engage in a process of predicting those actions and adjusting their own advertising behavior as a result.

This presents a particular challenge to candidates running in primaries. Such candidates are eager to respond to their eventual general election opponent, but in doing so risk losing the nomination contest in the primary. In a recent study, scholars show that statewide candidates facing a challenger in their primary focus their campaign advertising strategy on their primary challenger rather than their eventual general election challenger.[12]

In this November 2, 2010, photo, California Republican gubernatorial candidate Meg Whitman concedes the election at her election night party in Los Angeles. Dipping into their personal fortunes to finance a political campaign turned out to be a bad investment for several candidates trying to break into political office. Whitman took the steepest gamble, spending $142 million in her effort to become California's next governor.

SOURCE: AP Photo/Chris Carlson.

VOTING FOR STATE LEGISLATOR

This discussion has focused on gubernatorial elections, as there is more research in this area. Still, there are a number of things we can say about voting in elections for state legislature. As an overview, many of the same factors at the individual, state, and national levels influence how voters cast their ballots in state legislative elections in ways that are similar to how they impact voting for governor. However, there are certain institutional features of state legislative elections that set them apart from gubernatorial elections.

External Pressures on State Legislative Elections

One specific influence that has received attention from state legislative elections scholars is the influence of coattail effects from other electoral contests, particularly for president and governor. A coattail effect is defined as the tendency for a popular public official from a given political party to attract votes for other candidates of the same party. Research has demonstrated that voters with favorable images of the incumbent governor have a higher probability of voting for a state legislative candidate of the incumbent's party down the ticket. This effect is present both for races in which the incumbent governor is seeking reelection and for open seat gubernatorial elections. Presidential coattails have a similar effect on state legislative races. The president's party tends to gain seats proportionally to the presidential vote in that state and subsequently loses seats in the next midterm election in proportion to the previous presidential vote in that state.

However, the influence of external forces on state legislative elections is not automatic or equally felt across all state legislative chambers. Rather, the impact of external pressures is mediated through state legislative institutions, particularly state legislative professionalism. The professionalism of a state legislature is defined as an institutional design feature that forces the body of lawmakers into a mold that more closely resembles the U.S. House and Senate than a group of concerned citizens postulating about policy. (For more information about legislative professionalism, see Chapter 17.) Higher legislative professionalism has many implications for how the legislative chamber operates, including the fact that increasing professionalization establishes institutional boundaries that insulate members from external events and pressures. This means, for example, that as the level of professionalism of a particular state legislature increases, the effects of external state and national influences such as coattails from higher-level elections and national economic conditions on an incumbent legislator's chances for reelection lose their strength significantly.

The Incumbency Advantage

Another important feature of state legislative elections is the strong incumbency advantage that legislators enjoy. One part of this advantage, the "personal vote," is a segment of a legislator's voting bloc with whom he or she has built a personal (rather than party) reputation. (For more on this topic, see Connecting with Constituents box.) The personal vote is thought of as that share of an incumbent's vote total that is unique to him or her. It is generally accepted that a large fraction of the electoral advantage enjoyed by state legislative incumbents is owed to the personal vote. Past work has shown that incumbents devote extensive energy to developing personal relationships and establishing a larger personal vote in areas of their districts where they are electorally the most vulnerable. However, others argue that the personal vote should not be viewed only in terms of how incumbents extend their electoral support beyond the votes they should expect to receive based on partisanship. Rather, the personal vote should be considered more generally as resulting from the incumbents' performance while in office, and that performance might help the incumbents attract support outside of their partisan base and/or retain the support of their partisan base. This is another area ripe for further research.

Another facet of the incumbency advantage state legislators enjoy comes in the form of the scarcity of quality candidates to challenge incumbents. Incumbents have the upper hand of being able to amass such electorally beneficial assets as name recognition, powerful and visible leadership positions, and large "war chests" of campaign funds. Each of these benefits negatively impacts the likelihood that a quality candidate will emerge to challenge the incumbent. Because this is the case, there has been a steady decline in the proportion of marginal and contested seats in state legislatures over the last half-century.

The general lack of quality candidates in state legislative elections feeds into another component of the incumbency advantage: the number of uncontested seats in state legislative elections. In many state legislative districts, especially those in states with "low-value seats" characterized by less professionalized legislatures and lower levels of party competition, the proportion of seats that go uncontested is substantial. However, changing the type of district election rules measurably dampens this effect. Specifically, while incumbents still enjoy an electoral advantage in multimember districts, the proportion of seats that go uncontested in multimember districts is much lower than it is for single-member districts, meaning that incumbents in multimember and "free-for-all" districts are more vulnerable than those in traditional single-member districts because challengers are less deterred from throwing their hat into the ring.

CONNECTING WITH CONSTITUENTS

In his iconic 1978 book, *Home Style: House Members in Their Districts,* Richard Fenno posits that lawmakers have three main priorities while they hold elected office: to gain reelection, to gain power and influence in the legislature, and to pass what they consider to be good public policy.[1] To secure reelection, the vital strategy for the candidate on the campaign trail is to cultivate a sense of trust and the feeling that he or she can relate to voters in the district. Establishing this personal relationship with voters in a district and working to satisfy their demands is at the root of what most scholars mean when they describe an incumbent's ability to generate a personal vote. If candidates possess this trust of their constituents, it is much easier for them to legitimize themselves as capable leaders and justify the decisions they make in the legislature in pursuit of making good public policy and obtaining power.

A notion of trust between elected officials and voters can be forged in a few ways, the most prominent of which is for officials to be able to appear to relate to their constituents on a personal level. An official's ability to appear invested in the values of his or her constituents is essential for gaining voters' trust and, eventually, their votes. In a similar vein, studies have noted that personal attributes of candidates are, in many situations, measurably more important in a citizen's decision to vote for a candidate than policy issues. These personal characteristics assist politicians in appearing to identify with citizens; their vote-gaining effect is measurable, even across party lines. This leads to the conclusion that personal attributes could have a substantive effect alongside partisanship in the candidate evaluations of some voters. Therefore, politicians who can identify with voters based on personal traits increase their ability to connect with some voters who also share their partisanship, but also with some voters who do not share their partisanship but do share that other personal characteristic.

A new vein of research in this area has emerged that examines how candidates communicate with their constituents through speeches. An analysis of governors' state-of-the-state speeches, for example, shows that the general ideological orientation of a state's constituents, as well as their overall religious beliefs and values, are reflected in the frequency with which governors make references to religious themes.[2]

1. Richard F. Fenno, *Home Style: House Members in Their Districts* (New York: Longman, 1978).
2. Monica L. Moore, "Origins of Religious Language in Gubernatorial Speeches," master's thesis, University of North Carolina, 2012.

How do all of these factors aggregate up from individual decisions to determine who wins a state legislative election? Research on this topic underscores the deeply partisan character of state legislative races, but campaign spending is also a significant explanatory portion of predicting a winner. If a quality challenger with sufficient campaign resources steps up against an incumbent state legislator, the challenger's campaign spending has a greater effect on the voting outcome than does the incumbent's spending. Again, this does not mean that incumbent spending does not matter—just that the marginal impact of incumbent spending is much lower than it is for challenger spending. Interestingly, measures of an incumbent's job performance while in office are weak and inconsistent correlates of state legislative election outcomes, and incumbents who are ideologically positioned farther from the average citizen and toward their party's base are only slightly more likely to be challenged than other incumbents. These findings suggest that voters are not relying on a great deal of policy-related performance information when evaluating incumbent state legislators, or at least they are not doing so beyond what party labels already tell them about an incumbent.

CAMPAIGN FUND-RAISING

We devoted a fair amount of discussion to campaign spending in state elections, but another area ripe for research is the way campaigns raise and report their funds. As state governments have become more important in the larger policy-making process in many areas, and as they have begun to more closely resemble Congress in their professionalism, campaigns for seats within state legislatures have become more expensive and campaign finance laws more pertinent. Much of the research on state campaign finance expresses a normative concern about the inequality of funding across candidates and the negative consequences for democracy that may follow from this circumstance. Generally, all those who have done research in this area are concerned about whether or not campaign spending "buys votes," and almost always, they conclude that it does—whether it is by way of incumbency advantage, redistricting effects, or other contextual means—all with negative consequences for the basic principles of democracy.

While no reform is likely to level the financial playing field across the board for all candidates for state office, many states have put basic reforms in place to attempt to regulate campaign spending. By 1980, nearly every state required some sort of disclosure from candidates on their spending, half the states placed limits on individual contributions to campaigns, and sixteen states had set up some form of public funding for campaigns. By the mid-1990s, even more states had set up public funding systems, and states began to turn their attention toward regulating donations from political parties, unions, and political action committees (PACs).

While it is important that states have these campaign finance regulations, scholars are also interested in what electoral effects these laws have had. One challenge for measuring their impact is that it is nearly impossible to fully enforce these laws. It is difficult to monitor the behavior of campaigns and their contributors, enforcement and sanctions generally don't apply until after the election is over, and the regulatory agencies in charge of campaign finance enforcement are generally not given enough resources to adequately do their jobs. As a result, campaign finance disclosure laws do little to raise public awareness about the money spent in campaigns. In addition, while contribution limits are effective for limiting large donations from small interest groups, larger interest groups are able to circumvent this regulation and find other ways to influence the electoral process.

Citizens United and the States

The role of fund-raising and independent spending in state elections has been fundamentally altered by recent court decisions (*Citizens United v. Federal Election Commission* [2010]; *SpeechNow.org v. Federal Election Commission* [2010]).[13] These decisions paved the way for the formation of so-called super PACs that can raise and spend unlimited amounts of money from businesses, labor unions, associations, and individuals. According to the website OpenSecrets.org, as of November 4, 2012, there were 1,063 groups organized as super PACs that had reported a total of nearly $630 million in independent campaign expenditures.[14] While certainly a great deal of that spending focused on the presidential election that year, there were also multiple media reports of significant super PAC spending in gubernatorial, state legislative, and even state judicial campaigns in 2012. (See Super PACs in the States box for more on this question.) This is clearly an area in need of new research.

The one area of campaign finance policy reform that shows the most promise for achieving its intended goal in the states is the advent of public financing of elections. Most studies that sprang out of the 1990s on this topic concluded that public financing had no effect, or at best a small

SUPER PACS IN THE STATES

In its landmark decision in *Citizens United v. Federal Election Commission* (2010) the U.S. Supreme Court ruled that restrictions on independent political expenditures by individuals, corporations, and labor unions are unconstitutional infringements on freedom of speech. Corporations and unions were previously able to give any-size donations to 527 groups or "social-welfare groups," but these groups were not allowed to explicitly endorse a candidate, and they could not mention a candidate's name in an advertisement within sixty days of the general election. After *Citizens United,* any outside group can use unlimited donations from corporations and unions to make a direct case for who does or does not deserve one's vote, and they can do so with no time restrictions around Election Day. This change has not eliminated 527 groups and social-welfare groups, but it has given rise to a new type of group generally referred to as super PACs.

Leading up to the 2012 election, many feared that this decision would exacerbate two aspects of the electoral system that are generally viewed in a negative light: the growing amount of campaign spending in general, and the increasing influence of corporate power on the political process. After the election, however, only one of these predictions was proven true: the year 2012 was record for spending on the federal level—with reports of more than $6 billion spent—but this increased spending did not change the status quo much at the federal level, as both political parties raised massive sums, essentially balancing each other out in a sort of campaign-spending arms race.

However, evidence of the impact of super PACs on election results at the state level shows a stronger pattern. One study found evidence that *Citizens United* had a small but statistically significant effect of a positive bump in the probability of Republicans winning in state legislative elections, and numerous press accounts reported massive sums of money from outside groups being spent on state legislative and judicial campaigns.[1] This disparity in how the decision has impacted national versus state elections could be caused by many factors. It may be that super PACs do more specific targeting of funds to state-level races than they do at the national level. It may also be that super PAC spending has a greater impact on state races because those are generally lower-information races for voters. One thing is clear: the *Citizens United* decision has fundamentally altered the campaign finance landscape for state elections, creating a significant need for new scholarship in this area.

1. Tilman Klumpp, Hugo M. Mialon, and Michael A. Williams, "Money Talks: The Impact of *Citizens United* on State Elections," Emory Legal Studies Research Paper No. 12-218, at http://dx.doi.org/10.2139/ssrn.2123543.

positive effect, on leveling the playing field in state elections. However, in more recent years, the conclusions reached through research on this topic have shifted slightly into a more positive realm. For example, one recent study of the public financing systems in Arizona and Maine found a significant increase in competition in those state legislative districts in which the challengers accepted public funding.[15] Another possible consequence of public funding for elections is its potential to redirect a candidate's campaign efforts away from what some scholars call the "money chase," thereby freeing up time for other valuable campaign activities.

CONCLUSION

Scholars know a great deal about state elections. They know that individual-level, state-level, and national-level factors all combine to affect the types of candidates that emerge, what candidates do during their campaigns, and how voters respond to candidates. At the individual level, scholars know that partisanship plays a major role. At the state level, the performance of the incumbents, the performance of the state's economy, and the overall makeup of a state's population matter. At the national level, the biggest factor impinging on state politics is the level of support enjoyed by the president. Scholars know that incumbency matters, that legislative professionalism helps insulate legislative candidates from external political forces, and that campaign finance and spending are becoming increasingly important factors. They know that the laws defining voter eligibility and the ease of voter participation fundamentally affect the composition of the electorate. They know that strategic candidates respond both to their constituencies and to one another as they run their campaigns.

However, there remains a great deal that scholars do not understand well. Scholarly exploration of electoral contests for offices other than the governorship and state legislature is quite limited. Given changes in campaign finance and the removal of campaign restrictions by recent court decisions, we believe that particular attention should be devoted to judicial elections in the states. (See Chapter 21 for more discussion of how state judges are selected.) Furthermore, most of the research on campaign strategy is based on the analysis of either television advertising or the media coverage of campaigns. This limits what scholars know mostly to gubernatorial elections that are at least moderately contested. Scholars know much less about how candidates for the more than seven thousand state legislative seats conduct their campaigns and, thus, how voters respond to those campaigns. Finally, while a few studies have begun to explore the use of the Internet and new social media in state electoral politics, there is a vast gulf between what candidates, voters, and the media are doing with these technologies and what we understand of them as scholars. Thus the need for additional research is clear, and the opportunities for scholars to make significant contributions are abundant.

NOTES

1. Thomas M. Carsey and William D. Berry, "What's a Losing Party to Do? The Calculus of Contesting State Legislative Elections," *Public Choice,* forthcoming.
2. Jason Harold Windett, "State Effects and the Emergence and Success of Female Gubernatorial Candidates," *State Politics and Policy Quarterly* 11 (2011): 460–482.
3. For an overview, see Thad Kousser, *Term Limits and the Dismantling of State Legislative Professionalism* (New York: Cambridge University Press, 2005).
4. Michael P. McDonald, "Turnout Rate among Eligible Voters in the States, 1980–2000," *State Politics and Policy Quarterly* 2 (2002): 199–212.
5. Thomas Holbrook and Brianne Heidbreder, "Does Measurement Matter? The Case of VAP and VEP in Models of Voter Turnout in the United States," *State Politics and Policy Quarterly* 10 (2010): 157–179.
6. For overviews of these arguments, see S. E. Finkel and John G. Geer, "A Spot Check: Casting Doubt on the Demobilizing Effect of Attack Advertising," *American Journal of Political Science* 42 (1998): 573–595. See also Robert A. Jackson and Thomas M. Carsey, "U.S. Senate Campaigns, Negative Advertising, and Voter Mobilization in the 1998 Midterm Election," *Electoral Studies* 26 (2007): 180–195.
7. Harold F. Gosnell, *Getting Out the Vote: An Experiment in the Stimulation of Voting* (Chicago: University of Chicago Press, 1927); Alan S. Gerber and Donald P. Green, "The Effects of Canvassing, Direct Mail, and Telephone Contact on Voter Turnout: A Field Experiment," *American Political Science Review* 94 (2000): 653–663; Donald P. Green and Alan S. Gerber, *Get Out the Vote: How to Increase Voter Turnout,* 2nd ed. (Washington, DC: Brookings, 2008); Alan S. Gerber and Donald P. Green, *Field Experiments: Design, Analysis, and Interpretation* (New York: Norton, 2012).
8. Thomas M. Carsey and Gerald C. Wright, "State and National Factors in Gubernatorial and Senate Elections," *American Journal of Political Science* 42 (1998): 994–1002; rejoinder, 1008–1011.
9. Ibid. See also Lonna Rae Atkeson and Randall W. Partin, "Candidate Advertisements, Media Coverage, and Citizen Attitudes: The Agendas and Roles of Senators and Governors in a Federal System," *Political Research Quarterly* 54 (2001): 795–813.
10. Thomas M. Carsey, *Campaign Dynamics: The Race for Governor* (Ann Arbor: University of Michigan Press, 2000).

11. Thomas M. Carsey, Robert A. Jackson, Melissa Stewart, and James P. Nelson, "Strategic Candidates, Campaign Dynamics, and Campaign Advertising in Gubernatorial Races," *State Politics and Policy Quarterly* 11 (2011): 269–298.

12. Kevin K. Banda and Thomas M. Carsey, "Two Stage Elections, Strategic Candidates, and Agenda Convergence," paper presented at the twelfth annual meeting of the State Politics and Policy Conference, Houston, TX, February 16–18, 2012.

13. *Citizens United v. Federal Election Commission,* 558 U.S. 310 (2010); *SpeechNow.org v. Federal Election Commission,* 599 F.3d 686 (D.C. Cir., 2010).

14. This information was taken from the following website: www.opensecrets.org/pacs/superpacs.php.

15. Neil Malhotra, "The Impact of Public Financing on Electoral Competition: Evidence from Arizona and Maine," *State Politics and Policy Quarterly* 8 (2008): 263–281.

SUGGESTED READING

Alvarez, R. Michael. *Information and Elections.* Ann Arbor: University of Michigan Press, 1997.

Campbell, James. *The Presidential Pulse of Congressional Elections,* 2nd ed. Lexington: University Press of Kentucky, 1997.

Carsey, Thomas M. *Campaign Dynamics: The Race for Governor.* Ann Arbor: University of Michigan Press, 2000.

Cohen, Jeffrey E., ed. *Public Opinion in State Politics.* Stanford, CA: Stanford University Press, 2006.

Cox, Gary W., and Jonathan N. Katz. *Elbridge Gerry's Salamander: The Electoral Consequences of the Reapportionment Revolution.* New York: Cambridge University Press, 2002.

Gelman, Andrew. *Red State, Blue State, Rich State, Poor State: Why Americans Vote the Way They Do.* Princeton, NJ: Princeton University Press, 2008.

Hanmer, Michael J. *Discount Voting: Voter Registration Reforms and Their Effects.* New York: Cambridge University Press, 2009.

Key, V. O., Jr. *Southern Politics in State and Nation.* New York: Knopf, 1949.

La Raja, Raymond J. *Small Change: Money, Political Parties, and Campaign Finance Reform.* Ann Arbor: University of Michigan Press, 2008.

Malbin, Michael J., and Thomas Gais. *The Day after Reform: Sobering Campaign Finance Lessons from the American States.* New York: Rockefeller Institute Press, 1998.

McDonald, Michael P., and John Samples, eds. *The Marketplace of Democracy: Electoral Competition and American Politics.* Washington, DC: Brookings and Cato, 2006.

Morehouse, Sarah. *The Governor as Party Leader: Campaigning and Governing.* Ann Arbor: University of Michigan Press, 1998.

Rosenthal, Alan. *Engines of Democracy: Politics and Policymaking in State Legislatures.* Washington, DC: CQ Press, 2009.

Wright, Ralph G. *Inside the Statehouse: Lessons from the Speaker.* Washington, DC: CQ Press, 2005.

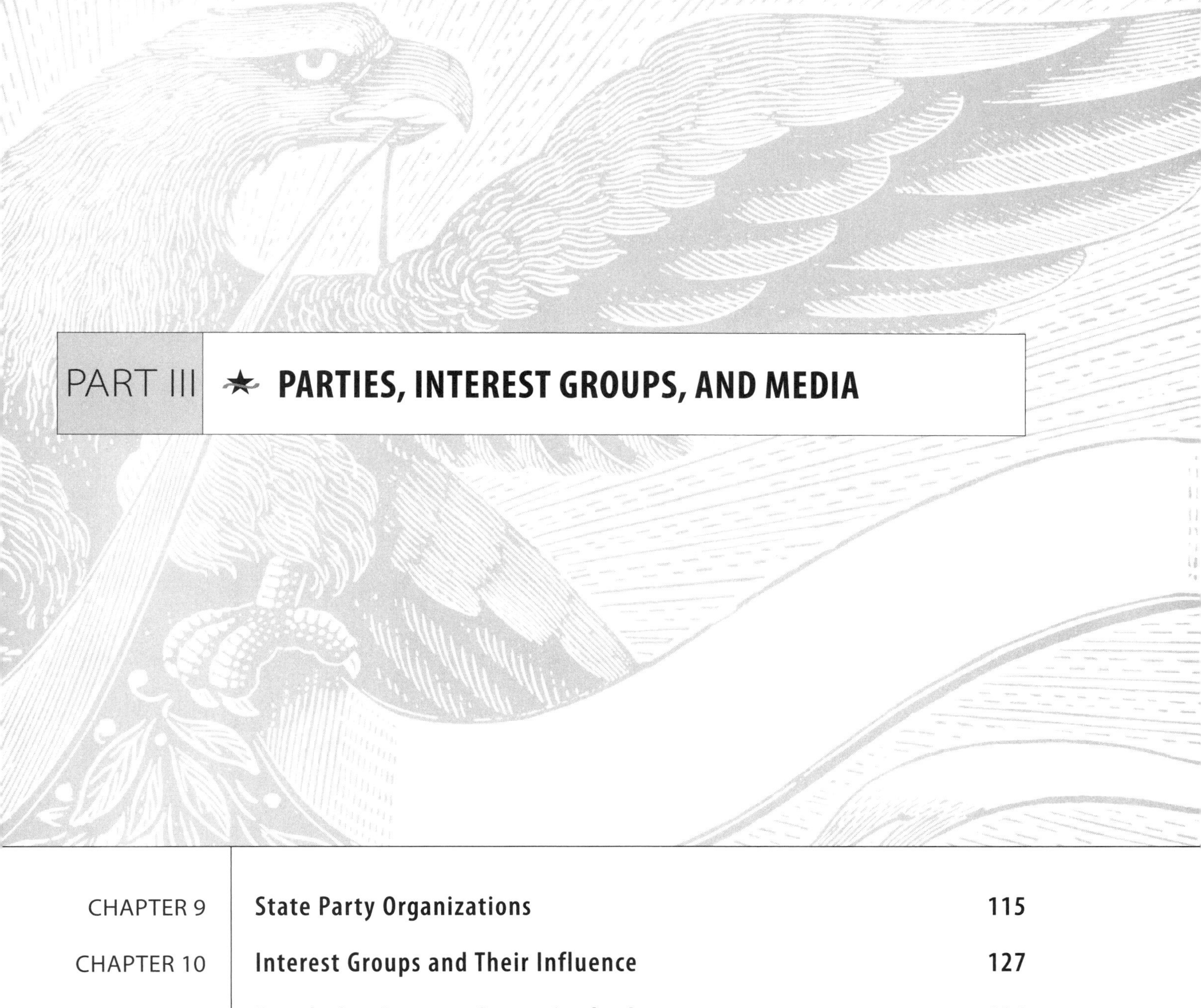

PART III ★ PARTIES, INTEREST GROUPS, AND MEDIA

Chapter 9

State Party Organizations

Paul S. Herrnson and Jeffrey A. Taylor

AMERICAN POLITICAL PARTIES ARE PRIMARILY electoral institutions. Throughout much of U.S. history, state party organizations have had a substantial impact on elections at the state, local, and federal levels of government. Among party organizations, state central committees assume the largest role in gubernatorial and other statewide elections.[1] Since the 1980s, legislative campaign committees (LCCs) have become the most important party organizations in elections to the state house.[2] While not as powerful as their predecessors, contemporary state party organizations continue to support candidates for state offices and work with local and national party organizations to elect candidates for other offices. They use several methods to accomplish these objectives, including some intended to bolster the campaigns of individual office seekers and others aimed at benefitting all candidates who appear on their state's ballot. By supporting party candidates on the campaign trail, state party organizations help build popular support for their priority issues and seek to create an environment that is conducive to enacting and implementing those priorities. A party's agenda setting and policy accomplishments, in turn, reinforce the loyalties of party identifiers and activists and create new loyalties among independent voters, which enhance the party's electoral prospects in ensuing elections.

This chapter surveys state party organizations from a broad perspective. First, it provides a review of the evolution of state party organizations. Next, it presents an overview of the structure and activities of contemporary state party organizations and their relationships with national and local party organizations. State laws, history, and other environmental factors have a major impact on these organizations' activities and associations with one another. The chapter also demonstrates the impact of these factors by comparing state party organizations in terms of their strength, their integration with other party organizations, and their influence over nominating procedures and the financing of campaigns.

ORGANIZATIONAL DEVELOPMENT

Party organizations at the national, state, and local level have shown a remarkable ability to adapt to change in the political environment and to remain influential in elections. Changes in the regulations governing the financing of campaigns, the selection of candidates, and the rules governing participation in party affairs have forced state party organizations to develop new methods and strategies in pursuit of their traditional goals. The power of state party committees has waxed and waned over the course of history.

The Golden Age of Political Parties

Despite receiving no formal mention in the U.S. Constitution, throughout much of the nation's history party organizations dominated the electoral process, determining in large part who appeared on the ballot and who showed up to vote on Election Day. Political parties dominated elections during their so-called golden age, roughly the latter half of the nineteenth century through the early twentieth century. In this era, state party organizations coordinated with national and local party committees, including the powerful machines that controlled politics in some parts of the country. The parties' ability to select candidates and their near monopoly over the resources needed to run campaigns made them a major force in politics.[3] Party leaders controlled nominations, coordinated the collection and dissemination of voter information, led mobilization efforts, and determined the distribution of resources to individual contests. When victorious, party leaders were able to use their influence over those they elected to direct the distribution of government jobs and contracts and provide their supporters with other favors.

During the golden age, most career politicians got their start in politics through contacts with state or local party officials. Party leaders identified and nurtured local talent and worked to place their protégés in elective and appointed offices. Candidates for most offices were selected through a party-run nominating caucus or convention attended by party activists who were selected, and more or less controlled, by party leaders. This meant that candidates had to appeal to party leaders to win the nomination and the place on the general election ballot that came with it. The party's dominance over candidate recruitment and selection meant that most career politicians developed strong connections to the party organization from the very start of their career.[4] The party's ability to dispense nominations meant that there was little incentive for an aspiring politician to assemble a campaign organization or run a contemporary-style campaign in order to win the nomination. It also resulted in most party nominees having to rely on their party to conduct the general election campaign.

Another source of party influence was rooted in party organizations' ability to structure the general election vote. In fact, party organizations literally wrote the ballots that their supporters cast. Unlike the contemporary period, government agencies were not involved in the design or distribution of ballots or the provision of voting machines that presented voters with candidates from which to choose. Rather, most voting was done with slips of paper that voters dropped into a ballot box. Given that a large portion of the electorate was illiterate, and thus unable to write down the names of their preferred candidates, party organizations were well positioned to help their supporters vote. The parties responded by circulating ballots that contained only the names of the party's nominees. As a result, those who voted with them on Election Day in essence were voting for a party slate rather than individual candidates.[5] Being listed on a party's ballot all but guaranteed a candidate the support of voters who identified with that party. This meant that in areas dominated by a single party virtually every party nominee would be elected. (See Chapter 7 for further discussion of ballot construction and election administration.)

The control party organizations enjoyed over most general election campaigns was another source of their influence. Parties were responsible for planning campaign strategies, raising money, recruiting volunteers, gauging public opinion, disseminating campaign propaganda, and mobilizing voters. Turning out voters was the parties' most important activity. Their ability to recruit armies of local volunteers made them highly effective at this effort. Precinct captains, ward leaders, and other party loyalists who were highly integrated into their communities collected information about their neighbors' political inclinations, policy preferences, practical concerns, and personal aspirations. They also provided their neighbors with factual information, political propaganda, and campaign promises designed to win their allegiance. Party-controlled newspapers further praised the virtues of their party's nominees and demonized their opponents. Party-sponsored rallies and picnics were used to whip up public support. Perhaps most important, party organizations were highly effective at delivering their supporters to the polls on Election Day.

Each level of the party organization was concerned with electing candidates to offices within their jurisdictions. Local machines prioritized local candidates. The Democratic National Committee (DNC) and Republican National Committee (RNC) cared first and foremost about electing a president. The principal concern of the Democratic Congressional Campaign Committee (DCCC) and National Republican Congressional Committee (NRCC) was the U.S. House elections. The Democratic Senatorial Campaign Committee (DSCC) and the National Republican Senatorial Committee (NRSC) focused on Senate contests. State party organizations concentrated their efforts on capturing state offices. Nevertheless, party organizations at different levels worked cooperatively to capitalize on the advantages each possessed. Local party machines were responsible for carrying out most grassroots campaign activities. National party committees played a critical role in setting the national campaign agenda, plotting national strategy, influencing the national press, and arranging for party dignitaries to travel to battleground locations, especially during presidential election years. State party organizations assumed an intermediary role. They gathered political information from local party committees, used it to plot strategy, and transferred a more digested version of it to national party committees. State parties also collected money from local party committees, as well as from individuals and groups employed by, seeking to do business with, or trying to influence state government. Some of the state party funds were distributed to affect competitive elections within the state, and others were transferred to party organizations at the national level. Depending on the nature of the competition within a state's borders and its implications for federal races, some states received support from the national parties while others did not.

During this era, most state party leaders worked closely with the "bosses" who ran the local political machines. The bosses' ability to turn out the vote in their localities enabled them to exert tremendous influence over decision makers in local and state government. It also provided them with clout over the private-sector organizations that had a stake in policymaking. As a result, the bosses were able to use their political muscle to provide public- and private-sector jobs and contracts to their activists and financial backers. They also were able to distribute financial relief, career and social opportunities, and other forms of assistance to low-income voters. Providing needy families and individuals with employment and other forms of assistance was central to winning voters' loyalties.

Reform and Environmental Change

Following the golden age, state governments assumed some of the traditional functions of the party organization and imposed regulations over many others. Combined with an increasingly well-educated electorate and the development of the mass-media communications that came to define the political campaigns of the mid- to late twentieth century, party organizations operated in a significantly different political environment than in the previous era. As the twentieth century progressed, political reforms, the rise of the social welfare state, and systemic changes weakened the parties' grip on the electoral process.

State governments enacted regulations to limit the control party organizations once held over the nominating process. The direct primary, introduced in Wisconsin in 1903, was a publicly conducted, state-administered election that enabled registered party voters—and, in some cases, others—to select party nominees. It replaced privately held, boss-dominated caucuses and conventions as a means for determining which candidates would be associated with the party on the general election ballot. By taking control over nominations away from party leaders, the direct primary helped change the entire focus of nominating contests. Rather than working to build support among the party bosses, aspiring politicians sought to amass personal followings among primary voters. To win the nomination a candidate would have to assemble his or her own campaign organization, financial backing, and volunteers. The candidate also would have to communicate a compelling message directly to voters. Participatory nominations encouraged voters to learn the qualifications of individual primary and general election candidates. The introduction of the Australian (secret) ballot in the late 1800s further encouraged voters to focus on the candidates. This official government-printed ballot, enacted with numerous other Progressive Era reforms intended to reduce party organizations' electoral dominance, included the names of all candidates who were competing in the general election and provided voters with an opportunity to choose among aspirants for different offices.[6]

From the late nineteenth to early twentieth centuries civil service reforms, also enacted as a result of the Progressive Movement, sought to prevent party leaders from rewarding their volunteers with the promise of public-sector jobs. These reforms also mandated competitive bidding for government-funded projects, making it difficult for party organizations to reward major contributors with lucrative government contracts. The loss of the patronage system forced party organizations to operate with fewer and less committed volunteers. Rather than motivate workers with tangible goods, party organizations were forced to appeal to volunteers motivated by ideology and principle.[7] This further limited roles in political campaigns and their political clout more generally.

Aaron Henry, chair of the Mississippi Freedom Democratic Party (MFDP) delegation, reading from a document before the Credentials Committee at the Democratic National Convention, Atlantic City, New Jersey, in August 1964. The MFDP was formed in 1964 as an alternative to the conservative, nearly all-white mainstream Democratic Party of Mississippi. It sought to have its own delegates recognized as the official Mississippi Democratic delegation. The national party refused; however, the MFDP forced a reform in the rules for delegate selection. Subsequently it merged with other progressive groups in the state to form the Loyal Democrats of Mississippi, which eventually displaced the segregationist group as the official Democratic delegation for the state.

SOURCE: Photo by Warren K. Leffler. Library of Congress Prints and Photographs Division, Washington, D.C. Call number LC-U9- 12470E-28 [P&P].

Beginning around the 1970s, the emergence of political consultants facilitated the development of candidate-run campaigns, allowing candidates to hire professionals to provide campaign assistance rather than rely on party officials.[8] These developments, along with the reform measures discussed above, helped transform election campaigns from party-focused, party-conducted affairs to events that revolved around individual candidates and their campaign organizations. The emergence of this candidate-centered campaign system weakened the party bosses' hold over candidates, elected officials, and political activists.

Demographic and cultural changes also contributed to the decline of machine-style politics and the rise of candidate-centered politics. Increased education and social mobility, and declining immigration contributed to the erosion of the close-knit, traditional ethnic neighborhoods that formed the core of the old-fashioned political machine's constituency. Growing preferences for movies, radio, and televised entertainment reduced the popularity of rallies, barbecues, and other forms of personal communication at which political machines excelled. These developments were accompanied by a general decline in the parties' ability to structure political choice. Voters began to turn toward nationally focused mass media and away from local party committees for their political information.

The decline of party organizations and their waning influence over decisions made by voters and some officeholders led mid-twentieth-century scholars and politicians to fear that parties might decline to the point where they would be unable to perform such traditional roles as building electoral and legislative coalitions, encouraging political participation, and transmitting democratic values through the political socialization of voters. In 1950 the Committee on Political Parties of the American Political Science Association, comprising the nation's leading scholars on the subject, reported that "the main trends of American politics have tended to out-flank the party system," resulting in disorganized party organizations that were unable to develop comprehensive party platforms and mobilize voters.[9] However, party organizations in the mid-twentieth century began to regain electoral influence as they learned to adapt to the new electoral environment.

CONTEMPORARY STATE PARTY ORGANIZATIONS

The rise of candidate-centered elections encouraged state and other party leaders to reassess their organizations' roles in the electoral process and search for new ways to help candidates win elections. During the second half of the twentieth century, many state party leaders took steps to modernize their organizations and develop new programs to promote the party's candidates. They also began to focus more on fund-raising. During the 1960s Republican and Democratic state party organizations increased the amounts they raised from individual donors, as well as from national party organizations and interest groups.[10] By 2008, Democratic and Republican state party central committees raised a total of $479 million, roughly $340 million more than in 1992. LCCs, first formed in the 1970s, soon became adept at fund-raising and had a significant role in state legislative elections in the decade that followed.

Larger budgets and more stable funding enabled many state parties to move their headquarters from temporary locations, such as the chair's home, into more permanent ones, including rented office space or party-owned buildings. It also enabled state party organizations to complement their coteries of volunteers with professional staffs skilled in fund-raising, targeting potential voters, polling, and political communications. By 1999, all but one party state central committee were housed in permanent headquarters, and all but seven employed a full-time executive director and other staff.[11] Most state parties also employed political consultants to assist with specialized campaign activities.[12] Contemporary party organizations also evolved into two-tiered organizations. The top tier, comprising the chair, other officers, and elected members, serves as a governing board that provides broad direction, oversight, and the political stature necessary to fund-raising. The next tier consists of the professional staff that implements the strategies and programs authorized by the elected membership.

Their institutional development enabled state parties to increase their candidate recruitment and campaign assistance programs, as well as more effectively coordinate their election efforts with national and local party organizations, allied interest groups, political consultants, political activists, and others who devote money or time to electoral politics. For example, the number of state party organizations that conducted candidate and campaign manager training seminars grew from just over half in the 1960s to more than 90 percent in 1999 (see Figure 9.1). The percentage of state parties publishing party newsletters and conducting voter identification programs and public opinion surveys also increased during this period. The temporary reduction that occurred between 1975 and 1980 is likely the result of substantial changes in federal campaign finance law. The Federal Election Campaign Act (FECA) of 1974, which restricted fund-raising and spending by federal party committees and candidates, initially made it very difficult for national and state party committees to transfer funds to one another or to conduct joint campaign efforts. It took a few years for party committees to adapt to the new restrictions, which were eased somewhat by amendments to the FECA in 1979.

Party-building programs introduced by the DNC, the DCCC, the DSCC, and their Republican counterparts contributed to the institutionalization of state party organizations. National party financial transfers, money, fund-raising assistance, office equipment, and staff training contributed to the modernization of state parties. This, in turn, enabled the state parties to organize seminars and campaign assistance programs for candidates for statewide offices and the state legislature. As the state parties developed their capacity to use voter research, polling data, and other strategic information, the national parties shared these resources with them.[13]

State party development was and continues to be somewhat uneven. Contemporary state party strength and campaign activities are associated with a number of factors. State party integration, the degree to which state party organizations receive assistance and work closely with the national parties, is associated with strong state parties.[14] A state's history and political culture are also important. States that have a long history of formidable

FIGURE 9.1 **Campaign Activities Performed by State Party Organizations, 1960–1999**

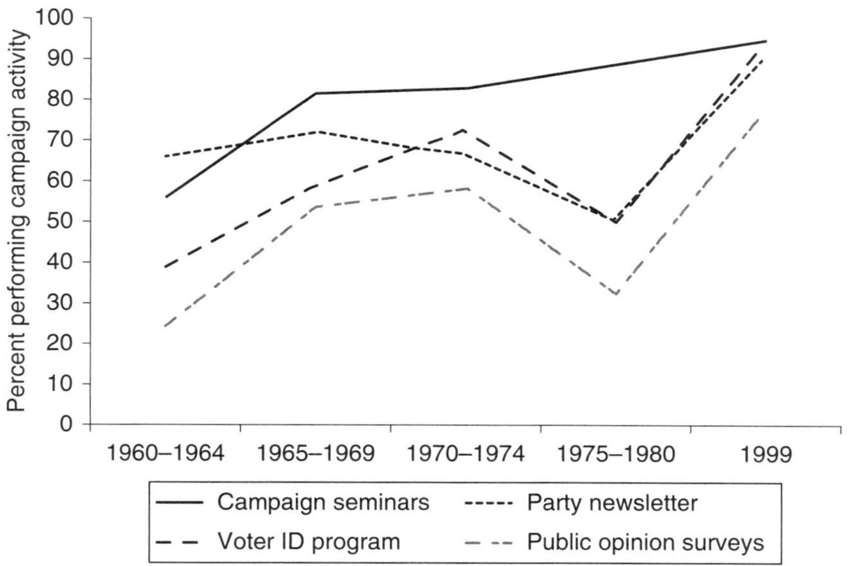

SOURCES: Data compiled from Cornelius P. Cotter, et al., "State Party Organizations, 1960–1980," ICPSR sudy no. 8281, Ann Arbor, MI; and John H. Aldrich, "Political Parties in a Critical Era," *American Politics Research* 27 (1999): 9–32.

party organizations, so-called traditional party organization states, tend to continue to have vibrant party organizations. Parties in these states, which include New Jersey and New York, are characterized by strong central leadership authority, regular support of candidates for a broad range of offices, and a reliance on material incentives to motivate volunteers. Other states that are traditionally home to weaker parties, such as Kansas, Nebraska, North Dakota, and South Dakota, consistently meet only a handful of these criteria and tend to be less influential in the electoral process.[15] Recent studies measuring the level of activity and professionalism of state central committees find significant variation in party strength (see Strong and Weak State Party Organizations box).

State laws also help to determine the strength of a party organization. Campaign finance regulations in some states limit the party's ability to support candidates. Following the enactment of the FECA, many state governments began to impose limits on contributions from political committees to candidates for state-level office. As of 2012, thirty-two states restricted the amounts state central committees can contribute directly to statewide, legislative, and judicial candidates. About two-thirds of states also regulate some aspects of the party organization's internal structure, including the selection of party leaders. The most intrusive state laws specify the number and frequency of party meetings. For example, California regulates the procedures for meetings and leadership appointments for its Democratic and Republican state central committee leaders. In addition to regulating party leadership selection, Oregon also requires party state central committees to hold at least one organizational meeting every twenty-five months.

Political competition also has a substantial impact on party organizational strength and activity. Not surprisingly, the weakest party organizations are found in one-party-dominated states, and the strongest ones are in states where neither party has a lock on most elective offices. For example, until the Voting Rights Act of 1965 laid the groundwork for meaningful two-party competition, active party organizations were largely absent from the South.[16] With the emergence of the region as a political battleground, party organizations in the South began to rank among the most highly developed in terms of professionalism, funding, and electoral activity.[17]

Candidate Recruitment

Contemporary state party organizations participate in candidate recruitment in a variety of ways. Barred from simply handing out nominations, parties in many states write the rules that structure the competition in nominating contests. Most candidates for elective office decide to run after consulting with their family members, friends, and other trusted advisers. Contemporary parties also influence the field of potential nominees. State party organizations begin their efforts by gathering information about the offices up for election and potential candidates for those offices. Given their primary goal to maximize the number of offices under their control, party leaders encourage highly

STRONG AND WEAK STATE PARTY ORGANIZATIONS

State parties vary both in their strength and the services they provide to candidates. A recent study evaluated state party central committees on the basis of fifteen criteria comprising campaign activities and institutional traits, including whether the campaigns recruited candidates for federal, state, and local office; conducted joint fund-raisers; coordinated registration drives with local and national party organizations; and employed a full-time chair and executive director. Republicans fielded their strongest state party organizations in Iowa and Ohio, and their weakest in New Hampshire. The strongest Democratic state party committee was located in Washington, and the weakest in Massachusetts.

State central committees in two states illustrate the variation in strength among state party organizations. The Republican Party of Florida ranked among the strongest because of its organizational development, financial prowess, and campaign efforts. It is led by a full-time state chair and executive director, and consistently works to recruit candidates for governor, other statewide offices, and the state legislature. The state central committee coordinates with national county party organizations to conduct traditional grassroots activities, such as registering voters and conducting get-out-the-vote drives. During the 2010 election cycle, it contributed $14 million to candidates for governor, other statewide offices, and the state house. The high degree of political competition in Florida is largely responsible for the strength of its Republican (and Democratic) state party organizations.

In contrast, the Democratic State Central Committee of Massachusetts ranked last among state party organizations, scoring only 3 out of a possible 15 points. It employed only a part-time state chair, and it does not actively recruit candidates for Congress, the governorship or other statewide offices, or for state legislative and local offices. It also is among only a handful of state central committees that do not routinely coordinate fund-raising, voter registration, or get-out-the-vote drives with county-level party organizations. During the 2010 elections, it contributed $5 million to Democratic candidates for governor, other statewide offices, and the state house. The Democratic Party's traditional dominance of Massachusetts politics goes a long way in explaining the organizational weakness of its Democratic State Central Committee. Simply put, the ease with which most Democratic candidates won their elections did little to encourage them, or Democratic Party activists, to invest their time or resources to develop a strong state party organization.

SOURCES: John H. Aldrich, Brad Gomez, and John D. Griffin, "State Party Organizations Study, 1999," cited in David H. Dulio and R. Sam Garrett, "Organizational Strength and Campaign Professionalism in State Parties," in *The State of the Parties*, 5th ed., John C. Green and David C. Coffey, eds. (New York: Rowman and Littlefield, 2007), 199–216; fund-raising data provided by the Federal Elections Commission and the National Institute on Money in State Politics, www.followthemoney.org.

qualified individuals to contest races for competitive seats. They make greater efforts when a strong candidate has not previously committed to enter such a contest.[18] State party organizations also devote some, albeit less, effort to encourage candidates to run in lopsided contests in order to build a farm team and strengthen local party organizations in these areas.

When recruiting candidates, state parties look for individuals with past experience in government, such as on a school board or a town or county council. The ability to fund a campaign, either with personal resources or from a network of backers, also is important. A positive reputation is another valuable quality. Name recognition and supportive voting and financial constituencies are important assets in a competitive primary or general election. Candidates who are divisive, have a questionable past, or may harm the prospects of a more electable primary contestant are sometimes discouraged from running for office.

Party organizations search most actively for candidates to challenge vulnerable incumbents or run for open seats.[19] These contests present prime opportunities for a state party to increase its representation in the state house. It is especially important for the party to field a quality challenger in these races because the choice of nominee usually has a big impact on the outcome of the general election. A party nominee with a checkered past or little to no political experience may lose a competitive general election that a seasoned and well-known politician would have won. State party organizations typically need to devote more effort to the recruitment of state legislative candidates than candidates for statewide offices, such as governor, attorney general, or U.S. senator. Elections for these high-profile offices usually draw fields of strong primary contestants—that is, unless the partisan composition of the state is so lopsided that few members of the minority party consider running for these offices.

State regulations have a significant impact on the conduct of party nominations. They can influence whether nominees are selected in primaries, caucuses, conventions, or some combination thereof. They also can determine if participation in these contests is limited to individuals who record a party affiliation when registering to vote, or if it is open to unaffiliated voters or even to voters registered with the opposing party.

Most states require that parties select their nominees using a direct primary. This process results in the candidate who wins a plurality of the vote receiving the nomination. Ten states, including seven in the South, mandate a runoff election between the top-two vote-getters when no primary candidate wins a majority of the vote. Runoff elections were originally used to keep African Americans from winning when two white candidates split the vote.[20] Runoffs also make it difficult for fringe candidates to receive a nomination.[21]

Sixteen states allow each party to choose the nominating method it will use to select its general election candidates. Some of the parties in these states use a direct primary, but others use more complex methods. In 2007, for example, the Virginia Republican State Central Committee decided to use a convention system that began with a primary to select convention delegates and ended with those delegates selecting the party's nominees. The party leaders' decision had ramifications for the political career of at least one powerful Virginia politician: Rep. Tom Davis III. Davis, a seven-term U.S. House member from northern Virginia who had chaired the House Government Reform Committee from 2003 to 2007 and the National Republican Congressional Committee from 1998 to 2002, had declared his candidacy for the U.S. Senate in September 2007. However, on learning that the GOP Senate nominee would be selected at a convention rather than a direct primary, he withdrew his candidacy for the Senate and resigned from the House to pursue a career in the private sector. Davis represented a moderate district in northern Virginia, and Republicans in the area continually supported him in the GOP primary. His decision to leave politics was based largely on his realization that the conservative ideologues who would dominate the convention would not select him as the party's nominee. This example demonstrates that rules influence who participates in the nomination process, which in turn affects the decision making of politicians, and ultimately affects who holds office. This case highlights that primaries typically advantage more moderate candidates, and conventions and caucuses tend to advantage ideologically extreme candidates.

Primary elections are conducted much like the general election. Voters cast ballots for their nominees in private voting booths, and the top vote-getters are awarded the nomination. Party caucuses operate differently. A party caucus is a meeting, typically during the evening or weekend, that may last several hours. Most famously used in Iowa as part of the presidential nominating process, the typical caucus includes time for debate and closing arguments from campaign representatives and local party officials. Participants make their decisions publicly by either writing their selections on a piece of paper or standing in a designated area. Because of the significant time commitment, only the most motivated voters attend. When selecting a nominee for president, caucus participants select delegates to attend county or state party conventions.

There are four basic types of primaries: open, closed, partially open, and top-two. Eleven states require primaries to be open to all registered voters, regardless of party affiliation. Another eleven states require primaries to be closed to all but individuals who register as party members. Partially open primaries are open to registered party members and unaffiliated voters (independents), and exclude voters registered with another party. Four states require top-two primaries, which provide all voters with a primary election ballot that lists all candidates, regardless of their party affiliation. For each office, voters select one candidate, and the top-two vote-getters appear on the general election ballot. Twenty-four states, including Alaska, give parties the flexibility to choose who can participate in their primary. In 2008 and 2010 the Alaska Democratic Party chose to

Protesters put signs around a bust of former Progressive Wisconsin governor and senator Robert "Fighting Bob" La Follette, in the state capitol in Madison, Wisconsin, on February 23, 2011. La Follette, who was a prominent Progressive figure in the late nineteenth and early twentieth century, championed labor and other workers' causes. The Wisconsin budget proposed by Republican governor Scott Walker in 2012 included cuts in benefits for state workers and took away many of their collective bargaining rights.

SOURCE: Brian Kersey/UPI/Newscom.

conduct open primaries; the GOP, by contrast, limited participation to registered Republicans only.

First used in Wisconsin in 1903, the open primary was introduced by a group of Progressive activists led by Republican governor Robert La Follette. The Progressives sought to allow nonpartisans to help select GOP nominees in order to weaken the influence of the party establishment and broaden support for La Follette's nomination for a second term. Critics of the open primary argue that they allow the non–party faithful to water down the decisions of "true" party loyalists, whereas proponents contend that they result in nominees who are more moderate and more representative of the voting population. Composed entirely of committed partisans, voters in closed primaries tend to be more ideologically extreme, leading some to argue that they select nominees who are at the ends of the ideological spectrum and contribute to polarization among elected officials. Supporters of the closed primary, however, argue that they contribute to stronger parties because party nominees are selected by and responsive to the party faithful. Top-two primaries make it more difficult for the party establishment to control who appears on the ballot.

Campaign Assistance Programs

Most contemporary party organizations possess the means to provide many of their nominees with substantial campaign assistance. Reflecting the candidate-centered nature of most elections, much of this help is targeted directly to candidates in close contests. However, some of it is intended to help all of the party's nominees whose names appear on the ballots in competitive locations within the state.[22] The latter form of assistance, sometimes referred to as the coordinated campaign, encompasses the traditional, grassroots strategies that have been the province of local party organizations since the golden age.

Candidate-focused party assistance typically consists of financial contributions, fund-raising assistance, help with hiring campaign consultants, gauging public opinion, voter targeting, issues and opposition research, campaign advertising, volunteer recruitment, and strategic advice. Parties also make independent advertisements consisting of direct mail, television and radio ads, and messages sent via the Internet and social media. This assistance does not go unnoticed by the candidates. Surveys of candidates show that they value the campaign support provided by their state

FROM BLANKET PRIMARY TO TOP-TWO PRIMARY

The blanket primary, first instituted in Washington State in 1935, provides voters with a ballot listing all potential nominees, regardless of party affiliation. Voters are allowed to select one candidate for each office, and the highest vote-getter from each party receives its nomination. Promoted by the Washington State Grange, a nonpartisan good-government organization, it was intended to give independent voters a voice in nominations, to prevent a return to machine-style politics, and to promote the selection of moderate candidates.

Blanket primaries were controversial. Opponents argued that they eliminated a party organization's right to define its members and control participation in its internal affairs, including selecting its nominees. In *California Democratic Party v. Jones* (2000),[1] the U.S. Supreme Court ruled that blanket primaries were unconstitutional because they restrict the party organization's freedom of association as protected by the First Amendment.

In the aftermath of the Court's decision, California, Nebraska, and Washington modified their blanket primary procedures by adopting the so-called top-two primary (also referred to as the nonpartisan primary or the jungle primary). Rather than resulting in the selection of one Republican and one Democratic nominee for each office, top-two primaries reserve a place on the general election ballot for the top-two vote-getters, regardless of their party affiliations. Louisiana has used a similar system since 1975, with one modification: if a primary candidate receives more than 50 percent of the vote, he or she is sworn into office, and no general election is held for that position. The top-two primary is unique because voters can select two nominees from the same party to compete in the general election. During the 2012 primary in California's 31st district, Pete Aguilar, a Democratic U.S. House candidate and a favorite of the Democratic Congressional Campaign Committee, failed to win enough votes to advance to the general election. This resulted in two Republican candidates, Gary Miller and California state senator Bob Dutton, competing against each other in the November election.

The top-two primary has generated much controversy, drawing many of the same criticisms as the blanket primary. Regardless, the Supreme Court upheld its constitutionality in *Washington State Grange v. Washington State Republican Party* (2008).[2]

SOURCES: Claudius O. Johnson, "The Washington Blanket Primary," *Pacific Northwest Quarterly* 33 (1942): 27–39; Tom Curry, "For Democrats, California's Top-Two Primary Brings Mixed Blessing," *NBC Politics*, June 6, 2012, www.nbcpolitics.nbcnews.com.

1. *California Democratic Party v. Jones*, 530 U.S. 567 (2000).

2. *Washington State Grange v. Washington State Republican Party*, 552 U.S. 442 (2008).

party organization. This is especially the case for candidates in hotly contested races.[23]

Nevertheless, it is important to recognize that party organizations do not dominate individual candidates' campaigns the way they did in the heyday of party politics. Although a state party organization may be the single largest contributor to some candidates, campaign finance regulations that limit the amounts parties can raise and spend have made it possible for individuals and interest groups to comprise the largest sources of funds in candidates' campaign coffers. Political action committees (PACs) have become particularly important to the financing of contemporary state elections. A PAC is an organization, usually sponsored by a corporation, trade association, labor union, or some other interest group, that collects money from individual (and sometimes organizational) donors and spends it in elections. In some states, such as Maryland, leadership PACs founded by state legislative leaders play a more important role than the LCCs in state legislative elections.

The amounts and sources from which a PAC can raise money and the sums it can spend vary by state. Nevertheless, some generalizations are possible: most PACs raise the majority of their funds from individuals, and most PAC expenditures take the form of contributions given directly to candidates. Moreover, most business-oriented PACs participate in elections to try to influence the policy-making process and thus give most of their contributions to incumbents, who have a high likelihood of reelection. Other PACs are motivated by salient partisan issues, and choose the candidates they support based largely upon their party affiliation, reputation, and record. In the aggregate, PACs (and other interest group entities, where legal) contribute substantially more to candidates for state office than do parties. However, interest group spending does not take place within a vacuum, and party organizations are often able to influence it. Because many interest groups and individuals rely on parties for information about individual candidates and their races, and recognize the importance of maintaining good relations with party leaders, state party organizations are able to funnel these donors' contributions to their targeted candidates.[24]

Given that many candidates for the state house, especially nonincumbents, have limited political experience and resources, party organizations can have a major impact on the conduct of their campaign. The LCCs' candidate-training programs help prepare candidates for the rigors of the campaign trail; their cash contributions often serve as seed money to form a campaign organization and raise additional funds; and their campaign service programs and strategic advice have a direct bearing on a candidate's ability to formulate and communicate an appealing message, present that message to loyal and undecided voters, and turn out supportive voters on Election Day. LCC transactional assistance, including help with fund-raising and outreach, helps candidates attract money, endorsements, and other resources from interest group and political elites who participate in elections. Most candidates for statewide office are seasoned politicians and do not require as much direct campaign assistance as state house candidates. Nevertheless, state party central committees assist these standard bearers in many aspects of campaigning, particularly fund-raising.

Coordinated and Independent Campaigns

The coordinated campaign is a massive voter registration and mobilization effort carried out by state, federal, and local party committees, and candidate campaigns. Interest groups that are aligned with a particular party also may participate. Cooperative in nature, coordinated campaigns are carried out in regions where a high turnout among party loyalists and swing voters could make the difference between election and defeat for party candidates up and down the ballot. The roles of those participating in the coordinated campaign vary according to their abilities and the circumstances in particular election cycles.

National party organizations usually provide most of the funding for coordinated campaigns and set national strategy. During the 2008 presidential election year, the DNC, RNC, DCCC, NRCC, DSCC, and NRSC transferred \$118 million to state party committees.[25] The DCCC, DSCC, and their Republican counterparts transfer funds to state party committees in states that are hosting competitive House and Senate contests. The 2010 Pennsylvania midterm elections exemplify well-funded coordinated campaigns involving national, state, and local party organizations. The election featured competitive races (less than a 15-point margin) for governor, one U.S. Senate seat, ten U.S. House seats, thirty-six seats for the state house of representatives, and one seat for the state senate. On the GOP side, the RNC, NRSC, and NRCC transferred over \$2.8 million to state and local Republican Party organizations in Pennsylvania, accounting for 12 percent of the \$24 million raised by the state's Republican Party and Republican LCCs. The Democrats also transferred large amounts of money to the state. The DNC, DSCC, and DCCC provided over \$4.2 million to Democratic state and local party organizations, constituting 30 percent of the \$14 million raised by the state's Democratic Party and Democratic LCCs.[26] Coordinated campaigns in battleground states in presidential election years typically involve much more expensive coordinated campaigns.

The national, congressional, and senatorial campaign committees also play substantial roles in setting strategy and providing data and technology in presidential and midterm election cycles. State party organizations assume the leadership role in coordinated campaigns that are conducted in election cycles that feature only state or local elections, or when few of their state's federal elections are competitive.

State party committees have a prominent role in setting up coordinated campaign headquarters, including determining where they will be located within their state. Working with candidates, local party committees, and allied interest groups, they rent office space and equipment, hire staff, recruit volunteers, and set the stage for their voter mobilization efforts. State parties participate in determining the parts of the state that will be the focus of the coordinated campaign efforts; the locations of rallies, fund-raisers, and other events; and the roles of different groups in collecting information from and disseminating it to voters and ensuring that party supporters turn out on Election Day. Because coordinated campaigns include many stakeholders and contemporary voters have several voting options, strategies and tactics are subject to many, sometimes heated, negotiations. Some discussions involve political priorities, such as whose name will appear most prominently on billboards, mail, direct-mail, and social media. Others are based on technology and local traditions. These include the relative effort to be devoted to encouraging absentee, early voting, and traditional Election Day voting; the types of appeals that are likely to be effective in different areas; and who should deliver those appeals. Regarding the last point, personal contacts are usually regarded as most effective,[27] but other considerations, such as the numbers and reliability of volunteers, may cause stakeholders to disagree over whether a candidate organization, local party, or interest group is best equipped to do the contacting. Union volunteers often take the lead in contacting other union members in the Democratic coordinated campaigns, and local business leaders often play prominent roles in contacting other business owners in Republican coordinated campaigns.

How important are the activities that state and other party organizations conduct in elections? There are many ways to address this question, but the most direct approach is to ask those who are the recipients of that assistance. Surveys of candidates for the state legislature demonstrate that the most valuable assistance provided by state party central committees are those commonly conducted by coordinated grassroots campaigns, including registration drives, encouraging likely voters to turn out, and transporting them to the polls on Election Day. Candidates considered LCCs to be more valuable than the central committee when it came to direct campaign assistance, such as providing demographic data, fund-raising, and devising campaign strategy. Candidates in competitive races were more likely to indicate that party organizations were helpful during the campaign. Incumbents, however, were more likely to rely on LCCs for help than the state central committee. Surprisingly, those running for open seats were less likely than others to respond that the party organization was valuable to the campaign effort.[28]

In addition to coordinated campaigns, state central committees and LCCs wage independent campaigns to communicate messages directly to voters without the candidates' knowledge or consent. Most of these messages are candidate comparisons or attacks that are intended to undermine an opponent.[29] One explanation for their overall negativity is that party operatives consider it easier to tear down an opponent than promote their own candidate. Another explanation is that they allow for a *de facto* division of labor that frees candidates to focus on a positive message and avoid being criticized for playing "dirty politics" and leaves it to the party (or allied interest groups) to do the mudslinging.[30] During the 2010 election cycle, Democratic and Republican state central committees and LCCs spent $16.2 million and $15 million on independent campaigns to influence state-level elections.[31]

The coordinated campaigns carried out by Florida's Democratic and Republican party organizations in 2010 exemplify those carried out by strong state party organizations in the midst of a heated election season. Florida's elections were among the most hotly contested in the nation. In addition to some high-profile elections for the governorship, six other statewide offices, and a U.S. Senate seat, the state hosted many competitive races for the U.S. House of Representatives, the state senate, the state house of representatives, and numerous local offices. Democratic and Republican party organizations were highly active in Florida, conducting coordinated grassroots and independent media campaigns to influence the many competitive contests on the ballot. The Florida Democratic State Central Committee led the Democrats' coordinated campaign, which included foot canvasses, telephone banks, and other direct voter contact activities designed to help the party's candidates. Special attention was paid to mobilizing Latino voters and helping voters who requested absentee ballots. The grassroots campaign was financed in part by $3.7 million transferred from the DNC and DCCC to the Florida Democratic State Central Committee, whose total spending during the 2010 election cycle exceeded $51 million, including $10 million in contributions to candidates for governor, other statewide offices, and the state house. The state central committee did not make any independent expenditures in 2010, but some of the local parties it helped fund spent about $10,800 on independent media campaigns and Democratic-leaning interest groups spent another $556,000. Most of these expenditures attacked Republicans in hotly contested races.[32]

As previously noted, Florida has a very strong Republican state party organization (see Strong and Weak State Party Organizations box), and in 2010 it was a major participant in the GOP's coordinated campaign, referred to as the Victory Program. Working with the RNC, the state central committee coordinated the voter identification, targeting, and mobilization efforts of Republican county party committees, local chapters of Young Republicans and College Republicans, and other local party organizations. The Victory Program focused on turning out Republican early, absentee, and Election Day voters. In support for these efforts, the RNC transferred $1 million, the NRCC $80,000, and the Republican Governors Association $8.3 million, respectively, to the Republican state central committee. The state central committee spent a total of $69.9 million in 2010, including $14 million in contributions to gubernatorial, other statewide, and state house candidates. As was the case with the Democrats, the Republican state central committee did not conduct an independent media campaign. However, the Republican State Leadership Committee, an allied interest, made $1.25 million in independent expenditures to influence Florida's statewide contests and close state legislative races.[33] Other GOP-leaning interest groups spent less money on their efforts.

CONCLUSION

American party organizations developed primarily in response to changes in their strategic environment, including political reforms, the introduction of new campaign technologies, and broad systematic changes in society. At the height of their power from the latter half of the nineteenth century through the early twentieth century, political parties selected candidates for office, dominated election campaigns, and commanded the loyalties of the government workers and others who volunteered for their organizations. They also commanded the votes of large swaths of the population. State party organizations were more influential than national party committees during this period. As their environment changed over the first half of the twentieth century, state parties had to adapt in order to maintain their influence. With the assistance of national party organizations, state parties eventually evolved into organizations that recruit candidates, provide campaign contributions and services, and directly communicate with voters through coordinated and independent campaigns. State laws, history, and political competition are among the factors that influence the development of state central committees and legislative campaigns committees, and the degrees to which they perform these functions.

For state party organizations, the period of renewal and development is far from over. Changes in state regulations governing the candidate selection processes, financial transactions, and voting procedures will present new challenges and possibilities. Shifts in their population, the ups and downs of electoral competition, the introduction of new technologies, and other societal changes also will influence their prospects and activities. They will likely continue to remain influential in elections, governance, and policymaking in the future.

NOTES

1. Malcom E. Jewell and Sarah M. Morehouse, *Political Parties and Elections in American States* (Washington, DC: CQ Press, 2001), 1–6.
2. Anthony Gierzynski, *Legislative Party Campaign Committees in the American States* (Lexington: University Press of Kentucky, 1992), 1–14.
3. Frank J. Sorauf, *Party Politics in America* (Boston: Little Brown, 1980).
4. Cornelius P. Cotter, et al., *Party Organizations in American Politics* (New York: Praeger, 1984), 31.
5. Jerrold G. Rusk, "The Effect of the Australian Ballot Reform on Split Ticket Voting: 1876–1908," *American Political Science Review* 64 (1970): 1220–1238.
6. Ibid.
7. Jewell and Morehouse, *Political Parties,* 83–85.
8. Larry J. Sabato, *The Rise of the Political Consultants* (New York: Basic Books, 1981).
9. Committee on Political Parties, "Toward a More Responsible Two-Party System," *American Political Science Review* 44 (1950): supplement.
10. John F. Bibby, *Politics, Parties, and Elections in America* (Belmont, CA: Wadsworth, 2000).
11. John H. Aldrich, Brad Gomez, and John D. Griffin, State Party Organizations Study, 1999, cited in David H. Dulio and R. Sam Garrett, "Organizational Strength and Campaign Professionalism in State Parties," in *The State of the Parties,* 5th ed., John C. Green and David C. Coffey, eds. (New York: Rowman and Littlefield, 2007), 199–216.
12. Cotter, et al. *Party Organizations in American Politics,* 21–22.
13. Ibid., 61–82.
14. Ibid., 67.
15. David Mayhew, *Placing Parties in American Politics* (Princeton, NJ: Princeton University Press, 1986), 17–23.
16. V. O. Key Jr., *American State Politics: An Introduction* (New York: Knopf, 1956), 20–51.
17. John H. Aldrich, "Southern Parties in State and Nation," *Journal of Politics* 62 (2000): 643–670.
18. Jewell and Morehouse. *Political Parties,* 52–57.
19. Ibid., 52–57.
20. Frank R. Parker, *Black Votes Count: Political Empowerment in Mississippi after 1965* (Chapel Hill: University of North Carolina Press, 1990).
21. Key, *American State Politics.*
22. Cotter, et al., *Party Organizations in American Politics,* 20.
23. Robert E. Hogan, "Candidate Perceptions of Political Party Campaign Activity in State Legislative Elections," *State Politics and Policy Quarterly* 2 (2002): 66–85.
24. John F. Bibby, "State Party Organizations: Strengthening and Adapting to Candidate-Centered Politics and Nationalization,"

in *The Parties Respond,* 4th ed., L. Sandy Maisel, ed. (Boulder: Westview, 2002).

25. Federal Election Commission, www.fec.gov.

26. National Institute on Money in State Politics, www.followthemoney.org.

27. Alan S. Gerber and Donald P. Green, "The Effects of Canvassing, Telephone Calls, and Direct Mail on Voter Turnout: A Field Experiment," *American Political Science Review* 94 (2000): 653–663.

28. Hogan, "Candidate Perceptions."

29. Michael M., Franz, Joel Rivlin, and Kenneth Goldstein, "Much More of the Same: Television Advertising Pre- and Post-BCRA," in *The Election after Reform: Money, Politics, and the Bipartisan Campaign Reform Act,* ed. Michael J. Malbin (Lanham, MD: Rowman and Littlefield).

30. Paul S. Herrnson, *Congressional Elections: Campaigning at Home and in Washington* (Washington, DC: CQ Press, 2012), 125.

31. National Institute on Money in State Politics, www.followthemoney.org.

32. Ibid.

33. Ibid.

SUGGESTED READING

Bibby, John F. *Politics, Parties, and Elections in America.* Belmont, CA: Wadsworth, 2000.

———. "State Party Organizations: Strengthening and Adapting to Candidate-Centered Politics and Nationalization." In *The Parties Respond,* 4th ed., L. Sandy Maisel, ed. Boulder, CO: Westview, 2002.

Cotter, Cornelius P., et al. *Party Organizations in American Politics.* New York: Praeger, 1984.

Dulio, David A., and R. Sam Garrett. "Organizational Strength and Campaign Professionalism in State Parties." In *The State of the Parties,* Lanham, MD: Rowman and Littlefield, 2007.

Gierzynski, Anthony. *Legislative Party Campaign Committees in the American States.* Lexington: University Press of Kentucky, 1992.

Herrnson, Paul S. *Party Campaigning in the 1980s.* Cambridge: Harvard University Press, 1988.

Hogan, Robert E. "Candidate Perceptions of Political Party Campaign Activity in State Legislative Elections." *State Politics and Policy Quarterly* 2 (2002): 66–85.

Jewell, Malcom E., and Sarah M. Morehouse. *Political Parties and Elections in American States,* 4th ed. Washington, DC: CQ Press, 2001.

Key, V. O., Jr. *American State Politics: An Introduction.* New York: Knopf, 1956.

La Raja, Raymond J. *Small Change: Money, Political Parties, and Campaign Finance Reform.* Ann Arbor: University of Michigan Press, 2008.

Malbin, Michael J., and Thomas L. Gais. *The Day after Reform: Sobering Campaign Finance Lessons from the American States.* New York: Rockefeller Institute Press, 1998.

Mayhew, David. *Placing Parties in American Politics.* Princeton, NJ: Princeton University Press, 1986.

Moncrief, Gary F., Peverill Squire, and Malcolm E. Jewell. *Who Runs for the Legislature?* Upper Saddle River, NJ: Prentice Hall, 2001.

Shay, Daniel M. *Transforming Democracy: Legislative Campaign Committees and Political Parties.* Albany: State University of New York Press, 1995.

Thompson, Joel A., and Gary F. Moncrief. *Campaign Finance in State Legislative Elections.* Washington, DC: CQ Press, 1998.

Chapter 10

Interest Groups and Their Influence

Peter L. Francia

On June 5, 2012, Gov. Scott Walker of Wisconsin celebrated a 7-point victory, 53 percent to 46 percent, in an election to have him recalled from office. Walker's win culminated a tumultuous sixteen-month period that began when Republicans in the Wisconsin state legislature submitted a controversial bill that stripped certain collective bargaining rights from most state employees. In reaction to the proposed legislation, public-sector unions organized mass demonstrations and protests that lasted several weeks, with picketing public school teachers, university teaching assistants, firefighters, and other state employees filling the streets near the state capitol in Madison. Despite sustained pressure and growing crowds of protestors, Republicans passed the governor's bill, and Walker signed the legislation into law on March 11, 2011.

Public-sector unions and their supporters responded by vowing to recall Republicans from office. After a successful campaign to gather the signatures needed to initiate several recall elections, organized labor and its allies succeeded in defeating three Republican state senators (two in August 2011 and one in June 2012), which shifted control of the state senate back to Democrats. However, in the highest-profile recall election of all, public-sector unions and their allies failed to oust their top target, Governor Walker. Assisting Walker in his victory was a pro-business and anti-union group, Americans for Prosperity, founded by the billionaire brothers David and Charles Koch, which helped Walker outspend his Democratic opponent, Tom Barrett, by a significant margin during the recall election.[1]

The high political drama that recently played out in Wisconsin underscores the significance of organized interests in state politics. Perhaps because of their importance and ubiquitous presence in the political process, polls show that a majority of the public believes the government does a poor job of promoting the well-being of all Americans ahead of the well-being of "special interests."[2] During the recent Wisconsin controversy, for example, some attacked organized labor for exerting too much influence on the Wisconsin political process and for putting the well-being of its members ahead of the larger interests of taxpayers in Wisconsin.[3] Others charged that the agenda of the very wealthy, led by the billionaire Koch brothers, was the foremost concern of Governor Walker in pushing his collective bargaining law.[4]

Yet, as this chapter will explain, the public's widespread belief that interest groups work against what is best for the average American is often too simplistic. The population of interest groups in state politics can be quite diverse, as can be the goals, strategies, and tactics of the various interest groups currently active in state politics. In short, interest groups undeniably occupy a central place in the political process, but the consequences of this involvement are more complex than what conventional wisdom often holds.

In the pages that follow, this chapter attempts to cut through some of the misconceptions about interest groups by (1) examining the current diversity of organized interests in state politics; (2) explaining the different goals, strategies, and tactics of various interest groups in state politics; and (3) offering proper perspective on the influence of interest groups in state politics.

DIVERSITY OF INTEREST GROUPS

In the 1830s, Alexis de Tocqueville wrote that the United States is the "one country in the world which, day in, day out, makes use of an unlimited freedom of political association."[5] Consistent with what de Tocqueville observed almost two centuries ago, Americans still commonly exercise their right to freedom of association. According to a recent study, three of every four Americans are active in voluntary groups, with the average American active in not just one, but multiple organizations.[6] Among organizations that can be properly called interest groups (i.e., associations of individuals or smaller organizations that engage in activity with a political purpose), some estimates indicate that there are as many as two hundred thousand in the United States.[7] Of these interest groups, about fifty thousand organizations and businesses have lobbyists, with approximately forty-six thousand paid lobbyists who are officially registered in the fifty states.[8]

Perhaps the simplest distinction among these many interest groups is their membership and composition. As one would expect, most interest groups are *membership associations* made up of individual people; however, some interest groups, known as *peak associations,* instead count other smaller organizations or firms as their members. The National Association of Manufacturers (NAM), for example, is a peak association comprised of eleven thousand manufacturing companies. Whether a membership association or a peak association, interest groups also can differ from one another in that some seek to advance the concerns of their immediate members only (i.e., private interest groups), whereas others work toward benefits that enrich the entire society (i.e., public interest groups). Environmental groups that fight to reduce air pollution and consumer groups that seek to protect the public from potentially dangerous products are examples of public interest groups.

Public interest groups, nonetheless, are not always universally supported by the public. For example, critics of environmental and consumer protection groups often complain that the actions of these organizations can be harmful to business and, by extension, the public as increased environmental and consumer regulations increase product costs, which reduce sales, profits, job creation, and ultimately the larger economy. Private interest groups, however, are typically what come to mind when Americans think of "special interests" because their narrow concerns often run counter to the overall public good. Ultimately, whether one is a defender or an opponent of a particular interest group often comes down simply to what specific interest the group claims to represent.

With literally thousands of interest groups active throughout the fifty states, there is certainly no shortage of groups for people to like or dislike. Because there are so many interest groups in the United States, each of these many interests would be too numerous to mention, and any specific list of interest groups would be difficult to compile given that the composition of interest group populations can differ substantially from state to state. Still, there are some categorizations that are applicable and helpful in describing the general types of interest groups that are most active in state politics. Political scientist Anthony Nownes offers perhaps the most useful typology, breaking interest groups into six manageable but distinct and comprehensive categories that include corporations and business firms, trade associations, labor unions, professional associations, governmental associations, and citizen groups.[9]

Corporations and Business Firms

Corporations and business firms are a common and significant source of influence in the political arena. Issues such as environmental regulations, tax rates, enterprise zones, government subsidies, government contracts, and labor rules are often at the center of the policy agenda for corporate and business interests. Because corporate and business interests are inextricably related to the economy as a whole, the concerns of corporations and business firms typically receive considerable attention from elected officials in state government, giving them what one scholar called a "privileged position."[10]

Nonetheless, it is worth noting that corporate and business interests are not always monolithic or cohesive. Corporations and businesses within an industry are ultimately competitors, and they sometimes work against one another when trying to influence government policy. If a specific firm can win certain targeted tax breaks for itself only, or secure a government contract, it can gain advantage over a rival business competitor. Moreover, different industries and areas of business hold varying degrees of power and influence in each of the fifty state governments—from the coal industry in West Virginia to the auto industry in Michigan to the oil industry in Texas. In other states with diverse economic interests, such as California, no one particular industry or business firm dominates the state. Instead, there is representation for multiple business interests.

While specific corporations and business firms may hold more power in one state than another, this does not necessarily mean that they limit their activities to only one state. The gaming industry, for instance, holds significant power and influence in the state of Nevada. However, a major player in the gaming industry, such as Caesar's Entertainment Corporation, is active not only in Nevada, but also lobbies elected officials across the nation, including those in state governments in Louisiana, Maryland, Massachusetts, and New Jersey, to name just a few places.

For business firms that specialize in an area of industry very specific to a certain region or state, political activity may be limited to one or two states. Icicle Seafoods, for example, harvests and processes wild Alaska salmon and other cold water seafood. Perhaps not surprisingly, its lobbying activity is limited to the Pacific Northwest states of Alaska and Washington.

In short, corporations and business firms share some common sets of general concerns and shared interests (e.g., reducing state regulatory requirements and lowering taxes). Yet there is significant variation among them that can lead to differences—both in terms of what some corporate and business groups seek from state government, and in how and where they go about trying to influence state government.

Trade Associations

Trade associations have interests that often overlap with those of corporations and business firms. The major difference between an interest group classified as a trade association and one that represents a corporation or business firm is in the membership of each. As described above, an interest group classified as a corporation/business firm represents a single corporation or business firm. A trade association, by comparison, often represents numerous business firms that come together in a voluntary partnership to advance their common interests. Because trade associations represent a wider set of business interests, their issues of concern are usually much broader than those of an interest group representing a single business firm or corporation.

Trade associations are among the most active of all interest groups in lobbying state governments. Perhaps the most influential trade associations are the various state and local chambers of commerce, which seek to promote the general interests of business (see Portrait of the U.S. Chamber of Commerce box). Many of these state chambers of commerce have been in existence for more than a century. The New Jersey Chamber of Commerce, for example, was established in 1911 with the help and support of famed inventor Thomas Edison. It has been active in organizing New Jersey businesses to provide a unified voice for business interests since its founding, and today is highly involved in state politics, fighting for what it describes as "pro-growth legislation" that "will make New Jersey more competitive and business friendly."[11]

Some trade associations have a more specific set of concerns and are often organized along a single industry, such as the American Petroleum Institute. Indeed, there is a trade association for almost every industry. Beer wholesalers have active state chapters of the Beer Wholesalers Association, for example, as do businesses that produce organic food, which have the Organic Trade Association. Some single-industry trade associations also wield more influence in some states than in others. The National Association of Wheat Growers, for example, is rather obviously more active in states where wheat production is greatest.

Ultimately, a trade association's value is that it provides individual business firms with power in numbers. While there are certainly cases of a single business firm wielding enough power to lobby a specific state government effectively on an important business issue, most business firms do not fit that description. When individual business firms organize together on an industry-wide basis into trade associations, however, their combined numbers can be substantial, as the efforts of trade associations like the Chamber of Commerce have proven throughout the fifty states.

Labor Unions

Labor unions are organizations of workers that bargain collectively with their employers for improvements in wages, benefits, working conditions, and other employment matters.

Labor unions also seek to improve the quality of life for workers by trying to influence government laws and policies. These policies can include labor-specific laws such as the minimum wage, or more general matters such as tax policy and civil rights legislation.

Workers with jobs in manufacturing, construction, mining, and transportation once dominated the union ranks. Today, however, the union membership has shifted largely to the public and service sectors. The National Education Association (NEA); the Service Employees International Union (SEIU); and the American Federation of State, County, and Municipal Employees (AFSCME) are presently three of the nation's largest unions. The NEA, in particular, plays an especially prominent role in state politics. With more than three million members and an annual budget that exceeds $300 million, it recently topped a list of the most influential interest groups that lobby state government.[12]

Of course, much like the interest groups that represent business firms and trade associations, the power and influence of labor unions can be quite different from state to state. The United Auto Workers (UAW), despite recent declines in membership, remains a viable political force in Michigan, where the auto industry is a major employer. UNITE HERE, which represents hotel, restaurant, gaming,

PORTRAIT OF THE U.S. CHAMBER OF COMMERCE

The U.S. Chamber of Commerce represents the interests of more than three million businesses, both large and small, in virtually every economic sector. There are active state and local chapters of the Chamber of Commerce across the nation. All are united in promoting and advocating for lower taxes and regulatory relief for businesses. In all fifty states, the Chamber of Commerce is a respected and formidable political force.

SOURCE: U.S. Chamber of Commerce's website, www.uschamber.com/about.

Johanna Sharrard counts signatures as she stacks minimum wage petitions on the floor of the AFL-CIO (American Federation of Labor and Congress of Industrial Organizations) labor union office in Lakewood, Colorado, on August 2, 2006. Petition drives are often launched by labor unions in order to influence labor-specific laws and policies.

SOURCE: Photo by Kathryn Scott Osler/*The Denver Post* via Getty Images.

apparel, and laundry workers, has a national presence but is especially strong in Nevada. And in West Virginia, where coal mining has long been one of the state's major industries, the United Mine Workers of America (UMWA), although presently in decline, is a union with a lengthy history of political activity in the state.

Overall, as of 2012, 14.4 million workers belonged to a labor union (with another 1.5 million workers whose jobs are covered by a union contract, but who do not report belonging to the union).[13] This number has dropped since the 1970s, when union membership exceeded 20 million workers, and today, just 12 percent of the U.S. workforce belongs to a labor union—the lowest rate of unionization in more than seven decades.[14] These national statistics, however, mask areas of union strength.

Nearly one-quarter of all workers in New York, for example, belong to a union.[15] Many other states in the Northeast also topped the national average by several points, which included Connecticut (17 percent), Rhode Island (17 percent), New Jersey (16 percent), Massachusetts (15 percent), and Pennsylvania (15 percent). Several states in the Midwest and Pacific West reached or exceeded 15 percent as well: Alaska (22 percent), Hawaii (22 percent), Washington (19 percent), Michigan (18 percent), Oregon (17 percent), Illinois (16 percent), Minnesota (15 percent), and Nevada (15 percent).

In sharp contrast, states in the South have exceptionally low rates of union membership: Louisiana (5 percent), Tennessee (5 percent), Virginia (5 percent), Georgia (4 percent), Arkansas (4 percent), North Carolina (3 percent), and South Carolina (3 percent). Many southern states, it should be noted, have right-to-work laws, which prohibit union membership as a condition of employment for workers who were not union members when hired. This explains at least partially why unionization is lower in the South, although several other factors may also play a role.[16] When taken together, the numbers suggest that although labor unions have undergone a national decline in membership, the strength or weakness of labor unions and the interest groups that represent them varies considerably from state to state.

Professional Associations

Professional associations represent individuals with careers in a common profession such as medicine or law. In many respects, professional associations are similar to trade associations. Both types of groups seek to represent a particular set of economic interests; however, a professional association differs from a trade association in that it usually organizes people rather than other smaller organizations or firms. Two of the most well-known professional associations are the American Medical Association (AMA), which represents doctors, and the American Bar Association (ABA), which represents lawyers. Many professional associations like the AMA and the ABA have state and local chapters that are active throughout the country.

Some professional associations are largely nonpolitical and focus mainly on efforts to educate, train, and issue standards of conduct and practice for the profession. Other professional associations, however, are very involved in politics. The extent of a professional association's political engagement varies not only from group to group, but can even vary for the same group from state to state based upon what each state's legislative agenda is at a particular time. When the state of Florida, for example, was working on a law protecting health care facilities against medical malpractice lawsuits in 2011, professional associations like the Florida Justice Association were especially active in lobbying, albeit unsuccessfully, against the bill.[17]

Perhaps the most striking feature of professional associations is how numerous and diverse they are. Indeed, there are professional associations active in state politics that represent not only doctors and lawyers, but also scientists, professors, insurance agents, public accountants, journalists, legal assistants, and optometrists, to name only a few. As one scholar noted, there are professional associations that represent virtually every economic sector, ranging from academics to zoologists.[18] In some cases, these professional associations represent a small, but very specific population, such as the National Association of Asian American Professionals (see Portrait of the National Association of Asian American Professionals box). Professional associations are especially active in state politics because licensing, regulations, and/or other requirements to practice in certain professions are almost always governed by state law and administered by state boards.

Governmental Associations

In state politics, governmental associations represent the interests of cities, counties, school districts, and even state and executive branch agencies. These governmental associations try to influence their respective state government because the decisions of the state legislature and governor can have a profound impact on the direction, wants, and needs of local government. Indeed, studies show that a high proportion of the legislation that state government introduces affects local government.[19]

A good example of a governmental association is any one of the various municipal leagues that exist across the nation. In North Carolina, municipal interests have a voice in the North Carolina League of Municipalities, which actively lobbies both the state and federal government. It also functions to help municipal officials share ideas about how to promote efficiency and improve the quality of local government services to meet the expectations and needs of citizens.

One of the challenges for any governmental association is that municipalities and local government interests can be quite varied. The North Carolina League of Municipalities, for instance, claims to represent "540 great hometowns."[20] The needs of a small, quiet beach resort community such as Atlantic Beach, North Carolina (population 1,495), are often quite different from those of a bustling city like Charlotte (population 731,424). Despite the different interests of rural, suburban, and urban communities, governmental associations are able to maintain a unified front on many issues, such as increased state funding for local transportation projects. To further promote unity, municipal leagues, such as the North Carolina League of Municipalities, do not have political action committees; nor do they engage in electoral activities. Even without a presence in partisan politics, governmental associations are still generally considered to be a legitimate source of influence on state government policymaking.[21]

Citizen Groups

Citizen groups, as the name implies, are organized by like-minded citizens who share a common set of political interests and concerns. What distinguishes a citizen group from a business group, labor union, or professional association is that its members are not motivated by interests that relate to their employment but by political ideology or a specific political cause. Some citizen groups are labeled "public interest" groups because they seek to provide public goods, which unlike private goods are available to everyone regardless of whether they are members of the group or not.

Many citizen or public interest groups are the products of social movements. As a political cause matures and evolves, "outsider" tactics—namely, protests—often give way to "insider" tactics such as lobbying and electoral politics. The feminist movement of the 1960s and 1970s, for example, gave rise to women's interest groups such as the National Organization for Women (NOW).

Citizen groups represent a myriad of different interests that include abortion rights, civil rights, environmental protection, gay rights, gun rights, property rights, the pro-life cause, smaller government and lower taxes, and numerous other political concerns that motivate citizens to take political action. There are even "good government" interest groups that, somewhat ironically, fight against the influence of interest groups. Some of the most well-known citizen groups include the National Rifle Association (NRA), AARP (formerly known as the American Association for

PORTRAIT OF THE NATIONAL ASSOCIATION OF ASIAN AMERICAN PROFESSIONALS

The National Association of Asian American Professionals (NAAAP) is an interest group of three thousand Asian American professionals. Chapters exist in the metropolitan areas of Atlanta, Boston, Chicago, Denver, Houston, New York City, Orange County in Southern California, Philadelphia, Raleigh-Durham, San Francisco, Seattle, and Washington, DC. The NAAAP works to promote Asian American leadership, including in politics, and provides career and professional development services for the Asian American community. It also has a history of defending the civil rights of Asian Americans. The NAAAP is a nonpartisan interest group.

SOURCE: The National Association of Asian American Professionals' website, www.naaap.org.

Retired Persons), and the National Association for the Advancement of Colored People (NAACP).

In state politics, the number and variation of citizen groups depends on the size and diversity of the state and its people. Large and multicultural states, such as California and New York, have citizen groups for virtually every interest and concern. By comparison, the most active and influential citizen groups in less populated states with citizens of similar backgrounds, such as Idaho and Wyoming, tend to reflect these states' more homogeneous populations.

GOALS, STRATEGIES, AND TACTICS

With so many different groups participating in state politics, each group must develop an effective political strategy so that its voice can be heard amid the large chorus of organized interests. In almost all instances, a group's political strategy is designed to advance a straightforward and simple goal: pressure elected officials in state government to pay attention to and then act upon the organization's specific policy and legislative objectives. There are several common strategic approaches that interest groups use to advance this goal in state politics: (1) elect like-minded candidates to public office; (2) directly lobby those already elected to office, especially those in positions of power; and (3) indirectly lobby officials in state government at the grassroots level.

Electoral Strategies and Tactics

Most interest groups involve themselves in campaigns and elections, although with a few exceptions. Governmental associations avoid electoral activities because such efforts are likely to alienate a good number of its members—half of whom would support Democrats and the other half of whom would support Republicans. However, for most corporations and business firms, labor unions, trade associations, professional associations, and citizen groups, electoral activities are an important part of how these groups go about trying to advance their interests in state government.

One of the first and most direct ways that interest groups attempt to influence elections is by recruiting candidates sympathetic to their concerns to run for office. In some cases, interest groups recruit promising local officeholders or perhaps someone from within their own membership to run for state office. The New Jersey State AFL-CIO, for example, has its own Labor Candidates School to help union members who become candidates wage competitive campaigns. Among its most notable accomplishments has been the rise of Steve Sweeney, a member of the Ironworkers Local Union #399, who is currently president of the state senate.

Interest groups also have several important resources at their disposal. Broadly speaking, these include monetary and personnel resources. Monetary resources refer to the contributions and expenditures that groups supply to candidates running for political office. Many interest groups form political action committees (PACs) to contribute money directly to candidates. PAC contributions can be important to candidates running for state office because they help purchase the services of pollsters, media consultants, and other campaign advisers.

Monetary resources can further purchase mass-media advertisements and internal communications, which interest groups often claim help to educate the public and/or their members about a specific issue or a candidate's position on an issue. Recent court rulings on campaign finance law have opened up new vehicles—527 groups, 501(c) groups, and super PACs—for interest groups to use for mass-media advertisements, provided that there is no coordination with a candidate's campaign (for definitions of these different groups, see Summarizing PACs, super PACs, 501(c) Groups, and 527 Groups box).[22] Although, 527 groups, 501(c) groups, and super PACs are more commonly known for their activities in federal elections, a few have become involved in state and local elections. In 2012, for example, conservative attorney James Bopp Jr. announced that his super PAC, USA Super-PAC, would spend money in a select number of state races.[23]

Personnel resources are a group's supply of people in the organization—its members, volunteers, and staff. These resources are important because interest groups that have several million members, such as the NRA (4.3 million members), are more likely to hold clout with elected officials in state government than much smaller groups like the NRA's rival, the Brady Campaign to Prevent Gun Violence (28,000 members). During elections especially, the ability of an interest group to provide volunteers to campaigns can be a valuable part of the so-called ground war during an election. Interest groups that can provide significant assistance with grassroots activities, such as voter registration and get-out-the-vote drives, mail and literature drops, and calls from telephone banks, can make a significant impact on the outcome of a close election.

The different ways that interest groups use these resources is determined to a large degree by each state's campaign finance laws. In some states, PACs can make unlimited campaign contributions to a candidate running for state office, making monetary resources an extremely valuable resource. In other states, PAC contributions are tightly regulated and limited, forcing interest groups to rely more on their personnel resources. (For more information on the regulation of interest groups, see Chapter 11.) Despite the differences in state campaign finance laws, interest groups generally tend to direct their political resources in a few different ways, as discussed later.

SUMMARIZING PACS, SUPER PACS, 501(C) GROUPS, AND 527 GROUPS

What is a PAC? A political action committee (PAC) is a legal entity formed by an interest group whose purpose is raising money for, and making contributions to, the campaigns of candidates for office.

What is a super PAC? A super PAC is similar to a PAC, but it remains completely independent of any candidate and agrees not to make contributions to a campaign. Because it is independent of any candidates and their campaigns, a super PAC, unlike a PAC, can raise unlimited amounts of money from potential donors and spend unlimited amounts of money during an election.

What are 501(c)(3), 501(c)(4), 501(c)(5), and 501(c)(6) groups? A 501(c)(3) group is a charitable organization that may accept unlimited donations, but it cannot attempt to influence legislation (i.e., lobby) as a substantial part of its activities, and it may not participate in partisan political campaign activities. 501(c)(4), 501(c)(5), and 501(c)(6) groups are similar to 501(c)(3) groups, but they may engage in unlimited lobbying and partisan political activity provided that neither activity is their primary purpose; 501(c)(4) groups are classified as "civic leagues" or "social welfare" organizations; 501(c)(5) groups are classified as "labor" or "agricultural" organizations; and 501(c)(6) groups are classified as "business leagues," "chambers of commerce," or "real estate boards."

What is a 527 group? A 527 group is a political committee, including political parties and candidate campaign committees. Some 527 organizations, however, avoid campaign finance regulations because they are focused on "issue education."

SOURCE: Adapted from Jody C. Baumgartner and Peter L. Francia, *Conventional Wisdom and American Elections: Exploding Myths, Exploring Misconceptions* (Lanham, MD: Rowman and Littlefield, 2010), Box 4.1, 56.

Targeting Resources

Monetary resources, notably PAC contributions, are often given disproportionately to incumbents, particularly those holding powerful positions in government, such as party leaders or the chairs of powerful committees in the state legislature. These incumbents frequently hail from electorally secure districts, all but guaranteeing that the interest group contributes to the winning candidate. An obvious motivation for this contribution is the hope that it will help the interest group gain access and perhaps some influence with these powerful members during the policy-making process. These access-oriented groups typically include those representing corporations and business firms as well as some trade associations.

In some cases, interest groups with access motives will contribute money to incumbents in competitive races because, as one scholar writes, "the more the members need the contributions, the more likely they are to respond gratefully later on."[24] However, access-oriented groups often hedge their bets in competitive elections by contributing money to both the incumbent and the challenger. This is a common strategy for groups flush with money—usually corporate and business interests, as well as some trade associations—that have the advantage of being able to spread their financial resources around to different candidates. In contrast, smaller interest groups with fewer monetary resources cannot afford the same luxury—and, in some cases, may not even form a PAC—because they lack the monetary resources to make significant campaign contributions.

Some interest groups, rather than pursuing access strategies, instead pursue ideological goals and, unlike access-oriented groups, are more willing to invest their monetary resources in the challengers of incumbents. The overriding purpose of this strategy is to replace legislators who consistently vote against the interests of the group and to reshape the overall ideological composition of state government from the legislature to the governor's mansion. Groups that follow this approach contribute most of their money to candidates in competitive elections and may even involve themselves in party primaries. They rarely make cross-party contributions, and because their members are typically devoted to a single cause or a strict ideology, they do not invest in candidates who oppose their group's positions on its core issues. These groups reject access strategies because they recognize that few legislators are likely to change their position on a controversial and well-known issue in exchange for a campaign contribution or expenditure.

Ideologically motivated groups include most citizen groups, as well as several professional groups and labor unions (although unions, to a lesser extent, do give some money for access purposes). Perhaps the best known of these groups is antitax crusader Grover Norquist's Americans for

AMERICANS FOR TAX REFORM'S TAXPAYER PROTECTION PLEDGE FOR STATE LEGISLATORS

TAXPAYER PROTECTION PLEDGE

I, ______________________, PLEDGE TO THE TAXPAYERS OF THE ______ DISTRICT OF THE STATE OF __________________ AND ALL THE PEOPLE OF THIS STATE THAT I WILL OPPOSE AND VOTE AGAINST ANY AND ALL EFFORTS TO INCREASE TAXES.

____
SIGNATURE

____
WITNESS

PLEASE SIGN AND RETURN TO:
AMERICANS FOR TAX REFORM
722 12TH ST., NW, 4TH FLOOR
WASHINGTON, DC 20005
FAX: 1-202-785-0261

____
DATE

____
WITNESS

The Taxpayer Protection Pledge is a project of Americans for Tax Reform (ATR). ATR works with taxpayer groups and activists around the country to ask all candidates and elected officials to make this important commitment to taxpayers. The national list of signers can be accessed at www.atr.org

SOURCE: Americans for Tax Reform's website, www.atr.org/userfiles/StatePledge.pdf.

Tax Reform (ATR). ATR requires candidates running for federal and state office to sign a written pledge swearing not to raise taxes in exchange for its support (see Americans for Tax Reform's Taxpayer Protection Pledge for State Legislators box). Politicians who refuse to sign the pledge or who sign the pledge but then later violate it after winning office are all but assured that ATR will support their opponents.

Groups such as ATR that look to make the most of their monetary resources frequently run advertisements using funds referred to as *independent expenditures.* These independent expenditures—often in the form of television and radio advertisements—are made without the candidate's knowledge or consent. There are no dollar limits on independent expenditures in any state. When the PAC of an interest group makes independent expenditures, it can expressly call for the election or defeat of a candidate. This is also true for an interest group's super PAC, which, unlike PACs in most states, has the extra advantage of being able to raise money in unlimited sums.

Interest groups that have 501(c) and 527 organizations face restrictions in expressly calling for the election or defeat of a candidate, but they can still craft issue advocacy advertisements that sometimes appear to be little more than thinly veiled campaign ads. Not surprisingly, interest groups typically use independent expenditures and issue advocacy advertisements in competitive races to accomplish ideological goals. In the rare instances when interest groups make independent expenditures or run issue advocacy ads in uncompetitive races, they are typically doing so to shape the issue agenda in an election.

Perhaps the most direct way that interest groups communicate their political intentions is by issuing endorsements of candidates. Some interest groups also provide scorecards and voter guides that evaluate candidates' support for the group's policy agenda. The NRA, for example, issues grades from "A" to "F." Other groups, such as the AFL-CIO's Committee on Political Education (COPE), provide legislator scorecards on a scale of 0 to 100. These scorecards, ratings, and voter guides are designed to mobilize the group's membership on behalf of candidates who receive the best evaluations.

The mobilization of a group's membership can be a valuable weapon in advancing ideological goals or in setting the issue agenda in an election. As the opening of this chapter discussed, interest groups, such as labor unions, can often accomplish this latter goal through protests and demonstrations. Though labor unions failed to stop Governor Walker from enacting his legislation or to remove him from office, they were able through protest to draw considerable attention to the issue of collective bargaining rights for state employees in the eventual recall elections that followed their protests.

Direct and Grassroots Lobbying

After elections end, interest groups continue their work to influence state government and public policy through both direct and grassroots lobbying. Direct lobbying refers to efforts by the lobbyist of an interest group, usually a paid professional but sometimes an amateur or volunteer, to inform and influence legislation through direct face-to-face communication with an official or staff member of government. While polls routinely indicate that the public holds a low opinion of lobbyists and even view them as a corruptive force in government, lobbyists themselves describe their job in a more innocuous way. As one California lobbyist explained, "I provide information; the other side does the same thing. It's up to lawmakers to sift through the material and make an informed decision."[25]

A lobbyist, of course, is not simply providing information to decision makers in government for altruistic motives; lobbyists provide information in an effort to influence and affect legislation in a way that benefits the interest group that the lobbyist represents. Indeed, lobbyists have become such a regular part of the legislative process in state government that some have dubbed them the "third house."[26] State lobbyists attempt to influence all branches of government, including executive agencies, the governor's office, the legislature, and in some instances even the state's judicial branch. They also regularly help to draft legislation, testify at legislative hearings, and communicate and build relations with the media. In rare but unfortunate instances, lobbyists can be as bad as their worst critics claim. For example, lobbyist Richard Lipsky pled guilty in 2012 to conspiracy charges for offering bribes to former New York state senator Carl Kruger.

Lipsky, of course, is not representative of most lobbyists. In fact, many interest groups generally do not even rely on contract lobbyists like Lipsky, but instead use in-house lobbyists or volunteer lobbyists. Though the contract lobbyist is what most people think of when asked about lobbying, these lobbyists make up 15 to 20 percent of all lobbyists in most states.[27] Contract lobbyists work for themselves and, as their title implies, are hired on a contractual basis by an interest group. These lobbyists are often former government officials, former government staffers, attorneys, or public relations specialists. Corporations and business firms as well as high-profile trade associations are the most likely to use contract lobbyists.

In-house lobbyists are more common than contract lobbyists in state politics. These lobbyists are often experts in a specialized area of policy that is important to an interest group. Many in-house lobbyists are part of an interest group's legislative department, or sometimes come simply from the top of the group's leadership, such as the president, executive director, or CEO. Rather than use the title "lobbyist," in-house lobbyists instead often take titles such as "government relations officer" or "legislative liaison."

Volunteer or amateur lobbyists are typically everyday citizens who are concerned deeply enough about a cause or issue that they decide to lobby state government without pay. The interest group Mothers Against Drunk Driving (MADD), for example, has had success using volunteer lobbyists to win stricter state penalties for the offense of driving while intoxicated or under the influence. Several years ago in Alaska, MADD volunteer lobbyist Cindy Cashen, who lost her father to a drunk driver, was described as "one of the most visible people at the Capitol [in Juneau]."[28] Volunteer lobbyists like Cashen try to impress upon government officials the moral responsibility they have to act upon a particular issue, such as drunk-driving laws.

Grassroots lobbying, in comparison with direct lobbying, operates in a slightly different way in that it seeks to influence legislation by shaping and influencing public opinion. A successful campaign not only wins over public opinion; it mobilizes significant numbers of citizens to contact their elected representatives, putting pressure on government officials to act on behalf of or against a proposed bill. Nearly all interest groups engage in grassroots lobbying and help in coordinating and financing grassroots political activity. Within the legislative departments of many state-chapter interest groups are Legislative Action Committees (LACs), which provide several services that promote grassroots lobbying. LACs, for example, compile voting records of legislators and communicate the group's positions on upcoming legislation and other pressing issues in an effort to keep their members informed about what is happening in state politics. In the age of electronic communications, interest groups increasingly rely on e-mail, text messages, blogs, and tweets to disseminate this information.

By educating their members about the political environment, it becomes easier for an interest group to convince its members to send an e-mail message, a text message, a fax, or a handwritten letter to a state legislator, or to picket and protest in a demonstration—all common parts of a grassroots lobbying effort. Interest group websites, such as the one for Planned Parenthood of Maryland, further assist these efforts with "Take Action" pages that offer information to its members about how to

Max Montrose of MedicinalMarijuana.TV and Colorado state senator Chris Romer discuss different points of support and dissent in House Bill 1284 during an April 27, 2010, grassroots lobbying tour of the capitol led by community organizers from Mile High NORML and the Colorado Coalition for Patients and Caregivers before public testimony on House Bill 1284 in the Old Supreme Court Chambers.

SOURCE: Photo by Joe Amon/*The Denver Post* via Getty Images.

contact elected officials.[29] In many cases, interest groups also provide pre-written letters and pre-scripted telephone talking points for their members to follow when contacting a state lawmaker's office.

Perhaps the most controversial type of grassroots lobbying is so-called astroturf lobbying, which refers to events that interest groups stage to give the false appearance of a spontaneous movement of everyday people in support of or in opposition to an issue or piece of legislation. Because astroturf lobbying is considered a form of fake grassroots lobbying, the term *astroturf lobbying* borrows from the fake grass used originally in the Houston Astrodome, known as astroturf. Many interest groups create or rely on front groups, also derisively called "sock puppet" groups,[30] to carry out astroturfing. The Center for Consumer Freedom, for example, represents the tobacco, alcohol beverage, and restaurant industries, although it would be difficult to know this from its name. Several years ago in Alaska, the vaguely named group Alaska's Future was set up by ExxonMobil, ConocoPhillips, and BP to oppose a state tax on gas line leases. In many instances, these front groups, such as Alaska's Future, dissolve once the group has accomplished or failed in its purpose to stop or enact a specific piece of legislation. The effectiveness of astroturf lobbying is unclear; however, there is some evidence, discussed in more detail in the next section, that suggests interest group actions, taken in total, have some impact on legislative actions in state government, although in a less corruptive way than the public often assumes.

THE INFLUENCE OF INTEREST GROUPS IN STATE POLITICS

Much of the political science research rejects the notion that interest groups can outright purchase a legislator with campaign contributions or other forms of assistance.[31] There are simply too many underlying factors and participants in the larger political process to isolate campaign contributions or the lobbying activities of a single interest group (or even several interest groups) as the cause of a bill's passage or defeat. Nonetheless, interest groups are also not powerless, and they can influence state politics in a few significant ways.

As already noted in the chapter, interest group electoral activities can influence the issue agenda in an election, and there is also general consensus that interest group contributions and campaign assistance can provide access to lawmakers. Some additional research suggests that interest group activities can affect lawmakers' legislative involvement and priorities.[32] More specifically in the arena of policymaking, interest groups and their lobbyists tend to be most influential on low-salience, nonideological, and narrow issues.[33] Indeed, it is highly unlikely for a lawmaker to go against the interests of his or her constituency and electoral base on a high-profile issue due to pressure from an interest group. Interest groups and lobbyists are also most likely to have an effect on legislation before it comes to a floor, such as through earmarks or amendments during committee markups.[34]

The power and influence of a specific group or organized interest, as mentioned in the first half of this chapter, tends to be based not only on each individual group's resources, but also on the political and economic environment of each state. The NRA, for example, is strongest in conservative states, especially in the South. Florida's Stand Your Ground law, which allows a person to use deadly force against someone if there is a reasonable belief of threat, drew national attention following the shooting death of Trayvon Martin, an unarmed, seventeen-year-old African American. Media accounts were quick to report that the controversial law was the product of the influence and lobbying efforts of the NRA in Florida.

Research from political scientist Lynda Powell further suggests that the influence of interest group campaign contributions can vary from state to state based on a number of institutional factors. Among several important findings, her results indicate that the influence of contributions increases in states with state legislators who earn higher levels of compensation and in states with a higher proportion of members who have ambition for higher office.[35] Powell adds that contributions to legislators get slightly less return in states with less populated districts, term limits, and highly educated constituencies.

Taken together, the power and influence of interest groups is less extensive and corruptive than what the public imagines, although crooked lobbyists like Lipsky do exist and reinforce the negative stereotypes that persist about lobbyists. Still, interest groups are significant in legitimately shaping some important aspects of the electoral and legislative process in state politics. Ultimately, interest group influence is situational and often multifaceted.

CONCLUSION

The first half of this chapter discussed the wide range and diversity of interest groups in state politics, illustrating that, despite widespread public condemnation for organized interests, virtually all Americans are represented by some type of special interest. The second half focused on how interest groups go about trying to advance the interests of their members. Although the public is deeply suspicious of lobbyists, with many people believing that lobbying activities are corruptive, the influence of interest groups in state politics is considerably more complex. When interest groups do affect the political process, they do so in ways ranging from shaping the issue agenda during an election, to determining which earmarks or words will appear in a bill, to influencing lawmakers' legislative priorities.

Interest groups do not, however, "buy" legislators' support on their issues of concern, as is commonly assumed. Indeed, as the Wisconsin controversy at the opening of this chapter illustrates, interest groups—even highly organized ones—sometimes lose their battles. Nonetheless, as the Wisconsin controversy also shows, virtually no significant decision or action taken by government can escape reaction from at least one of the many interest groups that populate the political environment of all fifty states. This makes interest groups impossible to ignore in the study of state politics.

NOTES

1. Phil Hirschkorn and Nancy Cordes, "A Record Amount of Money Spent on Wisconsin Recall," CBS News, June 6, 2012, www.cbsnews.com/8301-503544_162-57448678-503544/a-record-amount-of-money-spent-on-wisconsin-recall.

2. Associated Press/National Constitution Center/GfK poll, August 2011, retrieved July 14, 2012, from the iPOLL Databank, The Roper Center for Public Opinion Research, University of Connecticut.

3. James Sherk, "What Collective Bargaining Gets You," National Review Online, February 25, 2011, www.nationalreview.com/corner/260768/what-collective-bargaining-gets-you-james-sherk.

4. Eric Lipton, "Billionaire Brothers' Money Plays Role in Wisconsin Dispute," *New York Times,* February 21, 2011, www.nytimes.com/2011/02/22/us/22koch.html.

5. Alexis de Tocqueville, *Democracy in America,* ed. J. P. Mayer (New York: HarperPerennial, 1969), 520.

6. Lee Rainie, Kristen Purcell, and Aaron Smith, "The Social Side of the Internet," Pew Research Center, January 18, 2011, http://pewinternet.org/Reports/2011/The-Social-Side-of-the-Internet/Section-1/Overview.aspx.

7. Anthony J. Nownes, *Interest Groups in American Politics: Pressure and Power* (New York: Routledge, 2013).

8. Peggy Kerns, "Lobbying: A Big Business and Growing," National Conference of State Legislatures, January 2009, www.ncsl.org/legislatures-elections/ethicshome/lobbying-a-big-business-and-growing.aspx. See also Peggy Kerns, "States Identify Lobbyists," National Conference of State Legislatures, October 2010, www.ncsl.org/legislatures-elections/ethicshome/states-identify-lobbyists.aspx.

9. Anthony J. Nownes, "Interest Groups and State Politics," in *Guide to Interest Groups and Lobbying in the United States,* ed. Burdett A. Loomis, with Peter L. Francia and Dara Z. Strolovitch (Washington, DC: CQ Press, 2012), 445–455.

10. Charles E. Lindblom, *Politics and Markets: The World's Political Economic Systems* (New York: Basic Books, 1977).

11. New Jersey Chamber of Commerce, "Advocacy: Government Relations," www.njchamber.com/index.php/about-the-nj-chamber-of-commerce/advocacy.

12. Anthony J. Nownes, Clive S. Thomas, and Ronald J. Hrebenar, "Interest Groups in the States," in *Politics in the American States: A Comparative Analysis,* 9th ed., Virginia Gray and Russell L. Hanson, eds. (Washington, DC: CQ Press, 2008), 117.

13. Bureau of Labor Statistics, "Table 1. Union Affiliation of Employed Wage and Salary Workers by Selected Characteristics," January 23, 2013, www.bls.gov/news.release/union2.t01.htm.

14. Steven Greenhouse, "Union Membership in U.S. Fell to 70-Year Low Last Year," *New York Times,* January 21, 2011, www.nytimes.com/2011/01/22/business/22union.html.

15. Bureau of Labor Statistics, "Union Members Summary." Additional state union membership statistics also come from this source.

16. William Moore, "The Determinants and Effects of Right-to-Work Laws: A Review of the Recent Literature," *Journal of Labor Research* 19 (1998): 445–469. See also Morris M. Kleiner, "Intensity of Management Resistance: Understanding the Decline of Unionization in the Private Sector," *Journal of Labor Research* 22 (2001): 519–540; and John Godard, "The Exceptional Decline of the American Labor Movement," *Industrial and Labor Relations Review* 63 (2009): 82–108.

17. Lilly Rockwell, "Legal Protections for Nursing Homes Advance," *Sunshine State News,* April 2, 2011, www.sunshinestatenews.com/story/legal-protections-nursing-homes-advance.

18. Christopher M. Witko, "Professional Associations," in *Guide to Interest Groups and Lobbying,* ed. Burdett A. Loomis, 271–282.

19. Alan Rosenthal, *The Third House: Lobbyists and Lobbying in the States* (Washington, DC: CQ Press, 1993).

20. "About the League," North Carolina League of Municipalities, www.nclm.org/about/Pages/default.aspx.

21. Nownes, Thomas, and Hrebenar, "Interest Groups in the States."

22. See *Citizens United v. Federal Election Commission* (2010) and *SpeechNow.org v. Federal Election Commission* (2010).

23. Andy Kroll, "The Super-PAC Steamroller: Coming to a Town Near You!" *Mother Jones,* April 25, 2012, www.motherjones.com/politics/2012/04/super-pac-state-local-james-bopp.

24. Diana Evans, "Oil PACs and Aggressive Campaign Strategies," *Journal of Politics* 50 (1988), 1050.

25. Quoted in Peggy Kerns, "The Influence Business," National Conference of State Legislatures, January 2009, www.ncsl.org/Portals/1/Documents/magazine/articles/2009/09sljan09_lobby.pdf.

26. Rosenthal, *The Third House: Lobbyists and Lobbying in the States.*

27. Thomas and Hrebenar, "Interest Groups in the States," 142.

28. Bill McAllister, "Cindy Cashen: Still MADD, but Less Naïve," *Juneau Empire,* December 7, 2001, http://juneauempire.com/stories/120701/Loc_cashen.shtml.

29. See Planned Parenthood of Maryland, www.plannedparenthood.org/maryland/action-network-28629.htm.

30. The term *sock puppet group* is used, for example, by the Center for Responsible Lending, www.responsiblelending.org/media-center/center-for-straight-answers/astroturf-group-alert.html.

31. For a lengthy discussion on the effects of interest group contributions on congressional roll-call votes, see Frank R. Baumgartner and Beth Leech, *Basic Interests: The Importance of Groups in Politics and in Political Science* (Princeton, NJ: Princeton University Press, 1998), 13–17. See also Richard A. Smith, "Interest Group Influence in the U.S. Congress," *Legislative Studies Quarterly* 20 (1995), 91–97. For another excellent discussion on the issue, see John R. Wright, *Interest Groups and Congress: Lobbying, Contributions, and Influence* (New York: Longman, 2003), 136–149.

32. Richard L. Hall and Frank W. Wayman, "Buying Time: Moneyed Interests and the Mobilization of Bias in Congressional Subcommittees," *American Political Science Review* 84 (1990): 797–820.

33. Stacy B. Gordon, "All Votes Are Not Created Equal: Campaign Contributions and Critical Votes," *Journal of Politics* 63 (2001): 249–269.

34. Hall and Wayman, "Buying Time."

35. Lynda W. Powell, *The Influence of Campaign Contributions in State Legislatures: The Effects of Institutions and Politics* (Ann Arbor: University of Michigan Press, 2012).

SUGGESTED READING

Ainsworth, Scott H. *Analyzing Interest Groups: Group Influence on People and Policies.* New York: Norton, 2002.

Baumgartner, Frank R., Jeffrey M. Berry, Marie Hojnacki, David C. Kimball, and Beth L. Leech. *Lobbying and Policy Change: Who Wins, Who Loses, and Why.* Chicago: University of Chicago Press, 2009.

Baumgartner, Frank R., and Beth Leech. *Basic Interests: The Importance of Groups in Politics and in Political Science.* Princeton, NJ: Princeton University Press, 1998.

Berry, Jeffrey M. *The New Liberalism: The Rising Power of Citizen Groups.* Washington, DC: Brookings, 1999.

Berry, Jeffrey M., and Clyde Wilcox. *The Interest Group Society,* 5th ed. New York: Pearson-Longman, 2009.

Cigler, Allan J., and Burdett A. Loomis, eds. *Interest Group Politics,* 8th ed. Washington, DC: CQ Press, 2012.

Francia, Peter L. "Organized Interests: Evolution and Influence." In *The Oxford Handbook of American Elections and Political Behavior,* ed. Jan E. Leighley. New York: Oxford University Press, 2010.

Gray, Virginia, and David Lowery. *The Population Ecology of Interest Representation: Lobbying Communities in the American States.* Ann Arbor: University of Michigan Press, 1996.

Hrebenar, Ronald J. *Interest Group Politics in America,* 3rd ed. Armonk, NY: M. E. Sharpe, 1997.

Nownes, Anthony J. *Interest Groups in American Politics: Pressure and Power.* New York: Routledge, 2013.

———. "Interest Groups and State Politics." In *Interest Groups and Lobbying in the United States,* ed. Burdett A. Loomis, with Peter L. Francia and Dara Z. Strolovitch. Washington, DC: CQ Press, 2012.

Nownes, Anthony J., Clive S. Thomas, and Ronald J. Hrebenar. "Interest Groups in the States." In *Politics in the American States: A Comparative Analysis,* 9th ed., Virginia Gray and Russell L. Hanson, eds. Washington, DC: CQ Press, 2008.

Powell, Lynda W. *The Influence of Campaign Contributions in State Legislatures: The Effects of Institutions and Politics.* Ann Arbor: University of Michigan Press, 2012.

Rosenthal, Alan. *The Third House: Lobbyists and Lobbying in the States,* 2nd ed. Washington, DC: CQ Press, 2001.

Rozell, Mark J., Clyde Wilcox, and Michael M. Franz. *Interest Groups in American Campaigns: The New Face of Electioneering,* 3rd ed. New York: Oxford University Press, 2012.

Thompson, Joel A., and Gary F. Moncrief, eds. *Campaign Finance in State Legislative Elections.* Washington, DC: CQ Press, 1998.

Chapter 11

Regulating Interest Groups in the States

Christopher Witko

U.S. Constitutional guarantees of free association and the right to petition government ensure that organized interests will attempt to influence policy. Skeptical citizens, concerned that these "special interests" will use their resources to dominate government, undermine democracy, and push policies away from the common good, have led calls to place limits on interest group activities. In response, the states have enacted a variety of different laws limiting the conduct of organized interests. This chapter discusses these different types of interest group regulation, the determinants of their enactment, the effects these laws have on political and policy outcomes, and how federalism affects state regulation.

There is a deep tension in American thought regarding interest groups. Some thinkers have viewed them as an important means of promoting democracy and liberty, while others have viewed them as a threat to these values. James Madison argued that competition among competing factions—what we might call interest group conflict today—was essential to prevent tyranny of the majority. Later, many pluralist scholars writing in the post–World War II period argued that interest groups allowed democracy to persist in a large, modern country, albeit in a form quite different from the Jeffersonian ideal. But even as the pluralists were lauding "interest group democracy," critics such as E. E. Schattschneider were concerned that organized interests stymie the popular will as often as they advance it. Both of these perspectives have influenced the formation of interest group regulation at the state level, which acknowledges the importance of organized interests in our politics but seeks to place some limits on the activities of interest groups. These state regulations are also constrained by state and federal constitutional provisions.

TYPES OF STATE INTEREST GROUP REGULATION

Clive Thomas identifies three rationales for interest group regulation: the need to restore/maintain confidence in government; the need to prevent undue influence by wealthy interests; and the need to provide information about government activities to the public and media to aid in democratic decision making.[1] All states use some combination of requiring disclosure and actual prohibitions on certain group activities, but there is extensive variation in the stringency of these regulations. This chapter begins by discussing regulations that most directly affect organizations, along with some of the variation in their stringency across the states.

Lobbying and Ethics Laws

Lobbying laws regulate the practice of lobbying and place restrictions on the behavior of lobbyists and government officials, and regulate their interactions. (See also Chapter 17 for legislative ethics regulation.) Adam J. Newmark writes that "lobbying regulations are designed to curtail outright bribery and vote-buying but also to reduce the appearance of impropriety that reduces public trust in government." By the 1950s, thirty-eight states had some form of lobbying regulation, though the laws were lax by today's standards. The least invasive form of lobbying regulation simply requires organizations/individuals to register to lobby, though these laws are fairly easy to evade due to the difficulty of legally defining "lobbying." Other provisions of lobbying laws restrict the time, place, and manner of lobbying.[2]

Scholars have designed measures to systematically explore variation in lobbying laws across states, and it is significant. Cynthia Opheim first systematically measured the variation in lobbying regulations across states. Newmark created a measure and examined changes in regulation from 1990 to 2003. With a potential range of 0 to 18 on Newmark's measure, states ranged from 1 to 17. He finds that, though a handful of states have made their laws less stringent over time, most have increased stringency.[3] There are numerous dimensions along which state regulations vary. For example, states differ dramatically in terms of how they define the term *lobbyist,* with some states using a very broad definition and other states requiring many fewer types of individuals and interests to register as lobbyists. Some states place strict limits on lobbyist spending for entertaining legislators, while other states have fewer restrictions. States also regulate the relationships between lobbyists and executive branch officials, but there is little research into restrictions on lobbying governors, other elected or appointed executive branch officials, their staffs, or the bureaucracy.

Ethics laws "address potential conflicts between officials' private interests and their public duties."[4] The distinction between ethics and lobbying laws is not entirely clear, and sometimes they are used interchangeably. Yet ethics laws typically proscribe the behavior of public officials more directly than interest groups by, for example, limiting the types of gifts that officials can receive and requiring the disclosure of financial interests in private businesses or professions. The primary intention of ethics laws is to minimize, or at least publicize, the extent to which official decisions benefit the personal financial interests of government officials. Given that organized interests have often used gifts or payments to win favor, these laws also indirectly restrict organized interest behavior.

Campaign Finance Laws

Lobbying laws regulate interactions between interests and politicians after they are elected, and campaign finance laws regulate their interactions during campaigns. Campaign finance regulation generally refers to provisions of state law that (1) regulate candidate spending; (2) regulate the sources and amounts of contributions to candidates; and, in states with some public financing, (3) explain the mechanisms and manner of the public financing of elections. Like lobbying laws, there are both limits on behavior and disclosure requirements. Similarly, these laws are also intended to prevent actual corruption or the perception of corruption. In fact, the U.S. Supreme Court has largely justified the legality of limits on campaign donations with reference to preventing the appearance of corruption.[5] In some states there also appears to be a desire to make elections more competitive. Campaign finance has been widely regulated since the Progressive Era, but the post-Watergate era led to an explosion of campaign finance policy experimentation that continues to this day.

There is also tremendous variation across the states in terms of campaign finance laws, though again, the general trend has been one of increasing stringency over time. Unlike lobbying, which is clearly guaranteed in the Constitution, whether organized interests have a guaranteed "right" to donate money to politicians at all is contentious. The Supreme Court has equated political spending with free speech (*Buckley v. Valeo* [1976]), and therefore attempts to completely ban private contributions to candidates for office are illegal.

Nevertheless, though few states place aggregate limits on total organized interest campaign expenditures, most states do limit the amount of money that different types of organized interests can contribute to individual politicians. In some states, however, these limits are so high and riddled with loopholes that the amount of money that can be contributed to politicians is essentially unlimited. Similarly, while all states require some disclosure of campaign contributions, in many states the disclosure is not timely enough for media or opposing candidates to expose questionable finances during an election campaign, undermining these laws. As is true with lobbying laws, there is tremendous variation in campaign finance regulation across the states. Examining laws for the presence of twenty-two provisions, Christopher Witko found that states ranged from three to twenty.[6] There has been little research into the regulation of independent expenditures in the states, even though these expenditures are becoming increasingly important. Given Supreme Court rulings equating spending with free speech, there are likely to be serious limits on the extent to which states can restrict independent expenditures.

Few states have any public financing of election campaigns, which are generally intended to make elections more competitive. Minnesota and Wisconsin pioneered the use of public funding decades ago, but these early financing mechanisms have not kept pace with the ever-increasing amounts required for effective campaigns. A handful of states have gone very far toward complete public financing of elections with so-called clean election laws. These laws typically require candidates to raise small amounts of money from many donors, and once this threshold is met they receive public money in exchange for agreeing to abide by expenditure limits. The U.S. Supreme Court has consistently ruled that laws cannot compel candidates to participate in these types of financing plans, but by making participation in the funding system attractive to candidates, states can encourage them to voluntarily participate. Only a few states have passed clean election laws and spending limits, however, and there is variation in the content of these laws. Arizona, Connecticut, Maine, New Jersey, New Mexico, North Carolina, and Vermont have enacted some form of clean election law.[7]

Sunshine Laws

Campaign finance disclosure laws are intended to provide information regarding campaigns to the public and media. Sunshine laws have a similar goal. The term refers to regulations requiring that government business be conducted in an open, public manner and that records of decision making are made available to the public. It is most often applied to

Iowa governor Chet Culver signs a proclamation declaring March 11–17 to be Sunshine Week in Iowa, March 12, 2007, at the capitol in Des Moines, Iowa. Looking on is Carol Riha, chief of bureau for The Associated Press in Iowa. Sunshine Week is a national effort by journalists and concerned citizens to promote open government. The proclamation, submitted by The Associated Press, seeks to "educate all Americans about the importance of preserving our constitutionally guaranteed freedom of the press."

SOURCE: AP Photo/Steve Pope.

open-meeting/records or laws like the federal Freedom of Information Act (FOIA), and this is how the term is used in this chapter. Though intended to directly affect the behavior of public officials, these laws regulate the interactions of politicians and organized interests. The logic behind these laws is that, as Chief Justice Louis Brandeis famously stated, public exposure will prevent the corruption that concerned Progressives like himself.[8] Most states enacted these laws by the late 1970s.

Open meetings laws require advance public announcement and access by members of the public and media to legislative deliberations, such as committee hearings or floor debates. FOIA laws require the government to provide government documents to citizens. Given their role in the democratic process, legislatures are the most open institutions in government. By their nature, court deliberations are not automatically subject to the same level of public access. The executive branch, particularly in the gubernatorial deliberation process, falls somewhere in between, as governors can often credibly claim executive privilege for their communications with interest group leaders, though what exactly should be protected by executive privilege or open to the public is often controversial.

There are few studies of sunshine laws, but there may be greater uniformity across the states in this area of regulation, since they are less controversial than campaign finance or lobbying restrictions. One legal scholar notes, however, that while sunshine laws are widespread, they are also riddled with loopholes. Furthermore, these laws have failed to keep pace with new technologies. For example, states are grappling with how to handle e-mail or text messages, which did not even exist when state sunshine laws were originally enacted.[9]

The Tax Code

Sunshine laws that affect state interest groups are adopted at the state level, but both federal and state tax laws can influence the political activities of organized interests in the states. The tax code is not something that immediately comes to mind when considering the regulation of interest groups, but it has important implications for them. The federal tax code defines which nonprofit organizations can be considered tax exempt and places restrictions on the political activities of tax-exempt organizations. Many states use the tax-exempt determination made by the federal Internal Revenue Service (IRS) to determine state tax exemption status, and states often place restrictions on the political activities of tax-exempt organizations. If these organizations violate these prohibitions, they risk losing their tax-exempt status.

Furthermore, some federal prohibitions on political activities also apply to state and local political action. According to federal law, tax-exempt nonprofit organizations cannot advocate for any candidate for office at the federal, state, or local level. Prohibitions on lobbying for tax-exempt organizations are more complex and rely on technical interpretations of the term *lobbying* and the extent of an organization's involvement in lobbying activities. Tax-exempt nonprofit organizations can engage in lobbying if it does not comprise a "substantial portion" of their activities. In addition, lobbying is narrowly defined by the IRS as attempts to influence specific pieces of legislation in a legislative body. Nevertheless, the tax code does place some restrictions on the political behavior of nonprofit organizations.[10]

To conclude the discussion of the state regulation of interest groups, it is important to note that rigorous state regulation of one of these areas does not automatically imply stringent regulation in another area. Many states that have stringent campaign finance regulation do not have stringent lobbying regulation, and vice versa. Indeed, the correlation between Witko's campaign finance stringency index and Newmark's lobbying stringency index is a mere 0.11. The values on these indices for each state can be seen in Table 11.1.

TABLE 11.1 **State Lobbying and Campaign Finance Regulation Stringency**

State	Lobbying, 2003 (0–18)	Campaign finance, 2002 (0–22)	State	Lobbying, 2003 (0–18)	Campaign finance, 2002 (0–22)
Alabama	10	4	Montana	11	11
Alaska	15	11	Nebraska	8	7
Arizona	6	20	Nevada	10	11
Arkansas	9	14	New Hampshire	8	12
California	14	9	New Jersey	12	12
Colorado	13	13	New Mexico	8	9
Connecticut	13	12	New York	13	11
Delaware	8	9	North Carolina	6	13
Florida	11	13	North Dakota	1	6
Georgia	8	3	Ohio	11	16
Hawaii	12	14	Oklahoma	6	12
Idaho	10	13	Oregon	11	8
Illinois	6	4	Pennsylvania	10	10
Indiana	8	8	Rhode Island	10	16
Iowa	9	10	South Carolina	17	8
Kansas	10	10	South Dakota	7	8
Kentucky	14	14	Tennessee	9	9
Louisiana	9	12	Texas	15	4
Maine	15	12	Utah	13	9
Maryland	13	9	Vermont	11	9
Massachusetts	11	15	Virginia	6	7
Michigan	13	15	Washington	15	11
Minnesota	11	16	West Virginia	9	12
Mississippi	12	3	Wisconsin	13	17
Missouri	12	8	Wyoming	5	12

NOTE: These indices measure the stringency of state lobbying and campaign finance regulation, with higher values indicating more stringent laws. Newmark's lobbying index examines state laws for the presence of eighteen provisions, and Witko's campaign finance index does the same for twenty-two provisions of state campaign finance law. Both indices assign one point for each provision. Full details of the construction and properties of these indices can be found in Adam J. Newmark, "Measuring State Legislative Lobbying Regulation, 1990–2003," *State Politics and Policy Quarterly* 5 (2005): 182; Christopher Witko, "Measuring the Stringency of State Campaign Finance Regulation," *State Politics and Policy Quarterly* 5 (2005): 295–310.

SOURCES OF VARIATION IN INTEREST GROUP REGULATION ACROSS STATES

Interest group regulations are designed to curtail interest group influence, but they also often directly or incidentally regulate the behavior of politicians. For example, campaign finance laws require both interest groups and politicians to report their campaign financial transactions. Few people would choose to increase regulation of their own activities, and generally incumbents who have been successful under current regulations are hesitant to dramatically alter them.[11] Therefore, an interesting puzzle lies at the heart of understanding variation in interest group regulation: If all states regulate interest groups, and some states do so rather vigorously, why would politicians choose to regulate interest group conduct at all?

In part, this reflects that even very similar laws can affect politicians differently across different states and institutions, which affects their willingness to enact such laws. In other words, political self-interest calculations vary across states. For instance, where elections are less expensive, there is less resistance to enacting stringent campaign finance regulations. In addition, direct democracy, which allows the public and citizens groups to circumvent elected officials altogether, is important in the formation of interest group populations and, ultimately, interest group regulation.[12] Despite the differences between interest group regulation and other types of policy, the "usual suspects" in the policy determinants literature also shape interest group regulation: scandal, ideology/partisanship, political culture, and interest groups themselves.

Overcoming Resistance to Regulate: Scandals and Direct Democracy

Beth Rosenson argues that an agenda-setting model of policymaking explains the enactment of policies that contradict politicians' immediate self-interest. The public generally favors more restrictions on interest groups, but this issue is seldom very salient. Scandals can be important "focusing events" that shift public attention toward interest group regulation. There are several examples of major reforms following highly publicized scandals, and systematic studies show an association between scandals and the subsequent adoption of more stringent regulations.[13] In one case, following a federal investigation that uncovered serious ethical lapses in the dealings between legislators and lobbyists, South Carolina made its laws a great deal stricter.

While scandals can force politicians to overcome their reluctance to regulate their own behavior, direct democracy allows the public to enact policies by completely circumventing elected officials. In some states there are active good government groups that are focused on political reforms, and these groups have sometimes used the initiative to enact sweeping reforms. Direct democracy can potentially better align policy with public preferences any time the policy status quo favored by politicians differs substantially from that preferred by the public, and this is often the case with interest group regulations. Studies indicate that states with direct democracy are more likely to enact stringent campaign finance laws, and all of the states that have passed clean election laws have done so via the initiative, except Connecticut and Vermont. The effect of direct democracy on other types of interest group regulation has not been as systematically examined, but there are many examples of states passing other types of laws regulating interest groups via the initiative.[14]

"Normal" Policy Determinants

As is the case in other policy areas, the usual factors that influence state policy also influence interest group regulation. Daniel Elazar's conception of state political culture as moralistic, individualistic, or traditionalistic has fallen out of favor as an explanation of state policy outputs, but the states that Elazar categorized as moralistic appear to have more restrictive laws. For example, the moralistic states of Minnesota and Wisconsin were among the first to experiment with public financing of elections, and they currently have relatively stringent lobbying and campaign finance laws. Research shows that individualistic or traditionalistic states were less likely to adopt independent legislative ethics commissions in recent decades, but studies have not found the same effect on campaign finance reform.

A traditionalistic or individualistic culture is no guarantee of lax regulation. Following an infamous lobbying scandal in the early 1990s, South Carolina, a traditionalistic state, enacted some of the strictest lobbying laws in the country, but its campaign finance laws have remained weak (see "Operation Lost Trust" and Lobbying Reform in South Carolina box). In general, the traditionalistic states in the South have less stringent interest group regulation, which is what one would expect in states that have less of a desire to curtail the power of wealthy interests.[15]

In addition to political culture, state partisanship and ideology are common determinants of many types of laws; this also appears true for some types of laws regulating interest group behavior. One of the defining features of modern liberalism is a greater willingness to use government to address social problems, including the perceived problem of political inequality arising from the dominance of representative processes by organized interests. Since the American parties currently correspond largely with these ideological divisions (i.e., the Democrats are more liberal than the Republicans in all states), this means that in general politicians from the Democratic Party will be more supportive of restrictions on the behavior of interest groups. Since politicians of both parties and ideologies are often hesitant to enact restrictions on interest group behavior out of a concern for their own self-interest, however, the differences between liberal/Democratic and conservative/Republican states in this policy area may be more muted than in many other policy realms. Nevertheless, some studies find that liberal states are more likely to adopt stringent campaign finance regulations.[16]

As is true with other policies, organized interests also shape their own regulation. Though business interests are the most numerous organized interests, individual corporations generally have little incentive to expend their scarce resources on a "public good" by lobbying against regulations that will affect all organizations. Therefore, lobbying on such laws is dominated by ideological organized interests

"OPERATION LOST TRUST" AND LOBBYING REFORM IN SOUTH CAROLINA

In 1990 the FBI concluded "Operation Lost Trust" in South Carolina, which has been called the largest public corruption investigation in U.S. history. This investigation revealed the use of a widespread culture of questionable ethics and cash bribes from lobbyists in exchange for legislative favors. Several members of the legislature and a number of lobbyists ended up in prison as a result of the investigation. Following this scandal the state enacted tough new laws preventing lobbyists from giving gifts to legislatures. South Carolina is a traditionalistic state, with historically some of the weakest interest group regulations. Following this scandal, the state moved from having some of the least restrictive to some of the most restrictive lobbying laws, with both stringent limits on behavior and severe penalties for violating the law. It is now known as one of three "no cup of coffee states" (along with Massachusetts and Wisconsin) because legislators cannot even accept something of the value of a cup of coffee from lobbyists.

South Carolina may be an object lesson in the limits of interest group regulation and the ability of organized interests to circumvent laws, however. Though lobbyists can no longer buy legislators a cup of coffee, companies can apparently hire legislators to work for them directly. In the spring of 2012 Gov. Nikki Haley came under fire for lobbying a state agency on behalf of a company that hired her as an employee while she was serving as a state legislator—a practice that is widespread in the state, according to some observers. A current state legislator is alleged to have earned $160,000 from the South Carolina Association of Realtors and has sponsored a number of pieces of legislation desired by the group. Watchdogs are recommending another round of regulatory reform, and others are suggesting raising legislative pay from the approximately $22,000 so that legislators do not need to earn extra money with outside employment.

SOURCES: Schuyler Kropf, "Lost Trust Shook State 20 Years Ago," *Charleston Post and Courier*, July 5, 2010; Ginger Sampson and Peggy Kearns, "Gift Restrictions Laws for Legislators: It's Not a Physics Lesson," Eye on Ethics: Briefing Papers on Important Ethics Issues, National Conference of State Legislatures, June/July 2002, www.ncsl.org/legislatures-elections/ethicshome/ncsl-eye-on-ethics254.aspx; Adam J. Newmark, "Measuring State Legislative Lobbying Regulation, 1990–2003," *State Politics and Policy Quarterly* 5 (2005): 182; Renee Dudley, "Watchdogs Urge Scrutiny of SC Lawmakers' Business Ties," *Charleston Post and Courier*, June 11, 2012.

and associations representing numerous businesses, though individual corporations do sometimes lobby on these matters. As noted, good government groups, such as the League of Women Voters, also play a critical role in debates over interest group regulation, and statistical analyses indicate that states with stronger good government groups were more likely to adopt stringent campaign finance regulation in recent years.[17]

Finally, both horizontal and vertical diffusion can play an important role in the enactment of interest group regulation. Some scholars argue that a high-profile reform in neighboring states serves to set the agenda for reform; if a neighboring state adopts an independent ethics commission, then a state is more likely to adopt one, though studies are not consistent on this point. Following the federal campaign finance laws of the 1970s, many states enacted similar campaign finance laws, indicating that vertical diffusion may also take place in this policy area.[18]

CONSEQUENCES OF INTEREST GROUP REGULATION

The participants in policy debates over campaign finance tend to portray these conflicts as battles between good and evil. Good government groups think that the status quo breeds corruption and public cynicism, while opponents of regulation argue that reforms are a dire threat to liberty. In practice the effects of regulation on process, electoral, and policy outcomes are relatively unknown. Thomas noted three rationales for interest group regulation, and thus it is useful to ask whether interest group regulations accomplish these goals—preserving confidence and trust in government, preventing undue influence by wealthy interests, and making more information about government activities available to the public and media to aid in the decision making required in a democracy. Surprisingly, there are relatively few studies of the effects of interest group regulation, and they have focused mostly on campaign finance laws. Some of these studies are discussed here. Before turning to this research it is important to note that there are inherent limitations on the effect that regulations likely to pass constitutional muster can have on the status quo. One criticism of laws regulating interest groups is that precisely because they are usually resisted by politicians, they are largely symbolic even when they are enacted. The penalties for violating lobbying or campaign finance laws are almost always very light, and even if these laws are relatively stringent the agencies designed to enforce them are typically denied the resources to adequately do so. Even in states where reforms are passed via initiative, politicians often make decisions about agency resources.[19]

A more fundamental critique of regulating organized interests is that, due to the tremendous economic inequalities among different societal interests, these laws can have a very limited effect on political and policy outcomes. The right of organized political interests to form and lobby government is enshrined in the First Amendment to the U.S. Constitution, and no regulation can alter this fact. Thus, regardless of what restrictions are placed on lobbying, it will always be the case that wealthy interests will have more lobbyists. Within the campaign finance realms, some states have sought basically to remove private money from elections; but even assuming these laws withstand legal scrutiny in the coming years, they may ultimately do little to remove the money of wealthy interests from elections because there are countless different ways of spending money to influence elections. If one channel of influence is closed off, organized interests will find another. In the campaign finance literature this is known as the "hydraulic theory" of money because money, like water, will find its way into the system elsewhere. And research supports this view. Robert E. Hogan finds that in states with strict contribution limits, organized interests do contribute less money to candidates for office, but this leads them to increase expenditures on other forms of electioneering.[20] This does not mean that interest group regulation is irrelevant, but rather that the effects are likely to be relatively subtle.

Interest Group Regulation and Trust and Confidence in Government

The need to maintain or increase confidence in government is an important rationale for regulating interest group behavior. Scandals make it more likely that states will adopt laws regulating interest group behavior, suggesting that politicians believe that interest group regulation will restore confidence in government. And the Supreme Court has upheld the legality of interest group regulations with reference to this goal. Despite this apparently widespread belief, there is very little research examining this question at the state (or federal) level.

Research shows that strict campaign finance laws have an inconsistent effect on citizen efficacy, with some types of laws increasing efficacy and, puzzlingly, other types reducing it. Research shows that journalists in states with more stringent campaign finance laws perceive politics to be more, not less, corrupt. Public opinion scholars who study trust in government nationally seldom include variables measuring interest group regulation over time, which indicates that it is not viewed as a major determinant of trust in government. However, Marc J. Hetherington and Thomas J. Rudolph find that political scandals do reduce citizens' trust in government.[21] Thus, if regulation reduces scandal, there may be an indirect effect of regulation on trust in government. Unfortunately, there is little or no research into the question of whether stringent regulation actually reduces scandals.

Limiting the Influence of Wealthy Interests

One hope of reformers who urge the passage of laws regulating interest groups is that they will limit the ability of special interests to have "undue" influence in the policy process. Organized interests can shape policy either by influencing elections or by lobbying decision makers once they are in office (and, of course, many interests seek to do both). Thus the relevant questions are (1) What effect does interest group regulation have on the capacity of different organized interests? and (2) What effect does regulation have on the ability to influence policy or election outcomes?

Regulation and the Influence of Wealthy Interests in the Policy Process

Campaign finance regulation might influence the effectiveness of organized interest lobbying, since campaign contributions are typically used to gain access to important decision makers. Lobby regulation might potentially change the mix of interests represented in the lobbying community, or might change lobbyist-legislator interactions so that lobbying appeals are less successful. The most comprehensive studies make it appear that laws requiring interest groups to register in order to lobby have little effect on the size or composition of interest group communities, however. But there is some tentative evidence that more stringent lobby regulations do reduce the power of interest groups, since research shows that in states with more stringent lobbying regulations, state legislators perceive that interest groups are less powerful.[22] Research examining more direct rather than perceptual measures of group influence would be useful to provide more evidence on this question.

If lobbying by interest groups were less successful, this could lead to more responsiveness to the mass public. John Matsusaka examines the congruence between public opinion and policy on ten highly salient issues and finds that campaign finance laws did not have any significant effect on opinion-policy congruence, but Patrick Flavin finds that states with more stringent campaign finance regulation have less of a policy bias toward high social status groups. Furthermore, to the extent that campaign contribution limits reduce contributions from business, it seems that they would also likely reduce the influence of business in the policy process.[23]

Regulation and the Influence of Wealthy Interests in Elections

Campaign finance laws are obviously the most relevant type of regulation for election outcomes. Specifically, campaign finance laws might affect the ability of different candidates to fund-raise and may therefore result in different types of politicians being elected. They might also affect the ability of challengers to compete with incumbents. One criticism of a deregulated campaign finance system is that it protects incumbents who have succeeded in the current system and therefore preserves a bias in favor of the status quo, keeping new ideas out of the system and protecting entrenched interests. Thus it is thought that competitive elections and winning challengers are important to ensure democratic responsiveness. A number of studies thus assess how campaign finance laws affect the competitiveness of elections.

Campaign finance regulations can affect both the initial decision to run and the ability of challengers to make races competitive. Reformers often argue that relatively unregulated systems dissuade potentially good public servants from running because of the need to raise large amounts of money. They are also concerned that the need to raise large amounts of money prevents candidates from advocating for policies unpopular with wealthy interests. There has been little or no research done on the second question, but some studies find that more stringent campaign contribution limits and public financing of elections result in increased odds of incumbents facing a major-party challenger. Research on how laws may affect the ideology, quality of challengers, and other candidate attributes is needed.

Other studies have looked at how campaign finance laws affect the competitiveness of elections. While reformers often argue that more stringent regulation will make elections more competitive, critics point out that spending limits can make it harder for challengers to match the name recognition that incumbents enjoy, reducing competitiveness. Research is highly mixed on which of these views are accurate. Some studies find that candidate spending limits reduces the competitiveness of campaigns. Studies of campaign contribution limits indicate that they either have no effect on competitiveness or increase competitiveness. Interestingly, Thomas Stratmann and Francisco J. Castillo-Aparicio find that contribution limits have less of an effect on the margins for incumbents who actually participated in passing the limits, indicating that legislators certainly consider their own electoral self-interest when crafting such laws.[24]

Effect on the Amount of Information Available to the Public and Media

Finally, some regulations are intended to increase the amount of information available to the media, public, and electoral challengers. On this dimension there can be little doubt that these laws have been effective. The sources of campaign funding and lobbying activity are much more widely documented and known than in decades past, and this information is routinely used by journalists, good government groups, and candidates. Even prosecutors can use this information, as when campaign finance records at both the federal and state level were used to convict former U.S. House member Tom Delay, R-Texas, of money laundering. It is interesting to note that disclosure requirements were the type of campaign finance law that Flavin found to enhance the equality of representation.[25]

Nevertheless, there are many limits to disclosure laws. As already noted, many states do not require timely disclosure of campaign contributing and lobbying activities to ensure that voters have adequate information to evaluate candidates during a particular election campaign or policy debate. In addition, as is true with any other law, it is possible to circumvent disclosure laws with enough creativity. For instance, certain categories of tax-exempt groups are not required to disclose their donors, and some of these groups can legally produce issue advertisements—a practice that allows wealthy donors to circumvent campaign finance laws.

Overall, there are relatively few published studies examining the effects of interest group regulation on important outcomes, and most of these studies focus on the effects of campaign finance laws. Based on these studies it does seem that, on balance, more stringent regulation somewhat reduces the power of wealthy interests in the policy process and leads to more competitive elections. The findings are clearly inconsistent, however. Thus more study of how regulations affect these types of outcomes is needed. In addition, almost all of the studies examine outcomes within the past two decades. While this is understandable for data availability reasons, this approach limits variation in the key independent variables of interest since all states now have some laws regulating lobbying and campaign finance. To understand what politics would be like in a largely unregulated environment (which some critics prefer), historical studies that cover a longer time period at the state level would be needed.

FEDERALISM AND STATE INTEREST GROUP REGULATION

The very federal structure that makes state politics and the state-level regulation of interest groups meaningful creates interdependencies between the federal and state interest group regulatory regimes. States have the authority to make laws pertaining to their own elections and political processes, but the basic rights and liberties guaranteed by the U.S. Constitution must be observed by the states, meaning that federal court interpretations of the constitutionality of state regulations are a critical constraint on state policymakers. In addition, politicians active in one jurisdiction or level of government sometimes exploit weaknesses or loopholes in laws in another jurisdiction or level of government to achieve their political goals. Thus, like other policy realms, the regulation of interest groups is "federalized."

Sen. Geoffrey Gratwick, D-Maine, center, speaks at a Maine Citizens for Clean Elections rally in Augusta, Maine, on January 22, 2013. Dozens of activists called on legislators to make Maine the latest state to formally endorse a U.S. constitutional amendment they say will keep special interests from having an excessive impact on elections.

SOURCE: AP Photo/Glenn Adams.

U.S. Supreme Court Decisions and State Regulation

While laws limiting the activities of organized interests have existed at the federal level for decades, federal courts also have a history of being skeptical of attempts to regulate interest group conduct. In recent years, Supreme Court decisions on state campaign finance laws have been very controversial. The Court's equating of money and speech in the 1970s has placed fundamental limits on state and federal campaign finance schemes. Stating precisely what those limits are is an extremely difficult task, however, because of the evolving nature of decisions in this area of law. The Supreme Court has generally upheld the legality of campaign contribution limits and disclosure requirements. Laws limiting expenditures by candidates have generally been ruled unconstitutional, which is why most states have contribution limits and disclosure requirements, but fewer states have any types of spending limits. In recent years the Supreme Court has been increasingly skeptical of any regulation of campaign finance, and this has important implications for state laws.

The current U.S. Supreme Court seems to be revisiting what was thought to be settled law in the campaign finance realm. Clean election laws, the most comprehensive attempts to alter campaign finance laws in several decades, have not been looked upon favorably by the Court. For instance, provisions of the laws in both Arizona and Vermont have been ruled unconstitutional (see Federal Courts and State Campaign Finance Laws box). One of the most controversial Supreme Court decisions of recent years, *Citizens United v. Federal Election Commission* (2010), has significant implications for state campaign finance laws as well.[26] A number of states have laws often dating back to the Progressive Era preventing corporations and labor unions from using money from their general treasuries (as opposed to specific political action committees) on electoral or governmental activities. The decision in *Citizens United* essentially deems these laws unconstitutional limitations on free speech.

Some states have attempted to resist the implementation of these decisions. When Montana's 1912 law preventing unions and corporations from spending money from their treasuries on election campaigns was challenged, the Montana Supreme Court ruled that the precedent from *Citizens United* did not apply to state restrictions because of the unique history of corruption in Montana elections, but the U.S. Supreme Court summarily reversed the Montana court's decision based on the precedent from *Citizens United*[27] (see also Contested Definitions of Rights: Campaign Finance Reform box in Chapter 23). This represented a blow not only to Montana, but also to the twenty-two other states and the District of Columbia that had joined the suit along with Montana. *Citizens United* did not specifically apply to contributions to candidates (so states can still have laws limiting contributions from organizational general funds), but leading campaign finance experts think that the decision in *Citizens United* casts doubt on the legal justification for contribution limitations.[28] It is likely that this question will be litigated in coming years.

Venue Shopping: Strategic Politicians and Federal and State Interest Group Regulation

Actors seeking to influence politics in a federalist system have the ability to act at the level or unit of government that best allows them to accomplish their goals. Politicians and organized interests can choose to act at either the federal or state level of government, or even choose among the various states. And the regulatory differences across jurisdictions can make action in a given jurisdiction more or less attractive.

FEDERAL COURTS AND STATE CAMPAIGN FINANCE LAWS

While striking down hundred-year-old regulations of political expenditures by organized interests, the U.S. Supreme Court has limited the ability of the states to create new types of campaign finance regulation. Clean election laws, a recent attempt to fundamentally reshape the financing of elections, have been weakened significantly by U.S. Supreme Court decisions. In a decision released in the summer of 2011,[1] the Court struck down the matching provisions of Arizona's clean election law, dealing a major blow to the law's proponents. Candidates agreeing to abide by the clean election requirements must agree to spending limits in exchange for public funding, which raises problems for them if they face a self-financing wealthy challenger or privately financed challenger. Therefore, the Arizona law had a "matching" provision that permitted candidates facing privately financed candidates to receive additional money if that candidate's expenditures passed certain amounts. In a rather novel interpretation of the First Amendment to the U.S. Constitution, opponents of the law claimed that this matching fund provision had a chilling effect on their free speech because privately financed candidates would not want to spend higher amounts than the limits that triggered matching and enabled their opponents to receive matching funds. The Supreme Court agreed with this argument and struck down this provision of Arizona's clean election law as unconstitutional. The Court was careful to note that this ruling does not prevent the lump-sum payments given to candidates that are part of public financing systems. However, this decision clearly limits the attractiveness of public financing to candidates, who will rightly worry about being outspent by privately financed candidates. Parts of the Connecticut and Vermont clean elections laws have also been struck down as unconstitutional by federal courts.

SOURCES: Adam Liptak, "Justices Strike Down Arizona Campaign Finance Law," *New York Times*, June 27, 2011, www.nytimes.com/2011/06/28/us/politics/28campaign.html; Rachel Weiner, "Supreme Court's Montana Decision Strengthens Citizens United," *Washington Post*, June 25, 2012, www.washingtonpost.com/blogs/the-fix/post/supreme-courts-montana-decision-strengthens-citizens-united/2012/06/25/gJQA8Vln1V_blog.htm.

1. *Arizona Free Enterprise Club Freedom Club PAC v. Bennett*, 564 U.S._ (2011).

The area of law with the greatest flexibility is perhaps campaign finance because one does not have to be physically present in a particular location to contribute or spend money (whereas lobbying often involves face-to-face contact). The U.S. federal system allows politicians to choose among different states when establishing political committees to fund campaigns. In recent years politicians from around the country, including former New York governor George Pataki and former Arkansas governor Mike Huckabee, have established political action committees (PACs) in Virginia because of the state's lax campaign finance laws. These PACs had no relationship to Virginia politics other than being located in the state—Pataki's PAC only contributed $5,000 to one Virginia candidate in five years. Virginia was attractive because it is one of several states that does not place any limits on the amounts of money that individuals or organized interests can contribute to politicians. Thus politicians can engage in "venue shopping" due to the federalized system of regulation.[29]

State and federal politicians often have close working relationships with one another by virtue of being members of the same party or having served in the same political institution together at the state or federal level. Therefore, politicians can sometimes exploit weak interest group regulations at one level of government to achieve their goals in elections or policymaking at the other level of government. Prior to the passage in 2002 of the McCain-Feingold Act (P.L. 107–155), it was common for unregulated soft money donations to be given from federal party committees to state party committees for so-called party building activities. This money was often then used in support of federal and state candidates in close races. Thus we can see that interest group systems at either level are permeable, and that weak regulations at one level can frustrate stronger regulations at another.

CONCLUSION

Though interest groups are an important means of representation, the American public has often been skeptical of special interests. Rather than advancing democracy and preventing tyranny as a number of American thinkers from Madison to the pluralists argued, critics view organized interests as major impediments to democracy. Thus the states have sought to balance the representational role and constitutional rights of interest groups against the desire of the public to limit their power. Specifically, these regulations are generally intended to restore/maintain confidence in government, prevent undue influence by wealthy interests, and provide information about the political activities of organized interests to the public and media in order to allow the democratic process to hold groups and politicians accountable.

Naturally, politicians are somewhat reluctant to enact policies constraining their own behavior and that of their allied organized interests, or to provide detailed information about their activities. Despite this selfish motive, all states regulate the behavior of interest groups to some extent. Often these regulations are enacted by the use of direct democracy (see Chapter 6), which circumvents elected officials. But politicians will also enact meaningful regulation in response to a public outcry after scandals. And several of the factors that influence policies in other domains also influence the formation of interest group regulation (e.g., ideology, interest groups).

More research needs to be done on how these laws affect important political outcomes like public confidence in government and limiting the power of wealthy organized interests. It seems clear that more information is available to the public and media regarding interest group activity than ever before, and this is certainly a positive development. But when and how this information is used deserves further study. In terms of constraining the power of wealthy interests, on balance, research to date indicates that stringent lobbying and campaign finance laws do modestly reduce the power of wealthy interests and lead to more competitive elections. But the findings of these studies are by no means consistent, and it seems that the effect of interest group regulations on these outcomes varies considerably depending on the type and structure of the regulation in question. There is little evidence that interest group regulations restore or maintain confidence in government—which, ironically, is a major justification for these laws for the courts and reformers. There is very little research into this matter, however, and more should certainly be done.

In a federal system we must also be mindful of the fact that sometimes politicians can achieve their goals at either the state or the federal level and can even choose among different states, depending on which laws are more favorable. In addition, the power of the Supreme Court to determine what are lawful limitations on the behavior of politicians and organized interests is a constraint on some states that would prefer to go much further than federal or existing state regulation. Over the last century the regulation of interest groups has generally developed in the direction of increasing stringency. However, recent Supreme Court decisions make it fairly clear that this trend will not continue. There are often heated arguments by supporters and opponents of such regulations, and they are bound to continue. Responses to recent Supreme Court decisions again underscore these disagreements. Considering this controversy, social scientists should more systematically study the effect that interest group regulations have on important outcomes in order to better inform these debates, and to inform our theoretical understanding of how different policies shape political behavior, the representation of competing interests, elections, and policy outcomes.

NOTES

1. Clive S. Thomas, "Interest Group Regulation across the States: Rationale, Development, and Consequences," *Parliamentary Affairs* 51 (1998): 500–515.
2. Adam J. Newmark, "Measuring State Legislative Lobbying Regulation, 1990–2003," *State Politics and Policy Quarterly* 5 (2005): 182–191; Thomas, "Interest Group Regulation."
3. Newmark, "Lobbying Regulation"; Cynthia Opheim, "Explaining the Differences in State Lobby Regulation," *Western Political Quarterly* 44 (1991): 405–412.
4. Beth Rosenson, "The Costs and Benefits of Ethics Laws," *International Journal of Public Management* 8 (2005): 209–224, 229.
5. Donald A. Gross and Robert K. Goidel, *The States of Campaign Finance Reform* (Columbus: Ohio State University Press, 2003); Christopher Witko, "Measuring the Stringency of State Campaign Finance Regulation," *State Politics and Policy Quarterly* 5 (2005): 295–310; *Buckley v. Valeo,* 424 U.S. 1 (1976).
6. Witko, "Measuring the Stringency."
7. National Conference of State Legislatures, "Public Financing of Campaigns: An Overview," www.ncsl.org/legislatures-elections/elections/public-financing-of-campaigns-overview.aspx.
8. Louis D. Brandeis, *Other People's Money and How the Bankers Use It* (New York: Frederick A. Stokes, 1914).
9. Sandra F. Chance and Christina Locke, "The Government-in-the-Sunshine Law Then and Now: A Model for Implementing New Technologies Consistent with Florida's Position as a Leader in Open Government," *Florida State Law Review* 35 (2008): 245–270; Teresa D. Pupillo, "Changing Weather Forecast: Government in the Sunshine in the 1990's: An Analysis of State Sunshine Laws," *Washington University Legal Quarterly* 71 (1993): 1165–1187; Claire Heininger, "Gov. Corzine's Executive Privilege Faces Test," *Newark Star Ledger,* August 10, 2008, www.nj.com/news/index.ssf/2008/08/what_happened_to_andrew_clark.html.
10. Internal Revenue Service, "Lobbying," 2011, www.irs.gov/charities/article/0,,id=163392,00.html; Internal Revenue Service, "Revenue Ruling 2007-41," 2007, www.irs.gov/pub/irs-tege/rr2007-41.pdf; John Husted, Ohio Secretary of State, "Starting a Nonprofit in Ohio, www.sos.state.oh.us/sos/upload/publications/busserv/nonprofit.pdf.
11. John Pippen, Shaun Bowler, and Todd Donovan, "Election Reform and Direct Democracy: Campaign Finance Regulations in the American States," *American Politics Research* 30 (2002): 559–82; Beth Rosenson, "Against Their Apparent Self-Interest: The Authorization of Independent State Legislative Ethics Commissions, 1973–96," *State Politics and Policy Quarterly* 3 (2003): 42–65.
12. Pippen, Bowler, and Donovan, "Election Reform"; Witko, "Explaining Increases"; Frederick J. Boehmke, *The Indirect Effect of Direct Legislation: How Institutions Shape Interest Group Systems* (Columbus: Ohio State University Press, 2005).
13. Rosenson, "Against Their Apparent Self-Interest"; Newmark, "Lobbying Regulation"; Witko, "Explaining Increases."

14. Pippen, Bowler, and Donovan, "Election Reform"; Witko, "Explaining Increases."

15. Newmark, "Lobbying Regulation"; Rosenson, "Against Their Apparent Self-Interest"; Witko, "Explaining Increases"; Witko, "Measuring the Stringency"; Thomas, "Interest Group Regulation."

16. Pippen, Bowler, and Donovan, "Election Reform"; Witko, "Explaining Increases."

17. David Schultz, *Money, Politics, and Campaign Finance Reform in the American States* (Durham, NC: Carolina Academic Press, 2002).

18. Gross and Goidel, *The States,* 7–11; Rosenson, "Against Their Apparent Self-Interest"; Witko, "Explaining Increases."

19. Michael G. Malbin and Thomas L. Gais, *The Day after Reform: Sobering Campaign Finance Lessons from the American States* (Albany: Rockefeller Institute Press, 1998); Schultz, *Money, Politics;* Thomas, "Interest Group Regulation."

20. Robert E. Hogan, "State Campaign Finance Laws and Interest Group Electioneering Activities," *Journal of Politics* 67 (2005): 887–906.

21. David M. Primo and Jeffrey Milyo, "Campaign Finance Laws and Political Efficacy: Evidence from the States," *Election Law Journal* 5 (2006): 23–39; Marc J. Hetherington and Thomas J. Rudolph, "Priming, Performance, and the Dynamics of Political Trust," *Journal of Politics* 70 (2008): 498–512; Beth Rosenson, "The Effect of Political Reform Measures on Perceptions of Corruption," *Election Law Journal* 8 (2009): 31–46.

22. David Lowery and Virginia Gray, "How Some Rules Just Don't Matter: The Regulation of Lobbyists," *Public Choice* 91 (1997): 139–147; Joshua Ozymy, "Assessing the Impact of Legislative Lobbying Regulations on Interest Group Influence in U.S. State Legislatures," *State Politics and Policy Quarterly* 10 (2010): 397–420.

23. Patrick Flavin, "Campaign Finance Laws and Unequal Political Representation," paper presented at the annual meeting of the American Political Science Association (2011); John Matsusaka, "Popular Control of Public Policy: A Quantitative Approach," *Quarterly Journal of Political Science* 5 (2010): 133–167; Christopher Witko and Adam J. Newmark, "Business Mobilization and Public Policy in the U.S. States," *Social Science Quarterly* 86 (2005): 356–367.

24. Keith E. Hamm and Robert E. Hogan, "Campaign Finance Laws and Candidacy Decisions in State Legislative Elections," *Political Research Quarterly* 61 (2008): 458–467; Robert E. Hogan, "Challenger Emergence, Incumbent Success, and Electoral Accountability in State Legislative Elections," *Journal of Politics* 66 (2004): 128–1303; Donald A. Gross, Robert K. Goidel, and Todd G. Shields, "State Campaign Finance Regulations and Electoral Competition," *American Politics Research* 30 (2002): 143–165; Thomas Stratmann and Francisco J. Aparicio-Castillo, "Competition Policy for Elections: Do Campaign Contribution Limits Matter?" *Public Choice* 127 (2006): 177–206.

25. R. Jeffrey Smith, "Delay Indicted in Texas Finance Probe," *Washington Post,* September 29, 2005, www.washingtonpost.com/wp-dyn/content/article/2005/09/28/AR2005092800270.html; Flavin, "Campaign Finance Laws."

26. *Citizens United v. Federal Election Commission,* 588 U.S._ (2010).

27. *American Tradition Partnership v. Bullock,* 567 U.S._ (2012)

28. Richard L. Hasen, "*Citizens United* and the Illusion of Coherence," *Michigan Law Review* 109 (2011): 581–624.

29. Tim Craig, "Virginia Tightens Rules on PACs Formed by Out-of-State Politicians," *Washington Post,* May 8, 2007, Metro Section, www.washingtonpost.com/wp-dyn/content/article/2007/05/07/AR2007050701579.html; Frank R. Baumgartner and Bryan D. Jones, *Agendas and Instability in American Politics* (Chicago: University of Chicago Press, 1993).

SUGGESTED READING

Gross, Donald A., and Robert K. Goidel. *The States of Campaign Finance Reform.* Columbus: Ohio State University Press, 2003.

Hamm, Keith E., and Robert E. Hogan. "Campaign Finance Laws and Candidacy Decisions in State Legislative Elections." *Political Research Quarterly* 61 (2008): 458–467.

Hasen, Richard L. "*Citizens United* and the Illusion of Coherence." *Michigan Law Review* 109 (2011): 581–624.

Hogan, Robert E. "State Campaign Finance Laws and Interest Group Electioneering Activities." *Journal of Politics* 67 (2005): 887–906.

Malbin, Michael G., and Thomas L. Gais. *The Day after Reform: Sobering Campaign Finance Lessons from the American States.* Albany, NY: Rockefeller Institute Press, 1998.

Newmark, Adam J. "Measuring State Legislative Lobbying Regulation, 1990–2003." *State Politics and Policy Quarterly* 5 (2005): 182–191.

Rosenson, Beth. "Against Their Apparent Self-Interest: The Authorization of Independent State Legislative Ethics Commissions, 1973–96." *State Politics and Policy Quarterly* 3 (2003): 42–65.

Schultz, David. *Money, Politics, and Campaign Finance Reform in the American States.* Durham, NC: Carolina Academic Press, 2002.

Witko, Christopher. "Measuring the Stringency of State Campaign Finance Regulation." *State Politics and Policy Quarterly* 5 (2005): 295–310.

Chapter 12

Media Politics in the States

Martin Johnson

MASS MEDIA ARE ESSENTIAL TO SOCIAL and political systems. Members of the public usually have neither the time nor the inclination to monitor government directly. They rely on information conveyed by mass media to learn about the actions of government and officials and the outcomes of their actions and the proposals candidates make when seeking office. It is difficult to imagine a contemporary polity that could avoid reliance upon mass media to facilitate communication among constituents, representatives, and organized interests. Given their role linking the mass public and elite political actors, media are in a special position to influence audiences. Much scholarly and popular interest in the production and content of media messages is propelled in part by these potential effects.

In every U.S. state, a cadre of journalists sifts through the vast information about politics and government in the state capitol, filters and reports on what they learn through newspapers, magazines, television and radio broadcasts, and increasingly the Internet. In addition, candidates, political parties, and interest groups attempt to communicate with voters directly via advertising purchased in these same media outlets during political campaigns. Both journalism and advertising play a role in state politics.

However, the structure of the dominant forms of mainstream mass media in the United States militates against expansive coverage of state politics and government. Historically, the amount of information conventional news organizations could provide was fixed, limited by the length of a news broadcast or the size of a newspaper. The conventional wisdom of many scholars is that state government is a third priority after national and municipal news in local broadcasts and newspapers. For example, during the broadcast era prior to the current age of media choice marked by the expansion of cable television, national mainstream network news paid little attention to state governments.[1]

Broadcast television, in particular, is a poor fit to the American states. The United States is divided into 210 media markets—Designated Market Areas (DMAs)—the Nielsen Company identifies as part of rating the viewership of television programs. Each DMA comprises counties whose residents attend to the same television stations. Media markets traverse state lines, and they fragment and group electoral districts. Many people are familiar with living in a broadcast area composed of several congressional or state legislative districts. The Houston (Texas) media market, made up of nineteen counties, contains portions of at least twenty-five districts for the state house of representatives, according to the 2012 interim house redistricting plan. State legislative districts can also extend beyond a single media market. The eightieth assembly district of California contains portions of the Los Angeles, Palm Springs, and Yuma–El Centro DMAs. The odd fit between media markets and state legislative boundaries affects the prevalence of broadcast news coverage of state politics and the extent to which candidates target voters using broadcast advertising.

Of course, mass media have changed dramatically in the past twenty years. The expansion of twenty-four-hour cable news in the 1990s, including the development of more explicitly partisan news options in the Fox News Channel and MSNBC, means media pay more attention to the actions of public officials at all levels of the federal system. During the past decade, many important U.S. news stories have involved state government, including the following:

- The 2003 recall of California governor Gray Davis (D) and election of Arnold Schwarzenegger (R), whose celebrity and political positions made headlines throughout his time in office;
- The 2005 hurricane damage to New Orleans and the coast of several states along the Gulf of Mexico, as well as federal, state, and local government recovery efforts;
- State supreme court rulings, legislative acts, and ballot initiatives recognizing or failing to recognize same-sex marriage throughout the past decade; and

- Protests of state public employee unions against Wisconsin government in 2011 and their failed attempt to recall Gov. Scott Walker (R) in 2012.

The Internet and social media also provide new opportunities for the dissemination of information about state government. The states are more visible in this era of expanded media choice.

This chapter examines political communication and media politics in the states. It begins with the effects of mass media on political knowledge and opinion. Concerns about media effects motivate many questions about the political implications of mass media. From there, it explores the body of research investigating potential biases of news reporting in the states as well as the relationships between reporters and public officials. In addition, it examines how technological changes have affected state capitol press corps, both their overall size and makeup. Finally, the chapter considers variation in major institutions that govern relationships between reporters and sources—shield laws that may privilege the confidentiality of communication between reporters and sources as well as open government laws. Media politics in the states is a topic generally understudied but ripe for reconsideration due to technological changes and the rich variation observed across the United States.

MEDIA INFLUENCES ON VOTERS IN U.S. STATES

The most basic function of mass media is the transmission of information, allowing citizens to monitor government and punish and reward government officials accordingly—at all levels of government. Early theoretical understandings of media effects expressed concerns that mass communication also has a strong, direct influence on people, the "hypodermic needle" model of media influence. However, by the middle of the twentieth century, scholars understood mass media to have a more limited role. Audience members selectively expose themselves to media and actively interpret these messages for themselves, guided by their own predispositions about political and social issues. Contemporary understandings of how audiences interact with sources of information recognize this reality, but they identify other pervasive media effects. For example, news reports can affect the policy priorities voters have and how issues are defined.

There is little reason to think these basic human psychological and communication processes vary substantially across states or regions. Consequently, research on state-level media effects takes different forms, often focused on individual-level data. For example, researchers use opinion surveys conducted in single states, human subject experiments that invoke a political situation in a specific state, as well as data from several states. Many observational research designs may involve merging systematic content analysis of news reports or campaign messages to survey responses or observable behavior (e.g., election turnout) conditioned by state-level variations in the media environment. Importantly, these hypothesized general mechanisms often have implications for state government and how people understand intergovernmental relations in the United States.

Political Knowledge and Geography

In spite of the conventional understanding that news media downplay state politics, voters do learn about state politics from news outlets and campaign advertisements. People who consume news—any news—know more about state government and politics than those who do not.[2] However, people vary in the extent to which they acquire knowledge of state government as a function of at least their sources of news and where they reside. Audiences for news regard newspapers as providing more information about state government than broadcast news.[3]

Geography affects how much people learn about state government in at least two interesting ways. Proximity to the state capital matters. People who live in communities closer to the state house know more about state government than people living farther away typically know. In a 1990 political knowledge study of Virginia voters, residents of the area around Richmond, the state capital, were more likely to know the names of statewide elected officials, the timing of the legislative session, the party control of the legislative chambers, and policy facts than did people who lived in northern Virginia or the rest of the state. This is primarily due to differences in information environments and access to officials. In the Richmond area, news media have greater access to state officials, while reporters in other areas of the state lack easy access and find state government of less news value. This variation in access affects variation in how much information news outlets in different parts of the state provide.[4]

The disjoint between media markets and state boundaries also affects the acquisition of political knowledge. New Jersey illustrates the potential informational disadvantages presented by geography. The state is divided across two media markets, the New York and Philadelphia DMAs, which primarily target residents of other states and are more likely to cover the politics of these states—New York and Pennsylvania, respectively. Television stations in other media markets, like the nearby Hartford–New Haven DMA, provide programming for people residing in a single state and have no residents from a different state. People who live in media markets that are not divided across state lines are more likely to learn about their own state-level candidates than are people who live in markets that serve multiple states,[5] especially those media markets that primarily serve residents of a different state, like the New Jerseyans watching Philadelphia newscasts.

New Orleans, Louisiana, residents queue up to leave the city on September 1, 2005, after waiting days for rescue from the city after Hurricane Katrina struck the city. Evacuees in the Convention Center waited for days for government officials to rescue them from the shelter. Much of the media coverage of the event focused on this slow response, with some placing the blame on the federal government and others finding fault with the state government.

SOURCE: Gary I Rothstein/Icon SMI 534/Gary I Rothstein/Icon SMI/Newscom.

Agenda Setting and Framing

News media communicate issue priorities to the public and shape which problems people think government should be working to address, thus setting the political agenda. Early political communication research suggested support for this idea, identifying connections between local newspaper coverage of issues and the importance readers assigned to issues.[6] The theory behind agenda-setting research suggests that when people read more stories about the economy, they are more likely to view the economy as important. However, journalists also try to anticipate what people will think is important and interesting. Thus the correspondence between news and public issue salience could just be good journalism.

A stronger causal inference requires a more complicated research design. Data on news content and public opinion is collected at least at two points in time. Researchers estimate connections between earlier news content and public issue priorities at a later point in time, as well as the connection for the later news content and earlier public opinion about issue salience. The relative magnitude of these relationships provides more confidence about the extent to which news content affects public opinion about issues or vice versa. The most comprehensive study of agenda setting at the state level, including data from eighteen states across a twenty-two-year time span, suggests news media do shape public opinion about issue priorities at the state level.[7]

While news media influence what issues are on the public political agenda, media framing can also affect how a given issue is defined and thus which *aspects* of the issue members of the public deem important. This is important in a federal system because news media can inform whether a problem is perceived to be the responsibility of state or federal government. In the weeks after Hurricane Katrina devastated New Orleans and coastal Alabama, Louisiana, and Mississippi in 2005, local and national coverage of the storm was framed around blame for the slow government response to the crisis. People tended to castigate the federal government for a weak initial recovery effort. However, some news coverage alleged Louisiana governor Kathleen Blanco (D) had not properly requested aid from the administration of Republican president George W. Bush. People who consumed a greater quantity of news about recovery efforts were more likely to perceive that the state's failure to act had slowed the federal response because they were more likely to see news stories that framed the slow recovery as state government's fault.[8]

MEDIA BIAS, REAL AND PERCEIVED

Given the power news media have to inform the public, communicate issue priorities, and define issues and political institutions, it is worth asking whether they are fair and balanced in reporting news, or biased. This question has dominated a number of studies of political journalism at the state level. There are at least two approaches to the question. Some scholars investigate whether journalists themselves identify with political parties or ideologies, with the underlying assumption that reporters will articulate these political orientations in the stories they write. A second direction of research investigates news content itself for expressions of bias.

Liberal Reporters?

In general, state capitol reporters are more likely to identify themselves as liberals than to identify themselves as conservatives, like their peers working other news beats. The journalists who cover state government modally self-identify as moderates. Nonetheless, in terms of self-identification, single- and multiple-state surveys of capitol reporters suggest they lean to the left. However, the ideological landscape of state house reporters is more nuanced than simple allegations about their political leanings.

Reporters are, in a sense, representative of their states. The ideological orientations capitol reporters express correspond to the left-right balance of the states in which they work. So while reporters may generally be left-leaning, a state house reporter in a state with a more conservative public mood like Alabama will tend to be more conservative than one in a state with a liberal public mood such as Vermont. Furthermore, state capitol reporters who do not share *demographic* characteristics of their readers are less *ideologically* representative of these audiences. For example, white reporters who cover politics in a state with greater ethnic diversity and larger minority populations are less ideologically representative of their readers than they would be if they covered politics in a less diverse state.[9] Consequently, the characteristics of states and their residents also affect the extent to which reporters express a personal political viewpoint different from their readers.

Bias in News Content

There is less persuasive evidence that reporter political orientations influence the content of news stories about state government. Some studies appear to show news content biased toward Democratic candidates and officials, but others do not. Reporters reveal other types of biases in the news stories they write. For example, coverage of female candidates for governor may reflect gender stereotypes.[10] Reporters also seem to sympathize with their sources. During the implementation of legislative term limits, as their longtime trusted sources were being termed out of office, reporters were more likely to write negative stories on the issue, returning to a more neutral position following the implementation of term limits.[11]

State-level journalists also write about issues *for their audiences,* and exhibit patterns of what we might call bias reflective of that reality. A comparison of news stories about the same events, such as two high-profile gubernatorial elections, produced for state and national news organizations, will emphasize different themes. In 1989 reporters for Virginia newspapers covered the campaigns of then–lieutenant governor Douglas Wilder, a Democrat, and former attorney general Marshall Coleman, a Republican, differently. National news organizations were more likely to emphasize the historic nature of Wilder's potential service as the first African American elected governor in the United States since Reconstruction. This theme was not absent in state-level press accounts, but local reports were more likely to emphasize the substance of the campaign. Similarly, national media coverage of the 2003 California recall framed the campaign to replace Gov. Gray Davis (D) as a "circus," while news stories in state media focused more on the issues that led to the recall effort and election of Arnold Schwarzenegger (R).[12] These cases illustrate the fact that state political reporters are writing for readers who must make a practical decision in a specific state political context—whom to vote for. Readers in other states and the national journalists who wrote for them had none of the practical interest in voter decision making and thus focused more on the novelty of these stories.

RELATIONSHIPS BETWEEN REPORTERS AND OFFICIALS

How do reporters decide what to write about and how to write about it? In his classic study of relationships among elected officials, bureaucrats, and journalists, Delmer Dunn conducted in-depth interviews with reporters covering the Wisconsin state house. Many of his findings show commonalities among reporters at the state and national levels. He found that journalists authentically try to fulfill their responsibilities to transmit information, interpret government actions to help audiences understand them, and represent the public, even while stimulating officials to address public concerns with policy.[13] The choices reporters make over what stories to cover are affected by an intuitive set of criteria used to judge newsworthiness: the presence of conflict; changes that affect the lives of audience members; unique or novel events; and the involvement of focal personalities, such as the governor.

While journalists evaluate events as they happen in order to decide what to cover, they are influenced by colleagues in the press corps and in their news organizations. Differences across the states may affect the relative influence of a journalist's peers on his or her own news judgments. Because of the relatively smaller size of the press corps in Madison compared with Washington, DC, Dunn argued that reporters were more likely to reach agreement on what stories were important and how these events should be defined, leading to a more homogenous coverage of state government. In many states, including Wisconsin, reporters have offices located together in a single office or small cluster of offices. This also leads to a more direct set of social interactions among reporters themselves, producing more consistency in the news judgments of reporters for different news organizations. State capitols vary in the extent to which they gather or disperse the press corps. Reporters in state capitols that offer no centralized office space for reporters are likely to exert less influence on each other's judgments.

Many of the differences between state and federal reporter-official relations are also affected by the relative size of the political communities in these different settings—individual state governments, press corps, and bureaucracies are smaller than their analogs at the federal level. The need to maintain good relationships with sources, essential among members of the Washington press corps, is even more important to state house reporters because of the overall smaller number of potential sources. Reporters may be more likely to choose not to cover something that might embarrass or harm a source. Journalists "must weigh the disadvantages of losing a source against the advantages of writing the story," although they are reluctant to admit this.[14]

Expertise is also a concern with state house journalism. Dunn found that Wisconsin state house reporters had far less journalistic and political experience than Washington reporters. However, this has varied as well, with most states enjoying a wealth of knowledge and experience among members of the state capitol press corps. In fact, the onset of term limits in several states created an environment in many state capitols where some reporters might have more detailed knowledge of state legislative processes than some new legislators. However, the base of expertise in state capitol press corps is threatened by the staff reductions underway in many news organizations.

Florida governor Rick Scott takes a bite out of a chocolate-covered doughnut August 1, 2011, while talking with reporters in a first-of-its-kind informal session with the capitol press corps in his office at the state capitol in Tallahassee. Scott invited the press in for an hour of talks about government and politics, including some recollections about a doughnut shop he and his wife operated when they were just getting started in business. Such informal and interpersonal communications among state officials and members of the press can provide additional avenues for sharing information.

SOURCE: AP Photo/Tallahassee Democrat, Bill Cotterell.

Public Officials and the Press

Dunn extensively interviewed elected officials in the Wisconsin legislature and executive branch as well as agency leaders. Like their counterparts in national government, public officials communicate through news media for a variety of reasons. They want to earn publicity, of course, but also build support for their programs and proposals; notify the public of government actions; and provide "neutral" information, like job openings in government. Using journalists as a conduit for information is not limited to publication, however. Reporters may convey information interpersonally—essentially providing links among officials and other members of a state capitol community a sort of chain of gossip that lowers the cost of transmitting information. In addition to Dunn's work on Wisconsin reporters and officials, a number of scholars have made similar findings in Illinois, Indiana, New York, and elsewhere over time.[15]

Again, size matters here as well. Dunn finds some of these communication functions were less prevalent in Madison than they were in Washington, DC. For example, he claims that policymakers were less likely to float "trial balloons" among state house reporters, leaking policy ideas before formally presenting them as a legislative proposal or executive decision. At least during the 1960s, officials in the Wisconsin capitol found it easier to communicate with one another directly than did officials in Washington, DC. While state governments have grown in the past five decades, there is still a substantial size asymmetry between state and federal governments, suggesting that many of these differences related to press-government interactions still exist.

Officials and candidates try to shape media coverage and thus the agenda presented to the public. This gives rise to questions about whether media or these political elites serve as the ultimate agenda setter: Do officials drive the media agenda, or do mass media drive the issue priorities of *officials* in addition to influencing the public? Beyond their investigation of media agenda setting for the public, Yue Tan and David H. Weaver compare the connection between government issue priorities and media priorities over time for a small number of states—just three in their data set—and find that media agendas exert a stronger influence on policymakers than vice versa in two of them. In a larger sample of states with cross-sectional data only, they find stronger evidence of reciprocal agenda-setting effects in states with a moralistic political culture relative to states with individualistic political cultures. They argue that in moralistic states, political actors of each type (officials, journalists, and members of the public) are generally more responsive to one another.[16]

These patterns of influence also vary across types of elites or news organizations. In a case study of the 2005 Virginia gubernatorial campaign between Lt. Gov. Tim Kaine (D) and former attorney general Jerry Kilgore (R), the candidates influenced the agendas of two of four newspapers studied (*Roanoke Times* and *Virginian-Pilot* of Norfolk). Two other newspapers (*Richmond Times-Dispatch* and *Washington Post*) presented news with an issue agenda reciprocally related to the campaigns' priorities. These candidates found it easier to influence newspapers farther from the state capital (Roanoke and Norfolk) because the more distant newspapers have less experience covering politics than the more proximal ones typically do.[17]

In sum, it appears possible for officials and elites to influence news media organizations, and perhaps the public through them. However, this influence is not nearly as prevalent as many people assume: the news media themselves also influence the issue priorities of officials. The political culture of states, the size of the governmental community, and the experience of political reporters play the best-documented roles in moderating the influence of officials on journalists and vice versa.

Legislative Behavior and Televised State Government

The mere presence of mass media affects legislative behavior. Many state legislatures provide access to their proceedings with televised coverage comparable to the attention the U.S. House and Senate receive from the C-SPAN cable network, including live, gavel-to-gavel coverage of floor debates and committee hearings. Legislative proceedings may be viewed on cable television or over the Internet. The opportunity to view legislative action live has expanded tremendously with the increased availability of the Internet and cable television.

Visibility affects how lawmakers behave. In 1973 the Florida legislature pioneered a nightly television program, *Today in the Legislature,* working in conjunction with public television stations in the state, which has now expanded to a twenty-four-hour cable network. The visibility brought on by the introduction of television cameras in the chamber is credited with encouraging longer, grandstanding floor speeches.[18] When voters can watch lawmakers on television, it reduces the costs of comparing how they present themselves in the campaign with how they behave in office, arguably improving accountability. Candidates in states without televised legislatures have incentives to emphasize their reputations and party labels. In states with televised legislative proceedings, they have incentives to focus on specific positions, easily confirmed by watching floor deliberation.[19]

STATE PRESS CORPS

Cable television and the Internet make U.S. state governments more visible than they have been at any other time in U.S. history. However, in other ways the visibility of state government is on the decline. While many observers complain that newspaper attention to state government had never been all that high, fewer and fewer citizens are consuming information about their state governments in print form. During the past decade, traditional newspaper coverage of state politics has taken a steep decline due to the slow collapse of the newspaper industry. There is some hope that new media, including Internet-based professional news organizations, citizen reporting and commentary in the form of weblogs, and the expansion of onlookers sharing state government news via social media such as Twitter, will address the deficit of coverage left by news organizations that have reduced their commitments to covering the state house. However, the initial consensus is that these new forms of attention to state politics and policy have not quite yet filled these gaps. (See States Vary in How They Define Journalism in a Digital Age box.)

Decline of the Mainstream News Media

Periodically, the *American Journalism Review (AJR)* conducts a census of state capitol press corps. Its studies focus on bureaus for daily newspapers and newspaper chains and do not include wire services (e.g., Associated Press), specialty publications, bureaus for television or radio stations, weblogs, or nonprofit news organizations circulating content online. One of the main values of the census of newspaper bureaus this magazine provides is that it captures the trend in downsizing and bureau closure in state capitol bureaus. In 1999 the *AJR* census documented 533 state house reporters in 326 state capitol bureaus across the country; by 2009 *AJR* identified 355 reporters in 289 bureaus. This is a loss of about one-third of the newspaper journalists covering state capitols and more than one out of every ten bureaus.[20]

The number of reporters is declining at a rate faster than bureaus are closing due to at least two patterns of these cuts. Reductions in bureau staff are often experienced disproportionately by historically large news bureaus. The state house bureau for the Newark *Star-Ledger* showed twelve reporters in the 1999 *AJR* census and five in 2009, accounting for almost one-third of New Jersey's loss of capitol reporters over the decade. In addition, newspapers often nominally keep their state house bureau while substantially decreasing the number of full-time reporters, sometimes removing full-time staff entirely and sending journalists to cover the state house on a part-time or temporary basis, such as during the legislative session.

Rise of State House Bloggers

Even as mainstream traditional media attention to state government is on the wane, a coterie of reporters for new media—Internet-based news and opinion organizations, as well as citizen journalists—are becoming increasingly prevalent in the evolving state press corps. A National Council of

STATES VARY IN HOW THEY DEFINE JOURNALISM IN A DIGITAL AGE

Changes in media technology and news norms have created controversies in defining journalism and journalists. Online news organizations entering the state capitol press corps offer a novel publication method, but they also may have a different professional status and dissimilar commitments to journalistic norms such as objectivity. Some state politics blogs are maintained by individual citizens who may be quite knowledgeable about particular issues but have little formal journalism training. Other Web enterprises invest in professional reporting but have an expressed political orientation, like the progressive website The UpTake in Minnesota.[1] On the right, a number of websites like the Wisconsin Reporter, a self-described nonpartisan organization, have been founded across the states with the backing of the conservative nonprofit organization The Franklin Center for Government and Public Integrity.[2]

Most states officially recognize reporters and provide them access to state officials, especially legislators, beyond what is enjoyed by members of the general public. Credentialed reporters might be allowed into areas of a legislative chamber to which a constituent would not normally have access. In some states, the credentialing process is conducted by state officials, but in others it is organized by an association of journalists who are allowed to define their own membership. According to the National Conference of State Legislatures, many states make no distinction between online and traditional media in issuing press credentials. Others, including Mississippi, New Hampshire, and New Jersey, explicitly do not credential bloggers, although their treatment of journalists for online news organizations is less clear. Elsewhere, bloggers must demonstrate that they have a news outlet (Idaho), a nonpartisan online news service (Wyoming), or a blog for a traditional news outlet (Texas).[3]

State-level differences in the credentialing process mean similar online publications are treated differently in different states. The Wisconsin Reporter is a credentialed member of the Wisconsin Capitol Correspondents Association. However, the Capitol Correspondents Association in Idaho has been unwilling to credential the Idaho Freedom Foundation and its reporters from its www.IdahoReporter.com news website because of an insufficient separation between its advocacy and news reporting efforts.[4]

States also vary in their provision of physical space for reporters to work. Many state capitols offer office space to news media, either for rent or without charge. In 2010 Minnesota's The UpTake tried to rent space in the press room opened by the downsizing of the bureau for the *Duluth News Tribune* and other newspapers owned by Forum Communications. The progressive website's use of the space was protested by some press corps members, including a reporter from the Rochester (MN) *Post-Bulletin,* who argued the website staff was untrustworthy and partisan—"which compromises the efforts of all the media in that complex that have built their reputations over time," he wrote the state Department of Administration.[5] In response, the administration initially cancelled The UpTake's lease, although the website was eventually allowed to move into the space in January 2011.[6]

States also vary in their application of the journalist's privilege—protection from being compelled to reveal the names of sources or provide confidential information in court testimony—to reporters for Internet-based news organizations. One major issue is whether the privilege is designed to protect modes of communication or whether it protects the functions of journalists. In a 1986 New York district court ruling, reporters for the Hofstra University student newspaper were not allowed to invoke the journalist's privilege because even though they were engaged in newsgathering, they were not working as professional journalists for a newspaper with a paid circulation. In other states, television reporters have been denied access to journalists' privilege because the state's shield law narrowly defined its application to newspaper reporters. States are unevenly acting to keep up with changing technology.[7] For example, Arkansas amended its shield law in March 2011 to protect television and Internet reporters.

1. The UpTake, www.TheUptake.org.
2. Wisconsin Reporter, www.WisconsinReporter.com.
3. National Council of State Legislatures, "Media Access and Credentialing: A State-by-State Report," November 2011, www.ncsl.org/legislative-staff/lincs/media-access-in-legislatures.aspx.
4. Betsy Russell, "President's Column: Statehouse Reporting, the 1st Amendment, and More . . ." March 31, 2009, www.idahopressclub.org/presidents-column-8; Idaho Freedom Foundation, www.idahofreedom.net.
5. David Brauer, "Why Can't The Uptake Get a Capitol Press Office? April 9, 2010, *MinnPost,* www.minnpost.com/braublog/2010/04/why-cant-uptake-get-capitol-press-office.
6. The UpTake, "Citizen Media Now Has a Seat in the Capitol Press Room," www.theuptake.org/2011/01/19/citizen-media-now-has-a-seat-in-the-capitol-press-room.
7. Jason Shepard, "Bloggers after the Shield: Defining Journalism in Privilege Law," *Journal of Media Law and Ethics* 1 (2009): 186–216.

State Legislature's (NCSL) weblog, The Thicket at State Legislatures, provides links to 202 weblogs devoted to the politics and government of particular states.[21] The NCSL list includes at least one blog in every state, but a much larger number for several states, including Texas (twelve links), California (nine), and New York (eight). The Thicket undoubtedly underrepresents the scope of new media attention to state government, but it provides a useful point of reference. *Washington Post* blogger Chris Cillizza has also tracked the development of state politics blogs and Twitter feeds for reporters and observers covering state politics and government.[22] Many of these online news sources publish original journalism from professional reporters working in mainstream news organizations that have established a Web presence. Nonprofit organizations also develop websites to support and publish state and local investigative journalism. For example, the Texas Tribune was launched in November 2009 by a venture capitalist and two longtime Texas journalists, one a former editor of *Texas Monthly* magazine and the other a former capitol bureau reporter for the *Houston Chronicle* and editor of *Texas Weekly*, a well-known newsletter about the state's politics.[23] Some regard it and others, like Connecticut News Junkie, as having the potential to fill the gap left by the decline of traditional print journalism.[24]

The consensus, even among some state house journalists, is that online sources are valuable because they are able to cover stories that might otherwise be missed by the thinly spread remaining newspaper, wire service, television, and radio reporters. The NCSL conducted a survey of twenty-two state bloggers and thirty-two state house reporters in 2009, finding that a majority of both groups thought the growth of websites and blogs increased the amount of information available to readers about state government.[25] However, they do not yet fill the gap left by the decline of the newspaper press corps.

INSTITUTIONS REGULATING POLITICAL COMMUNICATION

As is true with so many aspects of state politics, institutions governing aspects of political communication vary substantially at the state level. To the chagrin of professional journalists, there is no national shield law to protect the confidentiality of information sources, notes, or other materials. In particular, states treat the confidentiality of a journalist's newsgathering activities and pre-publication work quite differently. As a result, some journalists may be subpoenaed and either compelled to testify or face contempt charges in one state but not another. States also vary on the extent of their transparency for reporters and the public—including the disclosure of campaign contributions, open meetings, and open records.

Shield Laws

The press has argued that the First Amendment to the U.S. Constitution guarantees their right to investigate and regulate the disclosure of information they collect, in addition to protecting their rights to express and publicize this information. In 1969 reporter Paul Branzburg wrote a story for the *Louisville* (KY) *Courier-Journal* about two young drug dealers, to whom he promised anonymity. More than a year later, he published an article about drug users in Frankfort, Kentucky. Both times he was subpoenaed to testify to a grand jury about the crimes he witnessed and identify his informants. Branzburg resisted these subpoenas, arguing that if he were to reveal his sources' identities, his reputation as a reporter would be damaged and others would be less likely to provide him useful information and chill the free flow of information.

In its 1972 *Branzburg v. Hayes* ruling, the U.S. Supreme Court refused to recognize a universal privilege for communication between reporters and sources, instead identifying a set of conditions under which reporters could potentially be compelled to testify.[26] This so-called *Branzburg* test allows courts to compel journalists to expose a confidential source or testify under three conditions—there is probable cause to believe the reporter has relevant information, the information can be obtained in no other way, and there is a compelling need for the information. In addition, the Court challenged states to develop their own standards for dealing with the treatment of information supplied confidentially to journalists. Several states already had laws of this nature at the time of the ruling. By 2011, forty states had passed shield laws, representing a great deal of institutional diversity.

Almost all shield laws, as well as legal precedent in states without shield statutes, allow journalists to protect the identity of informants—people who provide them information. In the 1960s, Kentucky afforded this kind of protection. The dispute in *Branzburg* revolved in part around whether the reporter could be compelled to divulge information about behavior he had witnessed and the people he saw committing those acts. Contemporary shield laws continue to vary state to state in their protection of what journalists have heard about violations of the law from their sources versus criminal behavior these reporters have witnessed directly.

Shield laws vary across other dimensions as well. They vary with regard to what material and communication may be protected. For example, some shield laws may extend beyond the protection of source identification and verbal communication between these sources and the reporter to protect a reporter's notes, drafts of stories, and other work product that are part of the process of newsgathering and preparation, while other shield laws may protect less of this material. Particularly relevant today is the fact that these protections also vary in their application to different types of media (e.g., reporters for newspapers, magazines, broadcast outlets, or Internet-based publications). There is also variation in the institutional settings in which the shield applies (e.g., courts, grand juries, or legislative hearings). Several states have catch-all shield laws that allow journalists to protect information and sources in a wide variety of situations—court proceedings, libel and defamation cases, legislative hearings, and grand juries. If a reporter can protect a source in court, but not in grand juries, the shield is qualitatively weaker than the protection a reporter can afford sources in states with multisetting shield laws.[27] In addition, shield laws vary in their explicit protection of sources to whom confidentiality has not been offered—about half of states with shield laws extend the journalist's privilege to these sources and the information they provide.[28]

Government Openness

Reporters are also affected by government openness. Campaign coverage is influenced by the extent of campaign disclosure. Reporters in states with more fulsome campaign disclosure are better able to cover how campaigns are funded.[29] Tracked by the Campaign Disclosure Project at the University of California, Los Angeles, states vary in the comprehensiveness of their campaign finance disclosure laws, the rigidity of requirements for the electronic filing of campaign reports, the availability of these reports to the public, and the usability of websites providing this information to the media and the public. For example, while all fifty states required the disclosure of campaign contributions, as of 2008, only thirty-six required the timely reporting of contributions immediately prior to the election. Six states did not require the reporting of independent expenditures, and of the forty-four that did, only twenty-seven required the timely reporting of expenditures made late in the campaign. These variations in campaign disclosure affect the ability of reporters to learn and identify the interests behind campaigns to their audiences.

States also express tremendous variation in open meetings laws, affecting the access reporters and other members of the public have to government proceedings and government records.[30] Most Americans assume a certain level of transparency in access to information and officials, but states vary in where meeting notices must be posted, how much notice must be given, the handling of requests for access to records, and a variety of dimensions of access. In addition, states vary in the punishments applicable for violation of laws related to open meetings and records. As of 2010, sixteen states, including Colorado and New York, provided no civil or criminal fines for violations of open meetings laws. The same number of states had no civil or criminal fines for open records law violations (including California and Ohio).[31]

CONCLUSION

Assessments of state media politics are due for reconsideration, in part because of the tremendous technological change mass media have seen in the last two decades. The expansion of Internet-based reporting, partisan news, and twenty-four-hour cable news networks brings new attention to state governments. While we know a great deal about state-level media effects, the content of state-level journalism, relationships between reporters and officials, and variation in institutions that regulate political communication in the states, much of this research predates these expansive media changes. Furthermore, while legal scholars, nonprofit organizations, and professional associations have done an excellent job describing the contours of variation in the regulation of media and expression in the states, much more research is needed to identify the effects of these institutions on the quality of democracy in the United States. Given the role mass media play linking people to government, this aspect of state politics is ripe for additional investigation.

NOTES

1. William T. Gormley Jr., "Television Coverage of State Government," *Public Opinion Quarterly* 42 (1978): 354–359; Doris A. Graber, "Flashlight Coverage: State News on National Broadcasts," *American Politics Quarterly* 17 (1989): 277–290; Doris A. Graber, "Swiss Cheese Journalism," *State Government News* 36 (1993): 19–21; Paul Simon, "Improving Statehouse Coverage," *Columbia Journalism Review* 12 (1973): 51–53.

2. Joey Reagan and Richard V. Ducey, "Effects of News Measure on Selection of State Government News Sources," *Journalism Quarterly* 60 (1983): 211–217.

3. Kim Fridkin Kahn, "Characteristics of Press Coverage in Senate and Gubernatorial Elections: Information Available to Voters," *Legislative Studies Quarterly* 20 (1995): 23–35; Reagan and Ducey, "Effects of News Measure on Selection of State Government News Sources."

4. Michael X. Delli Carpini and Scott Keeter, *What Americans Know about Politics and Why It Matters* (New Haven: Yale University Press, 1996), 211–213.

5. Charles Stewart III and Mark Reynolds, "Television Markets and U.S. Senate Elections," *Legislative Studies Quarterly* 15 (1990): 495–523.

6. Maxwell E. McCombs and Donald L. Shaw, "The Agenda-Setting Function of Mass Media," *Public Opinion Quarterly* 36 (1972): 176–187.

7. Yue Tan and David H. Weaver, "Local Media, Public Opinion, and State Legislative Policies: Agenda Setting at the State Level," *International Journal of Press/Politics* 14 (2009): 454–476.

8. Cherie D. Maestas, Lonna Rae Atkeson, Lisa Bryant, and Thomas Croon, "Shifting the Blame: Federalism, Causal Attribution, and Political Accountability Following Hurricane Katrina," *Publius: The Journal of Federalism* 38 (2008): 609–632.

9. Christopher A. Cooper and Martin Johnson, "Representative Reporters? Examining Journalists' Ideology in Context," *Social Science Quarterly* 90 (2009): 387–406.

10. Linda L. Fowler and Jennifer L. Lawless, "Looking for Sex in All the Wrong Places: Press Coverage and the Electoral Fortunes of Gubernatorial Candidates," *Perspectives on Politics* 7 (2009): 519–536.

11. Rick Farmer and Nathan S. Bigelow, "Term Limits Implementation in the News: Superficial or Biased?" in *The Test of Time: Coping with Legislative Term Limits,* ed. Rick Farmer, John David Rausch, and John C. Green (Lanham, MD: Lexington Books, 2003), 177–192.

12. Mark J. Rozell, "Local v. National Press Assessments of Virginia's 1989 Gubernatorial Campaign," *Polity* 24 (1991): 69–89; Martin Johnson, Chris Stout, Shaun Bowler, and Max Neiman, "*Cirque du Sacramento* and Weary Californians: State and National Coverage of the Recall Campaign," in *Clicker Politics: Essays on the California Recall,* ed. Shaun Bowler and Bruce Cain (New York: Prentice-Hall, 2005), 155–169.

13. Delmer Dunn, *Public Officials and the Press* (Reading, MA: Addison-Wesley, 1969), 7.

14. Ibid., 34.

15. Frederick Fico, "How Lawmakers Use Reporters: Differences in Specialization and Goals," *Journalism Quarterly* 61 (1984): 793–800, 821; Susan Herbst, *Reading Public Opinion: How Political Actors View the Democratic Process* (Chicago: University of Chicago Press, 1998); David Morgan, *The Capitol Press Corps: Newsmen and the Governing of New York State* (Westport, CT: Greenwood Press, 1978); Christopher A. Cooper, "Media Tactics in the State Legislature," *State Politics and Policy Quarterly* 2 (2002): 353–371.

16. Tan and Weaver, "Local Media, Public Opinion, and State Legislative Policies."

17. Scott W. Dunn, "Candidate and Media Agenda Setting in the 2005 Virginia Gubernatorial Election," *Journal of Communication* 56 (2009): 635–652.

18. David J. LeRoy, C. Edward Wotring, and Jack Lyle, "'Today in the Legislature': The Florida Story," *Journal of Communication* 24 (1974): 92–98; Debbie Salamone, "Where Political Junkies Tune In: Capitol TV Show Is Short on Thrills, Long on Pomp and Bluster," *Orlando Sentinel,* April 1, 1993.

19. W. Mark Crain and Brian Goff, *Televising Legislatures: Political Information Technology and Public Choice* (Boston: Kluwer Academic Publishers, 1988).

20. David Allan and Sinead O'Brien, "Capital News," *American Journalism Review* 21 (1999): 57–63; Jennifer Dorroh, "Statehouse Exodus," *American Journalism Review* 31 (2009): 20–35.

21. *The Thicket at State Legislatures,* http://ncsl.typepad.com/the_thicket.

22. Chris Cillizza, "The Fix's Best State-Based Political Blogs, 2011 Edition," *Washington Post,* August 2, 2011, www.washingtonpost.com/blogs/the-fix/post/the-fixs-best-state-based-political-blogs-2011-edition/2011/08/02/gIQApaWvpI_blog.html; Chris Cillizza, "The Fix's Best State-Based Political Tweeters," *Washington Post,* February 28, 2011, http://voices.washingtonpost.com/thefix/fix-notes/view-best-political-tweets-in.html.

23. *Texas Tribune,* www.texastribune.org.

24. Mark Lisheron, "Reloading at the Statehouse," *American Journalism Review* 32 (2010): 34–45; Rob Gurwitt, "Death and Life in the Pressroom," *Governing* magazine, January 2009; Belinda Lunscombe, "As Newsrooms Cut Back, Who Covers the Statehouse?" *Time* magazine, May 7, 2009; Connecticut News Junkie, www.ctnewsjunkie.com.

25. Edward Smith, "Disappearing Act: A Declining State Press Corps Leaves Readers Less Informed about Lawmakers' Efforts," *State Legislatures* 35 (2009): 28–31; Meagan Dorsch, "Blogs Fill Some of the Gaps," *State Legislatures* 35 (2009): 30; full results of supplemental surveys available at www.ncsl.org/press-room/sl-magazine-disappearing-act.aspx.

26. *Branzburg v. Hayes,* 408 U.S. 665 (1972).

27. Laurence B. Alexander and Leah G. Cooper, "Words That Shield: A Textual Analysis of the Journalist's Privilege," *Newspaper Research Journal* 18 (1997): 51–72.

28. Anthony Fargo, "The Journalist's Privilege for Nonconfidential Information in States with Shield Laws," *Communication Law and Policy* 4 (1999): 325–354.

29. Raymond J. La Raja, "Sunshine Laws and the Press: The Effect of Campaign Disclosure in News Reporting in the American States," *Election Law Journal* 6 (2007): 236–249.

30. Reporters Committee for Freedom of the Press, *Open Government Guide,* 6th ed. (Arlington, VA, 2011), www.rcfp.org/open-government-guide.

31. Daxton R. "Chip" Stewart, "Let the Sunshine In, or Else: An Examination of the 'Teeth' of State and Federal Open Meetings and Open Records Laws," *Communication Law and Policy* 15 (2010): 265–310.

SUGGESTED READINGS

Arceneaux, Kevin, and Martin Johnson. *Changing Minds or Changing Channels? Media Effects in the Era of Expanded Choice.* Chicago: University of Chicago Press, 2013.

Arnold, R. Douglas. *Congress, the Press, and Political Accountability.* Princeton, NJ: Princeton University Press, 2004.

Cook, Timothy E. *Governing with the News: The News Media as a Political Institution.* Chicago: University of Chicago Press, 1998.

Cooper, Christopher A. "Media Tactics in the State Legislature." *State Politics and Policy Quarterly* 2 (2003): 353–371.

Cooper, Christopher A., and Martin Johnson. "Representative Reporters? Examining Journalists' Ideology in Context." *Social Science Quarterly* 90 (2009): 387–406.

Delli Carpini, Michael X., and Scott Keeter. *What Americans Know about Politics and Why It Matters.* New Haven: Yale University Press, 1996.

Dorroh, Jennifer. "Statehouse Exodus." *American Journalism Review* 31 (2009): 20–35.

Dunn, Delmer D. *Public Officials and the Press.* Reading, MA: Addison-Wesley, 1969.

Fargo, Anthony L. "Analyzing Federal Shield Law Proposals: What Congress Can Learn from the States." *Communication Law and Policy* 11 (2006): 35–82.

Graber, Doris A. "Flashlight Coverage: State News on National Broadcasts." *American Politics Quarterly* 17 (1989): 277–290.

Herbst, Susan. *Reading Public Opinion: How Political Actors View the Democratic Process.* Chicago: University of Chicago Press, 1998.

Klapper, Joseph. *The Effects of Mass Media.* Glencoe, IL: The Free Press, 1960.

La Raja, Raymond J. "Sunshine Laws and the Press: The Effect of Campaign Disclosure in News Reporting in the American States." *Election Law Journal* 6 (2007): 236–249.

McCombs, Maxwell E., and Donald L. Shaw. "The Agenda-Setting Function of Mass Media." *Public Opinion Quarterly* 36 (1972): 176–187.

Morgan, David. *The Capitol Press Corps: Newsmen and the Governing of New York State.* Westport, CT: Greenwood Press, 1978.

Pew Center on the States. *Stateline: The Daily News Service of the Pew Center on the States,* www.pewstates.org/projects/stateline.

Renner, Tari, and G. Patrick Lynch. "A Little Knowledge Is a Dangerous Thing: What We Know about the Role of Media in State Politics," In *Media Power, Media Politics,* 2nd ed., Mark J. Rozell and Jeremy D. Mayer, eds. Lanham, MD: Rowman and Littlefield, 2008.

Reporters Committee for Freedom of the Press. 2011. *The Reporters Privilege,* www.rcfp.org/reporters-privilege.

Riffe, Daniel, Stephen Lacy, and Frederick Fico. *Analyzing Media Messages: Using Quantitative Content Analysis in Research.* Mahwah, NJ: Erlbaum, 1998.

Rosten, Leo C. *The Washington Correspondents.* New York: Harcourt, Brace and Company, 1937.

Tan, Yue, and David H. Weaver. "Local Media, Public Opinion, and State Legislative Policies: Agenda Setting at the State Level." *International Journal of Press/Politics* 14 (2009): 454–476.

PART IV ★ LEGISLATURES

Chapter 13

History and Development of State Legislatures, 1619 to 1961

Peverill Squire

STATE LEGISLATURES ARE THE PRODUCT OF A long evolutionary process, with their roots going back to the first colonial assembly that met in Virginia in 1619. Each of the colonies that became the original thirteen states had a colonial assembly that with relatively few changes was transformed into a state legislature following independence. In turn, those original state legislatures became the models for the U.S. Congress and all subsequent state legislatures.

This process has two noteworthy aspects. First, over time these legislatures became more complex organizations, with increasingly complex parliamentary rules and more elaborate decision-making structures, such as standing committee systems. Second, as new legislatures were established, they were fashioned in the image of legislatures of the time. Thus legislatures in younger states started their organizational development farther along than did legislatures in older states.

This chapter traces the structural development of state legislatures, examining their number of chambers and their membership sizes. It also gives attention to the evolution of organizational characteristics, notably parliamentary rules and standing committees. Finally, it reviews changes in the conditions of legislative service, with particular attention to salary and membership turnover. The goal is to explain how state legislatures had already changed as organizations prior to the professionalization revolution of the 1960s and 1970s.

THE COLONIAL ANTECEDENTS OF STATE LEGISLATURES

Legislative assemblies emerged in each of the American colonies relatively quickly after coming under English control, even though the colonies were settled by different groups of people at different times for different reasons. Virginia's first assembly was created because the failing colony's commercial managers hoped it would promote economic stability. Assemblies in Connecticut, Maryland, and Massachusetts were based in their early charters, but the impetus for their establishment came from the colonists. After the 1650s, it was thought that assemblies were essential structures for the development of successful societies; therefore each newly established colony was granted one.[1]

The Creation of Representative Assemblies and the Rise of Bicameralism

The early assemblies had to undergo two significant changes to become recognizable legislative institutions. First, they had to become representative bodies. In Virginia, the governor and his appointed councilors met from the beginning with two elected representatives from each of the colony's plantations and corporations. In New England, however, things were different; every freeman in each of those colonies participated in the "General Court" that made decisions. But the General Courts rapidly evolved into representative bodies as it became geographically impracticable for all freemen to participate in their frequent sessions. Thus across the northern colonies each town or county eventually came to elect representatives to speak on its behalf. Later assemblies were established as representative bodies from their start.[2]

The assemblies also had to evolve to become separate houses in bicameral legislatures. As discussed in the Dominance of Bicameralism box, bicameral legislatures emerged from unicameral bodies because of the critical distinction between councilors as appointed agents of the Crown or the colonies' proprietors and assembly members as elected agents of the colonies' freemen. Over many decades, their conflicting perspectives led the two groups to sit and deliberate apart. Except in Delaware and Pennsylvania, bicameralism became the established norm.

It is important to note that the decision to employ two houses was not an effort simply to imitate the British system. Bicameralism in the colonies differed in two essential ways. First, bicameralism emerged in England over representation of different social classes, while in America it was triggered

THE DOMINANCE OF BICAMERALISM

Initially, American legislatures consisted of a single body. The early colonial assemblies were composed of a governor, a council appointed to advise him, and either a colony's freemen or representatives elected to act on their behalf, all of whom sat together to make decisions. Thus they were not made in the image of the bicameral English Parliament with its hereditary House of Lords and elected House of Commons. But, over time, most of the colonial legislatures did, at different points and for different reasons, become bicameral legislatures, establishing a structure that is still in place in almost every state today.

Among the colonies, it was in Massachusetts that the council and the assembly first became unmistakably separate bodies. During the early 1630s, the appointed members of the council (the "magistrates") and the elected members of the assembly (the "deputies") developed divergent interests that led to conflicts between them. The most prominent dispute involved the case of a roving pig. A widow claimed that her sow had left her yard and wandered over to a sea captain's property, where it was killed. The widow sued for compensation. In deciding the case—many such judicial proceedings were conducted by legislatures at the time—the magistrates largely sided with the wealthy sea captain, while most of the deputies backed the financially strapped widow. This difference of opinion produced a split between the magistrates and deputies. In 1636 a working arrangement was reached between the council and the assembly requiring support from a majority of each group for a bill to pass and become a law. By 1644 the magistrates and the deputies were allowed to sit and deliberate apart, creating a bicameral legislature.

Most of the other colonial assemblies also became bicameral legislatures, although in some cases the split took decades to take place. By the time the final colonial assembly that would become a state legislature was created—Georgia, in 1855—bicameralism was the norm, and that body had two houses from its start. Bicameralism, however, was not universal; Pennsylvania started with two houses in 1682 but became unicameral with its new charter in 1701. And Delaware, which split off from Pennsylvania in 1704, was unicameral throughout its colonial existence.

An opportunity to revisit the question of how many houses to have was presented when the colonies declared their independence. In most of the new states there was relatively little thought given to the number of houses, and they simply maintained their existing bicameral systems. Of the eleven states that wrote constitutions, nine opted for bicameral legislatures. Additionally, both Connecticut and Rhode Island, which simply altered their existing charters, also continued their bicameral systems. The subject was, however, raised in a few places. In *Thoughts on Government,* John Adams argued that a unicameral legislature was unchecked and therefore prone to be "productive of hasty results and absurd judgments," a position most found persuasive. But in Pennsylvania, Benjamin Franklin successfully pushed for continuing that state's unicameral system, contending that bicameral legislatures were like putting one horse in front of a cart and another horse behind it, with the end result being that each horse pulls the cart in the opposite direction. Pennsylvania's constitution was the model for those subsequently adopted in Georgia and Vermont (which adopted a constitution in 1777 but was not admitted as a state until 1791), and both also created unicameral legislatures. Delaware, however, switched to a bicameral system in its 1776 constitution.

The dominance of bicameral legislatures soon became even more pronounced. The Georgia legislature became bicameral when the state adopted its second constitution in 1789, the change being motivated by a desire to bring the state into harmony with the design of Congress in the new federal Constitution. The following year Pennsylvania moved to a two-house system because of public discontent with its unicameral legislature. Vermont stayed with its single house until 1836, when voter unhappiness with the legislature's handling of a disputed gubernatorial election forced the change. Every state admitted since Vermont has entered the union with a bicameral legislature. Bicameralism was promoted because it was thought a second house prevented, or at least slowed down, the passage of bad legislation produced in response to fleeting political passions.

The only current deviation from bicameralism is in Nebraska, where voters in 1934 approved a constitutional amendment to create a unicameral legislature. Only the confluence of two extraordinary forces was able to overcome the American preference for bicameralism. One was the economic depression, which led Nebraskans to seek a less expensive legislative form. The other was the fanatical campaign of U.S. senator George Norris, R-Neb., for unicameralism, motivated by his hatred for what he saw as the lack of accountability and corrupt behavior in the conference committees appointed to resolve policy differences between the two houses in bicameral legislatures. Since then, however, every attempt to create a unicameral legislature in other states has failed.

by policy disagreements between groups holding office through different mechanisms. Second, the English House of Lords was a hereditary body and thus politically independent of both the Crown and the people. In contrast, council members in most of the colonies were appointees of the Crown or the proprietor and were politically dependent on them.[3]

The Role of the Colonial Assemblies

Some of the assemblies enjoyed the right to initiate legislation from their inception; others only gained that power over time. Eventually, they all came to be lawmaking bodies, passing legislation on a wide range of issues including economic regulation, election administration, law enforcement and justice, public welfare, taxation, and transportation. The assemblies successfully asserted parliamentary privilege for their members, protecting them in their public acts from retribution by the governor and royal officials. They also gained the right to establish their own procedural rules and to select their leaders.[4] The assemblies became so autonomous and successful that they were the main political engines pushing the colonies toward political independence.

Legislative Service in the Colonial Assemblies

The assemblies began as relatively small bodies, with membership sizes ranging from 10 members in New Jersey to 41 members in Pennsylvania. By the time of the Revolution, most were larger. There were, however, substantial differences in their sizes, from only 18 assembly members in Delaware to 138 members in Connecticut.

Over time the assemblies developed into institutions organized to meet the demands of their constituents. They relied heavily on petitions from the citizenry to set their agendas. As demands on them increased, the assemblies came to meet in longer sessions. In South Carolina, for example, it was customary for the assembly to meet for up to eight months a year, and when in session it met six days a week for six hours each day.[5] The assemblies acquired clerks to assist them in processing paperwork. After meeting in churches, taverns, school houses, private homes, and even barns, the assemblies eventually procured facilities dedicated to their use, providing them the space they needed to conduct their proceedings.

Assembly members in every colony save Georgia and South Carolina came to be paid for their services. Pay was instituted because of concerns about the willingness of potential lawmakers to serve given the financial burdens of doing so. In Rhode Island, for example, the colony's lawmakers initially received no compensation. But attendance proved to be such a problem that the decision was made to pay members to entice them to participate. To further encourage members to attend, most colonial assemblies also imposed a financial penalty for failing to show. What members got paid differed across the colonies, although it always came in the form of a per diem (daily wage). In both Maryland and Virginia, for example, members were initially paid in tobacco for each day the assembly was in session and for their travel to and from the meeting place. Later they came to be paid in shillings. Regardless of the currency used, the voters typically grumbled about the salaries paid while assembly members calculated that the sums were too little to cover their actual costs. It is, however, notable that salaries were established in the colonial assemblies at the same time their provision was being discontinued in Parliament.[6]

Despite the fact that the assemblies were both time demanding and poorly paid, over time, the institutions enjoyed increasingly stable memberships. From 1696 to 1775, turnover dropped in every assembly but New Jersey, and the decline was usually substantial. In the most extreme case, turnover in Pennsylvania dropped to a mean of 18 percent in the decade from 1766 to 1775 from a mean of 62 percent in the decade from 1696 to 1705. And well over half of the "new" members in later decades were actually former legislators returning to the institution. Thus by the early 1770s the assemblies enjoyed experienced memberships.[7]

The rules and procedures initially used by the assemblies were taken from those used in the English House of Commons. Over time, however, the assemblies elaborated on those rules, and they became more numerous, more complex, and less like those used in Parliament. In 1658 the Virginia House of Burgesses only had five rules, all of which centered on parliamentary protocol, but with a local twist: fines for violating accepted behaviors were specified in pounds of tobacco. Among the misbehaviors punished was appearing in the house "with overmuch drinke." By 1663, three more rules were added, including an antismoking ordinance punishing "every member that shall pipe it after the house is begun to be called over. . . ." By 1769, the house used twenty-eight rules, many of them unique to the colony. There were provisions requiring the clerk to read the orders of the day before the house proceeded to any other business and that all bills be taken up in the order they were introduced, unless the house decided otherwise. Specific quorum standards were set. One rule covered the process by which election contests were to be settled, while another explicitly banned the use of "Bribery, and other corrupt Practices" to gain election. In almost all of the colonial assemblies the rules became more complex over time, although they evolved somewhat differently in each, and each assembly devised distinctive procedures to process legislation.[8]

Initially, the assemblies exclusively used ad hoc committees created for each issue at each step of the legislative process; indeed, two were created on the first day of the initial Virginia General Assembly in 1619.[9] Over time, most of the assemblies came to establish standing committees to handle important topics that regularly appeared on their agendas. Standing committees never completely supplanted ad hoc committees, but their use became more pronounced over time in the assemblies outside of those in New England. They were particularly central to the legislative process in Virginia. By 1770, the House of Burgesses employed six standing committees. When bills were introduced they were referred to the appropriate standing committees; the committees then amended them before sending them on to the chamber's floor. The importance of standing committee systems in many of the assemblies is notable because, although their use was initially derived from counterparts in the English House of Commons, they disappeared in that body over the same time period their importance grew in most of the colonies. This is further evidence that colonial legislative systems evolved independently of their English parent.

THE FIRST STATE LEGISLATURES AND THEIR DEVELOPMENT IN THE EIGHTEENTH CENTURY

With independence, the colonial legislatures quickly became the new state legislatures. But what appears to be a seamless transition was actually interrupted briefly by the use of provincial congresses (called conventions in Maryland and Virginia) in most colonies. These congresses were unicameral bodies that exercised legislative, executive, and judicial functions during the interregnum between the colonial era and the establishment of the United States. When state constitutions were written, however, the state legislatures they created looked very much like their colonial predecessors and nothing like the provincial congresses.[10]

State Constitutions and the Legislatures

When the colonies declared their independence from Great Britain they were charged with writing constitutions to establish their new governments. They could have opted for completely new forms, but they chose instead only to tweak their existing structures. Indeed, Connecticut and Rhode Island continued to operate under their only cosmetically changed colonial charters until well into the nineteenth century. The eleven new states that wrote constitutions also made only minimal changes. This is understandable because, with the exception of Massachusetts, the new constitutions were written in haste and there was little time for reflection or invention.

As shown in Table 13.1, the original state legislatures emerged (almost) directly from their colonial predecessors. As noted in the Dominance of Bicameralism box, bicameralism continued to dominate, with eleven of the thirteen legislatures being established with two houses. The lower houses were essentially the colonial assemblies with new names. In New York's 1777 constitution the continuity was made explicit in Article IX: "That the General Assembly thus constituted shall chuse their own speaker, be judges of their own members, and proceed in doing business in like manner as the former Assemblies of the Colony of New York . . . did." The most noticeable change in the lower houses was a sizable increase in the number of seats compared with the colonial assemblies. Increased membership size was an effort to make them more representative, and most of the new seats came from previously unrepresented towns and inland areas. Increases in membership and representativeness had actually already occurred with the provincial congresses and were simply carried over to the new legislatures.[11]

TABLE 13.1 **Origin of State Legislatures**

State	State legislature first convened	Predecessor legislature(s) (years met)
Alabama	1819	territorial legislature (1818)
Alaska	1959	territorial legislature (1913–1958)
Arizona	1912	territorial legislature (1864–1909)
Arkansas	1836	territorial legislature (1820–1835)
California	1849	none
Colorado	1876	territorial legislature (1861–1876)
Connecticut	1776	colonial assembly (1637–1776)
Delaware	1776	colonial assembly (1704–1775)
Florida	1845	territorial legislature (1822–1845)
Georgia	1777	colonial assembly (1755–1776)
Hawaii	1959	territorial legislature (1901–1959), Republic of Hawaii legislature (1894–1898), Kingdom of Hawaii legislatures (1840–1892)
Idaho	1890	territorial legislature (1863–1889)
Illinois	1818	territorial legislature (1812–1818)
Indiana	1816	territorial legislature (1805–1816)
Iowa	1846	territorial legislature (1838–1846)

State	State legislature first convened	Predecessor legislature(s) (years met)
Kansas	1861	territorial legislature (1855–1861) and Free State Legislature (1856–1857)
Kentucky	1792	none
Louisiana	1812	(Orleans) territorial legislature (1804–1811)
Maine	1820	none, split from Massachusetts
Maryland	1777	colonial assembly (1637 or 1638–1774)
Massachusetts	1777	colonial assembly (1634–1777)
Michigan	1835	territorial legislature (1824–1835)
Minnesota	1857	territorial legislature (1849–1857)
Mississippi	1817	territorial legislature (1800–1817)
Missouri	1820	territorial legislature (1812–1820)
Montana	1889	territorial legislature (1864–1889)
Nebraska	1866	territorial legislature (1855–1867)
Nevada	1864	territorial legislature (1861–1864)
New Hampshire	1776	colonial assembly (1680–1775)
New Jersey	1776	colonial assembly (1668–1776)
New Mexico	1912	territorial legislature (1851–1909)
New York	1777	colonial assembly (1683–1775)
North Carolina	1777	colonial assembly (1665–1775)
North Dakota	1889	(Dakota) territorial legislature (1862–1889)
Ohio	1803	(Northwest) territorial legislature (1799–1801)
Oklahoma	1907	territorial legislature (1890–1905)
Oregon	1860	territorial legislature (1849–1859), provisional legislatures (1843–1849)
Pennsylvania	1776	colonial assembly (1682–1776)
Rhode Island	1776	colonial assembly (1647–1776)
South Carolina	1776	colonial assembly (1671–1775)
South Dakota	1890	(Dakota) territorial legislature (1862–1889)
Tennessee	1796	(Southwest) territorial legislature (1794–1795)
Texas	1846	Congress of the Republic of Texas (1836–1845)
Utah	1896	territorial legislature (1854–1895), General Assembly of Deseret (1849–1851)
Vermont	1791	Vermont General Assembly (1778–1791)
Virginia	1776	colonial assembly (1619–1775)
Washington	1889	territorial legislature (1854–1888)
West Virginia	1863	none, split from Virginia
Wisconsin	1848	territorial legislature (1836–1848)
Wyoming	1890	territorial legislature (1869–1890)

There was one substantial difference between the new state legislatures and the colonial bodies they replaced. In most of the colonies the upper house had been appointed; in the new state legislatures they became elected bodies. Calling them the senate was Thomas Jefferson's suggestion when Virginia's constitution was being written; the name was adopted and became the national standard.

The original state constitutions established three important relationships between the two legislative houses in bicameral systems that have carried through to the present. The first is that the upper house is always smaller than the lower house. The second is that the term of office for the upper house is as long as or longer than the term of office for the lower house. The final relationship is that qualifications for office imposed on the upper house, such as age, are as stringent as or more stringent than those imposed on the lower house. These relationships suggest that upper houses were intended to be fundamentally different from lower houses.

The initial size differences between the two houses were dramatic. In Maryland, for example, the senate had 15 seats while the lower house had 80 seats. The difference in Connecticut was even more pronounced, at 12 senate seats and 138 house seats. A few states gave members of both houses the same term of office. Thus in New Hampshire all state legislators had one-year terms, while in South Carolina they enjoyed two-year terms. In the other states lower house terms ranged from the traditional six-month terms in Connecticut and Rhode Island, to one-year terms everywhere else but South Carolina. Shorter terms of office were preferred because it was thought they promoted close contact between lawmakers and constituents, enhancing representation. Most of the new upper houses also had one-year terms, but several were granted longer terms, with Maryland's five-year term being the longest. Longer terms were favored for upper houses because they helped insulate lawmakers from political pressures.[12]

Constitutions also granted state legislatures several other important powers derived from their colonial experiences. Language allowing legislatures to select their own leaders appeared in nine constitutions, while five constitutions authorized legislatures to devise their own procedural rules. Control over their leaders and rules and procedures gave legislatures sway over their organizational evolution.

Another significant constitutional provision involved the power to originate tax legislation, authority the colonial assemblies had struggled to gain. Most of the new constitutions gave the lower house exclusive rights to initiate tax bills. Some of the constitutions went even further and forbade the upper house from amending tax bills, firmly rooting control over taxation in the hands of the larger and more representative lower houses.

There were minimal attempts to clearly delineate powers among separate branches of government. Only three constitutions (those of Massachusetts, New York, and South Carolina) gave their governor any form of a veto. Instead of creating governments with checks and balances, the initial constitutions established legislative supremacy.[13] Legislators could dominate governors and judges; in most states, all of those officials were elected by the legislature. Thus in 1786, when Rhode Island lawmakers disagreed with an important state supreme court decision, they simply refused to reappoint the offending judges and replaced them with men who would do their bidding.[14]

The Organizational Development of the New State Legislatures

There were obvious organizational continuities between the new state legislatures and their colonial predecessors. They generally used the same rules and had the same standing committees. Many customs also carried forward. At the beginning of each legislative session the New York General Assembly continued, as it had in the colonial assembly, to inform the governor "that the House are ready to proceed to business and wait His Excellency's *commands*." Such deferential form was maintained until 1823. A mace purchased in England for Virginia's colonial house Speaker continued to be used by the state's house Speaker until 1792, when it was decided that such "Kingly pomp" should be discarded.[15]

What was service in the new state legislatures like? Certainly, during the Revolution being a legislator may not have been appealing because had the British triumphed state legislators might have been tried as traitors. But there were also other things that made service unattractive. At a minimum, the legislatures met annually; thus time demands were not trivial. Salaries were not much of an enticement, with members being paid minimal per diems. During the 1770s and 1780s, New Hampshire paid its legislators six shillings for each day in session and four pence per mile traveled to and from the meeting place. While some legislatures had a permanent meeting location (Maryland, for example, always assembled in Annapolis), others were more nomadic (between 1777 and 1789 North Carolina's legislature met in seven different cities). Despite the apparent lack of incentives for service, membership turnover was not a problem. For instance, during the first decades of the New York General Assembly's existence only about a third of its members were new each session.[16]

THE DEVELOPMENT OF STATE LEGISLATURES DURING THE NINETEENTH CENTURY

The era of legislative supremacy did not last long. By the end of the eighteenth century, reservations were being expressed about the tremendous power invested in state legislatures. When the original states replaced their initial constitutions, which most eventually did, the newer documents included provisions that made governors and judges more independent of legislative control.[17] Explicit constraints on the legislature were imposed over the course of the nineteenth century. Among the procedural limitations imposed by state constitutions by the 1870s were restrictions on when bills could be introduced (three states), requirements that bills be confined to a single subject (nineteen states) and that they could not be reenacted only by reference to title or section (nineteen states), and mandates that all votes on final passage be taken by yeas and nays (twenty states).

State constitutions also came to place unambiguous limits on the sorts of special laws legislatures could pass. Special laws are measures designed for a narrow purpose and reference a particular place, person, or organization, and because of this they are prone to corruption. Article IV, Section 27, of the Missouri's 1865 constitution provides an example of the limitations placed on special bills with its long list of restrictions, among them prohibitions against "establishing, locating, altering the course, or affecting the construction of roads, or the building or repairing of bridges; or establishing, altering, or vacating any street, avenue, or alley in any city or town," and "extending the time for the assessment or collection of taxes, or otherwise relieving any assessor or collector of taxes from the due performance of his official duties. . . ." Limitations on the legislature's powers to pass special laws appeared in most nineteenth-century state constitutions.

Territorial Legislatures and Other Predecessor Institutions

The first thirteen state legislatures developed directly out of their colonial predecessors. The other thirty-seven state legislatures that would come to be established had different lineages, as shown in Table 13.1. A total of thirty-one state legislatures emerged from the territorial legislatures that preceded them. Territorial legislatures were created by the U.S. Congress as part of the governing structure it put in place when territories were established. Almost all of the territorial legislatures were bicameral. The exceptions were Orleans, which only briefly had a unicameral legislature, and Florida and Michigan, which Congress gave unicameral legislatures because it thought they were too poor to financially support two legislative houses. Congress eventually granted Florida a second house, but Michigan remained unicameral throughout its territorial existence. The territorial legislatures were important because their rules, committee structures, and occasionally personnel transferred over to the state legislatures that supplanted them.

Several of the territorial legislatures had been preceded by other legislative bodies that played important roles in their institutional evolution. In Oregon, for example, there were several iterations of a unicameral provisional legislature that made laws while the United States and Great Britain competed for political control of the area. Prior to the creation of the Utah Territory, Mormons founded the State of Deseret, complete with a bicameral general assembly. In Hawaii, the territorial legislature was preceded by several legislatures of the Kingdom of Hawaii, and a bicameral legislature was established under the Republic of Hawaii. Finally, in Kansas, a Free State Legislature arose not only to challenge the pro-slavery territorial legislature but ultimately to supplant it in the state legislature's evolutionary line.

There were six state legislatures that did not have a colonial or territorial predecessor. Both Vermont and Kentucky were admitted as states before Congress created the territorial system. Vermont, however, had an assembly for thirteen years prior to becoming a state, and that body became its state legislature. Maine and West Virginia were split off from Massachusetts and Virginia, respectively; Maine's new state legislature looked much like its parent, but West Virginia's drew on a number of different models. The state legislature in Texas was preceded by the bicameral Congress of the Texas Republic, and the two institutions shared rules, committee systems, and personnel. Finally, California became a state before any civilian territorial government could be established.[18]

Legislative Service during the Nineteenth Century

The size and shape of state legislatures changed over the course of the nineteenth century. Bicameralism dominated, with every new state legislature being established with two houses, and Vermont—the lone unicameral legislature at the beginning of the century—becoming bicameral in 1836. Bicameralism was endorsed because it was thought a two-house legislature promoted greater scrutiny of proposed laws.[19]

Legislative membership sizes fluctuated over the course of the century, but with a general upward trend. In New York, for example, in 1800 the senate had 43 seats. In 1802 the number of seats was reduced to 32, where it stayed until 1895, when it was increased to 50 seats. The number of seats in the lower house also bounced around: in 1800 it was 108; in 1802 it was lowered to 100; in 1808 it was increased to 112; and it boosted again to 126 in 1815, 128 in 1822, and finally 150 in 1895. In contrast, Pennsylvania experienced continual increases, with the upper house growing from 24 members in 1800 to 25 (1801), 31 (1808), 33 (1822), and 50 (1874). The lower house also grew dramatically, starting with 78 seats in 1800, reaching 100 by 1822, 201 by 1874, and 204 in 1888.

Membership size did decrease in a few legislatures, most notably in the Massachusetts House. Until 1857, the number of house members was a function of the number of towns in the state and how many of those towns in any particular year opted to cover the cost of sending their representatives to the legislature. Thus the house's membership size varied from session to session, reaching a high of 749 members in 1812 and a low of 160 members in 1822. By 1857, during a session in which 355 members were in attendance, it was determined that the membership was usually too large for the organization to function well. At that point the voters passed a constitutional amendment to cap the number of seats at 240. Virginia also cut back the size of its legislature, from a senate of 50 members and a lower house of 152 members in the middle of the century, to a senate of 40 members and a lower house of 100 members by the end of the century.

The contours of legislative service changed during the century. Legislative terms usually were lengthened. Among lower houses, in 1800 two states had six-month terms, thirteen states had one-year terms, and just Tennessee had two-year terms. By 1900, four states had one-year terms, thirty-nine states had two-year terms, and two states had four-year terms. Among upper houses, in 1800 six states had one-year terms, two had two-year terms, two had three-year terms, four had four-year terms, and Maryland gave its senators five-year terms. By 1900, two states had one-year terms, twelve had two-year terms, New Jersey gave its senators three-year terms, and thirty states had four-year terms. There were some twists and turns in this process; for instance, Maryland (1838–1850) and Texas (1869–1875) each briefly awarded their senators six-year terms before settling on four-year terms.[20] Longer terms were preferred because they meant elections could be held less frequently.

But term lengths also changed because legislatures came to meet less often. At the start of the nineteenth century, almost every state legislature met in annual sessions because those who wrote the original state constitutions thought frequent legislative meetings checked gubernatorial power and enhanced representation.[21] But a shift to biennial sessions occurred inexorably over the century. By 1832, three out of the twenty-four states limited their legislatures to meeting only every other year: Illinois, Missouri, and Tennessee, all of which were younger states that had established biennial sessions in their first constitutions. Delaware became the first of the original states to switch when it adopted biennial sessions in 1833. By 1900, only six of the forty-five states retained annual meetings, all of them from among the original thirteen states. Some states switched back and forth: Virginia adopted biennial sessions in 1850, returned to annual sessions in 1870, and then went back to meeting every other year in 1876, while Georgia adopted biennial sessions in 1877 but reverted to annual sessions in 1892. And Mississippi toyed with quadrennial sessions; starting in 1890 it scheduled its legislature to meet every fourth year, but allowed it to meet in regularly scheduled, limited special sessions at the two-year midpoint, effectively giving the legislature quasibiennial sessions. Longer periods between sessions became the national preference because it was reasoned that meeting less often reduced the number of laws the legislature passed and also reduced the cost to the state of having the legislature in session.

Although there had been debate over the issue, by the beginning of the nineteenth century every state paid its lawmakers a per diem for their service. None of the per diems was generous. In the 1830s the sums paid ranged from a low of $1.50 a day in the New England legislatures to a high of $4.00 in many of the southern states. Following Kentucky's lead in its first constitution, many states began setting their per diems in their state constitutions. This practice became dominant by the 1850s, taking control over their pay out of legislators' hands. In another innovation, in 1844 New Jersey began limiting the number of days its per diem would be given: $3 for the first forty days and then $1.50 for each additional day. This system gave lawmakers an incentive to conclude their business within the specified time period and limited their ability to pad their pay by extending sessions. Within a few years California, Illinois, Iowa, and New York employed similar systems.

The most notable change in legislative pay was introduced in Massachusetts in 1858 when it opted to pay its lawmakers an annual wage of $300 rather than a per diem. Pennsylvania quickly adopted the innovation and was paying its lawmakers $700 a year by 1860. By 1889, eleven states offered an annual salary, with New York setting the standard at $1,500. With the introduction of annual salaries the states began to differentiate themselves. In the early decades of the century there had been no systematic difference in legislative salaries between large, wealthy states and small, poorer states. By the end of the nineteenth century, the contrast was obvious, with the larger states paying their lawmakers considerably more.

Given the typically meager sums paid most legislators and the general drop in public regard for the institutions suggested by the constitutional constraints imposed on them, it is no surprise that over the nineteenth century state legislative memberships were highly unstable. Turnover had been relatively low toward the end of the eighteenth century, but then the pattern changed dramatically. For instance, during the first half of the century turnover in Connecticut, Georgia, and New York reached levels of between 70 percent and almost 100 percent. And these states were not exceptional. High levels of turnover were commonplace across all state legislatures during the antebellum period. In Arkansas, 93 percent of lower house members between 1836 and 1861 served only a single term.[22]

Turnover rates declined only slightly after the Civil War. Between 1886 and 1895, first-term members composed 68 percent of the Illinois House, 62 percent of the Iowa House, and 75 percent of the Wisconsin House. Turnover rates in the Ohio legislature in the 1880s and 1890s often reached close to 100 percent. Again, such figures were common.[23]

Some aspects of legislative service did improve during the nineteenth century. State legislatures acquired permanent facilities dedicated to their use. Indeed, four capitols built toward the very end of the eighteenth century and sixteen capitols constructed during the nineteenth century are still in use by state legislatures in the twenty-first century. Many early capitols were destroyed by fires. All were replaced by larger buildings that provided more space for legislators, staff, and other government offices. Other capitols were expanded to meet growing needs and upgraded with modern conveniences. In Minnesota's capitol gas lights replaced candles in 1866, and in 1871 a running water system was hooked up and steam heat replaced wood-burning stoves.

Despite fluctuations in legislative size, pay, term lengths, and turnover during the nineteenth century, the concept of permanent facilities for state legislatures took root. This print shows an 1896 competition drawing (not final design) for the state capitol building in Helena, Montana, with a busy street scene of carriages and coaches, and large groups of people standing on steps and at entrances to the building.

SOURCE: Library of Congress Reproduction Number LC-DIG-pga-03345; http://www.loc.gov/pictures/item/2006677661.

Assistance also improved. At the beginning of the nineteenth century state legislatures had little in the way of staff other than a clerk or two, a doorkeeper, and a sergeant-at-arms. The number of support staff grew over time, but only slowly. By 1858, the lower house in New York, which was a leader in building staff, employed a clerk, four deputy clerks, a librarian, an assistant librarian, a postmaster, and an assistant postmaster. By 1890, the number of staff had swelled considerably, to seventy-three positions. A number of posts were new, among them twelve committee clerks. By the last quarter of the century, more employees, including staff for at least some standing committees, were common in most state legislatures. Most clerks, however, were employed on a session-only basis, and in some legislatures they were hired and fired as needed, suggesting that the increase in their numbers was driven more by clerical needs and patronage desires than by informational demands. By the end of the century, however, the seeds of change were planted. Most notably, in 1890 the New York State Library established a legislative reference unit, the first of its kind in the nation. In 1892 the Massachusetts State Library took steps in a similar direction. Both organizations began to provide lawmakers the informational resources they needed to carry out their legislative responsibilities.[24]

The Institutionalization of State Legislatures: Rules and Standing Committee Systems

State legislatures became more complex organizations over the course of the nineteenth century. The development of legislative rules and procedures demonstrates this process. For example, in the Ohio House bill introduction procedures evolved significantly. During the early part of the nineteenth century, bills were introduced either by an individual by motion for leave (with a day's notice) or by order of the house on a report of a committee; most legislation was introduced by committees. By the 1860s, lawmakers were allowed to introduce legislation without leave of the house, and bills were about as likely to be introduced by an individual as by a committee. Similar transitions occurred in most other state legislatures.[25]

More generally, between 1818–1819 and 1888–1889 lower houses greatly increased the total number of rules under which they operated. In 1818–1819 the mean number of rules across the states was 37, with Delaware using the fewest at 16 and Massachusetts employing the most at 58. By 1888–1889, the mean number of rules had increased to 64, again with Delaware using the least at 26 and Massachusetts the most at 102. More important, toward the end of the century most legislatures employed sophisticated rules focused on managing the legislative process rather than on matters of parliamentary protocol.

Similar developments occurred with standing committees. By 1818 and 1819, every state legislature had at least a few standing committees—Connecticut had only 2 and the mean was 7—while several had a good number of them—Massachusetts used 17. Seven decades later, the mean number of standing committees had exploded to 33, with Delaware needing only 14 and Iowa and Michigan each naming 53. Importantly, by the end of the century standing committees were central to the legislative process in every state, with most enjoying substantial gate-keeping powers allowing them to kill legislation.

STATE LEGISLATURES FROM 1900 TO 1961: THE FIRST HINTS OF THE PROFESSIONALIZATION REVOLUTION

By the beginning of the twentieth century, state legislatures were quite different from what they had been one hundred years before. But even with all the positive changes, they suffered from one major flaw. In general, the public saw them as corrupt institutions, and it public had little confidence in them. At the same time, the decisions state legislatures made were central to the public. Most of the governmental policies that impacted daily life were decided by state legislatures, not the U.S. Congress. Thus voters began to demand more of their state legislators and the institutions in which they served. Because of this the seeds for legislative professionalization were planted and the first hints of improved member and institutional resources appeared.

The Beginnings of Professionalization: Increasing Member Pay, Legislative Sessions, and Staff Resources

In terms of basic structures, there were a few noticeable changes in state legislatures between 1901 and 1961. Perhaps the most significant occurred in Nebraska in 1934, when voters approved a constitutional amendment to create a unicameral legislature. At the same time, they also voted to make the legislature nonpartisan. (Minnesota's legislature was also elected without party labels at the time.) Being unicameral and nonpartisan made (and still makes) Nebraska's legislature distinctive.

Legislative membership sizes continued to increase in a majority of states. By 1960, upper houses in twenty-three states and lower houses in twenty-five states were larger than they had been in 1900. In some states the growth was substantial: the Georgia Senate grew to 54 seats from 44 seats, while the Georgia House expanded to 205 seats from 130 seats. Only the Idaho legislature was smaller in 1960 than it had been in 1900. Membership sizes tended to grow in response to increases in population.

The first half of the twentieth century also saw the trend toward longer legislative terms continue. For example, in 1947 New Jersey increased the term for its lower house from one year to two years, and for its upper house from three years to four years. By 1960, forty-five states gave their lower house members two-year terms, while the other states gave theirs four-year terms. At the upper house level thirteen states had two-year terms and thirty-seven had four-year terms. Longer terms reduced the cost of election administration while giving lawmakers more time to legislate between campaigns.

At the beginning of the twentieth century legislative salaries were low: the mean across the states was just under $250 a year. This was seen as a serious problem in many places. For instance, a 1904 *Atlantic Monthly* article observed, "We do not pay our legislators a living wage, certainly not a wage that can attract ability."[26] It was also thought that low pay encouraged corruption. Consequently, reform advocates campaigned for both higher wages and replacing per diems with annual salaries.

By the mid-1950s, the mean salary had increased to $1,188. Pay mechanisms had also changed. By the mid-part of the twentieth century, thirty-one states had done away with per diem payments in favor of offering a set salary. This change was associated with an increase in legislative pay in most states. The increase in pay appears to have had at least one important consequence: turnover rates began to decline noticeably, starting in the 1930s.

Over the course of the nineteenth century state legislatures had shifted from holding annual sessions to

State assemblies, such as the New York State Assembly shown here in Albany, New York, around 1913, are responsible for enacting state laws and policies. As more was demanded of state legislatures, many advocated for professionalization and additional resources.

SOURCE: Library of Congress Reproduction Number: LC-USZ62–95464; http://www.loc.gov/pictures/item/91482107.

biennial sessions. During the first half of the twentieth century they began to reverse course. By 1960, nineteen met annually. States began to move away from biennial sessions (or in the case of Alabama from quadrennial sessions, which it had in place during the century's first four decades) for one main reason: demands were increasing on legislatures, and meeting every other year did not allow them to respond expeditiously. Indeed, legislatures were regularly called into special sessions to address pressing problems.

At the beginning of the century no state legislature provided staff for individual lawmakers, and only limited assistance for committees. But, between 1900 and 1920, a number of states developed institutional staff resources. The most prominent was Wisconsin's Legislative Reference Bureau, which became a model for the other states and for the U.S. Congress as well. State legislatures also began to improve their informational resources in other ways. By the 1950s, clerical staff was provided to most committees in almost every state. Staff for individual members, however, was sparse: only Florida, Iowa, Missouri, Oregon, Pennsylvania, and Texas provided almost all of their lawmakers with clerical help. Most other states only provided members access to a secretarial pool.[27]

Finally, as organizations, state legislatures continued to evolve in terms of rules and standing committees. By the beginning of the twentieth century, parliamentary rules in most chambers were reasonably complex and sophisticated. They continued to grow in number, but only slowly. Innovations were focused on making the legislative process more efficient. A similar trend was evident with standing committee systems. At the start of the century they were bloated in most states. In 1915 the thirty-two-member Michigan Senate had sixty-five standing committees, fourteen of which dealt primarily with education issues. This sort of problem eventually forced most legislative houses to reduce their number of committees in the name of efficiency. Such reform was initially pursued in Wisconsin, and most other states followed suit. The rationale for the reduction was practical: "to facilitate their functioning and thereby expedite the whole legislative process."[28] Given these developments, by 1960 the effort to improve state legislatures enjoyed some momentum.

NOTES

1. Warren M. Billings, *A Little Parliament: The Virginia General Assembly in the Seventeenth Century* (Richmond: Library of Virginia, Jamestown 2007/Jamestown-Yorktown Foundation, 2004), 5–7; Michael Kammen, *Deputyes and Libertyes: The Origins of Representative Government in Colonial America* (New York: Knopf, 1969), 19, 32.

2. Maurice Klain, "A New Look at the Constituencies: The Need for a Recount and a Reappraisal," *American Political Science Review* 49 (1955): 1105–1119.

3. Robert Luce, *Legislative Assemblies* (Boston: Houghton Mifflin, 1924), 47–50; Jackson Turner Main, *The Upper House in Revolutionary America, 1763–1788* (Madison: University of Wisconsin Press, 1967), 3, 199–200.

4. Jack P. Greene, *The Quest for Power: The Lower Houses of Assembly in the Southern Royal Colonies, 1689–1776* (Chapel Hill: University of North Carolina Press, 1963), 216–219.

5. M. Eugene Sirmans, *Colonial South Carolina* (Chapel Hill: University of North Carolina Press, 1966), 241.

6. Peverill Squire, *The Evolution of American Legislatures: Colonies, Territories, and States, 1619–2009* (Ann Arbor: University of Michigan Press, 2012), 29–35.

7. Jack P. Greene, "Legislative Turnover in British America, 1696 to 1775: A Quantitative Analysis," *William and Mary Quarterly* 38 (1981): 442–463; Alan Tully, *William Penn's Legacy: Politics and Social Structure in Provincial Pennsylvania, 1726–1755* (Baltimore, MD: Johns Hopkins University Press, 1977), 181–182.

8. Squire, *The Evolution of American Legislatures*, 46–67.

9. William J. Van Schreeven and George H. Reese, eds., *Proceedings of the General Assembly of Virginia July 30–August 4, 1619 Written & Sent from Va. to England by Mr. John Pory Speaker of the First Representative Assembly in the New World* (Jamestown, VA: Jamestown Foundation of the Commonwealth of Virginia, 1969), 25–27.

10. Squire, *The Evolution of American Legislatures*, 71–83.

11. Main, *The Upper House in Revolutionary America;* Rosemarie Zagarii, *The Politics of Size* (Ithaca, NY: Cornell University Press, 1987), 42–43.

12. Peverill Squire and Keith E. Hamm, *101 Chambers: Congress, State Legislatures, and the Future of Legislative Studies* (Columbus: Ohio State University Press, 2005), 19–28.

13. Rogan Kersh, Suzanne B. Mettler, Grant D. Reeher, and Jeffrey M. Stonecash, "'More a Distinction of Words Than Things': The Evolution of Separated Powers in the American States," *Roger Williams University Law Review* 4 (1998): 5–49.

14. Arthur N. Holcombe, *State Government in the United States*, 3rd ed. (New York: Macmillan, 1931), 63.

15. Silvio A. Bedini, "The Mace and the Gavel: Symbols of Government in America," *Transactions of the American Philosophical Society* 87, Part 4 (1997): 1–21; Charles Z. Lincoln, *The Constitutional History of New York from the Beginning of the Colonial Period to the Year 1905, Showing the Origin, Development, and Judicial Construction of the Constitution*, vol. I (Rochester, NY: The Lawyers Co-operative, 1906), 576; Squire, *The Evolution of American Legislatures*, 89–93.

16. L. Ray Gunn, "The New York State Legislature: A Developmental Perspective: 1777–1846," *Social Science History* 4 (1980): 267–294.

17. Bayrd Still, "An Interpretation of the Statehood Process," *Mississippi Valley Historical Review* 23 (1936): 189–204; Gordon S. Wood, *Creation of the American Republic, 1776–1787* (Chapel Hill: University of North Carolina Press.1969), 446–453.

18. See Squire, *The Evolution of American Legislatures*, chap. 5.

19. Laura J. Scalia, *America's Jeffersonian Experiment: Remaking State Constitutions, 1820–1850* (DeKalb: Northern Illinois University Press, 1999), 107.

20. These data were gathered from Michael J. Dubin, *Party Affiliations in the State Legislatures: A Year by Year Summary, 1796–2006* (Jefferson, NC: McFarland and Company, 2007).

21. Squire and Hamm, *101 Chambers,* 68.

22. Donald A. DeBats, "An Uncertain Arena: The Georgia House of Representatives, 1808–1861," *Journal of Southern History* 56 (1990): 423–456; Clarence Deming, "Town Rule in Connecticut," *Political Science Quarterly* 4 (1889): 408–432; L. Ray Gunn, *The Decline of Authority: Public Economic Policy and Political Development in New York, 1800–1860* (Ithaca, NY: Cornell University Press, 1988), 75; Ralph A. Wooster, *The People in Power: Courthouse and Statehouse in the Lower South, 1850–1860* (Knoxville: University of Tennessee Press, 1969), 41–42; Ralph A. Wooster, *Politicians, Planters, and Plain Folk: Courthouse and Statehouse in the Upper South, 1850–1860* (Knoxville: University of Tennessee Press, 1975), 43.

23. Nancy Burns, Laura Evans, Gerald Gamm, and Corrine McConnaughy, "Pockets of Expertise: Institutional Capacity in Twentieth-Century State Legislatures," *Studies in American Political Development* 22 (2008): 229–248; Ballard C. Campbell, *Representative Democracy* (Cambridge: Harvard University Press, 1980), 228; David M. Gold, *Democracy in Session: A History of the Ohio General Assembly* (Athens: Ohio University Press, 2009), 53–54.

24. Samuel Rothstein, "The Origins of Legislative Reference Services in the United States," *Legislative Studies Quarterly* 15 (1990): 401–411; Squire, *The Evolution of American Legislatures,* 248–252.

25. H. W. Dodds, "Procedure in State Legislatures," *Annals of the American Academy of Political and Social Science* 17 (May supplement, 1918): 28; Gold, *Democracy in Session,* 119–120.

26. Samuel P. Orth, "Our State Legislatures," *Atlantic Monthly* 94 (1904): 728–739.

27. Belle Zeller, ed., *American State Legislatures* (New York: Crowell, 1954), 156–159.

28. John A. Perkins, "State Legislative Reorganization," *American Political Science Review* 40 (1946): 510–521.

SUGGESTED READING

Campbell, Ballard C. *Representative Democracy.* Cambridge: Harvard University Press, 1980.

Gold, David M. *Democracy in Session: A History of the Ohio General Assembly.* Athens, OH: Ohio University Press, 2009.

Goodsell, Charles T. *The American Statehouse: Interpreting Democracy's Temples.* Lawrence: University Press of Kansas, 2001.

Greene, Jack P. *The Quest for Power: The Lower Houses of Assembly in the Southern Royal Colonies, 1689–1776.* Chapel Hill: University of North Carolina Press, 1963.

Kammen, Michael. *Deputyes and Libertyes: The Origins of Representative Government in Colonial America.* New York: Knopf, 1969.

Luce, Robert. *Legislative Assemblies.* Boston: Houghton Mifflin, 1924.

Main, Jackson Turner. *The Upper House in Revolutionary America, 1763–1788.* Madison: University of Wisconsin Press, 1967.

Squire, Peverill. *The Evolution of American Legislatures: Colonies, Territories, and States, 1619–2009.* Ann Arbor: University of Michigan Press, 2012.

Squire, Peverill, and Keith E. Hamm. *101 Chambers: Congress, State Legislatures, and the Future of Legislative Studies.* Columbus: Ohio State University Press, 2005.

Zeller, Belle, ed. *American State Legislatures.* New York: Crowell, 1954.

Chapter 14

Districting

Michael P. McDonald

State legislators are elected from constituencies that are defined by geographic boundaries known as districts. Eligible voters who call a district home have the right to participate in elections to select its representatives. These district boundaries are redrawn periodically through a curious institution in democratic governance known as redistricting. In redistricting, elections are turned on their head when expert judgment is exercised to decide how to delineate the district boundaries that assign constituents to representatives. A clash of values often ensues when traditional principles, which may promote congruence of district and community boundaries while maintaining a pleasing district shape, run afoul of electoral goals, which may be affected by the inclusion or exclusion within a district of neighborhoods of particular partisan or racial character and even candidates' homes. Further heightening the tension among these values is the fact that in many states the persons tasked with redistricting are the same state legislators elected from the districts.

A storied history exists of politicians using redistricting to affect electoral outcomes. Patrick Henry supported a Virginia congressional redistricting plan designed to deny James Madison a seat in Congress. In 1812 the infamous gerrymander was given its name (see the Gerrymander box). Later, in the post-Reconstruction era in the South, districts were designed by white Southerners to deny effective representation for newly enfranchised African Americans. Together, these three types of gerrymanders are called incumbent, partisan, and racial gerrymanders, respectively.

Scholars have extensively debated gerrymandering's effectiveness to shape election outcomes, and even the historical record is mixed. Madison won election to his unfavorable district through an intensive campaign he waged at the urging of Thomas Jefferson. Yet a later president-to-be, Barack Obama, sought opportunities elsewhere after his home was drawn out of a congressional district for which he ran in 2000. The original gerrymander resulted in an antimajoritarian outcome where Federalists won a vote majority but barely more than a quarter of the seats, following the optimal partisan gerrymandering strategy that allocates an efficient level of partisan strength—not shaved too close as to make future elections competitive—among districts expected to be won by the party that controls redistricting and packing the opposition party into overwhelmingly safe districts. Yet greedy politicians have at times exceeded the optimal strategy, backfiring in what has been called a "dummymander." Where there is universal agreement is that race-conscious redistricting is effective at promoting or retarding minority representation. The Voting Rights Act of 1965 and its subsequent reauthorizations are credited with the election of thousands of minority candidates at the federal, state, and local levels, in areas where before there were none, although the future direction of voting rights is uncertain due to recent Supreme Court action.

Politicians' influence over redistricting is constrained. Federal and state constitutions and statutes describe how districts may be drawn and may build firewalls between politicians and line drawers. State variation in laws and who controls processes provide ample fodder for research. Scholars have even played an active role in redistricting, by devising and implementing legal tests and by peeling back the curtain on this arcane process that consumes politicians, but of which the public is largely unaware.

This chapter explores state legislative redistricting. It begins with an overview of the use of districts in state legislatures. It then describes redistricting criteria and institutions, paying particular attention to various commissions. Finally, it reviews scholarly work on the effects of these institutions, with some thoughts on future directions.

THE ORGANIZATION OF STATE LEGISLATIVE DISTRICTS

The U.S. Constitution largely leaves the organization of state legislative elections to the states, with some limited but

THE GERRYMANDER

In 1812 Massachusetts governor Elbridge Gerry's name was enshrined into American political lore when he signed into law a state senate redistricting plan devised by his Democratic-Republican Party. Senate president Samuel Dana was the likely author of the redistricting plan; however, the *Columbian Centinel* noted the bill originated from a House committee at the direction of House Speaker Joseph Story. Even today, only those in the map room know the true authors of a redistricting plan. The House committee approved two multimember senate districts that divided Essex County along town boundaries and would elect two and three at-large members. An amendment to form one Essex County district to elect five at-large members was proposed by Federalist committee members, but it was voted down.

According to the best historical account,[1] the Federalist paper, the *Weekly Messenger,* published a map of the offensive Essex County districts. The paper was displayed at a dinner party where, at the urging of guests, the artist Elkanah Tisdale drew wings onto the salamander-shaped district. (Imaginative Federalists also spied Governor Gerry's face in silhouette to the lower left of the district.) A poet, Richard Alsop, called the district a "Gerry-mander." Another apocryphal, poorly sourced account ascribes the cartoon to the celebrated painter Gilbert Stuart and the name to *Columbian Centinel* editor Benjamin Russell, but Russell denied these events. The image was quickly and widely reprinted in Federalist newspapers, and "gerrymander" briefly became slang for being tricked or deceived. As a cultural meme of its day, it is unsurprising that the gerrymander grew to such mythic proportions that historical figures like Stuart were woven into its tale.

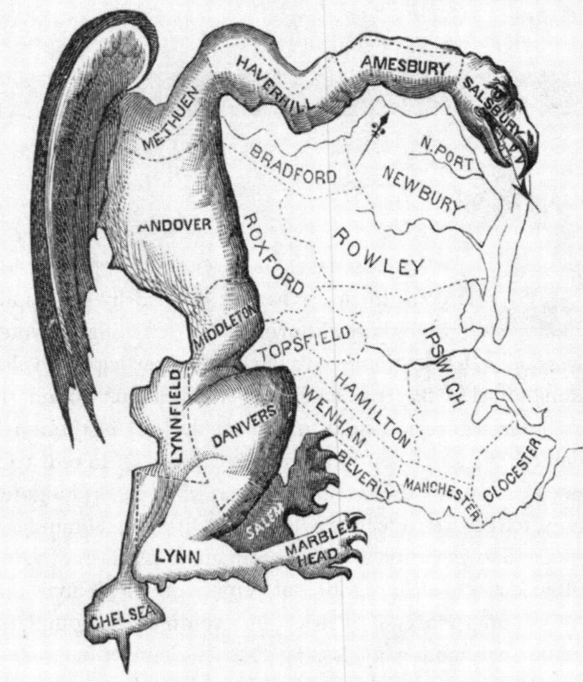

The term* gerrymander *was derived from this political cartoon. The district depicted was created by the Massachusetts legislature to favor the incumbent Democratic-Republican Party candidates of Gov. Elbridge Gerry over the Federalists in 1812.

SOURCE: Wikicommons: http://commons.wikimedia.org/wiki/File:The_Gerry-Mander.png.

The subject of the cartoon was a senate district drawn with a packing strategy in mind, to waste Federalist votes in a district they would win by an overwhelming margin. Federalist candidates in the district won as intended. Overall, the redistricting plan was brutally effective by limiting Federalists with a mere 27 percent of seats despite winning a narrow majority of votes in the next election. Yet the original gerrymander is now quaint in hindsight. It divided Essex County, but it kept its towns intact. Today, districts have been drawn that follow strip malls, road medians, and even the Colorado River as it flows through the Grand Canyon. Before one gets too offended, these examples all enhanced minority representation, which raises the question: Does shape alone define what is good and bad about a district?

1. John W. Dean, "The Gerrymander," *New England Historical and Genealogical Register* 46 (1892): 374–383.

consequential federal oversight. As of 2010, the United States had 6,888 state legislative districts, the most common being the single-member district. In Arizona, Idaho, North Dakota, South Dakota, and Washington the upper and lower legislative chambers share the same districts, with the lower chamber elected from multimember districts. The congruence of chambers' district boundaries is similar to a practice known as nesting, required or encouraged in fourteen states, whereby each upper chamber district wholly encapsulates two or more single-member lower chamber districts. Vermont and West Virginia have multimember districts for their upper and lower chambers. Maryland and New Hampshire use multimember districts for their lower chamber only. New Hampshire also employs what are known as floterial districts, where districts to the same chamber may overlap. The voting rules for these multimember districts vary; some hold separate at-large elections for each seat, whereas others employ bloc voting, whereby voters receive a number of votes equal to the number of seats and apportion them among the candidates.

States' legislative districts vary tremendously in their number and population. Pennsylvania's lower chamber has the most districts, 203. Although New Hampshire's lower chamber consists of 400 members, it currently has only 161 (often) multimember districts. The few single-member districts to that legislative body have the smallest populations among all states, an average of 3,291. At the other extreme, California's forty state senate districts have a greater population than its fifty-three congressional districts. The same is true for Texas's thirty-one state senate districts and thirty-six congressional districts. California's state senate districts have an average population of 931,349, compared with 702,905 for the congressional districts. Vermont's senate has the smallest number of districts; its thirty members are elected from thirteen districts. To put this another way, the state legislative district with the largest population is nearly three hundred times larger than the smallest district, and the state legislative chamber with the most districts has nearly sixteen times more districts than the chamber with the least.

Legislative body size is consequential when combined with redistricting constraints and a state's political geography. For example, Minnesota's senate has sixty-seven districts, and its house has 134 districts. Most Democratic-Farmer-Laborer Party voters are concentrated in Minneapolis. It is thus more difficult to unpack Democrats by bridging equal population districts from the urban core to the outlying Republican suburbs when drawing a house redistricting plan than a senate plan. This tendency has differing effects among states and legislative districts, since the distribution of partisans varies, as does the size of the legislative districts.

State constitutions may allow states to change the number of districts and the number of members assigned to their districts, or constitutional revision may adjust these numbers. These changes are implemented during redistricting, so they are a part of the process. Not much is known about these practices' political consequences. However, an anecdotal example illustrates that the size of a legislative body matters. In the 2012 state court case *Cohen v. Cuomo,* New York Democrats unsuccessfully argued that the state constitution required the state senate to maintain sixty-two districts, rather than increase to sixty-three districts; Republicans were perceived to benefit from the additional district.[1] As a consequence of changing state legislative body sizes and district magnitudes, a recent concise history of districting systems among state legislatures is challenging to compile.

STATE LEGISLATIVE REDISTRICTING REGULATION

District line drawers are constrained by state and federal constitutional and statutory regulations.[2] These regulations may be classified into three categories: institution-selecting, process-based, and outcome-based. Institution-selecting regulations affect who draws the lines, such as a legislature or commission. Process-based regulations constrain how district lines are drawn, such as requiring equal populations or respecting existing political boundaries. Outcome-based regulations attempt to affect a specific electoral outcome, such as the Voting Rights Act and state requirements for partisan fairness.

State legislative redistricting is more regulated than congressional redistricting. Perhaps this is so because state constitutions explicitly describe how their state legislatures are to be organized, including how state legislative districts are to be drawn. The U.S. Constitution delegates congressional redistricting to the states and allows federal government statutory regulation that could nullify state law, but it is not much used except with respect to minority representation that affects all districts and a requirement for single-member congressional districts. Of course, the U.S. Constitution's mandate for population equality is another important redistricting constraint.

State Legislative Redistricting Institutions: Institution-Selecting

Two types of redistricting institutions exist: those that follow the legislative process and those that use commissions at some stage. There are variants, particularly with regard to the role and membership of commissions. Because federal equal-population requirements require that redistricting be undertaken following a census, as do some state constitutions, state and federal courts may intervene if a state fails to redistrict or if a court finds constitutional defects.

Twenty-eight states use the regular legislative process to devise a redistricting bill that defines their state legislative districts. There are variants. North Carolina's legislature has sole responsibility. Florida's and Kansas's legislatures act without the governor's approval; however, the state supreme court verifies the constitutionality of adopted plans. Maryland's governor proposes plans to the legislature, which become law if the legislature fails to take action.

In Table 14.1, twenty-three states that use commissions for congressional or state legislative redistricting are presented. States may use a commission for only state legislative redistricting, only congressional redistricting, or both. They are classified into one of three types, in accordance with when and how they may take action, either as some step in the legislative process or separated from it. They are further classified by their membership and voting rules, which are critical to understanding how redistricting commissions behave. These procedures can be quite complex, which should caution scholars from assuming that all redistricting commissions behave similarly.

Commissions may have three roles. *Advisory* commissions propose plans to the legislature for its approval.

TABLE 14.1 **Redistricting Commissions in U.S. States**

State	Districts: Congress	Districts: Legislature	Type	Members: Initial	Members: Additional	Voting rule
Alaska		X	Standalone	Unbalanced partisan[a]		Majority
Arizona	X	X	Standalone	2 Dem, 2 Rep	At start, majority selects 1 other member	Majority
Arkansas		X	Standalone	Unbalanced partisan		Majority
California	X	X	Standalone	3 Dem, 3 Rep, 2 other	At start, majority constituting at least 2 Dem, 3 Rep, and 1 other selects 6 additional members: 2 Dem, 2 Rep, and 2 other	Supermajority, must include 3 of each type[b]
Colorado		X	Standalone	Unbalanced partisan[c]		Majority[d]
Connecticut	X	X	Backup[e]	Balanced partisan	At start, majority selects 1 member	
Hawaii	X	X	Standalone	Balanced partisan	At start, supermajority selects 1 member	Majority
Idaho	X	X	Standalone	Balanced partisan		Supermajority
Illinois		X	Backup	Balanced partisan	If majority cannot adopt plan, additional partisan member selected randomly	Majority
Indiana	X		Backup[f]	Unbalanced partisan		Majority
Iowa	X	X	Advisory[g]	Legislative staff		Advisory commission may propose 3 plans in succession; legislature approves with majority vote; third plan may be amended by regular legislative process
Maine		X	Advisory	Balanced partisan	At start, each group of partisans selects 1 "public" member; 2 public members then select 1 member	Legislature approves with supermajority vote[b]
Mississippi		X	Backup	Unbalanced partisan[h]		Majority
Missouri (senate)		X	Standalone	Balanced partisan		Supermajority[b]
Missouri (house)		X	Standalone	Balanced partisan		Supermajority[b]
Montana	X	X	Standalone	Balanced partisan	At start, majority selects 1 member; if majority fails, supreme court selects 1 member	Majority

State	Districts		Type	Members		Voting rule
	Congress	Legislature		Initial	Additional	
New Jersey	X		Standalone	Balanced partisan	Supermajority selects 1 member; if cannot, supreme court selects among 2 candidates receiving most votes	Majority
New Jersey		X	Standalone	Balanced partisan	If majority cannot adopt plan, supreme court selects 1 member	Majority
New York	X	X	Advisory[i]	4 Dem, 4 Rep	At start, at least 5 members select 2 other members	Advisory commission may propose 2 plans in succession; if second plan rejected, regular legislative process used[j]
Ohio	X	X	Advisory	Even number		Provides technical assistance only
Ohio		X	Standalone	Unbalanced partisan		Majority
Oklahoma		X	Backup	Balanced partisan		Majority
Oregon		X	Backup[k]	Secretary of state		Sole authority
Pennsylvania		X	Standalone	Balanced partisan	At start, majority selects 1 member; if majority fails, supreme court selects 1 member	Majority
Texas		X	Backup	Unbalanced partisan		Majority
Washington	X	X	Standalone	Balanced partisan		Supermajority[l]

NOTES:

a. Chief justice selects one of five members, who is pivotal if legislature and governorship controlled by different parties.

b. Supreme court draws districts if commission fails.

c. Chief justice selects four members, who are pivotal.

d. Supreme court automatically reviews plan.

e. A balanced partisan advisory commission advises the legislature, but has no formal map-drawing authority; legislature first attempts to adopt plan on a supermajority vote.

f. A standalone commission operating with same rules is convened if the state is without a valid redistricting plan, e.g., a court invalidating a plan.

g. An advisory commission advises legislative staff; initial membership is balanced partisan, majority selects one member.

h. Chief justice is chair, can be pivotal if two of four statewide elected officials serving on commission are of different parties.

i. Advisory commission exists by statute; constitutional revision currently underway to create substantially similar advisory commission.

j. Legislature approves with majority if chambers controlled by different parties, supermajority if one party controls both chambers.

k. Also draws plans if supreme court finds legislative plan unconstitutional.

l. Legislature may amend with supermajority vote.

Backup commissions engage if the legislative process fails to produce a plan. *Standalone* commissions are solely responsible for redistricting. With the exception of Maine, advisory commissions in three other states are semipermanent in that they exist by virtue of statute. They may be disbanded by new law. Legislatures commonly convene *ad hoc* advisory commissions, informally or by resolution, when redistricting is impending. A legal complexity is that a legislature cannot bind a future legislature, so in order to have legal force *ad hoc* redistricting procedures and criteria must be adopted in the session when a redistricting occurs.

Commissions are additionally classified according to their membership and voting rules. *Unbalanced partisan* commissions have an uneven number of commissioners—with a majority of one party or an even number with one party guaranteed to have a supermajority—who are either elected officials, legislative leaders, or their appointees. The distribution of Democrats and Republicans varies according to the party affiliation of elected officials. Of course, in rare instances minor-party candidates win statewide office, but these are discounted for parsimony. For example, the Arkansas Board of Apportionment consists of the governor, secretary of state, and attorney general, so the commission will consist of either three members of one party or two members of one party and one of the other.

Balanced partisan commissions begin with an even number of partisans. Some of these commissions, such as those in Idaho and Washington, adopt plans on a supermajority vote, explicitly requiring bipartisan consensus. Others, such as Hawaii and New Jersey's congressional commission, forge bipartisan compromise through the selection of an additional member; this is a weaker form of bipartisan compromise since the partisan members could deal among themselves without including the additional member. Yet others, such as those in Arizona, California, and New York (a process adopted following the most recent redistricting), attempt to remove partisan politics from the equation by selecting additional members that are not members of one of the two major political parties. Since the partisan composition of these three commissions is fixed, their composition is provided in Table 14.1.

At the outset, or when a commission fails to produce a plan, in some circumstances for Alaska, Colorado, Mississippi, Montana, and New Jersey's state legislative commissions a state supreme court might select pivotal members. For example, the majority and minority leaders of each chamber of the Colorado legislature select one member to the Colorado Reapportionment Commission, the governor selects three, and the chief justice selects four of the eleven members. In this case, the court's commissioners are pivotal and structure the commission's coalition formation. Since one party usually forms a winning coalition among these court-appointed commissioners, these commissions are classified as unbalanced partisan. New Jersey's exceptional experience with this framework is discussed below. When additional members are selected when a commission fails to adopt a plan, the failure may be a consequence of current members anticipating the partisan sympathies of future members, thus breaking deadlocks in their favor. Illinois's unique method involves randomly selecting among two different partisans when the Legislative Redistricting Commission deadlocks. The selection event is held in a public venue, where members of one side cheer while the others bury their heads in their hands after the selection is announced.

As the following discussion of commissions implies, redistricting outcomes may be predicted by institutions and players. When one party controls the legislative process a partisan gerrymander often results. However, a divided legislature does not necessarily result in gridlock over state legislative redistricting. Most frequently, it results in a bicameral logroll where the majority party of each chamber draws its own plan, and these plans are packaged together in one bill, which a governor will approve since his or her party has a stake in the outcome for one of the two chambers. This occurred, for example, in New York and Virginia during the post-2010 redistricting. Gridlock occurs more often when the governor is of a different party than a unified legislature. When gridlock occurs and the courts intervene, judges may choose a plan offered during the political process or, increasingly, draw their own plan. Regarding commissions, when one party controls the commission, a partisan gerrymander usually results. When bipartisan compromise is required—through supermajority rules or bipartisan consensus on the selection of additional members—commissions tend to protect all incumbents in a bipartisan gerrymander.

Sometimes political circumstances outside the regular process induce deviations from expected outcomes. For example, in the post-2000 redistricting, California Democrats, who controlled the state government, compromised with Republicans to institute a bipartisan incumbent-protection map when Republicans threatened to put a redistricting reform initiative on the ballot, which they did later in the decade anyway. The map locked in Democratic gains realized in the 1998 election. In the 1970s through the 1990s, a coalition of Republicans and Democratic African Americans worked against white Democrats on redistricting in southern state legislatures.

The question of control of the redistricting process is consequential to scholars who explore gerrymandering effects. Early studies of congressional redistricting coded control of the state government as equivalent to control of the redistricting process—a potentially erroneous assumption, given the existence of commissions and other complexities. Recent studies code outcomes, which creates a potential tautology when gerrymanders are identified by their expected electoral effects.

When commissions are designed to minimize political influence over the redistricting process, they may be considered "independent" to some degree. However, scholars have been surprisingly befuddled by commissions, on occasion labeling them collectively as independent of a legislature's politics. This organizational overview should disabuse such notions. Most commissions concentrate political power into party leaders; they do not remove politics from the equation. Backup commissions, all tending to have an unequal number of partisan members who select plans on a majority vote, are instructive of this dynamic. They serve to enact a plan when the legislature fails in its responsibilities in order to prevent court action; most were created in the wake of the 1960s legal turmoil discussed below. Indeed, these backup commissions invite political maneuvering when politicians in divided government situations anticipate their party will control a backup commission and balk at compromise during the regular legislative process.

Commissioners may be considered more "independent" when regulation is introduced to reduce political influence through regulation of commission membership. Alaska was the first to stipulate in Article IV, Section 6, of the state constitution that no commissioners "may be public employees or officials." Missouri was the first to restrict commissioners from running for office in the districts they draw. Arizona and California employ both of these regulations, along with complex vetting procedures that attempt to ensure that commissioners are not closely tied to politicians.

Arizona and California, along with Iowa and New Jersey, are generally considered by observers to be the most "independent" commissions. Reformers hold Arizona's and California's commissions in high regard: their commissions regulate membership, apply formal criteria to their decision making, solicit public input, and meet in public. Iowa's advisory commission is also regarded for its independence: nonpartisan legislative support staff draw redistricting plans (without public input) according to formal criteria and forward these plans to the legislature for approval. However, reformers do not advocate it as a reform model. Iowa's process is unlikely to work well in states with politicized support staff, it exists under statutes that can be revised easily, and the legislature could reject the advisory commission's plans to institute their own. New York will likely provides a test case for these assertions, as the state recently adopted by statute major components of the Iowa model for the post-2020 round of redistricting (a companion constitutional revision is in process). New Jersey's state legislative commission is perhaps an underappreciated model of independence. Here, an ostensibly nonpartisan ninth commission member appointed by the New Jersey Supreme Court has traditionally invited the even number and politically balanced partisan members to bid for his or her vote by proposing plans that best conform to a well-defined set of criteria that he or she proposes. All court-appointed members have been academics, starting with Donald Stokes, who initiated a tradition of including an objective measure of partisan fairness as a criterion.[3] The problem as a reform model of New Jersey and other states where the state supreme court may appoint pivotal members is that the commission operates "independently" as long as the court is willing to nominate good actors to it.

Lurking behind redistricting is potential court action. There is no reversion point for redistricting. States must produce a plan on a regular time schedule following the decennial federal census. If a plan is not forthcoming, a court will provide one. If the political parties hold beliefs about the likely action of a court, perhaps due to the ideological character of its judges, then the political party expecting to benefit from a court ruling may refuse to compromise in divided government situations. This was the scenario in Texas during the post-2000 congressional redistricting; legislative Democrats refused to negotiate with the governor in anticipation of a favorable court plan, which they did realize. Texas subsequently received much public attention after Republicans took control of the legislature and embarked upon a mid-decade redistricting in 2003. As the U.S. Supreme Court later ruled, there is no federal prohibition against such action. State law governs if a redistricting authority is allowed a second bite at the apple when a

Sen. Todd Staples, R-Palestine, is shown grasping his version of a congressional redistricting map for the state of Texas which was approved by the Senate Jurisprudence Committee on July 23, 2003, in Austin, Texas. The new congressional districts that were approved by the state legislature in the 2003 mid-decade redistricting gave the Texas GOP an advantage over Texas Democrats in Washington, with the Republicans gaining a majority of House seats.

SOURCE: AP Photo/Harry Cabluck.

court imposes a plan, or if states are allowed to redistrict at their discretion between censuses. Texas did not have such a state constitutional prohibition.

Even when a redistricting authority successfully adopts a plan, litigation often commences when political losers seek to reverse the outcome in court. Some state constitutions require court review as part of the regular process, and others streamline review by designating the state supreme court as the court of original jurisdiction for redistricting challenges. Increasingly, litigants have looked to state courts for relief over allegations of violations of state constitutional requirements, as state redistricting authorities have learned how to successfully navigate federal voting rights and equal population requirements.

State Legislative Redistricting Criteria: Process-Based

Process-based redistricting regulation attempts to constrain gerrymanders by describing how district lines are drawn. These criteria include drawing districts that are of equal population, contiguous, and compact; respect existing political boundaries, geographic features, communities of interest, and transportation and communication corridors; and maintain the core of the previous district, among others. Collectively, these criteria are known as traditional redistricting principles.

Historically, states imposed traditional redistricting principles on state legislative districts.[4] Redistricting was often synonymous with apportionment, the practice of apportioning districts to local government units based on population. State constitutions often either allocated districts to counties or townships by a proscribed formula or required that districts respect these existing boundaries in some manner. Population statistics were compiled from the federal or in some cases state-run censuses. Implicit in these practices are two traditional principles, population equality and respect for political subdivisions. States might also require contiguity, that all of a district's geography be connected, and compactness. Policymakers believed that these principles could check gerrymandering, and as the Oklahoma Supreme Court noted in the 1943 case *Jones v. Freeman,* state courts occasionally found that redistricting plans violated state constitutions.[5]

Where the state courts tread lightly, the U.S. Supreme Court feared to go, until 1962. *Baker v. Carr* was a watershed decision in which the Court first held that redistricting was a justiciable question not to be answered by politics alone. The issue at hand was malapportionment, or unequal district populations.[6] Malapportionment occurred when states apportioned legislative seats to counties or townships, with minimal or equal representation guaranteed to each political subdivision. Creeping malapportionment would also occur when a state failed to enact new redistricting plans over a long period of time. As a consequence, populous urban areas received less representation than sparsely populated rural areas. While *Baker* involved Tennessee's failure to redistrict its state legislature for over sixty years, Connecticut's lower chamber had perhaps the greatest malapportionment. The state's apportionment rule resulted in Hartford, a city with a population of more than 177,000, having the same representation as Union, a town of 261 persons.

Population disparities in Connecticut and elsewhere were not as severe near the time of the country's founding, when many of these apportionment rules were first enshrined into state constitutions. Still, the Founders were keenly aware of how apportionment affected the distribution of power with a state. For example, Jefferson proposed a rejected Virginia constitution that would have given more power to western localities by virtue of an apportionment formula based on population. Later, apportionment rules had clear antimajoritarian effects by allowing rural populations disproportional representation in state legislatures. When opportunities arose, rural interests would amend state constitutions to enshrine malapportionment schemes that were anticipated to favor their interests.

Connecticut was among many states where federal courts in the wake of *Baker* voided entire sections of state constitutions describing how legislative districts were to be drawn, thereby deemphasizing respect for political subdivisions as a redistricting principle. In response, many states revised their constitutions, and it was during this reactionary period that some states adopted commissions either as a sole redistricting authority or as a backup. Some states retained respect for political boundaries in their constitutions, and recent reforms have reintroduced them as a criterion; today, all but six states respect some political boundary, subordinate to federal requirements.[7] In cases such as *Gaffney v. Cummings,* the U.S. Supreme Court has allowed states leeway to balance other legitimate state goals against the federal equal population requirement, by allowing as much as a 10-percentage-point range in population deviations among the most and least populous state legislative districts.[8] Some states even impose tighter population deviation ranges than what the U.S. Constitution requires.

The U.S. Supreme Court remanded the *Baker* case to a lower court. The Court ruled in subsequent decisions in 1964—*Reynolds v. Sims* and *Wesberry v. Sanders*—that the Fourteenth Amendment to the U.S. Constitution mandated state legislative and congressional districts, respectively, to be of equal population.[9] At the time, observers cheered these rulings for ending the representation disparities between rural and urban areas. The new regime measurably shifted political power toward urban areas,[10] where minority communities were generally located. For this reason, Chief Justice Earl Warren called *Baker v. Carr* the most important case during his tenure on the Court,[11] over other notable civil rights cases such as *Brown v. Board of Education.*[12]

The reapportionment revolution dramatically changed redistricting, but it did not necessarily constrain partisan gerrymandering. Two noted scholars state, "population equality guarantees almost no form of fairness beyond numerical equality of population."[13] Another pair argue that "legislators learned how to take maximum advantage of the equal population requirement"[14] by using the equal population mandate as an excuse to segregate neighborhoods along political residential patterns. Candidates, like then–state senator Barack Obama, learned that lines could be drawn down to the city block to remove their homes from a rival's district. Consequentially, since the reapportionment revolution the number of political subdivisions split by districts has increased and districts' compactness has decreased.[15]

Thirty-seven states require that state legislative districts be compact. There are over thirty ways to measure district compactness,[16] but only Colorado formally defines compactness in Article V, Section 47(1), of its constitution and only a handful of other states have defined it by statute. Compactness is affected by a state's geography. The Census Bureau reports population data by census blocks, which are analogous to city blocks in urban areas, tend to follow natural features and roads in rural areas, and never cross political boundaries. States with lengthy coastlines; a substantial number of rivers, lakes, mountains, and other features; or oddly shaped localities have less compact districts than those where district lines can follow straight roads or county boundaries. As a consequence of these complexities, state courts rarely enforce state compactness requirements, and when they do they tend to rely on visual inspection of districts. The U.S. Supreme Court, in *Shaw v. Reno,* imposed a federal compactness requirement with respect to racial gerrymandering alone, finding that there must be a compelling state interest when drawing districts of "bizarre" shape that segregate persons by race.[17]

All states except Arkansas, Kentucky, and Rhode Island require that state legislative districts be contiguous to some degree, although this simple concept has been stretched to its limits. States have taken liberties as to what constitutes contiguity when districts stretch over water—what Article IV, Section 6(1), (3), of Hawaii's constitution refers to as "canoe districts"—by assigning an island to a district on a distant shore. Districts' contiguity is also challenged when they respect political boundaries of questionable contiguity. In the post-2010 redistricting, Virginia's 5th house district was connected at a point, what is termed "point contiguity," so that it could accommodate a point-contiguous piece of the city of Bristol. In the 2000s Wisconsin's 61st assembly district was functionally noncontiguous due to the assignment of a noncontiguous Racine city ward to the district; the state rectified this constitutional defect by declaring in statute that all wards are contiguous.

Contiguity, compactness, and respect for political subdivisions tap into a deeper concept of representation, which a federal court described as speaking to "relationships that are facilitated by shared interests in a political community."[18] Eighteen states require that districts respect communities of interest, which in practice may or may not coincide with political subdivisions, be contiguous, or be compact. Communities of interest may be defined by ethnic, cultural, economic, geographic, demographic, communication, and transportation factors, among others. State courts have on occasion found violations of communities of interest. However, the concept is fuzzy and thereby allows redistricting authorities wide latitude to decide what constitutes a community of interest. Better definitions are needed, and perhaps social media innovations will enable new and more concrete measures.

Ten states require that state legislative districts attempt to keep intact the previous district's core. Sometimes this is infeasible when within-state migration is so dramatic that drawing equal population districts requires collapsing one or more districts in one region so that they may be added to another. Population changes may also create what is known as a ripple effect, where like a dropped pebble's ripples on the surface of a pond, the changes to one district affect neighboring districts, and so on.

Respecting traditional redistricting principles may improve representation. Scholars have found that constituent-representative linkages are improved when district lines follow existing political boundaries or media markets.[19] Although there are outstanding legal issues regarding the ever-changing interpretation of federal requirements, states and localities have generally learned how to draw districts that meet federal voting rights law. Recent successful reform efforts in states such as Arizona, California, Florida, and New York suggest that litigation over state criteria will continue to increase.

State Legislative Redistricting Criteria: Outcome-Based

Where process-based regulation describes traditional redistricting criteria that can be directly measured and applied during redistricting, such as district compactness, outcome-based redistricting forecasts what may happen in proposed districts. Outcome-based criteria include the explicit electoral goals of partisan fairness, minority representation, and electoral competition. This is an area where social scientists shine when they apply their training to evaluate these goals, in their capacity as consultants to redistricting authorities, as expert witnesses during litigation, and even as commissioners.

In 1986 the U.S. Supreme Court, in *Davis v. Bandemer,* found partisan gerrymandering to be justiciable.[20] In subsequent litigation the swing justice on this matter, Justice Anthony Kennedy, has not found a standard that would trigger the Court to overturn a map on partisan gerrymandering grounds. Scholars have taken Justice Kennedy's reluctance as an invitation to devise standards grounded in well-established scholarly methods.[21] However, during the post-2010 census redistricting, federal courts found no violations of alleged partisan gerrymandering in Illinois, North Carolina, and Texas. With some states contemplating apportioning Electoral College votes among congressional districts instead of assigning them to the statewide winner, a move expected to favor Republicans, partisan gerrymandering may continue to be highly litigated.

With federal court action unlikely for the moment, reformers have looked elsewhere to cage the gerrymander. One method is to explicitly require political outcomes by law. Eight states have followed Hawaii's prohibition found in Article IV, Section 6, of the state constitution that "No district shall be so drawn as to unduly favor a person or faction." Arizona and Washington require that an effort be made to make districts competitive. Unlike the federal courts, state courts have on occasion enforced these state outcome-based criteria. Most recently, the Florida Supreme Court found a senate plan violated a state constitutional partisan fairness provision approved by voters in 2010.

Political parties execute gerrymanders by developing measures of the underlying partisan strength of districts by calculating previous vote totals for statewide offices within districts.[22] These statistics are then used to forecast election results within prospective districts. Another reform technique is to deny a redistricting authority election data. Arizona and Iowa forbid their commissions from access to political data at some stage of the redistricting process (a process-based regulation). The hope is that a politically blind redistricting that follows a proscribed set of *prima facie* neutral rules will result in a neutral outcome. Scholars have similarly proposed that traditional redistricting principles be used to prevent gerrymandering,[23] even recommending to program a computer to do the job, although technical challenges limit successful optimization algorithms to all but simple redistricting problems.[24]

Justice Byron White insightfully noted in *Gaffney* that "this politically mindless approach may produce, whether intended or not, the most grossly gerrymandered results." Frank Parker calls such gerrymandering that may occur when following traditional redistricting principles "second order bias," and provides an example of a locality implementing an unconstitutional racial gerrymander by equalizing districts' road mileage.[25] Scholars find that a compactness criterion tends to disfavor a geographically concentrated political party by inefficiently concentrating their voters in districts they will overwhelmingly win, such as the modern Democrats.[26] Similarly, there are limits to the number of competitive districts that can be drawn within a state. The degree of these tendencies is state-specific: factors include the size of the legislative districts and distribution of partisans across a state.

A technological innovation in the post-2010 redistricting is the widespread accessibility of redistricting software that enables nonexperts to draw legal redistricting plans. Reform advocates drew hundreds of legal redistricting plans at all levels of government, enabling robust comparisons against redistricting authorities' plans. These public plans confirm Democrats are generally inefficiently concentrated in urban cores, from a redistricting standpoint, when drawing districts favoring compactness and respect for local political boundaries. Comparisons of these public plans to those engineered by redistricting authorities demonstrate gerrymanders largely disregard criteria such as compactness and respect for local political boundaries. Furthermore, partisan fairness and district competitiveness can be balanced against traditional redistricting criteria. Doing so produces plans that in comparison to those that are adopted by redistricting authorities are equal or less in population deviation, are more compact, respect more political boundaries, are more politically fair, have more competitive districts, and even have equal or greater opportunities for minorities to elect candidates of their choice. Redistricting plans produced through political processes are often so far from optimum on these criteria that it is possible to both have and eat the proverbial cake.

As the following discussion indicates, an alternative approach to removing political considerations during plan development is to explicitly use electoral data to craft a fair political outcome—to use a tool of the gerrymander against it. Donald Stokes, when he was the ninth member of the New Jersey state legislative redistricting commission, used social science methodologies to evaluate partisan bias. A plan with no bias is one where a party that receives 50 percent of the vote averaged across the districts wins 50 percent of the seats (averaging is important to control for lower turnout, particularly among predominantly minority districts). Michael P. McDonald—the author of this chapter—used similar methodologies as a consultant to Arizona's commission post-2000 to recommend adjustments to increase district competition, which is also sometimes called responsiveness, or the change in seats for a given change in votes.

This may be a future direction of reform. Florida adopted partisan fairness criteria in 2010, and in the past decade Ohio reformers have twice placed unsuccessful redistricting reform ballot measures before voters that would create an independent commission that would consider partisan fairness and district competition. Ohio reformers can take heart that California adopted redistricting reform this past decade following previous failed attempts. Although California's criteria do not include partisan fairness or district competition, these were values that advocates favoring passage of the ballot initiative claimed would result from the reform. With the number of states dwindling where ballot initiatives can be used to reform redistricting, reform will likely be slow. Reform will have to come from elected officials in many states, and it may. New York governor Andrew Cuomo recently used his veto power to pressure the legislature to enact redistricting reform.

Ironically, despite intensive politics surrounding redistricting—legislatures deadlocked in special sessions, litigation, and reform efforts, all costing hundreds of millions of dollars each decade—the scholarly research is mixed regarding the effectiveness of partisan and incumbent protection gerrymandering. Many scholars find effects,[27] while others find little or none.[28] Recent scholarship has begun to resolve these conflicting findings. Even though legislators use redistricting to pad competitive *districts* with additional partisans to protect vulnerable seats or shore up a legislative majority,[29] *elections* tend to be more competitive immediately following a redistricting.[30] Confusion arises when scholars conflate the underlying partisanship of a district with election outcomes; the former can be affected by redistricting, the latter is determined by many factors outside of redistricting: candidate quality, scandal, and national and state mood, among others. Still, scholars have found that redistricting is related to election factors beyond district composition that create greater electoral volatility. Incumbents have lower incumbency advantage among the new, unfamiliar constituents added to their district,[31] which may then induce quality challengers to contest the temporarily vulnerable incumbents.[32] To put this another way, legislative elections are complex processes of which redistricting is but one component.

Perhaps the conflicting research is a reason why the federal courts have been reticent about adopting a gerrymandering standard. However, federal courts have enthusiastically embraced social science methodologies in another arena of redistricting law: minority voting rights. Sections 2 and 5 of the Voting Rights Act require states and localities to draw districts to promote racial and ethnic representation under certain circumstances. Section 2 applies nationally. The U.S. Supreme Court articulated in *Thornburg v. Gingles* that a district must be drawn to enable a minority community an opportunity to elect a candidate of its choice when a minority community is sufficiently large and compact, racially polarized voting is present, and there is a past history of discrimination.[33] In *Bartlett v. Strickland*, the Supreme Court stated that in order to have a Section 2 claim, plaintiffs must demonstrate it is possible to draw a district where the minority community is at least 50 percent of the voting-age population of the district.[34] Section 5 applies to certain "covered jurisdictions," located primarily in the South, and generally requires that when a change to an election law occurs, including redistricting, the ability of minorities to participate in the electoral process cannot be diminished, or retrogressed.

Recently, in *Shelby v. Holder*, the Supreme Court ruled that the formula for determining which jurisdictions are covered by Section 5 of the Voting Rights Act, found in Section 4, is out of date and unconstitutional. As a result, until Congress acts to revise the coverage formula, no jurisdictions are bound by Section 5. Section 2 is still operative, and through Section 2 litigation a few jurisdictions are bound by so-called "bail-in" provisions similar to Section 5, found in

Rep. Toby Barker, R-Hattiesburg, right, listens as Democratic representative Percy Watson, also of Hattiesburg, questions Mississippi House Legislative Reapportionment Committee chair Bill Denny, R-Jackson, over the proposed senate redistricting plan, May 3, 2012, in house chambers at the capitol in Jackson. The lawmakers voted 70–50 to approve the state senate plan, which increased the number of majority-black districts and reduced the number of split precincts. Both chambers already approved a new house map. Because of Mississippi's history of racial discrimination, the redistricting plans needed U.S. Justice Department approval to ensure the plans did not dilute minority voting strength.

SOURCE: AP Photo/Rogelio V. Solis.

Section 3 of the act. With Section 5 preventing many potentially discriminatory laws from being implemented, it remains to be seen if Section 2 alone can provide a sufficient deterrent for future electoral discrimination against minority communities.[35]

Social science methods are used in two voting rights areas. In the first, racial voting statistics are analyzed to determine compliance with the Voting Rights Act, to forecast if a current or proposed district will elect a minority candidate of choice. The secret ballot presents a difficulty because individuals' behavior cannot be observed directly; their behavior must be inferred from aggregate data, which are subject to what is known as the ecological inference problem. The statistical methodologies used widely today to "solve" this problem were developed in the 1950s, to which scholars have since proposed refinements.[36] In the second, historians conduct archival research to uncover past history of discrimination.

There is widespread agreement that the Voting Rights Act, for which the statistical methods play a small role, should be credited with the election of thousands of minorities to offices across the country. Where a scholarly debate arises is to what degree minority descriptive representation conflicts with their substantive representation. Minority opportunity districts tend to be the most Democratic of all districts, and thus potentially are an effective packing strategy for Republicans when drawing a district to elect a minority candidate of choice diminishes the number of districts where whites and minorities may form coalitions to elect candidates that generally support minorities' policy preferences.[37] Still, with Republicans now in control of many state governments where voting rights districts exist, they might find a cracking strategy to be effective, but are prevented from implementing such a strategy due to the Voting Rights Act. The effective demise of Section 5 means that some districts that might have been effective at electing a minority candidate of choice in the past will no longer be protected by the Voting Rights Act: those districts where the minority community comprises less than 50 percent of the voting-age population, but where the minority community was capable of electing a candidate of choice with sufficient crossover voting from other racial or ethnic groups.

While scholars agree that racial gerrymandering affects substantive racial representation, there is less agreement if redistricting affects the ideological polarization of Congress. A simple correlation of congressional ideological voting scores with districts' presidential vote reveals a positive correlation, as predicted by the Median Voter Theorem, with the most extreme ideological members tending to be elected from the safest districts.[38] However, even if every district were made to be perfectly competitive, there remains substantial ideological separation between the legislative party caucuses.[39] This latter observation is a static counterfactual, applied to current politics. If the conditional party government model is correct, an infusion of more moderates elected from competitive districts would result in a change in internal legislative rules that enforce party cohesion and ideological separation of the party caucuses. Still, the best evidence is that redistricting, like competitive elections, is but one component of a complex process that generally affects the quality of representation.

THE FUTURE OF STATE LEGISLATIVE REDISTRICTING SCHOLARSHIP

The public knows little about redistricting;[40] this is not surprising, given the public's overall meager political knowledge. State politics scholars have a similar lack of understanding about state legislative redistricting. Many studies cited in this chapter analyze congressional redistricting. Perhaps the profession can be forgiven for this lapse since state legislative district data has been difficult to obtain. The good news is that this is no longer true. The Census Bureau has recently collected and disseminated more state legislative district data, states are providing more data online, and even social scientists are offering data and software.[41]

This is an exciting time for the study of state legislative redistricting. Scholars can now test if the institutions that affect congressional redistricting similarly affect state legislative redistricting, and if the redistricting process has similar effects on politics as those observed at the federal level. There are good reasons to believe that new substantive findings will be discovered. With but two exceptions there are a much greater number of state legislative districts within each state, thereby offering more opportunities to finely slice and dice constituencies, and there is variation in district magnitude, which does not exist for single-member congressional districts. Recent data collection of state legislator roll-call voting has enabled reproduction of state legislative voting scores, which enable replication of the congressional polarization studies while leveraging the greater variability of state legislative districts. Finally, state legislative redistricting stakes are higher than congressional redistricting. No single state controls the fate of every congressional district, whereas state redistricting authorities are responsible for drawing their entire legislature. Where state legislators draw legislative districts, they draw their own districts, whereas congressional districts are represented by someone else. With greater motivation and opportunity to be observed in state legislative redistricting, perhaps state politics scholars will rediscover why the original gerrymander involved a state senate district.

NOTES

1. *Cohen v. Cuomo,* 19 N.Y.3d 196 (2012), 2012 NY Slip Op 3471, No. 135, Court of Appeals.

2. For a comprehensive review of federal and state rules, see Justin Levitt, *A Citizen's Guide to Redistricting,* 2010 ed. (New York: Brennan Center for Justice at New York University, 2010).

3. Donald E. Stokes, "Legislative Redistricting by the New Jersey Plan" (New Brunswick, NJ: Fund for New Jersey, 1993).

4. Micah Altman, "Traditional Districting Principles: Judicial Myths vs. Reality," *Social Science History* 22 (1998): 159–200; Robert B. McKay, *Reapportionment: The Law and Politics of Equal Representation* (New York: Twentieth Century Fund, 1965); Leroy Hardy, Alan Heslop, and Stuart Anderson, eds., *Reapportionment Politics: The History of Redistricting in the 50 States* (Beverly Hills, CA: Sage, 1981); Justin Levitt and Michael P. McDonald, "Taking the 'Re' out of Redistricting: State Constitutional Provisions on Redistricting Timing," *Georgetown Law Review* 95 (2007): 1247–1286.

5. *Jones v. Freeman,* 1943 OK 322, 146 P.2d 564.

6. *Baker v. Carr,* 369 U.S. 186 (1962).

7. For descriptions of state criteria discussed here, see Levitt, *A Citizen's Guide;* and National Conference of State Legislatures, *Redistricting Law 2010* (Washington, DC: National Conference of State Legislatures, 2009).

8. *Gaffney v. Cummings,* 412 U.S. 735 (1973).

9. *Reynolds v. Sims,* 377 U.S. 533 (1964); *Wesberry* v. *Sanders,* 376 U.S. 1 (1964).

10. Stephen Ansolabehere, Alan Gerber, and James Snyder, "Equal Votes, Equal Money: Court-Ordered Redistricting and Public Expenditures in the American States," *American Political Science Review* 96 (2002): 767–777.

11. Earl Warren, *The Memoirs of Earl Warren* (New York: Doubleday, 1977), 306.

12. *Brown v. Board of Education,* 347 U.S. 483 (1954).

13. Andrew Gelman and Gary King, "Enhancing Democracy through Legislative Redistricting," *American Political Science Review* 88 (1994): 541–559, 553.

14. Richard G. Niemi and Laura Winsky, "The Persistence of Partisan Redistricting Effects in Congressional Elections in the 1970s and 1980s," *Journal of Politics* 54 (1992): 565–572, 566.

15. Altman, "Traditional Districting Principles."

16. Richard G. Niemi, Bernard Grofman, Carl Carlucci, and Thomas Hofeller, "Measuring Compactness and the Role of a Compactness Standard in a Test for Partisan and Racial Gerrymandering," *Journal of Politics* 52 (1990): 1155–1181.

17. *Shaw v. Reno,* 509 U.S. 630 (1993).

18. *DeWitt v. Wilson,* 856 F. Supp 1409, 1414 (E.D. Cal 1994), summarily affirmed, 515 U.S. 1170 (1995).

19. Michael J. Ensley, Michael W. Tofias, and Scott de Marchi, "District Complexity as an Advantage in Congressional Elections," *American Journal of Political Science* 53 (2009): 990–1005; James M. Snyder Jr. and David Strömberg, "Press Coverage and Political Accountability," *Journal of Political Economy* 118 (2010): 355–408.

20. *Davis v. Bandemer,* 478 U.S. 109 (1986).

21. Bernard Grofman and Gary King, "The Future of Partisan Symmetry as a Judicial Test for Partisan Gerrymandering after *LULAC v. Perry,*" *Election Law Journal* 6 (2007): 2–35; Charles Backstrom, Samuel Krislov, and Leonard Robins, "Desperately Seeking Standards: The Court's Frustrating Attempts to Limit Political Gerrymandering," *PS: Political Science and Politics* 39 (2006): 409–415.

22. Statewide offices are favored since they are uncontaminated by district-specific campaign factors, such as a particularly strong incumbent who has warded off challengers or a weak incumbent who is the subject of a scandal. Scholars have proposed more sophisticated methods that seek to control for district-specific campaign effects. See Andrew Gelman and Gary King, "A Unified Method of Evaluating Electoral Systems and Redistricting Plans," *American Journal of Political Science* 38 (1994): 514–554.

23. Jonathan Winburn, *The Realities of Redistricting: Following the Rules and Limiting Gerrymandering in State Legislative Redistricting* (Lanham, MD: Lexington, 2008).

24. Micah Altman and Michael P. McDonald, "The Promise and Perils of Computers in Redistricting," *Duke Journal of Constitutional Law and Public Policy* 5 (2010): 69–112.

25. Frank R. Parker, *Black Votes Count* (Chapel Hill: University of North Carolina Press, 1990).

26. Peter J. Taylor, "Some Implications of the Spatial Organization of Elections," *Transactions of the Institute of British Geographers* 60 (1973): 121–136; Michael P. McDonald, *Midwest Mapping Project,* George Mason University Monograph, 2007; Jonathan Rodden and Jowei Chen, "Unintentional Gerrymandering: Political Geography and Electoral Bias in Legislatures," *Quarterly Journal of Political Science* (forthcoming).

27. E.g., Edward R. Tufte, "The Relationship between Seats and Votes in Two-Party Systems," *American Political Science Review* 67 (1973): 540–554; David Mayhew, "Congressional Representation: Theory and Practice of Drawing the Districts," in *Reapportionment in the 1970s,* ed. Nelson W. Polsby (Berkeley: University of California Press, 1971); Sam Hirsch, "The United States House of Unrepresentatives: What Went Wrong in the Latest Round of Congressional Redistricting," *Election Law Journal* 2 (2003): 179–216.

28. Alan I. Abramowitz, Brad Alexander, and Matthew Gunning, "Incumbency, Redistricting, and the Decline of Competition in U.S. House Elections," *Journal of Politics* 68 (2006): 75–88; Janet C. Campagna and Bernard Grofman, "Party Control and Partisan Bias in 1980s Congressional Redistricting," *Journal of Politics* 52 (1990): 1242–1257; Amihai Glazer, Bernard Grofman, and Marc Robbins, "Partisan and Incumbency Effects of 1970s Congressional Redistricting," *American Journal of Political Science* 31 (1987): 680–707.

29. Michael P. McDonald, "Redistricting and the Decline of Competitive Congressional Districts," in *Mobilizing Democracy: A Comparative Perspective on Institutional Barriers and Political Obstacles,* ed. Margaret Levi, James Johnson, Jack Knight, and Susan Stokes (New York: Russell Sage, 2008).

30. Gelman and King, "Enhancing Democracy through Legislative Redistricting."

31. Stephen Ansolabehere, James M. Snyder Jr., and Charles Stewart III, "Old Voters, New Voters, and the Personal Vote: Using Redistricting to Measure the Incumbency Advantage," *American Journal of Political Science* 44 (2000): 17–34; Scott W. Desposato and John R. Petrocik, "The Variable Incumbency Advantage: New Voters, Redistricting, and the Personal Vote," *American Journal of Political Science* 47 (2003): 18–32; cf. Jasjeet Sekhon and Rocio Titiunik, "When Natural Experiments Are Neither Natural Nor Experiments," *American Political Science Review* 106 (2012): 35–57.

32. Jamie L. Carson, Erik J. Engstrom, and Jason M. Roberts, "Redistricting, Candidate Entry, and the Politics of Nineteenth-Century U.S. House Elections," *American Journal of Political Science* 50 (2006): 283–293; Marc J. Hetherington, Bruce A. Larson,

and Suzanne Globetti, "The Redistricting Cycle and Strategic Candidate Decisions in U.S. House Races," *Journal of Politics* 65 (2003): 1221–1235.

33. *Thornburg v. Gingles,* 478 U.S. 30 (1986).

34. *Bartlett v. Strickland,* 556 U.S. 1 (2009).

35. *Shelby v. Holder,* 270 U.S.____ (2013).

36. Gary King, *A Solution to the Ecological Inference Problem* (Princeton, NJ: Princeton University Press, 1997); Ori Rosen, Wenxin Jiang, Gary King, and Martin A. Tanner, "Bayesian and Frequentist Inference for Ecological Inference," *Statistica Neerlandica* 55 (2002): 134–156.

37. Charles Cameron, David Epstein, and Sharyn O'Halloran, "Do Majority-Minority Districts Maximize Substantive Black Representation in Congress?" *American Political Science Review* 90 (1996): 794–812; David Lublin, "Racial Redistricting and African-American Representation: A Critique of 'Do Majority-Minority Districts Maximize Substantive Black Representation in Congress?'" *American Political Science Review* 93 (1999): 183–186.

38. Stephen Ansolabehere, James M. Snyder Jr., and Charles Stewart III, "Candidate Positioning in U.S. House Elections," *American Journal of Political Science* 45 (2001): 136–159.

39. Nolan McCarty, Keith T. Poole, and Howard Rosenthal, "Does Gerrymandering Cause Polarization?" *American Journal of Political Science* 53 (2009): 666–680.

40. Michael P. McDonald, "Reforming Redistricting," in *Democracy in the States: Experiments in Elections Reform,* ed. Bruce Cain, Todd Donovan, and Caroline Tolbert (Washington, DC: Brookings, 2008). When presented with reform options, voters tend to follow partisan cues; see Caroline J. Tolbert, Daniel A. Smith, and John C. Green, "Strategic Voting and Legislative Redistricting Reform," *Political Research Quarterly* 61 (2009): 92–109.

41. U.S. Census Bureau, "Redistricting Data," www.census.gov/rdo; Stephen Ansolabehere and Jonathan Rodden, "Election Data Archive Dataverse," http://projects.iq.harvard.edu/eda/data; Micah Altman and Michael P. McDonald, "Public Mapping Project," www.publicmapping.org.

SUGGESTED READING

Brunell, Thomas L. *Redistricting and Representation: Why Competitive Elections Are Bad for America.* New York: Routledge, 2008.

Bullock, Charles. *Redistricting: The Most Political Activity in America.* Lanham, MD: Rowman and Littlefield, 2010.

Butler, David, and Bruce E. Cain. *Congressional Redistricting: Comparative and Theoretical Perspectives.* New York, NY: Macmillan, 1992.

Cain, Bruce E. *The Reapportionment Puzzle.* Berkeley: University of California Press, 1984.

Cain, Bruce E., and Thomas Mann, eds. *Party Lines: Competition, Partisanship, and Congressional Redistricting.* Washington, DC: Brookings, 2005.

Canon, David. *Race, Redistricting, and Representation: The Unintended Consequences of Black-Majority Districts.* Chicago: University of Chicago Press, 1999.

Cox, Adam B. "Partisan Fairness and Redistricting Politics." *New York University Law Review* 70 (2004): 751–802.

Cox, Gary W., and Jonathan N. Katz. *Elbridge Gerry's Salamander: The Electoral Consequences of the Reapportionment Revolution.* Cambridge: Cambridge University Press, 2002.

Davidson, Chandler, and Bernard Grofman, eds. *Quiet Revolution in the South: The Impact of the Voting Rights Act, 1965–1990.* Princeton, NJ: Princeton University Press, 1994.

Grofman, Bernard, ed. *Race and Redistricting in the 1990s.* New York: Algora, 1998.

Grofman, Bernard, and Gary King. "The Future of Partisan Symmetry as a Judicial Test for Partisan Gerrymandering after *LULAC v. Perry.*" *Election Law Journal* 6 (2007): 2–35.

Hardy, Leroy, Alan Heslop, and Stuart Anderson, eds. *Reapportionment Politics: The History of Redistricting in the 50 States.* Beverly Hills, CA: Sage, 1981.

Herbert, Gerald, Paul Smith, Martina Vandenberg, and Michael DeSanctis. *The Realist's Guide to Redistricting: Avoiding the Legal Pitfalls,* 2nd ed. Washington, DC: American Bar Association, 2011.

Levitt, Justin. *A Citizen's Guide to Redistricting,* 2010 ed. New York: Brennan Center for Justice at New York University, 2010.

Lublin, David. *The Paradox of Representation.* Princeton, NJ: Princeton University Press, 1997.

McDonald, Michael P., and John Samples, eds. *The Marketplace of Democracy: Electoral Competition and American Politics.* Washington, DC: Brookings, 2006.

McKay, Robert B. *Reapportionment: The Law and Politics of Equal Representation.* New York: Twentieth Century Fund, 1965.

Owen, Guillermo, and Bernard N. Grofman. "Optimal Partisan Gerrymandering." *Political Geography Quarterly* 7 (1988): 5–22.

Polsby, Nelson W., ed. *Reapportionment in the 1970s.* Berkeley: University of California Press, 1971.

Winburn, Jonathan. *The Realities of Redistricting: Following the Rules and Limiting Gerrymandering in State Legislative Redistricting.* Lanham, MD: Lexington, 2008.

Chapter 15

Legislative Diversity

Beth Reingold

In terms of gender, race, and ethnicity, U.S. state legislatures are much more diverse today than in decades past. Forty years ago, one would have been hard-pressed to find anyone other than a white man serving in any of the ninety-nine chambers. In 1973, shortly after the passage of the Voting Rights Act of 1965 and only a year after Congress approved the Equal Rights Amendment, roughly 90 percent of state legislators charged with ratifying the ERA were white men. Today, not long after the historic election and reelection of the first black president and the groundbreaking (if not glass-ceiling-breaking) presidential and vice presidential runs of Hillary Clinton and Sarah Palin, approximately 67 percent, or two-thirds, of state legislators are white men. Though still underrepresented compared with their proportions in the overall population, women of all races and ethnicities, and minorities of both genders—African Americans, Latinos, Asian Americans, and Native Americans alike—have come a long way.

This chapter explores these changes in detail. It begins with a closer examination of the trends in state legislative diversification, for the pace and extent of change have varied quite a bit over time, across states, and across—and even within—groups. Explaining that variation—why change has occurred more or less slowly, and why some state legislatures have seen more change than others—is the topic of the second part of the chapter. Turning from the causes of change to the consequences of change, the third section examines the representational impact of the growing numbers of women and minorities in state legislatures. Do they make a difference, for women and minorities especially? Finally, the chapter concludes with a brief reflection on the implications of state legislative diversity not only for underrepresented groups in particular, but also for the role of gender, race, and ethnicity in American politics and society at large.

An illustration by Eric Hibbeler of Susanna Madora Salter, the first woman elected to any political office in the United States. On April 4, 1887, in the small Quaker town of Argonia, Kansas, Salter was elected mayor at just twenty-seven years of age, and only weeks after Kansas women had gained the right to vote in city elections. Nominated on the Prohibition Party ticket by several Argonia men as a joke, Salter surprised the group and received two-thirds of the votes. The first women elected to any state legislature were Clara Cressingham, Carrie C. Holly, and Frances Klock, who won election to the Colorado House of Representatives in 1894.

SOURCE: Hibbeler KRT/Newscom.

PATTERNS OF DIVERSITY

Women, African Americans, Latinos, Asian Americans, and Native Americans have all made significant gains in the past forty years. Yet there has been no singular trajectory of state legislative integration and diversification. (See Figures 15.1–15.3.) The number of female state legislators has increased five-fold (from 344 to 1,747, or from 4.5 percent of all legislators to 23.7) since the Center for American

Women in Politics (CAWP) started counting in the early 1970s. The number of black state legislators has tripled (from 198/2.6 percent to 622/8.4 percent) since the Joint Center for Political and Economic Studies (JCPES) started counting in the early 1970s as well. Over roughly the same time period, the number of Latinos more than tripled, going from 77 (1 percent) when Frank Lemus first collected a *National Roster of Spanish Surnamed Elected Officials* to the current 251 (3.4 percent) identified by the National Association of Latino Elected and Appointed Officials (NALEO).[1] Data on the numbers of Asian American and Native American legislators are not as extensive; but they too show impressive, yet somewhat different, gains. Since the mid-1990s, the number of Asian Americans has increased by about 60 percent (from 63/0.8 percent to 103/1.4 percent) and the number Native Americans has increased three-fold (from 26/0.3 percent to 79/1.1 percent).[2]

The pace of change has also varied across groups. Women's numerical representation in state legislatures increased steadily in the 1970s and 1980s, but has risen very little since then. Women occupy only 2 percent more legislative seats today than they did twenty years ago; but in 1983 they occupied almost 9 percent more seats than they did twenty years before. The number of black state legislators increased quite significantly in the early 1970s, early 1980s, and early 1990s especially. But in the latter half of the 1970s and 1980s, and from 1995 on, there was very little growth. At the same time, Latinos have experienced a relatively constant rate of growth, with a leveling off occurring only in the past few years. Too few data points are available for Asian American and Native American state legislators to observe rates of change over the same time span. But there are some indications that the former have experienced their largest representational gains in the last decade, while the latter experienced significant growth only between 2004 and 2008.

Equally remarkable is the variation in gender, racial, and ethnic diversity across the states. Today, women make up anywhere from 9 to 40 percent of legislators in any given state. Yet the same states that led and lagged behind in the 1960s still lead and lag.[3] South Carolina and several other states in the South have always been among those with the fewest women, while Arizona, Colorado, Connecticut, Vermont, and Washington have always been among those with the most. Most of the growth in black representation has occurred in southern state legislatures. Thus four of the five states with the largest African American delegations (22–28 percent) are in the Deep South (Alabama, Georgia, Mississippi, and South Carolina). Outside the South, there are only a few state legislatures with sizable (10–17 percent) black caucuses (Illinois, Michigan, New Jersey, New York, Ohio); and most (twenty, to be exact) have at least one chamber with no black legislators at all.[4]

Growth in Latino, Asian American, and Native American representation has been even more concentrated. Currently, four states (California, New Mexico, New York, and Texas) claim half of all Latino state legislators. Only two other states (Arizona and Nevada) have a Latino delegation of more than 10 percent; and a full fifteen have no Latino representatives at all. Similarly, two-thirds of Native American state legislators serving in 2012 can be found in only four states (Alaska, Hawaii, Montana, and Oklahoma). Up until the twenty-first century, the vast majority (at least 80 percent) of Asian American state legislators served in Hawaii. Even today, 57 percent serve in Hawaii and almost half the others (another 20 percent) can be found in only three other state legislatures (California, Maryland, and Washington). Nonetheless, in recent years, Latinos, Asian Americans, and Native Americans alike have broken numerous barriers and gained entry to many more state legislatures than before.

Tracing patterns of diversity along any single dimension (gender or race or ethnicity), however, often conceals very interesting differences within each group. Laurel Elder, for example, demonstrates that when patterns of women's representation in state legislatures are disaggregated by political party, "two starkly different dynamics" are revealed.[5] In the 1970s and 1980s, Democratic and Republican women experienced similar, steady gains. But, as Figure 15.1 illustrates, starting in the 1990s, the number of Republican women began to decline slightly, while the number of Democratic women continued to increase at the same, steady pace. Between 1987 and 2007, the percentage of women among Republican state legislators hardly changed (from 16.6 percent to 15.9 percent), while the percentage of women among Democrats doubled (from 15.1 percent to 31.9 percent).[6] The Republican surge in the 2010 midterm elections reversed these divergent trends, however. For the first time since the last Republican surge in the 1994 midterm elections, state legislatures (across the nation) saw a very significant increase in the number of Republican women and an equally dramatic decrease in the number of Democratic women. Thus the stagnant growth in the overall number of female state legislators over the past twenty years tells only part of the story.

Examining the intersections of gender, race, and ethnicity also uncovers a great deal more about the changing patterns of diversity in state legislatures.[7] Since the 1970s, the number of state legislative women of color has increased much more rapidly than those of white women and men of color. Indeed, women of color have been the engines behind many of the changes that have occurred. Most dramatically, black women account for all of the growth in the number of African American state legislators since the mid-1990s (see Figure 15.2). A similar pattern occurred among Latinos in the 1990s (see Figure 15.3). The first

FIGURE 15.1 **Number of Women in State Legislatures, 1981–2012**

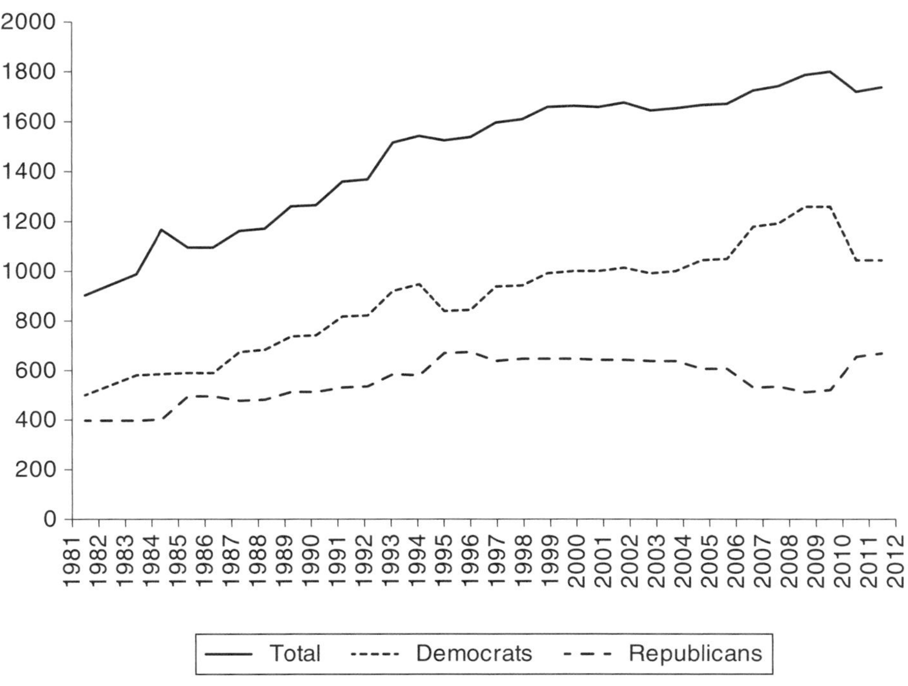

SOURCE: Center for Women in American Politics (CAWP).

decade of the twenty-first century also saw very little growth in the number of (all) women. But it was really the number of white women that remained stagnant while the number of women of color increased significantly. Adding partisanship to the mix renders an even more precise account: it was really the number of white *Republican* women that remained stagnant, while the numbers of white Democratic women, black women, and Latinas increased significantly. The result of this mixture of change and continuity is that, in state legislatures today, Democratic women are more racially/ethnically diverse than Democratic men, Republican men, or Republican women; and African Americans and Latinos are more gender diverse than are whites.

It is also worth noting that much of the increase in gender, racial, and ethnic diversity has taken place within the ranks of the Democratic Party. Among state legislative women, Democrats have outnumbered Republicans since the 1970s, sometimes by more than two to one. At the same time, the vast majority of Latinos and virtually all African Americans elected to state legislatures have been Democrats. Even in the wake of the 2010 elections, only 38 percent of women, 16 percent of Latinos, and 2 percent of African Americans serving in state legislatures were Republican.

DETERMINANTS OF DIVERSITY

There is, not surprisingly, no universal explanation for these complex patterns of gender, racial, and ethnic diversity in state legislatures. Indeed, women-and-politics scholars and race-and-ethnic-politics scholars each offer a fairly unique set of explanatory variables with which to understand the electoral fortunes of their respective groups. Nonetheless, there is a common theme: the waxing and waning of individual, organizational, and institutional biases over time and across states.

Research on women in politics focuses primarily on the puzzle of women's very slow entry into public office—that is, why there are (still) so few women in office compared with the general population. Most scholars employ a basic supply-and-demand framework to highlight the more or less insurmountable obstacles women face as candidates or potential candidates. Supply-side hypotheses stipulate there are too few women in the "eligibility pool" of willing and able candidates, for women have historically lagged behind men in accumulating assets usually associated with quality candidates (e.g., higher education, professional occupation, access to deep pockets). On the demand side, the thought or fear is that there are too few voters, donors, party leaders, or media outlets willing to actively support

FIGURE 15.2 **Number of African American State Legislators, 1971–2011**

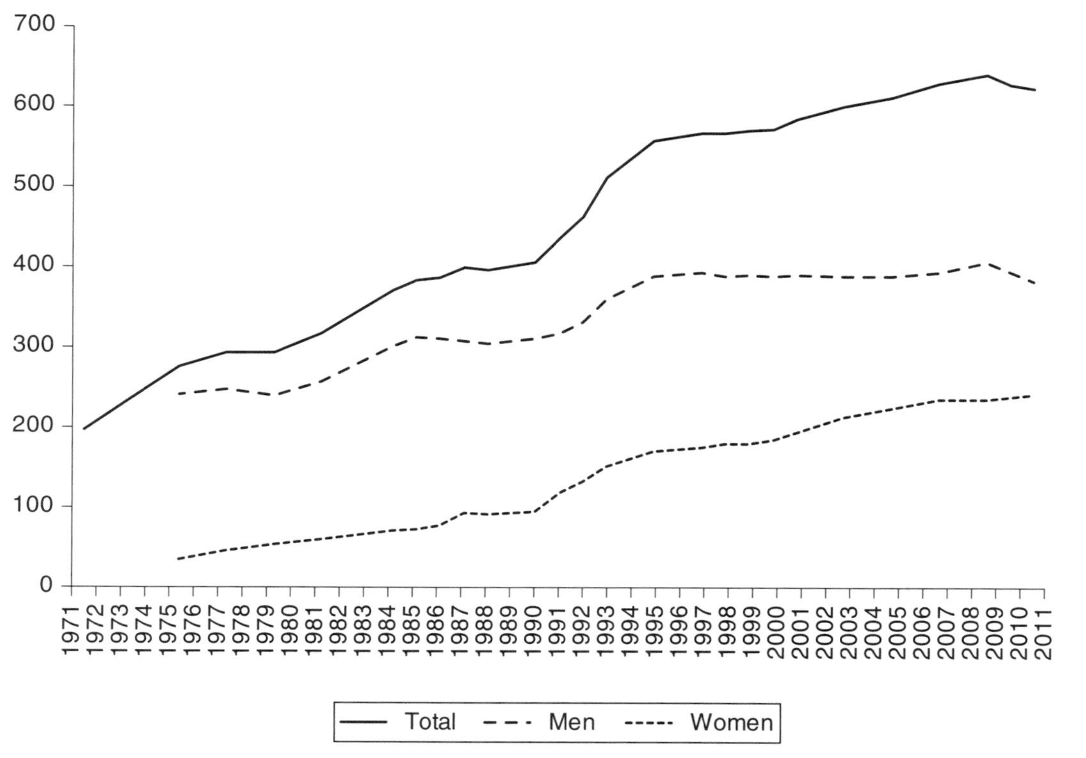

SOURCE: Joint Center for Political and Economic Studies (JCPES).

FIGURE 15.3 **Number of Latino/a State Legislators, 1984–2011**

SOURCE: National Association of Latino Elected and Appointed Officials (NALEO).

women in such leadership roles. And no doubt, limiting both supply and demand is the power of incumbency. Though there is greater turnover in state legislatures than in Congress, state legislative incumbents—the vast majority of whom are men—do not retire, run for higher office, or lose their reelection bids very often. Thus there are very few viable opportunities for women to run for open seats or against vulnerable incumbents.

Early research, in fact, concluded that incumbency was by far the greatest obstacle to women's representation (in state legislatures and elsewhere). Since the 1980s, it turns out, women who run for office are just as likely as men to succeed, all else being equal. When women run as incumbents, they are just as likely to win; when they challenge incumbents, they are just as likely to lose; and when women run for open seats, they face the same odds as men do (given the same partisan advantages or disadvantages). Nor are there any significant gender gaps in the margins by which women and men win or lose elections. And on the campaign trail, women raise just as much (sometimes more) money as similarly situated men do. Thus, researchers concluded, the problem was not demand-side gender biases, for voters, donors, and parties seemed quite willing to support viable female candidates. Rather, the primary problem was that there were too few opportunities (i.e., open seats or vulnerable incumbents) for women to run as viable candidates. And though more and more women were accumulating the educational, occupational, and political resources to make them credible candidates, there remained a supply-side shortage of women in the eligibility pool. Together, incumbency and shallow eligibility pools provided both an explanation for the steady, incremental gains in women's officeholding in previous decades and a prediction that those gains would continue for decades to come. Slowly but surely, as more male incumbents retire and as more women enter the eligibility pool, more women will get elected.

Such conclusions were roundly confirmed by the 1992 "Year of the Woman" elections, when women won office in unprecedented numbers, especially at the congressional level. For what was really remarkable about 1992 was not the rate at which women won elections, but—thanks to the combination of decennial redistricting, scandal-induced retirements, and anti-incumbent sentiments—the number of open seats and vulnerable incumbents. Motivated in part by the lack of women's representation revealed when Anita Hill brought allegations of sexual harassment to the confirmation hearings for Supreme Court nominee Clarence Thomas, record numbers of "eligible" women took advantage of the opportunities available and ran for public office.

Yet the turn of events soon after 1992, coupled with additional insight provided by state politics research, led scholars to take another, closer look at the array of opportunities and obstacles shaping women's representation. As noted above, the number of women getting elected to state legislatures did not continue increasing at the same steady pace. Instead, the rate of increase slowed considerably—*despite* the implementation of term limits in over a dozen states and *despite* the significant gains women continue to make in higher education, the professions, and thus the eligibility pool. States with term limits in effect have not seen any more gender diversity than have states where incumbency still reigns supreme. With or without term limits, many if not most open-seat state legislative races still fail to attract female candidates. Why?

Jennifer Lawless and Richard Fox's Citizen Political Ambition Study provides several clues.[8] Their 2001 and 2011 surveys of the nationwide eligibility pool (attorneys, business leaders, educators, and nongovernmental organization leaders) find that women are, indeed, much less likely than men even to consider running for office—even though they are equally qualified in terms of socioeconomic status and political experience. According to Lawless and Fox, women are so much more reluctant for two primary, mutually reinforcing reasons: they are less likely than their male counterparts to believe they are qualified to run for office, and they are less likely to receive any encouragement—or even suggestions—from others (friends, coworkers, family members, political activists, or party leaders) to do so. And, unlike most men in the eligibility pool, most eligible women will not consider throwing their hats in the ring unless they believe they are qualified or they receive such encouragement. Thus national surveys show that, among those who have won state legislative office, women are much less likely than men to have been "self-starters" whose initial decision to run for office was entirely their own.[9]

The fact that some state legislatures are more gender diverse than others suggests, however, that some environments are less daunting or more encouraging than others. Thus research seeking to explain that variation across states offers additional insight into the opportunities and obstacles facing women, in and out of politics. Kira Sanbonmatsu's study, for example, shows just how important state party leaders and organizations can be.[10] Women's representation in state legislatures suffers when state parties are more powerful and influential in the candidate recruitment and selection process. Rather than doubling their efforts to identify and support promising female candidates, many state party leaders either underestimate the viability of women as competitive candidates or simply look no further than their own, predominantly male social networks. In some states, at least, good ol' boy networks are alive and well.

Research also demonstrates that legislatures are more gender diverse in states with more liberal electorates and a moralistic—rather than traditionalistic—political culture. According to Daniel Elazar, who coined the terms, moralistic states value full democratic participation and a government that actively promotes the public good, while traditionalistic states—almost all of which are in the South—are more concerned with limiting governance to an established elite and preserving the status quo.[11] Liberal and/or moralistic states are thought to be fertile ground for women's representation for a variety of reasons. The greater openness to women in nontraditional gender roles, the political inclusiveness, and the preference for a more active welfare state may all work to make women (who tend to be more liberal than men) more willing to run for office and interest groups, party leaders, and voters more supportive of female candidates and officeholders (who are often assumed to be more liberal than their male counterparts). In such an environment, many more "eligible" women may see more advantages than disadvantages on the political horizon, feel more qualified or competitive, and receive more encouragement from others.

Other, more institutional features of state politics are thought to work in similar ways to reduce—or raise—the anxiety and risk so often associated with women's candidacies. A number of studies have found that "citizen" legislatures tend to have more women than more professionalized legislatures typically do. The theory is that legislatures that meet less frequently, pay less, and are less powerful may seem more accessible to and appropriate for women—as well as less desirable to and suitable for men. Similarly, much evidence suggests that states with at least some multimember districts (and the districts themselves) are more women-friendly than those that rely exclusively on single-member electoral arrangements; women may feel more confident running—and parties, voters, and others may feel more comfortable supporting them—when they are not the only possible winner.[12] Balancing the ticket, achieving more gender diversity, and sheer novelty may be easier or more appealing for everyone when they can support more than one candidate.

Explanations for the variation in minority representation in state legislatures, which have focused almost exclusively on the experience of African Americans and Latinos, seem at first glance less complicated and more dramatic. Standing in contrast to the multitude of everyday, de facto biases and oversights that discourage women from running for public office are the legacies of slavery, Jim Crow, racialized immigration quotas, lynching, race riots, and de jure disenfranchisement. In the study of minority representation, there is relatively little concern about the "pool" of willing and able candidates, and much more concern about voter suppression, racially polarized voting, and institutionalized electoral mechanisms (e.g., multimember, or at-large, districts in which substantial minority communities are overwhelmed by white majorities) that have intentionally denied minority voters the opportunity to vote for candidates of their choice. And in contrast to the decentralized, laissez faire attempts to encourage rather than require or guarantee women's candidacy (there has been, after all, no serious discussion of implementing quotas in the United States, though they have become increasingly popular worldwide) stands the Voting Rights Act of 1965 and subsequent amendments.

The story of minority representation in state legislatures (as well as local and national legislatures) is primarily the story of the Voting Rights Act and the long struggle to fully implement and enforce it. Once the most blatant barriers to minority voting rights (e.g., poll taxes) were removed, attention shifted in the 1970s and 1980s to the dilution of minority voting power via racial gerrymandering—the construction of electoral districts in ways that systematically privilege white voters and their preferred candidates—and the extension of voting rights protections to language minorities. The solution adopted by some state legislatures and eventually mandated by the U.S. Justice Department and Supreme Court was the abolishment of many majority-white multimember districts and the creation of majority-black and/or Latino, single-member districts. This two-pronged approach has been the key to minority representation ever since.

President Lyndon B. Johnson signs the Voting Rights Act of 1965 in a ceremony in the President's Room near the Senate chambers in Washington, D.C., August 6, 1965. Surrounding the president from left directly above his right hand, Vice President Hubert Humphrey; Speaker John McCormack; Rep. Emanuel Celler, D-N.Y.; first daughter Luci Johnson; and Sen. Everett Dirkson, R-Ill. Behind Humphrey is House Majority Leader Carl Albert of Oklahoma; and behind Celler is Sen. Carl Hayden, D-Ariz.

SOURCE: Associated Press.

Indeed, the bulk of the early research focused on the impact of the new single-member, majority-minority districts on minority representation in state legislatures, especially in the South. In one of the most powerful statements, Bernard Grofman and Lisa Handley asserted:

> [T]he number of blacks elected to office has increased because the number of majority black districts has increased, not because blacks are winning office in majority white districts. . . . [Furthermore,] the number of black districts has increased not because of redistricting based on population shifts reflected in the decennial census, but primarily because of the Voting Rights Acts of 1965 and 1982 amendments to that act.[13]

Thus it is no coincidence that the number of African Americans elected to state legislatures increased so significantly in the wake of decennial redistricting in the early 1970s, early 1980s, and early 1990s—practically the only time that new districts can be created (for whatever reason). Nor is it any coincidence that Latino representation in state legislatures has kept pace with Latino population growth—or that variation in minority representation across state legislatures today now tracks variation in state minority populations. As the most recent studies confirm, the size of the African American population is by far the most powerful determinant of African American representation in state legislatures, and the size of the Latino citizenry is by far the most powerful determinant of Latino representation. Voting Rights Act–empowered minority electorates can and almost always do elect minority candidates; little else seems to affect minority representation in state legislatures.[14]

The Voting Rights Act, or more precisely, the limitations of majority-minority districts, may even help explain why minority caucuses in state legislatures are still disproportionately small compared with minority populations in state electorates and why the number of African Americans in state legislatures has grown so little since the mid-1990s. There are only so many majority-minority districts one can draw, even with the best of intentions, given the size and geographic concentration of minority populations. Plus, majority-white electorates almost always elect white candidates. It seems there is little the Voting Rights Act and racial redistricting can do about racially polarized voting, a stagnating African American population of eligible voters and candidates (due in no small part to disproportionate incarceration rates and felony disenfranchisement), and geographically dispersed and politically diverse minority populations—especially since the Supreme Court began (in the mid-1990s) restricting the use of race and ethnicity in drawing district boundaries.

Scholars are just beginning to explore whether there are significant in-group differences in the paths to state legislative office. Elder reports that political opportunity structures in the states look and operate quite differently for Democratic and Republican women. Factors thought to facilitate women's entry into political leadership—such as larger workforce participation, women's interest groups, and term limits—are working only to the benefit of Democratic women; and factors thought to inhibit women's entry—such as legislative professionalism, the (growing) conservatism of state electorates, the influence of the Christian Right in party politics, and the strength of the state party organization—are working only to the detriment of Republican women. She and others suggest that, as the parties became more polarized on "issues concerning women's appropriate place in the private and public spheres" (among others), Democrats continued to support and welcome Democratic women into the state legislative fold while Republicans became increasingly inhospitable—especially toward more moderate Republican women seeking office.[15] It will be interesting to see whether the 2010 elections mark the beginning of the end of that trend.

Kathleen Bratton, Kerry Haynie, and Beth Reingold have also explored how gender, race, and ethnicity intersect on the way to state legislative office.[16] They find that white women's representation is lower in states with more conservative electorates, a traditionalistic political culture, a professionalized legislature, and strong party organizations—much as all the other research suggests is the case for all women. The presence of black women and Latinas in state legislatures, however, is almost entirely a function of their racial/ethnic group's share of the state population—as all the research suggests is the case for all blacks and Latinos. More generally, the electoral fortunes of African American women and men and those of Latinas and Latinos appear very closely linked; what affects one affects the other. But the same cannot be said of white women and women of color.

IMPACT OF DIVERSITY

The promise or hope that often accompanies women and minorities into public office is that they will "make a difference," especially for the underrepresented groups that share their social identities. Much research on the behavior of state legislative women, African Americans, and Latinos demonstrates that such expectations are well-founded. Throughout the policy-making process, and beyond, there are strong links between who state legislators are (descriptive representation) and for whom (or what) they act (substantive representation). Whether gender, racial, or ethnic diversity also affects legislative outcomes (or policy outputs) is not always clear, but it does seem eminently possible. Moreover, there is strong evidence that minorities who enjoy some degree of descriptive representation take notice and become more politically engaged and empowered. In all these ways, legislative diversity serves to enhance democratic representation and the civic interactions that make it possible.

With few exceptions, numerous studies document how state legislative women have been and continue to be more likely than their male colleagues to support and advocate policies that reflect and respond to women's interests, or the political concerns, needs, preferences, and perspectives often associated with women. In surveys and in roll-call votes, state legislators' policy preferences tend to reflect the gender gaps often found in public opinion. Though the gaps are fairly modest, female officials are more likely to take liberal positions on a wide variety of social welfare, civil rights, and public health and safety issues—just as women in general are. Women in state legislatures are also more likely to support proposals that advance women's rights, including reproductive rights and the Equal Rights Amendment, even though gender gaps on such issues in the electorate are often minimal. Importantly, these gender differences among state legislators cannot be attributed solely to differences in partisanship or constituencies. Even compared with men of the same party or with similar constituencies, women are often more liberal.

State legislative women are not simply more supportive of women's interests when they happen to come up. Rather, they are even more likely than their male counterparts to have put such issues on the legislative agenda in the first place. Analyses of bill sponsorship, committee assignments, surveys, and interviews show that female legislators care more and do more about women's issues or interests, whether they are defined strictly in terms of women's rights, opportunities, and bodies, or more broadly (and traditionally) in terms of women's greater concern for children, education, health, and social welfare. Moreover, women's leadership on women's issues is not contingent upon any sort of "critical mass." According to Kathleen Bratton, female lawmakers are not at all reluctant to introduce women's interest bills when they are only one of very few women in the legislature; and few slack off when surrounded by a larger group of female colleagues.[17] Research also suggests that state legislative women who advocate for women are quite effective, for—regardless of the subject matter—they are no less likely than their male colleagues to get their bills passed.

Nonetheless, it remains unclear whether gender diversity in state legislatures leads to or enables significant policy change on behalf of women. Studies that examine the impact of legislative women on state policy outcomes report mixed results, at best. On some issues, such as abortion and child support, female legislators can and do make a difference; but on other women's issues, such as domestic violence and women's health, female lawmakers have no discernible impact. The most comprehensive study to date finds that the percentage of women in state legislatures is associated with the adoption of only eight of the thirty-four women-friendly policies examined; and in three instances, the relationship is in the opposite direction (more women decreases the odds of adoption).[18]

In matters less directly related to policymaking, however, female state legislators make a difference in other ways. Compared with their male colleagues, women pay more attention to their constituents. For example, in two national surveys of state legislators (one in 1995, the other in 2002), women reported spending significantly more time than men did keeping in touch with constituents and helping constituents with their problems.[19] Again, such differences cannot be attributed to other factors likely to affect how legislators spend their time, such as professionalization, size of the constituency, or seniority. In a more recent follow-up survey, Rebekah Herrick finds that although women are no longer spending more time contacting constituents and doing casework, they still seem to be more engaged with or committed to their constituents.[20] While everyone puts in the now-requisite hours keeping in touch with and helping constituents with their problems, women go the extra mile by attending additional meetings with constituents and taking constituents into consideration in their policy-making activities.

Research on African American and Latino state legislators is not as extensive, but the findings and conclusions are equally, if not more, forceful. While a few of the earliest studies noted that minority state legislators tend to form more cohesive, liberal voting blocs and that black state legislators are more likely than whites—even white Democrats—to describe themselves as liberal, the lion's share of scholarly attention has focused on the agenda-setting activities and policy impact of African American and Latino state legislators.[21] According to these studies, minority lawmakers have made their mark on state policymaking, from start to finish, in ways that further their respective group's interests.

Kathleen Bratton and Kerry Haynie's analysis of agenda-setting behavior in six states across three decades reveals very strong links between black descriptive and substantive representation. Much like the case for women's representation, African American state legislators are more likely than others (even other Democrats and/or those with similar constituencies) to introduce measures that address black interests, whether such interests are defined narrowly in terms of combating racial discrimination or furthering the socioeconomic and political status of African Africans, or more broadly in terms of the quality and equity of education, health care, and welfare policy.[22] Black lawmakers are also more likely to seek and obtain the committee assignments that enable them to continue their policy-making efforts on behalf of African Americans.[23] Their efforts, however, are not always equally successful; in half the state legislatures examined, bills sponsored by black members are less likely to pass than those sponsored by white members of equal stature.

Bratton's more recent analysis of Latino representation in seven states also reveals very significant ethnic differences in agenda-setting behavior.[24] However, much like patterns seen in public opinion, Latino legislative leadership is most pronounced on issues related to immigration, language, and migrant labor. Latino legislators are no more or less likely than other, similarly situated legislators to introduce measures that might reflect broader interests in education, health, or welfare. Nor are they more likely to serve on such committees. Plus, no significant differences are found in the Florida legislature, where almost all Latino legislators are Republicans of Cuban descent (in contrast to the predominantly Democratic Latinos of Mexican and Puerto Rican descent in all other states). These patterns make sense, Bratton argues, given the diversity among Latinos and the fact that public opinion is less polarized along ethnic lines than along racial lines.

On a cautionary note, Bratton's research also suggests that further increases in state legislative racial diversity may not result in ever-increasing responsiveness to racial minorities.[25] Her analysis of legislative agenda setting over time shows that as the number of African American representatives increases, white legislators sponsor fewer black interest bills—as if transferring responsibility for doing so to their black colleagues. At the same time, the number of black interest measures sponsored by each African American legislator also drops—as if spreading the responsibility for a limited number of black interests more widely. The increasing presence of African Americans in state legislatures may also engender a backlash of sorts. White Republican lawmakers tend to introduce more measures *contrary* to black interests as their Democratic colleagues become more racially diverse. (Increasing gender diversity has no similar transference or backlash effects, according to Bratton.)

Nonetheless, numerous studies demonstrate that racial and ethnic diversity in state legislatures can result in very significant policy change on behalf of minority interests—at least, under certain conditions. Two independent analyses show that state expenditures for education, health care, and welfare increase as a result of greater African American descriptive representation in the legislature.[26] Some of these changes are quite dramatic. Chris Owens, for example, reports that the effect of a 4 percent increase in the number of black state legislators on state welfare spending is equivalent to the impact of two hundred thousand additional welfare recipients. Robert Preuhs's research demonstrates that both African American and Latino descriptive representation can raise welfare benefits and expenditures significantly—as long as minority representation is accompanied by minority incorporation into the ranks of legislative leadership.[27] In some cases, one vetopoint from a minority legislator in a formal leadership position may be all it takes to prevent policy adverse to minority interests.[28]

Finally, a number of recent studies show that the increased presence of minorities in state legislatures can have profound, empowering effects on minority constituents themselves. An innovative field experiment conducted by Daniel Butler and David Broockman indicates that African American constituents requesting help with voter registration receive differential treatment from their state representatives, depending on race/ethnicity. White legislators (Democrat and Republican alike) participating in the experiment were less likely to respond to a black constituent making such a request than a comparable white constituent, while minority legislators were much more likely to respond to the black constituent over the white constituent. Other studies show that descriptive representation in the state legislature (dyadic or collective) increases African American and Latino voter turnout and, among Latinos at least, alleviates feelings of political alienation.[29] Rene Rocha and colleagues further argue that collective representation in state legislatures is even more powerful than dyadic representation in Congress, especially for African American turnout.

Once again, in-depth research on the impact of diversity *within* groups of state legislators is sparse, but quite informative. Women-and-politics scholars have long recognized (often in passing) that even though legislative women in both parties are more likely than their male counterparts to act for women, significant partisan differences among women often remain. Not surprisingly, Democratic women in these studies are almost always more liberal on gender gap and women's rights issues than are their Republican counterparts. More recently, there are several indications that Republican women elected to state legislatures (and Congress) have become even more conservative—so much more conservative that they have effectively closed the gender gap between them and their male copartisans. Tracy Osborn argues that the policy impact of women in state legislatures is mediated through political parties.[30] Though they agree on the importance of representing women's interests, and they are more likely to do so than their male colleagues, Democratic and Republican women in state legislatures have very different ideas about what those interests are and how they are best addressed. Moreover, whose policy preferences and priorities get enacted depends heavily on which party controls the legislature.

Research that focuses on the activities and impact of state legislative women of color also recognizes how gender, race, and ethnicity can interact to mediate, condition, or otherwise complicate the impact of diversity in state legislatures. Most studies thus far suggest that women of color are uniquely situated to recognize how the demands for racial, ethnic, and gender representation, while not completely overlapping, often intersect and are likely to be mutually reinforcing. For example, Bratton, Haynie, and Reingold find that African American female lawmakers are uniquely responsive to both black interests and women's interests. They sponsor just as many black interest measures as do African American men, and just as many women's interest measures as do nonblack women; and they are more likely than any others to sponsor at least one black interest and one women's interest bill.[31] Luis Fraga and colleagues theorize that Latina public officials "are uniquely positioned to leverage the intersectionality of their ethnicity and gender" in ways that enable them "to be the most effective long term advocates on behalf of working class communities of color."[32] And, while some studies document the formidable obstacles women of color often face in white-male-dominated legislatures, others suggest that they are still able to make a difference.[33] Adrienne Smith and Beth Reingold argue, for instance, that it was women of color—rather than all African American or all Latino legislators—who had the strongest and most consistent mitigating effects on state welfare reform in the mid-1990s.[34]

UNDERSTANDING DIVERSITY

The story of state legislative diversity is, in so many ways, the story of gender, racial, and ethnic politics in the United States. The growing numbers of women and minorities elected to state legislatures are no doubt products of changing attitudes, relationships, cultures, and institutions of gender, race, and ethnicity in all walks of life—from the most personal to the most political. When and where those changes occur most dramatically we see the most significant gains in descriptive representation. Hence, states whose electorates, organizations, and institutions have grown most accustomed to women in the workforce, most amenable to women in power, and most open to social change are those that have the most women in the legislature. And only when states have been forced to abandon, one by one, the rigid customs and laws of racial-ethnic privilege, deprivation, and exclusion do we see minorities claim their rightful place among the governing elite in numbers that reflect (if not match) the general population. On the other hand, whenever and wherever change stalls or is blocked, state legislative diversity slows or even comes to a halt. Thus the stagnant growth in women's candidacy and election to public office reflects the many dimensions of the stalled gender revolution in American society; and the lack of minority officeholding outside the boundaries of majority-minority districts reflects the deep racial and ethnic divisions and entrenched inequalities that remain.

Just as the road to the state house is shaped by intersecting gender, racial, and ethnic regimes, so too is activity within. As outlined above, state legislative behavior is gendered and raced in ways that reflect and respond to the gendered and raced nature of political interests. Thus while increased legislative diversity often gives voice to previously underrepresented constituencies, its impact may be limited by other competing and often more powerful voices (inside and outside the state house). Plus, diversity—or descriptive representation—alone may not be enough; for policy change may require both presence and power in the legislature (see From Presence to Power box). Again, a complex array of opportunities and obstacles surround gender, racial, and ethnic diversity and the impact it has on policy and politics.

FROM PRESENCE TO POWER: DIVERSITY MEETS PARTY CONTROL AND POLITICAL GEOGRAPHY

When it comes to legislative diversity, sheer numbers may not always be enough. To have real influence over policy outcomes, racial/ethnic minorities and women must not only get elected to public office; oftentimes, they must also become members of the dominant governing coalition. In state legislative terms, that often means being part of the majority party—especially as party polarization makes bipartisan coalitions increasingly rare. In addition to having easier access to a majority of votes on their side, members of the majority party have almost exclusive access to the most influential leadership positions, including Speaker of the house, senate president, majority leader, and chair of committees that control state taxing and spending. It is from such positions that members of the majority party—individually and collectively—exert much of their agenda-setting and gatekeeping control.

Up until the 2010 midterm elections, most African American, Latino, and female state legislators were members of the majority parties in their states. Indeed, for many years while Democrats held sway in southern legislatures, almost all African American state legislators, themselves southern Democrats, enjoyed majority-party status. Following the 1994 elections, when Republicans gained control of their first three southern state legislative chambers, the percentage of black majority-party legislators fell from 99.5 (all but one) to 84. Even as late as 2010 (right before the elections), half of black state legislators in the South and 61 percent nationwide could claim majority-party status.[1] At the same time, 69 percent of Latinos and 64 percent of women in state legislatures were majority-party members,[2] as most of the predominantly Democratic Latino and female lawmakers served in states where Democrats held majority control.

Throughout the years, majority-party status and the access to positions of policy-making influence it granted played a crucial role in the policy impact of state legislative diversity. According to Robert R. Preuhs, for example, African American state legislators in the "racialized" South would have had no effect on welfare benefits in the 1980s and 1990s without it.[3] Similarly, legislative women—especially women of color—would have had little influence over welfare reform in the mid-1990s had they not been so well positioned.[4] And Latino legislators would have been powerless to stop English-only legislation from becoming law without such leadership positions.[5]

The Republican surge of 2010, however, severed many of these connections between legislative presence and policy-making power. Its impact is likely to be most dramatic and most serious for African American lawmakers in particular. As Republicans gained almost complete control over southern legislatures, only 5 percent of black legislators in the region retained their majority-party status. Even outside the South, the percentage of African American state lawmakers in the majority party fell from 81 to 54 percent. Thus, nationwide, only 29 percent can still claim majority-party status.

State legislative women have taken a hit as well. But because they are not as heavily Democratic as black officials are, nor are they as concentrated in the South or in other Republican-dominated states, their influence may not suffer as much. In the wake of the 2010 elections, the percentage of women in the majority party (nationwide) dropped 8 percentage points, to 56 percent. Losses were heaviest in the chambers where party control shifted from Democrats to Republicans, but not disproportionately heavy in chambers with the largest numbers of female members.

Latino state legislators, in contrast, have experienced practically no change in their majority-party status. In fact, there were as many majority-party Latino lawmakers in 2010 as in 2011 (167). The main reason is that Latino legislators are concentrated in states that were immune from the Republican surge. Indeed, only one chamber (the New York Senate) in the ten states with the largest Latino delegations experienced a shift from Democratic control to Republican. Most of the predominantly Democratic Latino legislators remain in Democratic-controlled chambers.

Clearly, the relationship between the numerical presence and policy-making power of minority legislators is highly contingent and complex. As recent events illustrate, the path to power depends on much more than numbers. Along the way, partisan dynamics and political geography play important, mediating roles—demonstrating once again that state legislative diversity cannot be fully understood in a political vacuum.

1. David A. Bositis, *Research Brief: Resegregation in Southern Politics?* (Washington, DC: Joint Center for Political and Economic Studies, 2011).
2. These and subsequent figures regarding Latino and female majority-party status are based on the author's analysis of data from the Center for American Women in Politics (CAWP) and the National Association of Latino Elected and Appointed Officials (NALEO).
3. Robert R. Preuhs, "The Conditional Effects of Minority Descriptive Representation: Black Legislators and Policy Influence in the American States," *Journal of Politics* 68 (2006): 585–599.
4. Beth Reingold and Adrienne R. Smith, "Welfare Policymaking and Intersections of Race, Ethnicity, and Gender in U.S. State Legislatures," *American Journal of Political Science* 56 (2012): 131–147.
5. Robert R. Preuhs, "Descriptive Representation, Legislative Leadership, and Direct Democracy: Latino Influence on English Only Laws in the States, 1984–2002," *State Politics and Policy Quarterly* 5 (2005): 203–224.

Equally important in understanding the history and future of state legislative diversity is the complex array of intersecting social and political cleavages. One cannot fully understand the trajectories of gender diversity, for example, in a vacuum devoid of race, ethnicity, and partisanship. Nor can one fully appreciate the workings of race and ethnicity without taking into account gender and partisan politics. Indeed, recent events and research suggest that the multiple dimensions of state legislative diversity are increasingly interdependent. As politics become more polarized, Republicans gain control of more state legislatures, and the numbers of state legislative women of color continue to grow, the fate and impact of state legislative women may depend more and more on which women—Democrats or Republicans, white, African American, or Latina—we consider. The fate and impact of African Americans and Latinos vying for state legislative office and influence may also depend more and more on which party is in control and which women are involved. But no matter how complicated things get, one lesson remains clear: gender, race, ethnicity, and partisanship all matter within state legislatures—precisely because they matter outside state legislatures.

NOTES

1. Frank C. Lemus, *National Roster of Spanish Surnamed Elected Officials* (Los Angeles: Aztlán Publications, 1974); *National Roster of Hispanic Elected Officials* (Washington, DC: National Association of Latino Elected and Appointed Officials [NALEO] Education Fund, various years, 1985–1993); *National Directory of Latino Elected Officials* (Los Angeles: NALEO Education Fund, various years since 1996). Current figures are available at www.naleo.org/directory.html.

2. See various editions of the *National Asian Pacific American Political Almanac*, UCLA Asian American Studies Center and the Asian Pacific American Institute for Congressional Studies; current figures are available from the National Asian Pacific American Caucus of State Legislators at www.napacsl.org/wordpress/?page_id=17. Data on the number of Native American state legislators were provided by the National Council of State Legislatures' State-Tribal Institute (personal communication, April 27, 2009) and the National Caucus of Native American State Legislators at www.nativeamericanlegislators.org/Public%20Documents/Caucus%20Membership.aspx.

3. Susan J. Carroll, "Commentary on Emmy E. Werner's 1968 Article, 'Women in the State Legislatures,'" *Political Research Quarterly* 61 (2008): 25–28.

4. David A. Bositis, *Research Brief: Resegregation in Southern Politics?* (Washington, DC: Joint Center for Political and Economic Studies, 2011).

5. Laurel Elder, "The Partisan Gap among Women State Legislators," *Journal of Women, Politics, and Policy* 33 (2012): 65.

6. Ibid., 68.

7. The figures cited in this paragraph are based on the author's analysis of data provided by CAWP, JCPES, and NALEO.

8. Jennifer L. Lawless and Richard L. Fox, *Men Rule: The Continued Under-Representation of Women in U.S. Politics* (Washington, DC: Women and Politics Institute, 2012).

9. Kira Sanbonmatsu, Susan J. Carroll, and Debbie Walsh, *Poised to Run: Women's Pathways to the State Legislatures* (New Brunswick, NJ: CAWP, Eagleton Institute of Politics, Rutgers University, 2009).

10. Kira Sanbonmatsu, *Where Women Run: Gender and Party in the American States* (Ann Arbor: University of Michigan Press, 2006).

11. Daniel J. Elazar, *American Federalism: A View from the States,* 3rd ed. (New York: Harper and Row, 1984).

12. R. Darcy, Susan Welch, and Janet Clark, *Women, Elections, and Representation,* 2nd ed. (Lincoln: University of Nebraska Press, 1994).

13. Bernard Grofman and Lisa Handley, "The Impact of the Voting Rights Act on Black Representation in Southern State Legislatures," *Legislative Studies Quarterly* 16 (1991): 112.

14. David Lublin, Thomas L. Brunell, Bernard Grofman, and Lisa Handley, "Has the Voting Rights Act Outlived Its Usefulness? In a Word, 'No.'" *Legislative Studies Quarterly* 34 (2009): 525–553.

15. Elder, "The Partisan Gap among Women State Legislators," 70.

16. Beth Reingold, Kathleen A. Bratton, and Kerry L. Haynie, "Descriptive Representation in State Legislatures and Intersections of Race, Ethnicity, and Gender" (unpublished manuscript, June 15, 2012).

17. Kathleen A. Bratton, "The Effect of Legislative Diversity on Agenda Setting: Evidence from Six State Legislatures," *American Politics Research* 30 (2002): 115–142; Kathleen A. Bratton, "Critical Mass Theory Revisited: The Behavior and Success of Token Women in State Legislatures," *Politics and Gender* 1 (2005): 97–125.

18. Kimberly Cowell-Meyers and Laura Langbein, "Linking Women's Descriptive and Substantive Representation in the United States," *Politics and Gender* 5 (2009): 491–518.

19. Michael J. Epstein, Richard G. Niemi, and Lynda W. Powell, "Do Women and Men State Legislators Differ?" In *Women and Elective Office: Past, Present, and Future,* 2nd ed., Sue Thomas and Clyde Wilcox, eds. (New York: Oxford University Press, 2005).

20. Rebekah Herrick, "Sex Differences in Constituent Engagement," *Social Science Quarterly* 91 (2010): 947–963.

21. Robert Harmel, Keith Hamm, and Robert Thompson, "Black Voting Cohesion and Distinctiveness in Three Southern Legislatures," *Social Science Quarterly* 64 (1983): 183–192; James Button and David Hedge, "Legislative Life in the 1990s: A Comparison of Black and White State Legislators," *Legislative Studies Quarterly* 21 (1996): 199–218.

22. Kathleen A. Bratton and Kerry L. Haynie, "Agenda Setting and Legislative Success in State Legislatures: The Effects of Gender and Race," *Journal of Politics* 61 (1999): 658–679.

23. Kerry L. Haynie, *African American Legislators in the American States* (New York: Columbia University Press, 2001).

24. Kathleen A. Bratton, "The Behavior and Success of Latino Legislators: Evidence from the States," *Social Science Quarterly* 87 (2006): 1136–1157.

25. Bratton, "The Effect of Legislative Diversity on Agenda Setting."

26. Haynie, *African American Legislators in the American States;* Chris T. Owens, "Black Substantive Representation in State Legislatures from 1971–1994," *Social Science Quarterly* 86 (2005): 779–791.

27. Robert R. Preuhs, "The Conditional Effects of Minority Descriptive Representation: Black Legislators and Policy Influence in the American States," *Journal of Politics* 68 (2006): 585–599; Robert R. Preuhs, "Descriptive Representation as a Mechanism to Mitigate Policy Backlash: Latino Incorporation and Welfare Policy in the American States," *Political Research Quarterly* 60 (2007): 277–292.

28. Robert R. Preuhs, "Descriptive Representation, Legislative Leadership, and Direct Democracy: Latino Influence on English Only Laws in the States, 1984–2002," *State Politics and Policy Quarterly* 5 (2005): 203–224.

29. Adrian D. Pantoja and Gary M. Segura, "Does Ethnicity Matter? Descriptive Representation in the Statehouse and Political Alienation among Latinos," *Social Science Quarterly* 84 (2003): 441–60; Rene R. Rocha, Caroline J. Tolbert, Daniel C. Bowen, and Christopher J. Clark, "Race and Turnout: Does Descriptive Representation in State Legislatures Increase Minority Voting?" *Political Research Quarterly* 63 (2010): 890–907.

30. Tracy L. Osborn, *How Women Represent Women: Political Parties, Gender, and Representation in the State Legislatures* (New York: Oxford University Press, 2012).

31. Kathleen A. Bratton, Kerry L. Haynie, and Beth Reingold, "Agenda Setting and African American Women in State Legislatures," *Journal of Women, Politics, and Policy* 28 (2006): 71–96.

32. Luis Ricardo Fraga, Valerie Martinez-Ebers, Linda Lopez, and Ricardo Ramírez, "Representing Gender *and* Ethnicity: Strategic Intersectionality," in *Legislative Women: Getting Elected, Getting Ahead,* ed. Beth Reingold (Boulder, CO: Lynne Rienner, 2008), 158.

33. Wendy G. Smooth, "Gender, Race, and the Exercise of Power and Influence," in Reingold, ed., *Legislative Women*; Byron D'Andrá Orey, Wendy Smooth, Kimberly S. Adams, and Kisha Harris-Clark, "Race *and* Gender Matter: Refining Models of Legislative Policy Making in State Legislatures," *Journal of Women, Politics, and Policy* 28 (2006): 97–119.

34. Beth Reingold and Adrienne R. Smith. "Welfare Policymaking and Intersections of Race, Ethnicity, and Gender in U.S. State Legislatures," *American Journal of Political Science* 56 (2012): 131–147.

SUGGESTED READING

Bratton, Kathleen A. "The Effect of Legislative Diversity on Agenda Setting: Evidence from Six State Legislatures." *American Politics Research* 30 (2002): 115–142.

Bratton, Kathleen A., and Kerry L. Haynie. "Agenda Setting and Legislative Success in State Legislatures: The Effects of Gender and Race." *Journal of Politics* 61 (1999): 658–679.

Bratton, Kathleen A., Kerry L. Haynie, and Beth Reingold. "Agenda Setting and African American Women in State Legislatures." *Journal of Women, Politics, and Policy* 28 (2006): 71–96.

Cowell-Meyers, Kimberly, and Laura Langbein. "Linking Women's Descriptive and Substantive Representation in the United States." *Politics and Gender* 5 (2009): 491–518.

Darcy, R., Susan Welch, and Janet Clark. *Women, Elections, and Representation,* 2nd ed. Lincoln: University of Nebraska Press, 1994.

Elder, Laurel. "The Partisan Gap among Women State Legislators." *Journal of Women, Politics, and Policy* 33 (2012): 65–85.

Haynie, Kerry L. *African American Legislators in the American States.* New York: Columbia University Press, 2001.

Lawless, Jennifer L., and Richard L. Fox. *It Still Takes a Candidate: Why Women Don't Run for Office.* New York: Cambridge University Press, 2010.

Lublin, David, Thomas L. Brunell, Bernard Grofman, and Lisa Handley. "Has the Voting Rights Act Outlived Its Usefulness? In a Word, 'No.'" *Legislative Studies Quarterly* 34 (2009): 525–553.

Osborn, Tracy L. *How Women Represent Women: Political Parties, Gender, and Representation in the State Legislatures.* New York: Oxford University Press, 2012.

Preuhs, Robert R. "The Conditional Effects of Minority Descriptive Representation: Black Legislators and Policy Influence in the American States." *Journal of Politics* 68 (2006): 585–599.

———. "Descriptive Representation as a Mechanism to Mitigate Policy Backlash: Latino Incorporation and Welfare Policy in the American States." *Political Research Quarterly* 60 (2007): 277–292.

Reingold, Beth, ed. *Legislative Women: Getting Elected, Getting Ahead.* Boulder, CO: Lynne Rienner, 2008.

———. *Representing Women: Sex, Gender, and Legislative Behavior in Arizona and California.* Chapel Hill: University of North Carolina Press, 2000.

Reingold, Beth, Kathleen A. Bratton, and Kerry L. Haynie. "Descriptive Representation in State Legislatures and Intersections of Race, Ethnicity, and Gender." Unpublished manuscript, June 15, 2012.

Reingold, Beth, and Adrienne R. Smith. "Welfare Policymaking and Intersections of Race, Ethnicity, and Gender in U.S. State Legislatures." *American Journal of Political Science* 56 (2012): 131–147.

Rocha, Rene R., Caroline J. Tolbert, Daniel C. Bowen, and Christopher J. Clark. "Race and Turnout: Does Descriptive Representation in State Legislatures Increase Minority Voting?" *Political Research Quarterly* 63 (2010): 890–907.

Sanbonmatsu, Kira. *Where Women Run: Gender and Party in the American States.* Ann Arbor: University of Michigan Press, 2006.

Thomas, Sue. *How Women Legislate.* New York: Oxford University Press, 1994.

Chapter 16

Leadership and Committee Organization

James Coleman Battista

THE FUNCTIONS OF LEGISLATIVE LEADERSHIP are generally organizational—leaders set the ground rules for the legislative process, affecting the fates of many bills at once. For political scientists, important questions about leaders include how much power legislatures grant to their leaders and how central a role leaders and parties play in the legislative process, and why we see variation. Committees are smaller, more specialized bodies within the legislature that generate recommendations for the larger chamber. Important questions about committees are who sits on the committee, who places legislators onto committees, how much authority committees are given to screen and modify bills, and why we see variation.

Leaders and committees (usually) share agenda power—the power to determine which bills the legislature will vote on, and in what form. This includes the power to prevent the legislature from voting on a bill that it would have approved. An important feature of leaders and committees in state legislatures is variation in the extent of their agenda control and other powers. How strong leaders are varies quite widely from state to state, as does the power and autonomy of committees. This variation allows researchers to better understand why different kinds of committee systems or different levels of leadership authority were chosen, and functions as a natural laboratory in which states can see the benefits and drawbacks of other systems of organization.

AGENDA POWER

A series of results from voting theory called "chaos theorems" prove that legislatures governed by simple majority rule are prone to instability. No matter what the legislature has chosen, there is always some change that a majority prefers—and if the legislature actually chooses that alternative, there is some *other* bill that a *different* majority prefers, and the cycle never ends. This instability gives agenda setters tremendous power. By choosing which votes will be allowed and in what order, clever and informed leadership can potentially ensure the passage of the outcome it likes best. Similarly, if committees are given independent authority over bills in their jurisdiction, they can limit the choices available to chamber leaders as they structure the voting process.

A recent example of agenda power came from Indiana, where in January 2012 the state senate passed SB 89, allowing school districts to require the teaching of creationist accounts of the origin of life. When the bill moved to the house in February, Speaker Brian Bosma sent the bill to the Rules Committee instead of the Education Committee. Under the rules and customs of the Indiana House, this effectively kept it from coming to a vote. Bosma indicated that he sent the bill to Rules to kill it, in part because even if it passed and became law it would surely be found unconstitutional after an expensive trial. In this case, his decision to refer the bill to Rules meant that it could not pass even though a majority would likely have voted for it if allowed to. In doing so, Bosma did not necessarily thwart the will of his fellow Republicans. If they preferred not to pass the bill, perhaps for reasons similar to Bosma's, but felt primary or general election pressure to vote for it, sending the bill to Rules achieved their goal of nonpassage without them having to vote against a bill that might have been popular at home.

Agenda power is not the only tool available to leaders and committees; nor is it their only responsibility. Leaders are (usually) charged with appointing members to committees or other positions (often including members of the minority party or parties as well), with managing the resources of the chamber, with serving as a referee in disputes among members, with gathering information about what members want to see in the legislative program, and so on. Committees are (usually) charged with researching bills to see what their likely effects would be, with eliminating bills that are obviously bad ideas (to the committee) before the chamber wastes its time on them, and with overseeing the performance of state agencies working in their jurisdictions.

LEADERSHIP AND PARTIES

All legislative chambers have some formal officer who is the official leader of the chamber, usually specified in the state's constitution. In some upper chambers, the state's lieutenant governor is formally the leader, but there is no guarantee that he or she will function in any more than a ceremonial capacity. In New York, for example, the lieutenant governor has fewer functions in the state senate beyond conducting ceremonial duties and breaking tie votes, while in Texas the lieutenant governor has historically been the actual, functional leader of the state senate and is often regarded as more powerful than the governor. However, the Texas lieutenant governor has this power because the Texas Senate has consistently *chosen* to accept the lieutenant governor's leadership. Leadership and parties are deeply intertwined, and it is almost always the case that the leadership of the *chamber* is the same as the leadership of the *majority party*, and that the chamber's leader is functionally elected by the majority party.

The power given to state legislative leaders varies by state, though there are difficulties in measuring concepts as abstract as power. However, the average state legislative leader is given substantially more formal authority than are modern Speakers of the U.S. House. Indeed, while most observers would considers U.S. Speakers Thomas Brackett Reed or Joseph Gurney Cannon to be the most powerful Speakers in the history of the United States, with powers often described as dictatorial, eleven leaders of state lower chambers had more formal authority over their chambers in 1995, and only six had less authority than did U.S. Speaker Dennis Hastert, who would be considered relatively powerful. If American legislatures can be characterized broadly as balancing power between leaders and committees, state legislatures usually tilt that balance toward the leadership.

What Do Leaders Do?

In early 2012, members of the Illinois General Assembly introduced two anti-abortion bills. One imposed requirements on clinics that would have shut down almost all abortion providers, while the other required (or required the offer of) a transvaginal ultrasound before a woman could receive an abortion. Illinois Speaker Michael Madigan, who supported the bills, faced a choice about which committee to refer the bill to, as the Illinois House had several committees that dealt with different aspects of health care—Health and Healthcare Disparities, Health Care Availability Access, Health Care Licenses, and Human Services, among others. Because the rules granted him sweeping authority over referrals, he actually chose to send the bill to none of the committees that dealt with health care. Instead, he referred the bills to the committee on Agriculture and Conservation. While the agriculture committee does not normally deal with health care issues (except for livestock) and presumably has not developed a store of expertise about health care, it did have one critical characteristic: its members were disproportionately conservative, and could be predicted to approve the bill. Indeed, the committee promptly reported both bills, though they did not become law.

This incident illustrates how leaders can use their organizational tools to shepherd their preferred bills through the legislative process. They can also deny such help to other bills, and ensure the failure of still others. Such management is leaders' most critical job. Most legislative leaders have strong referral powers, though not necessarily as sweeping as Madigan's. Referral powers are just one part of leaders' toolkits for managing legislative procedure and process, generally with an eye toward helping selected majority-party bills through the chamber. Another critical function leaders usually perform is appointing members to fill various offices in the chamber, such as committee members and committee chairs.

Appointment

In a 1995 study of lower chambers' rules, Richard Clucas found that forty-one of forty-nine lower-chamber leaders were granted the authority to name committee chairs, with ten of them also empowered to appoint most other chamber leaders.[1] In addition, most state Speakers were given the formal authority to name all committee members; the committees section of this chapter discusses this in more detail. The authority to appoint committee members and chairs gives the leader strong influence over how those committees go about their business and what decisions they are likely to make. Additionally, leaders can potentially use committee chairmanships to reward loyal members or punish rebels or even those personally disloyal to the leader. At the same time, though, the leader's decisions about appointments face real political constraints—disappointing too many members who expected to chair committees may result in falling support for the leader or even open rebellion.

Here again, the Illinois House provides a long-standing example of leadership's use of committee appointments as a leadership tool. In addition to having control over referrals, Speaker Madigan has long been known for using his leadership powers to frequently change the membership or leadership of committees, sometimes within a legislative session. This helped him ensure that decisions he viewed as important were being made by legislators he could trust to take his position, to the extent that it has been exceedingly rare for the Illinois legislature to pass a bill without Madigan's personal approval. While committees are powerful and autonomous agents by the terms of the Illinois House's formal rules, the Speaker's appointment power has rendered them, rather than independent centers of power, another tool the Speaker can use to control the agenda.

Procedure

Leaders also organize the legislative process. As just noted, one important tool most leaders have is referral. Most leaders have strong authority over which committee bills will be referred to, at least when there are multiple candidate committees, and many have the formal power to send bills to unrelated committees. The other main tool that leaders usually have over procedure is control of the calendar and scheduling. Control of the calendar, and the scheduling of votes, may seem like prosaic functions, but they are actually vital instruments of control—a bill that never receives a vote is one that cannot become law. Leaders may be able to exercise this power directly, or the power may be vested in a committee (typically a committee on rules) that is under the effective control of the leader. This power frequently verges on the absolute, though again it is important to remember that a leader who pushes forward alternatives his or her party prefers not to vote on might face growing opposition.

Maintaining Unity and Suppressing Obstruction

All of these tools help leaders maintain the unity of the majority party and limit the degree to which the minority can frustrate the majority's plans. By rewarding party loyalty with plum committee assignments, chairmanships, campaign support, or other resources, leaders have some capacity to apply pressure to their copartisans to toe the party line as decided in the party caucus.

Arguably more importantly, to the extent that leaders have control over procedure, they have some ability to arrange the legislative process so that rewards and punishments are less necessary. Control over the agenda means that the leadership can simply prevent votes in which majority members would be tempted to defect from the party.[2] In 1988 Colorado voters approved the GAVEL Amendment. Short for "Give a Vote to Every Legislator," the amendment required every bill to receive a hearing and every bill reported from committee to receive a floor vote, and it imposed sharp limits on leaders' agenda powers. As a consequence, the majority's "roll rate"—how frequently most of the majority party is on the losing side of a vote—more than tripled.[3] This implies that most of those votes had previously been suppressed by the leadership.

How Are Leaders Selected?

Usually, a legislative leader is effectively chosen by the majority party, and this choice is ratified by a vote in the chamber. The Minority Democratic Rule in Tennessee box presents a rare example of the leader being chosen by the minority, but this case depended on both a knife-edge majority and a sufficiently dissatisfied majority-party member. In practice, the decision about who will be leader is normally up to the members of the majority party, though "normally" is far from "always."

The selection process for legislative leaders creates two-way flows of influence and accountability. Leaders exert influence over ordinary rank-and-file legislators, applying pressure to vote the party line or building procedures that prevent them from casting votes they might prefer to cast. However, the simple fact that leaders are elected constrains how they use their power. A leader who consistently makes choices of which his or her copartisans disapprove, or who consistently disappoints copartisans seeking particular committee assignments, might find him- or herself a rank-and-file member at the start of the next session.

The threat of removal is emphatically not an idle one. In 2009 Republican Tom Craddick of the Texas House was removed as Speaker. Some majority Republicans felt that he had punished or threatened legislators too frequently and too severely. Other Republicans argued that his leadership had not produced the electoral victories Republicans in a GOP-trending state had expected and demanded: after the 2008 elections, Republicans retained only a slim majority of the house. In response, nearly all Democrats and a group of sixteen Republicans united behind Republican Joe Straus, who proceeded to appoint several Democrats to committee chairmanships. Similarly, in 1989 minority Republicans allied with urban Democrats to install Republican Joe Mavretic as Speaker instead of the incumbent Liston Ramsey, who urban and suburban Democrats felt privileged rural areas of the state. While legislative leaders are rarely removed, this is primarily the case because legislative leaders rarely make the strategic errors that lead to removal. Leaders usually can strongly influence the legislative process, but they can only lead to the extent that their chamber and party are willing to be led.

The power of removal, while rarely used, also implies that legislators' complaints of leaders abusing their powers might be met with some skepticism. To be sure, minority parties consistently protest that the use of agenda power is abusive or dictatorial, noting correctly that it does mean that many proposals are not even brought to a vote. Even within the majority, complaints can be common, but the fact that a leader has not been removed argues for the opposite conclusion—that he or she must have substantial support from the majority caucus, or else he or she would be replaced. However, this also illustrates how powerful a leader can be—the leader can push policy in his or her preferred direction until most majority members just barely prefer the leader to the work and uncertainty of assembling a new governing coalition.

Beyond these situations where a faction of the minority revolts, instances where the chamber leader is not the leader of the majority party are rare but do occur. The most obvious case is when there is no majority party, as in

MINORITY DEMOCRATIC RULE IN TENNESSEE

While the leader of a legislative chamber is almost always the leader of the majority party, there are exceptions. In Tennessee in 2009 the minority Democrats were able to control who attained the Speakership, in part through clever manipulation of the agenda.

In the 2008 state legislative elections in Tennessee, Republicans claimed a majority of seats for the first time since 1969, but the majority was razor-thin: fifty to forty-nine. Because the Republican leader, Jason Mumpower, had returned to office, the natural expectation was that Mumpower would be nominated by the Republicans; the Democrats would nominate the outgoing Speaker, Jimmy Naifeh; and Mumpower would be elected Speaker in a party-line vote. Such a practice is standard in American legislatures when they are not tied.

However, Naifeh remained the nominal leader until the incoming house was organized and had elected its own leadership. Naifeh made one critical change to the Tennessee House's normal rules: when the clerk of the house conducted the roll call to elect the Speaker, Naifeh instructed him to take the roll alphabetically by party rather than straightforwardly, with the Democrats voting first. When the time for nominations arose, the Republicans, as expected, nominated Mumpower their leader. The Democrats, however, did not nominate Naifeh. Instead, they nominated Republican Kent Williams.

Williams had several qualities that made him a particularly good choice for the Democrats in this context. First, he had previously voted to support the Democrat Naifeh in the 2007 election for the Speakership, by some accounts attempting to gain favor with the Democratic leadership in programs or other concrete goods for his district, so he had shown a clear willingness to work with Democrats when he felt it necessary. Second, some reported that he responded negatively to the Tennessee Republican Party chair's threats to seek primary opposition or even kick out of the party any member who did not vote for Mumpower.[1] Last and perhaps not least, Williams had the distinction of being alphabetically the last Republican legislator.

When the vote was taken—first the Democrats in alphabetical order and then the Republicans in alphabetical order—all forty-nine Democrats voted for Williams, and all forty-nine of the Republicans voting before Williams voted for Mumpower. This left Williams as the tie-breaking vote, and he chose to make himself Speaker rather than accept Mumpower as Speaker.

By all accounts, Williams then ran the house in a largely bipartisan fashion, which was far better for the now-minority Democrats than a straightforwardly Republican chamber would have been. This is, of course, the point of the exercise—by leveraging just one disaffected Republican in such a way that the choice before him or her was clear, the Democrats were able to secure a much more favorable legislative environment.

The victories for Williams and the Democrats were short-lived, however. Shortly after his selection as Speaker, the Tennessee Republicans ejected Williams from the party, though he was able to win reelection in 2010 as a "Carter County Republican." And the Republican tide in 2010 swept through Tennessee as well, which elected sixty-four Republicans (not counting Williams), who had the votes to elect Republican Beth Hartwell as the new Speaker over a straightforwardly partisan body. Williams then announced that he would not seek reelection in 2012.

1. Brad Schrade, "How Kent Williams Became the House's New Speaker: GOP Rift That Led to Election Surprise Has Deep Roots," *The Tennessean,* January 18, 2009, www.tennessean.com/article/20090118/NEWS0201/901180380.

nonpartisan Nebraska, or when the chamber is split evenly. It is also possible for prominent legislators to assemble personal, cross-party coalitions for their election to the leadership rather than a partisan one. Democrat Bill Clayton of the Texas House from 1975 to 1983 was well known for assembling a bipartisan backing coalition that would support his selection as Speaker in exchange for rewards such as committee chairmanships. Tom Craddick, noted earlier, had been first appointed a committee chair by Clayton.

Do Parties and Leaders Really Matter?

A key question that political scientists have considered is how much leaders and parties really matter. If partisans in a legislature share similar preferences, an argument goes, then we should see many party-line votes whether the leadership is strong or weak, simply because liberals take one side and conservatives the other.[4] If this is true, then how can we be sure that parties and leaders are really strong influences on the legislative process instead of just indicators of politics in a polarized era?

Gerald Wright and Brian Schaffner[5] compared the nonpartisan Nebraska legislature to the otherwise similar Kansas Senate. They found that in Kansas, legislators who took more liberal issue positions cast consistently more liberal votes, and vice versa, and liberals were consistently Democrats while conservatives were overwhelmingly Republicans. In Nebraska, however, more legislators' self-stated ideologies were utterly disconnected from their votes. In addition to the lack of a party cue, this made it very difficult for voters in Nebraska who wanted more liberal or conservative policies to figure out whom to choose. In short, organizing a legislature along partisan lines, with explicitly partisan leadership, seems to be an important component of

Rep. Tom Craddick, R-Midland, former Speaker of the Texas House, calls for the opening session of the 81st Texas legislature to be adjourned, in Austin, January 13, 2009. Having served as Speaker from 2003 to 2009, Craddick was removed as Speaker in January 2009 after losing the support of copartisans. New Speaker of the House Joe Straus, R-San Antonio, is in the background right.

SOURCE: AP Photo/Eric Gay.

providing a clear structure to the electorate so voters can evaluate legislative performance.

Why Are Some Leaders or Parties More Powerful Than Others?

Political scientists have tried to learn why some state legislatures have endowed their leaders with more power than others. To date, political scientists have used three methods to measure the strength of legislative leaders. Some researchers have analyzed the legislature's rules to determine the formal authority given to the leadership.[6] Other researchers have simply asked members of the legislature how much influence various actors have in the legislative process.[7] Still others have tried to capture party or leadership power by studying voting patterns. If Republican legislators with moderate preferences almost always vote with the most conservative Republicans, this implies stronger influence than we observe if moderates of both parties generally vote together.[8] The first and most surprising finding about leadership power is that tools and influence are only loosely related.[9] While this finding does make it difficult to speak of what influences leadership power overall, because something might enhance tools without increasing influence or vice versa, a few factors have emerged that are usually associated with stronger leadership.

First, stronger leadership is associated with the career aspirations of legislators.[10] In particular, "springboard" legislatures, where many members use a few terms of state legislative service as a platform from which to run for the U.S. House or statewide office, seem to have weaker leaders than "career" legislatures, where most members intend long service, or "dead-end" legislatures, where many members serve only a few terms. If members generally intend to move up and out of the legislature, then their career interests are served by relatively weak leaders who get out of their way and allow them to make a name for themselves. If, however, members generally intend to remain in the legislature as a career, then their career interests might best be served by a stronger leader who can help secure long-term outcomes favorable to the majority.

The effects of party competition are mixed. States with higher electoral party competition tend to give their legislative leadership more authority.[11] Similarly, legislatures where the party balance is closer show stronger party effects on voting,[12] and the majority grants the minority more procedural rights when the minority is smaller.[13] However, other research has found that larger majorities are associated with more influential leaders.[14]

While political scientists have made substantial strides in understanding why leaders have different levels of power, little or no modern research has looked at the effects of differences in leadership power in a comparative context. Does having institutionally very powerful leaders affect the policies selected by West Virginia or New York? Do the extensive grants of authority given to Illinois's Madigan lead Illinois to choose different policies than it would have with weaker leaders? There is no firm research to provide answers here. The best we can currently do is appeal to theory. To the extent that weaker leaders correspond to stronger committees, weaker leaders *should* lead to more decentralized policymaking: insurance policy made by people who happen to care about insurance (e.g., legislators who are or were employed in insurance, legislators who have faced serious problems with insurance companies), and so on. Stronger leaders and more centralized power, on the other hand, should lead to more majoritarian outcomes across policies—insurance laws that the average majority legislator might like better than the average legislator who particularly cares about insurance does, for example. Similarly, stronger leadership should simplify the process of bargaining between lower chambers, upper chambers, and governors. At least in theory, getting New York's "three men"—the governor, Speaker of the assembly, and majority leader of the senate—into a room to reach a compromise among their preferred alternatives should be more successful than a governor trying directly to deal with a multitude of committee chairs in both chambers. Again, however, there is little or no empirical research to tell us how well these theories map onto reality.

COMMITTEES

Committees are miniature legislatures within a legislature, smaller bodies that meet to consider legislation (among other duties) on a particular topic and generate recommendations of action for the entire chamber. State legislatures universally use systems of standing committees with fixed jurisdiction. Standing committees continue to exist at least throughout the session, and often across many sessions, rather than disbanding after they deal with some task appointed to them. "Fixed jurisdiction" means that the subject matter assigned to the committee remains more or less constant. However, it should be noted that leaders' referral powers may be strong enough, in theory and sometimes in practice, to send any bill to any committee, such as abortion bills to an agriculture committee.

One of the primary powers of committees in general is gatekeeping. Gatekeeping means that the chamber cannot (normally) vote on a bill unless and until the relevant committee has reported it and recommended passage. Gatekeeping gives committees a veto over bills in their jurisdiction, though their independent use of that veto depends on the relationship between committees and leaders. Gatekeeping also gives rise to the primary function of legislative committees—to kill bills before they can receive a vote on the floor.

What Do Committees Do?

Committees perform several functions in the legislature. They research bills, often holding hearings on the likely outcomes of a bill; screen bills so that only the best ones (from the committee's perspective) proceed to a vote; and shape bills before they proceed to a vote. Early research showed that effective committee systems were more likely in legislatures with more staff support, better interim support, and longer sessions.[15] Another important function of committees is oversight, whereby the legislature looks at how the state's bureaucratic agencies are implementing legislation, how successful that implementation has been, and what legislative changes or clarifications to the law might be necessary. Finally, political scientists have argued that committees can serve a more explicitly political function in assisting vote trades or compromises between and among bills.

Screening and Shaping

Screening is the process by which committees decide which bills to move forward to a chamber vote and which bills to reject prior to floor action. Screening eliminates or combines bills that substantially duplicate other bills, or programs that might cost too much, or bills that would likely violate the state or federal constitution, or bills that have so little support in the legislature that they could not possibly pass, or simply bills that seem like bad ideas to the committee. Screening is arguably the most important task that committees perform. First, no single legislator can become expert in all the various subjects the legislature deals with, but dividing into committees allows the legislature to split its information-gathering duties so that nobody has to become expert in more than a few areas, but every area has a few expert legislators. Second, dividing into committees means that the legislature can deal with many bills simultaneously, allowing it to efficiently consider far more bills than a committee-less system would permit.

As part of their legislative responsibilities, committees often hold public hearings. In this photo taken on January 29, 2002, in Denver, Colorado, the Colorado House Committee heard from two young constituents. The Medrano brothers, Noe Medrano (left), 12, Angevine Middle School, Lafayette, and Rolando Medrano (right), 10, Pioneer Elementary School, Lafayette, testify on an amendment to House Bill 1135, English Immersion Two Year, which would require kids that don't speak English to enroll in a two-year English immersion program. The amendment passed 6–4 but the bill failed.

SOURCE: Andy Cross/*The Denver Post* via Getty Images.

Shaping legislation is closely related to screening. Where screening is a simple binary yes/no operation, shaping legislation is more nuanced modification of one or more bills into a final bill that best reflects the committee's judgment. The single bill may combine what the committee thinks are the best aspects of multiple bills, and may be structured either as one of the original bills with some proposed amendments or as a new committee bill. A simple way to think about the shaping function is that it provides flexibility beyond basic gatekeeping, so that the bills that emerge from committee better reflect the committee's judgment and expertise.

Oversight

It is quite common for legislation to pass in vague terms, giving some state agency the responsibility and power to transform a vague statement of purpose such as protecting wetlands into a series of bureaucratic regulations that individuals can be punished for violating. Giving implementation over to agencies runs the risk that how the bill is implemented might better reflect the policy wishes of the governor, or of civil servants in the agency, than it does the legislature. Accordingly, legislatures try to examine how the agencies are implementing legislation, though they generally lack the strong and independent information-gathering capacity that congressional committees have. A secondary but also important function of oversight is to locate parts of enabling legislation that could be modified to enhance efficiency.

Assisting Logrolls

Screening and shaping are generally thought of as informational functions—the committee learns about a bill and informs the chamber what it has learned. However, political scientists have also considered committee functions that are more about interests and vote trades than information. Legislators might find it difficult to make agreements or compromises with one another across multiple bills because there are many opportunities to renege. Once their partners in the vote trade are no longer needed, it is easy for legislators to find a credible reason to back out of their side of an agreement, or to vote to kill the very program they had previously helped pass. Committees, constructed in a particular way, can make it easier for members to trust one another by limiting the opportunities members have to renege.[16] At the simplest level, if the agriculture committee is composed overwhelmingly of members from farm districts, then bills to take away a farm subsidy will die in committee. This makes it easier for legislators from farm districts to trust other legislators when they offer their votes on some other program in exchange for their partners' votes for a farm subsidy because they know that the subsidy will be difficult to remove once enacted. From this perspective, a committee system can lead to more compromises across bills, but those compromises, vote trades, or logrolls can be for good legislation or bad. An important quality of committees assisting logrolls is that their theoretical justification is built not on information or expertise but on interest. To the extent that they exist, these committees would not be a way for the chamber to learn about policy, but rather a way for the various economic interests represented in the chamber to find mutually acceptable compromises.

How Are Committees Set Up?

In most cases, legislative chambers are free to organize their committee systems in any way they see fit, though a few states impose constraints either in their constitutions or in statutes. This freedom means that chambers can have as many or few committees as makes sense to them, committees can be as large or small as they prefer, and committees can have as much or little power and authority as the chamber wishes to give them. Furthermore, legislatures are quite often willing to make substantial changes in the numbers of committees, though changes are less frequent in legislatures where committees are more important in the legislative process and where members tend to serve on the same committee in multiple terms.[17]

The number of committees varies quite strongly from one chamber to another. In 1999–2000 the Nevada Senate had only nine committees, while the Missouri House had fifty-six. Larger chambers tend to have more committees, if only because they can do so without spreading their legislators too thin, but it is not clear what effect the number of committees might have on policy. Similarly, the size of committees varies strongly. In 1999 the Joint Committee on Job Training in the Missouri legislature had only one member, while the Appropriations Committee of the Georgia House had sixty-nine, just over 38 percent of the chamber. In relative terms, the Appropriations Committee of the Oklahoma Senate was the largest, with just over 95 percent of legislators serving. Larger chambers tend to have committees with more members, but that are a smaller proportion of the chamber. However, as is the case with the number of committees, little research has been performed on the effects of committee size.

Generally, committees are organized by legislative chambers rather than the entire legislature. However, Connecticut, Maine, and Massachusetts rely on systems of joint committees, which have members from both chambers. The potential efficiency gains of a joint committee are obvious—having only one committee reduces the duplication of effort and resources between the two chambers. The potential downside to joint committees is that the resulting committee is no longer fully either chamber's. While some game-theoretic results indicate this should make little difference,[18] it remains possible that a servant of two masters might be less trustworthy (and less informationally efficient) than would a servant with just one. However, very little research has actually examined the effects of joint committees in a comparative context, so we do not actually know very much about how, if at all, they affect legislation.

How Are Committee Members Appointed?

The formal process of assigning members to committee is generally quite simple: as of 1995, thirty-six of forty-nine state lower-chamber leaders had the formal authority to appoint all members to committee, including members of the minority party or parties.[19] At the other extreme, the rules of the South Carolina Senate allow members to choose their own committee assignments, with the longest-serving senators choosing first. However, even in chambers in which the leader is granted sweeping authority over committee assignments, this does not mean that committee assignments are a simple and direct reflection of the leader's preferences. If committee assignments substantially disappoint enough members of the majority party, the leader could be removed. Leaders might well consider input from the minority leadership about their requested assignments, even if they are not formally required to, as a way of limiting the likelihood of payback if the current majority loses control of the chamber.

These informal constraints on leaders' choices about appointments mean that the rules themselves do not always provide firm guidance as to what *really* matters in committee appointments. Luckily, the National Conference of State Legislatures periodically surveys legislative clerks about what factors are important in committee assignments (among other details). All of the lower chambers that responded in the most recent survey (1996) indicated that legislators' preferences about their assignments were important considerations. Chamber seniority was a factor in 82 percent of chambers, while party and talent or competence were important in 77 percent. The remaining factors, in order from more commonly considered to rarely considered, were length of service on the committee and experience (70 percent each), the location of the district or legislator's occupation (57 percent each), and gender and ethnic balance (34 percent and 32 percent, respectively).

Who Sits on Committee?

Political scientists have performed a substantial amount of research on who sits on legislative committees. Committees are highly flexible institutions whose character can change radically simply by appointing different members. For example, imagine a baseball fan club creates a committee to generate a list of the greatest players in a way that requires substantial research on the players. If the committee consists of randomly sampled members from the fan club, its recommendations about the all-time greats should be very similar to the decisions the entire club would make if everyone could develop the necessary expertise.[20] If, however, the committee is made up entirely of fan club members from Boston, it is likely that the committee's recommendations will be biased, arguably unfairly, toward Red Sox players.

The important factor here is that the only difference between a committee designed to ferret out the truth and a committee designed to allow a biased group to enshrine their particular preferences is *who sits on the committee.* For similar reasons, political scientists have frequently examined how representative committees are of their parent chambers as a way to gauge to what extent they were created to learn and disseminate information versus allowing a narrower interest to have free rein over a committee's jurisdiction.

What we have learned is that state legislative committees have a very strong tendency to be ideologically representative of their parent chambers. Only a small percentage of committees are detectably more liberal or more conservative than a random sample of their chamber would be. This tells us that when gatekeeping or giving advice about the passage or rejection of a bill, the decisions they make and advice they give tend to be more or less unbiased instead of "too" liberal or "too" conservative.

However, we have also learned that state legislatures often appoint members with a stake in what their committee does—farmers to agriculture committees, teachers and professors to education committees, and so on. This tendency seems to be long-lasting, as it was first clearly identified in the 1980s.[21] More recent work shows that across a range of jurisdictions and states, there is a strong tendency toward appointing interested legislators.[22] However, using members' underlying expertise can be especially important for state legislatures, as they often lack the long sessions and information-gathering staff of the U.S. Congress. The danger is that farmers, educators, and so on might use their positions on committees either to enrich themselves at the expense of the state's electorate or provide biased information that equates a bill that is bad for farmers with one that is bad for the state. While current studies have not definitively resolved the question of whether appointing interested legislators taps their talent or unleashes their interests, limited findings provide better support for an origin in expertise and information.

As with many other issues, however, we do not know very much about the effects that representative and unrepresentative committees have on the legislative process. Do representative committees approve different bills than unrepresentative ones? Do unrepresentative committees cause more spending or more industry-friendly policies? These and related questions remain unanswered.

Committees across the States

Political scientists have examined several forms of variation in committee systems across the states, both in time-series and with cross-sectional snapshots of a single time. First and foremost, the power and autonomy of committees varies across state legislatures. Generally, political scientists have measured committee power or autonomy by studying the formal rules surrounding committees. These studies have found that committees are less autonomous when members have stronger "property rights" to remain on their chosen committees—that is, committees are given more authority when leadership has more control over their membership.[23]

A series of other studies examined what influences the ideological representativeness of committees or other aspects of who sits on which committee. Here, the rarity of ideologically biased committees has made study difficult, but studies have found that narrower majorities, the homogeneity of the majority party, and committees whose partisan split is similar to the chamber's are associated with more representative committees, and that greater uncertainty about the effects of policies gives committees more leeway to be somewhat unrepresentative.[24]

LEADERSHIP, PARTIES, AND COMMITTEES

Parties, leaders, and committees are deeply intertwined. The most obvious connection is that the committee system is, like the leadership, under the control of the majority party (or, rarely, some other organizing coalition). In practice, legislatures do not change the formal rules surrounding their committee systems very much or very often, so this control may be more in theory than practice. However, there is still good reason to expect that committee systems tend to further the interests of the majority party. For example, the leadership can potentially skew appointments to choice committees and committee chairmanships toward legislators more willing to toe the party line, or at least keep them from legislators known to have low party loyalty.

Perhaps the most important issue is the relative balance of power between leaders or parties and committees. It is important to note that an increase in the power or autonomy of committees does not *necessarily* imply that party leaders have become weaker, either absolutely or relatively; nor does an increase in the tools or influence of legislative leaders *necessarily* imply a reduction in the power or influence of committees or committee chairs. For example, one study found that states where term limits had begun to eject legislators had both less influential leaders and less influential committee chairs.[25] Early studies showed that the size of the majority party was critical—in chambers with overwhelming majority parties, leadership and the party caucus were less influential in decision making while committees were more important.[26] This finding is consistent with the idea that committee systems reflect the needs of the majority party—when the minority is too small to pose a realistic threat, legislators serve the parochial needs of their districts through committee action, but as the minority becomes more powerful, legislators cede more authority to the leadership to help maintain a united front against more effective opposition. More recent studies have shown that, all else being equal, more professionalized legislatures tend to have more influential leaders and less influential committee chairs.[27]

Another important area where parties and committees meet is in party representation on committees. Generally, committees are divided in approximately the same ratio as the chamber—if a chamber is 60 percent Democratic, most committees might be between 55 and 65 percent Democratic. However, this is only a general rule, and committees sometimes depart sharply from that ratio. As might be expected, this normally takes the form of the majority granting itself more seats than it would numerically "deserve." Majority overrepresentation is most common in chambers with narrow majorities, again consistent with the majority party shaping the committee system to meet its needs.[28] Overrepresentation of the minority party does occur, but more rarely, and seems to be concentrated in ethics committees, which are commonly split evenly irrespective of the party split of the chamber, and less important housekeeping committees such as internship committees.

CONCLUSION

The most important things to remember about parties, leaders, and committees are that they deeply affect the legislative process and that they are themselves objects of choice. Legislatures pass many bills that they would reject if they had different leadership, or differently organized committees, or even merely different legislators sitting on committee. And, conversely, many bills that are utterly dead on arrival in any given legislature could at least stand a reasonable chance of passage if the only change made was to its governing institutions. Explanations of why a bill passed, or failed, or never came to a vote should at least consider the actions (or inactions) of leaders and committee chairs. And, at the same time, these influential institutions are themselves more or less freely chosen by the legislatures they govern. Committee systems of standing committee with fixed jurisdiction were not handed down from Olympus; they were chosen, presumably because legislators have found that they adequately meet their needs. Taken together, when a bill fails because it was never voted upon, the likely conclusion is that this is because most legislators did not want to cast a vote on it.

NOTES

1. Richard A. Clucas, "Principal-Agent Theory and the Power of State House Speakers," *Legislative Studies Quarterly* 26 (2001): 319–338.

2. Gary W. Cox and Mathew McCubbins, *Setting the Agenda: Responsible Party Government in the U.S. House of Representatives* (Cambridge: Cambridge University Press, 2005).

3. Gary W. Cox, Thad Kousser, and Mathew D. McCubbins, "Party Power or Preferences? Quasi-Experimental Evidence from

American State Legislatures," *Journal of Politics* 72 (2010): 799–811.

4. Keith Krehbiel, "Where's the Party?" *British Journal of Political Science* 23 (1993): 235–266.

5. Gerald C. Wright and Brian F. Schaffner, "The Influence of Party: Evidence from the State Legislatures," *American Political Science Review* 96 (2002): 367–379.

6. Clucas, "Principal-Agent Theory."

7. Richard A. Clucas, "Legislative Professionalism and the Power of State House Leaders," *State Politics and Policy Quarterly* 7 (2007): 1–19.

8. James Battista and Jesse T. Richman, "Party Pressure in the U.S. State Legislatures," *Legislative Studies Quarterly* 36 (2011): 397–422.

9. James Battista, "Formal and Perceived Power in U.S. State Legislatures," *State Politics and Policy Quarterly* 11 (2011): 102–118.

10. Peverill Squire, "Member Career Opportunities and the Internal Organization of Legislatures," *Journal of Politics* 50 (1988): 726–744.

11. Clucas, "Principal-Agent Theory."

12. Battista and Richman, "Party Pressure."

13. Nancy Martorano, "Cohesion or Reciprocity? Majority Party Strength and Minority Party Procedural Rights in the Legislative Process," *State Politics and Policy Quarterly* 4 (2004): 55–73.

14. Clucas, "Legislative Professionalism."

15. Alan Rosenthal, *Legislative Performance in the States: Explorations of Committee Behavior* (New York: Free Press, 1974).

16. Barry R. Weingast and William J. Marshall, "The Industrial Organization of Congress; or, Why Legislatures, Like Firms, Are Not Organized as Markets," *Journal of Political Economy* 96 (1988): 132–163.

17. Keith E. Hamm and Ronald D. Hedlund, "Accounting for Change in the Number of State Legislative Committee Positions," *Legislative Studies Quarterly* 15 (1990): 201–226.

18. Vijay Krishna and J. Morgan, "A Model of Expertise," *Quarterly Journal of Economics* 116 (2001): 747–775.

19. Clucas, "Principal-Agent Theory."

20. Keith Krehbiel, *Information and Legislative Organization* (Ann Arbor: University of Michigan Press, 1991).

21. Keith E. Hamm, "The Role of 'Subgovernments' in U.S. State Policy Making: An Exploratory Analysis," *Legislative Studies Quarterly* 11 (1986): 321–351.

22. James Battista, "State Legislative Committees and Economic Connections: Expertise and Industry Service," *State Politics and Policy Quarterly* 12 (2012): 252–283; Keith E. Hamm, Ronald D. Hedlund, and Stephanie Shirley Post, "Committee Specialization in U.S. State Legislatures during the 20th Century: Do Legislatures Tap the Talents of Their Members?" *State Politics and Policy Quarterly* 11 (2011): 299–324.

23. Nancy Martorano, "Balancing Power: Committee System Autonomy and Legislative Organization," *Legislative Studies Quarterly* 31 (2006): 205–234.

24. James Battista, "Why Information? Choosing Committee Informativeness in U.S. State Legislatures," *Legislative Studies Quarterly* 34 (2009): 375–397; Jesse T. Richman, "Uncertainty and the Prevalence of Committee Outliers," *Legislative Studies Quarterly* 33 (2008): 323–347.

25. John M. Carey, Richard G. Niemi, Lynda W. Powell, and Gary F. Moncrief, "The Effects of Term Limits on State Legislatures: A New Survey of the 50 States," *Legislative Studies Quarterly* 31 (2006): 105–134.

26. Wayne Francis, "Leadership, Party Caucuses, and Committees in State Legislatures," *Legislative Studies Quarterly* 10 (1985): 243–257.

27. Carey, Niemi, Powell, and Moncrief, "The Effects of Term Limits."

28. Ronald D. Hedlund, Kevin Coombs, Nancy Martorano, and Keith E. Hamm, "Partisan Stacking on Legislative Committees," *Legislative Studies Quarterly* 34 (2011): 175–191.

SUGGESTED READING

Boyarsky, Bill. *Big Daddy: Jesse Unruh and the Art of Power Politics.* Berkeley: University of California Press, 2008.

Francis, Wayne. *The Legislative Committee Game.* Columbus: Ohio State University Press, 1989.

Loftus, Tom. *The Art of Legislative Politics.* Washington, DC: CQ Press, 1994.

Moncrief, Gary F., and Joel A. Thompson, eds. *Changing Patterns in State Legislative Careers.* Ann Arbor: University of Michigan Press, 1992.

Moncrief, Gary F., Joel A. Thompson, and Karl T. Kurtz. "The Old Statehouse, It Ain't What It Used To Be." *Legislative Studies Quarterly* 21 (1996): 57–72.

Rosenthal, Alan. *Engines of Democracy: Politics and Policymaking in State Legislatures.* Washington, DC: CQ Press, 2008.

———. *Legislative Performance in the States: Explorations of Committee Behavior.* New York: Free Press, 1974.

Squire, Peverill, and Keith E. Hamm. *101 Chambers: Congress, State Legislatures, and the Future of Legislative Studies.* Columbus: Ohio State University Press, 2005.

Wright, Gerald C., and Brian F. Schaffner. "The Influence of Party: Evidence from the State Legislatures." *American Political Science Review* 96 (2002): 367–379.

Wright, Ralph G. *Inside the Statehouse: Lessons from the Speaker.* Washington, DC: CQ Press, 2005.

Chapter 17

Legislative Reform

Alan Rosenthal

Like other institutions, state legislatures are constantly changing. Not all change should be thought of as legislative reform. Much of it—such as the digitalization of legislative records or the renovation of state capitols, for example—can be better understood as response to technology on the one hand and deterioration on the other. Much change occurs without conscious planning.

For present purposes, legislative reform is change that is intended and purposeful, even though some of the results may be unanticipated. Usually, the intent is to improve legislative structure, personnel, policy, process, or behavior. At every legislative session, and in virtually every legislative body, reforms are proposed and considered. A number of them are adopted. A new standing committee is established, a staff agency is reorganized, an ethics code is revised, a rule pertaining to floor debate is rescinded. These, however, are not the reforms that we shall address in this chapter. They are piecemeal and scattered. This doesn't mean that isolated cases are insignificant, but rather that the focus here is on recent patterns of legislative reform, which have had substantial and widespread effects in the American states. We shall consider three patterns or reform movements that have dominated the national scene from the 1960s to the present.

The first nationwide movement is that of legislative capacity building (also known as legislative modernization and legislative professionalization). This endeavor gathered steam in the early 1960s, peaked in the 1970s, and had run its course in most states by the 1980s. The second nationwide movement is that of legislative ethics regulation, which has been episodic but robust through the entire fifty years under study. The third is that of legislative deprofessionalization, a dominant current during the decade of the 1990s.

In examining state legislative reform movements, a number of questions will be addressed.[1] First, from where did the reforms or pressures for reform come? Essentially, the major impetus for change is either from inside or from outside the legislature. Second, what were the overall objectives of the reforms being advocated? This includes implicit as well as explicit objectives. Third, what constitutes the reform agenda? What proposals were advocated, how were they justified, and what counterarguments were made? Fourth, what reforms were adopted, and by what process? What were the results—for reform agendas and for the groups supporting and opposing these initiatives—and what factors led to success? Fifth, what effects or consequences have the adopted reforms had? Did they advance the objectives of the proponents, or not? Did they have unintended, as well as intended, consequences?

BUILDING LEGISLATIVE CAPACITY

Before the 1960s legislatures operated with relatively few resources. Political scientist Alexander Heard had described state legislatures as poorly organized; technically ill-equipped; lacking time, staff, and space; and with outmoded procedures and committee systems. "State legislatures," he summed up, "may be our most extreme example of institutional lag."[2]

The Organization of Reform

Heard's characterization took hold, although it exaggerated the primitive condition of state legislatures. Even in the prereform era, legislative capacity was being developed, albeit at a gradual pace. In the early 1900s legislative reference services were created to help draft bills, and by the 1930s legislative councils, the precursors of centralized staff agencies, were being established. And years before the surge of reform, California and New York furnished legislators with professional and secretarial staff assistance and district and capitol offices.

Scholars, journalists, and reform groups all agreed that legislatures were simply not up to the job. Still, the major impetus for the modernization movement came from within the ranks of legislators themselves. Jesse Unruh, the Democratic Speaker of the California General Assembly, was without doubt the driving force, first of reform in his own state and then of reform in legislatures across the country. Using his position as president of the National Conference of State Legislative Leaders, an organization of legislative leaders in nearly all the states, he exhorted colleagues to undertake capacity-building drives within their own legislative bodies. Other legislative leaders, such as Republicans W. Russell Arrington of Illinois and Robert Knowles of Wisconsin and Democrat Marvin Mandel of Maryland, signed on. Another organization, the National Legislative Conference, composed of rank-and-file legislators and members of legislative staffs, also joined the effort.

Foundations—principally the Ford Foundation and the Carnegie Corporation—funded a number of legislative reform projects. The American Political Science Association, the American Assembly, the National Municipal League, and the Council of State Governments all participated.

Unruh indirectly played a crucial role in building citizen support for the reform movement. Larry Margolis, his chief of staff, in 1965 became the first director of the Citizens Conference for State Legislatures (CCSL). The Conference helped organize state citizen groups around the country and conducted a program to increase public awareness of the need for legislative improvement. With a Ford grant, CCSL also conducted an evaluation study of the fifty state legislatures and made recommendations for their improvement. In a number of states, legislators and citizen representatives collaborated on special legislative study committees. In other places, legislators and citizens went their separate ways but wound up reinforcing one another's endeavors.

California Assembly Speaker Jesse M. Unruh, D-Los Angeles, shown here in Sacramento, California, on March 26, 1962, pushed for reform that would strengthen and professionalize the legislature, such as administrative staff, salary increases, and benefits.

SOURCE: Associated Press.

Reform Objectives

This legislative reform movement had as its principal objectives making the legislature modern, professional, efficient, and member-friendly. Such changes, it was thought, would help recruit and retain able individuals to legislative service and give them the wherewithal to do the job. Emphasis was on improving the lawmaking performance of legislatures, and giving members more of an opportunity to participate in a meaningful way. The model offered by reformers for the nation's legislatures—whether in Alabama, Idaho, Maine, or Oregon—was California, the legislature that came nearest to the full-time, highly professionalized, heavily staffed U.S. Congress.

One of the principal objectives of Unruh in particular was to strengthen the legislature vis-à-vis the executive. The growth of government in the first half of the twentieth century had enhanced the power of the executive. According to Unruh, who was well versed in the uses of power, "power flows toward efficiency."[3] So it was Unruh's objective that the legislature be able not only to scrutinize and ask the right questions of the governor's initiatives, but also to originate and innovate policy on its own.

In its evaluation report published in 1971, the Citizens Conference made seventy-three recommendations. They ran the gamut from those that had weighty implications, such as reducing the number of members in a legislative chamber, to those that were administrative in nature, such as requiring when bills would be available in printed form. The report included thirty-five recommendations for Wyoming, which was ranked at the bottom of CCSL's state ranking, and seventeen for California, which was ranked at the top.[4] Probably the most frequent recommendation, which was unanimously backed by insiders and outsiders alike, was to expand and/or increase professional staffing. Unruh had already provided each of his assembly members an administrative assistant and each of the standing committees consultants. He had added to the central staff agencies, such as the offices of legal counsel, legislative analyst, and legislative budget.

Elements of Success

The modernization movement succeeded mainly because of the combined efforts of both those inside and those outside the legislature. Legislative leaders, legislative rank and file, citizen and reform groups, foundations, and academics all did their parts. During the 1960s, at least thirty states undertook studies of the organization, staffing, and/or procedures of their legislatures. Additional studies were undertaken during the 1970s. Outside the legislature, citizens' campaigns took place in Georgia, Idaho, Iowa, Kentucky, Minnesota, Missouri, Montana, Oregon, Pennsylvania, Texas, and West Virginia. Inside the legislature, special interim committees or commissions were established to propose reforms. The Illinois legislature, for example, established its own commission, chaired by a Democratic legislator, Harold Katz. Legislatures in Arkansas, Connecticut, Florida, Maryland, Mississippi, Rhode Island, and Wisconsin commissioned the Eagleton Institute at Rutgers University to conduct studies and recommend how they could improve their organizations and procedures.

The times were propitious. Thanks in part to the appeal of President John F. Kennedy, the public's approval of government, Congress, and state legislatures, as recorded by opinion polls, was at its highest levels. Except for some of the more senior and conservative members, legislators appeared amenable to or enthusiastic for institution building. Many of them were the products of the legislative apportionments in the 1960s, which as a result of decisions of the U.S. Supreme Court increased suburban and urban representation at the expense of previously overrepresented rural areas. In Florida, for instance, a new generation of legislators, including a number of young attorneys who attended law school together at the University of Florida, agreed on the need to revitalize state government, and reconstruct the Florida legislature.

The environment for legislative capacity building could not have been more felicitous, but leadership still was essential. Unruh's work in 1961 on behalf of Proposition 1A in California was illustrative. He was able to raise funds for the initiative campaign from California lobbyists. Together with the California General Assembly's Republican leader, Bob Monagan, Unruh travelled around the state speaking to business and labor groups. It was a bipartisan effort, which was important not only in California but in many states. The two candidates for governor in 1966, Pat Brown and Ronald Reagan, were brought on board and the media were won over. The reform banner read: "Update the State! Brown, Reagan, Business-Labor All Say Yes on 1-A."[5]

Nationally, bipartisanship was a requirement. Locally, however, it did not always work, mainly because governors of both parties were not enthusiastic about strengthening the legislative branch. Legislators of the governor's party often were cross-pressured, some taking the side of their institution and others backing the statewide leader of their party. But the reform movement could not help but promote a spirit of legislative independence. In states such as Florida, Kentucky, and Virginia, which had traditionally been dominated by Democrats, the advent of Republican governors galvanized Democratic legislatures. Wisconsin, on the other hand, had been dominated by Republicans, but politics had become highly competitive, and in the early 1960s a Republican legislature confronting a Democratic executive prompted a drive among the legislative majority for a stronger legislature. In a few places, governors tried to block the legislature, thereby stoking the fires of independence. In Connecticut, for instance, the legislature by unanimous votes in each house overrode a governor's veto of an omnibus modernization bill.

Reform's Accomplishments

The reform movement resulted in significant legislative change in states across the nation.[6] In 1969 twenty-six states met annually; in 1985 thirty-seven did so. In the 1964–1965 bienniums, twenty-four legislatures spent one hundred or more legislative days in regular and special sessions; by

THE POLITICS OF RANKING STATE LEGISLATURES

The campaign for legislative reform had an impact in many states. The evaluation study by the Citizens Conference on State Legislatures (CCSL) was especially effective. In 1970, when CCSL was finishing up its project evaluating the fifty state legislatures, the author of this chapter on legislative reform, Alan Rosenthal, expressed doubts to Larry Margolis, who led CCSL, about the validity of the methodology being used. Rosenthal said that he did not believe that it was appropriate to give legislatures precise scores on about a hundred criteria, add the numbers together, and then rank the states from 1 to 50. At best, Rosenthal suggested, CCSL could group the states ordinally into three or four categories of legislative effectiveness. Margolis responded that only if each state were given a number to designate a precise ranking would anyone take CCSL's report seriously and adopt its recommendations.

A few years after the report was issued, and after each legislature was labeled with a ranking by the in-state media, Rosenthal met with Thomas Hunter Lowe, the Speaker of the Maryland House in Annapolis. Lowe detailed the reforms the Maryland General Assembly had made in response to the evaluation study. On parting, he restated, "We're not no. 20 anymore, we're no. 1."

Legislative leaders around the country were reacting in similar fashion. Many of them had been embarrassed by their low standing. They had to deal with the media's questions—what was the legislature going to do to improve itself and raise its ranking? In an effort to move up several notches, about four-fifths of the states, like Maryland, responded by adding staff, improving facilities, and adopting other recommendations. Margolis may have been on weak ground as a social scientist, but he knew what was required to get legislatures to pay attention to reform.

1979–1980 forty spent at least one hundred days, with twenty of them exceeding two hundred. By 1985 only nine states still set legislator compensation in their constitutions, instead of the twenty-four in the 1960s. The 1965 average annual salary of $3,900 had grown by 1979 to $14,000. In the 1960s offices for rank-and-file members were rare; by 1980 a majority of legislative bodies provided them, along with new legislator office buildings and renovated capitols. During the reform era, committee systems were streamlined. House committees were reduced in number in three-fourths of the states and senate committees in four-fifths. By the 1980s two out of three states had uniform committee rules, all had open committee meetings, and most were making use of standing committees during the interim period.

By 1980, legislatures had made tremendous gains in the variety and number of professional staff. Forty states provided staff for all committees, as compared with only eleven two decades earlier. Forty-three had permanent research agencies, as compared with only thirteen in the 1960s. In addition, legislatures established staff agencies to do program evaluation or performance auditing—in Hawaii in 1965, Minnesota in 1967, Connecticut and Kentucky in 1971, California in 1972, and Mississippi and Virginia in 1973.

Probably the most significant effect overall was to enhance the capacity of state legislatures, even the capacity of citizen legislatures in the smaller states. The additional time legislatures devoted to the job mattered, but the greatest boost to legislative capacity was from professional staffing, in terms of larger numbers and more specialized and proficient staffs. Leaders acquired greater staff support. Standing committees got the assistance they needed to do a better job studying, deliberating, and deciding on policy. Fiscal staffs and audit staffs offered legislatures additional technical competence. And individual members began to receive the staff assistance they needed to represent their constituents and fashion their own policy agendas.

Second-order effects of the reform movement are less obvious, but three seem of importance. First, democratization took place internally. As a result of getting more information and staff assistance, the ability of members to exercise power internally grew. Members could challenge their leadership, and they did. Finally, the opportunities of members for meaningful participation in the budget and lawmaking processes increased.

Second, as legislatures became more professionalized, so did the members. In the larger states, and to some degree in the medium-sized states as well, the old breed of citizen legislator, the part-time member with an outside career, was being replaced by professional politicians. The latter looked forward to careers in politics; what they did occupationally outside the legislature was secondary to what they were doing inside the legislature and what they might do to advance their political careers. Because of the capacity at the legislature's disposal and the higher salaries and better working conditions for individual members, a legislative seat became far more desirable than it was prior to reform. Members wanted to stay, at least until they could run for higher office. On average, only one out of ten departed voluntarily, and most of the incumbents who were left tended to win their races for reelection. Turnover declined substantially—in the case of lower houses from 33 percent in the 1960s to about 20 percent by the end of the 1980s.

Third, most legislators and observers would probably agree that as a result of the reform movement legislatures improved their performance. Benefitting from district offices and staff support, members in the more professionalized legislatures ratcheted up the job they did representing constituents and constituencies. This occurred particularly in constituent service and outreach activities by individual members. Policy products may not have changed dramatically, but the processes of lawmaking were based on more information, greater participation, more expert standing committees, and increased study and deliberation. And, for a while at least, feelings of legislative independence, a product of the reform movement, made legislatures more conscious of their responsibility to balance the power of governors.

LEGISLATIVE ETHICS REGULATION

The efforts associated with regulating legislative ethics are of a very different nature than those associated with the capacity-building movement. Ethics reform is less a movement, as such, and more of a continuing enterprise. Ethics was also part of the modernization movement in the 1960s and 1970s, because promotion of ethics tended to be part of any reform agenda. The media insisted on it. It appealed to the public. Legislators themselves were more than willing to support ethics regulation, if that was the price to be paid for their careers in politics and public service.

Why Legislatures Take on Ethics

Generally, ethics reform has been forced on legislatures from without, rather than summoned up from within. At the national level and in most of the states an array of organizations function as ethics watchdogs, monitoring the behavior of legislators and proposing ways to promote greater integrity by public officials and governmental institutions. Over the years Common Cause has been especially active, both nationally and through chapters in many states. Public Citizen and the League of Women Voters also are ardent advocates of ethics reform. Probably the most influential role in a persistent campaign has been that played by the media, which not only have been severe critics of the ethical behavior of legislators and legislatures, but also have succeeded in uncovering ethical malfeasance, misfeasance, and nonfeasance by members of state legislatures. The subject of ethics has its internal advocates as well, but they are a small minority of legislators. For the most part members, and especially those who have served a while, protest that they do not require special rules in order to behave ethically. They would prefer to avoid regulation, but usually avoidance is not possible for several reasons.

Legislators use ethics laws as a bargaining chip in their attempts to make other gains. In California, for example, Unruh in 1966 accepted the inclusion of a code of ethics in Proposition 1A, in return for salary increases and other benefits for legislators. The state also barred legislators from being awarded honoraria, in return for having legislative salaries set by an independent commission rather than by the legislature itself.

Often, ethics regulation cannot be avoided by legislatures if it is proposed by reform-minded governors such as Republican John Volpe in Massachusetts, and Republicans Thomas Dewey and George Pataki and Democrats Mario Cuomo and Andrew Cuomo in New York. Even if they haven't always persuaded their legislatures, governors have been able to keep ethics alive for the media.

Yet by far the greatest impetus for legislative ethics reform has been the misbehavior of legislators themselves. The success of the ongoing, yet intermittent, ethics reform movement has resulted from incidents of corruption, ethical misconduct, and scandals.

A chain of causation links scandal to law essentially as follows. A legislator is accused, indicted, or convicted in the criminal justice system or impugned in an investigative report, article, or commentary in the media. The story acquires legs, and reform groups press their ethics agendas with the legislature and the media. The public reacts with outrage, and soon legislators are hearing about the "scandal" from constituents when they return to their districts. The longer the story runs, the stronger the realization by legislative leaders that they need to enact additional ethics laws in order to assuage the media and pacify the public. More than anything else, pressures from events and from the outside compel legislatures to adopt reforms, so that they can put the scandal behind them and move on with their business of making laws.

In the states during the period from 1954 to 1996, as tracked by Beth Rosenson, scandal was the most critical influence in ethics reform.[7] Federal prosecutors and sting operations played a significant role in California, Illinois, Kentucky, Louisiana, South Carolina (see Chapter 11, "Operation Lost Trust and Lobbying Reform in South Carolina" box), Tennessee, and West Virginia, while local enforcement was key in Arizona and New Mexico. Scandals large, in Michigan, and small, in Minnesota, energized drives for additional laws. Where the statewide initiative existed, the urgency for legislatures to take action was even greater. In Massachusetts, for example, Common Cause's reform agenda made little headway until 1976, when two legislators were convicted of extortion. Common Cause began circulating an initiative for a statewide vote. The legislature acted preemptively, passing its own bill so that more extreme ethics restrictions would not be placed on the ballot for a vote by the electorate.

Components of Ethics Regulation

Implicitly, the objectives of legislatures in enacting ethics laws are to placate the media and the public, defend against partisan attack of members at election time, and be able to move on to regular lawmaking matters. The explicit objectives are to prevent unethical behavior by legislators, in particular using public office for private gain, and to build or restore public trust or confidence.

Ethics reform has been in addition to the surge of campaign finance regulation, which has imposed limits on contributions by individuals, political action committees (PACs), and political parties, and reporting requirements. More than half the states have placed restrictions on legislators receiving contributions during legislative sessions. And a number of states awarded public funds to legislative campaigns, including Connecticut, Georgia, and Maine, which provided flat grants to match small contributions.[8] While the states were attempting to bring campaign contributions under control, the following types of ethics reforms were also being adopted.

Ethics commissions. Nearly all the states have legislative ethics committees, in the senates or the houses or jointly. But as a result of scandals, almost half the states now have established independent ethics commissions with jurisdiction over legislator ethics as well as executive ethics (the most recent being in New York in 2011). These commissions can investigate complaints against legislators (or initiate investigations on their own) and report their findings and recommendations to the legislature for action.

Ethics codes. Most legislatures have adopted by statute or rule an ethics code for members. These codes lay out principles regarding public office, personal gain, and independence and impartiality. Many also maintain as a standard not only of behaving properly, but also of not giving the "appearance of impropriety."

Financial disclosure. Nearly every state has enacted the requirement that legislators make a public disclosure of their assets and sources of income. The rationale is that citizens ought to be able to infer for themselves whether lawmakers' private interests are affecting their public activities.

Common Cause executive director Phil West, right, listens as Rhode Island governor Don Carcieri (2003–2011), left, proposes a comprehensive public ethics reform plan on September 20, 2006. Carcieri asked the Ethics Commission to revise and strengthen ethics codes in order to close gaping loopholes in state ethics laws.

SOURCE: AP Photo/Stew Milne.

Lobbyist disclosure. All fifty states require lobbyists to register and file disclosure reports regarding clients and expenses. Many require specification of the expenditures made by lobbyists on the entertainment of legislators.

Gift restrictions. In 1957 Wisconsin passed the first "no cup of coffee" law, which prohibited legislators from taking anything of value from lobbyists and their principals. Today, gifts are banned in about a dozen states, although allowance is made for legislators to attend functions where all legislators (or all members of the senate, house, or a specific committee) are invited. In many other states there are limitations on the dollar amounts of gifts legislators can take on a single occasion per source or over the course of a year from one source. All gifts have to be reported. Reimbursed trips out of state by legislators have also been curtailed in a number of places.

Honoraria. Payment in return for speeches they deliver in connection with their public duties is banned in about half the states.

Conflicts of interest. Legislatures have adopted provisions to reduce the possibility that "citizen legislators" (who have employment outside the legislature) will act on behalf of their own personal, financial interest rather than for the benefit of the public and their constituents. Outside employment may be restricted, and members are expected to recuse themselves on issues where they feel they may be conflicted.

Nepotism. Nearly half the states now prohibit nepotism, thus doing away with the employment of relatives on legislators' office staffs.

Revolving door. To guard against an unethical use of influence while in office, more than half the states prevent legislators from employment as lobbyists immediately after leaving the legislature. Most require a moratorium of one year, but a few require legislators to defer employment as lobbyists for two years.

Ethics training. Most states now offer ethics training to legislators, and in some places to lobbyists as well. In a dozen states legislators are mandated to take the training. The training normally focuses on compliance with law.

Ethics counseling. Annual counseling by an attorney on the legislative staff is required in Maryland and New Jersey. The ethics counsel works off the financial disclosure form that legislators file to alert them to ethical issues that may confront them in their employment, investments, or in other positions they may hold.

Transparency. Of a somewhat different nature than the aforementioned ethics restrictions are the openness requirements that legislatures have been adopting. Since Florida's Government in the Sunshine Act passed in 1967, the states have adopted laws requiring that meetings of public bodies be open (except in certain specific situations). Along with opening up the processes of government, states also passed open public records acts making governmental information available on request. Transparency has been further promoted by legislative outreach activities by C-SPAN–type facilities and media coverage in the states.

What Difference Does It Make?

It is not possible to assess the effects of specific reforms. Consider campaign finance. Has it reduced corruption, or the appearance of corruption? At the federal and state levels, limits have been imposed on candidates and political parties. This, however, has led to a greater role in electoral politics for interest groups and political action committees. In assessing the impacts at the state level, Michael J. Malbin and Thomas L. Gais characterized such laws as having "unclear ends, incomplete implementation, and unforeseen consequences."[9] At both the federal and state levels, the attempt to control campaign spending has been largely unsuccessful, as participants in campaigns and elections have figured out how legally to get around restrictions and spend more than the advocates of such laws intended to be allowed.

Financial disclosure requirements provide a more specific example of unintended effects reforms may have. More information is made available to the media and to citizens, who can make their own inferences and draw their own conclusions about the integrity of individual legislators. The major consumers of such information, however, are political candidates and campaigns constructing a case against an incumbent. On the other side of the ledger, it is thought that intrusive disclosure requirements discourage a number of people from running for political office. Some people do not want it to be known publicly that they are relatively poor, and others do not want it to be known publicly that they are relatively wealthy.

Perhaps more important than anything else, capital cultures have changed.[10] The freewheeling and cozy relationships between lobbyists and legislators are no longer anything like those that existed in the 1960s and 1970s. Gift bans and gift disclosure requirements have been highly effective. Legislators now tend to avoid taking anything except campaign contributions. They do not want to risk the media, their constituents, or an opposing candidate exploiting a free meal to challenge their integrity. To some extent, socializing between legislators and lobbyists still occurs, but it is confined to large gatherings, fund-raisers, and receptions, rather than more intimate dinners or hunting or fishing trips that once were in fashion. (It should be noted that the transformation of capital cultures has come about not only because of ethics laws. New generations of legislators have less inclination to socialize—they work harder, and drink and party less.) On balance, no-cup-of-coffee laws and the like have made the process fairer and more ethical. Members can no longer live, as they once did, on the lobbyists' dime. Consider New Jersey, for instance, where so-called benefit passing never reached the scale of California, Florida, or Louisiana. In 1992, after disclosure was required, lobbyists spent $163,375 on public officials. In 2010 that figure was down to $7,476, and in 2011 it was down to $5,687. The latter figure averages out to $47 per legislator per year from the totality of lobbyists buying drinks or meals.

Although they are uncomfortable with ethics issues, leaders and members have adapted. Defensively, they provide for at least nominal training and ethics advising. Most important, the expectations today of most legislators are very different than they were in the 1960s. The existence of ethics codes and many regulations and examples of sanctions being brought against colleagues have led legislators to adjust to new standards and behave differently from their predecessors. They have little choice in the matter.

LEGISLATURES ARE NO LONGER ETHICALLY LAISSEZ-FAIRE

In the late 1980s an FBI sting operation, "Shrimpgate," led to the conviction of three Democratic members of the California Senate. The affair had a devastating effect on the legislature. A while later, in an interview with the senate president, David Roberti, Alan Rosenthal asked whether he could have done something beforehand that would have reined in his three members. Each had a reputation among Sacramento insiders of playing loose with the rules. Roberti responded that it wasn't his job to monitor the behavior of senators; it was to get votes for issues, and he needed the votes of all three of them to do so. His intervention, he believed, wouldn't have made a difference anyway; the three senators would have ignored his plea and continued the paths they had chosen. The pro tem would only have lost their support and come out a loser.

Just ten years later, evidence of unethical behavior was less likely to be swept under the rug. In Maryland in the late 1990s, for example, Mike Miller, the senate president, confronted one of the members of his leadership team after learning of questionable financial involvements on his part. The senator denied any wrongdoing. A little while later, in December 1997, an investigative report in the *Baltimore Sun* cited chapter and verse, and Miller immediately decided that action had to be taken—and taken quickly—to avoid the scandal's spilling over onto the legislative session that began in January and hurting the Democrats in November's gubernatorial and senatorial elections. Miller enlisted the Speaker of the house, and the two of them referred the case to the joint ethics committee and called for expeditious action. The committee found that the member had violated a number of public ethics laws. It made two recommendations: first, that the senate adopt a resolution to censure the member; second, that it consider a resolution to expel him. At the behest of the senate president, however, the senate took up the expulsion resolution first (so that members could not vote against it, claiming that they had already voted for censure). The resolution passed with more than the two-thirds required vote, and the senator was expelled.

Today, legislative leaders, realizing that misbehavior might inflict serious damage on the legislature, their party, and their colleagues—and that news about it is likely to spread quickly—believe that they cannot afford to ignore questionable behavior. Unlike Roberti in the 1980s, they indicate that they would have a heart-to-heart session with members who did not seem to know where the ethical line should be drawn. Such interventions might not always succeed, however, because challenged legislators might deny that they were doing anything illegal or unethical.

LEGISLATIVE DEPROFESSIONALIZATION

As if to prove the adage that for every action there is a reaction, the term-limits movement got down to serious business in the late 1980s, in part as a response to the legislative capacity building of the 1960s and 1970s. By professionalizing the legislature and making legislative careers more attractive, the movement created the conditions that spawned term limits. To growing numbers of people who distrusted politicians, citizen legislators were acceptable; they were expected to serve for a few years and then return full-time to their regular occupations. But professional legislators were something else; they would try to remain in office for entire careers.

Making legislatures full-time and professional had the intended effects. The job became more valuable. In states like California, Illinois, Massachusetts, Michigan, New York, and Pennsylvania, professional politicians took almost complete control of the legislative scene. Meanwhile, citizens were becoming less satisfied with their politics, politicians, and political institutions. The term-limits movement arose just as legislatures were losing the confidence of the public. When asked on a poll, people were still inclined to say they liked their own legislator, but they felt much less positive toward legislators collectively and toward the legislature as a political institution.

The Voters Decide

The motto of the organization U.S. Term Limits was "Citizen Legislators, *Not* Career Politicians." The objective was to rid the nation, and primarily the U.S. Congress, of career politicians. The argument for term limits went further. If legislators were limited in the number of terms they could serve, at the end of their tenure no one would be running with the advantages of incumbency. New people would be encouraged to run, and more would have a chance to be elected to open seats. In any case, newcomers with fresh ideas would replace cynical veterans who were in thrall to interest groups. Term-limited legislators, moreover, would not have to depend on special interests for political support; instead, they could faithfully represent their constituents.

Proponents asserted that legislators and legislatures would improve if career politicians were removed from the scene. The legislature would become a more diverse body of citizens, with more women and minorities in its ranks. Such a citizen legislature would pass better and fewer laws. For George Will, a leading proponent, term limits by sapping the electoral incentive would encourage legislators to think more broadly and more independently (in a Burkean sense) of the interests of the nation or state as a whole.[11]

The impetus for term limits came mainly from outside the legislature. Although five national groups, in particular U.S. Term Limits headed by Paul Jacob, became major players, the push for term limits was essentially a grassroots movement. Early proposals called for both congressional and legislative term limits to be enacted by the states, the principal target being Congress, the most professionalized and careerist legislative body of all. By 1995 twenty-two states had adopted term limits for members of Congress. But the U.S. Supreme Court, in *U.S. Term Limits Inc. v. Thornton* (1995), ruled that the U.S. Constitution did not allow the states to place restrictions on qualifications for federal office.[12] Only if the U.S. Constitution were amended could term limits be imposed on Congress, but this was too high a hurdle for the nascent uprising.

At the national level, Republican members generally favored term limits, and a limit on terms was one of the planks in Newt Gingrich's "Contract with America" of 1994. In the states, relatively few incumbent legislators (although more Republicans than Democrats) supported term limits for their legislatures. Ironically, the author of Proposition 140, which targeted career politicians in California, was Pete Schabarum, a Republican and former member of the assembly, who had held elective office for twenty-four years, and by 1990 claimed to be a "recovering politician."

Term limits were adopted for their legislatures by twenty-one states, but overruled by courts in Massachusetts, Oregon, Washington, and Wyoming, and subsequently repealed by legislatures in Idaho and Utah (where it had been passed as a statute and not a constitutional amendment). Today, they are in effect in fifteen states.

Of the twenty-one states that adopted term limits, only in Louisiana did the legislature make the choice without the pressure of a ballot proposition. The Utah legislature also adopted the change, but only because an initiative that was being readied for a ballot would have been more restrictive than the twelve-year senate and house terms the legislature enacted through the normal process. In all the other states, which provided for a constitutional and/or statutory initiative, proponents made an end-run around the legislature, seeking approval from the electorate. There was little organized opposition. Unions were against term limits, but neither they nor business played a large role. Legislators were afraid to take a stand on a measure the public clearly favored.

Term limits did not pass because rotation in office had a place in American history, when at the birth of the new Republic members voluntarily left Congress and state legislatures after a short time. Nor did limits pass because since 1951 the president of the United States had been term-limited by the Twenty-second Amendment to the U.S. Constitution, or that in more than half the states governors were term-limited. Nor did they pass because turnover was too low. (Indeed, in the ten years before the onset of term limits, from 50 to 94 percent of the members of the fifty state senates and 49 to 90 percent of the forty-nine state houses had turned over, allowing new blood to transfuse into the system.) They passed because voters had become angry with politics and politicians.

The Effects of Limits

Term limits, as they were adopted by legislatures in Louisiana and Utah, and by the popular adoption of initiative proposals elsewhere, came in a number of forms. One form related to whether limits were adopted as an amendment to the state constitution or as a simple statute. The second form related to whether the limits were "lifetime," which absolutely limited service in the legislature, or "consecutive," which allowed members who had served their terms to sit out an election and then run and serve again. The third form related to the number of terms or years that comprised the limit in each house of the legislature. In the fifteen states where term limits were in effect in 2013, members of senates are limited to eight years in eleven states and twelve years in two, and members of houses are limited to six years in three states, eight years in eight, and twelve years in two. In Nebraska's unicameral senate the cap is eight years, and in Oklahoma the total length of service for the two houses is twelve years.

The effects of term limits have been subject to extensive study by political scientists, providing the basis for the assessment here.[13] The movement has succeeded in one respect—that of curtailing legislative careers. Where term limits exist, legislative turnover has increased on average by about 14 percent, at the same time that there has been a slight decline in turnover in non-term-limited states. Few veterans can be found in a house of representatives anymore. Because a number of house members run for the other body when their terms expire, senates still have some experienced members. Legislators with fifteen or twenty years under their belts, the gray beards of yesteryear, are gone. These members are the ones who had been around long enough to be familiar with the issues and the processes, to know how to operate as lawmakers, to have memories of what happened in earlier years, and to have earned reputations as go-to legislators among their colleagues. They have been replaced by lawmakers who have to exit long before they can acquire comparable standing.

Besides shortening legislative careers, another objective of the proponents of term limits has been to deprofessionalize legislatures, which since the 1960s had been subject to galloping (or creeping) professionalization. Here, too, they can be credited with some success, even in the most professionalized places such as California and Michigan. As summed up by one political scientist, "For better or worse, legislatures that were redesigned by the professionalization movement have been revolutionized again by term limits."[14]

The third objective, that of replacing politicians with citizens, may have been achieved in part, but only in part. There is little doubt that the political careers of a number of people have been curtailed by term limits. When they leave the legislature, if no other political office is available, they return to their citizen pursuits. Yet the expectation that amateur and citizen legislators would replace professional and politician legislators in office has not been met. The people who run for the legislature in states with term limits are not very different from their predecessors. Nor are they different from their counterparts in non-term-limited states. They are people who like politics and are interested in carving out political careers for themselves. The term-limits movement did not rid legislatures of career politicians. It has just kept them from settling down with careers in the legislature; now they have to jump around from office to office and job to job.

Some advocates hoped and anticipated that term limits would make it easier for women and minorities to achieve legislative office. But this hasn't happened. Generally speaking, as national surveys show, there are no differences between term-limited and non-term-limited states, not only in members' minority status or gender, but also in their age, family income, religious affiliation, or ideology.

Although they do not differ demographically, term-limited legislators do vary in their orientations toward their jobs. They approach legislative service with a special sense of urgency, as is befitting their restricted statuses. They are impatient to get their agendas accomplished. Everything has to be done ASAP. The norm of apprenticeship was not strongly held before term limits; it is nonexistent in term-limited legislatures today. Freshman members chair standing committees, but they do not specialize; they do not have enough time ahead of them to make an investment in expertise worthwhile. Instead, their tendency is to hop from one committee to another, in order to ascend ladders of chamber influence and leadership.

The legislature as a functioning organization has felt effects. There has always been tension between the two houses, but under term limits the more experienced senate appears to have increased its influence vis-à-vis the less experienced house. The top legislative leaders, particularly of the majority party, are also weakened. Standing committees have been diminished. In California, for instance, there is less scrutiny of referred bills than before; fewer bills are screened out and fewer bills are amended before being reported out.[15] There is little reason any longer for nonmembers to defer to committees for judgment; consequently, committee recommendations carry little weight.

To some extent, activity and influence have moved to the floor of the chambers, where debate takes place and the fate of legislation is decided with less concern for the work a committee has done. To some extent, also, the business of deciding has shifted to the majority-party caucus. In Maine, for example, leaders do not give committees enough time to draft legislation and build consensus. Bills get decided in the majority-party caucus. Thus disagreements get resolved, not in a bipartisan setting that rewards expertise and deliberation, but in a partisan setting where political considerations play a larger role.

As for the effects of term limits on lobbyists, the picture is mixed or unclear. Proponents of the reform predicted that with legislators unable to plant roots, the strength of lobbyist–interest group–legislator alliances would diminish. This hasn't happened. Lobbyists and interest groups are no less important in the legislative process, although the job of lobbyists may be tougher because of the need constantly to build relationships with newly elected legislators.

What about the effects of term limits on the performance by legislatures of their major functions: representation, lawmaking, balancing the power of the governor, and maintenance of the legislature as an institution?

It is doubtful that term limits have impacted significantly on representatives serving their districts' interests or expressing their constituencies' views. Legislators still keep in close touch with their constituents and try in a variety of ways to help them out. On those few issues where a majority of constituents are in agreement on a position, legislators tend to agree as well; so they are able to reflect constituents' views. Whether term-limited or not, legislators perform the representational function well.

With less study and deliberation, diminished specialization, decreasing expertise, and insufficient knowledge, it would stand to reason that the legislature's performance of lawmaking would suffer. Inexperienced legislators make more mistakes, policy champions are fewer, perspectives are short-term. It is more difficult for legislative leaders to build consensus. The budget process, in particular, is less thorough than it had been. If the work and influence of standing committees are superseded by that of party caucuses, the process can be expected to become more partisan and more political, making interparty agreements tougher to reach.

The function that legislatures have had the most difficult time performing is balancing the power of the executive. For some time, governors have had the upper hand in their policy and budget dealings with legislatures. Among the governors' advantages are being single rather than multiple; being able to use the bully pulpit and lead issue campaigns; having the ability to formulate policy initiatives and budgets; being leader of one of the two major parties in the state; having a variety of rewards to dispense to legislators; and possessing the veto, line-item veto, or conditional (or amendatory) veto as a defensive (and, to a degree, offensive) weapon. The evidence is clear and consistent that, as a result of term limits, the legislature has lost further ground to the executive. That is what participants and observers think, and what researchers have found, particularly when it comes to the budget process and budget outcomes. This was not what the proponents of term limits wanted or expected to happen.

The fourth function performed by legislatures is less concrete. It pertains to institutional commitment, including the care and maintenance of the legislature as an institution.

INSTITUTIONALLY, GOVERNORS ARE THE WINNERS

Political scientists who have studied term limits generally agree that one of the principal effects of term limits is the loss of power by legislatures to governors. The turnover that results removes experienced and knowledgeable members who have acquired influence across the board or in particular policy domains. New members have neither the time nor incentive to become experts who can challenge the governor's policy people in departments and agencies. Strong legislative leadership might be able to challenge executive power, but in term-limited states leaders have been weakened vis-à-vis governors. They no longer have much experience before becoming leaders, and they have little time as top leaders to develop their skills as leaders. As soon as they take office, they have lame- duck status and consequently are less relevant to the careers of members. It can be hard for them to persuade members to follow their lead, especially when they are going in a direction that is different from that of the governor.

In interviewing former governors for a book he was writing, Alan Rosenthal was not surprised that they agreed with the research findings of political scientists. John Engler, a Republican from Michigan, who had served as senate majority leader before serving as governor from 1991–2003, summed up: "Term limits killed the legislature in Michigan." Former governors from Maine and Colorado are in accord, as is Republican Bob Taft of Ohio. The latter, interestingly, regards term limits as a mixed blessing for the executive. In his judgment, it is more difficult for governors with term-limited legislatures to take on tough issues that they might otherwise put on their agendas. That is because they can no longer depend on legislative leaders to do the heavy lifting. Leaders are not confident they can get their members on board when political risk is high. They don't have the clout they need. Moreover, according to Taft, it is more difficult to find knowledgeable legislators at any level to carry a governor's initiatives.

SOURCES: Richard J. Powell, "Executive-Legislative Relations," in *Institutional Change in American Politics: The Case of Term Limits*, ed. Karl Kurtz, Bruce Cain, and Richard G. Niemi (Ann Arbor: University of Michigan, 2002), 38–54; Alan Rosenthal, *The Best Job in Politics: Exploring How Governors Succeed as Policy Leaders* (Washington, DC: CQ Press, 2012), 32–33.

Institutional concern is relatively rare today. But it is noticeably lacking in term-limited legislatures, where members do not expect to remain for long and leaders have at most four years in top positions. The perspective is short-term, while an institutional perspective is long-term. The goal term-limited members shoot for is not a stronger legislature, which takes a while to accomplish, but the enactment of a program or bill and higher office or other office when their terms expire. The development of institutional commitment takes years and having increasing leadership responsibility, and even then the odds are against it developing. Term-limited legislators don't have their predecessors' luxury of time.

THE CONTINUING COURSE OF REFORM

Few, if any, state legislatures today are in a capacity-building mode. Most are retrenching. The term-limits movement has come to an end. Its effects are still being absorbed, but the adoption of term limits by other states or the repeal or liberalization of term limits in the fifteen states that enacted them is unlikely.

The other reform movement that we examined here—ethics regulation—continues to move along. National and state citizen groups keep advocating new and stronger regulation. The media editorialize along similar lines. Members, themselves, unwittingly help the cause of regulation by getting into trouble. Ethics reform will not go away, and certainly not while the public mood in many places is antipolitician and antipolitical.

Although no nationwide movements are underway currently, reform ideas still pop up in one place or another. Most continue to come from outside the legislature, although they have adherents inside as well. In some places, such as Michigan, the push is for a part-time citizen legislature. A few states, like Pennsylvania, think the process would improve if the number of members was reduced.

Other observers identify as an important problem the erosion of study and deliberation by legislatures. The weakening of committees and growing partisanship in many states are in part responsible for the deterioration of the process, which now focuses more on the political than the substantive aspects of policy. The ends have become more important than the means. While legislatures have become more responsive, many people question how responsible they are. Although they have responded to demands for the increases in programs and services, they have been reluctant to pay for them. Even the requirement that they balance their budgets has not averted structural deficits, and revenues from economic growth have not managed to save the day. Responsiveness pays off at the next election, but the payoffs from responsibility are longer-term and less concrete. What can legislatures do to achieve a balance between responsiveness on the one hand and responsibility on the other?

For those of an institutional bent, members' lack of commitment to the legislature as an independent branch of government in a separation-of-powers system is a serious problem. If legislators themselves show little concern, who can be expected to worry about their institution's well-being? The problem, of course, is devising ways to promote institutional commitment on the parts of members who are pulled in so many other and more immediate directions.

Growing numbers of Americans appear worried about the hyperpartisanship that currently characterizes national politics. Increasing partisanship and partisan conflict have been on the rise nationally since the 1970s. This trend grew in strength with the Republican takeover of Congress under the leadership of Newt Gingrich. It was going full steam during Barack Obama's first term in presidential office. A number of factors account for the hyperpartisanship in Washington. More competitive politics, ideological voters polarized along Democratic and Republican lines, changes in the nature of political campaigns, and the new media environment are among the most important ones.

A recent study examines partisanship at the state level. In the two least polarized legislatures, the Republicans in Rhode Island were more liberal than their compatriots elsewhere and the Democrats in Louisiana were more conservative than their compatriots elsewhere. Nationally, there was some overlap between the parties. For instance, the Democratic party of the Michigan legislature was more conservative than the Republican party in six other states, and the Republican party of the New York legislature was more liberal than the Democratic party in ten other states. Still, fifteen legislatures—including California, Texas, Washington, and Wisconsin—were reported to be more polarized than Congress.[16]

Efforts to reduce partisanship and partisan conflict in the states have gotten underway, although no national movements akin to the capacity-building or term-limits drives have developed as of yet. The potential, however, is there. Organizations such as Third Way are endeavoring to break the stranglehold that Republicans and Democrats now have on national politics. As far as state efforts are concerned, California is again in the vanguard.

Reformers believe that the political system in California exaggerates the strengths of the two parties, emphasizes the views of the more extreme partisan voters, and silences the voices of independents. As a consequence, conflict is endemic, stalemate is routine, and much of governance takes place in the campaigns for and against referenda on ballot initiatives. The argument made by reformers is that the system of redistricting by politicians, single-member districts, winner-take-all politics, and party primaries does not fairly represent the electorate, but instead overrepresent the extremes on the left and the right.[17]

Redistricting is a major target of reform throughout the nation, but perhaps the most dramatic changes have been made in California. Reformers in the Golden State believe that redistricting, conducted by the legislature, led to a lack of competition, control by the more extreme elements of one party or the other, and greater partisanship and polarization in the legislature. A California citizens commission, adopted by ballot initiative to do both legislative and congressional redistricting, is the most ambitious attempt yet to exorcise political factors and produce more competitive districts, ones in which those who are elected have to be responsive to voters of the other party, as well as to their own party bases.

The other major goal of California reformers has been to change the electoral system, one in which because of low turnout in both primary and general elections only about 10 percent of the electorate has been choosing more than half the legislators. In 1996 Proposition 198 established a blanket primary (which already existed in Alaska and Washington) in California, whereby all candidates were on the same ballot, open to all voters. The top vote-getter within each party advanced. The political parties challenged the blanket primary, and in 2000 the U.S. Supreme Court overturned it on the grounds that it violated the parties' First Amendment right to free association.[18] The struggle to break the grip of the parties on the electoral system did not stop with the Court's ruling. In 2004 a top-two-vote-getter (TTVG) initiative went on California's ballot, but it was rejected by the voters. Six years later it was adopted. This reform allows California voters to choose any candidate, regardless of party, in the primary. The top two, again regardless of party, advance to a runoff election that picks the winner.[19] Whether or not TTVG will moderate the two political parties and open the way for pragmatic solutions to the state's problems remains to be seen. Whether other states will follow California's path is also an open question.

As in the past, in the years ahead legislatures will be under pressure to reform themselves—to become more ethical, more representative, more responsive, more efficient, and more effective. Old nostrums and new remedies will be offered up. Which ones, if any, fuel a nationwide reform movement cannot be predicted with much confidence.

NOTES

1. This section draws on Alan Rosenthal, "Reform in State Legislatures," in *Encyclopedia of the American Legislative System,* ed. Joel H. Silbey (New York: Charles Scribner's Sons, 1994), 837–854.
2. Alexander Heard, ed., *State Legislatures in American Politics* (Englewood Cliffs, NJ: Prentice Hall, 1966), 3.
3. Donald G. Herzberg and Jesse Unruh, *Essays on the State Legislative Process* (New York: Holt, Rinehart, and Winston, 1970), 16–19.
4. John Burns, *The Sometime Governments* (New York: Bantam, 1971).
5. Bill Boyarsky, *Big Daddy: Jesse Unruh and the Art of Power Politics* (Berkeley: University of California Press, 2008), 167–169.
6. Advisory Commission on Intergovernmental Relations, *The Question of State Government Capability* (Washington, DC: The Commission, 1985).
7. Beth A. Rosenson, *The Shadowlands of Conduct: Ethics and State Politics* (Washington, DC: Georgetown University Press, 2005).
8. Michael J. Malbin, Peter W. Brusoe, and Brendan Glavin, *Public Financing of Elections after* Citizens United *and* Arizona Free Enterprise (Washington, DC: The Campaign Finance Institute, 2011).
9. Michael J. Malbin and Thomas L. Gais, *The Day after Reform* (Albany, NY: Rockefeller Institute Press, 1998), 179.
10. Alan Rosenthal, "The Effects of Legislative Ethics Law: An Institutional Perspective," in *Public Ethics and Governance: Standards and Practice in Comparative Perspective,* ed. Denis Saint Martin and Fred Thompson (Oxford: Elsevier, 2006), 155–177.
11. George F. Will, *Restoration: Congress, Term Limits, and the Recovery of the Deliberative Democracy* (New York: Free Press, 1993).
12. *U.S. Term Limits Inc. v. Thornton,* 514 U.S. 779 (1995).
13. See Karl Kurtz, Bruce Cain, and Richard G. Niemi, eds., *Institutional Change in American Politics: The Case of Term Limits* (Ann Arbor: University of Michigan, 2002); Thad Kousser, *Term Limits and the Dismantling of State Legislative Professionalism* (New York: Cambridge University Press, 2005); and Rick Farmer, Christopher Z. Mooney, Richard Powell, and John C. Green, eds., *Legislating without Experience: Case Studies in Legislative Term Limits* (Lanham, MD: Lexington Books, 2007).
14. Kousser, *Term Limits and the Dismantling of State Legislative Professionalism,* 203, 213.
15. Ibid., 51.
16. Boris Shor and Nolan McCarty, "The Ideological Mapping of American Legislatures," *American Political Science Review* 105 (August 2011): 530–551.
17. Joe Mathews and Mark Paul, *California Crackup* (Berkeley: University of California Press, 2010), 111–116.
18. *California Democratic Party v. Jones,* 530 U.S. 567 (2000).
19. Mathews and Paul, *California Crackup,* 111.

SUGGESTED READING

Advisory Commission on Intergovernmental Relations. *The Question of State Government Capability.* Washington, DC: The Commission, 1985.

Benjamin, Gerald, and Michael J. Malbin, eds. *Limiting Legislative Terms.* Washington, DC: Congressional Quarterly, 1992.

Boyarsky, Bill. *Big Daddy: Jesse Unruh and the Art of Power Politics.* Berkeley: University of California Press, 2008.

Brown, Richard E., ed. *The Effectiveness of Legislative Program Review.* New Brunswick, NJ: Transaction, 1979.

Burns, John. *The Sometime Governments.* New York: Bantam, 1971.

Citizens Conference on State Legislatures. *State Legislatures: An Evaluation of Their Effectiveness.* New York: Praeger, 1971.

Donovan, Todd, Daniel A. Smith, and Christopher Z. Mooney. *State and Local Politics: Institutions and Reform.* Belmont, CA: Wadsworth, 2009.

Farmer, Rick, Christopher Z. Mooney, Richard Powell, and John C. Green, eds. *Legislating without Experience: Case Studies in State Legislative Term Limits.* Lanham, MD: Lexington Books, 2007.

Herzberg, Donald G., and Alan Rosenthal, eds. *Strengthening the States: Essays on Legislative Reform.* New York: Doubleday, 1971.

Herzberg, Donald G., and Jesse Unruh. *Essays on the State Legislative Process.* New York: Holt, Rinehart, and Winston, 1970.

Kousser, Thad. *Term Limits and the Dismantling of State Legislative Professionalism.* New York: Cambridge University Press, 2005.

Kurtz, Karl, Bruce Cain, and Richard G. Niemi, eds. *Institutional Change in American Politics: The Case of Term Limits.* Ann Arbor: University of Michigan Press, 2002.

Malbin, Michael J., Peter W. Brusoe, and Brenden Glavin. *Public Financing of Elections after* Citizens United *and* Arizona Free Enterprise. Washington, DC: The Campaign Finance Institute, 2011.

Malbin, Michael J., and Thomas L. Gais. *The Day after Reform.* Albany, NY: Rockefeller Institute Press, 1998.

Mathews, Joe, and Mark Paul. *California Crackup.* Berkeley: University of California Press, 2010.

National Conference of State Legislatures, Center for Ethics in Government. *The State of State Legislative Ethics.* Denver: NCSL, July 2002.

Robinson, James A., ed. *State Legislative Innovation.* New York: Praeger, 1973.

Rosenson, Beth A. *The Shadowlands of Conduct: Ethics and State Politics.* Washington, DC: Georgetown University Press, 2005.

Rosenthal, Alan. *Drawing the Line: Legislative Ethics in the States.* Lincoln: University of Nebraska Press, 1996.

———. "The Effects of Legislative Ethics Law: An Institutional Perspective." In *Public Ethics and Governance: Standards and Practice in Comparative Perspective,* ed. Denis Saint-Martin and Fred Thompson. Oxford: Elsevier, 2006.

———. "Reform in State Legislatures." In *Encyclopedia of the American Legislative System,* ed. Joel H. Silbey. New York: Charles Scribner's Sons, 1994.

Rueter, Theodore. *The Minnesota House of Representatives and the Professionalization of Politics.* Lanham, MD: University Press of America, 1994.

Welch, Susan, and John G. Peters, eds. *Legislative Reform and Public Policy.* New York: Praeger, 1977.

Will, George F. *Restoration: Congress, Term Limits, and the Recovery of Deliberative Democracy.* New York: Free Press, 1993.

PART V ★ EXECUTIVE BRANCH

Chapter 18

Gubernatorial Backgrounds, History, Elections, Powers

Margaret R. Ferguson and Joseph J. Foy

Governors are the epicenter of politics in the American states. As the most visible, salient actors in state government, governors wield a considerable amount of legislative authority in addition to their administrative control over state bureaucracies.[1] Throughout the twentieth century, state executives began carving out a greater sphere of authority and political control across the United States, gaining the most significant ground in the 1950s and 1960s with constitutional reforms across the country that expanded gubernatorial autonomy and capacity. Likewise, with increasing federal authority being devolved to the states in the form of "new federalism" politics beginning in the 1970s, state executives began to command greater levels of influence in national political discussions. These changes in the political climate of the United States and in the office of the governor carried significant implications in redefining public expectations in relation to state executives. Governors began to emerge from their positions of subservience to state legislatures and take on new, more expansive roles as head of the executive branch—roles that include legislative and policy leader, head of party, representative of the popular will, prominent national figure, intergovernmental leader, and crisis manager.[2]

Increases in power and authority brought about concomitant increases in public scrutiny and expectation. Likewise, the expansion of state-level civil service agencies, along with the introduction of the merit system beginning in the late-nineteenth century, began to work both to empower and constrain state executives in their attempts to direct policy implementation and administrative functions throughout the state. In response to each of these demands, governors across the country have begun utilizing a variety of resources of power and influence in order to run their states.

This chapter begins with a description of the various powers—formal, informal, and quasiformal—possessed by governors to varying degrees throughout the states, and examines the impact of these powers on executive-legislative relations. Next, this chapter presents an overview of the democratic politics impacting state executives, including a look at gubernatorial selection and electoral checks in the form of recall elections. It then offers a

Founded in 1908, the National Governors Association is the collective voice of the nation's governors and one of Washington, DC's most respected public policy organizations. Its members are the governors of the fifty-five states, territories, and commonwealths. Louisiana governor Bobby Jindal speaks after the National Governors Association meeting at the White House in Washington, DC, on February 25, 2013.

SOURCE: REUTERS/Kevin Lamarque.

demographic profile of governors and the impact of diversity on policy discourse and outcomes. Finally, this chapter explores the changing nature of executive roles at the state level as such changes propel governors to the center stage of national politics.

GUBERNATORIAL POWER

In discussing the federal executive, Richard Neustadt famously proclaimed that all presidential power boils down to the "power to persuade."[3] This assessment of the presidency is of growing relevance to an understanding of gubernatorial politics across the American states. Due largely to a pronounced distrust of executive authority born out of abuses of colonial governors prior to the constitutional founding of the United States, most governors prior to the twentieth century were constrained by weak authority and hampered by the dominance of state legislatures. At the turn of the nineteenth century, states began amending their constitutions to allow for the popular election of state executives (as opposed to appointment by the legislature), and started to allow longer, multiple terms of service. Simultaneously, statutory changes, which included the delegation of new authority to boards and commissions under the purview of the executive branch, allowed many governors expanded jurisdiction over state policy. Following the trajectory of the presidency at the national level, the modern history of state politics has been an evolution of adding increased energy and authority in the executive.

Formal, Institutional Powers

Despite the national trend of expanding the political control of the executive branch, governors do not all share the same level of power. The formal powers assigned to the office derive from state constitutions and statutes. These powers establish the formal authority of the executive as an institution and are not tied to any single governor or administration. While creating a formal index to measure the institutional strength of state executives, Joseph Schlesinger noted that the difference in formal powers creates variable strength of governors across the states.[4] While some governors enjoy a considerable amount of strength, others enjoy only moderate levels, while still others have been left relatively weak (see Table 18.1).

Joseph Schlesinger, Thad Beyle, and Nelson Dometrius have each attempted to quantify the institutional dimensions of power available to governors as the basis for formulating an index of the formal powers of executives across the fifty states.[5] Though their measures differ somewhat in terms of dimensions of formal authority included, most scholars seem to support the more comprehensive measure provided by Beyle, which includes a ranking of

TABLE 18.1 **Governors' Institutional Powers, 2010**

State	Separately elected executive branch officials	Tenure potential	Appointment power	Budget power	Veto power	Party control	Overall institutional power (total/5)
Alabama	1.5	4	2.5	4	4	4	3.3
Alaska	2.5	4	3.5	5	2.5	3.5	3.5
Arizona	2	4	2.5	4	2.5	4	3.3
Arkansas	2	4	2	2	2	4	2.7
California	1	4	2	4	2.5	4	2.9
Colorado	4	4	3	2	2.5	3	3.1
Connecticut	4	5	3	2	2.5	4	3.4
Delaware	2	4	3	4	5	4	3.3
Florida	3	4	3	2	2.5	4	3.1
Georgia	1	4	1.5	5	2.5	4	3
Hawaii	5	4	2.5	2	5	5	3.9
Idaho	1	5	2	1	2.5	5	2.75
Illinois	4	5	3.5	2	5	4	3.9
Indiana	3	4	3.5	5	0	4	3.25
Iowa	3	5	3.5	2	2.5	3	3.2
Kansas	3	4	2.5	5	2.5	4	3.5
Kentucky	2.5	4	3	4	2.5	3	3.2

State	Separately elected executive branch officials	Tenure potential	Appointment power	Budget power	Veto power	Party control	Overall institutional power (total/5)
Louisiana	2	4	4	2	2	3	2.8
Maine	5	4	3	2	2	3.5	3.25
Maryland	4	4	3	5	5	4	4.2
Massachusetts	4	5	3	5	4	5	4.3
Michigan	4	4	3	4	4	4	3.8
Minnesota	4	5	3.5	2	2	4	3.4
Mississippi	3	4	2	5	5	3	3.7
Missouri	2	4	2.5	4	2.5	2	2.8
Montana	3	4	3	5	2.5	2	3.25
Nebraska	4	4	3	2	2.5	3	3.1
Nevada	2.5	4	2.5	5	0	4	3
New Hampshire	5	2	2.5	4	0	3	2.75
New Jersey	5	4	4	4	5	2	4
New Mexico	4	4	3.5	5	2.5	2	3.5
New York	4	5	3	2	5	3	3.7
North Carolina	3	4	2.5	2	1.5	2	2.5
North Dakota	3	5	3.5	5	2.5	4	3.8
Ohio	4	4	3	5	2.5	4	3.75
Oklahoma	1	4	1.5	2	2	4	2.4
Oregon	1.5	4	2	2	2.5	3	2.5
Pennsylvania	4	4	3	5	2.5	2	3.4
Rhode Island	4	4	3	2	0	1	2.3
South Carolina	1	4	2.5	2	2.5	4	2.7
South Dakota	3	4	3	5	3	4.5	3.75
Tennessee	2	4	4.5	2	2	4	2.75
Texas	2	5	1.5	2	2.5	4	2.8
Utah	4	5	3	2	2.5	5	3.6
Vermont	2	2	2.5	5	0	4	2.6
Virginia	2.5	3	3.5	5	3	3	3.3
Washington	1	5	4	5	5	4	4
West Virginia	2	4	3	5	2.5	4	3.4
Wisconsin	3	5	1.5	4	2.5	4	3.3
Wyoming	2	4	3	2	5	5	3.5
50-state average	2.9	4.1	2.85	3.5	2.65	3.7	3.3

NOTES:

Elected officials: 5 = only governor or governor/lieutenant governor team elected . . . 1 = numerous elected separately.

Tenure potential: 5 = unlimited four-year terms . . . 1 = 2 two-year terms.

Appointive power: 5 = governor alone appoints six major officials . . . 0 = all separately elected.

Budget power: 5 = governor has full responsibility for executive budget . . . 1 = shared responsibility, legislature has unlimited power to change.

Veto power: 5 = governor has item veto, special majority to override . . . 0 = no item veto.

Party control: 5 = governor's party has large majority in both houses . . . 1 = has a small minority in both houses.

SOURCE: Margaret R. Ferguson, "Governors and the Executive Branch," in *Politics in the American States: A Comparative Analysis,* 10th ed., Virginia Gray, Russell L. Hanson, and Thad Kousser, eds. (Washington, DC: CQ Press, 2013).

power based on the separate election of executive branch officials, the tenure potential of the governor, gubernatorial appointment power, executive control over the budget, veto authority, and overall party control (measured by congruence).

The institutional powers of the governor account for some of the variation in relative success of some governors to achieve policy and other goals during their tenure in office. States that are executive-centric (e.g., Maryland, Massachusetts, and New Jersey) have institutional executives that are given a considerable amount of statutory authority vis-à-vis the state legislature, while other states (e.g., North Carolina, North Dakota, and Rhode Island) have relatively weaker governors in terms of institutional capacity. Most states, however, hover somewhere in the middle, granting their governors authority to act along many dimensions but constraining them in other respects through institutional checks on power.

Informal, Personal Powers

In addition to those formal and quasiformal powers claimed by executives, governors are also individual people who bring with them to office differences according to how they view and attempt to exercise leadership. Applying Neustadtian logic about executive leadership, personal ability and skill are major factors in determining the strength or weakness of a governor. Often, state executives must draw upon informal powers—powers not specifically granted, but nevertheless used to gain political leverage—in order to direct policy and political activity. Their ability to do so enhances the possibility of attaining the outcomes they seek.[6] In fact, some analysts suggest that the informal, personal powers of the governor are more important than the formal, institutional powers.[7]

Though it is difficult to measure such idiosyncratic characteristics—the charisma, intellect, guile, oratorical skills, and determination—that help to create effective leaders, there are ways to capture several of the important informal dimensions of authority that combine to create an added dimension of personal power in the executive. For instance, a governor's electoral mandate gives considerable leverage (or creates significant constraint) when attempting to influence the state legislature, as does the ongoing evaluation of his or her job while in office in the form of gubernatorial performance ratings. Likewise, a governor's past political history, often referred to as his or her position on the "ambition ladder," provides some insight as to whether a governor has risen through the ranks of state government and has learned how to maneuver through a variety of organizations and offices given what is expected of those institutions. Finally, the personal future of a governor, captured by whether or not a governor is just beginning his or her term and whether he or she has the opportunity to seek reelection, can have an impact on the governor's overall ability to persuade the legislative branch or otherwise effectively pursue policy goals.

The personal powers of the governor—like the formal, institutional powers—can be combined to provide an evaluative measure of the relative strength of different governors across the United States (see Table 18.2). These informal measures, which are much more conditional and variable than the formal, institutional powers, help to provide insight into the environment in which each governor is operating. Such personal accounts help to explain why some governors are able to parlay their institutional capacities into successful policy outcomes while others struggle to achieve such programmatic victories even while possessing similar statutory authority. In some cases, even institutionally weak governors can be highly successful, given the right conditions and personal attributes.

Gubernatorial Power and Executive-Legislative Relations

Ultimately, all discussions of gubernatorial power and authority are aimed at trying more fully to understand the ability and capacity of an administration to achieve sought-after legislation from state legislatures and the effective implementation of those laws in accordance with executive demands. The high-profile status of governors, the ability to set and prioritize the legislative agenda in highly publicized moments like the annual State of the State address, and a willingness to work with or pressure members of their party in the legislature all help explain how governors have become dominant players in the legislative arena.

State executives are unique in comparison to the state legislatures in that the governor represents the entire state rather than a single district. The actions of governors often reflect their attempts at creating the largest possible voter base across the state, just as members of the legislature attempt to meet the demands of their constituencies within their voting districts. This sets governors apart from legislators in that they have a more diverse pool of voters that they can attempt to bring into their fold. Legislators have a much smaller support-target, and as such are more constrained than governors in the groups of people from whom they are seeking political support.[8]

The difference in primary constituencies is important in understanding executive-legislative relations. In dealing with the legislature, governors often do not find themselves dealing with unified majority and opposition groups. Instead, governors deal primarily with trying to control, or negotiate their way through, factions. Legislators must balance many interests. In the post-election phase, parties become less important identifiers of individual activity within the legislature, as representatives will continue to do what the party needs but also have a great

TABLE 18.2 **Personal Powers of the Governors, 2011**

State	Electoral mandate	Political ambition	Political future	Gubernatorial popularity	Overall personal power (total/4)
Alabama	5	5	5	na	4.0
Alaska	5	5	2	5	4.25
Arizona	5	5	3	3	4
Arkansas	5	1	3	5	3.5
California	5	5	5	3	4.5
Colorado	5	2	5	4	4
Connecticut	2	2	2	5	2.75
Delaware	5	5	5	na	5
Florida	2	1	5	2	2.5
Georgia	4	5	5	2	4
Hawaii	5	5	5	na	5
Idaho	4	5	5	3	4.25
Illinois	2	5	5	3	3.75
Indiana	5	5	3	4	4.25
Iowa	4	5	5	3	4.25
Kansas	5	5	5	4	4.75
Kentucky	5	5	4	4	4.5
Louisiana	5	5	4	4	4.5
Maine	2	5	5	3	3.75
Maryland	5	5	3	4	4.25
Massachusetts	2	1	5	3	2.75
Michigan	5	1	5	2	3.25
Minnesota	2	5	5	na	4
Mississippi	5	1	1	3	2.5
Missouri	5	5	5	3	4.5
Montana	5	1	1	na	1.75
Nebraska	5	5	3	5	4.5
Nevada	5	5	5	3	4.5
New Hampshire	4	1	5	5	3.75
New Jersey	3	5	5	3	4
New Mexico	4	5	5	4	4.5
New York	5	5	5	4	4.75
North Carolina	3	5	4	2	3.5
North Dakota	5	5	2	na	3

(Continued)

(Continued)

State	Electoral mandate	Political ambition	Political future	Gubernatorial popularity	Overall personal power (total/4)
Ohio	2	5	5	2	3.5
Oklahoma	5	5	5	na	5
Oregon	2	5	5	3	3.75
Pennsylvania	4	5	5	2	4
Rhode Island	2	5	5	2	3.5
South Carolina	3	5	5	2	3.75
South Dakota	5	5	5	na	5
Tennessee	5	5	5	3	4.5
Texas	5	5	5	5	5
Utah	5	5	5	5	5
Vermont	2	5	5	na	4
Virginia	5	5	3	3	4
Washington	3	5	5	1	3.5
West Virginia	5	5	5	3	4.5
Wisconsin	3	5	5	3	4
Wyoming	5	1	5	4	3.75
50-state average	4.1	4.2	4.1	3.3	3.8

NOTES:

Electoral mandate: 5 = landslide win . . . 1 = succeeded in office.

Political ambition: 5 = steady progression . . . 1 = in first elective office.

Political future: 5 = early in term, can run again . . . 1 = late in final term.

Gubernatorial popularity: 5 = over 60 percent job approval . . . 1 = less than 30 percent job approval; na = not available.

SOURCE: Margaret R. Ferguson, "Governors and the Executive Branch," in *Politics in the American States: A Comparative Analysis,* 10th ed., Virginia Gray, Russell L. Hanson, and Thad Kousser, eds. (Washington, DC: CQ Press, 2013).

deal of individual independence to do what they need to accomplish for reelection.[9] Likewise, the American system lends itself to having diverse groups that might not have anything in common other than party identification. This leads to a variety of unrelated (and sometimes competing) groups that fall under the umbrella of the same party, even though they may not agree with one another's position. These are all part of the reason why governors often find themselves dealing with various factions in the legislature rather than with unified party organizations. State legislatures also vary significantly in party organization. Some legislatures are very tightly organized around party akin to the U.S. Congress, while others are much less formally organized (see Chapter 16, Leadership and Committee Organization).

Quasiformal, Unilateral Powers

There are several potential avenues for understanding gubernatorial power beyond the powers formally expressed in state constitutions or statutes. One of the ways scholars have identified that executives exercise powers is through the use of quasiformal authority like executive orders, or policy statements and memoranda. These powers, though not explicitly defined through any formal legal designation, are claimed by executives as inherent to the office of the executive. The use of such powers is commonly referred to as "unilateral action" because they are often utilized as a way of influencing public policy implementation by the bureaucracy; therefore, they affect outcomes without the involvement of the other branches of government.

State Senate President Pro Tem Darrell Steinberg, D-Sacramento, left, discusses the agreement reached with Gov. Jerry Brown to finalize California's budget, at a capitol news conference in Sacramento, California, June 21, 2012. Although Democrats passed the main budget bill on a majority vote, the governor pressed for deeper cuts to welfare and other social services amid a projected $15.7 billion budget shortfall. Steinberg said the agreement makes changes to four social programs to minimize the impact on the poor. Seated second from left is state senator Mark Leno, D-San Francisco, chair of the senate budget committee.

SOURCE: Rich Pedroncelli, photographer; Associated Press.

The most public of such powers is the use of executive orders. Research on governors' executive orders has found that governors across the American states frequently employ executive orders, and their use spans a variety of functional areas. This demonstrates the importance of executive orders as an independent source of political power and a means of achieving the goals of the executive without having to maneuver through the legislative arena.[10]

Beyond executive orders, there are other quasiformal powers that have been exercised or claimed by executives. For example, some executives have used their authority as chief administrator to enter into contractual services with private-sector entities to deliver state services. This can have a direct impact on policy in the state. Likewise, some state executives have begun to use signing statements (written pronouncements directing bureaucratic interpretation of laws once signed) and policy memoranda (analyses by the executive interpreting policy and providing recommendations as to how agencies should work to implement such laws). Both such documents involve statements by the governor meant to clarify law, direct state agencies to take a particular course of action or to avoid others, or interpret law in a certain way. Neither requires the executive to work or negotiate with the legislature to achieve a desired outcome.[11] Very little is known about these techniques and their reach, but they appear to be widespread and largely unchecked by legislative or legal action. Signing statements have varying audiences: the public, the legislature, and the federal government, among others. Montana governor Brian Schweitzer noted that the state had been devastated by energy deregulation, and though he was signing the bill he had little confidence it would actually solve the problems at hand. Furthermore, he warned against the politics of the legislative process intruding into the rule-making process: "In the recent legislative process we have seen what special interests and well-moneyed obstruction can do to the business of running good government. I trust that we will not repeat that scenario in the rules process for HB25."[12] Upon signing a bill requiring health care providers to offer pregnant women a view of an ultrasound before performing an abortion, Gov. Robert McDonnell of Virginia asserted his anti-abortion credentials while also pointing out that he had insisted the legislature remove language mandating an internal ultrasound. Perhaps most colorfully, Gov. Edmund Brown Jr. issued a statement directed squarely at his colleagues in the legislature. Upon signing a bill allowing a dead mountain lion to be stuffed and displayed, he released the following statement: "This presumably important bill earned overwhelming support by both Republicans and Democrats. If only the same energetic bipartisan spirit could be applied to creating clean energy jobs and ending tax laws that send jobs out of state."[13]

The traditional literature exploring executive influence in public policy typically begins with the governor-as-chief-legislator model, which holds that if governors want to accomplish their goals in the policy arena they must effectively persuade the legislature to go along with them. From this perspective, the power of governors is defined in a Neustadtian fashion: influence derives from the power to persuade.[14] Most work on the gubernatorial policy leadership suggests that the importance of the institutional and personal powers of executives is wrapped up in their ability to wield control over the state legislature.[15]

The current literature on gubernatorial power provides a general framework for understanding the operations of the executive office, but it does not tell the whole story. Margaret R. Ferguson and Joseph J. Foy propose an alternative framework. For starters, the assumption that state legislatures are necessarily the option the governor turns to first when thinking about policy may be false. Governors may actually consider what actions they can pursue outside the legislative arena before turning to the legislature as a last resort. Why would this be the case? What predicts the use of quasiformal unilateral power as opposed to legislative leadership? Quite simply, working through the legislature formally is very time-consuming and difficult and can backfire, which harms the executive's efforts to control policy outcomes. Additionally, once the legislature becomes involved, it takes control. Other potential options are removed from the hands of the governor, and the legislature holds the power.

Interviews Ferguson and Foy conducted in Indiana test this alternative understanding of the exertion of gubernatorial power. It's not that governors avoid the legislature at all costs, or that governors never need to turn to the legislature to attain some policy victories. In those regards, the traditional assumptions guiding power seem right. Yet governors do not seem to act first and foremost as chief legislators when attempting to achieve policy goals. Instead, governors are first and foremost chief executives, and act accordingly whenever they are able.

Governors (in Indiana, at least) are highly attentive to when they must go to the legislature and when they can avoid it. Clearly, there are examples of gubernatorial policy goals for which legislative action is necessary. There are also

GOVERNORS AND GREENHOUSE GAS POLICY LEADERSHIP

For a variety of reasons, the federal government has largely been unwilling or unable to offer leadership in the arena of climate change, and particularly greenhouse gas emission reduction. In the late twentieth century, some state governors emerged as leaders in this arena. However, as the 2000s progressed, their successors sometimes acted to turn back these gubernatorial initiatives. While it is true that certain states have been out front in environmental policy, it is also the case that individual governors have made their own choices about leadership on climate change.

In 2003 Gov. George Pataki of New York began recruiting neighboring states to participate in the Regional Greenhouse Gas Initiative (RGGI). Initially seven, and ultimately ten, northeastern and Middle Atlantic states participated in this scheme to create carbon auctions in which carbon-based utilities bid for allowances to pollute. States are allotted a number of "carbon credits." If they do not need all of their credits because of in-state conservation or more efficient energy production, the state can auction the credits to inefficient states that need them. This mechanism helps to set a price for carbon production. Over time, the number of carbon credits released to each state is expected to decline, as the system demands more energy efficiency from all participants. The RGGI created the country's only operating cap-and-trade system to reduce greenhouse gas emissions.

In 2012 only nine states—Connecticut, Delaware, Maine, Maryland, Massachusetts, New Hampshire, New York, Rhode Island, and Vermont—were members of RGGI, as New Jersey governor Chris Christie acted unilaterally in 2011 to withdraw New Jersey from the compact despite the fact that the state had reaped large financial rewards from its participation. New Jersey's withdrawal is rather ironic in that New Jersey governor Thomas Kean was the first state executive to enact an executive order with a greenhouse gas limitation goal in 1989.

Other states chose to join the RGGI only after fits and starts. Massachusetts governor Jane Swift was an early leader on climate change policy, but her successor, Mitt Romney, took conflicting stances on climate change. He offered leadership in conservation at state agencies and universities, and he incorporated many small ideas, such as paperless systems, LEED (Leadership in Energy and Environmental Design) certification for buildings, and energy audits, into state practices. Romney also appointed a sustainability "czar" who led the roundtable process that proposed voluntary reductions in greenhouse gas emissions among Massachusetts industries. However, Governor Romney quickly moved away from climate change action at the time of the state plan's unveiling, speaking of his uncertainty that climate change existed, and failing to support and sign on to the RGGI, despite his czar's fundamental role in its construction. Deval Patrick was elected governor in 2006, as Romney turned his attention to national politics. Within his first year, Governor Patrick committed the state to the RGGI, and enacted E.O. 484, the Clean Energy and Efficient Buildings initiative. This action created uniform energy conservation standards for state facilities.[1]

The carbon market created by RGGI actually generated income. RGGI held its first auction of carbon allowances in September 2008. As of 2012, the auctions have raised more than $660 million for the member states. The system has not, however, worked exactly as planned. Membership in the compact requires that states set aside at least 25 percent of auction proceeds for reducing energy usage. As state economies struggled, governors in Maryland, New Hampshire, New Jersey, New York, and Rhode Island either tried or succeeded at redirecting the funds toward budget deficits (in violation of their predecessors' agreements).

In a quarterly auction, on June 9, 2012, compact member states raised $80.5 million. On that same day, New Hampshire lawmakers voted to use their state's expected $3.1 million share of the proceeds to help plug a $295 million budget hole. That move came after New York and New Jersey had staged even bigger raids on cap-and-trade funds. New York transferred $90 million out of a fund of auction proceeds and into its general fund. And New Jersey governor Christie planned to use $65 million from carbon-credit sales to help balance the state's budget (just before withdrawing from the compact). More recently, on June 5, 2013, 38.7 million carbon allowances were sold at auction, generating $124.4 million for reinvestment for member states.

1. See Brendan Burke and Margaret Ferguson, "Going Alone or Moving Together: Canadian and American Middle Tier Strategies on Climate Change," *Publius: The Journal of Federalism* 40 (2010): 436–459, for more about the role of governors in greenhouse gas policy.

times when the governor probably *could* avoid legislative action, but chooses to pursue it anyway. But there are many other instances—probably most, in fact—when the governor can choose to avoid the legislative arena and pursue a goal through some executive action or executive order. What explains which technique governors will employ in pursuing their policy goals? Which conditions enable a governor to act unilaterally and outside of the influence or direction of the legislature? Taken together, the interviews point to a handful of important variables. To begin, there are certain policy goals for which legal requirements mean legislative action is necessary.

Beyond the legal constraints, personal and political variables become important. First, the personal background and experiences of a governor help to determine how an executive will wield power vis-à-vis the legislature. Second, the party of a governor's predecessors also affects his or her decision making. Specifically, when governors follow a string of governors of the other party, they are often driven to achieve goals quickly and therefore to pursue unilateral action. Third, legislators are quite conscious of the governor's popularity in their districts and throughout the state; the ability of the governor to act independently of the legislature is encouraged by the legislature's willingness to "look the other way" when such power is exercised by a popular governor. Fourth, the lack of a full-time, professional legislature (in Indiana) offers the governor a great deal of flexibility to act outside of the legislative arena because the legislature is only in session for ninety-one days across the span of a two-year cycle. The governor can literally wait for the general assembly to leave town and then take action. Finally, party control of the legislature seems also to play an important role in influencing executive decisions to pursue action without first going through the legislature.

Even when governors lack strong formal power (as traditionally defined), and perhaps even when they lack a powerful personality or a particular skill at persuasion, they can exert a great deal of power if they choose (see Governors and Greenhouse Gas Policy Leadership box). Furthermore, short of court or legislative action (which is rare), there are few checks on this power. There are, however, occasional extraordinary responses to expansive assertions of gubernatorial power.

Recall Elections as External Check on Gubernatorial Authority

We noted above that governors who choose to exercise unilateral power can do so with very little risk of being thwarted. However, extraordinary cases arise when legislatures or courts act to limit gubernatorial power (see Governors Behaving Badly box). Even more unusual, voters might take matters into their own hands and attempt to limit gubernatorial power through electoral politics.

Although frequently invoked at local levels of state government, recall elections have been a rare occurrence at the state level—even rarer when involving state executives.[16]

GOVERNORS BEHAVING BADLY

The vast majority of governors serve the office with honesty and integrity. But certain states seem to have particular dispositions toward corruption. Illinois and Louisiana come to mind. When it comes to the governorship, Illinois's case is the most extreme.

Gov. Rod Blagojevich in 2008 famously proclaimed that the U.S. Senate seat vacated by newly elected president Barack Obama was too valuable to be "given away for free." Blagojevich was ultimately impeached by the Illinois House, convicted by the state senate, and removed from office. He was also convicted of eleven counts related to the vacant U.S. Senate seat and six counts related to fund-raising extortion of a hospital executive. He was sentenced to fourteen years in prison. This latest episode is not particularly unusual in Illinois politics. Six Illinois governors have been charged with crimes during or after their governorships. Blagojevich was the fourth governor convicted since the 1960s. His immediate predecessor, George Ryan, was convicted in 2006 of eighteen felony counts, including racketeering conspiracy, tax and mail fraud, and lying to the FBI for taking illegal cash payments while secretary of state and governor. He is in prison serving a six-and-a-half-year sentence. Gov. Dan Walker (1973–1977) served eighteen months in prison after being convicted of bank fraud (on charges not related to his time in office), and Gov. Otto Kerner (1961–1978) was convicted of seventeen counts of bribery, conspiracy, perjury, and income-tax charges from his time as governor and received three years in prison and a $50,000 fine in 1973. Two additional governors were indicted but not convicted.

Louisiana governor Edwin Edwards once bragged that he had been indicted six times but never convicted! Indeed, when Edwards ran for his fourth term against former head of the Ku Klux Klan David Duke, a popular bumper sticker read "Vote for the Crook: It's Important." In 2001 he finally was convicted and sentenced to ten years in prison for racketeering. Interestingly, Duke was also later convicted of mail fraud, making the Louisiana gubernatorial race in 1991 the only one in which both candidates were later imprisoned. Edwards was released from prison in 2011, and his supporters petitioned President Obama to pardon him so that he might run for a fifth term as governor (having failed to secure such a pardon from President George W. Bush). President Obama similarly took no action on the request.

To some degree, these two states seem to accept a certain amount of corruption from their political officials. But it could be that even these two states have had enough of such bad behavior. As state governments play ever larger roles in our federal system, the states cannot afford *not* to take the integrity of their chief executives seriously.

Only nineteen states allow them for state offices, and several have specific limits to the grounds upon which a recall can be initiated.[17] Even where there are no restrictions on the grounds for recall, the guidelines for all recall elections suggest that they should be used only in extraordinary circumstances. Apart from those recalls attempted on a municipal level, Michigan and Oregon became the first to adopt recall procedures for state officials in 1908. Since then, there have been twenty-four state legislative recall elections involving thirty-two state legislators, but only two successful elections to recall state executives. In 1921 North Dakota voters successfully recalled Gov. Lynn Frazier and two other officials (the attorney general and commissioner of agriculture), and in 2003 the voters of California successfully recalled Gov. Gray Davis. In 1988, though enough signatures had been gathered, Arizona governor Evan Mecham was impeached and convicted of obstruction of justice and misuse of public funds prior to a recall election against him.[18] Most recently, in Wisconsin, amid a flurry of recall elections in 2011 and 2012 involving thirteen state senators (including the senate majority leader), over nine hundred thousand verified signatures were gathered to initiate recall elections against Gov. Scott Walker and Lt. Gov. Rebecca Kleefisch. Walker and Kleefisch survived their respective recalls, both winning approximately 53 percent of the vote over their Democrat challengers. However, the various recall elections did swing control of the state senate from Republican to Democrat, thereby eliminating unified party control.

Recall elections use direct democracy as an external check on gubernatorial authority along two dimensions. First, such efforts can be invoked by the electorate when they perceive governors to be abusing the power of the office and subverting the legitimate processes of the state. Second, recall efforts may be initiated if the voters of a state feel as though the governor is engaging in political "overreach" by pursuing extreme policies well outside the perceived mandate of the electorate. In both cases, and as gubernatorial power becomes more concentrated and governors increasingly pursue unilateral powers to act without consultation or cooperation with the legislature, the potential use of recall elections is an important consideration for governors as they attempt to achieve desired policy goals. The reach of unilateral power, while great, is not unlimited.

GUBERNATORIAL CAMPAIGNS AND ELECTIONS

The direct election of governors that was initiated in most states in the early twentieth century emboldened governors and offered them a source of countervailing strength vis-à-vis the legislature. With this change, governors could mobilize the party apparatus and ultimately build their own campaign structures in the quest for election and reelection. All of this means that gubernatorial campaigns have been ever more professionalized and ever more expensive. Though the costs of campaigns vary widely by the size of a state and the costs of media markets, large states predictably have expensive gubernatorial campaigns. Texas, for example, has seen average costs rise to close to $60 million since the mid-2000s. Other states with unusually high spending are less obvious. Formerly one-party states have seen significant growth as true two-party competition has become the norm. For example, Virginia ($32.7 million), Florida ($28.7 million), North Carolina ($23.2 million), and Louisiana ($22.9 million) have seen the average cost of their governors' races escalate dramatically over the last five election cycles (1990–2010).

Gubernatorial campaigning has followed the trajectory of more professionalized campaigns seen in races for other high offices. With the transformation of

Protestors sleep on the floor of the state capitol rotunda in Madison, Wisconsin, during demonstrations in March 2011 against Gov. Scott Walker's "Wisconsin budget repair bill." The Wisconsin legislature passed the measure, which virtually eliminated collective bargaining by public employee unions except police and firefighters, but it was strongly opposed by unions and their allies. Opponents received enough support to force a recall election on June 5, 2012, a first for a governor in the state of Wisconsin and only the third gubernatorial recall in U.S. history. Walker successfully kept his seat as governor, making him the first U.S. governor to have successfully kept the seat as governor in a recall election.

SOURCE: Allen Fredrickson, photographer; SMI/Newscom.

state political parties and the decline of party identification among voters, candidates can no longer depend on the party regulars to deliver the needed votes. Candidates must build their own campaigns from the ground up. And they must spend money on new and expensive technologies. While candidates still spend a lot of time "on the ground" holding rallies and town hall–type meetings, they increasingly turn to mass media. Some, such as television advertising, have been around for a long time. But candidates today also turn to new media and social networking. These sources are potentially less costly, but their effects are still relatively unproven. Meanwhile, chunks of the war chest still go to twentieth-century strategies as well: opinion polls, political consultants, direct-mail persuasion, fund-raising, and telephone banks.[19]

Governors' races are generally more expensive when political parties are weak, an open seat is up, the race is highly contested from nomination to general election, or there is a partisan shift as a result of the election or an incumbent is unseated. Which of these factors is the most significant probably varies not only by state but also by candidate and by circumstances. The recent trend toward self-financed candidates such as Meg Whitman in California (who spent $144 million of her own money in the 2010 governor's race but lost) has also inflated costs.[20]

Candidates cannot avoid the "arms race"; inevitably, in most races the candidate who spends the most wins the election. It is also true, however, that candidates with the greatest chance at winning can also typically raise the most money—so the relationship is not as straightforward as it might first appear. The relationship between spending and votes for incumbents is exaggerated and largely disappears once incumbent popularity is considered.[21] Research indicates that campaign spending differentially impacts different types of candidates. Spending is most effective for in-party candidates, indicating that raising more money does not necessarily level the playing field for the out-party challenger.[22]

Governor and Lieutenant Governor Ticketing

In all states except New Jersey, governors must contend with other statewide elected officials who may or may not share the governor's party affiliation and policy goals. The lieutenant governor is perhaps the most important. In some states, the lieutenant governor serves as the governor's handpicked partner (much like the vice president), but in other states the lieutenant governor is elected separately and may not even share a party affiliation. Forty states popularly elect their lieutenant governors. In twenty-four of those the gubernatorial candidate chooses the lieutenant governor, who most likely shares a party affiliation and general political orientation with the governor. In the remaining sixteen states in which lieutenant governors are elected, they are chosen separately from the governor. In this scenario, candidates put themselves forward for election, and voters might choose governors and lieutenant governors who are of different parties. While some might view this as a positive means of limiting the power of government, it also adds a level of difficulty to the job of being governor, as the governor cannot depend on his or her lieutenant to share policy preferences and cannot necessarily mobilize the lieutenant governor to help pursue policy goals.[23] Even when voters choose governors and lieutenant governors from the same party, the fact that they were elected separately means that the two do not share electoral fortunes, and therefore the governor lacks the influence that such a shared fate tends to provide.

To add further complexity to the picture, the power of the lieutenant governor varies somewhat across the states. In most cases the lieutenant governor acts as the president of the senate and typically has the power to cast a tie-breaking vote. However, in a handful of states, lieutenant governors actually function as the true leader of the senate. Seven states give the lieutenant governor the power to assign members to committees. In each of these states (Alabama, Georgia, Mississippi, Rhode Island, Texas, Vermont, and West Virginia) the lieutenant governor and governor are elected separately. Twelve states give the lieutenant governor the power to refer bills to committees. In four of these states (Massachusetts, New Mexico, North Dakota, and Pennsylvania) the governor and lieutenant governor are elected on a ticket, so this power might be very useful for gubernatorial legislative agendas. In the remaining states (Alabama, Georgia, Mississippi, South Carolina, South Dakota, Texas, Vermont, and West Virginia) this amounts to an independent source of power for a lieutenant governor, which in some cases nearly supplants the governor as legislative leader.[24] (See also Chapter 16, Leadership and Committee Organization.)

GUBERNATORIAL DEMOGRAPHICS

The governorship for most of the nation's history, like high-level offices across the country, was long the bastion of white males. Today, governors are somewhat more reflective of the diversity of the country. No longer is the governor's chair a spot only for white males. In 2012 six women held the governorship, though two of them (Bev Purdue of North Carolina and Christine Gregoire of Washington) chose not to seek reelection. And over half the states have had at least one female governor. As of 2013, there are two Latino governors: Susana Martinez of New Mexico (that state's first female governor) and Brian Sandoval of Nevada. Three African American men have served as governor since Douglas Wilder was elected in Virginia in 1990. African American David Paterson of New York (who is also the only legally blind governor to date) succeeded to the office upon the resignation of Eliot Spitzer in 2008. Deval Patrick of Massachusetts is the only African American governor as of 2013. Bobby Jindal of Louisiana and Nikki Haley of South Carolina are the first two Indian American governors. Despite these promising developments, much remains unchanged. The gubernatorial elections in 2012 were in fact noteworthy for the lack of diversity of candidates. Each major-party candidate in the nine gubernatorial elections in 2012 was a white male.

While it is clear that the "face" of the governorship has changed, it is less clear what effect, if any, greater diversity in the governors' mansions has on the policies states adopt. Thirty years ago, political scientist Larry Sabato asserted in his book *Goodbye to Good-Time Charlie* that "modern" governors were no longer mere figureheads. They were better educated, more ambitious, and empowered by changes in their institutional powers, all of which meant that governors were, in fact, finally true leaders of their states. It is hard to say at this point that we can similarly bid farewell in any meaningful way to the white male–dominated politics of the past. Certainly, modern governors are more "descriptively representative" of their citizenry. Whether their leadership has progressed to substantive representation remains unclear.

Some research has examined whether and in what ways female governors are different from their male counterparts. For example, female governors as a whole express different notions of power than do their male colleagues. As feminist theory would predict, female governors are more likely than men to express a "feminine," "power to" orientation to politics. Surprisingly, however, they also express high levels of the more traditional (and stereotypically masculine) notion of hierarchical "power over." Such expressions of power have been demonstrated to result in greater success for governors, so these studies taken together bode well for the success of female governors as legislative leaders.[25] As for other underrepresented groups, there are unfortunately too few minority governors as yet to systematically examine whether their leadership is different from other governors.

FROM THE GOVERNOR'S MANSION TO THE WHITE HOUSE: A PATHWAY TO THE PRESIDENCY

Today, governors are routinely considered as potential presidential or vice-presidential candidates. Governors are more successful than other high-profile officials, such as senators, in getting the parties' nomination.[26] The 2012 Republican nominee, Mitt Romney, is but the most recent example of a governor getting his party's nod for the presidency. This has not always been the case. In the early Republic, vice presidents and secretaries of state were more likely than governors to become president. In fact, no sitting state executive was elected president from George Washington to Ulysses S. Grant. However, in the period from Rutherford B. Hayes to Franklin D. Roosevelt, presidents were twice as likely as previously to have had prior state executive experience. In all, seventeen of the forty-four presidents were former governors, including the five presidents who preceded Barack Obama. Indeed, the 2008 presidential election was unusual in that it pitted two senators against each other.

Governors turned president are common in the modern period. But some argue that their impact is even greater than sheer numbers. Saladin Ambar asserts that governor-presidents actually built the American governorship by defining the meaning of the modern executive: "Empowered yet distant, state executives built a set of practices and theories that ultimately shaped presidential behavior and, indeed, made acceptable a broad executive-centered approach to governance in America. Modern executive power was being created in the states first—from the ground up."[27] Ambar demonstrates that the elements we identify today with the "modern presidency," features such as leadership of the legislative branch, party leadership, emphasis on press relations, etc., actually grew out of the changing nature of executive leadership in the states. Governors became presidents, and in turn transformed the presidency.

CONCLUSION

The governorship has changed and become emboldened and empowered. Modern governors are key leaders in the state and the nation. They are spokespersons for their parties in the national media. They have more tools at their disposal and larger and more professional staffs. They are the true leaders of their states. If one thinks of power in the states as sometimes being a tug of war, no institution in the modern period has more strength than that of the governor. Research indicates that professionalized legislatures (which might shun gubernatorial leadership in exchange for internal leaders) actually look to governors for leadership more than do their less professional counterparts. Furthermore, in states where term limits have been imposed on legislators, governors have made even greater gains at the expense of legislative leaders setting the states' agendas (see Chapter 17, Legislative Reform). They lack the internal institutional knowledge to develop strong leaders and offer compelling policy alternatives.

Much like the role of the presidency in the nation, the state chief executive is the centerpiece of state governments. This centrality brings with it enhanced scrutiny and growing public expectations for performance. Thomas Cronin and Michael Genovese identify nine "paradoxes" of the American presidency. These highlight a variety of ways in which the desires and expectations for the presidency held by the American people sometimes contradict one another and routinely set the president up for failure. Most essentially, they argue that "Americans demand powerful presidential leadership that solves the nation's problems. Yet we are inherently suspicious of strong centralized leadership and the abuse of power."[28] Modern governors seem likely to struggle with these contradictions as well. The more we look to them for leadership, the greater are the chances that they will not be able to live up to our expectations.

NOTES

1. Charles Barrilleaux and Michael Berkman, "Do Governors Matter? Budgeting Rules and the Politics of State Policy Making," *Political Science Quarterly* 118 (2003): 409–417; Thad Beyle and Lynn Muchmore, eds., *Being Governor: The View from the Office* (Durham, NC: Duke Policy Studies, Duke University Press, 1983); Larry Sabato, *Goodbye to Good-Time Charlie* (Washington, DC: Congressional Quarterly, 1983).

2. Margaret R. Ferguson, "Governors and the Executive Branch," in *Politics in the American States: A Comparative Analysis,* 10th ed., Virginia Gray, Russell L. Hanson, and Thad Kousser, eds. (Washington, DC: CQ Press, 2013); E. Lee Bernick lists the top formal and informal roles of the governor in order of importance as (1) budget formation, (2) popular support, (3) administrative control (appointment power, influence of the administrative bureaucracy, etc.), (4) veto, (5) mass media, (6) prestige of office, (7) personal contact with legislators, (8) party leader, (9) personal characteristics, (10) public relations, (11) patronage, (12) bargaining skills, (13) legislative message, and (14) administration of programs in district; see E. Lee Bernick, "Gubernatorial Tools: Formal v. Informal," *Journal of Politics* 41 (1979): 656–664.

3. Richard E. Neustadt, *Presidential Power: The Politics of Leadership from Roosevelt to Reagan,* rev. ed. (New York: Free Press, 1990).

4. Joseph A. Schlesinger, "The Politics of the Executive," in Herbert Jacob and Kenneth Vines, eds., *Politics in the American States: A Comparative Analysis* (Boston: Little, Brown, 1965).

5. Ibid., Nelson C. Dometrius, "Changing Gubernatorial Power: The Measure vs. Reality," *Western Political Quarterly* 40 (1987): 319–333; Nelson C. Dometrius, "Measuring Gubernatorial Power," *Journal of Politics,* 41 (1979): 589–610.

6. Coleman Ransone, *The American Governorship* (Westport, CT: Greenwood, 1985); Sarah Morehouse, *State Politics, Party, and Policy* (New York: Holt, Rinehart, and Winston, 1981); E. Lee Bernick, "Gubernatorial Tools."

7. Margaret R. Ferguson, "Chief Executive Success in the Legislative Arena," *State Politics and Policy Quarterly* 3 (2003): 158–182.

8. In "Do Governors Matter?" Barrilleaux and Berkman find evidence that suggests that governors who enjoy high approval ratings and are considered to be electorally safe are more likely to support the constituency-specific spending measures called for by individual legislators than those who are insecure in their possibility of reelection. However, their research indicates that, in general, governors are more likely to support budgetary measures that optimize statewide benefits rather than benefiting a limited number of people in a single district.

9. According to David Mayhew, "It should be obvious that if they wanted to, American congressmen could immediately and permanently array themselves in disciplined legions for the purpose of programmatic combat. They do not. Every now and then a member does emit a Wilsonian call for program and cohesion, but these exhortations fail to arouse much member interest. The fact is that the enactment of party programs is electorally not very important to members (although some may find it important to take positions on programs)." Mayhew, *Congress: The Electoral Connection* (New Haven: Yale University Press, 1974), 98–99.

10. Margaret R. Ferguson and Cynthia J. Bowling, "Executive Orders and Administrative Control," *Public Administration Review* 68 (supplement, 2008): S20–28. In discussing executive orders the authors note, "Some of these areas are largely symbolic or ceremonial, ideas commonly associated with the chief of state role of governors. Most, however, are more substantive in nature, creating or reorganizing governmental entities or directing particular executive action" (S21).

11. Margaret R. Ferguson and Joseph J. Foy, "Unilateral Power: Beyond Executive Orders," Paper presented at the annual meeting of the Midwest Political Science Association, March 31–April 3, 2011, Chicago, IL.

12. Signing Statement, Office of the Governor, State of Montana, May 14, 2007.

13. Signing Statement, Office of the Governor, State of California, September 30, 2011.

14. Alan Rosenthal, *Governors and Legislatures: Contending Powers* (Washington, DC: Congressional Quarterly, 1990); Robert E. Crew Jr. and Gregory Weiher, "Gubernatorial Popularity in Three States: A Preliminary Model," *Social Science Journal* 33 (1996): 39–54.

15. Thad Beyle, "Governors: Elections, Power, and Priorities," *Book of the States 2002* (Lexington, KY: Council of State Governments, 2002); Jay Barth and Margaret R. Ferguson, "American Governors and Their Constituents: The Relationship between Gubernatorial Personality and Public Approval," *State Politics and Policy Quarterly* 2 (2002): 268–282; Ferguson, "Chief Executive Success."

16. Thomas Cronin estimates that four thousand to five thousand recall elections have occurred at the local level in the United States, with an even greater number of petitions circulated unsuccessfully. See Cronin, *Direct Democracy: The Politics of Initiative, Referendum, and Recall* (Cambridge, MA: Harvard University Press, 1999).

17. Virginia allows "recall trials" in which the recall process can be initiated by citizens, but those efforts merely begin legal proceedings that ultimately must be decided in the state courts.

18. National Conference of State Legislatures, "History and Use of the Recall in the United States," Recall of State Officials, www.ncsl.org/default.aspx?tabid=16581.

19. Ferguson, "Governors and the Executive Branch."

20. Ibid.

21. Kedron Bardwell, "Reevaluating Spending in Gubernatorial Races: Job Approval as a Baseline for Spending Effects," *Political Research Quarterly* 58 (2005): 97–105.

22. Randall W. Partin, "Assessing the Impact of Campaign Spending in Governors' Races," *Political Research Quarterly* 55 (2002): 213–233.

23. Margaret R. Ferguson, *The Executive Branch of State Government: People, Process, and Politics* (Santa Barbara, CA: ABC CLIO, 2006).

24. Ibid.

25. Jay Barth and Margaret R. Ferguson, "Gender and Gubernatorial Personality," *Women and Politics* 24 (2002): 63–82.

26. Nate Silver, "The Governors' Advantage in Presidential Races Is Bigger Than You Thought," *New York Times*, June 15, 2011, http://fivethirtyeight.blogs.nytimes.com/2011/06/15/the-governors-advantage-in-presidential-races-is-bigger-than-you-thought.

27. Saladin Ambar, *How Governors Built the Modern American Presidency* (Philadelphia: University of Pennsylvania Press, 2012), 8.

28. Thomas E. Cronin, and Michael A. Genovese, *The Paradoxes of the American Presidency*, 3rd ed. (New York: Oxford University Press, 2010).

SUGGESTED READING

Beyle, Thad L., ed. *Governors in Hard Times*. Washington, DC: Congressional Quarterly, 1992.

Clynch, Edward J., and Thomas P. Lauth. *Governors, Legislatures, and Budgets*. New York: Greenwood, 1991.

Ferguson, Margaret R. *The Executive Branch of State Government: People, Process, and Politics*. Santa Barbara, CA: ABC CLIO, 2006.

Kousser, Thad, and Justin Phillips. *The Power of American Governors: Winning on Budgets and Losing on Policy*. Cambridge: Cambridge University Press, 2012.

Leal, David L. *Electing America's Governors: The Politics of Executive Elections*. Basingstoke, UK: Palgrave Macmillan, 2006.

Rosenthal, Alan. *The Best Job in Politics: Exploring how Governors Succeed as Policy Leaders*. Washington, DC: CQ Press, 2013.

Shribnick, Ethan G. *A Legacy of Innovation: Governors and Public Policy*. Philadelphia: University of Pennsylvania Press, 2008.

———. *A Legacy of Leadership: Governors and American History*. Philadelphia: University of Pennsylvania Press, 2008.

van Assendelft, Laura A. *Governors, Agenda Setting, and Divided Government*. Lanham, MD: University Press of America, 1997.

Chapter 19

Bureaucracy

Cynthia Bowling

If one were trying to capture the nature of U.S. governance from one location, the observer would only need to stand inside the offices of any state administrative agency. From this vantage point, policy decisions are made and programs implemented within the vast web of intergovernmental relationships. State government administration is, quite simply, the nexus in which policies created at all three levels of the federal system (national, state, and local) are put into action.

When Congress makes policies, more often than not, state agencies coordinate the day-to-day implementation. State Boards of Education interpret the guidelines and assess the progress local schools make under national No Child Left Behind mandates. Secretaries of state and election divisions help local officials manage the statewide voter registration rolls required by the Help America Vote Act. On the other hand, local governments depend on state government policymakers and administrators to put local programs into action. Federal funds flow through state administration to localities for programs as varied as educational assistance for disabled children, day care for the elderly, or community development. Administrators reallocate funds from the state budget to help pay local schoolteachers. Many guidelines and regulations for local programs and implementation of federal initiatives are developed by state administrators as intermediaries in the federal system.

States are much more than the fulcrum of federalism, however. A state can create myriad governmental policies and programs for the safety and well-being of its own citizens under the auspices of state constitutions. Although No Child Left Behind mandates some state activities, it is a state's own Board of Education that creates the majority of policies for its schools, including teacher qualifications, funding, and curricula. California pushed past federal guidelines to create more rigid environmental regulations than are federally mandated. Moreover, states often venture into policymaking even in areas where many people argue they should not go. While still under scrutiny from state and federal courts, several states, most notably Alabama and Arizona, have passed their own versions of immigration regulations. During the 2012 November elections, Colorado and Washington legalized the use of small amounts of marijuana, directly contradicting federal law. Within two weeks of the passage of the "pot" policies, Washington state attorneys had already begun to drop drug violation charges. State government creates and implements directly in all policy arenas where power is neither given specifically to the national government nor prohibited to the states by the Tenth Amendment to the U.S. Constitution.

All in all, more than five million individuals are employed by state governments to implement policy, develop programs, or produce (and follow) governmental procedures. Who are these administrators? Who leads state organizations, and what are their qualifications? In what areas do state agencies operate? How do they interact with elected officials, citizens, and clientele groups? How do administrators perform the tasks of government, and how are they held accountable? This chapter provides an overview to the functions of state government bureaucracy, the administrators who undertake these challenges, and the practices of state administration.

THE SCOPE OF STATE ADMINISTRATION

The roles and responsibilities of state government emerge from citizen demands and the unique position states hold in American federalism. Although some view American federalism as a hierarchy, with the localities situated under the rule of state governments and the national government at the top, the reality is that state legislatures pass more laws than the U.S. Congress, and state administrations implement more programs directly to citizens than federal bureaucracies. The true division of responsibilities between the national and state government is more of a blur than a smooth demarcation, with both levels of government implementing policies across almost all functional areas. For example, within the education policy area, state administration implements federal guidelines, creates its own education programs, receives and allocates national funding to local schools, reallocates state revenue across localities to hire teachers, and oversees the functioning of local school districts. The same intergovernmental dance is repeated in all policy areas, including social services, state security, and criminal justice. But how did state administrators come to play these roles in American federalism?

Evolution and Expansion of State Government Responsibilities

Understanding state-level bureaucracy requires understanding the unique history of evolving public demands on state government and the institutional structures created to meet citizens' needs. The last 150 years of state administration can be viewed as a cycle of reactive responses to internal and external demands. In the earliest years of this country, state government provided few direct services to its citizens. Early citizen demands occurred primarily at the lowest levels, as towns or cities responded to the most basic needs created from industrialization and urbanization—safety and sanitation. As populations grew, federal- and state-level action became necessary. The Industrial Revolution initiated waves of state economic development, increasing populations prompted state agricultural and transportation programs, and the end of the Civil War demonstrated the need for veterans' services. The turn of the twentieth century called for water and transit regulation, while economic shifts expanded social services and education provisions. After World War II, better highways, welfare programs, and educational opportunities were needed. Over the last two decades, new demands have emerged. For instance, the terrorist attacks on September 11, 2001, and the creation of the Homeland Security federal cabinet department initiated the creation of *state* security agencies. Internal demands include input from state citizens, interest groups, and local governments. External demands from federal initiatives also necessitated institutions at the state level to provide the services.

Table 19.1 demonstrates the scope of responsibilities state governments have undertaken by listing the "generations" in which significant administrative departments were created in a majority of the states. Almost half of the agencies listed were in place by the 1950s, with about forty more added in the next two decades as needs arose. The first generation of agencies responded to demands in the first part of the twentieth century. In the 1960s, technological advances and industrialization brought the need for state regulations on air quality, and the grants provided by the national war on poverty spawned departments of state-federal relations. States created departments in the 1970s to assist minority and women's rights efforts. Over the last

TABLE 19.1 **Scope and Growth of State Administrative Agencies, by Decade (1959–2010)**

A. First-generation agencies (1950s)

1. Adjutant General
2. Aeronautics
3. Aging
4. Agriculture
5. Alcoholic Beverage Control
6. Attorney General
7. Banking
8. Budgeting
9. Child Welfare
10. Corrections
11. Education (State School Officer)
12. Emergency Management (Civil Defense)
13. Employment Services
14. Fire Marshal
15. Fish and Game
16. Food (Inspection/Purity)
17. Forestry
18. Geology
19. Health
20. Higher Education
21. Highway Patrol
22. Highways
23. Insurance
24. Labor
25. Labor Arbitration and Mediation
26. Library
27. Mining
28. Mental Health (and Retardations)
29. Motor Vehicles
30. Oil and Gas
31. Parks and Recreation
32. Parole
33. Personnel
34. Planning
35. Post Audit
36. Public Utility Regulation
37. Purchasing
38. Revenue
39. Secretary of State
40. Securities (Regulation)
41. Soil Conservation
42. Solid Waste (Sanitation)
43. Tourism (Advertising)
44. Treasurer
45. Unemployment (Compensation) Insurance
46. Veterans Affairs
47. Vocational Education
48. Water Quality
49. Water Resources
50. Welfare
51. Workers' Compensation

B. Second-generation agencies (1960s)

1. Administration
2. Air Quality
3. Commerce
4. Community Affairs
5. Comptroller
6. Court Administration
7. Criminal Justice Planning
8. Economic (Industrial) Development
9. Federal-State Relations
10. Highway Safety
11. Juvenile Rehabilitation (Delinquency)
12. Law Enforcement (State Police)
13. Natural Resources

C. Third-generation agencies (1970s)

1. Alcohol and Drug Abuse
2. Archives
3. Arts Council
4. Child Labor
5. Civil Rights
6. Consumer Affairs (Consumer Protection)
7. Energy Resources
8. Environment (Protection)
9. Ethics
10. Exceptional Children (Special Education)
11. Fair Employment (Equal Opportunity)
12. Finance
13. Historic Preservation
14. Housing Finance
15. Human Resources/Services
16. Manpower
17. Mass Transit
18. Medicaid
19. Occupational Health and Safety
20. Public Lands
21. Railroad
22. Savings and Loan
23. Social Services
24. State-Local Relations
25. Telecommunication
26. Transportation
27. Veterinarian
28. Vocational Rehabilitation
29. Women's Commissions
30. Information

D. Fourth-generation agencies (1980s)

1. Boating Law Administration
2. Emergency Medical Services
3. Employee Relations
4. Employee Services
5. Ground Water Management
6. Hazardous Waste
7. Horse Racing
8. International Trade
9. Licensing (Occupational/Professional)
10. Small and Minority Business
11. State Fair
12. Training and Development
13. Underground Storage Tanks
14. Vital Statistics
15. Weights and Measures

E. Fifth-generation agencies (1990s)

1. Building Codes
2. Child Support Enforcement
3. Crime Victims Compensation
4. Development Disabled
5. Facilities Management
6. Fleet Management
7. Gaming (Regulation)
8. Lobby Law Administration

F. Millennial agencies (2000s)

1. Campaign Finance
2. Lottery
3. Public Defender
4. Public Safety
5. Recycling
6. State Data Center
7. State Security

G. Emergent agencies (present in twenty or more states, but less than thirty-eight in 2010)

1. Borders Management
2. Coastal Zone Management
3. Native American (Tribal) Affairs
4. Ombudsman

SOURCE: Based on listings in *Book of the States*, Supplement 2, "State Administrative Officials Classified by Functions" (Lexington, KY: Council of State Governments, 1959, 1969, 1979, 1989, 1999, and 2010). Agency names are listed if the agency existed in thirty-eight or more states for the respective decades. Agency names/titles vary slightly from decade to decade.

thirty years, agencies to oversee state lotteries, security from domestic terrorism, and border control have emerged. Today, almost all public problems are addressed by one or more state organizations.

Another aspect of state administrative evolution is reflected by the reorganizations and reforms that occurred during the same time periods. With the piecemeal nature of state growth, organizing and overseeing state activities became increasingly more difficult. For instance, at one point in the early twentieth century, New York functioned with over 150 different agencies. In 1926 New York reorganized to limit the number of departments to 25 and placing agencies into functional areas. This process was repeated in over twenty more states. Throughout the last century, continuous cycles of administrative reform have occurred. The Progressive Reform Movement around the turn of the twentieth century addressed the blatant patronage systems in all levels of government by instituting merit systems, hiring rules, and tenure to protect administrators from undue political influence. Later, the Brownlow Commission in 1937 and the Hoover Commissions in 1949 and 1953 urged executive control of administration. The growth of gubernatorial staff and resources, along with administrative reorganizations, aided state government's evolution into the more familiar executive branches we see today.[1]

Over the past few decades, an increased emphasis on improving management processes has occurred. Georgia governor Jimmy Carter (D) introduced zero-based budgeting in the 1970s to more effectively allocate state resources. Total quality management and quality circles sought to improve information flow and productivity across levels of bureaucracy. Reinventing government initiatives in states lauded increasing efficiency in government by "contracting out" state services. The current wave of Republican governors elected across the country in 2010 have focused on reducing "waste" in government and scaling back state services. Thus administration in the states has included cycles of expansion in response to citizen demand and federal policies mirrored by corresponding initiatives to maintain order of Hydra-esque state bureaucracies.

Growing State Government: By the Numbers

The enlarging scope of state administration has been mirrored by the size of state government. State budgets have increased exponentially since World War II. State expenditures from all fifty states increased from about $10 billion in 1948 to $25 billion around 1960, an increase of about 250 percent over a single decade. Less than thirty years later, total state expenditures were $400 billion in 1987, almost doubled to $725 billion in 1995, and topped $1 trillion by 2000. Expenditures have continued to grow steadily. Although state revenue declined in 2009 and 2010, spending by the states has continued to grow an average of about 6 percent with the use of federal stimulus money during the 2009–2011 recession. Today, the states together spend more than $1.7 trillion a year.[2]

While state budgets have increased consistently, state employment seems to have reached a plateau. During the 1980s, total state employment increased more than 25 percent. In the 1990s, increases averaged only about 6 percent. Currently, total state employees (full and part-time) number about five million, growing only by about four hundred thousand people over the last two decades. However, as shown in the brief table below, public employment growth in the individual states has varied significantly since the early 1990s, from an almost 10 percent decrease in Illinois to an almost 50 percent increase in Nevada.[3]

Percentage growth in employees	Number of states	State examples
No growth/decrease	7	Illinois, Indiana, Louisiana
1–10% growth	14	Alabama, Maine, Virginia
11–20% growth	14	Connecticut, Iowa, Wyoming
More than 20% growth	15	Arizona, Nevada, North Carolina

Thus state administration provides an ever-changing and expanding array of services, spends trillions of dollars, and employs millions of individuals. Who are these bureaucrats? Who does the work of the states?

WHO ARE STATE ADMINISTRATORS?

Elected Administrators

In the executive branch of state government, everyone can be considered an administrator. The governor is often chiefly regarded as an elected policy advocate and decision maker in the legislative process, signing or vetoing state legislation. However, the governor may also be called the "chief administrator" of the state bureaucracy. He or she is vested with ensuring the implementation of all laws and resulting rules and policies. Nominally, the governor sits atop a typical bureaucratic hierarchy. In reality, however, other elected and appointed officials share policy and program efforts.

In addition to the governor, many states elect some other officials by statewide vote. The most common separately elected officials are lieutenant governors, attorneys general, treasurers, and secretaries of state. Typically, these officials are termed "process officials," overseeing staff functions for the entire state. Additionally, some states elect several other top officials, such as commissioners of agriculture, transportation department secretaries, or school board heads. In these cases, each actor may have his or her own electoral mandates and individual policy preferences.

Most states (forty-four) elect a lieutenant governor, who in many ways functions similarly to the vice president of the United States. He or she is next in line for the governorship and performs various administrative and legislative functions. In many states the lieutenant governor is also a legislative officer, capable of setting the agenda and rules for state legislatures, introducing legislation, and/or casting votes. In about half of the American states, the governor and lieutenant governor are elected together—the governor chooses a lieutenant governor with whom to run. In these cases, the two tend to share basic ideological values, and thus conflict is limited. The lieutenant governor is often a member of the governor's cabinet and assigned to boards or commissions to act as policy adviser. However, in nineteen other states, the governor and lieutenant governor are elected separately and may or may not be from the same political party. In Tennessee and West Virginia, members of the state senate choose a legislative president or Speaker who also is considered the lieutenant governor. When this split-executive situation occurs, the governor may lose power to advocate for particular policies to a lieutenant governor that can directly shape the legislative agenda. Typically, lieutenant governors do not share broad administrative authority over state agencies; however, in a few states particular administrative actions are assigned to the office. For instance, lieutenant governors may serve on a state budget commission (Delaware), as the chief elections officer (Utah), or as the director of commerce (Indiana).

A few other high-ranking process officials are often elected separately. A vast majority of the forty-seven secretaries of state in the United States are elected in partisan elections. The secretaries of state can be thought of as the most "administrative" of the statewide elected officials. The secretary of state is typically a recorder of licenses for businesses and professionals; a publisher of state laws; and an archivist of state, and local, records. Typically, the secretary of state is considered a nonpartisan state actor. One area has become very important in the last decade and calls for the most apolitical and fair processes—elections. A vast majority of secretaries of state have professionalized and streamlined election divisions in their states. However, a few have been accused of making administrative decisions with a political bias. For instance, during the 2012 presidential election, the Republican secretary of state in Ohio was accused of limiting early voting in districts with Democratic majorities. Though this decision was soon changed, if these actions were indeed motivated by partisan interests, they are a perfect example of the perils of electing bureaucratic actors in partisan races who may act not with neutral competence but with political goals.

Attorneys general are the top legal advisers in the states, offering opinions to other state and local officials, defending the states against lawsuits, and prosecuting state law breakers. A vast majority (43 percent) are popularly elected. Attorneys general play an important role for other agency heads. State officials are vested with implementing and enforcing federal and state laws that are often broad and unclear. Sometimes, state and federal legislation even conflicts. In these cases, agency executives often seek guidance from their attorney general. The attorney general is then in a position to defend agency actions, especially when agencies are brought to court for alleged violations of federal law.

Other elected actors include officials involved in the budget or finance areas of state government. Treasurers are responsible for cash management and investment in states. This includes ensuring that the state's general fund or other trust funds have sufficient money to flow to state agencies as appropriated in the budget. Furthermore, the treasurer typically oversees debt and investment. Comptrollers are typically the accountants for the states. Only sixteen states elect their comptroller; in other states, the comptroller is appointed by the governor or director of the finance or budget departments. Comptrollers record money transactions and ensure that money is used in compliance with generally accepted governmental accounting principles. Finally, state auditors provide independent reviews of cash flow management and accounting records. They are elected in seventeen states; appointed by the legislature in another third of the states; or appointed by governors, commissions, or department heads.[4]

Separately elected lieutenant governors can hinder policy agenda setting and advocacy. Attorneys general also can disrupt gubernatorial control by issuing advisory opinions in contradiction with gubernatorial preference. However, the actors mentioned above generally do not disrupt the governor's ability to oversee the executive organizations in state government. They assist with the day-to-day management functions of government to ensure that other agencies can perform their tasks. But this is not always the case with popularly elected, partisan officials in charge of particular functional areas of state activities.

All together, over three hundred separately elected officials may serve in twelve major offices in the fifty states. In these cases, the governor must share policymaking and oversight functions with department heads who can also claim an electoral mandate to pursue particular policy directions. The major policy officials, who are often separately elected, oversee state corrections, K–12 education, health services, transportation, public utility regulation, and/or welfare services. Governors in some states—for instance, Hawaii, Maine, New Hampshire, or New Jersey—do not share power; the governor and lieutenant governor, running together, are the only statewide officials elected. Alternatively, in states including Alabama, California, Georgia, Idaho, Oklahoma, and Washington, the governor is elected along with seven or more other officials.[5] In all of the states, even with elected and appointed department officials, other state agency heads—those directly managing specific agencies—provide the majority of the direct policy interpretation and implementation. These agency heads, their midlevel managers, and other state employees are typically who we define as "bureaucrats" in the executive branch.

Characteristics and Careers of Other State Administrators

One way of describing top-level state administrators is in terms of qualifications and professionalism. Education, experience, and career paths all contribute to agency heads' ability to be policy leaders and implementers. Over the past forty years, agency heads have become increasingly more capable, possessing higher levels of education and more years of experience than ever before.[6] Currently, three in four state agency heads have at least a master's degree, with 23 percent having a PhD or other terminal degree. Forty years ago, only about 40 percent had graduate degrees. Today's agency heads have worked in state government an average of eighteen years, and within their current agencies for thirteen years. They have probably been the agency head for about six years, and almost half rose through the ranks of that agency. In 1968 agency heads had served in state government for only about ten years and typically had spent only about six years in their current agency. Today's state agency heads are also familiar with other types of organizations. Almost two-thirds have held positions in a private company, and a slightly smaller number in nonprofit organizations.[7] They are extremely well qualified, experienced, and invested in the business of state administration. All in all, agency heads are equipped to lead in their particular policy fields and connected to an array of agencies within and outside of state government.

Another perspective examines the ability of state agency heads to effectively advocate and create policy for all citizens. The concept of bureaucratic representation considers the degree to which governmental administrations mirror the public through demographic characteristics *(passive representation)* and represent the needs of various citizens through *active representation* of their interests. Especially, administrators who work with the public daily as "street level bureaucrats" and are the face of state government should in some ways reflect the individuals they serve.

The five million employees of the fifty states seem to be a cross-section of citizens. According to 2009 data from the Equal Employment Opportunity Commission (EEOC), state employees are approximately 48 percent male and 52 percent female (see Table 19.2). They are 69 percent white; about 20 percent African American; 7 percent Hispanic; and about 4 percent other minorities, including Asians and Native Americans. Whites hold the percentage of state jobs approximately proportional to their overall population, African Americans hold a slightly higher proportion of state employment positions (20 percent) than their U.S. population of about 13 percent, and Hispanics hold fewer state jobs than their 16 percent of the total population would suggest. While women and African Americans are appropriately represented, Hispanics, the fastest growing group in the United States, still have much ground to gain in state government.

Salary data, though, indicate more disparity in terms of gender and ethnicity. Diversity lessens as position responsibilities and salaries increase. The glass ceiling, for many individuals, is barely cracked and definitely not yet broken. Table 19.2 notes that men, especially white men, are noticeably more prominent in the highest-paid positions. Only 10 percent of the women working in state government earn over $70,000, compared with 18 percent of men. African Americans face even harder glass ceilings, with about two-thirds in part-time, clerical, or lower-level supervisory positions, and only 7 percent in the highest-salary category. Hispanics, though underrepresented overall in state government, are more likely than African Americans to reach parity with whites in employment levels and salaries.[8]

Now, focus on just the state agency heads—executives directly under department heads who often have the largest impact on policy interpretation and implementation. Despite these initial data from the EEOC, other studies indicate that top-level agency leaders are more diverse in terms of gender than in other realms of public or private employment.[9] Women are now 28 percent of state agency heads; they are still underrepresented but have made significant strides into the executive arena. However, overall numbers of minorities in state agency head positions have remained stagnant since the 1970s, at around 6 percent. As minorities, when aggregated, will soon become more than half of the U.S. population, the fact that the proportion of minorities leading state agencies is virtually unchanged since 1978 is especially troubling for democratic governance. Given the challenges of immigration and growing pressure on governmental services, it becomes entirely appropriate to ask

TABLE 19.2 **Salaries of State Employees, by Race and Gender**

	Male	Female	White	African American	Hispanic
All employees (100%)	48%	52%	69%	20%	7%
Salary levels	**Male**	**Female**	**White**	**African American**	**Hispanic**
Less than $25,000	6%	11%	6%	16%	8%
$25,000 to $42,999	36	46	39	50	47
$43,000 to $69,999	40	33	39	27	33
More than $70,000	18	10	16	7	12
Totals	100%	100%	100%	100%	100%
Median salaries[a]	$47,500	$40,200	$45,500	$36,600	$41,200

NOTES: Table calculated from 2009 data from the Equal Employment Opportunity Commission; *N* = 2,189,331.

a. Additionally, although only about 3 percent of state employees identify themselves as Asian, one in four Asians have salaries over $70,000, with a median wage for Asian Americans of $53,000.

SOURCE: Equal Employment Opportunity Commission, 2009 data.

whether the unique needs of different ethnic groups can be brought to decision makers' agendas and appropriately addressed in public policy when they are directly represented by so few agency executives of their own ethnicity. Furthermore, the absence of any notable growth in minority numbers for over thirty years raises credible concerns of racism and elitism within governmental appointment and hiring processes.

Merit Systems and Public Unionization

State administrators also operate within a unique employment framework. The civil service system stemmed originally from the Progressive Reform Movement and the federal Pendleton Act. Prior to this time, public administrators were most often given administrative positions based on "who" not "what" they knew and allegiance to particular elected officials. The 1883 Pendleton Act created the civil service commission that would hire federal employees based on merit and job qualifications. The states followed this lead. New York (1883) and Massachusetts (1884) immediately created merit systems. Today, all states are federally required to have merit-based systems for a sizable portion of their employees, particularly those involved with administering federal aid. Most states have comprehensive systems that cover a majority of their employees. The civil service system ensures recruitment, selection, and promotion based on knowledge and skills; conducts regular employee reviews; and creates pay schedules and incentive systems. Civil service promotes neutral competence and creates job security to allow state administrators to perform their jobs with limited interference from politicized, elected officials.[10]

Even with job protection, the salaries and benefits received by state employees have been, and still are in many cases, lower than those in similar positions in the private sector. With the recognition of public-private employment disparities, distrust of merit systems, and an inability to influence management rulings and grievance processes, public employees began to form their own unions to address these issues. In 1932 one of the main public-sector unions, the American Federation of State, County, and Municipal Employees (AFSCME), began organizing in Madison, Wisconsin. Later, in 1959, Wisconsin became the first state to allow collective bargaining for state employees. Although some local and state employees had engaged in collective activities previously, public-sector unions grew extensively in the 1950s, 1960s, and 1970s as federal legislation granted collective bargaining rights to federal workers. Today, forty-two states specifically allow at least some of their employees (e.g., teachers, firefighters, and social service workers) to engage in collective bargaining. While private-sector union membership has decreased drastically over the last half-century to about 6 percent of workers, approximately 40 percent of public employees either belong to a union or are represented through collective bargaining activities.[11] Across the United States, public employees' union membership differs vastly, with northern and midwestern states more unionized than southern states. Below, the states with the lowest and highest percentages of public-sector employees belonging to a union or utilizing collective bargaining agreements are shown.[12]

Public-sector unions engage in three main activities for their members. The first is collective bargaining. While

Public sector union membership in states

Highest percentage	Lowest percentage
Connecticut (66)	Georgia (12)
Massachusetts (64)	North Carolina (13)
Rhode Island (64)	Arkansas (13)
Oregon (63)	Louisiana (14)
Minnesota (62)	Mississippi (15)
California (60)	South Carolina (15)
New Jersey (60)	Wyoming (16)
Pennsylvania (57)	Idaho (17)
Alaska (56)	Virginia (17)
Maine (56)	Tennessee (20)

merit systems address methods for hiring, promotion, and normalizing salaries, many of these decisions are not addressed with the employees themselves. Thus unions give public employees a collective representation with state government leaders. However, unlike private-sector unions, public unions are more limited in what they can address. Only a slight majority of states allow bargaining on compensation levels, although benefits are slightly more negotiable. The effects of compensation bargaining, though, are limited. On average, public-sector unions have raised wages for their members only by about 4–8 percent compared with non-unionized workers.[13] They have been more successful in improving benefits and pensions. Furthermore, unions promote employee representation on issues of work rules and processes as well as conflict resolution and grievance procedures.

A second purpose of public-sector unions is to give public employees a collective "face" to present to the public. Often, public workers are disdainfully called "bureaucrats" or only "good enough for government work." Public unions help provide an identity for administrators that can be promoted in the public square, especially when unions apply political pressure at the bargaining table. When Gov. Scott Walker (R) of Wisconsin began a budgetary and political campaign against public-sector workers early in 2012, unions and their members acted quickly to surround the state capitol building, protesting his actions and making their jobs and faces known to the public. With the current fiscal crisis in the states and political rhetoric over public employee salaries and benefits increasing, these packages are now the target of government cutbacks. Republican governors especially have taken on public-sector unions in the name of fiscal containment. Union membership has begun to decline under new rules and statutes limiting union power and salary/pension improvements. The New Faces of Union Busting? box discusses these conflicts in more depth.

Finally, unions are at their core an interest group. Unions promote the interests of their membership. They offer selective incentives to potential members to increase their enrollments. For example, teachers belonging to the National Education Association receive free legal counsel. Police and firefighters may receive additional insurance benefits by joining their unions. Public-sector unions actively pursue policies that will improve not just their own interests but often lead to votes that protect government budgets. When public-sector workers vote as a block, they can have a strong impact on election outcomes, particularly at the state and local levels. When they place their campaign money behind political candidates, the impact can be even greater.

WHAT STATE ADMINISTRATORS DO

State administrators play multiple roles. First, state administrators are *policy experts*. Agency heads and career officials help forecast policy problems and advise governors and legislators. Second, state administrators *implement* federal and state policy, creating rules and regulations to guide service provision. Third, administrators also play *management* roles, carrying out the day-to-day functions of the

Union members, supporters, and labor leaders protest Illinois governor Pat Quinn's position during contract negotiations between the state and the American Federation of State, County and Municipal Employees, on Governor's Day, August 15, 2012, at the Illinois State Fair in Springfield, Illinois.

SOURCE: Seth Perlman/Associated Press.

THE NEW FACES OF UNION BUSTING?

In early 2011 a peculiar drama erupted in Wisconsin, the state that had been an early leader in public-sector unions and collective bargaining. Newly elected governor Scott Walker (R) began his term by targeting public-sector unions for increasing the cost of state and local government to unsustainable levels. Using Wisconsin's $140 million budget deficit as a backdrop, on February 11, 2011, Walker initiated his "budget repair bill." Fiscally, this bill essentially ended collective bargaining rights for salaries as well as increased employee contributions to insurance and benefit plans. However, in the eyes of union members, many citizens, and the Democratic Party, the bargaining limitations were accompanied by additional measures they claimed were purely aimed at union busting, such as eliminating payroll deductions for union dues, requiring annual certification of unions by its members, and limiting the ability to strike. Even as public union leaders indicated their willingness to negotiate with officials, Governor Walker and the Republican legislature continued to push for anti-union legislation and benefit cuts.

Here, the story gets even stranger. The nation watched as the television media showed union members and their supporters, conservatively estimated at over a hundred thousand protesters, surrounding the Wisconsin state capitol building. Even more interesting were the interviews with Wisconsin Democratic legislators from a location in Illinois, where they had fled to avoid being summoned into the senate. Without a quorum, budget bills could not be brought to a vote. A couple of weeks later, through some sketchy legislative maneuvering, the anti-union portions of the bill were passed quickly through the Wisconsin legislature. The next day, the first lawsuit was filed in state court. The Supreme Court of Wisconsin, in a 4–3 vote, upheld the state law restricting public-sector collective bargaining rights by finding that no laws had been broken in the passage of the bill. However, the Madison teachers union then filed another lawsuit, claiming that its right to equal protection is denied by Act 10, among other constitutional issues. A district judge agreed, and the law did not go into effect. The governor has appealed, and the Supreme Court of Wisconsin will likely hear the case in the fall of 2013, this time on constitutional as opposed to procedural issues. There are also other challenges to the law in several other courts, so the issue is still not settled. Meanwhile, in June 2012 Governor Walker infamously was subjected to a recall vote almost as soon as legally allowed. Although he ultimately won the recall vote, Walker still has challenges ahead, both legal and political.

Though the Wisconsin battle was definitely the most interesting scenario, it was not the only recent battle between Republican governors and public-sector unions. In 2005, on his first day in office, Indiana governor Mitch Daniels (R) rescinded collective bargaining rights for state workers. Indiana now ranks near the bottom states for public employee average pay. In 2012 New Jersey governor Chris Christie (R) signed an executive order limiting public-sector unions' political contributions, then went forward with plans for a wage freeze, limitations on future pensions, and increasing employee contributions for health care.

Although Governors Walker, Daniels, and Christie seem to be the "poster boys" in fights against public-sector unions, the same battles are raging in other states—California, Michigan, Ohio, and New York, for example. Are these conflicts really about the devastating effect of personnel costs on state and local budgets? Or do governors, especially but not exclusively Republican, want to limit the political clout unions wield on elections and policy decisions?

The answer is probably a bit of both. Public employee salaries are probably not the issue. Although low-skilled workers may earn slightly more than their private-sector counterparts, most higher-skilled or professional public employees do not. Benefits, though, tend to be better for government employees. A vast majority of public employees have defined pension plans and relatively low-cost insurance benefits, which unions have bargained for (and received) in lieu of salary increases in parity with the private sector. These pensions, though, have been improperly managed in terms of contributions and outlays, and the poor economy has taken its toll on trust funds. When schoolteachers continue to receive free or low-cost ($1 to $20 per month) health insurance, government budgets do skyrocket with insurance premium increases. Politically, though, Republicans have made unions and public employees the scapegoats for state and local budgetary woes more likely caused by slow economic growth, lost tax revenue, and falling interest from trust funds. When citizens are struggling to make ends meet, with fewer jobs, lower salaries, and lost pensions, it is easy to blame inefficient bureaucrats whose pockets are lined with tax dollars.

However, the blame game must stop, and common sense must prevail. Otherwise, this political battle will continue to rage, with scapegoats instead of solutions and reactive policy instead of proper planning. Do we really want to portray state bureaucrats as overpaid, overzealous union strikers, and governors or state legislators as the mustachioed, flamboyant union busters in a scene from the movie *Gangs of New York?*

state's "business" by hiring service providers, allocating expenditures, keeping records, and managing large programmatic operations. Fourth, state administration may function as a knowledge "node" or nexus, interacting with federal, state, and local officials as well as private and nonprofit organizations to coordinate policy and program activities. Finally, many state administrators function as *street-level bureaucrats*, providing services directly to citizens, such as education, social services, unemployment assistance, or public safety. State administration is not simply a holding place for nameless bureaucrats but rather a source of knowledge, service, and action.

The American State Administrators Project (ASAP) has surveyed state agency heads twice a decade beginning in 1964. Data from the 2008 ASAP provide an in-depth look at the attributes, attitudes, and activities of agency executives.[14] To complement the general description of the roles administrators play, ASAP asked agency heads how their time was spent. On average, agency executives spend about half of their time on routine administration. This includes budget processes, human resource functions, and coordinating operating activities—the management role mentioned above. Agency executives report that the rest of their time is divided between two broader functions—policy development and promoting public support. Policy development activities include conducting analyses and advising other governmental actors about public problems, potential issues, and policy solutions. Agency heads can act either as policy advocates, promoting a particular policy agenda, or as neutral experts, discussing the implications of different policy choices. Executives also help develop the more detailed processes that are needed to execute laws. Overall, about one-quarter of their time is devoted to the inner workings of policy analysis, decision making, and implementation.

The final fourth of administrative time is used for the more "political side" of policy execution. Norton Long once suggested that power was "the lifeblood of administration."[15] Thus state executives need the support of the citizens to whom they provide services. In this way, agency heads can cultivate the political support to advocate for particular policies favorable to their clientele as well as defend against budget cuts or service reductions. Though scholars often state that administrators develop policy, implement programs, and manage organizations, the ASAP data show that gaining public support and cooperation is vital to these activities. In fact, research indicates that more effective and efficient agencies may be linked to the development of public support and policy development but negatively correlated to time spent on managerial activities.[16] When administrators spend more time on routine internal administration, activities that may support agency policies or garner resources for the organization are forgone.

Because of their role in coordinating different levels of government and relevant groups, ASAP also asked administrators to identify how often they were in contact with a variety of actors. The results below also show the frequency of contact with potential agency supporters:

Percentage of Agency Heads Reporting Daily or Weekly Contact with:

Governor	12%	Governor's staff	46%
Legislators	34	Legislative staff	32
Personnel in other agencies	66	Officials in other states	25
Citizens at large	60	Clientele groups	59
Local officials	28	National officials	13

By a large margin, more contact occurs with personnel in other agencies, citizens, and clientele groups than with other administrative actors. Typically, administrators coordinate agency activities or develop policy with personnel in other agencies. Interacting with citizens and clientele groups typically involves policy development and analysis as well as developing support from these groups. Evidence also indicates that agency executives, whether in their roles of policy expert, implementer, or political advocate, have a strong impact on those with whom they interact. Even though contact between administrators, governors, and legislators is infrequent, over 85 percent of administrators report influencing the governor; about 80 percent of these perceive having a moderate or high impact. Almost 94 percent of agency heads report influencing the legislature, with almost four-fifths of them reporting a moderate to high impact. One can also not ignore the very strong impact of the administrator on his or her agency's clientele groups. About 85 percent report influencing their clientele groups, the vast majority indicating at least moderate impact of their influence. State agency heads are definitely not wallflowers, and they have strong perceptions of their own efficacy in state activities.[17]

Executing State Programs: Capacity, Contracting, and Collaboration

The primary purpose of state bureaucracy seems simple enough—to implement state policies through regulation and programs. While the purpose is generally straightforward, accomplishing goals is not. In addition to the actions and interactions of administrators noted previously, program implementation depends on a state government's administrative capacity.

In essence, bureaucratic capacity is the ability of a state's administrative branch to fulfill the goals and intent of legislation and resulting policies. Defining capacity explicitly is a bit trickier. Ann Bowman and Richard Kearney broadly defined capacity as the "ability to respond effectively to change, make decisions efficiently, effectively, and responsively, and manage conflict."[18] The authors then examined the parts of administration that have been targeted by reform, identifying four dimensions of executive capacity: staffing/spending, coordination mechanisms, executive power, and the centralization of authority. Following this vein, Jeffrey Brudney et al. used ASAP to examine the extent to which reinvention reforms had been integrated into state administrative structures during the 1990s.[19] The reforms included decentralization of decision making, greater discretion for managers in spending and procurement, training programs, the use of strategic planning, benchmarks, quality improvement programs, and the simplification of human resource rules. The reinvention efforts in states were in many ways about lessening hierarchical structures and centralized power. More recently, the New Public Management administrative reform movement is focused on performance outputs, outcomes, and measurement.

Helen Tucker, bottom, and Sherry Butler, bottom left, take calls at a state-run call center April 6, 2004, in Everetts, North Carolina. Although many states have turned to outsourcing to deliver services, North Carolina lawmakers agreed to spend $1.2 million to hire thirty new people to answer food stamp questions at the call center instead of outsourcing to workers in India.

SOURCE: AP Photo/Bob Jordan.

Patricia Ingraham and her colleagues[20] discussed four operational areas that are important for administrative capacity—the quality of management systems, leadership, coordination across systems, and a results-oriented focus. They argue further that financial systems, human resource management, and information technology are all important. Related to Ingraham et al.'s work, the Government Performance Project (GPP), in 1999, 2001, 2005, and 2008, undertook the task of "grading the states." The GPP examined each state's structures and processes in four key areas—people, money, infrastructure (coordination), and information. As the "Grading the States 2008" report states, "A focus on these critical areas helps ensure that states' policy decisions and practices actually deliver their intended outcomes."[21] And, as their GPP grades reflect, some states performed better than others. The overall best performers were Utah, Virginia, and Washington. Some of the worst were Alaska, California, and New Hampshire. Thus the ability to govern—to carry out policies to their intended outcomes—is dependent upon the capacity of administrators and administrative structures in each state. Moreover, leadership, intra- and intergovernmental relationships, and coordination among administrators and agencies are also integral to administrative capacity.

Two ways in which state agencies increase or extend their capacity is through contracting out public service provision and collaborating with other organizations. Over the past two decades, state governments have increasingly contracted with private and nonprofit organizations for delivery of governmental services, including portions of Medicaid, prison systems, educational endeavors, and transportation. According to the 2008 ASAP, almost two-thirds of state agency heads are using contracting as a method of service delivery. Of the contracting agencies, 57 percent work with other government entities, 70 percent contract with nonprofit service providers, and 80 percent pay private businesses for services. As widespread as contracting is, agency heads report mixed results. Only a slight majority perceive improved quality of services and responsiveness, 40 percent report improved accountability, and only about one-quarter report decreased costs. In many ways, contracting is more of an ideological approach to state government than a proven, more efficient way to provide services.

While agency heads have a variety of perceptions about the impact of outsourcing, the other method of extending agency capacity—collaboration—seems to be more widely used and positively viewed by administrators. A vast majority (86 percent) of state agencies collaborate to provide services; over four-fifths of these work with other government entities or nonprofit organizations. About 62 percent collaborate with private-sector organizations. Overwhelmingly and uniformly, more than four-fifths of agency heads report increased scope and quality of public services and better achievement of agency goals through collaboration. Moreover, agency executives report that three out of four citizens are more satisfied with collaborative arrangements. While both contracting and collaboration extend administrative capacity, collaborative efforts seem to be the more successful approach.

PERFORMANCE, ACCOUNTABILITY, AND TECHNOLOGY

Measuring State Performance

Performance measurement is not a new phenomenon. Businesses have been measuring performance for many years, delineating costs per unit produced or returns on investment. Applying business techniques to governmental performance is also not new, dating back to Scientific Management at the turn of the twentieth century. Performance measurement for governmental organizations came into national prominence in the 1990s with the Clinton administration and quickly spread through state and local governments.

For businesses, most elements—inputs, outputs, cost ratios, and outcomes—can be readily measured. For governments, the process of measuring performance is no less important but much more complex. Performance measures are utilized in some way by a vast majority of the states. In 2008 the National Association of State Budget Officers (NASBO) reported that forty states collected program-level performance measures for a wide variety of purposes. For instance, Vermont is required by law to use output and outcome indicators in the executive budget submission. Florida agencies identify goals and performance measures in their long-term planning. Although the use of performance measures in states is widespread, how they are used and the range of agencies reporting indicators varies.[22] Here, we focus on state performance measures as tools used (1) for accountability and transparency; (2) during the budget process; and (3) to promote achievements and increases in positive governmental outputs and outcomes.

First, performance measures are a powerful tool in democratic governance. The promotion of accountability and transparency is a dominant theme in state government, especially with the significant fiscal stress in the past four years. One way to measure governmental outputs or outcomes is to let the public decide. This process translates to governmental accountability. Creating goals for governmental organizations and measuring the degree of their achievement help elected officials determine if administrators are reaching established objectives. Furthermore, citizens can judge whether elected officials are producing the results they promised during their campaigns. The GPP discussed earlier focused on inputs. Citizens also need direct measures of their state's efficiency, output, and outcomes. If citizens can readily access performance indicators of state activities, then a "transparent" government exists. Citizens may readily access information, make judgments, and take actions to ensure administrative integrity and efficiency.

A second goal of performance measurement is efficiency. For state government, this may mean determining whether public resources are used in a way that achieves the most output or outcome for each tax dollar. This goal is primarily accomplished through the state budgeting process, where using performance measures when allocating resources improves efficiency by coupling the appropriation of funds to the services provided. For example, an agency requesting additional funds should note the extent to which indicators of performance should increase with the use of the resources. NASBO reports that almost four-fifths (thirty-nine) of the fifty states are required to include performance measures as part of an agency's budget request.

How are performance indicators used by elected officials? Two-thirds of administrators in states employing performance features in the budget process noted that the governor or central budget office utilized these performance measures. On the other hand, only about half of the agency heads in these states felt that the legislature used performance reports in its decision making.[23] In other words, the extent to which performance indicators are translated from the agency requests to the governor's budget submission and subsequent financial decisions varies greatly. States can report performance measures throughout the entire budget document (Iowa, Kentucky, and Tennessee) or only in one section devoted to performance (Kansas, Mississippi, and Virginia). In a few states, performance measures are reported only in a separate, stand-alone document. In the case of Alabama, performance measures are created, used when agencies request funds, reported on the Alabama website, and even reviewed regularly, but they are not necessarily and/or directly informing legislative budget decisions and allocations.

Third, performance measurement can also function as a planning and recording tool. *Strategic planning* is now a common term in state government administration, yet states vary significantly in the focus and extent of planning. Some states do no statewide planning at all. Other states have a formalized state-level strategic plan that integrates agency-level goals. Where state-level strategic planning occurs, performance measurement is almost always utilized and reported in conjunction with the plan. Whether or not they are integrated statewide, a majority of agencies across the states create goals and objectives for performance and attempt to measure their progress. Many then publish these objectives and/or report measures of performance to the public.

E-Government

The twenty-first century is the "digital age." Since the 1990s the Internet has unleashed a new wave of information resources, social networking, and business exchanges. State government is no stranger to these trends.

First, state government websites now contain access points for all types of information. One of the best examples relates to the performance measures discussed above. In a 2011 analysis of sixteen states' websites, Bowling found that thirteen of the states displayed agency goals in conjunction with the indicators of agency performance. Thus administrators, elected officials, and citizens could easily compare the initial goals to the achievements of these objectives. In a majority of the states, performance measures are shown across multiple years—the last year's goals and achievements, the current year's goals and achievements, and the next year's goals. A few states displayed comparative benchmarking, providing their own measures of performance in different areas to similar measures in other states or to a national or regional average. Thus one important part of getting information to citizens is related to the push for performance measurement and citizens' calls for more efficiency in governance.

Much more information is also included on state websites. Meetings open to the public are posted on state calendars. Links to agency phone or e-mail contact information allow citizens easier access to personal interactions with administrators. State websites also post general guides to administrative processes, such as renewing a driver's license. Other sites allow citizens to access more personal information—for example, birth or death records and court dates.

Second, state governments, surprisingly, operate as social networks. Some states have actual Twitter feeds, Facebook accounts, or links through other sites. For example, the state of Virginia's website provides a "social media directory," with links to Twitter, Facebook, and other social sites affiliated with state agencies on its main webpage. Other states take on the roles of these social networks. The most basic aspects of these state sites simply provide information and photographs of important state events, gubernatorial travels or speeches, or statements from agency officials. Some governors and legislators operate their own blogs, providing their own opinions on state issues. In return, states and/or their agencies often have online suggestion boxes, allowing citizens to voice their own thoughts or concerns. Social networking via a state's website has become not only an effective but a legitimized form of governmental communication.

Finally, and perhaps most important for governmental administration, is the use of e-government to conduct the state's business. States are increasingly providing citizens the opportunity for service provision through the Internet. Citizens can apply for driver's, business, fishing, or occupational licenses online. State human resource departments post job openings and take job applications online. Some states allow citizens to apply for social services via a governmental website, such as Temporary Assistance for Needy Families (TANF); Women, Infant, and Children's services (WIC); or temporary disability or unemployment services. Millions of people pay their state and federal taxes each year online.

Perhaps one of the most promising future e-government services is voter registration and elections. Already, states update and operate statewide voter registration databases. Voter registration services and absentee ballot provision through the Internet were tested in multiple states for the 2012 elections, with few reported problems. This is especially important for service members or citizens who are overseas during election time. E-voting is almost instantaneous, as opposed to the paper and postal services, by which ballots can take weeks to arrive at election offices. If e-voting services continue, citizens in every state will have greater access to participate in electoral processes. Not everyone thinks voting should be this accessible; they fear widespread fraud or the inclusion of citizens who may not have voted in the past, which could potentially change the expected outcomes of elections. However, e-voting seems almost inevitable.

However one perceives digital government services, one main shortcoming exists: although e-government encourages participation in governmental processes, a "digital divide" exists within states and localities. Unfortunately, only citizens who are connected to and comfortable with the Internet have access to these new routes of engagement and participation. Those least likely to participate in government are again left behind. The spreading use of e-government services makes shrinking the digital divide an important goal for broadening democracy and creating effective and efficient state services.

CONCLUSION

This chapter has revealed many administrative facets of state government. State government employees are more representative and more educated than they were just twenty years ago, though there is still room for improvement. Administrators play important policy roles as experts, analysts, and advisers. They interact with governors, legislators, staff, and citizens to change or improve state services. These employees provide a broad array of governmental services through hundreds of agencies and departments. They implement public programs through direct state services or collaboration and contracting with private businesses, nonprofit organizations, or other levels of government. Through increases in the use of goal setting, performance evaluation, and e-governance, state administration is more responsive to the public and responsible with public funds than ever before. Even when fiscal stress threatens government services and citizens are frustrated by the inaction of federal and state legislatures, state administration trudges on, sometimes surges on, to professionally govern with and for its citizens.

NOTES

1. Cynthia J. Bowling, "State Government Administration: The Impact of Reform Movements," in *Encyclopedia of Public Administration and Public Policy*, ed. John Gargan (New York: Marcel Dekker, 2003). See also Ann O'M. Bowman and Richard C. Kearney, *The Resurgence of the States* (Englewood Cliffs, NJ: Prentice Hall, 1986).

2. National Association of State Budget Officers and National Governors Association, *The Fiscal Survey of the States* (Washington, DC: NASBO and NGA, 2012); and National Association of State Budget Officers, *State Expenditure Report 2010: Examining Fiscal 2009–2011 State Spending* (Washington, DC: NASBO, 2010).

3. United States Census Bureau. Employment estimates adapted from the *Census of Governments* 1992, 1997, 2002, 2007, and 2011, www.census.gov/govs/cog2012/.

4. Cynthia J. Bowling, "The Role of the Executive Branch in State Politics," in *About the U.S. State Government: The Executive Branch,* ed. Margaret R. Ferguson (Santa Barbara: ABC-CLIO, 2006).

5. Margaret Ferguson, "Governors and the Executive Branch," in *Politics in the American States: A Comparative Analysis,* 10th ed., Virginia Gray, Russell L. Hanson, and Thad Kousser, eds. (Washington, DC: CQ Press, 2012).

6. Cynthia J. Bowling and Deil S. Wright, "Change and Continuity in State Administration: Administrative Leadership across Four Decades," *Public Administration Review* 58 (1998): 429–441.

7. Cynthia J. Bowling and Deil S. Wright, data from the American State Administrators Project, 1964–2008. For information on this project and data, see Jeffrey Brudney, Cynthia J. Bowling, and Deil S. Wright, "Continuity and Change in Public Administration across the Fifty States: Linking Practice, Theory, and Research through the American State Administrators Project, 1964–2008" (e-version), *Public Administration Review* (January/February 2010).

8. Equal Employment Opportunity Commission, State and Local Government Employment (EEO-4), National Employment Summary, 2009, www.eeoc.gov/eeoc/statistics/employment/jobpat-ee04/2009/table3/table3_1_state_.html.

9. Christine Kelleher, Cynthia J. Bowling, Jennifer Jones, and Deil S. Wright, "Women in State Governments: Gender Representation in Legislative, Administrative, and Other Institutions of American Society," in *Book of the States,* ed. Keon Chi (Lexington, KY: Council of State Governments, 2006).

10. Ann O'M. Bowman and Richard C. Kearney, *State and Local Government,* 8th ed. (Boston: Wadsworth. 2012).

11. Ibid.

12. Barry T. Hirsch and David A. Macpherson, "Union Membership and Coverage Database from the Current Population Survey: Note," *Industrial and Labor Relations Review* 56 (2003): 349–354. Adapted from current data taken from unionstats.com.

13. Bowman and Kearney, *State and Local Government.*

14. Brudney, Bowling, and Wright, "Continuity and Change in Public Administration."

15. Norton E. Long, "Power and Administration," *Public Administration Review* 9 (1949): 257–264.

16. Willow Jacobson, Christine Palus, and Cynthia Bowling, "A Woman's Touch? Gendered Management and Performance in State Administration," *Journal of Public Administration Research and Theory* 20 (2010): 477–504.

17. Brudney, Bowling, and Wright, "Continuity and Change in Public Administration"; American State Administrators Project, original data analysis.

18. Ann O'M. Bowman and Richard C. Kearney, "Dimensions of State Government Capability," *Western Political Quarterly* 41 (1988): 341–362.

19. Jeffrey L. Brudney, F. Ted Hebert, and Deil S. Wright, "Reinventing Government in the American States: Measuring and Explaining Administrative Reform," *Public Administration Review* 59 (1999): 19–30.

20. Patricia W. Ingraham, Philip G. Joyce, and Amy Kneedler Donahue, *Government Performance: Why Management Matters* (Baltimore, MD: Johns Hopkins University Press, 2003).

21. Government Performance Project, "Grading the States 2008," www.pewstates.org/projects/government-performance-project-328600.

22. National Association of State Budget Officers, *Budget Processes in the States* (Washington, DC: NASBO, 2008).

23. American State Administrators Project, original data.

SUGGESTED READING

Bowling, Cynthia J. "State Government Administration: The Impact of Reform Movements." In *Encyclopedia of Public Administration and Public Policy,* ed. John Gargan. New York: Marcel Dekker, 2003.

Bowling, Cynthia J., Christine Kelleher, Jennifer Jones, and Deil S. Wright. "Cracked Ceilings, Firmer Floors, and Weakening Walls: Trends and Patterns in Gender Representation among Executives Leading American State Agencies, 1970–2000." *Public Administration Review* 66 (2006): 823–836.

Bowling, Cynthia J., and Deil S. Wright. "Change and Continuity in State Administration: Administrative Leadership across Four Decades." *Public Administration Review* 58 (1998): 429–441.

Bowman, Ann O'M., and Richard C. Kearney. *The Resurgence of the States.* Englewood Cliffs, NJ: Prentice Hall, 1986.

———. *State and Local Government,* 8th ed. Boston: Wadsworth, 2012.

Brudney, Jeffrey L., Cynthia J. Bowling, and Deil S. Wright. "Continuity and Change in Public Administration across the Fifty States: Linking Practice, Theory, and Research through the American State Administrators Project, 1964–2008" (e-version). *Public Administration Review* (January/February 2010).

Brudney, Jeffrey L., F. Ted Hebert, and Deil S. Wright. "Reinventing Government in the American States: Measuring and Explaining Administrative Reform." *Public Administration Review* 59 (1999): 19–30.

Brudney, Jeffrey L., and Deil S. Wright. "Revisiting Administrative Reform in the American State: The Status of Reinventing Government in the 1990s." *Public Administration Review* 62 (2002): 353–361.

Ferguson, Margaret. "Governors and the Executive Branch." In *Politics in the American States: A Comparative Analysis,* 10th ed., Virginia Gray, Russell L. Hanson, and Thad Kousser, eds. Washington, DC: CQ Press, 2013.

Government Performance Project. "Grading the States 2008," www.pewstates.org/projects/government-performance-project-328600.

Ingraham, Patricia W., Philip G. Joyce, and Amy Kneedler Donahue. *Government Performance: Why Management Matters.* Baltimore, MD: Johns Hopkins University Press, 2003.

Jacobson, Willow, Christine Palus, and Cynthia Bowling. "A Woman's Touch? Gendered Management and Performance in State Administration." *Journal of Public Administration Research and Theory* 20 (2010): 477–504.

Kelleher, Christine, Cynthia J. Bowling, Jennifer Jones, and Deil S. Wright. "Women in State Governments: Gender Representation in Legislative, Administrative, and Other Institutions of American Society." In *Book of the States,* ed. Keon Chi. Lexington, KY: Council of State Governments, 2006.

Long, Norton E. "Bureaucracy and Constitutionalism." *American Political Science Review* 46 (1951): 808–818.

———. "Power and Administration." *Public Administration Review* 9 (1949): 257–264.

National Association of State Budget Officers. *Budget Processes in the States.* Washington, DC: NASBO, 2008.

National Association of State Budget Officers and National Governors Association. *The Fiscal Survey of the States.* Washington, DC: NASBO and NGA, 2012.

Weber, Ronald E., and Paul Brace, eds. *American State and Local Politics: Directions for the 21st Century.* London: Chatham House, 1999.

Wright, Deil. "Executive Leadership in State Administration: Interplay of Gubernatorial, Legislative, and Administrative Power." *Midwest Journal of Political Science* 11 (1967): 1–26.

PART VI ★ COURTS

Chapter 20

Organization and Structure of State Courts

Paul Brace

IN THE CONTEMPORARY AMERICAN STATES, THERE are in excess of twenty thousand courts spread over a host of functions and geographical and substantive jurisdictions. In fact, no two states share identical court structures. In numbers and diversity, state court structures present a lot to comprehend, rendering detailed treatments of each court structure incomprehensible for practical purposes. While a state-by-state cataloging of the many differences in state court structures is possible, this would hardly serve the purpose of promoting understanding of the basis for this tremendous diversity. The strategy of this chapter is to illustrate the basic legal traditions and subsequent historical processes that adapted these traditions to fit initial conditions of settlement and subsequent developments within states. Ultimately, state court structures reflect a pragmatic hybridization of traditions and conditions—political, economic, social—resulting in differentially stable and unstable structural features over the course of history in the court systems of the American states.

This chapter begins with some basic understandings of law and the functions of courts in general. This is followed by considering historical contexts: the manner in which law and courts emerged during colonization, the effects of statehood and national expansion, and important forces promoting new contingencies and structural adaptations in select or many states. The interplay of tradition and historical forces then serves as a foundation for exploring diversity in contemporary state court structures. Rather than reflecting grand, rational designs, these structures are more typically a hodgepodge of traditions differentially modified to fit the needs of changed conditions by interests within the states. In most states, traditional anachronisms coincide with partly or wholly realized historical reforms driven by the concerns and interests of various groups of the moment. This discussion concludes with a review of some of the evidence concerning the effects of state judicial structure on judicial behavior and outcomes.

LAW

In a brief discussion, we cannot reasonably investigate the history of law, which is ancient and extensive. Most fundamentally, law is a system of rules enforced by institutions of government to govern behavior. In theory and in practice, the sources of law are varied. To some, the fundamental foundations of law are as embodied in nature, where others believe all law is man-made. Moreover, the production of operative law can be from legislatures in the form of codes (civil law), or from courts based upon their decisions and precedents (common law).

The original foundation of American law and legal process is English common law.[1] Within common law, the highest source of law was not a legislative statute but a "general custom" reflected in the decisions of common law judges. Common law was judge-made law: molded, refined, and changed in the crucible of actual decision, and handed down from generation to generation in the form of reported cases. These laws reflected the values and attitudes of the English people, maintained by judges' reliance on precedent but also modified in response to changing times and patterns of litigation.

While built on the foundations of English common law, many features of the American experience were decidedly different from those addressed by English common law precedents, and much adaptation was necessary both in law and in legal institutions.[2] Moreover, other European traditions from Spain, France, and the Netherlands left civil law legacies in some regions of North America that would ultimately be absorbed into the United States. In the end, English common law was the dominant but not exclusive influence on American law; but it was not a rigid template. The spirit of common law, if not the particulars, promoted adaptation to particular legal contingencies and alternative legal traditions, resulting in much diversity in structure and practice driven by pragmatism.

THE BASIC ELEMENTS OF AMERICAN JUDICIAL PROCESS

In contemporary America, national and state constitutions contain the most fundamental laws. Among other things, contemporary constitutions provide for independent judiciaries, legislatures, and executives. State constitutions also provide the grounds for many legal appeals that state appellate courts address.

Like the federal judiciary, state courts reside within systems of separated powers with comparable functions and limitations. Most fundamentally, courts are independent representatives of the state or community engaged when there is a dispute and at least one of the parties seeks resolution through the court. Courts are passive, reactive institutions: courts may only act on issues brought to them, their focus is largely confined to the issues brought by the litigants, and consequently they act to resolve discrete anomalies in general laws on a case-by-case basis, unlike legislatures that produce comprehensive laws addressing general disputes.

The other central distinguishing feature of contemporary state courts is that they have neither the "purse nor the sword" to enforce compliance with their decisions: where legislatures and executives wield resources to produce positive incentives or negative sanctions, courts must rely on other institutions, or the citizenry, to ensure compliance with their decisions. To make independent as opposed to acquiescent judgments, where compliance might be resisted, courts require the perception of legitimacy among the citizenry and other political actors. When courts are perceived as legitimate, disappointments with specific unpopular decisions do not necessarily destroy overall approval of the judicial institution. Legitimacy is particularly important for courts because a central purpose of an independent judiciary is to maintain minority rights within a majoritarian system, especially those rights that allow political minorities to compete for political power.[3]

There are many disputes in any state, but for courts to act, a party or parties have to pursue resolution in courts. This requires (1) legal grounds for the dispute; (2) a means for litigants to pursue judicial resolution; and (3) a sufficient supply of courts to pursue their disputes. Constitutions, statutes, regulations, or judicial precedents establish the legal grounds for a dispute. Getting to court is an expensive process, and the majority of private disputes are resolved pretrial because the expected costs outweigh the expected benefits of a trial. In criminal cases, prosecutors, almost universally burdened by a surplus of potential cases, must weigh the costs of prosecution of a criminal charge against the alternative of allowing a plea bargain to a lesser charge. Because they are passive institutions, the structure of state court systems establishing the number of courts, their jurisdictions, and the methods for recruiting judges critically determine the perceptions that shape who uses the courts, the types of questions raised, and ultimately the actions that are central to judicial power.

THE ORIGINS OF LAW AND LEGAL PROCESS IN AMERICA

After the fifteenth century, Britain, France, the Netherlands, and Spain sought to exploit the riches of North America. Unlike military conquests for gold and other precious metals, many North American riches, such as tobacco, required investment and labor to cultivate. A critical imperative was creating conditions that could secure investor confidence in the new colonies and attract settlers to provide needed labor. In British colonies, after a period of trial and error, "law" became the solution: the problem was convincing prospective investors or settlers that their interests would enjoy basic protections from avarice and caprice.

The process of how law first emerged in the Virginia Colony is instructive. The colony was a business endeavor, not an exercise in governance. Initially, it was set up as a monopoly that controlled all assets, including land; regulated even minute economic transactions within the colony to ensure that profits accrued to the Virginia Company, and not individuals; and required settlers to work for the colony and not themselves, using coercion instead of free-market incentives. The results were disastrous: settlers were idle, conflict raged within, and threats loomed from native populations without. Starvation was rampant.

Idleness and conflict rendered the commercial venture a disaster. To address this problem, the Company imposed Sir Thomas Dale's *Lawes Divine, Moral and Martial* in 1611.[4] Dale's Code was only more oppressive than it was arbitrary in its brutal punishments. It imposed the death penalty for any individuals engaging in exchange, theft, sedition, sodomy, and numerous other crimes. Whipping, tongue piercing, cutting off of ears or arms, binding, and similar savage punishments were inflicted for improper dumping of laundry water, an unclean residence, or having a bed an inappropriate height off the floor. Perhaps most notably, the Code went to great lengths to specify punishments for idleness.

While seeking to impose order, this Code discouraged migration to the colony and was quickly abandoned in 1619 when it was announced that free settlers would live under the same free laws of England. In addition, to attract new settlers and reduce the need for importing costly provisions from England, private property was offered to colonists. With expanded private property and enterprise came a host of new questions and grounds for disputes over property rights and commercial activity.

The common law of England would be the foundation for the colonies. The building blocks of common law were precedents established in past decisions developed from formal adversarial legal processes containing trial by jury, the writ (documents petitioners needed to set legal processes in motion), the summons (a formal notice for a defendant to appear in court), written pleadings (the petitioners' legal arguments), and oral testimony.

England's common law was complex and commonly ill-suited to the particulars of Virginia or the legal skills of those trying to apply it. The practice and substance of common law was narrow: it was overwhelmingly aristocratic law developed by the Royal Courts of Justice that handled the legal problems of a tiny group of gentry and nobility drawn from the top of English society, principally concerning land. It could not address the substance or scope of vital features of the colonial setting: broader land ownership and participation in commerce; broad use of contracts of indentured migrants; and, most notably, the institution of slavery, which was not addressed at all. There were few to no lawyers in Virginia early on, and legal practice and process would develop from the vague familiarities of those involved with general or local English legal traditions with which they were familiar. In sum, there could be no simple and direct reception of the law or legal institutions and practices from England. The result was a hybridization of law and legal institutions to fit local needs, interests, and backgrounds. Other English colonies would repeat this pattern. They developed diverse laws, lawmaking processes, and legal practices that paralleled Virginia but also reflected unique contingencies operating within.[5] In general, the colonies began with simple, undifferentiated structures and later developed more complex systems, with more division of labor.

Colonial challenges were many, and they began in a perilous legal vacuum. Nascent popular assemblies were only beginning to produce legal statutes, and England's common law precedents were little understood and ill-suited in many instances. The early development of colonial legal institutions, processes, and laws was not driven by high-minded concepts of freedom, liberty, or popular consent. Instead, order, profit, and the accumulation of wealth for settlers and investors drove the transformation of the colony's law. The rule of law mattered less because of its particular content and more because its content was known, fixed, and not subject to arbitrary change. The colonists developed their courts in the pragmatic pursuit of order within the context of local conditions, yielding tremendous diversity in judicial institutions, practices, and laws. These colonial legal traditions would be a fundamental element shaping the distinctiveness and independence of what would become states after the Revolution.

MAJOR HISTORICAL INFLUENCES ON STATE COURT STRUCTURES

Statehood and Constitutions

The original states had in theory the option to write or not write constitutions. In actuality, states embarked on constitution-making earlier than the federal government. A first order of business in the new states was to pass reception statutes, maintaining adherence to the legal principles developed before the Revolution where they did not conflict with their new constitutions. No two state constitutions were ever exactly alike, yet none was purely innovative. States routinely copied one another, and popular clauses or provisions tended to spread everywhere. Rather than reinventing the wheel, new states found it efficient to borrow selectively from other (state or federal) constitutions to fit their particular needs. The hybridized common law colonial legal traditions were largely mimicked by new states but adapted to their particular needs.

The Northwest Ordinance (1787) explicitly imposed common law on the lands of the American frontier, but not without notable resistance in some territories. These territories, formerly controlled by France, the Netherlands, and Spain, had operated under civil-law legal systems reflecting these countries' legal traditions. In general, the role of the judiciary in civil law systems was much more subordinate than in England's common law traditions. Civil law judges were afforded less discretion in determining the law: they were part of large bureaucracies intended for administering colonial possessions. These territories would become Alabama, Arizona, Arkansas, California, Florida, Illinois, Indiana, Louisiana, Michigan, Mississippi, Missouri, New Mexico, and Texas, and some of their civil law traditions linger to this day. Moreover, recent research suggests that civil law experiences had a lasting impact on the future balance of power between legislatures and courts in these states. Research on contemporary state court systems indicates that states with civil law origins exhibit lower levels of judicial independence than common law states, and were more likely to adopt intermediate appellate courts than were common law states.[6]

The early constitutions not only varied in content; they would also differ in resilience. Unlike the U.S. Constitution, many (but not all) state constitutions have been replaced over the course of the nation's history. Consequently, the foundations of the judicial power within states and attendant structural features have changed, as have many of the fundamental laws under which courts operate. State constitutions also vary substantially in their length and policy content. (For the number of constitutions per state, along with other details, see Chapter 2.)

Taken together, we may broadly assay the complex of forces shaping the foundations of state court structures. The adaptation of vague notions of English common law filtered through initial conditions of settlement that reflected both the needs and interests of initial settlers. Hybrid structures and processes to legitimize local processes that established traditions carried through the Revolution and initial statehood. The fundamentals—adversarial, trial, appeal, hierarchy, judicial independence—were codified in the U.S.

Constitution, and similar if nonetheless distinctive forms within the states. New states would expand the basic common law foundations and often mimicked the constitutions of existing states. This process was not uniform, however, as civil law territories proved resistant to the common law model, and these traditions have left a lingering impact on contemporary state court structures.

Governmental Reforms

The experience of the former colonies with royal governors and the judges they appointed to Crown courts promoted an initial aversion to these institutions and a strong commitment to legislative institutions. Governors were made institutionally weak, and judges were appointed and retained (or not) by legislatures. At its founding, America was overwhelmingly a nation comprised of insular local communities, isolated by distance and primitive means of transportation and communication. The dominant concern of most state governments in this period was the promotion of infrastructure to better integrate outlying areas into the economy by lowering transportation costs.

Transportation infrastructure was commonly pursued through state public finance to build roads and bridges, and later, steamships and railroads. State legislatures, reluctant to pass taxes, pursued these endeavors through special corporations conferring benefits on private contractors, and massive debt financing. Legislatures took on massive unsecured debts and conferred many special privileges on private firms to produce infrastructure transportation projects in roads and canals, and later, steamboats and railroads. This led to an economic revolution in some vicinities, but in others the projects were ill-conceived and unsuccessful: the enticing politics of unsecured debt financing was not consistent with realities in the economics of infrastructure operations. Ultimately, this public finance came to a crashing halt with the economic depression that began in 1839 as many states defaulted on their debts. A severely depressed economy and the retreat of vitally needed foreign capital created a crisis of legitimacy for states resulting in calls for fundamental reforms in government.

Widespread legal reform resulted between 1842 and 1852; eleven states adopted new constitutions placing greater limits on government power generally, and legislative power more specifically.[7] The focus of much of these reform efforts was directed at state legislatures, seen as causing the crisis. Logrolling had produced undisciplined indebtedness and expenditure, as well as many monopolies and special privileges for private actors.

Due to fear of the corruption of legislatures and the corrosive effects of unchecked power, constitutions became more rigid, codifying super laws that precluded legislative norms; new state constitutions replaced legislative dominance with more balanced and differentiated government, with each branch identified by its function. Governments became more differentiated; courts assumed a larger, more independent role. Dissatisfaction with legislative politics created a vacuum in state governance, and courts assumed new and growing power over legislation. Questions about controlling state government and separation of powers coincided with interests in popular control, much of it stimulated by Jacksonian impulses to hold those in power electorally accountable. As judicial power grew, reformers had a different interest: they were interested in freeing courts from legislatures and governors, and many states instituted judicial elections to provide courts with an independent power base.[8]

This period left many lasting legacies. Revolutions in transportation and communication would radically transform the localized economies of the earliest period. This created new private endeavors of increasing scope and power that would play a growing role in law and litigation thereafter.[9] Constitutional change created new opportunities for judicial power, and change in judicial selection would produce a stronger political foundation for their authority. While it would take until the latter part of the nineteenth century, this heightened independence would allow judicial review of legislative actions to flower, with state supreme courts being bolder and more inventive than federal courts.

Legal Codification and Court Modernization Movements

The common law and its substantive and procedural traditions provided critical foundations for law in America, yet common law was huge and shapeless, with principles extracted from a jungle of words. The codification movement sought to remedy this situation by identifying basic rules of law and assembling them in a simple and sensible code.

Other judicial reforms were embodied in what has been called the "court modernization agenda," which included the following: (1) consolidated, simplified, and standardized trial and appellate court structures; (2) centralized systems of court management and administration; (3) rationalized court rulemaking and standardized procedures; (4) centralized court budgeting; (5) full state funding of state and local courts; (6) formal structures and procedures for disciplining and removing judges for misbehavior or disability; and (7) the nonpartisan "Missouri" or "Merit Plan" of judicial selection.[10]

States variously ignored codification or modernization agendas, adopted selected elements, or embraced one or both comprehensively. Moreover, these movements persist in many states today. Combining the complete, partial, or lack of reform across the states with their already variegated state court systems, the result is a seemingly mystifying level of differences in state court systems.

THE STRUCTURE OF CONTEMPORARY STATE COURTS

As noted, state courts were initiated as hybrids. Subsequent events, political conflicts, and variable adoptions of reforms have culminated in structures with variable emphases on geographical and functional specialization, and notable differences in the relative dependence of courts on other political institutions or voters. These patterns are evident in both state trial and appellate court structures. In a brief presentation, it would be impossible to illustrate all of the structural differences in state courts. Instead, some select but important differences are described below.

Table 20.1 illustrates some of the major state court reforms. From the nation's inception, states have experimented with their court structures, including methods of selecting judges and the relative power of courts. Table 20.2 illustrates the resulting variation in judicial selection systems currently operating in the American states: eight systems currently operate among the states, and more than one system operates in some states. (For more on judicial selection, see Chapter 21.)

TABLE 20.1 **Notable Innovations or Reforms of State Court Structures**

Year	Feature	State
1777	Judicial election	Vermont
1840–1850s	Constitutional revisions weakening legislatures	11 states
1847	Partisan judicial elections	New York
1848	Legal codification	New York
1875	Special appellate court	Missouri
1877	Creation of intermediate appellate court	Illinois
1911	Nonpartisan judicial elections	California, Ohio
1940	Merit selection	Missouri

SOURCE: David B. Rottman and Shauna M. Strickland, U.S. Department of Justice, Office of Justice Programs, Bureau of Justice Statistics, "State Court Organization," August 15, 2006, http://bjs.ojp.usdoj.gov/index.cfm?ty=pbdetail&iid=1204.

TABLE 20.2 **Judicial Selection Today**

State Judicial Selection Systems as of 1990	
System	**State**
Appointment by governor	Maine, Massachusetts, New Hampshire, New Jersey
Appointment by legislature	Rhode Island, South Carolina, Virginia
Partisan election	Alabama, Arkansas, Mississippi, North Carolina, Tennessee, Texas, West Virginia
Nonpartisan election	Georgia, Idaho, Kentucky, Louisiana, Michigan, Minnesota, Montana, Nevada, North Dakota, Ohio, Oregon, Washington, Wisconsin
Appointment by governor from list assembled by nonpartisan nominating commission	Connecticut, Delaware, New York
Initial appointment by governor, retention via uncontested retention election	California, Vermont
Initial partisan election, retention via uncontested retention election	Illinois, Pennsylvania
Merit plan	Alaska, Arizona, Colorado, Florida, Hawaii, Indiana, Iowa, Kansas, Maryland, Missouri, Nebraska, New Mexico, Oklahoma, South Dakota, Utah, Wyoming

SOURCE: David B. Rottman and Shauna M. Strickland, U.S. Department of Justice, Office of Justice Programs, Bureau of Justice Statistics, "State Court Organization," August 15, 2006, http://bjs.ojp.usdoj.gov/index.cfm?ty=pbdetail&iid=1204.

Figure 20.1 illustrates the vast differences in size and jurisdiction of state trial courts. The smallest trial court system is in South Dakota, with 38 trial courts. Contrast this with Texas, with 3,074 trial courts. Not surprisingly, the number of trial courts correlates with state population (r = .74). State variation in trial court organization and in limited jurisdiction trial courts is also vast: in most states, the number of trial courts that are functionally or geographically limited exceeds that of general jurisdiction trial courts; California, Illinois, Iowa, and Minnesota have only general jurisdiction trial courts. States also exhibit substantial variability in types of state trial courts and use of specialty courts, as illustrated in Chapter 22.

It is common to classify state appellate court structures into two categories: those with and without intermediate appellate courts. Inspection of Table 20.3 reveals much more diversity in these structures. All states have single courts of last resort (COLRs) except Oklahoma and Texas, which have two COLRs with functional specializations in criminal and civil cases. Eleven states have no intermediate appellate courts, four states have two intermediate appellate courts, and the remaining states have one intermediate appellate court.

State appellate court structures have also been differentially sensitive to geographic concerns. Nine states select their COLRs based on geography, and fourteen states select their intermediate appellate courts on a geographic basis. Additionally, eight COLRs and nineteen intermediate appellate courts meet based on geographic as opposed to at-large locations.

Some state appellate courts also have functional specializations. As noted above, Oklahoma and Texas have separate COLRs for criminal and civil appeals. Six states have intermediate appellate courts (IACs) with functionally specialized jurisdictions. Alabama and Oklahoma have IACs devoted to civil appeals, Alabama and Tennessee have IACs specializing in criminal appeals, and Maryland has an IAC devoted to special appeals.

Table 20.4 presents differences in the size, terms of office, and authority to issue advisory opinions of state appellate courts. The number of judges serving on state supreme courts varies from five to nine members; the terms of office on appellate courts range from six years to life. In ten states, their supreme courts have the authority to issue advisory opinions to legislatures, commenting on the constitutionality of proposed measures. Rather than passing a law and waiting for a legal challenge to its constitutionality, this advisory procedure can help to resolve these issues before finalizing a law.

Differences in state court appellate systems also appear in the governance of state judicial branches (see Table 20.5). Thirty-four states designate the chief justice of their state supreme court as the formal head of their judicial branch, fifteen states designate their state supreme courts as a whole as heads of their judicial branch, and Utah has a judicial council to perform this role. Beyond this, states differ in the formal basis for this authority: in thirty-five states this authority is established in their state constitutions, while in fifteen states this authority is established by legislative statute.

Considering state court structures comprehensively, there are clearly many more differences than similarities. Trial structures differ dramatically in size, functions, and geographic consideration. Above this, closer inspection of state appellate court structures reveals that rather than two (or three) basic types; there are instead eighteen different combinations of appellate court structures when geographic and functional specializations are taken into consideration. Differences in court structures only multiply when the methods for selecting judges (see Table 20.2), the size and terms of office (Table 20.3), and formal basis for leading state judiciaries (Table 20.5) are considered. In sum, there is such substantial variation in function, geographic attention, method of selection, and governance as to render no two states' court structures alike.

SOME EFFECTS OF COURT STRUCTURE

Clearly, state court structures differ in many ways: size, jurisdiction (general, geographical, and functional), appellate structure, professionalization, and methods of selection, among others. The important question is whether these differences are mere historical or state idiosyncrasies, akin to state flowers or state birds, or if structural differences among the states significantly influence judicial processes and outcomes. While the enormous diversity of state court systems yields a vast array of untapped questions about state court structural effects, a substantial and growing body of scholarship provides evidence that state court structures play a significant role in shaping the operations and influence of state judiciaries.

State courts are defined by state constitutions, and these constitutions also serve as the basis for litigant claims in trials and appeals. Initial research indicates that variations in civil litigation are significantly increased when state constitutions contain more particularistic policy content.[11] State constitutional provisions also shape state supreme court decision making in death penalty cases.[12]

We have learned that state court systems are highly decentralized, with differing connections to local geography. In their study of medium-sized trial courts, James Eisenstein, Roy B. Flemming, and Peter Nardulli observe that local political influences and community values affect these courts in many ways. Local officials determine their resources, make up their staff, and manage operations so as to fit local needs. In combination, norms shaped by local

FIGURE 20.1 **Number and Jurisdictions of State Trial Courts**

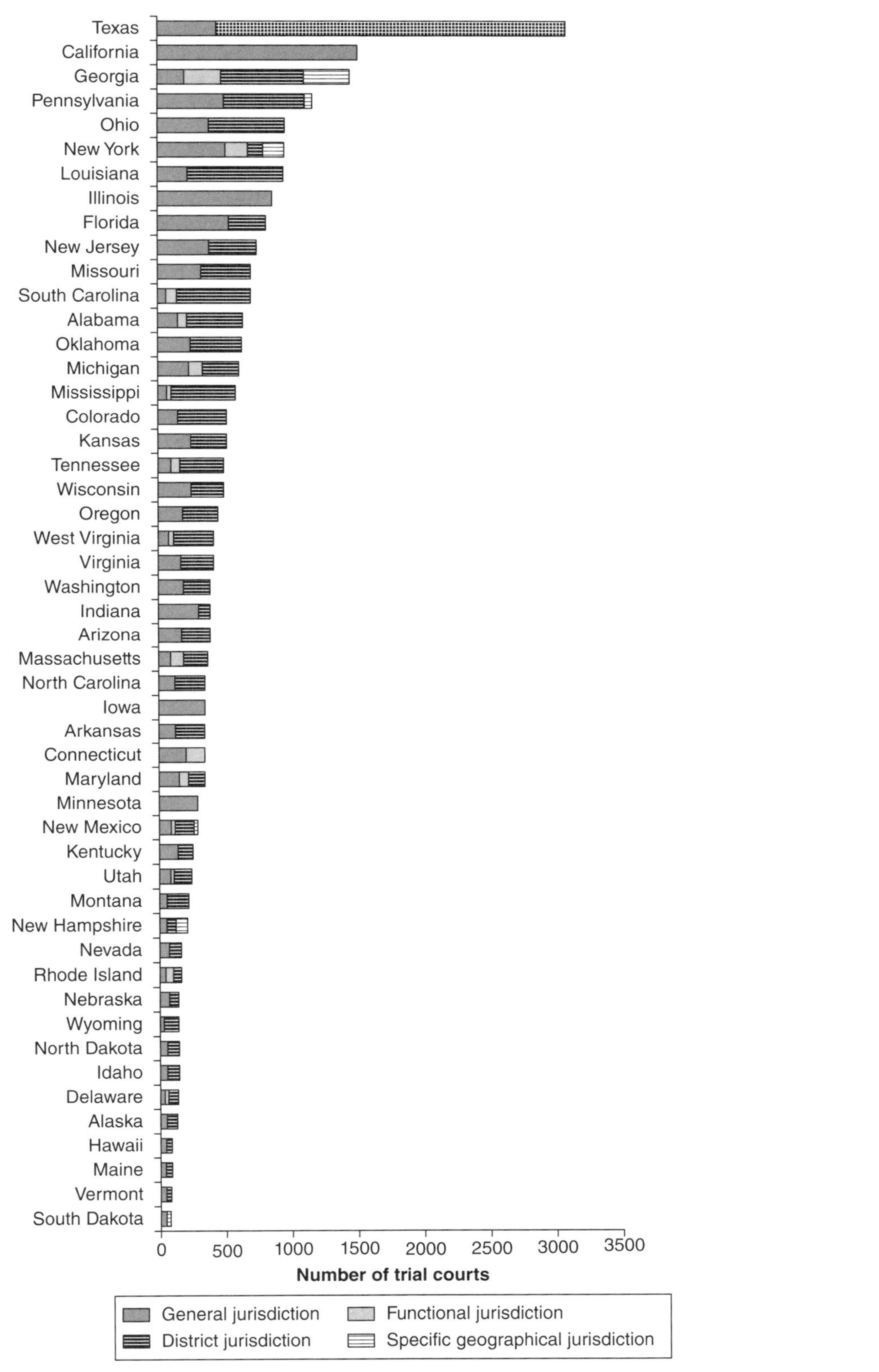

SOURCE: David B. Rottman and Shauna M. Strickland, U.S. Department of Justice, Office of Justice Programs, Bureau of Justice Statistics, "State Court Organization," August 15, 2006, http://bjs.ojp.usdoj.gov/index.cfm?ty=pbdetail&iid=1204.

TABLE 20.3 **State Appellate Court Structure and Jurisdiction**

State	Number of courts of last resort	Number of intermediate appellate courts	Court(s) of last resort selected by geography	Intermediate appellate courts selected by geography	Court(s) of last resort meet by geography	Intermediate appellate courts meet by geography
Delaware	1	0	N	NA	N	NA
Maine	1	0	N	NA	N	NA
Montana	1	0	N	NA	N	NA
North Dakota	1	0	N	NA	N	NA
New Hampshire	1	0	N	NA	N	NA
Nevada	1	0	N	NA	N	NA
Rhode Island	1	0	N	NA	N	NA
Vermont	1	0	N	NA	N	NA
West Virginia	1	0	N	NA	N	NA
Wyoming	1	0	N	NA	N	NA
South Dakota	1	0	Y	NA	N	NA
Arkansas	1	1	N	N	N	N
Arizona	1	1	N	N	N	N
Connecticut	1	1	N	N	N	N
Georgia	1	1	N	N	N	N
Hawaii	1	1	N	N	N	N
Iowa	1	1	N	N	N	N
Massachusetts	1	1	N	N	N	N
North Carolina	1	1	N	N	N	N
Ohio	1	1	N	N	N	N
Oregon	1	1	N	N	N	N
South Carolina	1	1	N	N	N	N
Utah	1	1	N	N	N	N
Kansas	1	1	N	N	N	Y
Minnesota	1	1	N	N	N	Y
New Jersey	1	1	N	N	N	Y
New Mexico	1	1	N	N	N	Y
New York	1	1	N	N	N	Y
Virginia	1	1	N	N	N	Y
Alaska	1	1	N	N	Y	N
Colorado	1	1	N	N	Y	N
Idaho	1	1	N	N	Y	Y
California	1	1	N	N	Y	Y
Missouri	1	1	N	Y	N	N

State	Number of courts of last resort	Number of intermediate appellate courts	Court(s) of last resort selected by geography	Intermediate appellate courts selected by geography	Court(s) of last resort meet by geography	Intermediate appellate courts meet by geography
Michigan	1	1	N	Y	N	Y
Washington	1	1	N	Y	N	Y
Wisconsin	1	1	N	Y	N	Y
Florida	1	1	Y	Y	N	Y
Kentucky	1	1	Y	Y	N	Y
Louisiana	1	1	Y	Y	N	Y
Maryland	1	1	Y	Y	N	N
Mississippi	1	1	Y	Y	N	N
Nebraska	1	1	Y	Y	N	N
Illinois	1	1	Y	Y	Y	Y
Alabama	1	2	N	N	N	N
Indiana	1	2	N	Y	N	N
Pennsylvania	1	2	N	N	Y	Y
Tennessee	1	2	N	N	Y	Y
Oklahoma	2	1	Y	Y	N	Y
Texas	2	1	N	Y	Y	Y

SOURCE: David B. Rottman and Shauna M. Strickland, U.S. Department of Justice, Office of Justice Programs, Bureau of Justice Statistics, "State Court Organization," August 15, 2006, http://bjs.ojp.usdoj.gov/index.cfm?ty=pbdetail&iid=1204.

attorneys, clerks, and other court personnel create a local legal culture that influences court operations.[13]

States differ substantially in the basic structural features of their courts. The presence of intermediate appellate courts significantly affects variations in court outcomes.[14] Numerous studies indicate that state court structure influences the levels of consensus on courts.[15] Research also reveals that state court structure influences the types of cases litigated and the outcomes of those cases.[16] Structural differences in state supreme courts such as how they are selected and the presence of intermediate appellate courts, among others, influence their policy-making powers and the conditions under which they review and invalidate state laws.[17]

We also observed considerable variation in the procedures used for selecting judges in the states. A long and growing

Nevada Supreme Court chief justice Kristina Pickering addresses state lawmakers at the Legislative Building in Carson City, Nevada, on March 1, 2013. Pickering's address focused on the work of Nevada's trial courts, the supreme court, and the importance of an intermediate appellate court as proposed in a pending constitutional amendment.

SOURCE: AP Photo/Cathleen Allison.

TABLE 20.4 **Number of Appellate Court Judges, Terms of Office, and Advisory Opinion Authority**

State	Type of court	Court name	Number of judges	Length of term (years)	Number of supreme court members	Supreme Court offers advisory opinions about legislation
Alabama	SC	Supreme Court	9	6	9	Y
	IA	Court of Civil Appeals	5	6		
	IA	Court of Criminal Appeals	5	6		
Alaska	SC	Supreme Court	5	10	5	N
	IA	Court of Appeals	3	8		
Arizona	SC	Supreme Court	5	6	5	N
	IA	Court of Appeals	22	6		
Arkansas	SC	Supreme Court	7	8	7	N
	IA	Court of Appeals	12	8		
California	SC	Supreme Court	7	12	7	N
	IA	Courts of Appeal	88	12		
Colorado	SC	Supreme Court	7	10	7	Y
	IA	Court of Appeals	16	8		
Connecticut	SC	Supreme Court	7	8	7	N
	IA	Appellate Court	9	8		
Delaware	SC	Supreme Court	5	12	5	Y
Florida	SC	Supreme Court	7	6	7	Y
	IA	District Courts of Appeal	62	6		
Georgia	SC	Supreme Court	7	6	7	N
	IA	Court of Appeals	12	6		
Hawaii	SC	Supreme Court	5	10	5	N
	IA	Intermediate Court of Appeals	6	10		
Idaho	SC	Supreme Court	5	6	5	N
	IA	Court of Appeals	3	6		
Illinois	SC	Supreme Court	7	10	7	N
	IA	Appellate Court	53	10		
Indiana	SC	Supreme Court	5	Up to 12	5	N
	IA	Court of Appeals	15	Up to 12		
	IA	Tax Court	1	Up to 12		
Iowa	SC	Supreme Court	7	8	9	N
	IA	Court of Appeals	9	6		
Kansas	SC	Supreme Court	7	6	7	N
	IA	Court of Appeals	12	4		

State	Type of court	Court name	Number of judges	Length of term (years)	Number of supreme court members	Supreme Court offers advisory opinions about legislation
Kentucky	SC	Supreme Court	7	8	7	N
	IA	Court of Appeals	14	8		
Louisiana	SC	Supreme Court	7	10	7	N
	IA	Courts of Appeal	53	10		
Maine	SC	Supreme Judicial Court	7	7	7	Y
Maryland	SC	Court of Appeals	7	10	7	N
	IA	Court of Special Appeals	13	10		
Massachusetts	SC	Supreme Judicial Court	7	Until age 70	7	Y
	IA	Appeals Court	28	Until age 70		
Michigan	SC	Supreme Court	7	8	7	Y
	IA	Court of Appeals	28	6		
Minnesota	SC	Supreme Court	7	6	7	N
	IA	Court of Appeals	16	6		
Mississippi	SC	Supreme Court	9	8	9	N
	IA	Court of Appeals	10	8		
Missouri	SC	Supreme Court	7	12	7	N
	IA	Court of Appeals	32	12		
Montana	SC	Supreme Court	7	8	7	N
Nebraska	SC	Supreme Court	7	At least 3	7	N
	IA	Court of Appeals	6	At least 3		
Nevada	SC	Supreme Court	7	6	5	N
New Hampshire	SC	Supreme Court	5	5	5	Y
New Jersey	SC	Supreme Court	7	7 (+ tenure)	7	N
	IA	Superior Court, Appellate Div.	35	7 (+ tenure)		
New Mexico	SC	Supreme Court	5	8	5	N
	IA	Court of Appeals	10	8		
New York	SC	Court of Appeals	7	14	7	N
	IA	Supreme Court, Appellate Div.	57	5 or duration		
North Carolina	SC	Supreme Court	7	8	7	N
	IA	Court of Appeals	15	8		
North Dakota	SC	Supreme Court	5	10	5	N

(Continued)

(Continued)

State	Type of court	Court name	Number of judges	Length of term (years)	Number of supreme court members	Supreme Court offers advisory opinions about legislation
Ohio	SC	Supreme Court	7	6	7	N
	IA	Courts of Appeals	68	6		
Oklahoma	SC	Supreme Court	9	6	9	N
	SC	Court of Criminal Appeals	5	6		
	IA	Court of Civil Appeals	10	6		
Oregon	SC	Supreme Court	7	6	7	N
	IA	Court of Appeals	10	6		
Pennsylvania	SC	Supreme Court	7	10	7	N
	IA	Superior Court	23	10		
	IA	Commonwealth Court	9	10		
	IA	Court of Appeals	39	16		
Rhode Island	SC	Supreme Court	5	Life	5	Y
South Carolina	SC	Supreme Court	5	10	5	N
	IA	Court of Appeals	10	6		
South Dakota	SC	Supreme Court	5	8	5	Y
Tennessee	SC	Supreme Court	5	8	5	N
	SC	Court of Appeals	12	8		
	IA	Court of Criminal Appeals	12	8		
Texas	SC	Supreme Court	9	6	9	N
	SC	Court of Criminal Appeals	9	6		
	IA	Courts of Appeals	80	6		
Utah	SC	Supreme Court	5	10	5	N
	IA	Court of Appeals	7	6		
Vermont	SC	Supreme Court	5	6	5	N
Virginia	SC	Supreme Court	7	12	7	N
	IA	Court of Appeals	11	8		
Washington	SC	Supreme Court	9	6	9	N
	IA	Courts of Appeals	22	6		
West Virginia	SC	Supreme Court of Appeals	5	12	5	N
Wisconsin	SC	Supreme Court	7	10	7	N
	IA	Court of Appeals	16	6		
Wyoming	SC	Supreme Court	5	8	5	N

SOURCE: David B. Rottman and Shauna M. Strickland, U.S. Department of Justice, Office of Justice Programs, Bureau of Justice Statistics, "State Court Organization," August 15, 2006, http://bjs.ojp.usdoj.gov/index.cfm?ty=pbdetail&iid=1204.

TABLE 20.5 **Governance of the Judicial Branch**

State	Who is the head of the judicial branch?			What authority establishes the head of the judicial branch?			Source of authority
	Supreme court chief justice	Supreme court	Other	Constitution	Statute	Other	
Alabama	X			X			AL Const. AM 328 § 6.10
Alaska	X			X			AK Const. Art IV § 16
Arizona	X			X			AZ Const. Art VI § 3
Arkansas		X		X			AR Const. Amend. 80
California	X			X			CA Const. Art VI § 6
Colorado	X			X			CO Const. Art VI § 5
Connecticut	X				X		C.G.S. § 51-1b(a)
Delaware	X			X			DE Const. Art IV § 13
Florida	X			X			FL Const. Art V § 2
Georgia		X		X			GA Const. Art 6 § 9 Para. 1
Hawaii	X			X			HI Const. Art VI § 6
Idaho		X		X			ID Const. Art 5 § 2
Illinois	X			X			IL Const. Art 6 § 16
Indiana	X			X	X		IN Const. Art VII § 3
Iowa		X		X	X		IA Const. Art V § 4; Iowa Code § 602.1201
Kansas	X			X	X		KS Const. Art III § 1; K.S. § 20101
Kentucky	X			X			KY Const. § 110(5(b)
Louisiana	X			X			LA Const. Art V § 6
Maine	X				X		4 M.R.S.A. § 1
Maryland	X			X			MD Const. Art IV § 18B
Massachusetts		X		X	X		MGL C.h. 211 § 3; MA Const. Pt. I, Art 29
Michigan		X		X			MI Const. Art VI § 3-4
Minnesota	X				X		MS § 2.724 Subd. 4
Mississippi	X				X		MSC § 9-3-61; V9-3-39; § 9-21-3
Missouri		X		X			MO Const. Art V § 4
Montana		X		X			MT Const. Art VII § 2
Nebraska	X			X			NE Const. Art V § 1
Nevada	X			X			NV Const. Art VI § 19
New Hampshire	X			X			NH Const. Pt. 2 Art. 73-A
New Jersey	X			X			NJ Const. Art 6 § 7 Pt. 1
New Mexico		X		X			NM Const. Art 6 § 3
New York	X			X			NY Const. Art VI § 28
North Carolina		X		X	X		NC Const. Art IV § 13; NCGS § 7A 33, 34
North Dakota	X			X	X		ND Const. Art VI, 33; NDCC § 27-02-05.1
Ohio	X			X			OH Const. Art IV § 5

(Continued)

(Continued)

State	Who is the head of the judicial branch?			What authority establishes the head of the judicial branch?			Source of authority
	Supreme court chief justice	Supreme court	Other	Constitution	Statute	Other	
Oklahoma	X			X			OK Const. Art 7 § 6
Oregon	X				X		ORS § 1.002 (1)
Pennsylvania		X		X			PA Const. Art V § 10; 42 Pa.C.S. Sec. 1701
Rhode Island	X				X		RI GL § 8-15-2
South Carolina	X			X			SC Const. Art V § 4
South Dakota	X			X			SD Const. Art V § 11
Tennessee		X			X	Judicial branch rule	TCA 16-3-501-502; S. Ct. R. 11
Texas		X		X	X		TX Const. Art 5 § 31; TX Gov't Code Ch. 74
Utah			Judicial Council	X			UT Const. Art 8 § 12
Vermont		X		X			VT Const. Ch. II § 30
Virginia	X			X			VA Const. Art VI § 4
Washington		X		X			WA Const. Art 4 § 1
West Virginia	X			X			WV Const. Art 8 § 3
Wisconsin	X			X			WI Const. Art 7 § 4 (3)
Wyoming	X			X	X		WY Const. Art 5 § 2; W.S. § 52-102

SOURCE: David B. Rottman and Shauna M. Strickland, U.S. Department of Justice, Office of Justice Programs, Bureau of Justice Statistics, "State Court Organization," August 15, 2006, http://bjs.ojp.usdoj.gov/index.cfm?ty=pbdetail&iid=1204.

body of research indicates judicial selection systems make judges more or less independent from other political institutions, or the electorate. In general, elections condition the effects of legal and external influences on courts, selecting judges that are consistent with state electoral and ideological environments.[18] (For more on the effects of judicial selection methods, see Chapter 21.)

Court resources are an important component of court professionalization, shown to vary dramatically among states.[19] Numerous empirical studies underscore the significance of state court professionalism on various dimensions of court performance. The reputation of state supreme courts,[20] their intensity of citation between other courts,[21] and their informational capacity and civil case decisions are conditioned by their professionalization.[22]

Combined, these and other studies provide compelling evidence that state courts are influenced by external and internal structures that shape their legal environments, their jurisdictions, the manner in which judges are recruited, and their resources. These attributes, in turn, are shown to significantly influence the issues state courts address, outcomes, levels of consensus, court reputations, and their transmission of precedent.

The outputs of courts are central: they reveal the scope, quantity, and quality of their activities and capture a major dimension of judicial power within the states. This brief survey of empirical research on court structures makes it clear that these structures shape the volume of their activities, the issues they address, the direction and degree of consensus of their decisions, the legal impact of those decisions, and their comparative reputations. While not the exclusive determinant of state judicial activities and power, state court structures are central elements that condition the scope of their influence.

CONCLUSION

State court structures share fundamental origins in common law derived from functional needs for dispute settlement; however, they reflect vast differences in details stemming from the initial conditions of settlement and the varying impact of subsequent innovations in governance generally, and in adjudication specifically, spanning over two centuries of thought about governance in state politics. The final product is state court systems that are differentially sensitive to functional and geographic specializations, and to alternative concerns about judicial independence.

The structural characteristics of state court systems evolving from these distinctive patterns of institutional development are consequential. Judicial outcomes are shaped by the characteristics of the judges selected to serve in these systems and by the institutional constraints operating on these judges. Moreover, state court structures condition the degree of consensus among judges about those outcomes, or the clarity of law. Beyond this, patterns of litigation are more than a simple sample of justiciable disputes within states; they reflect strategic considerations by litigants shaped by the institutional designs of their state court structures.

In the end, today's judicial outcomes are at least partly a reflection of the cumulative effect of history on the institutional development of state court structures. For a state's resident today with a potentially justiciable issue, the fate of this dispute will reflect the supply of courts; their jurisdictions; the proclivities of the judges serving on those courts; the appellate structure of those courts; and how these alternative courts are, or are not, constrained by judge selection, appellate structure, and other institutional contingencies. State court structures may be more or less attractive for litigants, drawing certain types of cases while discouraging others, ultimately producing case outcomes that reflect the strategies of litigants, and mixtures of judge preferences, the law, and the conditioning effects of institutional structures on the judges producing those outcomes.

NOTES

1. This history of American law is voluminous. This summary is derived from Lawrence Friedman, *A History of American Law,* 3rd ed. (New York: Simon and Schuster, 2005); Kermit L. Hall and Peter Karsten, *Magic Mirror: Law in American History* (New York: Oxford University Press, 1989); William E. Nelson, *Americanization of the Common Law: The Impact of Legal Change on Massachusetts Society, 1760–1830* (Cambridge, MA: Harvard University Press, 1975).

2. For the adoption of common law in America, see Nelson, *Americanization of the Common Law.*

3. For a review of the extensive literature on legitimacy, see James Gibson, *The Campaigns of Judges and the Legitimacy of Courts: Do Judicial Elections Really Stink?* (Chicago: University of Chicago Press, forthcoming).

4. For Dale's Code and the adoption of common law in America, see D. T. Konig, "Dale's Laws and the Non-Common Law Origins of Criminal Justice in Virginia," *American Journal of Legal History* 26 (1982): 354–375.

5. On legal cartography, see Christopher Tomlins, "The Legal Cartography of Colonization, the Legal Polyphony of Settlement: English Intrusions on the American Mainland in the Seventeenth Century," *Law and Social Inquiry* 26 (2001): 315–372; for legal origins, see Edward L. Glaeser and Andrei Shleifer, "Legal Origins," *Quarterly Journal of Economics* 117 (2002): 1193–1229.

6. Daniel Berkowitz and Karen B. Clay, *The Evolution of a Nation: How Geography and Law Shaped the American States* (Princeton, NJ: Princeton University Press, 2012).

7. John Wallis, "Constitutions, Corporations, and Corruption: American States and Constitutional Change, 1842 to 1852," *Journal of Economic History* 65 (2009): 211–256.

8. On the development of state judicial independence, see Andrew Hanssen, "Learning about Judicial Independence: Institutional Change in the State Courts," *Journal of Legal Studies* 33 (2004): 431–473.

9. Major events and patterns of state economic development, and related literature, are reviewed in Paul Brace, "State Economic Development," in *Oxford Handbook of State and Local Government,* ed. Donald Haider-Markel (New York: Oxford University Press, 2011).

10. Phillip Dubois, "The Politics of Innovation in State Courts: The Merit Plan of Judicial Selection," *Publius: The Journal of Federalism* 20 (1990): 23–42.

11. Paul Brace and Brent D. Boyea, "State Supreme Courts and Civil Litigation," *Albany Law Review* 75 (2010): 1441–1458.

12. Paul Brace and Brent D. Boyea, "State Public Opinion, the Death Penalty, and the Practice of Electing Judges," *American Journal of Political Science* 52 (2008): 360–372.

13. James Eisenstein, Roy B. Flemming, and Peter Nardulli, *The Contours of Justice: Communities and Their Courts* (Boston: Little, Brown, 1988).

14. See, e.g., Burton M. Atkins and Henry R. Glick, "Environmental and Structural Variables as Determinants of Issues in State Courts of Last Resort," *American Journal of Political Science* 20 (1976): 97–115; also see numerous studies by Brace and Hall.

15. Melinda Gann Hall, "Constituency Influence in State Supreme Courts: Conceptual Notes and a Case Study," *Journal of Politics* 49 (1987): 117–124; Melinda Gann Hall and Paul Brace, "Order in the Courts: A Neo-Institutional Approach to Judicial Consensus," *Western Political Quarterly* 42 (1989): 391–407; Brent D. Boyea, "Linking Judicial Selection to Consensus: An Analysis of Ideological Diversity," *American Politics Research* 35 (2007): 643–670.

16. E.g., Harold W. Elder, "Property Rights, Structures, and Criminal Courts," *International Review of Law and Economics* 7 (1987): 21–32; Andrew Hanssen, "Learning about Judicial Independence: Institutional Change in the State Courts," *Journal of Legal Studies* 33 (2004): 431–473; Jeffrey Yates, Holley Tankersley, and Paul Brace, "Assessing the Impact of State Judicial Structures on Citizen Litigiousness," *Political Research Quarterly* 63 (2010): 796–810; Paul Brace, Jeffrey Yates, and Brent D. Boyea, "Judges, Litigants, and the Design of Courts," *Law and Society Review* (forthcoming).

17. Laura Langer, *Judicial Review in State Supreme Courts: A Comparative Study* (Albany: State University of New York Press, 2002); Berkowitz and Clay, *The Evolution of a Nation.*

18. E.g., Paul Brace and Melinda Gann Hall, "The Interplay of Preferences, Case Facts, Context, and Rules in the Politics of Judicial Choice," *Journal of Politics* 59 (1997): 1206–1231; Gregory A. Huber and Sanford Gordon, "Accountability and Coercion: Is Justice Blind When It Runs for Office?" *American Journal of Political Science* 48 (2004): 247–263; Paul Brace and Brent D. Boyea, "State Public Opinion, the Death Penalty, and the Practice of Electing Judges," *American Journal of Political Science* 52 (2008): 360–372; Richard P. Caldarone, Brandes Canes-Wrone, and Tom S. Clark, "Partisan Labels and Democratic Accountability: An Analysis of State Supreme Court Abortion Decisions," *Journal of Politics* 71 (2009): 560–573.

19. Peverill Squire, "Measuring the Professionalization of U.S. State Courts of Last Resort," *State Politics and Policy Quarterly* 8 (2008): 223–238.

20. Gregory A. Caldeira, "On the Reputation of State Supreme Courts," *Political Behavior* 5 (1983): 83–108.

21. Gregory A. Caldeira, "The Transmission of Legal Precedent: A Study of State Supreme Courts," *American Political Science Review* 79 (1985): 178–194.

22. Paul Brace and Melinda Gann Hall, "'Haves' versus 'Have-Nots' in State Supreme Courts: Allocating Docket Space in Power Asymmetric Cases," *Law and Society Review* 35 (2001): 393–417.

SUGGESTED READING

Atkins, Burton M., and Henry R. Glick. "Environmental and Structural Variables as Determinants of Issues in State Courts of Last Resort." *American Journal of Political Science* 20 (1976): 97–115.

Berkowitz, Daniel, and Karen B. Clay. *The Evolution of a Nation: How Geography and Law Shaped the American States.* Princeton, NJ: Princeton University Press, 2012.

Boyea, Brent D. "Linking Judicial Selection to Consensus: An Analysis of Ideological Diversity." *American Politics Research* 35 (2007): 643–670.

Brace, Paul. "State Economic Development." In *Oxford Handbook of State and Local Government,* ed. Donald Haider-Markel. Oxford: Oxford University Press, 2011.

Brace, Paul, and Brent D. Boyea. "State Public Opinion, the Death Penalty, and the Practice of Electing Judges." *American Journal of Political Science* 52 (2008): 360–372.

———. "State Supreme Courts and Civil Litigation." *Albany Law Review* 75 (2010): 1441–1458.

Brace, Paul, and Melinda Gann Hall. "'Haves' versus 'Have Nots' in State Supreme Courts: Allocating Docket Space and Wins in Power Asymmetric Cases." *Law and Society Review* 35 (2001): 393–417.

———. "Integrated Models of Judicial Dissent." *Journal of Politics* 55 (1993): 914–935.

———. "The Interplay of Preferences, Case Facts, Context, and Rules in the Politics of Judicial Choice." *Journal of Politics* 59 (1997): 1206–1231.

———. "State Supreme Courts and American Democracy." In *The Judiciary and American Democracy,* ed. Kermit Hall and Kevin McGuire. Oxford: Oxford University Press, 2005.

Brace, Paul, Jeffrey Yates, and Brent Boyea. "The Effects of Case Selection, Judge Ideology, and Institutional Structure in Tort Litigation in State Supreme Courts." *Law and Society Review* (forthcoming).

Caldarone, Richard P., Brandes Canes-Wrone, and Tom S. Clark. "Partisan Labels and Democratic Accountability: An Analysis of State Supreme Court Abortion Decisions." *Journal of Politics* 71 (2009): 560–573.

Caldeira, Gregory A. "On the Reputation of State Supreme Courts." *Political Behavior* 5 (1983): 83–108.

———. "The Transmission of Legal Precedent: A Study of State Supreme Courts." *American Political Science Review* 79 (1985): 178–194.

Dubois, Philip L. "The Politics of Innovation in State Courts: The Merit Plan of Judicial Selection." *Publius: The Journal of Federalism* 20 (1990): 23–42.

Elder, Harold W. "Property Rights, Structures, and Criminal Courts." *International Review of Law and Economics* 7 (1987): 21–32.

Friedman, Lawrence M. *A History of American Law,* 3rd ed. New York: Simon and Schuster, 2005.

Gibson, James. *The Campaigns of Judges and the Legitimacy of Courts: Do Judicial Elections Really Stink?* Chicago: University of Chicago Press (forthcoming).

Glaeser, Edward L., and Andrei Shleifer. "Legal Origins." *Quarterly Journal of Economics* 117: 1193–1229.

Hall, Kermit L., and Peter Karsten. *Magic Mirror: Law in American History.* New York: Oxford University Press, 1989.

Hall, Melinda Gann. "Constituency Influence in State Supreme Courts: Conceptual Notes and a Case Study." *Journal of Politics* 49 (1987): 117–124.

Hall, Melinda Gann, and Paul Brace. "Order in the Courts: A Neo-Institutional Approach to Judicial Consensus." *Western Political Quarterly* 42 (1989): 391–407.

Hanssen, Andrew. "Learning about Judicial Independence: Institutional Change in the State Courts." *Journal of Legal Studies* 33 (2004): 431–473.

Huber, Gregory A., and Sanford Gordon. "Accountability and Coercion: Is Justice Blind When It Runs for Office?" *American Journal of Political Science* 48 (2004): 247–263.

Konig, D. T. "Dale's Laws and the Non-Common Law Origins of Criminal Justice in Virginia." *American Journal of Legal History* 26 (1982): 354–375.

Kritzer, Herbert M., Paul Brace, Melinda Gann Hall, and Brent D. Boyea. "The Business of State Supreme Courts, Revisited." *Journal of Empirical Legal Studies* 4 (2007): 427–439.

Langer, Laura. *Judicial Review in State Supreme Courts: A Comparative Study.* Albany: State University of New York Press, 2002.

Maddex, Robert L. *State Constitutions of the United States.* Washington, DC: CQ Press, 1998.

Nelson, William E. *Americanization of the Common Law: The Impact of Legal Change on Massachusetts Society, 1760–1830.* Cambridge, MA: Harvard University Press, 1975.

Rottman, David B., and Shauna M. Strickland. "State Court Organization." U.S. Department of Justice, Office of Justice Programs, Bureau of Justice Statistics, August 15, 2006, http://bjs.ojp.usdoj.gov/index.cfm?ty=pbdetail&iid=1204.

Tomlins, Christopher. "The Legal Cartography of Colonization, the Legal Polyphony of Settlement: English Intrusions on the American Mainland in the Seventeenth Century." *Law and Social Inquiry* 26 (2001): 315–372.

Wallis, John. "Constitutions, Corporations, and Corruption: American States and Constitutional Change, 1842 to 1852." *Journal of Economic History* 65 (2009): 211–256.

Yates, Jeffrey, Holley Tankersley, and Paul Brace. "Assessing the Impact of State Judicial Structures on Citizen Litigiousness." *Political Research Quarterly* 63 (2010): 796–810.

Chapter 21

Judicial Selection and Retention of State Court Judges

Meghan E. Leonard and Laura Carlson

State courts adjudicate the majority of disputes in this country, and most of this work is done by elected judges. As of 2012, there were 10,712 state judges, and 9,512 of them will face some type of election to remain in office; there are only seven states in which judges do not face reelection or retention elections, which are uncontested elections where voters are asked to vote "yes" to retain the judge, or "no" not to retain the judge. The choice of selection and retention method, and especially the question of whether judges should be elected, has been a frequent and long-standing stimulus of judicial reform, led by both legal practitioners and politicians; it continues to be the subject of some of the most contentious debates across the country. More recently, these normative questions have ignited scholarly debate on the consequences of different selection and retention methods across state courts. Much of the debate, scholarly or otherwise, centers on a simple dichotomous distinction—elected versus appointed judges.

Appointment or election is the simplest way to categorize state judicial selection systems; however, there are important differences in the methods for selecting and retaining judges across states, and these methods also vary within states, across levels of court. For example, some states elect the members of the state's highest court and appoint judges that serve on lower appellate and trial courts. These distinctions are important to recognize and often make the appointed versus elected dichotomy too simplistic. Nonetheless, despite the idiosyncrasies of each state's judicial selection and retention method, there are some key elements shared by certain systems. These commonalities allow us to identify eight general types of judicial selection and retention systems used for state high court justices, intermediate appellate court judges, and/or trial court judges: gubernatorial appointment; gubernatorial appointment from a list of candidates supplied by a nonpartisan nominating commission; gubernatorial appointment followed by uncontested retention elections; legislative appointment; partisan election; partisan election followed by uncontested retention elections; nonpartisan election; and merit selection (see Table 20. 2 in Chapter 20 for general categorization of states).

In this chapter, a synthesis of the literature will show that discussions about judicial selection and retention should not be categorized as a simple dichotomy, but rather understood as a multifaceted issue. Adding to the complexity of judicial selection and retention is the transformed environment in which judges attain and retain seats on state courts. This change is especially important to understand because it has occurred to some degree across all types of judicial elections, including retention elections, which are a common component of merit selection systems and other appointment systems. Judicial elections, once considered low-visible races, are now conceptualized as more consequential than previously suspected, and they garner increased and national media attention. Indeed, these races now arguably operate much the same way as legislative elections; they have an incumbency advantage, strategic challengers, and informed vote choices. This new conceptualization, based on more systematic examination of judicial elections, has allowed scholars to explore more completely the broader implications of state judicial selection and retention methods. The increased saliency of these contests further permits scholarly inquiry on how campaigns alter information levels in elections and the effect of changing contextual cues on voting behavior.[1]

Much of this transformation can be attributed to the role of money and increased media attention in these races. Money plays an important part, especially in lower-information, lower-salience judicial elections, because it allows judicial candidates to give voters much more information than the voters may have had in the past. Another sign of a significantly changed environment, even for appointed judges, is the explosion of social media usage by state judges and court administrators. According to the National Center for State Courts, by the end of 2011, nine state high courts used Twitter, and in ten other states lower courts or their administrative offices used Twitter, Facebook, and/or YouTube. In addition to money and social media, recent decisions by the U.S. Supreme Court and lower courts have played a vital role in reshaping the landscape of judicial elections in particular and selection and retention more broadly.

This transformed environment is central to an understanding of judicial selection and retention because it advances our knowledge about how selection and retention likely shape who runs for office; who votes for them; and, perhaps most important, how judges and judicial candidates campaign for office. A broader understanding of judicial selection and retention also includes scholarly analysis of how these procedures alter the institutional legitimacy afforded to courts. This chapter begins by discussing the role of money and television advertisements in judicial elections, followed by a brief overview of key court decisions that have contributed to the changed nature of judicial elections. Next, this chapter discusses the extant literature that addresses various effects of judicial selection and retention on judges and courts, and offers an assessment of the scholarly works that link selection and retention methods to the politicization of the judicial branch. Finally, some conclusions about what we know and need to know about judicial selection and retention are offered.

MONEY, MEDIA, AND ADVERTISING IN JUDICIAL ELECTIONS

Today, twenty-two states elect their high court justices in competitive elections, sixteen hold retention elections for their state high court justices, and thirty-nine elect lower court judges.[2] As money and television advertisements have become ubiquitous in judicial elections, public and political scrutiny of judicial selection and retention methods has become a hotly debated issue. Policy clashes among state courts, state legislatures, and federal courts continue to rise as legislators and higher courts attempt to understand and constrain the role of media and money in judicial elections. As noted earlier, low levels of voter awareness, and scant information about judicial candidates, once fostered a characterization of these elections as unimportant in the democratic process; however, fast-forward to the new millennium and the landscape for judicial elections could not have undergone a more radical change.

Much of this change can be attributed to the pervasive role of money, television advertisements, and media in these races. Many examples highlight this significant growth. Between 1993 and 2006, the median amount of campaign funds raised by a judicial candidate increased by almost 90 percent, from about $130,000 to about $250,000. While these figures reflect a dramatic increase in the flow of money in judicial elections, some state high court races included candidate spending of more than $1 million, most often in states where judges are chosen on partisan ballots. In her report on money in judicial races, Nina Totenberg notes that the 2006 race for chief justice in Alabama cost more than $6.2 million. Even in nonpartisan races, where the party affiliation of the candidate is not identified on the ballot, state high court races attracted significantly more dollars in 2006 than in 1996. The most expensive nonpartisan race in 2006 was in Georgia, where the cost of winning a seat on the state's highest court was just over $1.3 million; yet in 1996, the winning candidate for a seat on Ohio's Supreme Court spent only $483,302. The increased spending does not seem to be an aberration; by the fall of 2008 judicial candidates raised $29.4 million. Moreover, during 2007–2008, eighty-four candidates for state high court seats raised $43.8 million, with five states setting records for fund-raising.[3]

Not only has the cost of judicial elections grown significantly over the past three decades, but the campaigns have also undergone a serious transformation. For example, in 2000 television advertisements for judicial candidates ran in just four (22 percent) of the eighteen states with contested elections. Four years later, in 2006, television ads were utilized in 91 percent of the eleven states with contested elections. Candidates in Alabama, Georgia, and Ohio spent the most money on television ads in 2006; however, interest groups alone spent over $2.7 million for television ads in the races for seats on the Washington Supreme Court. Perhaps most convincing of the changing nature of the electoral environment in judicial races is that in 2000 there were 22,646 total television ads, compared with 121,646 in 2006. The Justice at Stake campaign, a judicial reform group, found that over $19 million was spent on television advertising in the 2008 judicial races. In 2012 estimates of total spending on television advertisements marked another all-time record in the forty-six contestable races for state high court seats.

Alicia Bannon, counsel in the Brennan Center for Justice's Democracy Program at the New York University School of Law, broadly commented on the 2012 races: "Judicial elections this year were characterized by attack ads, record-breaking spending, and outsized influence by special interests." Beyond television advertisements, super PACs, specialized interest groups, and political parties are turning to media outlets such as YouTube, Facebook, and Twitter to support, or more often attack, judicial candidates. Direct mailings have also become a significant factor in judicial elections. Super PACs spent millions in 2011 and 2012 on direct mailings in many contested races around the country. In North Carolina, early estimates showed that a few super PACs spent over $500,000 on postcards in the state's 2012 high court race between Justice Paul Newby and Judge

Samuel James Ervin IV. Similarly, in Wisconsin, special interests spent close to $4 million on judicial candidates running in 2011, with much of the money spent on negative television ads and direct mailings.[4]

Retention elections have also been transformed by money and television advertisements. Judges confronting a retention election were once considered holders of safe seats; these elections were considered a simple formality of the merit selection system and some other variants of appointive systems. Yet in the past several years, controversial decisions on same-sex marriage, abortion, and school financing, to name a few, coupled with the influx of media and money, have changed many of these "safe elections" into real contests. In the past few years, judges in states such as Colorado, Florida, and Illinois faced strong campaigns to vote "no" on many of the judges up for retention. As the 2010 Iowa Retention Elections box illustrates, a significant amount of money was raised and spent to unseat justices on the Iowa Supreme Court, who faced a retention election in 2010. Adam Skaggs, a lawyer with the Brennan Center for Justice, commented, "These cases suggest that the same type of arms-race spending in other contested elections is now beginning to impact previously quiet judicial elections." For the twenty-five state high court justices running in the 2012 retention elections in thirteen states, estimates of total spending on television advertisements marked another all-time record.[5]

What remains unknown, however, is whether what happened in Iowa and other states is simply rebellion against a single decision, not likely to happen again, or the beginning of a trend where more money is spent to oust justices as they face retention election. Due to the generally uncompetitive nature of these elections, little systematic research has been done. In fact, many studies group retention elections with partisan or nonpartisan elections, given that it is likely the case that the retention elections themselves are not all that different from contested elections. In fact, Melinda Gann Hall finds that voters in retention elections are responsive to similar contextual forces and political conditions present in partisan and nonpartisan elections.[6]

While much has been said about the changing nature of these elections, an important insight gained by recent scholarship is that the increased presence of campaign expenditures across all three types of elections (i.e., partisan, nonpartisan, retention) is generally more beneficial for nonincumbents. One of the main components of the incumbency advantage in congressional elections is name recognition. In judicial elections, this incumbency advantage is more tenuous because many judges are initially appointed and only later confront some type of election to remain in office. Studies of judicial elections provide a natural experiment for examining not only the role of media and money in a changing electoral environment, but the role of institutional rules on electoral outcomes.[7]

COURT DECISIONS REGARDING JUDICIAL CAMPAIGNS

In response to controversy over judicial selection and electioneering activities, a series of state and lower federal court cases emerged. Ultimately, the U.S. Supreme Court intervened, and two decisions became especially relevant to understanding the transformed environment in which judges are selected and retained: *Republican Party of Minnesota v. White* (2002) and *Citizens United v. Federal Election Committee* (2010). *Caperton v. Massey* (2009) is a third case that has contributed to the changing nature of judicial elections, and more generally, campaign contributions and judicial impartiality (see *Caperton v. Massey* [2009] Handling Judicial Bias box for a brief summary of the *Caperton* decision).[8]

The Model Code of Judicial Conduct adopted by the American Bar Association (ABA) in 1990 provides rules on how judges should conduct themselves on the bench, in public, and when running for a judicial office. Following the lead of the ABA, many states adopted codes of conduct,

2010 IOWA RETENTION ELECTIONS

In 2010 three Iowa Supreme Court justices were up for retention election: Justices Marsha Ternus, David Baker, and Michael Streit. These justices had joined a unanimous decision in 2009 that legalized same-sex marriage in Iowa. This prompted a powerful campaign to encourage Iowans to vote "no" on the retention of these justices. This election brought to the forefront the arguments for and against judicial elections, and highlighted the increased presence of money in retention elections specifically. According to the National Institute for Money in State Politics, more than $1.4 million was spent on the state supreme court elections in 2010, and of that more than $990,000 was spent on the campaign against these justices. All three lost their bid for retention.

SOURCE: Kevin McNellis, "Independent Spending in Iowa, 2006–2010," National Institute on Money in State Politics, October 27, 2011, followthemoney.org/press/ReportView,phtml?r=464.

Caroline Kennedy, second from right, applauds as the recipients of the 2012 John F. Kennedy Profile in Courage Awards hold their lanterns. From left are Michael Streit, former Iowa Supreme Court justice; Marsha Ternus, former chief justice of the Iowa Supreme Court; David Baker, former Iowa Supreme Court justice; and Robert Ford, right, U.S. ambassador to Syria. The justices, all of whom were removed from office by Iowa voters after they voted to legalize same-sex marriage, were honored for "the political courage and judicial independence each demonstrated in setting aside popular opinion to uphold the basic freedoms and security guaranteed to all citizens under the Iowa constitution."

SOURCE: Elise Amendola/AP/Corbis.

which sought to limit or restrict the actions of judges and judicial candidates that could be seen as harmful to the court. In what is referred to as an "announce clause," Minnesota's Code of Judicial Conduct, like that of many other states, prohibited judicial candidates from discussing issues that could come before them if elected. In *Republican Party of Minnesota v. White*, the U.S. Supreme Court invalidated Minnesota's announce clause, which prohibited candidates from announcing their opinions on legal issues that were likely to come before the court. The decision in the *White* case was denounced by judicial reform organizations. In response, twenty-seven states updated their judicial codes of conduct, with twenty states adopting the ABA's 2007 amended announce clause.[9]

Far from settling the issue of conduct in judicial elections, the *White* decision prompted several more legal questions and suits. The challenges that arose after the *White* decision focused on other clauses in the judicial codes of conduct that restricted campaign behavior. These include commitments and disqualification clauses, endorsement clauses, and pledges or promises clauses. While the text of these clauses varies from state to state, they generally prohibit the solicitation of campaign funds; a pledge or promise to adjudicate a particular result; endorsements from political parties in nonpartisan elections;

CAPERTON V. MASSEY (2009) HANDLING JUDICIAL BIAS

West Virginia Supreme Court justice Brent Benjamin ran for reelection and received close to $3 million from the "And for the Sake of the Kids" political action committee (PAC). This PAC was headed by Don Blankenship, the CEO of the A. T. Massey Coal Company. After winning the election, Justice Benjamin participated in a case involving the Massey Coal Company and voted in favor of Massey. The outcome of the case overturned a $50 million verdict against the Massey Coal Company. In *Caperton v. Massey*, the U.S. Supreme Court was asked whether or not Justice Benjamin, and judges more generally, should recuse themselves in cases where they received significant campaign contributions from a party to the case. Justice Anthony Kennedy wrote the opinion for the Court, and found that when there is a "probability of bias" such as in Justice Benjamin's case, a justice must recuse him- or herself in order to not violate due process.[1] The 5–4 decision ignited debate over judicial selection and retention, and in particular, judicial impartiality; it also triggered congressional hearings on judicial recusals and prompted nine states as of 2013 to develop or redefine recusal rules. For example, in 2011, New York restricted case assignment to a judge if that judge had received $2,500 or more from a party in the case, or if a judge received $3,500 or more from the attorneys, their firms, and their clients collectively. Recusal reform in the wake of *Caperton* is likely to continue as more states adopt rules to define when justices who have been recipients of campaign contributions should recuse themselves.

SOURCES: Brennan Center for Justice, "Judicial Recusal Reform—Two Years after *Caperton*," brennancenter.org/content/resource/judicial_recusal_reform_two_years_after_caperton; Dmitry Bam, "Understanding *Caperton:* Judicial Disqualification under the Due Process Clause," *McGeorge Law Review* 42 (2010): 65–83.

1. *Caperton v. A. T. Massey Coal Co., Inc.*, 556 U.S. __ (2009).

TABLE 21.1 **Significant Court Decisions on Judicial Codes of Campaign Conduct after *Republican Party of Minnesota v. White* (2002)**

Case name	Year decided	Court	Judicial campaign issue	Outcome
Bauer v. Shepard	2011	7th Circuit Court of Appeals	Indiana pledges and promises and commit clauses[1]	Pledges and promises and commit clauses are constitutional.
Yost v. Stout	2008	Federal District Court for Kansas	Kansas code: solicitation clause[2]	Prohibition of solicitation of campaign contributions is unconstitutional.
Simes v. Judicial Discipline and Disability Commission	2007	Arkansas Supreme Court	Arkansas code: solicitation clause	Solicitation limitations are constitutional.
Pennsylvania Family Institute v. Celluci	2007	Federal District Court for Eastern District of Pennsylvania	Pennsylvania code: pledges and promises and commit clauses	Pledges and promises and commit clauses are constitutional.
Wolfson v. Brammer	2006	Federal District Court for Arizona	Arizona code: pledges and promises clause	Pledges and promises clause is constitutional.
Kansas Judicial Watch v. Stout	2006	Federal District Court for Kansas	Kansas pledges and promises and commit clauses	Injunction issued against enforcement of clauses, but not directly overturned or determined to be unconstitutional.
In Re Kinsey	2003	Florida Supreme Court	Florida pledges and promises and commit clauses	Pledges and promises and commit clauses are constitutional.

NOTES:

1. Pledges and promises and commit clauses forbid statements that commit or appear to commit candidates to positions on cases, controversies, or issues that are likely to come before the court.

2. Solicitation limitations restrict judicial candidates from personally soliciting contributions for their campaigns.

SOURCE: Brennan Center for Justice at New York University Law School, "Summaries of Relevant Cases Decided since *Republican Party of Minnesota v. White*," www.brennancenter.org/content/resource/summaries_of_relevant_cases_decided_since_republican_party_of_minnesota_v_w.

prohibitions of endorsements of political candidates by judges; and also new recusal rules as a result of the *Caperton* decision. In this chapter, it would not be possible to discuss the multitude of decisions after *White*. Instead some of the more significant cases are summarized in Table 21.1.

Citizens United v. Federal Elections Commission (2010) was another landmark case in which the U.S. Supreme Court addressed electioneering activities. While the Court's decision in *Citizens United* did not directly affect any state law, it raised constitutional questions about laws that restricted corporate spending in judicial elections in twenty-four states. In *Citizens United*, the Court held that government may not restrict corporations or unions from making independent expenditures to support or oppose individual candidates in an election. Despite being widely criticized, the Supreme Court affirmed *Citizens United* in June 2012 with a per curiam opinion in *American Tradition Partnership, Inc. v. Bullock* (2012), where it overturned a decision of the Montana Supreme Court that was in direct conflict with the precedent set in *Citizens United*.[10] The reaction from scholars and judicial reformers to the Supreme Court's decisions in *White*, *Caperton*, and *Citizens United* was decidedly mixed. However, scholars have sought to assess how these decisions actually may have changed or affected judicial campaigns and judicial elections.

In many ways it is too early to determine the effects of *Citizens United* and *Caperton*. However, there is a growing body of literature assessing the post-*White* elections. In a recent article by Chris W. Bonneau, Melinda Gann Hall, and Matthew J. Streb, the authors summarize some of these scholarly findings and conclude that scholars have found few statistically significant changes pre- and post-2002. For example, the quality of challengers that are drawn by incumbents in these elections has not changed. In state supreme court and intermediate appellate court elections, contestation, competition, spending, and ballot roll-off are all consistent pre- and post-*White*.[11] While some things stayed the same, other important factors have changed since the *White*

"Citizens United to Kill Democracy." Imaginative protest signs were ubiquitous among the several hundred thousand who attended a "Rally to Restore Sanity and/or Fear" on the National Mall organized by Comedy Central talk show hosts Jon Stewart and Stephen Colbert in Washington, DC, on Saturday, October 30, 2010. This man protests the recent U.S. Supreme Court **Citizens United** ***decision, which opened up unlimited campaign funding for corporations.***

SOURCE: Jeff Malet Photography/Newscom.

decision. Hall and Bonneau find that attack ads and liberalized speech codes mobilize the electorate in judicial campaigns. Codes of conduct that allow candidates freer speech "increase the propensity to vote in state supreme court elections in a powerful way."[12] Thus, while there have only been a few election cycles since the *White* decision, some of the effects many worried about have not materialized and other interesting findings have been shown. Given the more recent Supreme Court decisions, there is still much to learn about the changing nature of judicial elections in response to these significant cases.

One line of inquiry that has received increased attention, especially in response to the *Caperton* decision, is the relationship between campaign dollars and judicial votes. There is strong evidence, for example, that campaign money has been shown to be an important contributor to success in judicial elections.[13] However, we do not have many systematic evaluations of the hypothesis that campaign contributions by attorneys, or a party in the suit, lead to favorable outcomes for the attorneys. Damon M. Cann's two-stage analysis of money and votes on the Georgia Supreme Court tackles this question. He finds evidence that as the amount of contributions from liberal (or conservative) attorneys increases, the probability of the justice voting liberal (or conservative) increases. Cann concludes that due to this relationship between money and votes, competitive judicial elections may seriously compromise the independence of the judiciary. Indeed, Cann is among the first to test these linkages with scientific scrutiny; however, the evidence is limited to a single state and a single year. It is this line of inquiry where more data will help advance our understanding of the role money plays in judicial voting.[14]

JUDICIAL ELECTIONS: OUTCOMES

Competition, Winning, and Challengers

Electioneering activities and, in particular, the influx of money and media have altered judicial elections, but scholarly studies have only recently begun to examine whether or not they have changed voters and candidates. Marie Hojnacki and Lawrence Baum were among the first to document changes in the character of judicial elections as a result of large-scale campaigns, more media attention, and more policy discussions.[15] Among the most comprehensive studies of voters in judicial elections is Hall's study of ballot roll-off in 654 state high court elections in thirty-eight states from 1980 to 2000. Hall found that voters respond to important cues such as incumbency and competition, and that the type of judicial elections (i.e., partisan, nonpartisan, retention) significantly influences participation rates. Partisan elections seem to stimulate participation and improve voter accuracy about justices' preferences. Hall's study demonstrates that factors that influence participation in state high court elections are comparable to those that influence voter turnout for other offices.[16] In this area, scholars have probed more deeply to look at the demographics of those who vote, the consequences of roll-off, and the linkages judicial selection provides between the judiciary and the electorate.

More recent studies of state high court elections have also documented electoral competition in judicial races. Bonneau, for example, finds that in most election cycles from 1990 through 2000, the percentage of incumbent defeats in state supreme court elections was higher than for other state or federal offices. The presence of quality challengers in judicial elections is one reason why these races have become more visible and more competitive. Increased scholarly attention has thus focused on when and why quality challengers emerged and the impact quality challengers had on the electoral success of incumbents in state high court elections.[17] This scholarship has highlighted some important parallels to congressional races. For example, Bonneau and Hall conclude that competition in state court elections is very predictable from factors such as the characteristics of the individual incumbent, as well as state-level indicators and the institutional context. When predicting quality challengers, they find that if incumbents are new appointees or if their previous election was close, quality challengers are more likely to emerge. Also similar to congressional elections, Bonneau finds that incumbent defeats can be predicted by the characteristics of the campaign (i.e., spending ratio), the characteristics of the incumbent, and the political context of the state. Like studies that have established quality challengers fare better in congressional elections, scholarly research on judicial elections documents a similar phenomenon.[18]

While many of the conclusions drawn from congressional races are reinforced in the work by judicial scholars who have studied state high court elections, there are some important differences. Taken together, researchers find that institutional arrangements and contextual forces, such as the type of the election (partisan versus nonpartisan), the size of the constituency (statewide versus district elections), and the salary of the justices are important factors in predicting the emergence of quality challengers in state high court elections. Moreover, there are many similarities with open-seat elections in the congressional literature; however, an important departure from these contests is that there is no evidence, at least to date, that open-seat races on state high courts are related to the state's partisan climate.[19]

Elections and Diversity on the Bench

In addition to quality challengers, incumbency advantage, and effectiveness of electioneering activities, another consideration, especially in the last decade, has been on whether selection and retention influence gender diversity on these state high court benches. Mark S. Hurwitz and Drew Noble Lanier emphasize the importance of examining the characteristics of those serving on appellate courts, though they do not find any links between judicial characteristics and decision making. Nor do they find a relationship between method of selection and gender composition on these high courts. However, Kathleen A. Bratton and Rorie Spill offer some limited evidence that states with appointment systems are more likely to have a woman serving on that bench than do states with elective systems.[20]

There are many important reasons to explore the composition of state high courts. For example, Bonneau argues that judicial characteristics of these benches affect decision making and permit an examination of representation. Although these studies have contributed to a larger political dialogue regarding the democratic nature of the judiciary, Laura Langer and Teena Wilhelm argue that it is necessary to examine whether the ideological tenor of the leaders on state high courts varies systematically across elected versus appointed courts.[21] Despite the amount of attention devoted to the relationship between method of selection and composition of state high courts, debates over whether elected courts are significantly more diverse across gender and race, or whether elected courts are comprised of justices with lower legal qualifications compared with appointed courts, remain unresolved in the literature. Similarly, scholarship that focuses on the chief justices of the state supreme courts has emphasized recruitment and its impact on judicial behavior. As Langer et al. note, one of the problems with this body of literature is that the focus is on the end part of the selection process—that is, who is on the bench, rather than who is a candidate for the bench. Scant attention to the latter is in large part due to limited information about potential nominees in appointment systems and the initial and complete pool of candidates in the preelection stages of elected systems.[22]

Voting Behavior of Elected Judges Compared with Appointed Judges

Another question that has received attention by judicial scholars is whether elected or appointed systems influence judicial behavior on state high courts. A predominant conclusion in this area of research is that judicial behavior indeed varies across methods of judicial selection and retention. In particular, scholarly research on this subject provides overwhelming evidence that state high courts are responsive to public opinion when the members of these institutions are elected rather than appointed. In a series of articles, Paul Brace and Melinda Gann Hall consider the conditioning effect of selection methods on judicial behavior in death penalty cases. They find that justices behave differently when faced with the possibility of electoral sanctions or when they have been exposed to the partisan process of recruitment. Hall's earlier work also demonstrated that while voters in judicial elections are generally uninformed, justices nonetheless believe that citizens are aware of some of their decisions. In another important study, Gregory A. Huber and Sanford C. Gordon find that trial court judges alter their behavior by increasing the severity of sentences as reelection nears. The findings in this study indicate that even in the low-information setting of retention elections in ten-year intervals, judges appear to respond to potential electoral consequences.[23]

Generally, past research has shown that justices who are elected make decisions in such a way as to avoid losing their seat on the bench in the next election. Langer finds that on state supreme courts, justices vote their sincere preferences when they are more insulated from political pressures and vote strategically when the selection and retention method along with institutional rules create more possibilities for retaliation from either the public or other branches of government.[24] More recently, Brace and Boyea find that the voting behavior of elected justices on state high courts is tied directly (and indirectly) to public opinion toward the death penalty. Specifically, Brace and Brent Boyea find that "elections and strong public opinion exert a notable and significant direct influence on judge decision making in these [death penalty] cases."[25] In an examination of abortion decisions on state supreme courts, Richard P. Caldarone, Brandice Canes-Wrone, and Tom S. Clark find that justices who face nonpartisan elections are even more responsive to public opinion.[26]

In many ways, appointed systems are treated in the literature as a singular alternative to electoral or merit selection. In these systems, justices are appointed by either the governor or the state legislature, and many stand for some sort of confirmation in at least one house of the state legislature. Typically, these justices serve longer terms, and in a few states serve lifetime appointments (or to a predetermined retirement age). However, there are few studies that examine either the selection or decision making of appointed justices on their own. What we do know is that many of these justices must face reappointment by either the governor or the state legislature, and that this constrains their decision making. Specifically, scholars have found that while elected justices evince strategic behavior in voting while being responsive to the public, those justices who are appointed are strategic as they consider the preferences of the other branches of government when making decisions.[27]

JUDICIAL SELECTION AND RETENTION, JUDICIAL LEGITIMACY, AND PUBLIC CONFIDENCE

At the heart of the debate over how we should select and retain justices on state supreme courts is the role elections might play in the public's confidence in the court. Judicial reformers worry that elections hurt the impartiality of judges, or at least the appearance of such. Scholars have examined how individual citizens view their state courts, and the role elections play in affecting the legitimacy of a state supreme court. Knowledge of the courts, experience with the courts, age, race, and gender have all been found to shape an individual's trust and confidence in the state courts.[28] Specifically, initial research found that partisan elections hurt the public's perception of their state courts. For example, Sara C. Benesh finds that citizens in states with partisan elections are more likely to have "only a little" confidence in their state courts, and they are less likely to have a "great deal of confidence." Others find similar support for this conclusion, and these studies have also shown more specifically that when citizens express concern about campaign contributions in elections, they show significantly less support for their state courts.[29]

However, more recently scholars have found that the link between elections and legitimacy is more complicated than previously thought. Using a series of experiments, researchers have made direct connections between elections and campaigning and their effects on legitimacy.[30] When judges receive campaign contributions from an individual who has direct interests before the court, citizens view this as bias and perceive the court to be less legitimate. Campaigning for office also has been shown to affect the legitimacy of the court, but in some unexpected ways. Judges expressing policy views—where a candidate states a position on an issue but makes no claims about future decisions—during a campaign does not hurt the legitimacy of a court; however, judges expressing policy promises—where a candidate states he or she will decide on an issue in a certain way—does. In fact, policy views and some information provided by advertisements during the course of a campaign for judicial office may actually enhance the legitimacy of state supreme courts. Far from the assumption that elections hurt legitimacy, "elections are beneficial to courts, because they are the one means by which citizens are stimulated to think about the accountability of the judiciary, which seems to be favored by a large portion of the American people."[31] In other words, elections are legitimacy-conferring institutions under some circumstances. While elections may provide some legitimacy to judicial institutions, electioneering activities may in fact hurt the court's public support.

CONCLUSION

Given that more than 88 percent of all state judges must face reelection at some point via partisan, nonpartisan, or retention election, the focus of many scholars studying state judicial selection and retention has changed to reflect a newly transformed electoral environment.[32] Once categorized as less visible and mundane, judicial elections, including retention races, are now at the forefront of public, political, and scholarly discussions. As we note, much of this transformation can be attributed to the role of money in the selection and retention of judges, along with an increased amount of media attention and type of media attention on judges, opinions, and judicial elections. Systematic scholarly evaluations of judicial selection and retention have even broader implications as this debate becomes more politicized across the country. For the past decade, during almost every legislative session states have reconsidered whether and how to change the way judges are selected and retained. In 2012, three states in particular made national news as voters in Arizona, Florida, and Missouri rejected measures to change the merit selection systems currently operating in their states. The primary question before state legislators is whether judges should be held accountable to the public, and thus elected, or whether judges should be more independent from the electorate, and thus appointed. However, around the country, electioneering activities and the increased role of money and media in the judicial arena have prompted even more questions about the selection and retention of state judges. The legitimacy of and public confidence in state courts, which were once considered a given, are now in question as concerns about representativeness, independence, and judicial impartiality are raised.

Systematic examinations of state court elections and campaigns have advanced the science of politics both theoretically and methodologically and opened new paths of political inquiry about elections across all three branches of government. While there have been tremendous gains in our knowledge of judicial selection and retention, the subfield's movement forward has been slower in linking electioneering activities and campaign contributions with judicial decisions and, more generally, judicial legitimacy. Much of what we know in these areas is based on empirical findings from single-state studies; multistate studies of limited time frame; or multistate and single-state studies that isolate judicial elections and campaigns from other governmental activities, including other elections. We would benefit from future research that makes these links, as well as research that examines how rule changes set out by the Supreme Court in *Citizens United, Caperton,* and *White* might affect races for the bench in the future. What we know for certain is that the choice of judicial selection and retention methods has consequences, and that the debate over how to select and retain judges on state courts will continue. Future research will be critical to the advancement of a more complete understanding of this multifaceted issue.

NOTES

1. Melinda Gann Hall, "State Supreme Courts in American Democracy: Probing the Myths of Judicial Reform," *American Political Science Review* 95 (2001): 315–30; Melinda Gann Hall and Chris W. Bonneau, "Does Quality Matter? Challengers in State Supreme Court Elections," *American Journal of Political Science* 50 (2006): 20–33.

2. Compiled by the authors from American Judicature Society webpage and National Center for State Courts.

3. See Carmen Lo, Katie Londenberg, and David Nims, "Spending in Judicial Elections: State Trends in the Wake of *Citizens United,*" California Assembly Judicial Committee, 2011; James Sample, Adam Skaggs, Jonathan Blitzer, and Linda Casey, "The New Politics of Judicial Elections, 2000–2009: A Decade of Change," for the Justice at Stake Campaign and the Brennan Center for Justice, 2010, www.justiceatstake.org/media/cms/JASNPJEDecade ONLINE_ 8E7FD3FEB83E3.pdf.

4. Sample et al., "New Politics of Judicial Elections." See also the Brennan Center for Justice, November 7, 2012, press release, "Judicial Election TV Spending Sets New Record, Yet Voters Reject Campaigns to Politicize the Judiciary"; Brennan Center for Justice Analysis on "Judicial Public Financing in Wisconsin—2011," April 5, 2011, www.brennancenter.org/content/resource/judicial_public_financing_in_wisconsin_2011.

5. See the Brennan Center for Justice, November 7, 2012, press release.

6. See e.g., Paul Brace and Brent Boyea, "State Public Opinion, the Death Penalty, and the Practice of Electing Judges," *American Journal of Political Science* 52 (2008): 360–372; Hall, "State Supreme Courts in American Democracy"; see also Peverill Squire and Eric R. A. N. Smith, "The Effect of Partisan Information on Voters in Nonpartisan Elections," *Journal of Politics* 50 (1988): 169–179.

7. Chris W. Bonneau, "Electoral Verdicts: Incumbent Defeats in State Supreme Court Elections," *American Politics Research* 33 (2005): 818–841; Chris W. Bonneau, "What Price Justice(s)? Understanding Campaign Spending in State Supreme Court Elections," *State Politics and Policy Quarterly* 5 (2005): 107–125; Chris W. Bonneau, "Patterns of Campaign Spending and Electoral Competition in State Supreme Court Elections," *Justice System Journal* 25 (2005): 21–38; Chris W. Bonneau and Melinda Gann Hall, *In Defense of Judicial Elections* (New York: Routledge, 2009).

8. *Republican Party of Minnesota v. White,* 536 U.S. 765 (2002); *Citizens United v. Federal Election Committee,* 558 U.S. __ (2010); *Caperton v. A. T. Massey Coal Co., Inc.,* 556 U.S. __ (2009).

9. See Cynthia Gray, "Developments Following *Republican Party of Minnesota v. White,* 536 U.S. 765 (2002)," www.ajs.org/files/9613/6484/9233/DevelopmentsafterWhite.pdf; see also Chris W. Bonneau and Damon M. Cann, "Campaign Spending, Diminishing Marginal Returns, and Campaign Finance Restrictions in Judicial Elections," *Journal of Politics* 73 (2011): 1267–1280.

10. *American Tradition Partnership, Inc. v. Bullock,* 567 U.S. __ (2012).

11. Chris W. Bonneau, Melinda Gann Hall, and Matthew J. Streb, "White Noise: The Unrealized Effects of *Republican Party of Minnesota v. White* on Judicial Elections," *Justice System Journal* 32 (2011): 247–268, 264–266; Bonneau and Hall, *In Defense of Judicial Elections.*

12. Melinda Gann Hall and Chris W. Bonneau, "Attack Advertising, the *White* Decision, and Voter Participation in State Supreme Court Elections," *Political Research Quarterly* (forthcoming).

13. Damon M. Cann, "Justice for Sale? Campaign Contributions and Judicial Decisionmaking," *State Politics and Policy Quarterly* 7 (2007): 281–297; Madhavi M. McCall and Michael A. McCall, "Campaign Contributions, Judicial Decisions, and the Texas Supreme Court: Assessing the Appearance of Impropriety," *Judicature* 90 (2007): 214–225. See, e.g., Chris W. Bonneau, "The Effects of Campaign Spending in State Supreme Court Elections," *Political Research Quarterly* 60 (2007): 489–499.

14. Cann, "Justice for Sale?"

15. Marie Hojnacki and Lawrence Baum, "'New-Style' Judicial Campaigns and the Voters: Economic Issues and Union Members in Ohio," *Political Research Quarterly* 45 (1992): 921–948.

16. Melinda Gann Hall, "Voting in State Supreme Court Elections: Competition and Context as Democratic Incentives," *Journal of Politics* 69 (2007): 1147–1159; Melinda Gann Hall, "Voluntary Retirements from State Supreme Courts: Assessing Democratic Pressures to Relinquish the Bench," *Journal of Politics* 63 (2001): 1112–1140.

17. Chris W. Bonneau, "Electoral Verdicts."

18. Chris W. Bonneau and Melinda Gann Hall, "Predicting Challengers in State Supreme Court Elections: Context and the Politics of Institutional Design," *Political Research Quarterly* 56 (2003): 337–349; Bonneau, "Electoral Verdicts." For legislative elections, see Alan I. Abramowitz, "Incumbency, Campaign Spending, and the Decline of Competition in U.S. House Elections," *Journal of Politics* 53 (1991): 34–56; Gary Jacobson, "Strategic Politicians and the Dynamics of House Elections, 1946–1986,"

American Political Science Review 83 (1989): 773–793; see also Hall and Bonneau, "Does Quality Matter?"

19. Bonneau and Hall, "Predicting Challengers in State Supreme Court Elections"; Hall and Bonneau, "Does Quality Matter?"; Bonneau, "What Price Justice(s)?"; Chris W. Bonneau, "Vacancies on the Bench: Open Seat Elections for State Supreme Courts," *Justice System Journal* 27 (2006): 143–159.

20. Mark S. Hurwitz and Drew Noble Lanier, "Explaining Judicial Diversity: The Differential Ability of Women and Minorities to Attain Seats on State Supreme and Appellate Courts," *State Politics and Policy Quarterly* 3 (2003): 329–352; see also Nicholas O. Alozie, "Selection Methods and the Recruitment of Women to State Courts of Last Resort," *Social Science Quarterly* 77 (1996): 110–126; but also see Kathleen A. Bratton and Rorie Spill, "Existing Diversity and Judicial Selection: The Role of the Appointment Method in Establishing Gender Diversity in State Supreme Courts," *Social Science Quarterly* 83 (2002): 504–518.

21. Chris W. Bonneau, "The Composition of State Supreme Courts, 2000," *Judicature* 85 (2001): 26–31; Laura Langer and Teena Wilhelm, "The Ideology of State Supreme Court Justices," *Judicature* 89 (2005): 78–86.

22. Laura Langer, Jody McMullen, Nicholas P. Ray, and Daniel D. Stratton, "Recruitment of Chief Justices on State Supreme Courts: A Choice between Institutional and Personal Goals," *Journal of Politics* 65 (2003): 656–675.

23. Paul Brace and Melinda Gann Hall, "The Interplay of Preferences, Case Facts, Context, and Rules in the Politics of Judicial Choice," *Journal of Politics* 59 (1997): 1206–1231; Melinda Gann Hall, "Electoral Politics and Strategic Voting in State Supreme Courts," *Journal of Politics* 54 (1992): 427–446; Paul Brace and Melinda Gann Hall, "Integrated Models of Judicial Dissent," *Journal of Politics* 55 (1993): 914–935; Gregory A. Huber and Sanford C. Gordon, "Accountability and Coercion: Is Justice Blind When It Runs for Office?" *American Journal of Political Science* 48 (2004): 247–263.

24. Laura Langer, *Judicial Review in State Supreme Courts: A Comparative Study* (Albany: State University of New York Press, 2002).

25. Brace and Boyea, "State Public Opinion, the Death Penalty."

26. Richard P. Caldarone, Brandice Canes-Wrone, and Tom S. Clark, "Partisan Labels and Democratic Accountability: An Analysis of State Supreme Court Abortion Decisions," *Journal of Politics* 71 (2009): 560–573.

27. Brace and Boyea, "State Public Opinion, the Death Penalty"; Langer, *Judicial Review in State Supreme Courts;* Langer, "Strategic Considerations and Judicial Review: The Case of Workers' Compensation Laws in the American States," *Public Choice* 116 (2003): 55–78.

28. Christine A. Kelleher and Jennifer Wolak, "Explaining Public Confidence in the Branches of State Government," *Political Research Quarterly* 60 (2007): 707–721; James P. Wenzel, Shaun Bowler, and David J. Lanoue, "The Sources of Public Confidence in State Courts: Experience and Institutions," *American Politics Research* 31 (2003): 191–211; Sara C. Benesh, "Understanding Public Confidence in American Courts," *Journal of Politics* 68 (2006): 697–707.

29. See also Damon M. Cann and Jeff Yates, "Homegrown Institutional Legitimacy: Assessing Citizens' Diffuse Support for State Courts," *American Politics Research* 36 (2008): 297–329.

30. James L. Gibson, "Challenges to the Impartiality of State Supreme Courts: Legitimacy Theory and 'New-Style' Judicial Campaigns," *American Political Science Review* 102 (2008): 59–75; James L. Gibson, "Campaigning for the Bench: The Corrosive Effects of Campaign Speech?" *Law and Society Review* 42 (2008): 899–927; James L. Gibson, "'New-Style' Judicial Campaigns and the Legitimacy of State High Courts," *Journal of Politics* 71 (2009): 1285–1304.

31. James L. Gibson, Jeffrey A. Gottfried, Michael X. Delli Carpini, and Kathleen Hall Jamieson, "The Effects of Judicial Campaign Activity on the Legitimacy of Courts: A Survey-Based Experiment, Pennsylvania, 2007," *Political Research Quarterly* 64 (2011): 545–588, 553.

32. Compiled by the authors from the American Judicature Society website, www.judicialselection.us/judicial_selection/methods/selection_of_judges.cfm?state.

SUGGESTED READING

Bonneau, Chris W., and Melinda Gann Hall. *In Defense of Judicial Elections.* New York: Routledge, 2009.

Bonneau, Chris W., Melinda Gann Hall, and Matthew J. Streb. "White Noise: The Unrealized Effects of *Republican Party of Minnesota v. White* on Judicial Elections." *Justice System Journal* 32 (2011): 247–268.

Brace, Paul, and Brent Boyea. "State Public Opinion, the Death Penalty, and the Practice of Electing Judges." *American Journal of Political Science* 52 (2008): 360–372.

Brace, Paul, and Melinda Gann Hall. "Integrated Models of Judicial Dissent." *Journal of Politics* 55 (1993): 914–935.

Caldarone, Richard P., Brandice Canes-Wrone, and Tom S. Clark. "Partisan Labels and Democratic Accountability: An Analysis of State Supreme Court Abortion Decisions." *Journal of Politics* 71 (2009): 560–573.

Cann, Damon M. "Justice for Sale? Campaign Contributions and Judicial Decisionmaking." *State Politics and Policy Quarterly* 7 (2007): 281–297.

Cann, Damon M., and Jeff Yates. "Homegrown Institutional Legitimacy: Assessing Citizens' Diffuse Support for State Courts." *American Politics Research* 36 (2008): 297–329.

Gibson, James L. "Challenges to the Impartiality of State Supreme Courts: Legitimacy Theory and 'New-Style' Judicial Campaigns." *American Political Science Review* 102 (2008): 59–75.

Gibson, James L., Jeffrey A. Gottfried, Michael X. Delli Carpini, and Kathleen Hall Jamieson. "The Effects of Judicial Campaign Activity on the Legitimacy of Courts: A Survey-Based Experiment, Pennsylvania, 2007." *Political Research Quarterly* 64 (2011): 545–588.

Hall, Melinda Gann. "State Supreme Courts in American Democracy: Probing the Myths of Judicial Reform." *American Political Science Review* 95 (2001): 315–330.

Hall, Melinda Gann, and Chris W. Bonneau. "Does Quality Matter? Challengers in State Supreme Court Elections." *American Journal of Political Science* 50 (2006): 20–33.

Huber, Gregory A., and Sanford C. Gordon. "Accountability and Coercion: Is Justice Blind When It Runs for Office?" *American Journal of Political Science* 48 (2004): 247–263.

Hurwitz, Mark S., and Drew Noble Lanier. "Explaining Judicial Diversity: The Differential Ability of Women and Minorities to Attain Seats on State Supreme and Appellate Courts." *State Politics and Policy Quarterly* 3 (2003): 329–352.

Langer, Laura. *Judicial Review in State Supreme Courts: A Comparative Study.* Albany: State University of New York Press, 2002.

Langer, Laura, and Teena Wilhelm. "State Supreme Courts as Policymakers." In *Rethinking U.S. Judicial Politics*, ed. Mark Miller. New York: Oxford University Press, 2008.

Sample, James, Adam Skaggs, Jonathan Blitzer, and Linda Casey. "The New Politics of Judicial Elections, 2000–2009: A Decade of Change." For the Justice at Stake Campaign and the Brennan Center for Justice, 2010, www.justiceatstake.org/media/cms.

Streb, Matthew J. *Running for Judge: The Rising Political, Financial, and Legal Stakes of Judicial Elections.* New York: New York University Press, 2007.

Chapter 22

Specialization in the Courts

Lawrence Baum

MANY OF THE JUDGES WHO SERVE ON state courts hear a wide array of cases. In that respect they fit the traditional image of judges as generalists. But there is also a good deal of specialization in state court systems, primarily at the trial level. Among the many types of specialized courts are juvenile courts, drug courts, mental health courts, probate courts, and business courts.

This chapter examines the phenomenon of judicial specialization in the states. It surveys specialization in state courts, examines the reasons for its use, and probes its success in achieving its purposes.

A SURVEY OF JUDICIAL SPECIALIZATION

For judges, specialization can take two general forms. In the first, for some period of time a judge hears only one category of cases that is defined by its subject matter. In the second, a judge usually hears a full range of cases, but during part of each week or month the judge focuses on a specific category. The category in which a judge specializes full-time or part-time can vary a good deal in its scope. The broadest specialization is in civil cases, a category so diverse that we might not consider it a specialization at all. Somewhat narrower are fields such as criminal law and domestic relations. Some specializations are quite narrow, such as prosecutions for gun offenses.

Some judicial specialization is mandated by a state constitution or by legislation. Some is established by the courts themselves, most often by administrative action within a specific court. Specialization can fall at different points along a spectrum based on its formality and permanence.

At one end of the spectrum are the separate specialized courts that are established by state law.[1] Virtually all judicial specialization at the appellate level takes this form. Oklahoma and Texas each have two supreme courts to hear civil and criminal cases (called the Supreme Court and the Court of Criminal Appeals), and Alabama and Tennessee have a similar separation between intermediate appellate courts. Also at the intermediate level, Indiana has a court that specializes in tax cases, and Pennsylvania's Commonwealth Court specializes in cases in which the state or local governments are involved.

State laws have created numerous specialized courts at the trial level. To take a few examples, states have courts that hear cases involving land (Massachusetts), water rights (Colorado and Montana), workers' compensation (three states), taxes (four states), and environmental issues (Vermont). Fifteen states have probate courts, which handle the estates of people who have died and other matters such as guardianships and commitments to mental institutions. And half the states have trial courts that hear only criminal cases, most of them municipal courts with jurisdiction over misdemeanor offenses.

Next along the spectrum are specialized units within trial courts that are established by law or that courts have maintained for a long period of time. Under Ohio law, for instance, most counties have separate probate courts within their Courts of Common Pleas, and many counties have courts within Common Pleas to handle probate, juvenile, or domestic relations—sometimes combinations of two or three of those areas. Across the country, many trial courts have long-standing divisions within them to hear certain kinds of cases, such as criminal or traffic cases. Although these divisions could be eliminated by a court at any time, in practice they are something close to permanent.

At the other end of the spectrum are specialized units that are created to address specific needs. A wide array of such courts has been created in various times and places. The need might be for a way to address a social problem more successfully. Alternatively, a rising tide of cases in one field might be shunted to a special unit to process them more rapidly. Some of these units move along the spectrum as they become institutionalized by law or practice. Others disappear within a short time.

Specialization of trial court judges is largely a function of a court's size. The more judges who sit on a court, the more practical it is to assign certain judges full-time to hear one type of case. In courts with only a few judges, specialization typically takes the more limited form of a part-time focus on certain types of cases by one or more of those judges. As a result, specialization is typically at its highest level in big cities.

When specialized courts or court units are established by law, judges are often elected or appointed to those courts in the same way that judges are chosen for other courts. Voters in most Ohio counties choose judges for the general unit of their Court of Common Pleas and for one or more specialized units of Common Pleas. When courts create their own specialized units, judges typically are chosen for those units by chief judges or other judges with administrative responsibilities, though judges' own preferences to serve or not to serve are often taken into account. Some specialized units are staffed not by judges but by "parajudges," typically called magistrates, referees, or commissioners, who are hired by the court to serve in those subordinate roles. That is a standard practice for traffic courts.

Because most judicial specialization is not mandated by law, the level of specialization in courts and court systems is fluid. In the country as a whole, state trial courts have become more specialized over time, largely through action by courts themselves. In part, that change reflects growth in the number of judges that facilitates specialization. In part, it reflects the success of movements that advocated certain types of specialization. The most important movements have been those that favored "socialized" courts during the Progressive Era of the early twentieth century and "problem-solving" courts in the period since the 1980s. Both movements, discussed later in this chapter, were efforts to make courts more effective in attacking crime and the social problems that underlie it.

It is difficult to summarize how much specialization exists in state trial courts. One difficulty, suggested by the discussion so far, is definitional: Is a judge a specialist if she rotates between civil and criminal cases every few months or years? If a judge presides over juvenile court in a locality but spends most of his days on other cases, is he a specialist in juvenile cases?

A second difficulty lies in the lack of comprehensive data on judicial specialization. One study does show that a great many judges specialize in a particular field at a given time. That study was based on a 1977 survey of judges in general jurisdiction trial courts, courts that handle the more serious criminal and civil cases. In those courts about two of five judges were hearing only one type of case at the time of the survey. A majority of those judges were assigned to the broad category of civil cases. But even if we set aside specialization in civil cases, one in six judges on general jurisdiction courts was still hearing only one type of case—primarily criminal.[2] Because other types of trial courts have higher levels of specialization, both those proportions underestimated the extent of specialization by trial judges. Nor did the survey identify part-time specialization by judges.

For the reasons discussed earlier, almost surely there is more specialization of trial judges today than there was in 1977. One thing is clear: if specialization means that a judge at a given time is not hearing a representative sample of the cases that come to court in a state, there is a great deal of specialization in state trial courts.

REASONS FOR SPECIALIZATION

In the United States there is widespread support for the idea that judges should be generalists, and many judges prize their status as generalists. In light of that support, why is there so much specialization within state court systems? Two considerations underlie judicial specialization. The first is the belief that courts will function better—more efficiently and effectively—with some degree of specialization. The second is the belief that specialization will produce different and better judicial policies.

Efficiency and Effectiveness

In government and society as a whole, specialization is viewed very positively. Most people take it for granted that specialized personnel will perform better than people who try to do a broad range of tasks. People are regularly hired or assigned to a particular job because they have relevant expertise. Even if they do not, we usually assume that someone who carries out a narrow set of tasks will develop expertise and thus effectiveness in doing those tasks. Furthermore, specialists in a particular job are expected to perform with greater efficiency than the person who moves from job to job. That set of beliefs underlies the factory assembly line. It is also reflected in the professions. Individual attorneys typically specialize in a few of the many fields of law, and many work in only one narrow area.

From that perspective, it is striking that most levels of the courts feature only limited specialization. Although there are important specialized federal courts, judges on the major courts at each level of the federal judiciary are all generalists. With the exceptions described earlier, the same is true of state appellate courts. This dominance of generalist courts reflects both tradition and the positive image of the generalist judge.

Thus state trial courts stand out from other levels of the courts for the extent of specialization. The reason for this difference seems to be that they have several attributes that make specialization especially attractive. One attribute is the large number of judges in many trial courts, which makes it practical to divide cases among judges by subject. The Superior Court in Los Angeles County has more than five hundred judges, referees, and commissioners. Because different kinds of cases involve different sets of lawyers and other participants, it is convenient to concentrate particular kinds in their own courtrooms. That is especially true of criminal cases. And urban trial courts often suffer from overloads of cases, so they must give a high priority to rapid processing of cases in the same way that many bureaucratic agencies do. As in the bureaucracy, then, the people who set the structure of judges' work may take it for granted that work should be allocated by subject matter when doing so would seem to enhance efficiency and effectiveness.

Those potential benefits of specialization are especially attractive when a crisis arises. Such a crisis occurred in some trial courts in the 1970s and 1980s, when the number of prosecutions for drug offenses increased enormously. Looking for ways to keep up with the caseload, court administrators in cities such as Chicago and New York assigned some judges to hear only drug cases in the hope that they could process these cases rapidly. Similarly, in 2010 the Florida legislature set up special courts to deal with the backlog of foreclosure cases that resulted from the collapse of the housing market.

A different kind of concern with efficiency and effectiveness has motivated the creation of courts to serve the business community. State policymakers often try to attract businesses to their state in order to generate jobs and tax revenue. In that effort they adopt policies that range from subsidies for the building of manufacturing plants to lenient regulations of business practices.

Judicial specialization is another policy that states have used to appeal to businesses. The connection between specialized courts and attracting business activity is not obvious, but historical circumstance has created

THE DELAWARE COURT OF CHANCERY

The Court of Chancery operated in Great Britain for several centuries. It is perhaps best known in the United States as the setting for the seemingly endless dispute over a will in Charles Dickens's novel *Bleak House*. The British court was a model for similar courts in America. Most of those courts have disappeared, but Delaware, Mississippi, and Tennessee still have chancery courts. Because of other developments in Delaware, its Court of Chancery plays an especially important role in the state.

The Delaware Court of Chancery hears cases on the equity side of an old legal distinction between "law" and "equity," and equity jurisdiction is somewhat miscellaneous. The fields in which the Chancery Court works include real estate, commercial law, contracts, and trusts and estates, among others. It is the court's jurisdiction over corporate law that makes it especially important to the state.

Because of changes in its own laws and those of New Jersey, early in the twentieth century Delaware became the primary legal home for U.S. corporations. It has retained that status, and today a majority of all publicly held companies and of the five hundred largest companies are incorporated in Delaware.[1] That is a remarkable position for a small state (Delaware's population is around nine hundred thousand), and it has been a significant boon to the state's economy and its government revenues.

Delaware gained its dominant position through policies that corporate officials found attractive, and the state's leaders today adhere to policies that are intended to maintain that position. The courts are part of that effort. The Chancery Court is widely viewed as expert in corporate law. Some of its judges practiced in that field before their appointments, and the large numbers of corporate cases that it hears provide an opportunity for judges to gain expertise during their judicial service. The state supreme court, which hears appeals from Chancery decisions, is seen as having the same strengths. In turn, it is thought, this expertise is one of the advantages that attract corporate officials to incorporate in Delaware: cases that arise over the governance of corporations will be handled efficiently and effectively, and the law of corporations has a stability that may be lacking in other states.

Experts in corporate law and other observers generally agree that the Chancery Court is one attraction of the state to corporate leaders. But some of them argue that this attraction is not simply a matter of efficiency and effectiveness. As they see it, the Delaware courts adopt policies that favor corporate management over stockholders and other groups on issues such as the rules that govern hostile takeover efforts. Since it is management that decides where to incorporate and to do business, they argue, these policies buttress Delaware's special status. In contrast, defenders of the Delaware courts argue that their judges give considerable weight to the interests of stockholders. The pattern of Delaware decisions in corporate law gives some support to both of these competing views.

The role of the Chancery Court in maintaining Delaware's enviable position as a site of corporations is impossible to ascertain. There appears to be a widespread perception that the state's courts handle corporate cases very well, but it is uncertain whether that perception has an independent impact on choices about where to incorporate and about the location of business activity. In any event, the belief that the Chancery Court serves the state's economic interests ensures that the court will continue to exist in the foreseeable future.

SOURCES: William T. Quillen and Michael Hanrahan, "A Short History of the Delaware Court of Chancery—1792–1992," *Delaware Journal of Corporate Law* 18 (1993): 819–866; various journal articles.

1. Delaware Division of Corporations, http://corp.delaware.gov/.

that connection. As described in the Delaware Court of Chancery box, it is widely perceived that the expertise of the Delaware Court of Chancery in corporate law has assisted Delaware in maintaining its position as the leading home of corporations in the United States. Since 1993, legislators and judges in nineteen states have tried to emulate Delaware's success in a small way by establishing trial courts and court divisions that specialize in cases involving the business community. Most of these courts serve certain cities within the state rather than the state as a whole.

The jurisdiction of these courts differs. Some hear a wide range of cases involving the governance of individual businesses and disputes between businesses. Others hear only types of cases that are regarded as unusually complex. Advocates for business courts hope that these courts will be perceived as expert in business matters and that this perception will attract business activity and incorporations to their state.

Shaping Judicial Policy

An effort to foster efficiency and effectiveness through judicial specialization can affect the outcomes of cases and the policies that courts make through their interpretations of the law. In Chicago and New York City, for instance, creation of drug courts to deal with backlogs of cases resulted in more favorable plea bargains to defendants as a means to resolve cases more quickly.[3] In that situation, the effects of specialization on court outputs are a by-product of other goals. But, quite frequently, specialization is used deliberately to shape the policies of state trial courts.

Typically, this process begins when people within the court system or outside it become dissatisfied with the way that courts handle a particular type of case. Such dissatisfaction can lead to a wide range of prescriptions. One common prescription is to create a specialized court unit for that type of case and to give the unit a mission to deal with those cases in a new way. Often, the judges for the specialized unit are chosen for their commitment to that mission.

In the federal courts, that process has occurred in several different areas of law, and it is largely responsible for the creation of specialized courts such as the Court of Federal Claims and the Court of Appeals for the Federal Circuit. In the states, it occurs primarily on the criminal side of trial courts' work.

One source of dissatisfaction with the courts' handling of criminal cases is a perception that they are too lenient in dealing with a particular kind of offense. Among the possible responses is creation of a court unit for those cases, giving it a mission to treat defendants with greater severity. The creation of such a unit in itself can signal to its participants that they should take these cases seriously. Sometimes a judge who seems to be inclined toward severity is selected to preside over the unit, giving some assurance that the court's mission will be followed.

This was the primary goal behind creation of gun courts in several cities, including Baltimore, Milwaukee, and New York. The first of these courts was established in Providence in 1994. The court was set up by the Rhode Island legislature at the behest of the mayor of Providence, who felt that the courts were not serious enough about enforcing laws that prohibited the possession and use of guns under certain circumstances. The judge who was selected to preside over the gun court had a reputation as tough on crime. Indeed, it was reported that he had sentenced one defendant to death despite the absence of capital punishment in Rhode Island.

Other courts have been established with similar goals in particular places. One such court was the "Eagles Court" that set up shop in 1997 in the football stadium in which the Philadelphia Eagles

Judge Seamus P. McCaffery helps Judge Louis J. Presenza with his robe shortly before they opened the courtroom at Veterans Stadium on November 30, 1997. The judges heard cases from fans who were arrested for disorderly conduct during the Philadelphia Eagles game against the Cincinnati Bengals. McCaffery presided at the first ad hoc court established at the stadium on November 23 to help control drunk and rowdy fans.

SOURCE: blj/Photo by Barbara L.

played. Unhappy with the behavior of some fans at games, the local authorities placed a judge in the stadium to try and then sentence miscreants quickly. Over the years, Chicago has been home to a good many courts with the mission of bringing greater rigor to enforcement of laws against particular types of criminal offenses. The range of such courts is described in the Crime and Specialized Courts in Chicago box.

A great many specialized court units have arisen from the campaign for socialized courts during the Progressive Era and the ongoing campaign for problem-solving courts. Each of these movements has sought to change the outcomes of criminal cases, but in a more complex way than simply imposing more rigorous sanctions on wrongdoers. Rather, as the term *problem-solving* suggests, the goal is to identify the problems that result in criminal behavior and to find solutions to them. Determining guilt or innocence is less important than changing offenders so that they will not commit future crimes.

The prototype for courts that embody this approach was juvenile courts, the first of the socialized courts and the most widespread of all courts with a relatively narrow specialization. The original juvenile court was created in Chicago in 1899, and action by courts and state legislatures spread juvenile courts across the country. By the time of a 1918 survey, the great majority of cities with populations of twenty-five thousand or more had "specially organized" juvenile courts.[4]

The primary impetus behind the juvenile courts was the belief that young people who commit criminal offenses should be regarded as victims of social conditions rather than wrongdoers. Supporters of the juvenile courts thought that courts should focus on treating the problems of juvenile offenders rather than adjudicating guilt and punishing those who are found guilty. The judge and supporting personnel in the court would help offenders overcome the conditions that led to their undesirable behavior, making use of expert knowledge about the appropriate treatment. In line with this idea, the young people who came into court would not be regarded as criminal defendants, and the standard procedures of criminal courts would largely be dispensed with.

CRIME AND SPECIALIZED COURTS IN CHICAGO

Historian Michael Willrich called Progressive Era Chicago a "city of courts."[1] Willrich was referring to Chicago's pioneering role in creating specialized units within its municipal court to address social problems, what became known as socialized courts. The juvenile court was invented in Chicago in 1899, and Chicago also had a Court of Domestic Relations, a Morals Courts, and a Boys' Court (for young men who were too old for juvenile court). These courts differed in their orientations, but all were aimed at using innovative approaches to deal with particular kinds of crimes or offenders.

These socialized courts represent only one aspect of the proliferation of specialized courts in Chicago. Like the municipal court of past eras, the Chicago circuit court today is a court with broad jurisdiction that is divided into smaller units to hear specific types of cases. To a considerable degree, this division of labor is designed to achieve greater efficiency and to match judges' expertise with their work. But it offers other benefits, including the opportunity to assign areas of law with the most politically sensitive cases to judges who are considered reliable by local authorities.

Historically, a recurrent phenomenon in Chicago was the creation of court units to overcome perceived leniency in the handling of particular crimes. The idea was to assign one or more judges to cases involving an offense in order to impose more severe sanctions on the people committing that offense and thereby strengthen the law's deterrent effect. Over time, this goal resulted in the establishment—among others—of a gambling court, a racket court, a smokers court, a perjury and vagrancy court, and an auto theft court. These courts were generally short-lived, reflecting the rise and decline of concern about a particular type of criminal offense.

Courts of this type could be successful only if the judges who staffed them were committed to their mission, and the court administrators who assigned judges to units sometimes showed considerable ingenuity in identifying appropriate judges. After a speeders' court was created in 1913, a sympathetic observer reported that its first judge was one "who did not own an automobile and who was not owned by the owner of any automobile."[2] Two decades later, local authorities sought to combat hay fever, and one step they took was creation of a weed court to punish violators of the ordinance requiring that property owners cut their ragweed. The judge chosen to serve on the court was thought not only to be "retributive" but also to suffer from hay fever.[3] In a symbolically fitting episode, the opening of the weed court was delayed when the judge had to leave town because of an attack of hay fever. It is a reasonable guess that on his return, he meted out significant sanctions to the defendants who came before him.

SOURCES: Sources cited in the footnotes; various articles in the *Chicago Tribune*.

1. Michael Willrich, *City of Courts: Socializing Justice in Progressive Era Chicago* (New York: Cambridge University Press, 2003).
2. Herbert Harley, "Business Management for the Courts," *Virginia Law Review* 5 (1917): 11.
3. Albert Lepawsky, *The Judicial System of Metropolitan Chicago* (Chicago: University of Chicago Press, 1932), 167.

This idea was appealing to many people, especially those in the Progressive Movement of the early twentieth century. In the absence of a significant opposition movement, they were able to secure the widespread adoption of the juvenile court idea. Their success was permanent: juvenile courts with judges assigned to them full-time or part-time are a standard feature of state trial courts a century after they first became popular.

The closest counterparts to the juvenile courts are several types that have grown out of the current movement for problem-solving courts, including drug courts, mental health courts, and veterans' treatment courts. That movement reflects widespread frustration with the perceived failure of ordinary criminal courts to prevent recidivism, new criminal behavior after an individual has gone through the court system. The movement has strong advocates within the courts, including officials in state court systems such as New York and Ohio, and the federal government provides monetary support for some types of problem-solving courts. Within individual courts, individual judges often play a key role in creating and sustaining a problem-solving court.

Drug courts were the original type of problem-solving court, and they have served as a model for some other types. The first problem-solving drug court (as distinguished from the earlier courts that focused on clearing backlogs of drug cases) was founded in Miami in 1989. Since then this institution has spread widely. By one count there were more than 2,600 drug courts in 2012, including variants such as juvenile drug courts.[5] That number indicates that a substantial portion of the country has some kind of drug court. A national group, the National Association of Drug Court Professionals, supports existing drug courts and seeks to foster new ones. Some of these courts work with people accused of violating drug laws, but the emphasis has been on other (usually nonviolent) offenses that are committed by people who are addicted to drugs. Some drug courts and separate DWI (Driving While Intoxicated) courts include offenders with addictions to alcohol.

Drug courts do not adjudicate guilt. Defendants enter drug court programs after they plead guilty or after a prosecutor agrees to defer prosecution. The court's focus is designed to help offenders overcome their drug problems through cooperative efforts by judges, attorneys, and other court personnel. Offenders who enter drug court programs are supervised intensively and make frequent appearances in court. Drug courts provide strong support for offenders but also require that they adhere to the behavioral goals set for them. Offenders who fail to do so may be moved back into regular criminal proceedings.

No other type of problem-solving court is nearly as common as drug courts. Of the other types, the one that has diffused most widely is mental health courts. These courts are aimed at addressing the mental health problems that underlie the criminal behavior of some individuals. They are quite diverse in form, but they share the same general orientation toward treatment that characterizes drug courts. In recent years courts in many cities have created units that hear cases in which the defendants are military veterans. These courts are discussed in the Courts for Veterans box.

Both the socialized and problem-solving labels have been stretched considerably, and sometimes they are applied to courts whose main goal is to strengthen enforcement of the law. In the era of socialized courts, the prime example was the domestic relations courts that were instituted in several large cities. Unlike courts with the same name today, these domestic relations courts were criminal courts, with the primary mission of collecting money from fathers who had failed to meet their legal duty of financial support to their families.

Among the problem-solving courts, domestic violence courts exemplify an orientation toward strong enforcement of the law. About two hundred domestic violence courts have been created, with the primary mission of enforcing

A session of a newly created court for veterans was held November 18, 2010, in West Palm Beach, Florida, before Judge Ted Booras. Here, Rocco Zito (who says he was in the Marines for four years) appears before the judge on cocaine possession charges.

SOURCE: Bruce R. Bennett/*The Palm Beach Post*/ZUMAPRESS.com.

COURTS FOR VETERANS

In 1989 a San Diego trial court established a homeless court that was aimed at helping homeless military veterans deal with misdemeanor charges that were pending against them. The idea was to resolve the charges with plea bargains and, in the process, get veterans to participate in a program that was designed to address their problems. The homeless court met only occasionally. After receiving a federal grant in 1999, it held regular monthly sessions in homeless shelters.

The idea of a homeless court won support in some other communities, primarily in California, and by 2007 there were about three dozen homeless courts. In San Diego and other cities, homeless courts served nonveterans as well as military veterans.

In 2008 a judge in Buffalo established a veterans' treatment court that was designed specifically to help military veterans who had become criminal defendants. That judge already served in a drug court and a mental health court. His innovation gained a good deal of favorable publicity, and judges in other cities began to follow his example. At the end of 2011, there were around one hundred veterans' treatment courts across the country. Funding from federal agencies has facilitated the creation and operation of these courts.

If criminal defendants as a group are one of the less popular segments of the population, military veterans are among the most popular. When veterans commit relatively minor criminal offenses, especially if those offenses seem to stem from the problems they face as veterans, it is easy for people in the courts to sympathize with them. Thus the emphasis in veterans' courts has been on helping defendants to deal with their problems rather than on punishing them for their offenses. As in other problem-solving courts, defendants can receive attention and treatment over a long period of time. Other veterans often play a supportive role in the court.

With the rapid diffusion of veterans' treatment courts, they still exist in only a small proportion of all locations with trial courts. The costs of the intensive efforts that they make on behalf of defendants limit the number of places they can be set up and the numbers of veterans they can serve. That limitation applies to any court that follows a problem-solving model which diverges from the standard, rapid processing of criminal cases in most courts.

SOURCES: Kristina Shevory, "Prisoners of War: Why Should Vets Get Their Own Court System?" *The Atlantic*, December 2011, 18, 20, 21; various newspaper articles.

laws against domestic violence more rigorously. Some of these courts handle criminal prosecutions; others deal with civil protection orders. Some domestic violence courts make efforts to treat offenders in ways that are similar to drug courts. Overall, however, the emphasis is on strong enforcement of laws against domestic violence. Similarly, the environmental courts that exist primarily in the South have the mission of helping to secure strong enforcement of laws relating to protection of the environment, broadly defined.

Community courts, another type of problem-solving court, have been set up in a few dozen cities since 1993. As their generic name may suggest, community courts take different forms. But their focus is generally on the needs of what one commentary called "a victimized community"[6] within a city rather than on the problems of defendants. Often, the emphasis is on dealing more effectively with "nuisance" or "quality-of-life" crimes such as loitering that make a neighborhood unattractive. Some of these courts were created primarily at the initiative of businesses that were negatively affected by the prevalence of minor crimes, and community courts in Manhattan and St. Louis were funded in part by local businesses.

Thus most specialized units that focus on particular kinds of criminal offenses have been created to achieve different outcomes and court policies in criminal cases. In turn, changing what courts do has been viewed as a means to address social problems that are connected with crime.

THE SUCCESS OF JUDICIAL SPECIALIZATION

Of the goals that have motivated judicial specialization in the states, the most straightforward is enhancing court efficiency. Simple as it would seem to measure achievement of that goal, we actually know little about the effects of specialization on efficiency. The same is true of effectiveness in handling cases, in part because effectiveness is difficult to measure.

For the business courts that have been inspired by the Delaware Court of Chancery, efficiency and effectiveness are viewed as means to the end of keeping companies in the state or attracting others to come. As discussed in the Delaware Court of Chancery box, it is difficult to isolate the impact of Chancery on Delaware's status as home of corporations from other state policies. It appears, however, that the court plays a secondary but significant role. Creation of business-oriented courts in other states seems unlikely to have a similar impact. In the absence of the other conditions that exist in Delaware, increased effectiveness in handling business-related cases probably has little effect on decisions about where to locate businesses.[7]

The most important questions about the impact of state specialized courts relate to the courts that were created to shape judicial policy in some category of criminal cases. In turn, changes in judicial policy are a means to address social problems, problems that range from the narrow (such as unruly behavior in a stadium) to the broad (such as drug addiction). On the basis of the incomplete but meaningful information we have, the success of judicial specialization in shaping judicial policy and addressing social problems can be examined.

Judicial Policy

When a specialized criminal court is given a mission, will it carry out that mission? In the short run, the prospects are generally good. One reason is that the judges who initially serve in such a court usually have a personal commitment to the mission. These assignments are usually made within the judiciary, and frequently judges more or less assign themselves because of their enthusiasm for a court's goals. The judges who staffed the early juvenile courts and drug courts were often the primary advocates for creation of those units within their courts.

Furthermore, other people in the court and interested parties outside court are often enthusiastic supporters of the court's mission. Like judges, prosecutors and public defenders who join a new drug court generally believe in the problem-solving approach that drug courts are intended to take. People outside the courts sometimes reinforce a court's mission, as has been true of local businesses and residents for community courts.

Some specialized units exist for only a limited time, often because they were intended to be temporary. With a court that continues for a lengthy period, the initial impetus behind its mission is not always maintained. Interest and scrutiny from outside the court are likely to wane, so that the court becomes more autonomous. Continued adherence to a mission then depends heavily on the views and commitment of judges.

Over time, judges who begin with great enthusiasm for their court's mission may lose some of that enthusiasm. This is especially true when the mission requires that judges give close and extended attention to individual defendants, as drug courts and mental health courts do. That kind of mission can wear judges down, just as it can with people who work in social service agencies.

A bigger problem is the assignment of judges who have no particular commitment to a court's mission. The more widespread and long-lasting a type of court is, the more likely that outcome is to occur. The history of juvenile courts best illustrates that process. When juvenile courts spread across the country, they came to some courts in which no judge was enthusiastic about handling juvenile cases in a new way. And over the course of the twentieth century, juvenile courts increasingly slid back from the original model in which young offenders were viewed as people to be treated for their problems to the traditional criminal model of defendants to be judged and punished. This backsliding ultimately led the U.S. Supreme Court to demand that juveniles be given most of the procedural rights that were provided for adult defendants.[8] As the Court collectively saw it, juveniles originally had been deprived of those rights in the cause of serving their interests under the treatment model. Since the treatment model had atrophied, the rights should be restored.

Because drug courts have not spread as widely or lasted as long as juvenile courts, they have adhered more closely to their original mission. But it is already clear that some of the judges who serve in drug courts do not share the vision of the people who developed the drug court model. The most vivid example is a Georgia judge whose harsh and punitive treatment of drug court defendants was brought to light by a national radio show. After the state judicial conduct commission charged the judge with misconduct for her courtroom conduct, she resigned her position in 2011.[9]

Atrophy of organizational missions over time is not unique to specialized courts. Students of bureaucracy have pointed to a similar process in administrative agencies that begin with strong mandates to adopt particular lines of policy. The image of a regulatory agency that initially regulates an industry with zeal and then becomes "captured" by that industry, although often exaggerated, reflects a reality of administrative behavior.

This process is not inevitable. Within the judiciary, many juvenile courts continue to function as the inventors of that institution intended, and the same may be true of drug courts and veterans' treatment courts decades into the future. The sense of satisfaction that judges often say they get from following the problem-solving model rather than the conventional approach to criminal cases is a powerful force. But keeping those institutions focused on their original missions is not always an easy process.

Addressing Social Problems

The goals behind the creation of specialized courts differ considerably in their ambition. Courts set up to deal with backlogs of drug prosecutions or foreclosure cases are asked to solve a relatively simple and straightforward problem. But the socialized courts established in the early twentieth century and the problem-solving courts of the current era have been mandated to address difficult and complex social problems.

Juvenile courts, the earliest courts of this type, had highly ambitious goals. For the young people who came before them, juvenile courts were intended not only to prevent future criminal activity by them but also to improve their life prospects. The far-reaching goals of these courts were reflected in their gaining jurisdiction over "offenses" that would not be criminal for adults and over young people who were abused and neglected rather than charged with wrongdoing.

Although they are more limited in their reach, some problem-solving courts have similar aims. Working with people addicted to drugs, those suffering from mental illnesses, or military veterans whose service has put them in difficult circumstances, these courts are intended to address both short-term and long-term problems of the offenders who are their clients. In effect, these kinds of courts are efforts to rehabilitate criminal defendants, though that term is not often used.

The term *rehabilitation* is avoided because it came to be viewed with suspicion. For most of the twentieth century, rehabilitation was a central goal of the criminal justice system. Judges gave heavy weight to the potential for rehabilitation when they sentenced defendants, and parole boards were established to base prisoners' release dates on their success in achieving rehabilitation. But the belief that rehabilitation could be effective gradually declined. In part for that reason, a movement developed to base criminal sentences on the severity of the offense and the defendant's prior record rather than on potential rehabilitation. That movement succeeded in making fundamental changes in sentencing rules for federal courts and many states.

Can problem-solving courts overcome the difficulties that led to the decline in rehabilitation as a goal? Advocates of these courts argue that they represent a new approach, one in which offenders are kept under close scrutiny and given strong support in their efforts to overcome their problems. There is already a body of research evaluating the success of drug courts and some research on mental health courts. This research gives some reason for hope that the problem-solving approach can be effective, but the evidence is mixed.

Problem-solving courts of a particular type may be most effective when they are small in number and work with limited numbers of offenders. When they are small it number, it is more likely that the judges, attorneys, and other personnel who serve in them will be dedicated to their missions. When they work with a limited number of offenders, they can concentrate their limited resources on those offenders.

Resources are a significant issue because the high level of attention and effort given to defendants in problem-solving courts is expensive. (If these courts reduce the number of people who are sentenced to prison, they can save the penal system considerable money, but those savings do not necessarily come back to the courts.) Federal money helps to maintain problem-solving courts, and court systems in some states aid trial courts in establishing and maintaining these courts. Even so, scarcity of resources limits the numbers of offenders who can enter problem-solving courts.

Most problem-solving courts do handle small numbers of cases. This reality has led some commentators to refer to problem-solving courts as "boutique courts." That label has a negative connotation that may be inappropriate, but it captures an important reality. According to a 2005 estimate, at that time drug courts were dealing with only 4 percent of the "at-risk arrestee population."[10] If drug courts can improve the prospects of 4 percent of this group, that is not a trivial accomplishment. But at best, drug courts and other courts that fit under the problem-solving label can serve as a small part of the solution to the problems of the groups with which they work.

CONCLUSION

Specialization in state courts varies in many respects—official and unofficial, permanent and temporary, full-time and part-time, broad and narrow. Some forms of specialization, such as rotation of judges between criminal and civil cases, seem routine and unremarkable. Others, such as concentration of domestic violence or environmental cases in a single courtroom, are potentially more consequential.

Taken as a whole, the considerable degree of specialization in state trial courts represents a departure from the traditional image of the generalist judge who hears the full range of cases that come to court. If that image represents an ideal, to a degree the states have rejected that ideal. Rather, for reasons that range from an interest in greater efficiency to an interest in addressing social problems, policymakers within and outside the courts frequently opt for specialization.

Within state government, of course, specialization is hardly unique to courts. The bureaucracy is divided into agencies by subject matter, and individual employees within agencies are often highly specialized in their responsibilities. Legislators vote on a wide range of issues, but they do much of their work in committees that deal with particular types of issues. In this respect, as in many others, the judiciary has more in common with the other branches than it seems to have at first glance.

NOTES

1. These courts are shown in the State Court Structure Charts at the website of the Court Statistics Project, www.courtstatistics.org/Other-Pages/State_Court_Structure_Charts.aspx.

2. John Paul Ryan, Allan Ashman, Bruce D. Sales, and Sandra Shane-DuBow, *American Trial Judges: Their Work Styles and Performance* (New York: Free Press, 1980), 23.

3. See Barbara E. Smith et al., "Burning the Midnight Oil: An Examination of Cook County's Night Drug Court," *Justice System Journal* 17 (1994): 41–52.

4. Evelina Belden, *Courts in the United States Hearing Children's Cases* (Washington, DC: Government Printing Office, 1920), 29–30.

5. National Association of Drug Court Professionals, "Types of Drug Courts," www.nadcp.org/learn/what-are-drug-courts/models.

6. Jeffrey Fagan and Victoria Malkin, "Theorizing Community Justice through Community Courts," *Fordham Law Journal* 30 (2003): 902.

7. John F. Coyle, "Business Cases and Interstate Competition," *William and Mary Law Review* 53 (2012): 1915–1983.

8. *Kent v. United States,* 383 U.S. 541 (1966); In *re Gault,* 387 U.S. 1 (1967).

9. Robbie Brown, "Georgia Judge Accused of Misconduct Will Resign," *New York Times,* December 21, 2011, A27.

10. Avinash Singh Bhati, John K. Roman, and Aaron Chalfin, *To Treat or Not to Treat: Evidence on the Prospects of Expanding Treatment to Drug-Involved Offenders* (Washington, DC: Urban Institute, 2008), 33.

SUGGESTED READING

Bach, Mitchell L., and Lee Applebaum. "A History of the Creation and Jurisdiction of Business Courts in the Last Decade." *The Business Lawyer* 60 (2004): 147–275.

Baum, Lawrence. *Specializing the Courts.* Chicago: University of Chicago Press, 2011.

Berman, Greg, and John Feinblatt, with Sarah Glaser. *Good Courts: The Case for Problem-Solving Justice.* New York: The New Press, 2005.

Butts, Jeffrey A., and John Roman, eds. *Juvenile Drug Courts and Teen Substance Abuse.* Washington, DC: Urban Institute Press, 2004.

Casey, Pamela M., and David B. Rottman. "Problem-Solving Courts: Models and Trends." *Justice System Journal* 26 (2005): 35–56.

Coyle, John F. "Business Courts and Interstate Competition." *William and Mary Law Review* 53 (2012): 1915–1983.

Fagan, Jeffrey, and Victoria Malkin. "Theorizing Community Justice through Community Courts." *Fordham Law Journal* 30 (2003): 897–953.

Getis, Victoria. *The Juvenile Court and the Progressives.* Urbana: University of Illinois Press, 2000.

McCoy, Candace. "The Politics of Problem-Solving: An Overview of the Origins and Development of Therapeutic Courts." *American Criminal Law Review* 40 (2003): 1513–1539.

Mirchandani, Rekha. "What's So Special about Specialized Courts? The State and Social Change in Salt Lake City's Domestic Violence Courts." *Law and Society Review* 39 (2005): 379–417.

Nolan, James L., Jr. *Reinventing Justice: The American Drug Court Movement.* Princeton, NJ: Princeton University Press, 2001.

Quillen, William T., and Michael Hanrahan. "A Short History of the Delaware Court of Chancery—1792–1992." *Delaware Journal of Corporate Law* 18 (1993): 819–866.

Rottman, David B. *Community Courts: Prospects and Limits.* Williamsburg: National Center for State Courts, 2002.

Ryerson, Ellen. *The Best-Laid Plans: America's Juvenile Court Experiment.* New York: Hill and Wang.

Sviridoff, Michele, David B. Rottman, Brian Ostrom, and Richard Curtis. *Dispensing Justice Locally: The Implementation and Effects of the Midtown Community Court.* Amsterdam: Harwood Academic Publishers, 2000.

Tanenhaus, David S. *Juvenile Justice in the Making.* New York: Oxford University Press, 2004.

Tsai, Betsy. "The Trend toward Specialized Domestic Violence Courts: Improvements on an Effective Innovation." *Fordham Law Review* 68 (2000): 1285–1327.

Willrich, Michael. *City of Courts: Socializing Justice in Progressive Era Chicago.* New York: Cambridge University Press, 2003.

Winick, Bruce J., and David B. Wexler, eds. *Judging in a Therapeutic Key: Therapeutic Jurisprudence and the Courts.* Durham: Carolina Academic Press, 2003.

Chapter 23

Courts and the Initiative and Referendum Process

Kenneth P. Miller and Aditya Pai

DIRECT CITIZEN PARTICIPATION IN lawmaking is a defining characteristic of state government. While the United States is one of the world's few advanced democracies that has never held a national referendum on a policy or constitutional issue, the individual states have developed a strong tradition of democratic participation through popular referendums. In nearly every state, the referendum procedure gives the people the power to approve or reject proposals presented to them by state legislatures and state constitutional conventions.[1] More radically, as described in Chapter 6, states that have adopted the direct initiative process empower citizens to enact laws without any substantive participation by representatives. In these states, a citizen activist, interest group, or coalition can draft a new law or state constitutional amendment (or both) and gather enough petition signatures to place the question on the ballot and submit it to the people for their approval or rejection.

As direct citizen lawmaking has expanded in recent decades, some states have developed what may be considered *hybrid* systems of government—part representative, part direct—with institutional dynamics unlike the traditional textbook model of three-branch checks and balances. Through the initiative process, citizens in these states regularly bypass, override, and marginalize state legislatures on important policy issues. Citizen lawmaking, however, cannot bypass the courts. Judicial review—the power to invalidate a law that, in a court's view, violates either the federal or state constitution—extends to all laws, including those enacted directly by the people. The courts thus operate the strongest institutional check on direct popular rule.

Moreover, the judicial power has expanded over time. The U.S. Supreme Court has recognized and enforced a growing sphere of federal constitutional rights, particularly in the areas of equal protection, due process, privacy, free speech, and criminal procedure and punishment. Since the 1970s, many state supreme courts have also actively expanded the judicial power by defining and enforcing some state constitutional rights beyond federal minimums.[2] Courts have thereby shifted many policy questions from majoritarian political processes to the judicial arena.

The concurrent rise of direct democracy and the judicial power—one purely majoritarian, the other countermajoritarian—has thus produced novel forms of checks and balances. In examining these dynamics, one must ask: Have courts, in fact, countered direct democracy? The short answer is "yes," but the full story is more complex. An accurate assessment requires us to consider the various ways courts have interacted with direct democracy. Courts have defended the institutions of direct democracy against various threats, but they have also partially or completely struck down many citizen-enacted laws. In addition, courts play a part in administering the initiative system's preelection procedures—a task that varies from state to state.

Understanding the relationship between direct democracy and the courts does not stop with the judicial check on citizen lawmaking. One must also ask: Have the people used direct democracy to counter the judiciary when they believe it has overreached? Again, the answer is "yes," but only under certain circumstances.

The interplay between direct democracy and the courts has become an increasingly important feature of state government with consequences for taxes, term limits, campaign finance reform, criminal procedure and punishment, abortion, affirmative action, same-sex marriage, and many other controversial policies. More fundamentally, the conflict raises questions about the proper scope of popular sovereignty and judicial power in a constitutional system. This chapter explores these dynamics and their implications.

JUDICIAL RESPONSE TO DIRECT DEMOCRACY

The concept of direct citizen lawmaking through the initiative process was introduced in the United States in the late nineteenth century. After much debate, a critical mass

Students hoping for a repeal of California's Proposition 209 hold signs as they protest outside of the Ninth U.S. Circuit Court of Appeals on February 13, 2012, in San Francisco, California. The federal appeals court heard arguments in a lawsuit seeking to overturn Proposition 209, a voter-approved measure that prohibits affirmative action at state universities, and in April 2012 upheld the affirmative action ban.

SOURCE: Photo by Justin Sullivan/Getty Images.

developed in favor of direct democracy in some parts of the country, especially in the West. By 1918, twenty states and many more local jurisdictions empowered their citizens to enact laws directly. Today, twenty-four states have adopted the initiative process. The initiative process has been used more frequently in some states than in others, but has become increasingly important in a growing number of states since the 1970s[3] (see Chapter 6, Initiative and Referendum). Over time, courts have developed a complicated relationship with direct democracy. First, courts have protected the people's power to enact laws directly by invalidating various efforts to abolish or restrict the process. Second, courts have assumed a regulatory function by reviewing preelection procedures and technical requirements. And third, courts have exercised a heavy check on direct democracy by invalidating individual initiatives at high rates. This section explores these various judicial interactions with direct popular rule.

Judicial Protection of the Initiative Process

Courts have protected the institution of direct citizen lawmaking from various attacks. When the initiative process was first introduced in the states, opponents argued that it violated the federal Constitution's Article IV guarantee clause, which reads: "The United States shall guarantee to every State in this Union a Republican Form of Government[.]" In a series of court challenges, opponents contended that direct democracy impermissibly bypassed republican government, which they defined as *representative* democracy, and that laws enacted through the initiative process were illegitimate and void.

The issue reached the U.S. Supreme Court in *Pacific States Telephone and Telegraph Company v. Oregon* (1912).[4] In a unanimous decision, the Court was unwilling to embrace the opponents' Article IV challenge, ruling that the issue was a nonjusticiable political question outside the Court's purview. The Supreme Court thus effectively protected the process of direct citizen lawmaking at the state and local level from court challenges on federal constitutional grounds. That outcome conferred constitutional legitimacy on the new devices of direct democracy. Individual initiatives would face legal challenges, but the constitutional validity of the process itself was now secure.

More recently, courts have invalidated many efforts by state legislatures to restrict the initiative process. Legislatures have sought to limit contributions to ballot measure campaigns, ban payments to signature gatherers, require petitioners to be registered to vote in the state, and limit the locations where petitioners can operate. If allowed to stand, these restrictions could seriously inhibit direct citizen lawmaking. The courts, however, have frequently struck down these limitations. For example, in *Meyer v. Grant* (1988), the U.S. Supreme Court declared that initiative sponsors have a First Amendment right to pay persons to collect signatures on initiative petitions.[5] Courts have also invalidated laws requiring petitioners to reside or be registered to vote in the state or county where they are circulating initiative petitions, or requiring petitioners to disclose their status as paid signature gatherers by wearing a badge or by other means. Through these and other related decisions, courts have protected the exercise of direct democracy from restrictive regulations.

Judicial Administration of the Initiative Process

Courts also supervise preelection procedures for qualifying individual measures for the ballot. Here, judicial protection of direct democracy has been less consistent. Aggressive preelection enforcement of procedural rules and technical substantive requirements can significantly constrain the initiative power. Unsurprisingly, then, initiative opponents have often pursued preelection lawsuits to attempt to kill measures before they reach the ballot. Preelection challenges to initiatives fall into three categories. The first type challenges the measure for failure to comply with procedural rules of the initiative process, such as the form of the petition, the sufficiency of signatures, and the language of the title and summary. Most states permit preelection review of procedural compliance; in many states, this review is mandatory. The second type of preelection challenge claims improper subject matter, such as multiple subjects. Courts in most states will review these types of challenges before the election. Finally, some preelection challenges attack the initiative on substantive constitutional grounds. On purely procedural matters, such as challenges to the sufficiency of petition signatures, courts have generally interpreted the requirements liberally to prevent a measure's opponent from exploiting technicalities to block an initiative. But when an initiative challenge involves both procedural and substantive elements, the courts have provided less protection.

Consider preelection review of ballot titles and summaries. In most initiative states, a title board, the attorney general, or the secretary of state has initial responsibility for drafting an initiative's title and summary. If interested parties object to the wording, they can challenge it in court. The judicial preelection role varies considerably from state to state. Some courts have shown great deference toward the drafting agency's decisions; others have become enmeshed in lengthy disputes over the text of ballot titles. The Oregon high court's docket, for instance, became clogged with ballot title disputes in the 1990s, with several parties appealing ninety-two of the titles certified by the attorney general's office. The court rewrote half of these titles—fully one-fifth of its decisions involved these disputes.[6] The titling process in several states, including Arizona, Colorado, and Washington, has also become increasingly litigious. The greatest controversies have arisen in states such as Florida, where proponents write their own ballot titles and courts have blocked initiatives from the ballot on the grounds that the title was inadequate. In addition, as discussed further below, some courts have also used preelection review of the initiative's compliance with the single-subject rule to block measures from the ballot. The evidence thus indicates that some state courts have offered significant resistance to direct democracy through the preelection enforcement of rules for the initiative process.

A related issue is whether courts should rule on the substantive validity of an initiative prior to the election. Courts in most initiative states are reluctant to resolve these questions before the people have a chance to vote on the measure—and, possibly, reject it. Although some courts have invalidated initiatives before the election, they have more often exercised the judicial check after people have voted. This principle of restraint is based on the doctrine of "ripeness"—the general rule against advisory opinions and other related concerns of separation of powers and judicial economy. However, courts in several states have rejected this view. In Arkansas, Missouri, Montana, Nebraska, Oklahoma, and Utah, courts will consider constitutional challenges to initiatives before the election. In Florida, the state constitution actually mandates this form of preelection review. Many judges and legal scholars also believe courts should be willing to intervene before the election to remove unconstitutional initiatives from the ballot.

Judicial Check on Voter-Approved Initiatives

The courts' most consequential ongoing interaction with direct democracy is postelection review. Through this power, courts have exercised a strong check on the initiative process across states and over time. Analysis of postelection challenges to voter-approved initiatives shows that substantial percentages of voter-approved initiatives have been challenged and invalidated.

Overview

Data from high-use initiative states (California, Oregon, Colorado, Washington, and Arizona) show that during the first century of citizen lawmaking (1904–2008), more than 40 percent of initiatives faced postelection challenges. After 1970, the rates sharply increased, with more than half of all initiatives adopted from 1970 through the end of the 1990s facing postelection judicial review. Initiative litigation reached all-time highs in the 1990s in both absolute and percentage terms. Postelection challenges were also common in the other initiative states and remained high in the post-2000 period.[7]

Invalidations of citizen-enacted laws provide even better evidence of the judicial check on direct democracy. The data show that courts invalidated, either in part or entirely, nearly one-fifth of all voter-approved initiatives in the high-use initiative states. Moreover, invalidation rates increased dramatically between the 1960s and the 1990s, as the conflict between citizen lawmakers and courts intensified. Courts invalidated, in whole or in part, over 30 percent of all initiatives adopted in these states during the 1990s. As initiative use rose to historic highs in the 1990s, the rate of initiative challenges and invalidations rose with it. Indeed, the litigation record suggests that the judicial check on direct democracy has more than kept pace with the dramatic expansion in citizen lawmaking over the past several decades.

State versus Federal Courts

When challenging an initiative, attorneys need to decide whether to file the case in state or federal court. Whereas state courts have general subject matter jurisdiction and can hear claims arising under *either* federal or state law, federal courts are constrained by the limits of federal subject matter jurisdiction. As a consequence, an initiative's opponents may pursue a federal court challenge only if the case presents a federal question. In the early decades of the initiative process, opponents routinely challenged initiatives in state courts, even when the case raised federal constitutional issues. Beginning in the 1980s, however, opponents increasingly turned to the federal courts when the option was available. The strategic shift yielded mixed results. The record shows that federal courts have been somewhat more likely than state courts to invalidate a challenged initiative. However, when federal courts have found a constitutional violation, they have been more likely to sever the invalid provisions and allow the remainder of the initiative to stand, while state courts have more frequently invalidated the initiative in its entirety. Thus, while federal judges have more frequently checked voter-approved initiatives, state judges have delivered a stronger check when they intervene.

Legal Bases of Initiative Challenges and Invalidations

The legal challenges to initiatives have been fought in two broad arenas of constitutional law: rights and powers. Rights-based challenges have most frequently alleged that the initiative violated state or federal constitutional protections of property, contract, speech, petition, association, due process, equal protection, or the cluster of rights governing criminal prosecutions. Powers-based challenges, by contrast, have most often claimed that the measure violated federal constitutional provisions such as the Article I qualifications clauses, the Article IV guarantee of republican government clause, or the Article VI supremacy clause, or state constitutional provisions related to the powers of government institutions or the scope of the initiative process.

Opponents have attacked initiatives more frequently on powers- than rights-based theories, but courts have been more receptive to rights-based challenges. When ruling that an initiative violates a constitutional right, courts have more frequently invoked federal than state constitutional rights. In cases involving disputes over powers, courts have most frequently struck down initiatives for violating state constitutional provisions concerning separation of powers, the powers of representative institutions, or limitations on the initiative process such as the rule that an initiative may contain only one subject.

Outcomes by Initiative Subject Matter

Broad developments in constitutional law have created variations in litigation outcomes depending on the subject matter of the initiative. Over the past several decades, initiatives that have addressed contested areas of rights such as political speech (especially regulation of campaign contributions and expenditures), abortion, criminal procedure and punishment, and the rights of racial and other minorities have been most frequently challenged and invalidated, whereas measures related to taxing, government spending, environmental protection, and economic regulation have faced less opposition in the courts.

Some postelection challenges are highly predictable. For example, campaign finance reform initiatives are almost always challenged—and often at least partially invalidated—on federal First Amendment grounds (see Contested Definitions of Rights: Campaign Finance Reform box). Similarly, initiatives that place restrictions on abortion have always faced constitutional challenges. Nearly three-fourths of voter-approved initiatives related to criminal procedure and punishment have been challenged after the election, usually in the context of criminal appeals. Courts have upheld many of these initiatives against constitutional attack, including some very tough measures such as California's "three-strikes-and-you're-out" sentencing law. Yet courts have also invalidated several crime measures in whole or in part, on a range of state and federal constitutional grounds. Initiatives that arguably limit the rights of certain minority groups—including racial minorities, immigrants, non–English speakers, and gays and lesbians—will likely face court challenges, usually on federal equal protection grounds. The outcomes in these types of cases have been mixed. Courts have upheld some measures (such as bans on affirmative action and bilingual education), but have struck down others, such as Colorado's Amendment 2 of 1992, which sought to broadly prohibit laws granting protected status to persons based on their sexual orientation.

In cases involving government powers, state-level initiatives that have sought to alter government institutions or the relationship between state and federal powers have taken a heavy toll in the courts. The most notable examples come from the term-limits movement of the 1990s. During that decade, voters in more than twenty states adopted initiatives and referendums aimed at limiting the terms of federal elected officials, state elected officials, or both. Courts invalidated most of these citizen efforts to restrict the terms of elected representatives (see Conflicts over Government Powers: Term Limits box). Courts have also invalidated several initiatives on topics such as immigration reform on the basis that federal law preempts the citizen-enacted state law.

Standards of Judicial Review

Judges and legal scholars have debated the appropriate standards for judicial review of initiatives: Should courts treat initiatives the same way they would a law enacted by a legislature, or should they use different standards when reviewing citizen-enacted law?

CONTESTED DEFINITIONS OF RIGHTS: CAMPAIGN FINANCE REFORM

Conflicts between the people and the courts often involve disputes over the scope of constitutional rights in areas ranging from criminal procedure and punishment to race, abortion, and marriage. One of the most frequently contested areas involves the right to free speech in the context of campaign contributions or expenditures. Over time, the people have supported many ballot measures designed to regulate money in politics. Courts, however, have frequently invalidated such measures on the grounds that political contributions and expenditures are a form of "speech" and are protected by the First Amendment to the U.S. Constitution or equivalent provisions of state constitutions. A recent case from Montana, *American Tradition Partnership, Inc. v. Bullock* (2012), illustrates these dynamics.[1]

Montana voters approved the state's Corrupt Political Practices Act as a citizen's initiative in 1912. Among other things, the act states that a "corporation may not make . . . an expenditure in connection with a candidate or a political party that supports or opposes a candidate or a political party." This ban on corporate political contributions was rendered vulnerable by the U.S. Supreme Court's controversial decision in *Citizens United v. Federal Election Commission* (2010), the case that struck down on First Amendment grounds a ban on independent expenditures in federal elections by corporations and labor unions.[2]

American Tradition Partnership (ATP), a conservative 501(c)4 advocacy group, challenged the Montana law, and in 2011 the case reached the Montana Supreme Court. The question presented was whether the right recognized in *Citizens United* applied here, or whether Montana could permissibly ban corporate political contributions.

The Montana Supreme Court, in a 5–2 ruling, upheld the law. The court determined that the measure survived "strict scrutiny" because Montana's unique context and history of corruption justified the ban in ways not contemplated by *Citizens United.* American Tradition Partnership then sought review from the U.S. Supreme Court. American Tradition Partnership contended that the Montana Supreme Court's refusal to follow *Citizens United* was such an obvious error that it merited the Court's summary reversal. Montana attorney general Steve Bullock urged the justices to uphold his state's ban on corporate political spending. The record, Bullock argued, showed the Montana Corrupt Practices Act imposed far different obligations, and therefore affected corporate speech in a far different manner, than the federal law at issue in *Citizens United.*

In a 5–4 decision that broke along the same lines as *Citizens United,* the U.S. Supreme Court reversed the Montana Supreme Court, holding that the Montana ban violated the First Amendment. The dissenting justices, led by Justice Stephen Breyer, argued that *Citizens United* should get new scrutiny in the light of its effect on campaign finance, but the majority rejected this view. Notably, the Court reaffirmed a broad and controversial reading of the First Amendment in a way that thwarted the people of Montana's desire to secure other values, such as reducing the threat of political corruption posed by corporate spending.

The ruling in *American Tradition Partnership, Inc. v. Bullock* demonstrates the growing scope of judicial review and the limits of citizens' checks on federal courts. While the people can overturn a state court's interpretation of state constitutional law through state constitutional amendment, it is almost impossible to overturn a decision of the U.S. Supreme Court on a question of federal constitutional law. Some supporters of robust campaign finance reform have called for an amendment to the U.S. Constitution to reverse the Court's interpretation of the rights of political contributors, but the hurdles presented by the federal Constitution's amendment process are almost certainly too high.

1. *American Tradition Partnership, Inc. v. Bullock,* 132 S. Ct. 2490 (2012).
2. *Citizens United v. Federal Election Commission,* 558 U.S. 50 (2010).

This debate is driven by the distinctive nature of the judicial check on direct democracy. When a court strikes down a voter-approved initiative, it is not checking a department of representative government; it is checking the people themselves. Although the prevailing rule is that courts should review an initiative no differently than they would other laws, a range of voices have proposed alternative standards of review. Some have argued courts should exercise *more* deference when reviewing initiatives than they do when reviewing ordinary legislation; others have pushed for *less* deference to initiatives.

The theory that courts should exercise greater deference when reviewing initiatives relies almost exclusively on the principle of popular sovereignty. Citizens have not only the right to make laws, the argument runs, but also a sovereign and reserved right to do so—superior to any power they delegate to the legislature. Courts should thus exercise maximum restraint when reviewing the validity of the laws people directly enact. This view enjoys little support in the contemporary legal academy, but some judges have embraced it. U.S. Supreme Court justice Hugo Black was a prominent example. In *Reitman v. Mulkey* (1967), a case testing the constitutional validity of California's Proposition 14 of 1964, Justice Black suggested that the challenge should have less force "because here, it's moving in the direction of letting the people of the State—the voters of the State—establish their policy, which is as near to a democracy as you can get."[8] Several state judges have expressed similar deferential attitudes when reviewing citizen-enacted laws.

CONFLICTS OVER GOVERNMENT POWERS: TERM LIMITS

In the early 1990s, an antigovernment mood spread through much of the nation and helped spur the term-limits movement. Many citizens concluded that periodic elections no longer provided a sufficient popular check on representatives. Term limits, they argued, were necessary to curtail long-term incumbency. A movement thus gathered momentum to impose mandatory term limits on both state elected officials and members of Congress. The term-limits movement, however, quickly revealed a divide between citizens and their representatives. In 1990 a national poll showed that citizens supported term limits for members of Congress by a 61–21 percent margin. By contrast, 66 percent of U.S. House members opposed them.

Facing opposition from state and national legislators, the movement decided to bypass representatives and impose term limits directly, through the initiative process, in every state where that was an option. Citizen lawmakers in Oklahoma first approved term-limits measures in September 1990 by a 67 percent vote. Over the next two years, voters approved term-limits measures in Arizona, Arkansas, Florida, Michigan, Missouri, Montana, Nebraska, North Dakota, Ohio, Oregon, South Dakota, and Wyoming. Support for term limits continued to build. By 1995, twenty-one states had adopted term limits on state elected officials and twenty-three states had imposed limits on their representatives in Congress. In almost every case, the changes occurred through the initiative process. This wave of term-limits initiatives greatly contributed to the high rates of initiative use in the 1990s and was one of the most successful political mobilizations in U.S. history. Many members of Congress, however, looked to the Supreme Court to strike down the voter-imposed limitations on their terms. Article I of the U.S. Constitution provides a short list of qualifications for representatives and senators related to age, citizenship, and residency. Were these qualifications exclusive, or could states add additional qualifications? The Supreme Court's decision in *U.S. Term Limits v. Thornton* (1995) would settle the question.[1]

The test case emerged from Arkansas. In November 1992, voters in Arkansas had joined the term-limits movement by adopting Amendment 73—an initiative that placed limits on both members of Congress and state elected officials. The voters approved the initiative by a 67–33 percent margin. Soon after the election, term-limits opponents challenged the measure; two years later, the case reached the U.S. Supreme Court. In May 1996, by a 5–4 vote, the Court declared state-imposed congressional term limits unconstitutional.

The heart of the decision focused on institutional powers: states simply did not have the authority to enact term limits on federal offices. Writing for the majority, Justice John Paul Stevens explained that "allowing the several States to adopt term limits for congressional service would effect a fundamental change in the constitutional framework." The only permissible way to establish congressional term limits was through the federal constitutional amendment procedures set forth in Article V.

U.S. Term Limits was one of the most countermajoritarian decisions in the Court's history, and demonstrated how the Court can—in a single opinion—invalidate initiatives adopted by citizens in several states. In one stroke, the Court invalidated laws adopted by twenty-three states, overriding the will of nearly twenty-five million American citizens. State supreme courts also invalidated term-limit laws on state elected officials on other theories. And although term limits on state elected officials survive in fifteen states (see Chapter 17), the courts put a major damper on this popular citizen-driven movement.

1. *U.S. Term Limits v. Thornton*, 514 U.S. 779 (1995).

The theory that courts should give less deference to citizen-enacted laws rests on very different premises. The proponents of heightened scrutiny of ballot measures celebrate the courts as strong guardians of rights and denigrate the initiative process. Most in this camp contend that direct democracy is too democratic—that is, it too easily translates majority sentiments into law and endangers the rights of unpopular individuals or minority groups. Scholars including Derrick A. Bell and Julian N. Eule have called for heightened scrutiny of direct democracy, or at least a "hard look" on particular kinds of initiatives most likely to limit minority rights.[9] In sum, these debates over the standard of review for initiatives are motivated by conflicting attitudes regarding the appropriate scope of direct democracy in relation to judicial power.

Strict Enforcement of Initiative Rules

Judicial attitudes toward the initiative sometimes reveal themselves in cases interpreting and enforcing a state's rules for citizen lawmaking. State court judges can interpret such rules in divergent ways, and a court's attitude toward the initiative process can sometimes be discerned by how strictly it enforces them. In recent decades, a number of state supreme court judges have grown concerned about the increasing power of the initiative process and concluded that new interpretations of state constitutional law are necessary to constrain direct citizen lawmaking. They have explored several avenues, including the *single-subject rule*, the *separate-vote requirement*, and the *no-revision rule*.

The single-subject rule offers courts in several states the opportunity to strike down citizen-enacted laws on technical grounds. Three-fourths of the initiative states have a version of the single-subject rule, such as Colorado's version, which states that "if a measure contains more than one subject . . . [it] shall not be submitted to the people for adoption or rejection at the polls."[10] As legal scholar Daniel Hays Lowenstein has noted, the malleability of the term *subject* makes the rule a potentially severe constraint on the initiative power because a court can determine that almost any measure contains multiple "subjects."[11] Most courts have generally opted for a liberal interpretation of the rule. The California Supreme Court has been particularly consistent in rejecting nearly all single-subject attacks against initiatives, even when the measures have contained multiple, loosely related elements. Courts in states such as Colorado and Florida, however, have used strict enforcement of the single-subject rule to invalidate many initiatives. In one notable example, the Florida Supreme Court invalidated a series of proposed initiatives to ban state-sponsored affirmative action on the grounds that they violated the state's single-subject rule, even though comparable initiatives were permitted in other states, including California, Michigan, and Washington.

Similarly, courts in some states, including Montana and Oregon, have strictly enforced a rule called the separate-vote requirement for state constitutional amendments. This rule stipulates that when two or more constitutional amendments are submitted to the voters in the same election, they must be voted on separately. As the Oregon Supreme Court demonstrated in *Armatta v. Kitzhaber* (1998), enforcement of the separate-vote rule can spark intense controversy.[12] That court invoked the rule to invalidate a victims' rights initiative, Measure 40 of 1996. The court held that the separate-vote requirement is a "narrower restriction than the requirement that a proposed amendment embrace only one subject." Soon after *Armatta,* the Montana Supreme Court followed Oregon's lead when it invalidated Constitutional Initiative 75 of 1998, a voter-approved initiative requiring voter approval for tax increases, on the basis that it violated Montana's separate-vote requirement.[13]

Meanwhile, in California, initiative opponents have urged the state supreme court to limit the state's initiative power through strict enforcement of the no-revision rule. That rule stipulates that certain constitutional changes can be effected only through a constitutional revision, not by an amendment. The rule is important because constitutional revisions require the participation of the legislature. In one landmark case, the California Supreme Court declared that portions of a 1990 victims' rights initiative violated the no-revision rule by restricting the state courts' ability to interpret state constitutional rights beyond federal constitutional minimums.[14] But in most other cases, the California Supreme Court has refused to invalidate other initiatives as "revisions." It declined to hold that initiatives restoring capital punishment, restricting state taxing power, or limiting the terms of state legislators so fundamentally changed the state constitutional design that they were revisory rather than amendatory. More recently, in *Strauss v. Horton* (2009), the California Supreme Court rejected an appeal to invoke the rule to invalidate Proposition 8 of 2008, the amendment limiting marriage to a man and a woman. The court concluded that "the constitutional change embodied in proposition 8 . . . by no means makes such a far-reaching change in the California constitution as to amount to a constitutional revision."[15]

These examples demonstrate that courts can interpret and enforce various rules governing use of the initiative process in ways that either accommodate or constrain direct citizen lawmaking. Some urge courts to use strict enforcement of these rules to rein in the initiative process, but others allege that aggressive enforcement amounts to a subjective, standardless judicial veto—exceeding the courts' legitimate power of judicial review.

THE PEOPLE'S CHECKS ON COURTS

As the foregoing discussion demonstrates, courts have exercised an extensive and powerful check on direct democracy by invalidating a substantial number of citizen initiatives. Do the people exercise a reciprocal check on courts? The answer differs at the federal and state levels. While the people have almost no direct ability to constrain federal judicial power, they can and do exercise meaningful, direct constraints on state courts.

Federal versus State Courts

The people have little power over federal courts because the U.S. Constitution promotes judicial independence—that is, it insulates federal judges from popular control. Article III of the Constitution provides that federal judges be selected by the president with the advice and consent of the Senate, and thereafter enjoy tenure for life. Congress may impeach federal judges, but the people have no direct power to remove judges from the federal bench. Moreover, it is exceptionally difficult for the people to override federal court decisions that interpret the U.S. Constitution. The extremely high hurdles for amending the Constitution protect judicial interpretations from popular reversal and mean that when the Supreme Court issues a controversial ruling on a question of federal constitutional law, its decision is effectively final.

By contrast, state constitutions allow the people to hold judges accountable to the popular will. The procedures for judicial selection and retention vary from state to state, but almost all states give the people a direct vote in either the election or confirmation of judges and provide opportunities for the people to remove judges through regular elections, judicial recall, or both (see Chapter 21). Moreover, the people have the ability to override state court decisions interpreting state constitutions through constitutional amendment. As noted above, in almost every state, constitutions can be amended through referendums placed on the ballot by state legislatures, and in some states, the people can directly propose and adopt state constitutional amendments through the initiative process. These procedures make state constitutions much easier to amend than the federal Constitution. As a consequence, when a state court issues a controversial decision on a contested question of state constitutional law, the people can amend their constitution to override the court's judgment.

Contests over the Definition of Rights

Popular efforts to exercise a democratic check on courts have most often arisen in controversies over the definition or scope of rights. In the American constitutional system, courts bear important responsibility for enforcing the rights contained in state or federal constitutions, even if doing so invalidates a law that enjoys strong majority support. This remarkable judicial power can be abused, however, if judges reach beyond what a constitution mandates in order to substitute their own policy preferences for those embodied in existing laws.

Judicial interpretation and enforcement of constitutional rights is often hotly contested, in part because there is much disagreement regarding the scope of rights and in part because the distinction between a right and a mere interest is highly consequential. Once established, a new right trumps other competing values that may be of great importance but lack the status that "right" confers.[16] Given these stakes, Americans have long debated whether the courts should bear sole responsibility for defining the scope of constitutional rights, or whether the people should also be able to participate in this task.

Over a century ago, the conflict between courts and popular majorities became acute when courts expanded the definition of economic rights, including "liberty of contract," to overturn progressive social and economic regulations such as workers' compensation and maximum hours laws. At that time, progressive reformers led by Theodore Roosevelt railed against conservative judges and proposed ways for the people to overturn judicial decisions through popular votes. During his campaign for the presidency in 1912, Roosevelt advocated what he called a "recall of judicial decisions." Under his plan, if a state court declared a law unconstitutional, the people of the state could circulate a petition to "recall" the decision. If the people approved the court's ruling, it would stand; if they opposed it, the ruling would be void.[17] This procedure was briefly adopted in one state (Colorado), but never implemented. The initiative constitutional amendment procedure, however, achieves much the same purpose. If the people disapprove of a state court interpretation of their state constitution, they can adopt a constitutional amendment to override the court's decision. In states that lack the initiative process, the legislature must propose the amendment to override the court. In either case, the people, rather than the courts, have the last word on the definition of state constitutional rights and other questions of state constitutional law.

By the 1970s, conflicts over the definition of rights had established a pattern. The U.S. Supreme Court defined a "floor" of federal constitutional rights that courts protected against violation by either the federal government or the states. While states were compelled to follow these decisions and not restrict rights *below* this minimum standard, they could choose to expand rights *above* the floor. And, indeed, every state supreme court has interpreted its state constitution in ways that establish state constitutional rights beyond the federal constitutional minimum. In this sphere of state constitutional rights, however, the people can use the tools of initiative and referendum to exercise a check on judicial power. Indeed, in numerous instances, the people have used initiatives and legislative referendums to reverse state court decisions to expand rights beyond federal constitutional minimums, in a range of areas including racial desegregation (involving court-ordered busing in public schools), capital punishment, criminal procedure, abortion, and same-sex marriage.

Capital Punishment and Other Controversies

A controversy in California over the validity of the death penalty provides an example of how the people can overturn a major state court ruling on a contested issue of state constitutional rights. In the 1960s, a number of legal scholars and rights activists began asserting that the death penalty is *per se* unconstitutional. The U.S. Supreme Court was unwilling to adopt that view, but in 1972 the California Supreme Court, in the case of *People v. Anderson,* declared that capital punishment violates the *state* constitution.[18] The state court's ruling was highly consequential. It overturned the death sentences of over one hundred inmates on California's death row, including the notorious mass murderer Charles Manson and Sirhan Sirhan, the assassin of Sen. Robert F. Kennedy. It also prohibited future executions in California.

In its decision, the court reasoned that the California Constitution's prohibition on cruel or unusual punishments should be interpreted more broadly than the federal Constitution's Eighth Amendment. By finding a right against execution in the state constitution, the California Supreme Court insulated the ruling from review by the U.S. Supreme Court (federal courts generally do not review a state court's interpretation of state law), but it also exposed the decision to attack by the people through a citizen-initiated state constitutional amendment.

Public opposition to the court's *Anderson* decision quickly turned into popular countermobilization. A coalition of law-and-order groups prepared an initiative constitutional amendment to reverse *Anderson* and restore capital punishment in the state. Proponents quickly collected enough signatures to qualify the measure for the November ballot as Proposition 17. The initiative proposed to amend the state constitution to override explicitly the California Supreme Court's *Anderson* ruling, so that the death penalty "shall not be deemed to be, or to constitute, infliction of cruel and unusual punishments." In November 1972—less than nine months after the court's decision—Californians approved Proposition 17 by a decisive 2–1 vote. Through the power of initiative constitutional amendment, the citizens of California reversed a controversial new constitutional right and enforced the popular will regarding the constitutional validity of capital punishment.

The people in several states have used initiative and referendum to exercise similar checks on state court expansion of rights. In Massachusetts (1982) and Oregon (1984), voters adopted initiative constitutional amendments to overturn state supreme court decisions invalidating the death penalty. In California (1979), voters used the initiative process to override a state supreme court decision that mandated desegregative busing for public school students beyond federal mandates. In California (1982 and 1990) and in Florida (1982), citizens adopted initiative constitutional amendments reversing several state supreme court decisions that expanded rights of criminal defendants beyond federal minimums. In Colorado (1984), Arkansas (1988), and Florida (2004), voters adopted state constitutional amendments to override state supreme court decisions that expanded abortion rights beyond the federal standard.

The Battle over Marriage

The most widespread use of the initiative and referendum to override or preempt state court decisions emerged in the battle over the definition of marriage (also see Chapter 27, Moral Issues). The pattern of judicial action and popular countermobilization began in the 1990s when the Hawaii Supreme Court declared that the state's limitation of marriage to a man and a woman was suspect under the state constitution. The Hawaii legislature drafted an amendment to the state constitution to counter the court's decision by specifically authorizing the legislature to affirm the traditional definition of marriage. Hawaii voters approved the amendment by a 69–31 percent margin.

In 2003 the Massachusetts Supreme Judicial Court issued a landmark decision in *Goodridge v. Department of Public Health,* establishing a new state constitutional right of same-sex couples to marry.[19] Similar decisions followed in California, Connecticut, and Iowa. Meanwhile, advocates of traditional marriage pursued a state-by-state strategy of overriding or preempting such decisions through state constitutional amendments.

Over the course of two decades, voters in more than thirty states approved constitutional amendments that either expressly limited the definition of marriage to a union between a man and a woman or, in Hawaii's case, authorized the legislature to do so.[20] Most of the amendments came in 2004–2006, in the wake of the 2003 *Goodridge* decision. Some of the amendments focused only on the definition of marriage; others also prohibited the establishment of other legal arrangements substantially similar to marriage, such as domestic partnerships or civil unions.

While the Massachusetts court's decision in *Goodridge* helped trigger preemptive constitutional amendments in many states, voters in Massachusetts itself were unable to vote on the marriage issue. Soon after the court handed down its ruling, proponents of traditional marriage attempted to override the decision by amending

Marcia Hams, left, and her partner, Susan Shepard, right, cut a celebratory wedding cake in the mayor's chambers of the Cambridge Town Hall in Cambridge, Massachusetts. The lesbian couple was the first to be issued a marriage license in the state after Massachusetts became the first state in the United States to legally sanction same-sex marriage based on a ruling by the Massachusetts Supreme Judicial Court. In Goodridge v. Department of Public Health, *issued on November 18, 2003, the court gave the state legislature 180 days to arrange for the issuance of marriage licenses to same-sex couples, and the City of Cambridge began taking applications one minute after midnight on May 17, 2004.*

SOURCE: EPA/CJ GUNTHER.

the Massachusetts Constitution through the initiative process. The state legislature, however, prevented the amendment from reaching the ballot. Because Massachusetts lacks a direct form of initiative constitutional amendment, its citizens do not have the same ability as citizens in some other states to bypass the legislature and submit an amendment directly to the people for the approval or rejection. As a consequence, Massachusetts voters did not have a direct, up-or-down vote on extending marriage rights to same-sex couples. The same was true for voters in Connecticut and Iowa, other states where courts recognized a state constitutional right of same-sex couples to marry.

The story was different in California, where citizens have access to a direct form of initiative constitutional amendment. Under that system, proponents of an amendment can submit it directly to voters. In early 2008, before the California Supreme Court held in *In re Marriage Cases* that same-sex couples have a state constitutional right to marry,[21] proponents of traditional marriage were already circulating petitions for an initiative designed to embed the traditional definition of marriage in the state constitution. The measure qualified for the ballot and, in November 2008, six months after the court's ruling, voters approved the amendment, known as Proposition 8, by a 52–48 margin.

The differences between the Massachusetts and California experiences demonstrate that state-level rules can have substantive consequences. In states like California, with a direct form of initiative constitutional amendment process, citizens have greater ability to override state courts and to shape state constitutional interpretation than do citizens in some other states.

It is important to emphasize that the state marriage amendments can constrain the power of *state* supreme courts to invoke *state* constitutions to establish a right of same-sex couples to marry. A U.S. Supreme Court ruling that same-sex couples have a *federal* constitutional right to marry would override state constitutional amendments adopted by the people. In *Hollingsworth v. Perry* (2013), the Supreme Court declined to determine the federal constitutional validity of such laws.[22] Instead, the Court held that the proponents of California's Proposition 8, a 2008 California state initiative constitutional amendment defining marriage as a union between a man and a woman, lacked standing to defend it against a challenge in federal court when California state officials refused to do so. The practical effect of the *Hollingsworth* decision was to let stand a federal trial court judge's ruling declaring Proposition 8 unconstitutional—an outcome limited to that state.[23]

As these examples indicate, the people have used initiative and referendum to exercise a check on state courts when they seek to recognize new rights beyond what the federal Constitution requires. This popular check on state courts operates within the limits of federal constitutional law: as long as the people operate within federal limits, they can use initiative and referendum to participate in defining state constitutional rights—and, indeed, can override state courts and have the last word on these hotly contested questions.

CONCLUSION

The initiative and referendum have added a majoritarian element to state governments, especially in states where citizens most actively exercise the initiative process. Conversely, courts have often used the power of judicial review to limit majorities and promote minority interests. As these countervailing forces have become more powerful, it is not surprising that they have come into frequent conflict. Both state and federal courts have exercised a heavy check on direct citizen lawmaking and, in some instances, the people have used the tools of direct democracy to limit the power of state courts, especially when those courts have expanded contested rights beyond federal constitutional minimums.

Unlike the legislative process, which is designed to promote consensus building, compromise, and partial victories, both direct democracy and activist courts offer stakeholders the chance to achieve one-sided outcomes. The rise of direct democracy and the judicial power has thus contributed to the polarization of politics on a range of issues. While this polarization is, indeed, cause for concern, the problem is partially mitigated because the conflicts are confined to individual states operating within a federal system and constrained by the federal Constitution. Within these constraints, state-level battles between the people and the courts have produced new institutional arrangements, definitions of rights, and other policies—a form of conflict that will likely shape state government in many states, for better or for worse, for years to come.

NOTES

1. Delaware is the only state where the legislature may amend the state constitution without submitting the changes to the people for their approval or rejection. Delaware Constitution, Article XVI.

2. Robert F. Williams, *The Law of American State Constitutions* (New York: Oxford University Press, 2009).

3. Kenneth P. Miller, *Direct Democracy and the Courts* (New York: Cambridge University Press, 2009); see also the Miller-Rose Institute Initiative Database, available at www.cmc.edu/rose.

4. *Pacific States Telephone and Telegraph Company v. Oregon,* 223 U.S. 118 (1912).

5. *Meyer v. Grant,* 486 U.S. 414 (1988).

6. Richard J. Ellis, *Democratic Delusions: The Initiative Process in America* (Lawrence: University Press of Kansas, 2002).

7. Miller, *Direct Democracy and the Courts, supra* note 3, chap. 4.

8. *Reitman v. Mulkey,* 387 U.S. 369 (1967).

9. Derrick A. Bell Jr., "The Referendum: Democracy's Barrier to Racial Equality," *Washington Law Review* 54 (1978): 1; Julian N. Eule, "Judicial Review of Direct Democracy," *Yale Law Journal* 99 (1990): 1503.

10. Colorado Constitution, Article V, Section 1 (5.5).

11. Daniel Hays Lowenstein, "Initiatives and the New Single Subject Rule," *Election Law Journal* 1 (2002): 35.

12. *Armatta v. Kitzhaber,* 327 Ore. 250 (1998).

13. *Marshall v. State ex rel. Cooney,* 293 Mont. 274 (1999).

14. *Raven v. Deukmejian,* 52 Cal.3d 336 (1990).

15. *Strauss v. Horton,* 46 Cal.4th 364 (2009).

16. Douglas S. Reed, "Popular Constitutionalism: Toward a Theory of State Constitutional Meanings," *Rutgers Law Journal* 30 (2001): 871.

17. Theodore Roosevelt, "A Charter of Democracy: Address before the Ohio Constitutional Convention," Columbus, Ohio, February 21, 1912, www.theodorerooseveltcenter.org/.

18. *People v. Anderson,* 6 Cal.3d 628 (1972).

19. *Goodridge v. Department of Public Health,* 440 Mass. 309 (2003).

20. In 2012 the movement to use the state constitutional amendment process to defend the traditional definition of marriage faced increased opposition. While voters in North Carolina approved such an amendment by 61–39 percent, voters in Minnesota rejected one by 53–47 percent. Meanwhile, in 2012 voters in Maine, Maryland, and Washington State approved nonconstitutional ballot measures that effectively authorized same-sex marriage in those states.

21. *In re Marriage Cases,* 43 Cal.4th 757 (2008).

22. *Hollingsworth v. Perry,* 570 U.S. __ (2013).

23. The Supreme Court's decision in *Hollingsworth* that Proposition 8's proponents lacked standing to defend the law in federal court when state officials refused to do so presents a new constraint on the people's power to enact law directly. Voters often adopt initiatives that state officials oppose. Now, on at least some issues, state officials may be able to "veto" voter-approved initiatives by declining to defend them if they are challenged in federal court after the election. The Court left for a later day the decision whether to declare unconstitutional all state laws denying legal recognition of same-sex marriages. Such a decision could be democratically overturned only through an amendment to the federal Constitution—an unlikely prospect, considering the stringent requirements for federal constitutional amendment.

SUGGESTED READING

Brennan, William J., Jr. "State Constitutions and the Protection of Individual Rights." *Harvard Law Review* 90 (1977): 489.

Cronin, Thomas E. *Direct Democracy: The Politics of Initiative, Referendum, and Recall.* Cambridge, MA: Harvard University Press, 1989.

Dinan, John J. *The American State Constitutional Tradition.* Lawrence: University Press of Kansas, 2006.

Ellis, Richard J. *Democratic Delusions: The Initiative Process in America.* Lawrence: University Press of Kansas, 2002.

Eule, Julian N. "Judicial Review of Direct Democracy," *Yale Law Journal* 99 (1990): 1503.

Glendon, Mary Anne. *Rights Talk: The Impoverishment of Public Discourse.* New York: Free Press, 1991.

Miller, Kenneth P. *Direct Democracy and the Courts.* New York: Cambridge University Press, 2009.

Reed, Douglas S. "Popular Constitutionalism: Toward a Theory of State Constitutional Meanings." *Rutgers Law Journal* 30 (1999): 871.

Ross, William G. *A Muted Fury: Populists, Progressives, and Labor Unions Confront the Courts, 1890–1937.* Princeton, NJ: Princeton University Press, 1994.

Sabato, Larry J., Howard R. Ernst, and Bruce A. Larson, eds. *Dangerous Democracy? The Battle over Ballot Initiatives in America.* Lanham, MD: Rowman and Littlefield, 2001.

Tarr, G. Alan. *Understanding State Constitutions.* Princeton, NJ: Princeton University Press, 1998.

Tarr, G. Alan, ed. *Constitutional Politics in the States: Contemporary Controversies and Historical Patterns.* Westport, CT: Greenwood, 1996.

Waters, M. Dane, ed. *Initiative and Referendum Almanac.* Durham, NC: Carolina Academic Press, 2003.

Williams, Robert F. *The Law of American State Constitutions.* New York: Oxford University Press, 2009.

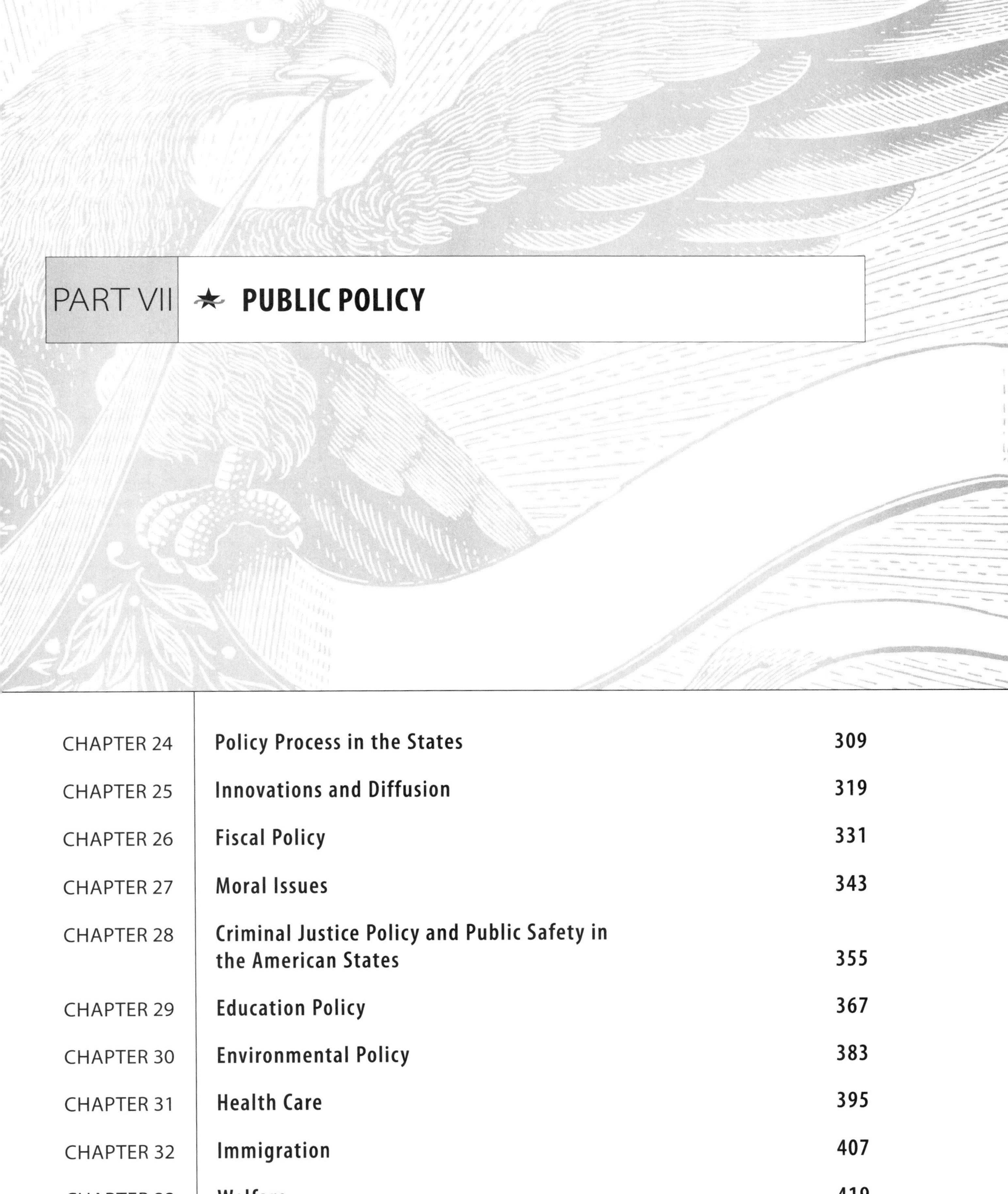

PART VII ★ PUBLIC POLICY

Chapter 24

Policy Process in the States

Lilliard Richardson

GIVEN THE COMPLEXITY OF INSTITUTIONS, processes, and political actors in the states, how does a social problem become a political issue that emerges as a new policy or a policy reform? At any given time, there are a multitude of social conditions, such as poverty, drug abuse, environmental degradation, or slow economic growth, that could merit the attention of state political leaders, but generally only a few issues at a time are actively under consideration for major policy change.

Potential policy changes face an environment of considerable time constraints, resource constraints, and information constraints. Yet state legislatures in most states meet for only a few months a year, most legislators do not serve full-time, and legislative staff is fairly limited in most states. Governors have more time and typically more staff than do legislators, but they have far less support than the president and yet face many of the same domestic issues. State courts are burdened with a huge volume of criminal cases that consume most of the judicial resources in a state, but they also have been embroiled in a number of important controversies involving education, the environment, and morality policy. Furthermore, because of ballot measures available in many states, voters are more directly drawn into the policy process at the state level than at the national level, but voters have very limited interest in politics and limited knowledge of policies and processes, and they have very limited choices available through the ballot process. These constraints on major state political actors make the policy process even more challenging at the state level. And yet, as we shall see, most of the major policy process theories have not been tested extensively at the state level.

Multiple theories have been proposed to examine how policies emerge and work their way through the political system. At one time, the policy stages heuristic was the dominant approach, but it has been criticized for an absence of "causal drivers" that would help one understand how policy would make it through the system and for defining the process in distinct steps whereas the real process is much messier.[1] Another approach has been to assess how policies spread from state to state. (Theories of diffusion are discussed in Chapter 25.)

Four theories have been dominant in the policy literature over the past couple of decades: institutional analysis and development, multiple policy streams, advocacy coalition framework, and punctuated equilibrium. In general, the theories, much of the supporting empirical research, and case studies used to illuminate the theories have been based in national politics rather than state politics, but the theories could also help us understand how policies emerge from complex state political systems. The purpose of this chapter is to provide an overview of the basic features of each theoretical lens, to describe the forms of evidence used to support the theories, and to pose questions about applying each theory to state politics.

INSTITUTIONAL ANALYSIS AND DEVELOPMENT

Based on a rational choice approach, institutional analysis and development (IAD) theory focuses attention on institutional arrangements and the incentives they create for human behavior. Methodological individualism is central to the approach, and the fundamental questions relate to collective choice problems in which individual incentives for behavior are not in alignment with optimal social outcomes.

One particular issue of concern is a common pool resource, which is a resource that is difficult to exclude anyone from using and as a consequence is subject to overuse, pollution, or congestion problems unless collective action is taken. One classic example is an ocean fishery, which anyone with a boat can consume for free but that can be overfished if each participant takes too much, resulting in depleted stocks and worse long-term outcomes for the group. A variety of natural resources, such as clean air, species survival, and watersheds, can be common pool

This photo, taken September 2, 2009, shows commercial fishing boats tied up at the Port of Brookings-Harbor, Oregon. The Pacific Fishery Management Council, which regulates sport and commercial fishing in federal waters off the West Coast, has adopted an ecosystem management plan to help it take into account impacts on the whole ocean in making decisions on fishing seasons, catch quotas, and other issues. Management plans such as this are often instituted to address the issue of common pool resources, whereby collective action is needed to prevent problematic consequences associated with their nonexclusive use.

SOURCE: AP Photo/Jeff Barnard.

resources, but manmade structures such as irrigation systems or open source collaborations can also be plagued by similar incentives for overuse. The IAD literature has largely focused on governance structures for these common pool resources and how institutions can help shift individual incentives away from noncooperative, suboptimal equilibria into more cooperative equilibria with potential for greater collective benefits for the involved players.

Elinor Ostrom's development of this topic since the 1970s earned her a 2009 Nobel Prize in Economic Sciences, and her 1990 book, *Governing the Commons,* firmly established this framework. Across a number of studies, Ostrom and her colleagues have explored a variety of ways humans have taken collective action to manage common pool resources. One important distinction is that some of these structures have been more in the form of norms of behavior for individuals, but in many other situations formal institutions have been created to monitor behavior and impose sanctions on those who violate expectations. These institutions are not always formal governmental structures, and in some cases they may even be more implicit structures that require the researcher to examine the "rules in use" rather than the "rules in form." Furthermore, these rules in use may be found mostly at the local or micro level of governance, but they are nested in larger systems of rules and institutions at the macro level (such as constitutional rules).

One crucial concept is the "action arena," which is the social space where various policy actors in and out of government interact, utilize different resources, and attempt to shape policy outcomes. The rules in use, local social environment, information availability, social structure, and players' beliefs about how these factors work together shape the interactions and ultimately the policy outcomes. While game theory or neoclassical economic theory can be used to model individual behavior, the IAD approach has more typically relied on bounded rationality in which individuals do not have complete information and do not have the time or resources to engage in an exhaustive search of alternative policies or their likely outcomes.

The IAD literature has examined a wide variety of institutional arrangements, but typically state institutions have been more a part of the mix than of particular interest. Much of the work has focused on environmental policy issues, and studies have examined issues such as fisheries, collaborative watershed partnerships, and interstate water compacts. State legislatures, state agencies, and state courts are important players in these political settings, but variations in state institutions and the political science literature on these institutions have not been explicitly incorporated into these studies. For example, a state may be the geographic space for an action arena so a state's rules and institutions could matter, but they have not been tested extensively or in comparative context. Furthermore, the model incorporates the idea that the attributes of a community, such as the local political culture and the level of trust, shape the rules used, the need for monitoring and sanctions, as well as the acquisition of information about a public problem, but the variation in culture across the states and the scholarly work on this variation have not been fully explored.[2]

In one of the few studies to explicitly explore the linkage between state institutions and variation in policy using this approach, an analysis of water management policy in Arizona, California, and Colorado finds that differing state laws and regulations, administrative structures, and legal frameworks have produced divergent water management policies and outcomes.[3] The work shows how states could be relevant case studies for this approach, and it suggests how states can be important action arenas for policy.

Another recent concern in this literature has been the idea of how to depict policy designs in a systematic way

Professor Elinor Ostrom, left, receives the Nobel Prize in Economic Sciences from King Carl XVI Gustaf of Sweden during the 2009 Nobel Prize awards ceremony in Stockholm, Sweden. Ostrom, who died in 2012, received the award for her research on how people create rules and institutions that allow for the equitable management of shared resources.

SOURCE: AP Photo/Scanpix/Jonas Ekstromer/Pool.

using the "grammar" built into institutional outputs such as statutes, regulations, and rulings, and some of this analysis has relied on state policies.[4] One recent study examined an abortion bill in Georgia. The authors use a coding scheme to describe the legislation that draws attention to whether a component helped set up a rule creating sanctions for certain kinds of behavior, a norm establishing incentives for desired behaviors, or a strategy for planning based on expectations for individual behavior responding to these rules and norms. Another recent study advanced this idea with an assessment of aquaculture policies in Colorado. Neither study assesses the effect of any particular state features, but they show how their grammar analysis could be done with other state policies.

Another major question for the IAD framework is whether it can extend beyond the case of common pool resources and its focus on policy issues related to resource management and environmental policy. For the model to have relevance to state policy processes, it needs to explain a wide range of social, health, and education issues. A limited number of studies have examined education policy, childcare policy, and social welfare policies; these studies find different forms of governance in these policy areas, so it suggests this would be a fruitful avenue for research.[5]

These studies of policies outside of the common pool resource framework have shown important differences. For example, one important distinction for policies is that goods with information asymmetry, such as the case of childcare in which parents cannot completely monitor performance, face different coordination problems than common pool resources. Many of the issues facing the states, such as nursing home care, indigent health care, and education, are characterized by this information asymmetry for the consumers of the services. One possible way to deal with this information asymmetry is to rely on nonprofits or faith-based organizations to remove the profit motive that could induce shirking behavior. In turn, differing governance structures may affect service delivery. Clearly, the states show considerable variation in their reliance on differing governance structures across policy areas, and this could be a fertile area of research.

MULTIPLE POLICY STREAMS

John Kingdon first posited the approach now known as multiple policy streams (MPS) in his 1984 book, *Agendas, Alternatives, and Public Policies.* Most of the applications of the theory have been for national politics rather than state politics, even though the framework is broad enough to apply to the states. Kingdon argues that there are three separate streams influencing the policy process: (1) the problems stream, which includes the various social conditions seen by at least some political actors as problematic and needing coordinated collective action; (2) the politics stream, which includes the public mood, the interest group environment, campaigns and elections, and partisan control of institutions; and (3) the policy stream, in which political entrepreneurs advocate solutions for dealing with various social conditions. At times, a window of opportunity opens in which the three streams interact to form new policies, and it can occur somewhat randomly, through a "complex adaptive system." Kingdon's model builds on the earlier Garbage Can Theory, which assumes a high level of ambiguity in a dynamic process with changing players, poorly defined problems, unclear goals, and uncertainty about how inputs lead to different policy outputs.[6]

In this view, state policymakers with limited resources face a bewildering array of statistics about social conditions, institutional feedback from agencies, interest group demands, public opinion, media coverage of social issues, constituency demands, and events that provide shocks to the system. Political entrepreneurs, from inside of government or outside, help draw attention to a particular set of social problems and pull the streams together in what theorists call "coupling." In some cases, the entrepreneur for a particular issue may be an elected official, such as a governor or powerful state legislator, but in other cases it may be an agency director or an interest group leader. In some instances, political entrepreneurs may engage in "problem surfing," in which they attempt to attach a preferred solution to an available policy problem in another policy issue area as the opportunity arises. In general, the public mood, partisan control of political institutions, and budgetary conditions may limit which solutions are feasible, but the policy choice that emerges is largely random. Therefore, policy outputs are not necessarily rational or a product of institutional design.[7]

The multiple policy streams approach has been criticized on several dimensions. One of the main criticisms is that it does not help explain when a policy window will open or when a policy reform will develop once a window opens. A second concern is that it does not produce testable hypotheses. Furthermore, others have criticized the random nature of the model, and its lack of definitive answers for policy analysis.[8] A recent expansion of the model has added three assumptions: (1) policymakers have considerable time constraints; (2) streams are largely independent; and (3) political systems deal with multiple issues at the same time in parallel, but decisions are serial in nature because policymakers can only consider a limited number of issues at a time—therefore the decision process can appear to be "quite abrupt and disorderly."[9]

While Kingdon's work focused on national policymaking and others have applied the multiple streams approach to parliamentary systems in Europe, a few studies have tested or applied this theory to policy issues in the states. Examining education policies in Texas, a survey of school superintendents examines the assumption of different participant types in separate streams, but the study finds contradictory evidence that superintendents regularly cross between the problem stream and the policy stream rather than working exclusively in just one stream.[10] Other studies have used the MPS approach to examine agenda setting in a variety of policy contexts: higher education decentralization efforts in Arkansas, Hawaii, and Illinois; child obesity policy development in Arkansas; and reading policy in California, Michigan, and Texas.[11]

In a more explicit attempt to incorporate states into the MPS approach, Erik Ness and Molly A. Mistretta expand the basic model by adding a "policy milieu" stream that includes state legislative and state administrative structure as a factor shaping policy formation, and they argue that the policy milieu "accounts for organizational structures and characteristics of the state government and state higher education system, such as professionalism of the state legislature, strength of governor's powers, and level of campus autonomy."[12] In particular, they examine higher education policy and governance to compare policy design related to the use of lottery proceeds in the states of North Carolina and Tennessee and merit aid for higher education students in New Mexico, Tennessee, and West Virginia. They argue that the revised MPS model more accurately characterizes the policy process in these cases than does the advocacy coalition framework, to which we now turn.

ADVOCACY COALITION FRAMEWORK

P. A. Sabatier and H.C. Jenkins-Smith introduced the Advocacy Coalition Framework (ACF) in their 1993 book, *Policy Change and Learning: An Advocacy Coalition Approach*, and further developed the approach in a series of single-authored and coauthored articles.[13] The ACF starts with the assumptions that policy is incredibly complex, that interested participants must specialize to have any impact on policy, that a variety of players with strong beliefs about policy are involved, and that it is best to examine policy change over a long period of time, such as a decade or more. Policy experts working in policy-specific subsystems form the coalitions at the heart of the ACF, and coalitions form around a system of core beliefs about the nature of problems, the values at stake, and the causal factors underlying problems. In this view, most policymaking is essentially a negotiation among advocates within the policy subsystem, and participants will seek out allies with similar beliefs to form coalitions to control policy, but dynamic changes in partisan control of institutions, societal structures, and intrusions from other policy subsystems can contribute to major policy changes over time.

One of the challenges for a researcher applying this framework to a policy area is the scope of the policy subsystem. There is considerable potential for policy subsystems to overlap into the domain of other subsystems, such as alcohol abuse problems affecting transportation through drinking and driving, crime policy through intimate violence, and health policy because of the complications of chronic alcohol abuse. Policy subsystems may also be nested within larger subsystems, such as traffic safety policies fitting within the larger criminal justice subsystem, as well as the larger transportation policy subsystem. Multiple layers of government only add to the complexity.

Coalitions form around a core set of beliefs, and policy systems typically have from two to five coalitions. Coordination problems are always a challenge for groups trying to coordinate actions, but the ACF argues that a core set of beliefs helps create trust and burden sharing among participants in a coalition. In addition, distrust of rival coalitions, stronger memories of losses than wins, and overemphasis on the evil tactics of the opponents may help coalitions work together. The level of coordination and the types of activities can vary widely, and there is considerable research on how networks and coalitions work together.

Coalitions can also be dynamic, and the structure and members of the coalition can change over time. Studies have examined the level of group homogeneity in various policy subsystems, how homogeneity affects trust within the coalition, and whether it affects the ability of the coalition to effect policy change. In general, homogenous coalitions may be more stable and trusting, but they may be too narrow to achieve policy change. On the other hand, expansion of the coalition risks conflict over the core values holding the coalition together. Policy learning within the subsystem is also crucial to policy change in the ACF as adaptation is important for coalitions to survive and thrive, but this also has potential to affect coalition composition and support as well.

Another concern among ACF scholars is the impact of shocks external and internal to the coalition, and how changes in public opinion or other changes in the political topography influence coalition dynamics. In particular, focusing events can cause a "salience disruption" within the coalition. Because salience disruptions involve events drawing considerable attention from the public and elected officials, the subsystem may be opened to new players. Potential threats may emerge to how things have been done, but there is also potential for additional resources and attention to the core social problems of interest to the subsystem. Alternatively, political entrepreneurs may create internal shocks to the policy subsystem by creating "dimension shifts" in which policy tools are taken from one policy area into another. Political entrepreneurs may strategically create linkages across subsystems to help bring about policy changes.[14]

Much of the early work on the ACF was national in nature, with some federalism aspects extending to the states, but much of the recent work has moved into the global arena. ACF applications have analyzed watershed, air pollution, land management, and other environmental concerns, where the policy subsystems are often geographically limited to one region. These often involve one or more state governments, but states are typically not the focus of these studies. In addition, much of the ACF research has focused on environmental issues that often transcend borders, but among the many publications applying this approach, some have examined subjects such as taxation, health, morality policy, and education, which are also important areas of concern in the states.

The ACF has not directly built state institutions or processes into the model, but it has been used to examine policies in the states.[15] Typically, such studies use qualitative methods, especially semistructured interviews or elite surveys, to apply the approach. Generally, state officials are in the sample along with local and national officials as well as nongovernmental stakeholders, but state institutions and processes are not explicitly incorporated. Some of the results suggest that structural differences in states could be important for the approach to consider, but they are not directly tested. For example, the ACF has been used to explain the sharply divergent policies of Arizona and Texas in allowing in-state tuition for undocumented students graduating from state high schools.[16] The study suggests that the presence of the citizen initiative in Arizona but not in Texas affected the policy outcomes. Although the evidence is limited to this one case study comparison, the ballot measure could be an important challenge to the model's premise that coalitions in the policy subsystem largely determine policy over the long term, and it is an important difference between the state and national policy environments that could contribute to stronger theory.

Another component of the model that could be different for states is that many studies have been conducted at the national level in Western democracies, and typically they have examined established policy subsystems that have been in existence for decades. Alternatively, fewer studies have applied the model to less mature policy subsystems, such as less developed nations or American states. States with more professionalized legislatures, such as California or New York, may have policy subsystems similar to the established national systems, but in states with citizen legislatures, such as New Hampshire or North Dakota, the policy subsystems may be less developed and therefore more heavily influenced from the outside.

States pose additional challenges to the theory. Do state advocacy coalitions develop around core values unique to a state, or are they typically just local branches of the national policy coalitions? What strains in networks might develop as a result of local differences relative to national coalitions? In addition, policy learning is at the core of the ACF, and it may be especially important in the states as they borrow ideas from other states through diffusion (see Chapter 25), through national conferences and training events within their networks, or via best practices developed by coalition allies in other states. Finally, one of the core ideas of the ACF is that policy expertise and policy information are key resources within a coalition and in policy debates, and clearly the information environment is very different in the less professionalized states than in Washington, DC, so how would this affect the applicability of the model?

PUNCTUATED EQUILIBRIUM

The punctuated equilibrium (PE) approach was largely initiated by Frank R. Baumgartner and Bryan D. Jones in a 1993 book, and they have expanded on and clarified the model in a series of articles and a second edition of the book in 2009. The PE approach relies on two basic observations about public policy. There are often long periods of relative stasis in which policy changes very little, but these periods of calm can be followed by abrupt and sometimes radical change in a short period of time.

The first observation about stasis is built on the theory of incrementalism, which argues that one might hope that administrators would regularly conduct exhaustive searches of the policy environment to determine public problems, find possible alternatives to fix such problems, and determine how these alternatives affect policy goals, but the opportunity costs in terms of time, energy, and resources suggest such searches are not feasible.[17] Rather, policymakers engage in a succession of limited searches that result in minor tweaks of policy based on a limited set of alternatives under consideration. Furthermore, broader assessments of underlying goals or values are not only costly but also potentially divisive, so most policy searches will seek to advance a limited set of goals with small changes in policies.

This view of incrementalism has also been particularly important in explaining budgetary politics.[18] In essence, the budget one sees today is typically the best predictor of tomorrow's budget. This year's budget is a baseline for next year's budget, and programmatic changes will be relative to the baseline. Limitations on time and energy would pose problems for a comprehensive assessment of an entire budget, so it is more realistic to expect that elected officials overseeing agency requests would make small relative changes in the main budget along with more intensive considerations of smaller components of the budget from time to time. Incremental drift is likely, and such models assume that agency managers will seek to expand the power and resources available to the organization, so we will generally expect to see an upward drift in budgets.

Scholars have questioned the incrementalism model on a number of grounds related to theory, measurement, and vagueness of concepts,[19] but Baumgartner and Jones also point out that it ignored the second observation from above—although they may be rare, sudden major policy changes do happen. While stasis or incrementalism may be dominant for long periods of time, there are major shifts in policy or budgets from time to time. Relying on models borrowed from evolutionary biology, PE models argue that environmental pressures sometimes build up such that bigger change can occur. Policy monopolies, which are comprised of a small group of decision makers focused on a particular policy issue, typically hold sway during periods of stasis, but various environmental factors can challenge this control.

External shocks to the system, such as natural disasters, industrial accidents, stock market crashes, or other sudden events covered widely in the media, can be "focusing events" that create considerable activity in the political system that may result in major policy change.[20] Focusing events shine light on an issue, and potential challengers to the policy monopoly can use this attention to change the policy image associated with the issue, change the tone of debate, and possibly change the problem definition. Policy change may occur at such times. The issue attention cycle, however, suggests that attention will wane at some point as the media, the public, and elected officials begin to focus on other events or issues, and policymaking in a particular area will return to an equilibrium of relative stasis controlled largely by the policy experts in a given policy subsystem. Much of the early empirical work on the theory focused on patterns of media attention to issues and how the attention cycle operated.

In addition to sudden external events leading to punctuated equilibrium, challengers to the policy monopoly can attempt to bring about policy change by expanding or changing the venue for a policy debate. Although the policy monopoly may have control over the relevant institutions given the existing problem definition, a shift in the policy image may allow a policy to be considered under the jurisdiction of other institutions, such as allowing a bill to be considered by a different legislative committee that may not be dominated by those in the policy monopoly or even shifts between levels of government.

Considerable attention has been devoted to identifying whether the observed distribution of policy outputs is consistent with the expectations of the PE approach. In particular, the theory suggests that the pattern of policy outputs (e.g., budget growth in percentages) will show a rather slender but steep mountain of data in the range from 0 to 2 percent, very little observed change in the midrange, and fat tails of the distribution where large changes occur in a punctuated equilibrium. This pattern, referred to as a leptokurtic distribution, has been observed in various settings.[21]

Critics of the PE theory point out that while there is considerable evidence of leptokurtic distributions in policy outputs, the theory is not as strong in identifying the factors explaining why one external shock leads to policy change but another may not; when punctuations will emerge; how inputs are related to particular outputs; and, most important, which policies will be the product of an equilibrium. Others have argued that the theory lacks the causal mechanisms for when an issue moves from stasis to punctuation, and in this view punctuated equilibrium is more of a metaphor than a theory.[22]

While the theory has been tested and applied to a number of policy areas at the national level, it has received less attention at the state level. Studies find that states with more powerful governors, in terms of veto powers and agenda-setting powers, experience more pronounced budgetary punctuations, and that budget categories with more extreme punctuations show less growth in the long term.[23] An application of this theory to budgetary data for Texas school districts finds that more bureaucratic systems adjust budgets more quickly to reflect information. Using the same data, another study shows that organizational centralization increases the likelihood of large budgetary changes, but organizational size increases the chances of stasis.[24] Another study demonstrated that states with more administrative reorganizations avoid larger punctuations in administrative organization.[25]

Although the PE approach may fit state policy processes, it is not clear that it would. For example, in a study of state incarceration rates, punctuations were found, but not necessarily at the beginning or end of periods of growth or decline in incarceration rates as expected. Furthermore, national mood seemed to be more important in explaining growth patterns than any given state factors, but the study suggests that much of the variation in rates was not explained by punctuations or the national mood.[26] A different study (of state tobacco policy) found that despite considerable efforts by health advocates, no punctuations occurred in nine states during the period from 1990 to 2006.[27] It is notable that these two studies examined policy outputs rather than budgets as in many of the other state studies previously mentioned. Given similar findings with studies exploring policy outputs, this difference in methodological approach may provide a challenge to the theory, but it could also be that states pose a different test.

As mentioned previously, Jones and Baumgartner provided a more formal explication of a model of choice for public policy to extend the PE approach. They argue that the PE model as originally developed was a model of policymaking but not a theory of decision making, and they seek to remedy this with a more formal model. Building on theories of bounded rationality and studies of congressional policy action in committees, they argue that information is abundant in Washington, but attention is scarce.[28]

This key assumption of their model may be valid for national politics, but it is clearly less true for state policymakers where attention and information are often scarce. If this assumption does not hold, does the model accurately represent decision making in the states, and how does the model need to be revised? Alternatively, the simulation work supporting the model depends on differential weights attached to different clues in the environment, and this may actually be more prevalent for part-time or term-limited state legislators who do not have the time to consider a range of factors.

An additional challenge could be that policy monopolies may be more difficult to maintain in term-limited states and less professionalized legislatures, where turnover is far more prevalent than at the national level. State scholarship could help inform the application of the model in many ways. Work on interest groups in the states (see Chapter 10), the role of media in covering state politics (Chapter 12), and committee organization in state legislatures (Chapter 16) could inform policy scholars about the richness of the information environment in the state policy process. The variation across states on these dimensions, as well as the differences across states in institutions such as term limits and ballot measures, could provide considerable empirical leverage for the assessment of the PE approach.

CONCLUSION

In some ways these approaches compete with one another, but the MPS, ACF, and PE frameworks share some common elements and have been grouped together as "synthetic" approaches.[29] Each one sees some random elements in the process, assumes bounded rationality for the participants in the policy process, examines long-term changes for a policy issue, and involves some degree of policy learning over time.

Furthermore, the role of the political entrepreneur is a common element of the three synthetic approaches. A considerable literature has developed around this concept of the political entrepreneur as a crucial component of policy change, and it has been used in conjunction with each of these approaches.[30] The policy process is dynamic, fluid, and often constrained for long periods of time, and each of the three models sees an important role for change agents that can move policy change forward. There has been little research on the role of political entrepreneurs in the states or how they might cross state borders to influence change, and this could be a rich source of research into how various state institutions shape political entrepreneurship.

Another element that transcends the three synthetic approaches is the potential role for shocks to the system. Whether treated as salience disruptions in the ACF or focusing events in the multiple streams and punctuated equilibrium approaches, disasters and crises can create opportunities for change. Such events may attract media attention, allow new players into the system, and permit solutions from other policy areas to be considered. The approaches vary somewhat in how it occurs, but a common element is that political entrepreneurs can take advantage of these opportunities to reframe the policy definition, change the nature of the debate, or push the decision to another policy arena.

One of the enduring questions across the four models is how well they apply to the states. Studies applying these theories to policies in the states have often applied two or three of them to an issue, and the results vary as to which one offers the most analytic traction. One of the key issues is how well the assumptions of each of the models apply to the states. In particular, state policymakers face far more constraints in terms of information, time, staff, and financial resources than do national policymakers at the heart of these theories. States also face different institutional constraints, such as term limits and balanced budget requirements that shape policy adoption. In addition, states have federal pressure to conform to federal mandates via fiscal federalism. Furthermore, in about half the states, policymakers must deal with the ramifications of ballot measures. The combination of these constraints as well as the different political cultures across the states provide a considerable challenge for these theories of the policy process.

NOTES

1. Peter deLeon, "The Stages Approach to the Policy Process: What Has It Done? Where Is It Going?" in *Theories of the Policy Process,* ed. P. A. Sabatier (Boulder, CO: Westview, 1999); P. A. Sabatier, "The Need for Better Theories," in *Theories of the Policy Process,* 2nd ed., P. A. Sabatier, ed. (Boulder, CO: Westview, 2007).

2. Scott D. Hardy and Tomas M. Koontz, "Rules for Collaboration: Institutional Analysis of Group Membership and Levels of Action in Watershed Partnerships," *Policy Studies Journal* 37 (2009): 393–414; Edella Schlager and Tanya Heikkila, "Resolving Water Conflicts: A Comparative Analysis of Interstate River Compacts," *Policy Studies Journal* 37 (2009): 367–392.

3. William Blomquist, Edella Schlager, and Tanya Heikkila, *Common Waters, Diverging Streams* (Washington, DC: Resources for the Future, 2004).

4. Xavier Basurto, Gordon Kingsley, Kelly McQueen, Mshadoni Smith, and Christopher M. Weible, "A Systematic Approach to Institutional Analysis: Applying Crawford and Ostrom's Grammar," *Political Research Quarterly* 63 (2010): 523–537; Saba Siddiki, Christopher M. Weible, Xavier Basurto, and J. Calanni, "Dissecting Policy Designs: An Application of the Institutional Grammar Tool," *Policy Studies Journal* 39 (2011), 79–103; Saba Siddiki, Xavier Basurto, and Christopher M. Weible, "Using the Institutional Grammar Tool to Understand Regulatory Compliance: The Case of Colorado Aquaculture," *Regulation and Governance* 6 (2012): 167–188.

5. Elinor Ostrom, "Institutional Rational Choice: An Assessment of the Institutional Analysis and Development Framework," in P.A. Sabatier, ed., *Theories of the Policy Process;* Elinor Ostrom, "Institutional Analysis and Framework," *Policy Studies Journal* 39 (2011): 7–27; Brenda K. Bushouse, "Governance Structures: Using IAD to Understand Variation in Service Delivery for Club Goods with Information Asymmetry," *Policy Studies Journal* 39 (2011): 99–113; Michael D. McGinnis, "Networks of Adjacent Action Situations in Polycentric Governance," *Policy Studies Journal* 39 (2011): 51–78.

6. Michael Cohen, James March, and Johan P. Olsen, "A Garbage Can Model of Organizational Choice," *Administrative Sciences Quarterly* 17 (1972): 1–25.

7. Jessica E. Boscarino, "Surfing for Problems: Advocacy Group Strategy in U.S. Forestry Policy," *Policy Studies Journal* 37 (2009): 415–434; Nikolaos Zahariadis, "Ambiguity and Choice in European Public Policy," *Journal of European Public Policy* 15 (2008): 514–530.

8. Robert F. Durant and Paul F. Diehl, "Agendas, Alternatives, and Public Policy: Lessons from the U.S. Foreign Policy Arena," *Journal of Public Policy* 9 (1989): 179–205; Gary Mucciaroni, "The Garbage Can Model and the Study of Policy Making: A Critique," *Polity* 24 (1992): 459–482.

9. Nikolaos Zahariadis, "The Multiple Streams Framework: Structure, Limitations, Prospects," in Sabatier, ed., *Theories of the Policy Process.*

10. Scott E. Robinson and Warren S. Eller, "Participation in Policy Streams: Testing the Separation of Problems and Solutions in Subnational Policy Systems," *Policy Studies Journal* 38 (2010): 199–216.

11. M. K. McLendon, "Setting the Governmental Agenda for State Decentralization of Higher Education," *Journal of Higher Education* 74 (2003): 479–515; Rebekah L. Craig, Holly C. Felix, Jada F. Walker, and Martha M. Phillips, "Public Health Professionals as Policy Entrepreneurs: Arkansas's Childhood Obesity Policy Experience," *American Journal of Public Health* 100 (2010): 2047–2052; Tamara V. Young, Thomas V. Shepley, and Mengli Song, "Understanding Agenda Setting in State Educational Policy: An Application of Kingdon's Multiple Streams Model to the Formation of State Reading Policy," *Education Policy Analysis Archives* 18 (2010): 1–19.

12. Erik Ness, "The Politics of Determining Merit Aid Eligibility Criteria: An Analysis of the Policy Process," *Journal of Higher Education* 81 (2010): 33–60; Erik Ness and Molly A. Mistretta, "Policy Adoption in North Carolina and Tennessee: A Comparative Case Study of Lottery Beneficiaries," *Review of Higher Education* 32 (2009): 489–514.

13. P. A. Sabatier and H. C. Jenkins-Smith, eds. *Policy Change and Learning: An Advocacy Coalition Approach* (Boulder, CO: Westview, 1993); P. A. Sabatier and H. C. Jenkins-Smith, "The Advocacy Coalition Framework: An Assessment," in Sabatier, *Theories of the Policy Process*; P. A. Sabatier and C. M. Weible, "The Advocacy Coalition Framework: Innovations and Clarifications," in Sabatier, ed., *Theories of the Policy Process;* C. M. Weible, P. A. Sabatier, H. C. Jenkins-Smith, D. Nohrstedt, A. D. Henry, and Peter deLeon, "A Quarter Century of the Advocacy Coalition Framework: An Introduction to the Special Issue," *Policy Studies Journal* 38 (2011): 349–360.

14. C. M. Weible, P. A. Sabatier, and Kelly McQueen, "Themes and Variations: Taking Stock of the Advocacy Coalition Framework," *Policy Studies Journal* 37 (2009): 121–140; Michael D. Jones and Hank C. Jenkins-Smith, "Trans-Subsystem Dynamics: Policy Topography, Mass Opinion, and Policy Change," *Policy Studies Journal* 37 (2009): 37–58.

15. C. M. Weible and P. A. Sabatier, "Comparing Policy Networks: Marine Protected Areas in California," *Policy Studies Journal* 33 (2005): 181–201; Weible et al., "A Quarter Century of the Advocacy Coalition Framework."

16. K. J. Dougherty, H. K Nienhusser, and B. E. Vega, "Undocumented Immigrants and State Higher Education Policy: The Politics of In-State Tuition Eligibility in Texas and Arizona," *Review of Higher Education* 34 (2010): 123–173.

17. Charles Lindblom, "The Science of Muddling Through," *Public Administration Review* 19 (1959): 79–88.

18. Aaron Wildavsky, *The Politics of the Budgetary Process* (Boston: Little, Brown, 1964).

19. John F. Padgett, "Bounded Rationality in Budgetary Research," *American Political Science Review* 74 (1980): 354–372; William D. Berry, "The Confusing Case of Budgetary Incrementalism: Too Many Meanings for a Single Concept," *Journal of Politics*

52 (1990): 167–196; Bryan D. Jones and Frank R. Baumgartner, "A Model of Choice for Public Policy," *Journal of Public Administration Research and Theory* 15 (2005): 325–351.

20. Thomas Birkland, *After Disaster: Agenda Setting, Public Policy, and Focusing Events* (Washington, DC: Georgetown University Press, 1997).

21. Bryan D. Jones, Tracy Sulkin, and Heather A. Larsen, "Policy Punctuations in American Political Institutions," *American Political Science Review* 97 (2003): 151–169; James L. True, Bryan D. Jones, and Frank R. Baumgartner, "Punctuated-Equilibrium Theory: Explaining Stability and Change in Public Policymaking," in Sabatier, ed., *Theories of the Policy Process.*

22. Peter John, "Is There Life after Policy Streams, Advocacy Coalitions, and Punctuations: Using Evolutionary Theory to Explain Policy Change?" *Policy Studies Journal* 31 (2003): 481–498; David Prindle, "Stephen Jay Gould as a Political Theorist," *Politics and the Life Sciences* 25 (2006): 2–14.

23. Christian Breunig and Chris Koski, "Punctuated Budgets and Governors' Institutional Powers," *American Politics Research* 37 (2009): 1116–1138; Christian Breunig and Chris Koski, "The Tortoise or the Hare? Incrementalism, Punctuations, and Their Consequences," *Policy Studies Journal* 40 (2012): 45–68; Christian Breunig, Chris Koski, and Peter B. Mortensen, "Stability and Punctuations in Public Spending: A Comparative Study of Budget Functions," *Journal of Public Administration Research and Theory* 20 (2010): 703–722.

24. Scott E. Robinson, "Punctuated Equilibria, Bureaucratization, and School Budgets," *Policy Studies Journal* 32 (2004): 25–40; Scott E. Robinson, Floun'say Caver, Kenneth J. Meier, and Laurence J. O'Toole Jr., "Explaining Policy Punctuations: Bureaucratization and Budget Change," *American Journal of Political Science* 51 (2007): 140–150.

25. Michael Berkman and Christopher Reenock, "Incremental Consolidation and Comprehensive Reorganization of American State Executive Branches," *American Journal of Political Science* 48 (2004): 796–812.

26. Anne Larason Schneider, "Patterns of Change in the Use of Imprisonment in the American States: An Integration of Path Dependence, Punctuated Equilibrium, and Policy Design Approaches," *Political Research Quarterly* 59 (2006): 457–470.

27. Michael Givel, "Assessing Material and Symbolic Variations in Punctuated Equilibrium and Public Policy Output Patterns," *Review of Policy Research* 25 (2008): 547–561.

28. Bryan D. Jones and Frank R. Baumgartner, "A Model of Choice for Public Policy," *Journal of Public Administration Research and Theory* 15 (2005): 325–351.

29. John, "Is There Life after Policy Streams?"

30. M. Mintrom and P. Norman, "Policy Entrepreneurship and Policy Change," *Policy Studies Journal* 37 (2009): 649–667; M. Mintrom and S. Vergari, "Advocacy Coalitions, Policy Entrepreneurs, and Policy Changes," *Policy Studies Journal* 24 (1996): 420–434.

SUGGESTED READING

Baumgartner, Frank R., and Bryan D. Jones. *Agendas and Instability in American Politics,* 2nd ed. Chicago: University of Chicago Press, 2009.

Birkland, Thomas. *After Disaster: Agenda Setting, Public Policy, and Focusing Events.* Washington, DC: Georgetown University Press, 1997.

Jones, Bryan D., and Frank R. Baumgartner. "A Model of Choice for Public Policy." *Journal of Public Administration Research and Theory* 15 (2005): 325–351.

Jones, Bryan D., Tracy Sulkin, and Heather A. Larsen. "Policy Punctuations in American Political Institutions." *American Political Science Review* 97 (2003): 151–169.

Kingdon, John W. *Agendas, Alternatives, and Public Policies,* 2nd ed. New York: Addison-Wesley, 1995.

Lindblom, Charles. "The Science of Muddling Through." *Public Administration Review* 19 (1959): 79–88.

Ostrom, Elinor. *Governing the Commons: The Evolution of Institutions for Collective Action.* Cambridge: Cambridge University Press, 1990.

Ostrom, Elinor, Roy Gardner, and James Walker. *Rules, Games, and Common-Pool Resources.* Ann Arbor: University of Michigan Press, 1994.

Sabatier, Paul A. *Theories of the Policy Process,* 2nd ed. Boulder, CO: Westview, 2007.

Sabatier, Paul A., and Hank C. Jenkins-Smith. *Policy Change and Learning: An Advocacy Coalition Approach.* Boulder, CO: Westview, 1993.

Weible, C. M., P. A. Sabatier, H. C. Jenkins-Smith, D. Nohrstedt, A. D. Henry, and Peter deLeon. "A Quarter Century of the Advocacy Coalition Framework: An Introduction to the Special Issue." *Policy Studies Journal* 38 (2011): 349–360.

Chapter 25

Innovations and Diffusion

Andrew Karch

"IT IS ONE OF THE HAPPY INCIDENTS OF THE federal system," Supreme Court justice Louis Brandeis wrote in a famous 1932 dissent, "that a state may, if its citizens choose, serve as a laboratory; and try novel social and economic experiments without risk to the rest of the country."[1] Since this landmark dissent, the fifty states have regularly been referred to as laboratories of democracy. Liberal and conservative jurists have cited this metaphor dozens of times, and actors from across the political spectrum have invoked it to describe the states' innovative potential. The metaphor refers to the two crucial ideas that this chapter addresses.

The first idea is that states are potential innovators that can develop new and untested solutions to emerging societal problems. If officials are dissatisfied with patterns of academic achievement, levels of air pollution, trends in crime rates, or other conditions within their jurisdiction, they can attempt to address them by adopting programs that have never been tried in the state. These policy innovations need not be new in an objective sense, and they might already exist in several other jurisdictions. By convention, however, if decision makers perceive a policy as new, then it qualifies as an innovation.[2] Most studies that examine this topic in the context of the fifty states focus on their relative innovativeness. Are some states inherently more innovative than others? The first section of this chapter examines this question, focusing on the effort to identify both the states that are most receptive to new policy approaches and the demographic, socioeconomic, and political factors that correlate with this openness.

Subsequent sections of the chapter turn to a second idea invoked, at least implicitly, in Brandeis's dissent. Policy innovations can diffuse or spread from one jurisdiction to another. The laboratories of democracy metaphor implies a rational, trial-and-error dynamic through which public policies are evaluated along a set of objective or political dimensions. If evaluators agree that the policies achieve their programmatic or political goals, then other states might adopt them. Diffusion, in other words, is a process of learning or emulation during which decision makers look to other states as models to be followed or avoided. It occurs when the existence of an innovation in Jurisdiction A significantly affects the likelihood that it will be adopted in Jurisdiction B. Diffusion is not merely the fact of increasing incidence; it implies movement from the source of an innovation to an adopter. The chief analytical challenge for state politics scholars is to distinguish between independent actions that lead to policy convergence from an interdependent policy-making process in which state officials learn from one another's experiments.[3]

The scholarly literature on policy diffusion is vast, reflecting its centrality to the state politics subfield of political science. Indeed, state politics scholars have examined the diffusion of innovative public policies in such diverse arenas as health care, education, criminal justice, economic development, environmental protection, and many others.[4] As a result, they have gained significant insight into the different reasons why diffusion occurs; the varied diffusion mechanisms that help transfer new policy ideas from one jurisdiction to another; and the important ways in which the content of public policies influences, and is influenced by, the diffusion process. This chapter turns to those three topics after examining existing research on innovativeness.

THE QUESTION OF INNOVATIVENESS

Is innovativeness a durable and meaningful state characteristic? In 1969 the seminal research of Jack Walker first drew scholarly attention to the question of whether some states are more innovative than others. At a time when most studies of state politics examined program expenditures, Walker constructed a composite innovativeness score based on the speed with which states initiated eighty-eight programs in twelve different issue areas. The states that received the highest scores were described as innovative due to their tendency to adopt new programs more rapidly than their peers.[5]

The measurement of state innovativeness became a topic of considerable interest, and two distinct strategies emerged. Several scholars based innovativeness scores on the speed with which policymakers endorsed a set of programs, typically combining original data with a reexamination of some of the programs that Walker had investigated. Other scholars conducted surveys in which they asked state officials to identify the most and least innovative states, both generally and in the context of specific issues. These studies converged in identifying several demographic correlates of innovativeness, about which more will be said shortly. They also highlighted a series of interrelated conceptual and methodological issues that caused interest in the topic to decline by the early 1980s.

Critics questioned whether innovativeness was a meaningful concept. They pointed specifically to variation across policies and over time. States that tended to be early adopters in certain programmatic areas were laggards in others. For example, states that led the way in adopting new approaches to civil rights did not adopt innovations in education policy with the same speed. State rankings also seemed to be affected by the governmental entity responsible for decision making; studies that identified legislative and judicial innovators reached different conclusions. Temporal variation was another prominent theme. Critics of the innovativeness concept contended that the most consistent early adopters depended on the time period under examination. Within a decade of Walker's path-breaking study, both his supporters and his detractors seemed to agree that innovativeness was issue- and time-specific. This variation led some critics to question the usefulness of innovativeness as a political concept.[6]

It also invoked methodological concerns. If innovativeness varied across policy areas and over time, then the states identified as leaders and laggards might depend on the sample of policy innovations examined. Thousands of policies had diffused among the states, making it possible that existing measures were based on sets of programs that were somehow unrepresentative. Sampling was a critical issue, and scholars struggled to devise criteria for issue selection that seemed reasonable and appropriate. Some asserted that the problem could be addressed by developing broad indices that represented the full spectrum of state government activity. Others claimed that, regardless of which policies were included, scholars should be careful about drawing inferences on the basis of a single study. Interest in innovativeness research declined as scholars struggled to resolve these conceptual and methodological debates.

Recently, scholars have returned to the study of innovativeness. Most contemporary analyses develop indices based on the speed with which state officials adopted a set of programs, the approach pioneered by Walker. They attempt to overcome the obstacles that hamstrung earlier research by incorporating a larger number of policy innovations, examining variation across policy types,[7] accounting for the fact that the policies being studied have not been adopted by all existing states at the time of analysis, and developing innovativeness scores that can vary over time.[8] Despite their impressive breadth and increased methodological sophistication, however, the studies remain subject to concerns about representativeness because they rely on convenience-based approaches to sampling.

The two waves of state innovativeness research converge in at least one important respect. Scholars generally agree on the factors that correlate with this characteristic. Virtually every study of innovativeness highlights the influence of slack resources. Slack resources enable lawmakers to experiment with innovative programs because policy failures will not be fatal, whereas decision makers who operate without such slack might guard their limited resources more carefully.[9] Resource availability is a critical determinant of the ability to innovate because it enables potential innovators to overcome the hurdles that they will inevitably confront.[10] Two common indicators of state capacity are fiscal strength and legislative professionalism, both of which have been shown to facilitate the early adoption of policy innovations.

Scholars have also linked innovativeness to various demographic and political factors. State size, typically measured in terms of population, is often viewed as an indicator of resource availability, and multiple studies have found that innovativeness is correlated with size, urbanization, and education levels. In terms of politics, states with higher levels of political competition seem to be more receptive to innovations. A competitive environment fosters innovation by making elected officials more responsive to citizen concerns and by producing fluidity and turnover in the political system. The ideological environment is another influential political factor. Liberal states display a general openness to policy change and activity, whereas conservative states tend to be less receptive to changes in the status quo.

In an era of heightened policy activity at the state level, the recent revitalization of innovativeness research is a promising development. The breadth and increased sophistication of recent studies promise to illuminate whether some states are inherently more innovative than others, and this recent wave of research highlights many of the same correlates of innovativeness as did its predecessors. One key analytical challenge remains, however. Scholars must address the long-standing concern about representativeness that has bedeviled this literature for over four decades. Given the inherent difficulty of choosing a representative set of policies, they must continue to think carefully about case selection. Turning to alternative forms of state-level activity might provide an out-of-sample test of the innovativeness concept. If states vary in systematic and predictable ways in their receptivity to innovative policy approaches, then existing measures should have some predictive power outside the context in which they were devised. Scholars might gain analytical leverage by examining diverse forms of state activity. Evaluating whether similar states serve as leaders and whether similar factors correlate with receptivity to new ideas in other contexts might give scholars more confidence that innovativeness captures a meaningful and durable state characteristic.

WHY DOES DIFFUSION OCCUR?

The question of why policy innovations diffuse among the states is deceptively simple. Diffusion can occur for multiple reasons, and only recently have scholars begun to distinguish among them. This attention to multiple factors represents a major analytical shift. It has long been recognized that policymakers are more likely to draw lessons from some states than others, and that the political circumstances in which they find themselves can affect the examples upon which they rely. The main emphasis in most diffusion research, however, has been upon geographic proximity. Most studies assume that policies in nearby states provide a model upon which officials can draw and, perhaps more problematically, that this model makes policy adoption more likely.[11]

A common statistical proxy for the impact of proximity is the proportion of a state's bordering neighbors in which a policy innovation has already been adopted. Other studies modify this strategy by examining regional adoptions rather than focusing solely on a state's neighbors. Some scholars have argued that the statistical significance of this proxy variable is *prima facie* evidence that diffusion occurred. The absence of such statistical significance, in contrast, is sometimes interpreted to suggest that state officials were not affected by developments in other jurisdictions.

There are many reasons why geographic proximity might affect the diffusion process. It might facilitate the development of communications networks through which policy-relevant information spreads. Lawmakers in nearby states might be especially likely to discuss policies with one another, enabling programs in the same region to have a disproportionate impact on their decision making. Overlapping media markets can also alert residents and government officials to the existence of innovative programs in nearby states. For example, the reach of the Boston media market means that developments in Massachusetts are likely to become known in Maine, New Hampshire, and Rhode Island. Finally, officials might be especially inclined to use nearby states as models because they are likely to be culturally and demographically similar to their own states. This dynamic highlights the central analytical challenge for diffusion research, namely, distinguishing policy convergence from the learning and emulation that is characteristic of diffusion.

The preceding list is not exhaustive, but it suggests several reasons why geographic proximity could drive the spread of innovative policies. The notion that diffusion is driven primarily by geography has been roundly criticized, however. Critics argue that proximity might be less influential in the early twenty-first century than it was previously due to dramatic changes in communications and transportation technology. New lines of communication extend beyond regional boundaries and make it easier for officials to acquire policy-relevant information from and about far-flung states. National forces like the media and professional networks that operate through conferences and professional associations might be more important than developments in nearby states. The diffusion process might therefore be better described as a national process than as one driven by geographic proximity.

One challenge for diffusion research is to specify the conditions under which it will be driven by geographic proximity and to demonstrate the source of this relationship more convincingly. Even when the aforementioned proxy for proximity is found to have a statistically meaningful impact on the adoption of policy innovations, it does not reveal whether this link is due to close communications networks, overlapping media markets, the shared attributes of nearby states, or something else. In an era of technological interconnectedness, the role of proximity should be treated as an empirical question.

In light of the potential shortcomings of the traditional emphasis on geographic proximity, one of the most promising developments in diffusion research is the heightened attention that has been paid to other sources. For example, a policy might diffuse because officials believe that failing to adopt it will put their state at a competitive disadvantage. They may feel pressure to keep up with their colleagues. In those cases, diffusion is driven by interstate competition, a dynamic often associated with economic development programs and other policies with implications for state revenue. If businesses and citizens are attracted to places with the most favorable ratio of taxes paid to services received, then state lawmakers operate under the implicit threat that they will relocate if they believe that this ratio is no longer favorable. Officials might feel pressure to adopt a policy innovation that exists elsewhere if they think that its absence affects their state's relative attractiveness.

States might also compete to be less attractive to an undesirable group. If a state offers more generous welfare programs than its neighbor, for example, it might attract welfare recipients from that neighbor. As a result, the adoption of more stringent policies in one state might cause its neighbors to follow suit in a dynamic that has been described as a "race to the bottom." This competition to repel undesirables might sometimes explain why policy diffusion occurs. A similar "race" is possible in the context of environmental protection, tax policy, and other issues with the potential to affect firms' locational decisions.

A few studies examine the impact of interstate competition. Thus far the focus has been primarily upon policies that affect individuals, such as lotteries. State lawmakers appear to be influenced by the existence of lotteries in nearby states because they lose out on potential revenue when their own residents travel out of state to purchase lottery tickets. A recent analysis suggests that the size and location of policy-relevant populations within a state's neighbors generate a competition effect on the diffusion of state lotteries.[12] Examinations of other policy innovations, including Indian gaming compacts and antismoking regulations (see The Diffusion of Antismoking Policies box), have also found evidence of interstate competition.

The recent attention devoted to interstate competition is a promising development. It offers a theoretically compelling explanation of why innovative policies spread from one state to another. Thus far scholars have focused on competition among nearby states, and one potential avenue for future research is to examine issues where competition is not necessarily a matter of geography. Capital mobility, for example, means that states often engage in a nationwide competition to entice businesses to locate within their borders. Scholars must theorize carefully both about the conditions under which competition is likely to occur and about the type of competition that is likely to emerge if they are to build effectively on existing research.

Diffusion might also be driven by a process of imitation during which state officials engage in a national search for policy models. Imitation is distinct from learning because it occurs when state officials focus on the other government that adopted the policy rather than on the action that the other government has taken.[13] Imitation-driven diffusion occurs when decision makers adopt innovations because they want their jurisdictions to be viewed as favorably as those that are seen as leaders. It also occurs when officials believe that they share a policy-relevant characteristic with an early adopter and, therefore, believe that they ought to enact it too.

Imitation suggests that "closeness" can be determined by a political, demographic, or economic resemblance. Decision makers might believe that they have more in common with their far-flung colleagues than they do with their colleagues in nearby states. Ideological and resource similarities have been linked to the diffusion process. One study concluded that the ideological position of previous adopters affected the enactment of lotteries, academic bankruptcy laws, and criminal sentencing guidelines.[14] Similarly, an analysis of the Children's Health Insurance Program (CHIP) found that officials followed the example set by states with similar partisan and ideological leanings, state-level demographics, and budgetary situations.[15] These studies help answer the fundamental question of why diffusion occurs. They suggest that policy innovations spread because lawmakers imitate their colleagues who operate in similar environments. This possibility was initially raised by studies emphasizing geographic proximity, but neighboring states are not the only ones where such overlap is potentially influential.

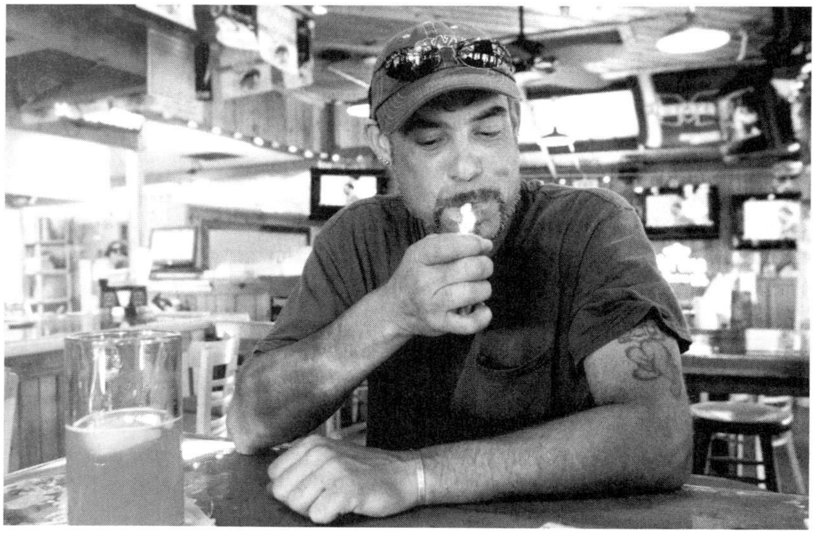

Finally, policies can diffuse because state officials view existing versions as successful. This emulation process occurs when lawmakers believe they should adopt a policy because it will allow them to achieve a substantive objective. Their decisions are based upon the perceived success of a policy rather than the attributes of the states in which it has already been adopted. Emulation also implies that officials will learn from unsuccessful policy experiments by not enacting them, but this possibility has received less attention. Emulation resonates with the idea

Roger Rice, from North Carolina, smokes at a restaurant in Horn Lake, Mississippi. A statewide ban on smoking in all bars and restaurants in North Carolina took effect in 2010, but as of early 2013, a statewide smoking ban had not diffused to Mississippi, where state legislators left it to local governments to decide whether to allow smoking in bars and restaurants.

SOURCE: © Stan Carroll/ZUMA Press/Corbis.

THE DIFFUSION OF ANTISMOKING POLICIES

Thousands of innovative policy ideas have diffused among the American states in recent decades, and it would be foolish to identify any single episode as representative. Yet the diffusion of antismoking policies illustrates many of the themes discussed in this chapter and offers an opportunity to look more closely at the distinctive political forces that can influence the spread of policy innovations. Various public health concerns, including the number of Americans who die each year of tobacco-related causes and the dangers of secondhand smoke, have been used to justify restrictions on tobacco products. States and cities across the country have enacted these restrictions in recent decades.

The diffusion of antismoking policies illustrates four themes that appear in this chapter. First, it displays how policy innovations often contain multiple components. State policymakers who wished to address this public health issue had a variety of options from which to choose. They could restrict access to cigarettes by making it more difficult for young people, especially teenagers, to purchase them (youth access laws). Many states passed laws restricting sales of individual cigarettes or those outside the original manufactured full packages with this goal in mind. Another option was to adopt "clean indoor air laws" that restricted or banned smoking in government buildings or placed similar limitations on smoking in restaurants and other public places. As a result, asking simply whether states adopted an antismoking policy overlooks the manifold ways in which state policies differed from one another.

Second, the different components of antismoking policies illustrate the varied speeds with which innovations diffuse. In 1975 Minnesota became the first state to adopt clean indoor air laws both for government buildings and for restaurants. Over the next four years, eight states adopted the restrictions for government buildings and seven states adopted them for restaurants. The years from 1985 to 1990 were a period of heightened activity, with twenty states adopting government building restrictions and sixteen states adopting restaurant restrictions. In short, both policies followed the standard S-curve often associated with the diffusion of innovations. By 2000, forty states had adopted government building restrictions, while thirty-two had adopted restaurant restrictions. The diffusion of youth access restrictions, in contrast, proceeded more slowly. In 1981 Texas became the first state to adopt them, but by 1990 only three other states had followed suit. There was a burst of activity from 1993 to 1997, when twenty states adopted the youth access restrictions, and by 2000 they existed in thirty-one states.

Third, the diffusion of antismoking policies among the states also illustrates how many different forces can drive the spread of innovative programs. Geographic proximity appears to have influenced the spread of antismoking policies. States whose neighbors had previously adopted the aforementioned restrictions were themselves more likely to do so. One analysis concludes that this relationship was driven by changes in public opinion. The existence of a policy in a neighboring state encouraged the aggregate opinions of state residents to change in a more supportive direction, spurring their elected leaders to adopt similar policies.[1] A study of policy change at the urban level found evidence that officials in smaller cities were especially influenced by imitation and competition.[2]

Finally, the emergence and spread of antismoking policies suggest that the effect of these political forces is a conditional one. An analysis of the interactive relationship between urban and state-level policies, for example, suggests that state officials were more likely to learn from urban experiences in states with high legislative professionalism and interest group activism. In other words, health organizations served as a conduit for the diffusion of youth access restrictions, transporting this innovative policy idea from the city level to the state level.[3] Scholarship on antismoking policies, in sum, illustrates how heightened attention to diffusion mechanisms, the reasons why diffusion occurs, and the content of what is spreading can offer broader lessons.

1. Juliana Pacheco, "The Social Contagion Model: Exploring the Role of Public Opinion on the Diffusion of Antismoking Legislation across the United States," *Journal of Politics* 74 (2012): 187–202.
2. Charles R. Shipan and Craig Volden, "Bottom-Up Federalism: The Diffusion of Antismoking Policies from U.S. Cities to States," *American Journal of Political Science* 50 (2006): 825–843.
3. Charles R. Shipan and Craig Volden, "The Mechanisms of Policy Diffusion," *American Journal of Political Science* 52 (2008): 840–857.

that the states can serve as laboratories of democracy in which lawmakers experiment with innovative policy approaches. An innovation's success drives its diffusion through a process of social learning, whereas unsuccessful innovations will not diffuse.

The diffusion of a successful innovation will not be affected by geographic proximity. Thus the emerging emphasis on emulation implicitly recognizes that officials can engage in a national search for models upon which to draw. Perhaps the most compelling illustration of emulation-driven diffusion is the aforementioned study of CHIP. It combines interviews of program administrators with a sophisticated statistical analysis to identify the objectives that officials pursued, and it finds that successful states are more likely to be emulated regardless of their location.[16]

At the same time, however, the study highlights the practical challenges involved in identifying emulation-driven diffusion. It can be difficult to evaluate public policies on objective criteria because policymakers either disagree on the appropriate metric for evaluation or agree on the metric but disagree on the amount of change that would constitute "success." Elected officials might also

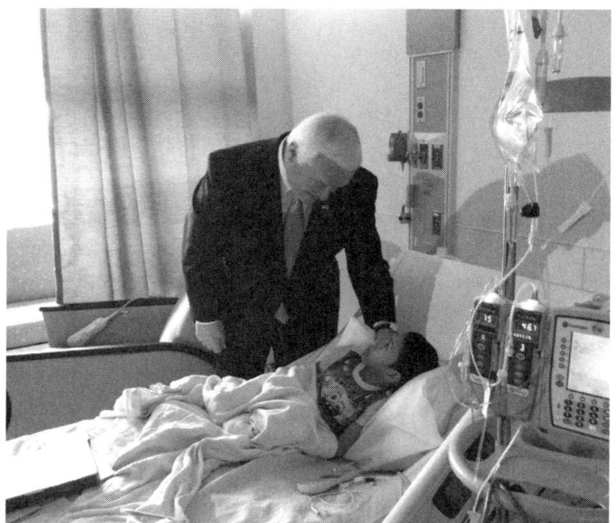

Pennsylvania governor Tom Corbett stops to talk to seven-year-old patient Jonathan Ortiz while taking a tour of Penn State Hershey Children's Hospital to highlight a 2013 proposal to expand a state health insurance program for low-income children. Pennsylvania's Children's Health Insurance Program, begun in 1992, served as a model for the program Congress enacted five years later.

SOURCE: AP Photo/Marc Levy.

emphasize the political impact of a policy at the expense of substantive outcomes. Ongoing debates about the effectiveness of such educational reforms as charter schools and school choice illustrate these challenges. While emulation offers a compelling explanation of why diffusion occurs, its relevance is likely to vary across policies.

In sum, public policies can diffuse for many reasons. Political scientists have only recently moved beyond their conventional emphasis on geographic proximity and distinguished among these driving forces. Policies can diffuse through interstate competition, in which lawmakers feel pressure to enact an innovation that exists elsewhere because it affects their state's relative attractiveness. Policies can diffuse through a process of imitation, in which officials want their jurisdictions to be viewed as favorably by those that are seen as leaders or believe that they share a policy-relevant trait with the jurisdictions that have already adopted them. Finally, policies can diffuse through a process of emulation, in which officials learn from the successes and failures of others, adopting programs that have been successful elsewhere. Competition, imitation, and emulation help explain why diffusion occurs, and several studies make theoretically valuable contributions by demonstrating their potential impact.

The next logical step in this line of research is to specify the conditions under which each of these dynamics is most likely to occur. For example, competition might influence the diffusion of policies that have significant cross-border externalities, such as economic development innovations, but it might not affect the diffusion of programs whose primary impact is symbolic. In contrast, one form of imitation, the use of ideological or partisan cues, might influence the diffusion of policies whose impact is uncertain or about which there are intense partisan disputes. Finally, given the inherent difficulty of evaluating many innovations, emulation or policy learning might be especially likely to occur in relatively nonpolitical settings that receive limited public attention. It is also important to acknowledge that the diffusion of any individual policy innovation might be driven by a combination of these forces, making it imperative to assess their relative contributions.[17]

DIFFUSION MECHANISMS AND THE POLICY-MAKING PROCESS

As has already been noted, the chief analytical challenge for those interested in policy diffusion is to distinguish between simple policy convergence and the interactive dynamic that constitutes diffusion. *Diffusion* is about the movement of a policy across jurisdictional boundaries, whereas *adoption* represents the decision to establish it in an individual jurisdiction. This distinction is often blurred, and sometimes the two terms are used interchangeably. Consequently, another promising development in diffusion research is the emerging emphasis on political forces that operate in multiple jurisdictions and are therefore capable of transporting new policy ideas across state lines. Due to their geographic reach, these political forces are potential diffusion mechanisms. The recent focus on these mechanisms promotes a better understanding of why some innovations spread widely and others remained confined to a smaller number of jurisdictions.

Another way to distinguish between adoption and diffusion is to adopt a process-oriented approach. Historically, most diffusion studies focused exclusively on the adoption decision. This approach shed significant light on the political, economic, and demographic correlates of adoption, but it did not illuminate the political processes through which innovations diffuse from one state to another. For example, it neglected the processes through which officials become aware of policy innovations, gather information about them, and amend them. If the most influential forces vary across these diverse policy-making stages, studies that examine only enactment may underestimate the impact of certain forces while overestimating the impact of others. Examining a wider range of outcomes makes it possible to focus more intently on diffusion mechanisms and to understand how their impact varies across stages of the policy-making process. This section profiles several causal forces and their relationship to a "process-oriented" approach.[18]

The national government, with its ability to simultaneously affect policymaking in multiple states, is a potent diffusion mechanism. It can influence both the content of state political agendas and whether state policymakers decide to adopt a specific innovation. When national policymaking affects state policymaking in either of these ways, diffusion becomes a vertical process.

National government activity affects the agenda-setting process by encouraging state officials to focus on certain issues rather than others. Its primary contribution is to raise the political profile of a policy innovation through its actions. State officials operate under considerable time constraints, and they are often drawn to visible, salient policies. National political campaigns and policy debates rank among the most visible elements of American politics, so time-pressed state officials who are looking for cues about "hot" political issues sometimes use national developments as a measure of what is on the agenda. Even when national debates are unresolved, they often garner sufficient attention to cause certain alternatives to be seriously considered. An analysis of embryonic stem cell research policy suggests, for example, that President George W. Bush's nationally televised address and his veto of congressional legislation increased both the likelihood that state officials would introduce related bills in a given year and the number of bills they introduced.[19] National government activity can also facilitate the dissemination of policy-relevant information by encouraging the formation of policy networks.[20]

National government officials also have several tools at their disposal to influence state officials' decisions about whether to adopt a policy innovation. Financial incentives represent an especially direct and powerful tool, and they cause public policies to diffuse more widely and more rapidly. National officials can also affect diffusion by providing money for demonstration projects and through the approval of waiver requests for state-run, federally funded programs like Medicaid. Nonfinancial forms of national government intervention also exist. For example, national officials can send signals to the states concerning their preferences and the potential for future action.[21] In sum, national government intervention can influence state political agendas, the resources officials consult to gather information, and the decision to endorse or reject specific innovations. For more on vertical diffusion, see Chapter 1, Federalism and Intergovernmental Relations.

Policy entrepreneurs represent a second diffusion mechanism. They may be elected officials, executive agency officials, or private citizens, such as representatives of the business community or policy activists. They can facilitate policy diffusion because they either operate or have professional connections in more than one state. Networking across state lines allows policy entrepreneurs to learn about the details and effects of policies that exist elsewhere. They can then use technical and political information to sell their ideas to politicians and the public. Thus policy entrepreneurs are willing to devote their time, knowledge, and energy to a political cause, serving both as informational resources and advocates for the policies they favor.

Relatively few diffusion studies have assessed the impact of policy entrepreneurs, despite repeated calls to grant them a more prominent role. One barrier to research on this topic is the inherent difficulty of constructing valid and feasible state-level measures of entrepreneurial activity. Policy entrepreneurs are idiosyncratic, and that makes large sample studies of them extremely difficult. A national survey to identify entrepreneurial activity in the context of school-choice educational reform represents an especially promising example.[22] It suggests that policy entrepreneurs are better able to place their preferred policy on the agenda than to facilitate its adoption, a pattern that underlines the importance of looking beyond adoption patterns in diffusion research.

Like the national government and policy entrepreneurs, national organizations can transport policy innovations across state lines. In fact, some interest groups and professional associations view the dissemination of policy-relevant information as a key part of their organizational missions. For example, think tanks and policy research institutes publish books, periodicals, and policy briefs and host conferences that facilitate the development of professional networks. Interest groups and professional associations rely on many of the same tools. The underlying goal of all of these activities is to update decision makers about innovative programs and their political and substantive impact. The dissemination of information is a critical, albeit often overlooked, component of the diffusion process. Late adopters can enact a policy that exists elsewhere without any knowledge of existing programs, but state officials must be aware of and interested in developments in other jurisdictions for diffusion to occur.

Several organizations provide state officials with information about developments across the country. Professional associations like the Council of State Governments, the National Conference of State Legislatures, and the National Governors Association are active on a wide array of policy issues. Survey evidence suggests that legislative leaders value the information that these groups disseminate.[23] Recently, the American Legislative Exchange Council, a group of conservative lawmakers and policy advocates, has successfully promoted both awareness of and the adoption of several new policies at the state level. Founded in 1973, the organization focuses primarily on economic policy, but it has also been linked to controversial "Stand Your Ground" laws and voter identification legislation. Other national organizations have been linked to the diffusion of innovations like living-wage laws, same-sex marriage bans, and health care reform.

Understanding which mechanisms spark diffusion episodes will enable scholars to explain variation in the number and geographic distribution of the states in which specific innovations exist. The increased attention that diffusion mechanisms have recently received suggests several productive avenues for future research. Scholars should investigate the conditions under which specific mechanisms are most likely to affect diffusion; their impact may depend on the type of innovation involved. Professional associations might be especially influential when less salient administrative reforms are under consideration, while policy entrepreneurs and interest groups might have a more significant impact in other contexts.

Another potential avenue for future research is to examine the impact of various causal mechanisms during different policy-making stages. The political forces that place an innovation on the agenda might not be the same as the ones that spur officials to adopt it. For example, policy entrepreneurs and professional associations might affect the agenda or disseminate policy-relevant information, but they are unlikely to influence the adoption decision because they do not represent the intrastate constituencies to which elected officials must respond. Most existing diffusion research focuses on adoption at the expense of the agenda-setting and information generation, but the recent turn toward causal mechanisms provides an opportunity to incorporate information about the policy-making process into diffusion research.[24] A process-based approach promises to shed significant light on many overlooked facets of policy diffusion.

POLICY CONTENT AND THE DIFFUSION OF INNOVATIONS

When state officials endorse a policy that exists elsewhere, they do not have to copy it exactly. They can make any changes that they deem necessary. During this customization process, they can make adjustments to account for the political, economic, and demographic traits of their states, or they can alter the inherited template based on the experiences of early adopters. Studies of these adaptations, like all diffusion studies, must be particularly attentive to the relative influence of internal and external forces on the policies that state officials ultimately endorse. Policy innovations typically take on various forms in the states in which they are adopted, and sometimes this variation can be profound. Moreover, content differences at the adoption stage can be further extended as the policies are implemented and revisited.

Most diffusion research, however, simply treats all adoptions as identical. This problematic oversight is due, in part, to the use of event history analysis, the conventional statistical means through which scholars have modeled policy adoption at the state level. Event history analysis offers numerous statistical advantages, and its widespread use has facilitated comparability across studies of state policymaking.[25] Most of these studies focus on whether and when a policy innovation was adopted, using a dichotomous dependent variable that indicates whether it was adopted in a given state in a given year. The question of policy content remains outside the scope of the analysis, meaning that it simply cannot answer the question of why innovations take on a variety of forms in the states in which they gain enactment.

Treating policy content as an outcome of interest requires an alternative approach. Fortunately, several options exist. Some of them are best described as modifications to the standard event history approach, whereas others use ordinary least squares regression or event count frameworks to assess policy scope.[26] Many different analytical strategies can be used to examine policies that involve multiple components. These approaches enable scholars to study the presence or level of specific provisions, permitting a richer understanding of policy variation. They must be accompanied, however, by additional theorizing about the political forces that are responsible for policy variation.

The primary theoretical framework through which scholars have assessed policy content is conscious reinvention, a systematic process by which later adopters learn from the experiences of early adopters. The primary research question that has been examined is whether later adopters establish more or less expansive policies than leaders, or whether they engage in wholesale borrowing. A few studies have examined the hypothesis that later adopters enact more expansive policies, speculating that early models provide political or administrative lessons that enable later adopters to expand on their efforts. Thus reinvention might cause laggard states to adopt policies with the most innovative and expansive provisions.

Despite their laudable attention to policy content, existing studies tend to treat reinvention as a mechanical process. They largely ignore potential political and policy-relevant factors as well as the many reasons why late adopters might endorse less expansive versions of a policy. If early adopters experience unforeseen administrative difficulties, later adopters might conclude that the policy will not be manageable unless its scope is reduced. Alternatively, the policy might generate a political backlash that gives later adopters pause. Controversial laws tend to become less comprehensive over time, while noncontroversial laws tend to become more expansive.[27] Other conditions and forces might also affect reinvention, and scholars have barely scratched the surface of its potential contribution to our understanding of diffusion.

Policy content is not only an outcome to be explained, however. It can also affect the diffusion process itself. For example, policy content can influence the types of groups that are active. Even minor variations in policy content can affect the mobilization of specific constituencies, as when religious fundamentalists had a substantial impact on the adoption of general funds lotteries but not on the adoption of education funds lotteries.[28] As discussed earlier, technical administrative policies might spark the engagement of professional associations, whereas interest groups might be more likely to influence debates about publicly salient programs. In short, policy content might affect which political actors mobilize for action, leading to a better understanding of why diffusion occurs and the role of specific diffusion mechanisms.

The impact of policy content on the diffusion process has recently received substantial scholarly attention. These analyses attempt to explain the varying speed with which innovative policies diffuse among the states, recognizing that some policies diffuse very rapidly rather than in the familiar S-shaped pattern that is frequently associated with an incremental learning process. Salience and complexity seem especially important. High-salience policies tend to diffuse more rapidly than do low-salience policies. Complex policies that require technocratic analysis, in contrast, tend to diffuse more slowly than do policies that require little policy expertise.[29] Thus morality policies characterized by elevated issue attention, low complexity, and high emotional appeal are more prone to rapid diffusion episodes than are regulatory policies that are characterized by high technical complexity and low salience.[30] Other policy characteristics have the potential to affect diffusion. A recent examination of criminal justice policy innovations found that state officials were especially likely to learn from their peers when policies produced results that could be easily observed, but that they were less likely to learn from their peers both when they could conduct their own limited experiments and when the policies were too complex for such learning to be of much use.[31]

The relationship between policy content and diffusion merits a prominent place in diffusion studies. Future research should continue to examine both the reasons why existing versions of a policy can vary so significantly and the ways in which the attributes of an innovation affect the diffusion process. After all, observers are interested not only in the mere incidence of diffusion but also in what is being diffused. The recent focus on policy content in diffusion research is a positive development, but many key questions remain unaddressed.

CONCLUSION

The fifty states are often described as laboratories of democracy. Observers have long marveled at state officials' ability to devise innovative solutions to emerging societal problems and at the spread of these new policy ideas from state to state, both of which are invoked by this famous metaphor. Since the publication of Walker's seminal article in 1969, the study of policy innovations and their diffusion has been a central component of the state politics subfield of political science. Recently, diffusion scholars have made numerous theoretical and empirical advances, and the recent revitalization of research on innovativeness promises to produce similar insights. Reaching this potential, however, will require that scholars address several analytical challenges.

In examining the spread of innovative policies, political scientists must continue to move beyond the conventional focus on geographic proximity. Policy diffusion might occur because officials feel competitive pressures to enact a policy that exists elsewhere, because they imitate the policy choices of their counterparts in states that share a policy-relevant characteristic, or because they emulate successful policies. In none of these cases would geographic proximity be determinative. Similarly, several recent studies have illustrated the impact of such diffusion mechanisms as the national government, policy entrepreneurs, and national organizations. These political forces are capable of transporting policy lessons across state lines and, once again, their influence is not constrained by geography. Now that we have a better appreciation for the range of forces and actors with the potential to affect policy diffusion, the next theoretical and empirical challenge is to isolate the conditions under which they are most likely to be influential. Their impact might depend on the type of policy innovation being considered as well as the stage of the policy-making process in which officials are engaged. The political forces that influence the adoption decision might differ from those that cause an innovation to be considered, that disseminate information about it, or that affect how officials adapt the existing policy template.

Scholars must also devote more attention to policy content, both as an outcome to be explained and as a factor that affects the spread of innovative policies. State officials can customize policies to fit their jurisdictions, and they can learn from the experiences of early adopters. Policies that are nominally the same might vary in substantively meaningful ways. One promising development is the seriousness with which these differences have been treated. Scholars have also highlighted how the attributes of a policy innovation can affect both the mobilization of specific constituencies and the speed with which it diffuses. Salient and complex policies seem to diffuse more rapidly than do policies that are less well-known and require greater technical expertise.

Addressing the issues highlighted in this chapter may require innovative analytical approaches. Event history analysis has been the standard way to model diffusion for more than two decades, but modified versions of this approach and alternative strategies like event count models are likely to prove illuminating. Qualitative evidence can also be used to examine the impact of specific diffusion mechanisms or to assess the availability and use of policy-relevant information. Intensive case studies of individual innovations or states might help scholars distinguish policy convergence from interdependent decision making, the key analytical challenge for future research. The ideal approach would be a combined one. By triangulating their findings, researchers can purge their studies of the biases that can exist when only one source of evidence is employed.

Regardless of the empirical approach they employ, scholars should consider the broader implications of their findings. Understanding how political forces influence the development and spread of policy innovations is an especially meaningful issue during an era in which the policy repertoire of the states continues to expand. Moreover, diffusion can occur in both domestic and international settings, so the theoretical and empirical advances that are made in the study of state-level diffusion might have implications for other branches of political science.

NOTES

1. *New State Ice Co. v. Liebmann,* 285 U.S. 262 (1932).
2. This definition of innovation has been employed in fields ranging from anthropology and rural sociology to marketing and public health. See Everett M. Rogers, *Diffusion of Innovations,* 4th ed. (New York: Free Press, 1995).
3. Craig Volden, Michael M. Ting, and Daniel P. Carpenter, "A Formal Model of Learning and Policy Diffusion," *American Political Science Review* 102 (2008): 319–332.
4. For a recent literature review see Andrew Karch, "Emerging Issues and Future Directions in State Policy Diffusion Research," *State Politics and Policy Quarterly* 7 (2007): 54–80. This chapter updates and expands upon many themes in that review.
5. Jack L. Walker Jr., "The Diffusion of Innovations among the American States," *American Political Science Review* 63 (1969): 880–899.
6. Virginia Gray, "Innovation in the States: A Diffusion Study," *American Political Science Review* 67 (1973): 1174–1185.
7. Graeme Boushey, *Policy Diffusion Dynamics in America* (New York: Cambridge University Press, 2010).
8. Frederick J. Boehmke and Paul Skinner, "State Policy Innovativeness Revisited," *State Politics and Policy Quarterly* (forthcoming).
9. Rogers, *Diffusion of Innovations.*
10. Lawrence B. Mohr, "Determinants of Innovation in Organizations," *American Political Science Review* 63 (1969): 111–126.
11. Christopher Z. Mooney, "Modeling Regional Effects on State Policy Diffusion," *Political Research Quarterly* 54 (2001): 103–124.
12. William D. Berry and Brady Baybeck, "Using Geographic Information Systems to Study Interstate Competition," *American Political Science Review* 99 (2005): 505–520.
13. Charles R. Shipan and Craig Volden, "The Mechanisms of Policy Diffusion," *American Journal of Political Science* 52 (2008): 840–857.
14. Lawrence J. Grossback, Sean Nicholson-Crotty, and David A. M. Peterson, "Ideology and Learning in Policy Diffusion," *American Politics Research* 32 (2004): 521–545.
15. Craig Volden, "States as Policy Laboratories: Emulating Success in the Children's Health Insurance Program," *American Journal of Political Science* 50 (2006): 294–312.
16. Ibid.
17. Shipan and Volden, "The Mechanisms of Policy Diffusion."
18. Andrew Karch, *Democratic Laboratories: Policy Diffusion among the American States* (Ann Arbor: University of Michigan Press, 2007).
19. Andrew Karch, "Vertical Diffusion and the Policymaking Process: The Politics of Embryonic Stem Cell Research," *Political Research Quarterly* 65 (2012): 48–61.
20. Karen Mossberger, *The Politics of Ideas and the Spread of Enterprise Zones* (Washington, DC: Georgetown University Press, 2000).
21. Mahalley D. Allen, Carrie Pettus, and Donald P. Haider-Markel, "Making the National Local: Specifying the Conditions for National Government Influence on State Policymaking," *State Politics and Policy Quarterly* 4 (2004): 318–344.
22. Michael Mintrom, *Policy Entrepreneurs and School Choice* (Washington, DC: Georgetown University Press, 2000).
23. Jill Clark and Thomas H. Little, "National Organizations as Sources of Information for State Legislative Leaders," *State and Local Government Review* 24 (2002): 38–44.
24. Steven J. Balla, "Interstate Professional Associations and the Diffusion of Policy Innovations," *American Politics Research* 39 (2001): 221–245.
25. Frances Stokes Berry and William D. Berry, "State Lottery Adoptions as Policy Innovations: An Event History Analysis," *American Political Science Review* 84 (1990): 395–415.
26. Frederick J. Boehmke, "Approaches to Modeling the Adoption and Diffusion of Policies with Multiple Components," *State Politics and Policy Quarterly* 9 (2009): 229–252.
27. Scott P. Hays, "Influences on Reinvention during the Diffusion of Innovations," *Political Research Quarterly* 49 (1996): 631–650.
28. Patrick A. Pierce and Donald E. Miller, "Variations in the Diffusion of State Lottery Adoptions: How Revenue Dedication Changes Morality Politics," *Policy Studies Journal* 27 (1999): 696–706.
29. Sean Nicholson-Crotty, "The Politics of Diffusion: Public Policy in the American States," *Journal of Politics* 71 (2009): 192–205.
30. Boushey, *Policy Diffusion Dynamics in America.*
31. Todd Makse and Craig Volden, "The Role of Policy Attributes in the Diffusion of Innovations," *Journal of Politics* 73 (2011): 108–124.

SUGGESTED READING

Allen, Mahalley D., Carrie Pettus, and Donald P. Haider-Markel. "Making the National Local: Specifying the Conditions for National Government Influence on State Policymaking." *State Politics and Policy Quarterly* 4 (2004): 318–344.

Balla, Steven J. "Interstate Professional Associations and the Diffusion of Policy Innovations." *American Politics Research* 39 (2001): 221–245.

Berry, Frances Stokes, and William D. Berry. "State Lottery Adoptions as Policy Innovations: An Event History Analysis." *American Political Science Review* 84 (1990): 395–415.

Berry, William D., and Brady Baybeck. "Using Geographic Information Systems to Study Interstate Competition." *American Political Science Review* 99 (2005): 505–520.

Boehmke, Frederick J. "Approaches to Modeling the Adoption and Diffusion of Policies with Multiple Components." *State Politics and Policy Quarterly* 9 (2009): 229–252.

Boehmke, Frederick J., and Paul Skinner. "State Policy Innovativeness Revisited." *State Politics and Policy Quarterly* (forthcoming).

Boushey, Graeme. *Policy Diffusion Dynamics in America*. New York: Cambridge University Press, 2010.

Clark, Jill, and Thomas H. Little. "National Organizations as Sources of Information for State Legislative Leaders." *State and Local Government Review* 24 (2002): 38–44.

Gray, Virginia. "Innovation in the States: A Diffusion Study." *American Political Science Review* 67 (1973): 1174–1185.

Grossback, Lawrence J., Sean Nicholson-Crotty, and David A. M. Peterson. "Ideology and Learning in Policy Diffusion." *American Politics Research* 32 (2004): 521–545.

Hays, Scott P. "Influences on Reinvention during the Diffusion of Innovations." *Political Research Quarterly* 49 (1996): 631–650.

Karch, Andrew. *Democratic Laboratories: Policy Diffusion among the American States*. Ann Arbor: University of Michigan Press, 2007.

———. "Emerging Issues and Future Directions in State Policy Diffusion Research." *State Politics and Policy Quarterly* 7 (2007): 54–80.

———. "Vertical Diffusion and the Policymaking Process: The Politics of Embryonic Stem Cell Research." *Political Research Quarterly* 65 (2012): 48–61.

Makse, Todd, and Craig Volden. "The Role of Policy Attributes in the Diffusion of Innovations." *Journal of Politics* 73 (2011): 108–124.

Mintrom, Michael. *Policy Entrepreneurs and School Choice*. Washington, DC: Georgetown University Press, 2000.

Mohr, Lawrence B. "Determinants of Innovation in Organizations." *American Political Science Review* 63 (1969): 111–126.

Mooney, Christopher Z. "Modeling Regional Effects on State Policy Diffusion." *Political Research Quarterly* 54 (2001): 103–124.

Mossberger, Karen. *The Politics of Ideas and the Spread of Enterprise Zones*. Washington, DC: Georgetown University Press, 2000.

Nicholson-Crotty, Sean. "The Politics of Diffusion: Public Policy in the American States." *Journal of Politics* 71 (2009): 192–205.

Pierce, Patrick A., and Donald E. Miller. "Variations in the Diffusion of State Lottery Adoptions: How Revenue Dedication Changes Morality Politics." *Policy Studies Journal* 27 (1999): 696–706.

Rogers, Everett M. 1995. *Diffusion of Innovations,* 4th ed. New York: The Free Press.

Shipan, Charles R., and Craig Volden. "The Mechanisms of Policy Diffusion." *American Journal of Political Science* 52 (2008): 840–857.

Volden, Craig. "States as Policy Laboratories: Emulating Success in the Children's Health Insurance Program." *American Journal of Political Science* 50 (2006): 294–312.

Volden, Craig, Michael M. Ting, and Daniel P. Carpenter. "A Formal Model of Learning and Policy Diffusion." *American Political Science Review* 102 (2008): 319–332.

Walker, Jack L., Jr. "The Diffusion of Innovations among the American States." *American Political Science Review* 63 (1969): 880–899.

Chapter 26

Fiscal Policy

James E. Alt, Soledad Artiz Prillaman, and David Dreyer Lassen

STATE FISCAL POLICY DEALS WITH GOVERNMENT revenues (taxes, fees, transfers from other levels of government, and other sources of income), spending (which includes transfers to local government, administration of public services, and cash transfers to individuals and businesses), and borrowing. The first part of this chapter lays out definitions and facts, illustrating major developments in recent years in each of these areas. For any given year, the budget is a detailed fiscal plan setting forth the intentions of the government (governor and legislature) for financing and spending money on public projects. The budget emerges each year through a political process of legislation, lobbying, and bargaining. Understanding that process, which varies across the states in important ways that influence policy outcomes, is the subject of the second part of the chapter.

Budgets emerge under a set of rules—practices, statutory laws, and constitutional provisions embodied in budget institutions—and these institutions, like budgets, vary across the states. This is valuable to a scholar of American politics: there is only one president, one Congress, and one U.S. economy, but there are fifty states, with governors, legislatures, and economies. So if we want to understand how fiscal policy affects the economy, such as by stabilizing the economy and offsetting a recession, we can turn to the states for evidence. The final part of the chapter analyzes research on how state budget institutions affect fiscal policy and related political outcomes like elections.

FISCAL SCOPE, SCALE, AND BALANCE

The scale, or size, of states' budgets varies significantly across states and across time. Fiscal scale reflects a balance between desired levels of spending and the cost of collecting the necessary revenues, which stem from tax collections and intergovernmental transfers. Over the past fifty years, state budgets experienced major changes. As Figure 26.1a demonstrates, state revenues and expenditures in constant dollars more than doubled from 1960 to 2010: in nominal dollars the figure for 2010 would be over $6,000. As is also evident, the growth of spending as a share of income is slower: from roughly 7 percent to 12 percent over the past fifty years (see Figure 26.1b). By contrast, the growth of overall federal spending is faster: ten percentage points as a share of income from 1960 to 2010 if Medicare and Social Security are included. Despite this change in fiscal scale, states mostly maintained fiscal balance, as shown in Figure 26.1c. The impact of economic shocks and recessions (1970s, 1990s, 2008) that increase deficits is very clear in this figure. Figure 26.1d also demonstrates that state debt differs from national debt in important and clear ways, with much less volatility and much lower levels. Achieving balance between revenues and expenditures, while targeting a particular fiscal scale, is of key importance to state fiscal policymakers.

Composition of Revenues

Intergovernmental Transfers

A major source of state revenue comes from the federal government through direct intergovernmental grants. In 2006 over 20 percent of states' revenues derived from federal intergovernmental grants and transfers. This marked a sharp increase in the allocation of federal dollars to the states, despite an overall decrease in federal spending. From 1995 to 2010 states became more reliant on federal transfers, with the average percentage of revenues from federal spending increasing by eight percentage points.

Generally, federal grants target the promotion of particular programs and policies, such as Medicare or highway expansion. Also known as categorical grants, these tied transfers allow the federal government to influence the budgets and policy decisions of the states directly. Federal matching grants, a subset of categorical grants, provide an incentive for state governments to increase expenditures on a specific program, with the federal government allocating grant money relative to the amount

FIGURE 26.1 **State Fiscal Scale, Balance, and Debt**

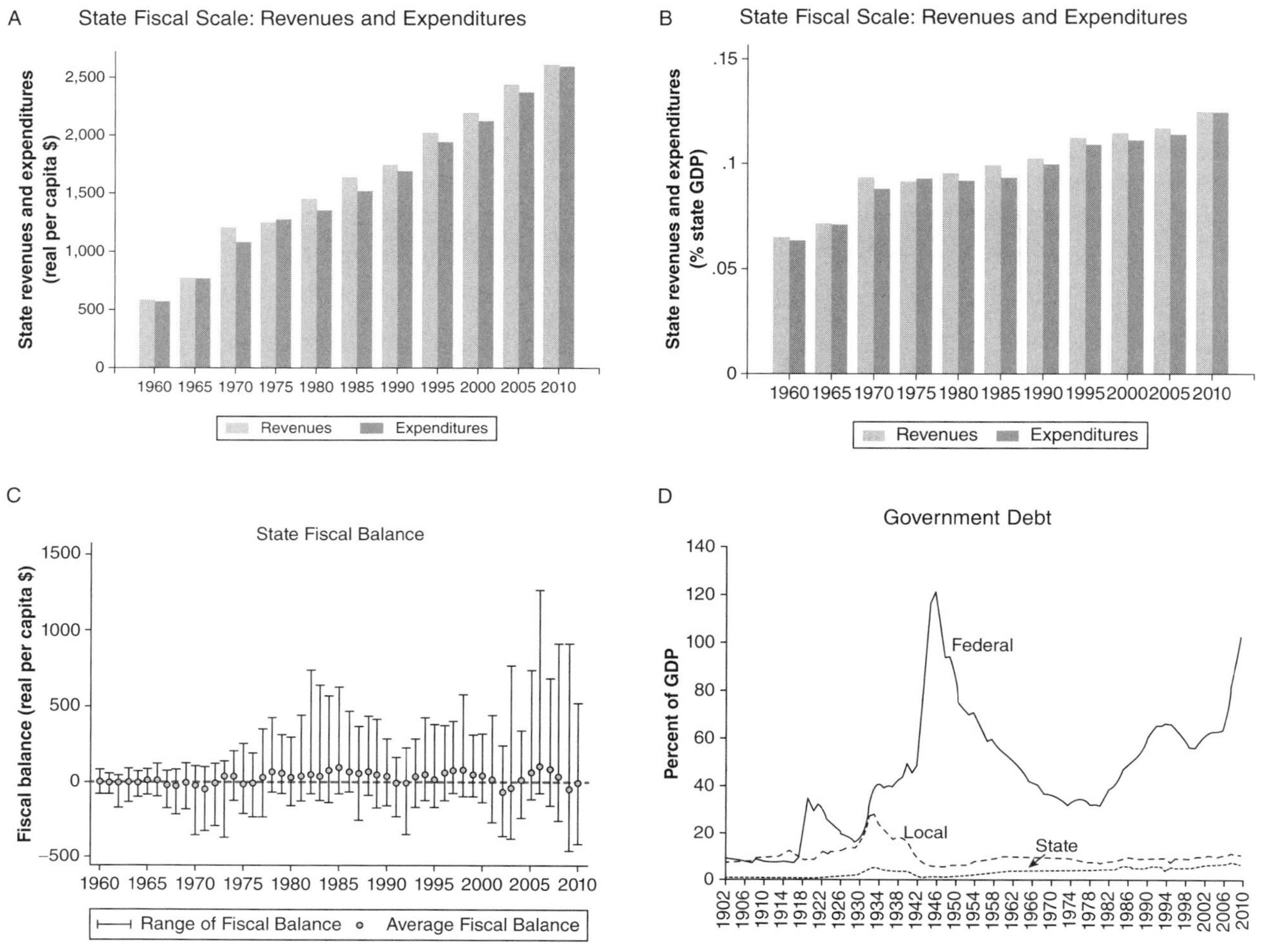

NOTE: Balance figure omits Alaska because of extreme surpluses resulting from oil price spikes.

SOURCE: State Government Finances; U.S. Bureau of Economic Analysis, Bureau of Labor Statistics.

spent by the state. A second major type of grant provided by the federal government to a state is a block grant. Block grants have fewer restrictions and give states greater discretion in their allocation.

Program support is not the only way that the federal government plays a significant role in state fiscal politics. The federal government also plays an indirect role in state budgeting through court-ordered standards, regulations, and mandates with which states have to comply. These requirements are costly and have a significant impact on the level, distribution, and growth of state revenues and expenditures. Federal grants-in-aid depress state tax effort, regardless of whether the program is heavily monitored or has a matching requirement.[1] Federal and state fiscal policies remain fundamentally intertwined (see Current Controversies: Fiscal Federalism box).

Own-Source Revenues

The majority of a state's revenues are collected by the state itself through tax receipts. States levy income, sales, property, and other taxes to fund the social services they provide (see Current Controversies: Taxes box). The two primary sources of revenue for the states are the income and sales taxes, with property taxes mostly funding local governments. Since Wisconsin first introduced an income tax in 1911, nearly every state adopted a state personal or corporate income tax, excluding only five states. Forty-one states directly tax personal income, two states (New Hampshire and Tennessee) tax personal income from investments, and two states (Alaska and Florida) only tax corporate income. The income tax is traditionally a progressive tax, with higher tax rates for higher-income brackets. Proponents of the income tax argue that public opinion polls find this form

CURRENT CONTROVERSIES: FISCAL FEDERALISM

FEDERAL DEFICIT REDUCTION PLANS

In 2011 the federal government vocalized a serious concern regarding the growing federal deficit. Along with these concerns, President Barack Obama outlined a federal deficit reduction plan. With over 20 percent of states' revenues coming from federal grants, state policymakers are concerned that their budgets will be cut. In particular, states are concerned that a disproportionate amount of funding will be cut for discretionary grants. This could also include some cuts in funding to large welfare programs, which would pose an additional challenge to state policymakers.[1]

MEDICAID AND HEALTH CARE REFORM

In 2010 Medicaid surpassed elementary and secondary education in becoming the largest component of state spending, and the cost of Medicaid is expected to continue to grow. As a result, state policymakers have faced significant challenges in budgeting for Medicaid. While the Supreme Court upheld the Patient Protection and Affordable Care Act and the individual mandate for insurance, it conceded that Congress cannot withhold Medicaid funding to states for not expanding eligibility. States have jurisdiction over Medicaid expansion, but cuts in federal support mean that twice as many states plan cuts in eligibility and payment rates for FY 2013.

HIGHER EDUCATION CUTS, TUITION RISING

State spending on higher education has fallen from 13 percent of total spending to 10 percent of total spending from 1998 to 2011. Public universities and colleges in California have been hit the hardest, with 2011 experiencing over a 21 percent rise in tuition and fees. The increasing costs of higher education and the decrease in state support have made it more difficult to receive an affordable education. Over the past twenty years, the cost of higher education has increased by over 130 percent, while median incomes have remained virtually the same.

PENSION COMMITMENTS AND REDUCTIONS

States spend about 3 percent of their budgets on retirement system contributions. Since the fall of financial markets in 2007, many experts have worried about the ability of states to meet their pension obligations. Some estimate that state pension programs could be as much as $1 trillion underfunded. In 2004, 79 percent of cities surveyed said that their pension funds were not doing well. State public pension systems showed positive earnings in 2010, which was a significant improvement over the $700 billion in losses from 2009. Despite this gain, in 2011 Detroit and other localities approved and executed pension cuts.

TRANSPORTATION

With federal transportation funds from the 2009 American Recovery and Reinvestment Act gone, states spent the first half of 2009 readjusting budgets and plans for infrastructure development. Many states turned their focus to maintenance rather than expansion. In response to these budgeting concerns, Ohio and Virginia are working with private contractors and are beginning to forge transportation privatization plans. However, in July 2012 Congress passed a transportation authorization bill, the Moving Ahead for Progress in the 21st Century Act (MAP-21), providing over $100 billion funding for transportation projects and giving states greater control.

1. Scott Pattison and Ben Husch, "Impact on States of Federal Deficit Reduction," National Association of State Budget Officers, October 5, 2011.

of taxation more politically acceptable; opponents, however, suggest that this could act as a work disincentive, ultimately affecting investment, savings, and economic growth.

The adoption of sales taxes began during the Great Depression era to fund the growth of social programs. To date, forty-five states employ a sales tax. Unlike the income tax, the sales tax is traditionally a regressive tax, since people with lower earnings spend a greater percentage of their income on the direct consumption of goods and the associated sales taxes. From the perspective of policymakers, voters find sales taxes more acceptable because the burden of the tax is disbursed over time, as compared with a lump sum property tax. The sales tax, however, is not a stable source of revenue because of its tie to the sale of goods, which fluctuates with the economic business cycle.

Selective sales (excise) taxes, such as those on cigarettes, tobacco, or motor fuel, also provide a major source of state revenue. Alaska, for example, generates a large portion of its revenues from the taxation of natural resources. State governments often earmark revenue from selective sales taxes for specific programs, such as spending on highways and transportation. Sin taxes, a subset of excise taxes, tax the consumption of goods that society wishes to discourage, like tobacco. Dependent on the supply and demand of these goods, selective sales taxes can have a substantial impact on the fiscal scale of a state.

In recent years, with the economic recession and in many cases one or another of a variety of tax and expenditure limits (discussed ahead), states turned to direct charges and user fees as additional sources of revenue.

These fees are imposed directly on the services they fund, and users are charged immediately upon consumption of the good or service, such as for higher education, highways, or professional licensing. The use of direct charges has become more popular, as they stimulate revenue without raising taxes: a politically acceptable move. Supporters of these fees argue that they directly impose the cost of a service on those who consume it, rather than dispersing the cost across the population in the form of a tax. Fees, like sin taxes, can discourage the consumption of scarce resources like water and other utilities. Many voters began to oppose user fees as they became more widely used. For example, for the 2011–2012 academic year California saw the highest increase in tuition and fees at public universities, with growth of over 8 percent. Since both low- and high-income groups pay the same flat fee for the use of these services or goods, this represents a shift toward a much more regressive revenue source (one in which the greater burden falls on lower-income brackets), at least relative to income taxes.

Student demonstrators sit and block the Bruin Plaza walkway on the University of California Los Angeles (UCLA) campus as the UC Board of Regents meets in Los Angeles, November 28, 2011. UCLA students were protesting against the possible increase in tuition fees, pepper-spraying of student protesters by University of California Davis police, and other issues related to Occupy Wall Street protests. States may turn to user fees, such as tuition, as means of raising additional revenue without increasing taxes.

SOURCE: REUTERS/Danny Moloshok.

Unlike most federal transfers, which the federal government predesignates for particular programs, state policymakers have much more discretion in the allocation

CURRENT CONTROVERSIES: TAXES

SIN TAXES AND LOTTERIES

During the economic recession, states turned to sin taxes, and particularly taxes on cigarettes, to fill budget gaps. In 2010 some states raised the tax on a pack of cigarettes by over $1.00. Taxes on cigarettes vary significantly across states, with South Carolina taxing only a few cents a pack and Rhode Island taxing nearly $3.50 a pack. In fact, over 10 percent of Rhode Island's revenues come from gambling and another 4 percent derive from cigarette sales. State revenues from lottery sales continue to grow in the forty-two states, with total revenues topping $60 billion in 2008. Most revenues from lottery sales are earmarked for education (North Carolina raised one-third of revenue for education through lottery sales), while tax revenues from cigarettes tend to be earmarked for health care.

INTERNET SALES AND TAXATION

Until recently, Internet-only sales companies, like Amazon.com or Overstock.com, were exempt from charging sales taxes on online purchases. One estimate showed that states lost over $8 million in sales tax revenue in 2008 to online sales. With the exponential growth of Internet sales and substantial decline in sales tax revenues, several states decided to collect sales taxes on Internet goods. Sales tax collections rose by only 1.2 percent in 2011, considerably less than the 4.7 percent rise in consumer spending. By the end of 2013, over thirteen states will have implemented laws forcing the payment of sales tax on Internet goods.

BUSINESS AND JOB INCENTIVES

Over the past several years, states have used their powers of fiscal policy to create incentives for businesses regarding where to locate (see also Chapter 4, Interstate Interactions). Particularly, states hope to encourage business entry through business-targeted tax cuts. Recently, Oregon passed a new law that permits technology companies to forgo paying taxes on intangible assets, such as their brand. Facebook, Apple, Google, and Amazon will all benefit from this new law. Similar programs, such as the Missouri Quality Jobs program, provide tax cuts to businesses that promise to create a minimum number of jobs. States intend to use these incentive programs and tax breaks to bring in new jobs and encourage economic growth. However, as is the case with the Missouri Quality Jobs program, these incentive schemes may not reap the economic rewards desired.

of own-source revenues. Most of this revenue goes toward funding statewide programs, with education and welfare traditionally receiving over 50 percent of the budget. Similar to federal transfers, state governments disperse a portion of their revenues to local governments. Over the last two decades, states have spent more on welfare and decreased their funding for highways, without making substantial changes to their composition of expenditures.

Sources of Variation

No two states are identical in their approach to fiscal policy. States have freedom to tax as much or as little as they want and to allocate their budget how they want within the confines of their constitutional limitations. However, environmental factors constrain these decisions. Demographic conditions, such as population size, age, and wealth, directly affect the potential scale of a state government. States with large and wealthy populations will bring in more tax revenue than those with small or poor populations. The demographic profile of a state may also affect how the state chooses to allocate its funds. Other constraints like the availability of natural resources affect the scale of government and may affect the tax structure adopted. Moreover, states are in "tax competition" with their neighbors who offer higher or lower rates. States are vulnerable to the economic cycle, where balanced budget rules compel states to cut spending during recessions to match declining tax receipts (see Budgeting in Hard Times box). Finally, politics play a major role in variation across the states and across time. Interest groups constrain fiscal policy, particularly regarding the allocation of federal grants. However, scholars highlight the effect of public preferences and political parties in determining states' fiscal policies.

Public Preferences and Discourse

In many states, the budget process allows, in principle, for the general public to be informed, through webcasts and

BUDGETING IN HARD TIMES

Economic recessions hit state fiscal policy hard. Incomes decline so revenues decline. Taxes become volatile. State government tax revenues are hit hard. In the most recent recession, real gross domestic product (GDP) fell by about 5 percent, while the consumption of items typically covered by state sales taxes fell by 11 percent, making this the largest collapse in state revenues to date. From 2009 to 2012, budget shortfalls have totaled more than $540 billion. "Rainy day" funds, barely rebuilt since the previous recession, were cut in half within two years. By 2010–2011, two "natural resource" states (Alaska and Texas) accounted for half the remaining balances. The variety of constraints states face—limits on taxes, spending, and debt—made prompt adjustment more necessary but also more difficult. Unsurprisingly, while many states raised income and sales taxes, some experimented with fees and lotteries, considered novel extensions of sales taxes to previously untaxed services, or turned to gimmicks to balance the budget. These included deferring expenditures to the next fiscal year, shifting expenses to or borrowing from other entities, or selling assets, like California's 2010 sale (and leaseback) of two dozen government buildings, with long-term liabilities incurred in return for a quick injection of needed cash. In response, states have become much more dependent on federal support. However, this dependence on federal revenues introduced more uncertainty into budgeting: when a lower-than-expected Medicaid reimbursement rate was introduced in early 2011, revenue forecasts went awry, unbalancing budgets. Problems with revenue cumulated and expanded.

Some costs also increased, making state finances unsustainable. Medicaid enrollments expanded, and mandated rising expenditures for unemployment compensation, medical assistance, income support, and food stamps added to budget deficits. Entitlements also increased costs when, for example, unemployed workers and their families exhausted health insurance benefits and turned to safety net services. Spending fell by about 10 percent over two years, a decline not seen since the early 1980s. Budgets in many programs were cut, and some programs disappeared entirely. In 2012 Pennsylvania stopped all funding for the General Assistance Program, a last-resort, temporary program supporting the sick and disabled. Cuts would have been larger except for the injection of federal dollars under the American Recovery and Reinvestment Act. Borrowing to finance the act was also federal, allowing states to keep debt down. States attempted to shift the burden of some spending by shifting responsibilities (and reducing transfers) to local governments, which were themselves having the same difficulties with shrinking property tax revenues that states had with declining sales and income tax revenues. Case studies of individual states from the fiscally conservative Georgia and Virginia to the more liberal ones like Connecticut and Massachusetts tell much the same story: cuts in spending, depletion of reserves, delay of execution through federal subsidies, and acceleration of problems when the subsidies ran out. The financial crisis in Illinois, where there is a projected cash deficit of over $27 billion in the next ten years, exemplifies the difficulties states face during hard times. In the end, more states run deficits. General fund balances shrink and disappear, and more debt is issued. The whole system of governance of state fiscal policy appears to be struggling, if not completely broken or broke.[1]

1. James K. Conant, "Introductions: The 'Great Recession,' State Budgets, and State Budget," *Public Budgeting and Finance* 30 (2010): 1–14.; Richard Ravitch and Paul Volker, "Report of the State Budget Crisis Task Force," *State Budget Crisis Task Force,* July, 2012, 1–110, www.statebudgetcrisis.org/wpcms/wp-content/images/Report-of-the-State-Budget-Crisis-Task-Force-Full.pdf.

minutes from budget committee meetings, and involved, for example, in the form of public hearings. This can take the form of legislative public budget hearings, as in New York State, where committees hold public hearings on various budget topics. Recently, state-level watchdog organizations, which attempt to provide citizens with accurate information on state and local government, have arisen with the sole goal of promoting "a vibrant, well-informed electorate and a more transparent government."[2]

Citizens and voters have strong opinions and preferences regarding state fiscal policy. How much these preferences enter into the decision-making process of policymakers remains an area of great debate. Limited information, interest groups, and legislative structure can all inhibit congruence between majority opinion and policy decisions.[3] Many scholars and citizens argue that vocal and prominent minorities can have more policy influence than the majority. In fact, John G. Matsusaka found that only 59 percent of the time states passed policies in line with majority opinion. Of the ten policy areas he examined, the two representing fiscal policy had slightly higher congruency with majority opinion: between 63 and 70 percent. Given that random policy selection is represented by 50 percent congruence, this demonstrates that the public's influence on fiscal policy decisions is limited.

In some states, institutions exist to encourage the representation of public preferences in the policy decision-making process. The initiative, established in twenty-four states, not only increases citizen participation in politics, but also directly affects state fiscal policy. Matsusaka[4] demonstrates that states with the initiative both spent and taxed less and that these policies were in line with majority public opinion. States with the initiative were also more likely to decentralize spending to local governments and to raise more money from user fees and less from taxes, as compared with states without the initiative. (See also Chapter 6, Initiative and Referendum.)

Parties

The news, political advertising, and common belief tell us that parties matter: Democrats tax more, Republicans spend less, etc. Despite this seemingly basic idea, academics have debated this issue for years. Do parties matter, or is what we see and think simply an artifact of the institutions by which they are constrained? David M. Primo[5] argues just this: the political institutional framework of a state dictates the behavior of parties and politicians. For example, he finds that states with conservative governors tend to spend more than states with liberal governors, contingent on the existence of spending limits. In fact, he finds that parties in the legislature have no impact on fiscal scale, regardless of institutional environment.

However, Timothy Besley and Anne Case[6] find that the higher the fraction of seats held by Democrats in the legislature, all else being equal, the higher are state taxes and spending per capita. Others find that the party of the governor does not matter after accounting for the legislative atmosphere. States where Democrats control the legislature had significantly higher tax burdens than did their Republican counterparts, suggesting that Democrats target a larger fiscal scale.[7] Not only does fiscal scale differ between Democrats and Republicans, but also parties respond differently to changes in the fiscal environment. Given a budget surplus, Republican-led legislatures react more sharply and decrease revenues more than Democratic majorities.

THE BUDGET PROCESS

Budgets are separated into operating budgets and capital budgets. Operating budgets establish the legal basis/foundation for the operation of state agencies or programs, and can consist of one or several appropriations bills, while capital budgets govern major, long-term investments, including state infrastructure. Operating budgets are divided into a general fund, consisting of money that can be used at the discretion of the governor and legislature, and special or nongeneral funds, typically revenues that are earmarked for specific use; for example, gasoline and motor vehicle taxes can be earmarked for use on transportation programs. Capital budgeting items are often debt financed, through bond issuance, and not subjected to balanced budget requirements; indeed, capital budgeting owes its existence largely to states having trouble financing long-term investments within the confines of these requirements.

The process by which a budget is prepared, formulated, decided, and carried out shares several features across states; but, at the same time, it differs in important dimensions. Every step of the budget process has the potential to be subject to political negotiations and institutional restrictions, from the determination of the starting point of the budget, the baseline, revenue forecasts, overall budget transparency, and legislative (dis)agreement with divided government, to gubernatorial vetoes and budget deadlocks. Overall, the process by which a state budget is developed and decided has important implications for final outcomes.

Budgets can be annual or biennial, and in all but four states fiscal years begin on July 1; twenty-one states use a biennial budget cycle, and two use a combination. Of the twenty-one states with biennial budgets, twelve have legislatures that meet every year and often reopen the budget if necessary. Even in states with annual budgets, however, mid-year adjustments may be necessary. Particularly in times of fiscal crisis, revenue shortfalls may turn out to be substantially more serious than projected in the budget preparation phase.

Revenue Forecasting

In a typical state, the state budget office collects agency appropriations requests, prepared under guidelines from the governor about the desired direction and composition of state expenditures to achieve political goals, and square these, often in an iterative process involving substantive review and evaluations, with revenue projections. Revenue projections involve estimating how different tax bases, and thus revenues under current policy, will evolve over the coming budget period. This can be a contentious process, as estimates—and therefore, ultimately, the scope for expenditures—depend crucially on assumptions about the future economic climate of both the state and the nation, assumptions that can potentially be manipulated to serve political goals. States differ across many dimensions: who decides on the assumptions used in the revenue forecast, who actually carries out the revenue forecast, whether forecasts are decided upon under consensus, who revises projections (to include more up-to-date information late in the budget phase), whether such revisions are binding, and the years projected beyond the current budget cycle. While forecasting revenues beyond the current cycle is subject to increasing uncertainty, it is obviously important to the extent that appropriations involve spending beyond the current term. Research suggests that the details of revenue projections are important for outcomes, but much remains to be done.[8]

Due to the centrality of revenue projections for the state budget process, who has responsibility is potentially important for revenue projections. Two main traditions exist. In some states, revenue projections are mainly part of the governor's budget proposal and do not involve other actors. In other states, the legislative branch or a nonpartisan agency has, or shares, responsibility for projections.

Making sure that expenditures are in line with (estimated) revenues is all the more important due to the existence of important institutional restrictions on the budget formulation: balanced budget requirements, tax-and-expenditure limits and limits on borrowing, debt issuance, and debt service. In particular, since the governor in all but a handful of states must submit a balanced budget, projections about future tax revenue become essential in defining the scope for gubernatorial possibilities. With a finalized budget proposal in hand, this budget proposal is presented to the legislature.

Formal Budget Powers and Deadlines

Upon receipt of the governor's budget proposal, the legislature refers the proposal (at this point denoted a budget bill) to committees. Committees discuss the bill, often hold public hearings, and may introduce amendments. After a comprehensive review in appropriations committees both in the lower house and the state senate, the—possibly amended—budget bills are brought to the floor of the two chambers. In case of disagreement between chambers (perhaps controlled by majorities from different political parties), negotiations continue, oftentimes in conference committees. Once agreed upon, the entire legislature sends the amended budget back to the governor to be signed. Most states have a deadline (either a date or specific number of weeks or sessions) for presenting a completed budget to the governor. For example, the California state constitution requires the state legislature to pass a budget by June 15. (See Late Budgets box for a discussion of the reasons and costs of late budgets.) The division of budgetary powers between the governor and the legislature varies greatly across states. In some states, governors enjoy unilateral policy-making authority over budgetary formulation, resulting in complete executive budgetary control, while in other states, governors have little budgetary control, as authority is shared with legislatures or other institutional actors. In past decades, governors' institutional dominance over the budgetary process has diminished.[9] Furthermore, real budget authority may differ from formal powers. Under unified governments, governors tend to take additional responsibility for the budget, resulting in faster fiscal adjustment toward partisan target fiscal scale: between one-quarter and one-third of the way to their ideal point in two years. Under divided government the legislative party shifts fiscal scale in its desired direction,[10] but it does so more slowly than in unified governments. Divided government can also increase the risk to investors, resulting in lower bond ratings and diminished availability of debt.[11]

Finally, upon receipt of the legislative budget, the governor can sign the budget. However, in most states, the governor has the right to veto proposals from the legislature; in some states this right extends to vetoing specific items, the line-item veto. If items, or entire budgets, are vetoed, a qualified majority—often two-thirds—in the legislature can often override the veto; but if not, and disagreement persists, the budget may be delayed beyond the fiscal year deadline.

State Government Debt

If expenditures exceed current revenues already at the budgeting stage, it is possible for state governments to run a deficit and, in turn, issue debt. However, while debt is commonly used in order to finance long-term investments in the capital budget, issuing debt to cover operational expenses is much more controversial. As Figure 26.1d suggests, this results in much lower levels of debt at the state level, as compared with federal and local government. Only a handful of states have no constitutional or statutory policies to limit authorized debt in place, while one state, Indiana, does not

LATE BUDGETS

In hard times, politics, economics, institutions, and fiscal management come together in the form of increased conflict and delayed, sometimes long-delayed, budgets. For FY 2010, nine states began the year without a finalized budget. When is a late budget more likely? The first answer given is, when the fiscal circumstances of the state are not strong. In budgeting for 2010, states had to reconcile a decline in revenues of over $145 billion as a result of the prevailing economic recession. Moreover, divided government increases the risk of delay in all circumstances. California is notorious for budget gridlock: from 1950 to 2008, the budget was adopted late nearly half of the time. How long are these delays? This involves many factors, but they can be up to several months. Researchers agree that divided government increases the expected duration of stalemate. The expected duration is higher in fiscal downturns than in upswings of similar magnitude: having more revenue rather than less coming in is an easier problem to solve. For instance, increasing unemployment leads to a longer budget negotiation process, increases the risk of missing budget deadlines, and prolongs periods with no budget in place. Even so, other things being equal, changes in fiscal circumstances, regardless of direction, also increase the expected duration by making the bargaining between politicians more difficult. Higher political costs shorten budget delays. When the absence of a timely budget produces a government shutdown, the threat of that outcome brings the bargaining to a close sooner. In Minnesota, for example, the 2011 government shutdown resulted in lost revenue of $2.3 million a week just from lost lottery revenue alone. Since 2002, five states have faced similar government shutdowns and similar losses. Higher political costs are also present in election years and shorten the duration of delayed budgets. Soft or hard deadlines that require the legislature to end its regular session before the end of the fiscal year also limit the occurrence of late budgets.

What are the costs of late budgets, apart from the appearance of poor fiscal management? There are electoral consequences for governors and state legislators. We find that legislatures face significant negative electoral consequences of not finishing a budget on time, though governors are penalized only under unified governments. Members of the majority party see their reelection probabilities reduced by something like 5–6 percent, if all budgets in the session have been late. For the minority the penalty is about half as large, but it is still there. In general, electoral penalties are larger where legislators' responsibility for delay is clear: clarity is reduced by divided government and also depends on supermajority requirements and seat share margins. There are also consequences for the state and the taxpayer in the form of higher state government borrowing costs. A month-long budget delay, in the long run, raises a state's interest costs by only two basis points, and states with large reserves or a budget surplus face small or no costs. On the other hand, states running a deficit on average face an impact of about nine basis points, and the impact of budget delay increases during election years.[1]

1. See Carl Klarner, Justin Phillips, and Matt Muckler, "Overcoming Fiscal Gridlock: Institutions and Budget Bargaining," *Journal of Politics* 74 (2012): 992–1009; and Asger Andersen, David Dreyer Lassen, and Lasse Holbøll Westh Nielsen, "Late Budgets," *American Economic Journal* 4 (2012): 1–40.

allow general obligation debt at all. Between these two extremes, restrictions on the authorization of debt, sometimes constitutional, sometimes statutory, typically take the form of a numerical rule expressed as a percentage of current and past tax revenues or measured relative to the general fund or state personal income. In most states, such rules are accompanied by policies to limit debt service, the payment of interest.

In addition to institutional constraints, state government debt issuance is also subject to two additional types of constraints: popular consent, in that in some states debt cannot be issued without the explicit consent of voters, and capital markets. When states have to finance government deficits by issuing bonds, the yield on such bonds is determined on capital markets and reflects the perceived ability of state governments to meet their obligations, given their institutional framework. Recent research suggests that state reserves, budget institutions, and fiscal governance systematically affect bond premiums.

RECENT RESEARCH: THE IMPACT OF INSTITUTIONS AND RULES ON BUDGET POLITICS

The states offer researchers variation on institutions like the transparency of the budget process. They also have unique political institutions for fiscal policy unseen at the national level. These include balanced budget requirements; limits on taxes, spending, and debt issuance; supermajority requirements; the ballot initiatives; and the item veto, which did exist briefly at the national level before being held unconstitutional. We want to consider the effect of these institutions on fiscal policy. Important research reviews appeared about a decade ago; we review the results and update where necessary.[12]

Fiscal institutions like antideficit rules can affect deficits and fiscal policy in several ways. One is a direct effect: they constrain the actions that can legally be undertaken by fiscal policymakers, as well as affect their incentives to take those actions. Indirectly, these actions affect bond market participants' perceptions of the state and thus affect its borrowing costs. Moreover, electoral accountability forces politicians to face voter sanctions for their actions. Both bond market participants and voters face problems of informing themselves and coordinating actions. Hence the existence and functioning of rules for fiscal policy is also inevitably bound up with the transparency of state budget institutions, and with the incentives and ability of politicians to manipulate fiscal quantities to augment reelection prospects.

Above, we mentioned how important political parties are in state fiscal policy. Party differences show up most clearly, however, when a single party controls both the executive and the legislature. Besley and Case also found significant effects of party competition on total taxes per capita and for workers' compensation, both of which were significantly lower, the greater the party competition in the state. But party control is complicated by the possibility that high competitiveness leads to divided government. As above, the relative bargaining power of the executive and legislature depends on whether, and how, government is divided, as well as factors relating to the relative patience of the bargainers, like years remaining in the governor's term. Governors have more influence when one or both chambers of the legislature are controlled by their copartisans. Care is needed to differentiate the effects of partisan preferences, divided government, and institutions, as we discuss below.

Moreover, early research suggested that other state-level fiscal institutions affected the size of state government, the incidence of fiscal deficits, and the level and composition of state borrowing. Tax and expenditure limits reduced government spending as a fraction of state income. State antideficit laws reduced the average size of state budget deficits. States with constitutional restrictions on the legislature's power to issue general obligation debt issued less debt than did those without such limits, though as a consequence the former relied more heavily on revenue bonds and similar "off-budget" debt. These are facts, but causality is not so clear: Do these differences arise because of the institutions, or do the institutions exist because citizens of the states preferred to create institutions that bring about these outcomes? With institutions like the initiative, but also with frequently shifting institutions like transparency, this becomes a central question.

Budget Process Transparency

Transparency of government principally refers to ease of extracting information in a timely fashion. In state budgeting, transparency is important to citizen-stakeholders, as well as the advocates and analysts who use budget information, because it decreases the cost to acquire accurate information on government processes. In various sources, James E. Alt and David Dreyer Lassen develop a transparency index from several indicators involving simplicity (an annual cycle, a single budget bill), clear meanings and standards (use of generally accepted accounting principles, binding forecasts, no open-ended appropriations), lack of bias (bills written by a nonpartisan staff, forecasts not solely prepared by the executive), and informativeness (inclusion of performance measures and multiyear forecasts). Most states now require performance measures, use multiyear forecasting, and require a legislative forecast, while less than a third require generally accepted accounting principles (GAAP) reporting. Some states have only two or three of these institutions, while a handful like Iowa and Michigan have more or less all. Transparency has generally increased in recent years, particularly with the popularity of performance measures.

For instance, while state governments have always had auditors, they now have to issue comprehensive annual financial reports (CAFRs) in accordance with Statement No. 34 of the Governmental Accounting Standards Board. CAFRs evaluate financial condition and net worth and provide information on the many special funds outside the "budget." State laws mandating public input in local budgeting are another aspect of transparency. Recent innovations include online availability of information about subsidies, contracts, and lobbying, among others, but these remain controversial. In May 2011, Montana governor Brian Schweitzer (D) vetoed plans to create a website that would let citizens track state government spending. He explained that the cost of the website was excessive and would provide no return to the taxpayers, who in his view already had ample access to information about the state budget.

Greater budget transparency across states leads to greater confidence (job approval) in incumbents and popularity of government. Other things being equal, this in turn increases the scale of government (taxes or spending), since transparency increases citizens' confidence in politicians as agents handling their tax dollars. Lower levels of debt are also associated with higher transparency. The connection from transparency to higher taxes and spending with lower debt runs through the connection between transparency and the reelection of incumbents. While budget transparency does not have a direct effect on reelection, more budget transparency dampens the negative effect of tax increases on the retention of incumbent governors because voters are better able to understand the justification for the increases.[13] This, in turn, reduces the incentive for politicians to manipulate fiscal quantities, like the deficit, for reelection purposes: deficits timed to be effective boosts to spending before elections, with the balance restored after the election. Indeed, research shows that the electoral-cyclical variation of state deficits does not vary with budget transparency, though there is evidence of less manipulation where the penetration of mass media is greater. Very recent research also suggests that bond rating agencies use the broader, government-wide information provided in CAFRs, even though their writing still focuses on the general fund.

Quantitative evidence and case studies of reform show that both politics and fiscal outcomes affect the level of transparency. States that are politically polarized and have highly competitive legislatures tend to choose higher levels of budget transparency. Fiscal imbalance, in the form of higher surpluses or deficits, also contributes to higher transparency. However, the presence of divided government reduces this effect: divided government could make it less likely that, for example, a governor can increase transparency under good budget performance to look good to observers. However, there is no systematic evidence of a connection between the years in which gubernatorial elections occur and changes in any of the government transparency measures.

Balanced Budget Laws

Most states have several constitutional and statutory provisions that touch on budget balance, and no state has nothing at all—though a few, like Vermont and Wyoming, do not have much. Research on balanced budget rules attempts to discern the effect of these institutions and struggles to find a uniform definition of when these laws are effective or "stringent," even though most of the rules (Tennessee is the exception), whether statutory or constitutional, have been in place for decades or even over a century. However, studies often contradict one another in assigning "legal stringency" in up to a quarter of cases, because some are ambiguous. For example, Colorado's constitution both prohibits expenditures in excess of tax revenue and allows the state to issue debt "to provide for casual deficiencies" in the event that a deficit does occur.[14]

Nevertheless, most scholars agree that the most bite is not in requiring the drafting or even passage of a balanced budget, but in what happens at the end of the fiscal year, when a variety of provisions ensure that deficits are not incurred, specify very limited conditions under which deficits may be carried over to the next fiscal year, or require a shutdown of government. Laws affecting the end of the fiscal year are most likely to be effective (if sufficiently transparent in their requirements) by forcing explicit recognition of last year's shortfalls in next year's plans. A consensus of sources suggests that (minimally) about a third of the states have "no carryover" (NOCA) provisions.

Partly because of the conflicting indicators, there is little consensus on the cyclical economic effects of NOCA provisions. Some early work inferred that fiscal discipline came at the cost of less flexibility: strict balanced budget rules inhibited or constrained the use of fiscal policy for stabilization, resulting in greater volatility of state economies. It was also shown that states with relatively tight antideficit rules adjusted more quickly when revenues fell short of expectations or expenditures exceeded projections. However, this was mostly true of states with unified party government, while states with split legislatures adjusted less regardless of the legal situation. This may be why more recent work suggests that NOCA laws make state fiscal policy more stable: the economy is less volatile (at least in large states) because quicker adjustment keeps bad situations from getting out of hand.

It is generally accepted that stringent balanced budget requirements are associated with lower state expenditures, taxes, deficits, and debt, and with greater state savings in the form of a general fund balance. Some believe that the effectiveness of NOCA laws depends on another institution: independent or elected courts. However, it is rare to find cases where courts have enforced government shutdowns as an ultimate sanction. It appears likely that at least some of the savings in public-sector costs work through less costly debt service, not only because debt is lower but also because, where NOCA laws exist, credit ratings are higher and thus interest rates are lower. While many states and their courts explicitly offer politicians wiggle room, the operation of bond markets gives politicians an incentive to maintain orderly fiscal policies, which brings lower operating costs and thus more funds to spend elsewhere.[15]

There is no evidence that NOCA laws affect the retention of incumbents by reducing the electoral cost of raising taxes, as in the case of transparency discussed above. But NOCA laws do have an electoral effect. The electoral budget cycle described above should be larger in states without NOCA rules than in those with those rules, if the rules are effective in limiting politicians' incentives and ability to run deficits and thus manipulate the timing of spending for electoral purposes. Indeed, the cycle is larger under no rules than under rules; this difference is the biggest single contextual difference in the magnitude of political budget cycles.

Tax, Expenditure, and Debt Limits

Tax and expenditure limitations (TELs) fall into three broad categories: (1) indexed limits on the growth of revenues or expenditures, for example, to the population growth rate; (2) requirements that voters approve all new taxes; and (3) supermajority conditions that require anywhere between three-fifths and three-quarters of the legislature to approve tax increases.[16] In 2008, thirty-three states in all had one or more of these limits. Of these thirty-three, thirty states had indexed limits on revenues, spending, or both, while seventeen required voter approval, supermajorities, or both (though five required a simple majority if the governor had declared a state of emergency). About half the states with index limitations restricted the growth in state expenditures to the growth rate in personal income averaged over some previous period; others indexed to a specified percentage of state income or to an index of population growth and inflation; and a few restricted the absolute expenditure growth rate. Half of the limits in place are constitutional; the rest are statutory. Spending on capital projects is usually excluded from limits, as are federally funded projects. Recently, thirty-nine states allowed issuing general obligation debt, and thirty of these had some form of debt limits. At one extreme, these varied from outright prohibitions on guaranteed long-term debt to those requiring referendum approval. At the other, the weakest restrictions are revenue-based limitations or some kind of supermajority voting requirement in the legislature. Generally, all these limits exist where whatever they were designed to fix was more of a problem: the 1840s origins of debt limits lie in the expansion of state debts, and the rapid expansion of TELs in the 1970s and 1990s followed periods of growth in state taxes and spending.

The effects of limits have also long been the same: they are more likely to cause politicians to shift than to cut. With the initial passage of debt limits, borrowing for infrastructure projects shifted from states to local governments in the nineteenth century. Modern debt limits are circumvented by issuing complex or specialized bonds or through the growth of special districts and the use of these other public authorities in issuing debt, and courts have generally supported this desire of elected politicians. Worse, debt limits in the face of revenue shortages can impel states to use one-off remedies like selling assets, often incurring significant long-term costs if the assets are subsequently leased back.

TELs also have not generally worked as their proponents had hoped. This is partly due to technical reasons: some indexing schemes leave the TEL cap above the states' revenues or expenditures. More often, TELs have proven ineffective because state officials evade them by raising money through fees or other levies exempt from the limit, and again courts have generally supported this. Revenue limits are associated with higher interest costs and expenditure limits with lower costs because they lead to higher credit ratings. Supermajority vote requirements (which date back to 1934 but are mostly recent) can reduce at least some kinds of state taxes. A problem with supermajority limits is that they can create divided party government, which in turn can produce delayed budgets, prolonged deficits, and lower credit ratings.

Other Institutions

States have other institutions that affect the budget process: the item veto, rainy day or stabilization funds, and mandated spending. There has not been a great deal of research on these institutions in the last decade, and what there is supports nuanced conclusions like those above. The effects of the item veto depend on the distribution of preferences of politicians in the budget process, and possibly on the presence of divided government. Stabilization funds may produce better bond ratings, but whether or not they do so depends on technical details like the rules constraining withdrawals from the funds. Moreover, rainy day funds are not immune from the political budget cycle discussed above, where they can be raided by politicians faced with reelection or economic hard times.[17] Reelection pressures can also lead politicians to defer liabilities like absence and pension compensation from state employment, which surges before elections. Mandates are often not funded, creating ongoing fiscal problems, but courts have tended to privilege mandated spending over other rules like NOCA laws.

NOTES

1. Sean Nicholson-Crotty, "Fiscal Federalism and Tax Effort in the U.S. States," *State Politics and Policy Quarterly* 8 (2008): 109–126.

2. Over nineteen states have already implemented these watchdog groups. See watchdog.org.

3. John G. Matsusaka, "Popular Control of Public Policy: A Quantitative Approach," *Quarterly Journal of Political Science* 5 (2010): 133–167.

4. John G. Matsusaka, *For the Many or the Few: The Initiative Process, Public Policy, and American Democracy* (Chicago: University of Chicago Press, 2004).

5. David M. Primo, "Stop Us before We Spend Again: Institutional Constraints on Government Spending," *Economics and Politics* 18 (2006): 269–312.

6. Timothy Besley and Anne Case, "Political Institutions and Policy Choices: Evidence from the United States," *Journal of Economic Literature* 41 (2003): 7–73.

7. James E. Alt and Robert C. Lowry, "A Dynamic Model of State Budget Outcomes under Divided Partisan Government," *Journal of Politics* 62 (2000): 1035–1069.

8. Robert C. Lowry, "Fiscal Policy in the American States," in *Politics in the American States: A Comparative Analysis* (Washington, DC: CQ Press, 2008).

9. George Krause and Benjamin Melusky, "Concentrated Powers: Unilateral Executive Authority and Fiscal Policymaking in the American States," *Journal of Politics* 74 (January 2012): 98–112, analyzes unilateral executive authority over the budget (control over revenue projections and budgetary formulation).

10. Alt and Lowry, "A Dynamic Model of State Budget Outcomes."

11. See Skip Krueger and Robert W. Walker, "Divided Government, Political Turnover, and State Bond Ratings," *Public Finance Review* 36 (2008): 259–286.

12. In addition to Besley and Case, "Political Institutions and Policy Choices," see Brian Knight and Arik Levinson, "Fiscal Institutions in U.S. States," in Rolf Strauch and Jürgen von Hagen, eds.,

Institutions, Politics, and Fiscal Policy (New York: Springer, 1999); and Alberto Alesina and Roberto Perotti, "Budget Deficits and Budget Institutions," in J. M. Poterba and J. von Hagen, eds., *Fiscal Institutions and Fiscal Performance* (Chicago, University of Chicago Press, 1999), 13–36.

13. James E. Alt and Robert C. Lowry, "Transparency and Accountability: Empirical Results for U.S. States," *Journal of Theoretical Politics* 22 (2010): 379–406.

14. Yilin Hou and Daniel L Smith, "A Framework for Understanding State Balanced Budget Requirement Systems: Reexamining Distinctive Features and an Operational Definition," *Public Budgeting and Finance* 25 (2006): 22–45.

15. R. C. Lowry and J. E. Alt, "A Visible Hand? Bond Markets, Political Parties, Balanced Budget Laws, and State Government Debt," *Economics and Politics* 13 (2001): 377–394.

16. See Thad Kousser, Mathew D. McCubbins, and Ellen Moule, "For Whom the TEL Tolls: Can State Tax and Expenditure Limits Effectively Reduce Spending?" *State Politics and Policy Quarterly* 8 (2008): 331–361; and C. L. Johnson and K. A. Kriz, "Fiscal Institutions, Credit Ratings, and Borrowing Costs," *Public Budgeting and Finance* 25 (2005): 84–103.

17. L. Van Lent, "Discussion of the Influence of Elections on the Accounting Choices of Governmental Entities," *Journal of Accounting Research* 50 (2012): 477–494.

SUGGESTED READING

Alt, James E., and Robert C Lowry. "Divided Government, Fiscal Institutions, and Budget Deficits: Evidence from the States." *American Political Science Review* 88 (1994): 811–828.

Baicker, Katherine, Jeffrey Clemens, and Monica Singhal. "The Rise of the States: U.S. Fiscal Decentralization in the Postwar Period." *Journal of Public Economics* (2012): 1–13.

Besley, Timothy, and Anne Case. "Political Institutions and Policy Choices: Evidence from the United States." *Journal of Economic Literature* 41 (2003): 7–73.

Donovan, Todd, Christopher Mooney, and Daniel Smith. *State and Local Politics: Institutions and Reform*. Belmont, CA: Wadsworth, 2010.

Dye, Richard F., Nancy W. Hudspeth, and David F. Merriman. "Transparency in State Budgets: A Search for Best Practices." Chicago, IL: Institute of Government and Public Affairs, 2011.

Fisher, Ronald C. *State and Local Public Finance*. Mason, OH: Thomson South-Western, 2007.

Garrett, Elizabeth, Elizabeth Graddy, and Howell Jackson, eds. *Fiscal Challenges: An Interdisciplinary Approach to Budget and Policy*. New York: Cambridge University Press, 2008.

Hines, James R., Jr. "State Fiscal Policies and Transitory Income Fluctuations." *Brookings Papers on Economic Activity*, 2010, 313–350.

Kiewiet, D. Roderick, and Kristin Szakaly. "Constitutional Restrictions on Borrowing: Analysis of State Bonded Indebtedness." *Journal of Economics, Law, and Organization* 12 (1996): 62–97.

Kousser, Thad, and Justin Phillips. *The Power of American Governors*. New York: Cambridge University Press, 2012.

Chapter 27

Moral Issues

Laura S. Hussey

WHAT COUNTS AS A *MORAL ISSUE* CAN be disputed, but this term often calls to mind debates over controversial personal conduct such as abortion, homosexual relations, gambling, alcohol and drug use or abuse, pornography, and teen premarital sex. Moral issues consume a large portion of state policy agendas. Some scholars have argued that many of these issues share a distinct style of politics, called the politics of morality policy, so that the factors that drive policymaking on these issues are different from those that drive policy in other areas (see Is Morality Policy Really about Morality? box). Study of moral issues policymaking is therefore central to the study of state politics and policy.

This chapter explores moral issues politics and policy in the American states. It begins by sketching and explaining the state of moral issues federalism. It then offers detailed description and analysis of state policymaking on four moral issues: abortion, same-sex unions and other gay rights policies, physician-assisted suicide, and gambling. These policy profiles explain the rise of each issue on state policy agendas and the scope of state, relative to federal, authority on each issue. They also identify salient debates within each issue area, summarize states' policy choices on these matters, discuss important contributors to these policy choices, and share findings from research on select policy outcomes.

STATES: THE MAIN ARENAS FOR MORAL ISSUES POLICYMAKING

It is impossible to understand the status of morality policy without looking at the policy choices of the fifty states. Most criminal law and family law is state law. Despite a growing federal role, states remain the chief policymakers in several other areas as well that often serve as contexts for moral debate, such as education (e.g., how should schools teach sex education?) and health care.

The importance of states for moral issues policymaking flows from the Tenth Amendment to the U.S. Constitution, which reserves to the states (and/or

IS MORALITY POLICY REALLY ABOUT MORALITY?

Prominent morality policy scholars have argued that issues qualify as morality policy not because of their topic but because of their political characteristics. One important characteristic they identify is that at least one side of the debate must portray an issue in terms of sin and/or threats to its most fundamental values. Gary Mucciaroni reads these definitions to suggest that advocates' framing of an issue in moral terms is what matters. Based on analysis of debates over gay rights policy in ten states (and Congress), he concluded that morality was not an important part of arguments against same-sex marriage, civil unions, and nondiscrimination measures, which are often considered to be classic morality policy issues. Opponents instead cited pragmatic arguments about the implementation and consequences of gay rights policy as well as statements about the role of government.[1] (Note a similar phenomenon in advocates' arguments for other issues discussed in this chapter.) While inclined to believe that these arguments were sincere, Mucciaroni suggested that advocates may also have been strategically limiting morality talk in order to appeal to moderates.

1. Gary Mucciaroni, "Are Debates about 'Morality Policy' Really about Morality? Framing Opposition to Gay and Lesbian Rights," *Policy Studies Journal* 39 (2011).

individuals) authority over those powers not given to the federal government. The Tenth Amendment is also the source of states' so-called police powers, which concern their authority to regulate to protect public health, safety, and morals. Over time, federal activity has expanded substantially into policy areas traditionally considered to be states' domain. Nonetheless, there are important philosophical and practical reasons why states remain especially significant for moral issues policymaking. Among them, in a heterogeneous polity, state control over morality policymaking facilitates closer correspondence between public policy and public values—a democratic norm and a source of stability—than would national control. Attempts to nationally aggregate diverse citizen views on salient and polarizing issues can also produce gridlock. Policies concerning moral issues are thus easier to pass at the state level, where there is likely to be greater homogeneity of values, partisanship, ideology, religion, socioeconomic status, race and ethnicity, and other characteristics that affect public policymaking. There are indeed important state differences on a key input to moral issues policymaking: public opinion. Pooled over 1999–2008, support for same-sex marriage, for example, ranged from 23 percent in Alabama and Mississippi to 56 percent in Massachusetts.[1]

National interests respond opportunistically to this situation in ways that further heighten states' importance as moral issues policy arenas. Leading policy process theories posit that the U.S. federal system gives interests many opportunities to "venue-shop"— that is, to push their policy proposals in those settings where prospects for enactment are most favorable. Donald Haider-Markel has offered evidence that policymaking on same-sex marriage reflects this kind of behavior.[2] Institutions of direct democracy, which states but not the federal government have to different degrees, also invite national interest groups into state arenas.

Once one or more states enact a new policy idea, adoption of that policy by other states becomes theoretically more likely; political scientists refer to the process by which policies spread throughout the states as "policy diffusion." Among other reasons, this may happen because the policy change induces competition among states, or because it provides information to the public and policymakers about the effects of a reform considered to be controversial or experimental. Plausibly, early victories in sympathetic states can also increase the momentum of and resources available to an interest group, help advocates hone their arguments, and warm up publics and policymakers to proposals that are initially controversial, perhaps increasing the likelihood of eventual policy adoption at the national level. (For more on policy diffusion, see Chapter 25.)

Even if less active than the states, the federal government has been far from inactive on these issues. Federal elected officials, like their state counterparts, want to appear responsive to their constituents' most important concerns. Interest groups may perceive that a national policy will be faster, less expensive, and more effective than doing battle in fifty states. Policy heterogeneity may also present practical problems. In addition, some advocates find the policy choices some states would make on their own to be unacceptable in light of their moral principles or their ideas about civil liberties and the scope of government power; indeed, advocates often claim that moral issues policies present constitutional questions, facilitating their consideration by federal courts.

As in other issue areas, the federal government has often responded by specifying minimum conditions that state public policy must meet, leaving the rest of the details to state discretion. The scope of discretion left to states on moral issues varies widely; of the four issues profiled in this chapter, states are most constrained when it comes to abortion policy and least when it comes to physician-assisted suicide. Christopher Mooney argues that rather than settling an issue, federal action on moral issues can increase its contentiousness and the demand for state policy change. The linkage between state opinion and public policy is disrupted, activists mobilize, and the losing side seeks another venue where its odds will be favorable.[3]

Issues qualifying as morality policy, among other things, are easy for citizens to understand, highly salient, and characterized by high levels of citizen involvement. As a result, public opinion should be a particularly important determinant of states' morality policy choices. Morality policy also invokes core values and is resistant to compromise; moral issues policymaking should then also feature a prominent role for religion and for single-issue, policy-motivated groups that cannot give up the fight. Because morality policy concerns values that are deeply held and often behavior that tends to be private, some also argue that it is hard to enforce.[4] This is an important limitation to assessing the effectiveness of moral issues policy; nonetheless, a growing body of literature offers some evidence for and against various claims of policy advocates and opponents.

ABORTION

Abortion was broadly illegal in the American states from the nineteenth century until the 1960s. Beginning with Mississippi in 1966, however, states began to loosen their abortion regulations, allowing abortion to be performed legally under an increasing number of circumstances. Overall, eighteen states liberalized their abortion laws over 1966–1972.[5] While this pre-*Roe v. Wade* abortion policy reform was initially framed as a medical matter, a broader range of ideological and religious actors began entering both sides of the debate in the late 1960s, resulting in the reframing of abortion as a moral issue.

Members of the Crow Wing County Chapter of Minnesota Citizens Concerned for Life march in subzero temperatures in Brainerd, Minnesota, on January 22, 2013, the fortieth anniversary of the U.S. Supreme Court's* Roe v. Wade *decision. Although the* Roe *decision established a federal constitutional right for a woman to obtain an abortion, it did not completely eliminate states' involvement in the abortion issue, as the Court allowed states to regulate abortion procedures.

SOURCE: AP Photo/*Brainerd Dispatch,* Steve Kohls.

The Federal Role in State Abortion Policy

Roe v. Wade, decided by the U.S. Supreme Court in 1973, nullified most state regulation of abortion.[6] The Court asserted the existence of a constitutional right to privacy that encompassed a woman's right to obtain an abortion; thus state laws prohibiting abortion except in cases of danger to the life of mother, like the Texas law at issue in the case, violated the due process clause of the Fourteenth Amendment to the U.S. Constitution. Leaving open a window for limited state regulation of the abortion procedure, the Court acknowledged a state interest in protecting women's health as well as a state interest in the protection of the unborn that grew weightier as pregnancy advanced. The majority opinion in *Roe* authorized some state regulation of abortion after the third month of pregnancy in the name of protecting women's health. It also appeared to authorize the prohibition of abortion after viability, the point at which it is scientifically possible for life to be sustained outside the womb, so long as abortion was still permitted when a physician deemed it necessary to protect the life or health of a woman. A companion case decided by the Court on the same day, however, *Doe v. Bolton,*[7] defined "health" as encompassing "all factors—physical, emotional, psychological, familial, and the woman's age—relevant to the wellbeing of the patient," meaning that abortion would have to be legal in every state for all nine months of pregnancy.

The question of how states could regulate (legal) abortion returned to the Supreme Court many times after *Roe v. Wade.* While the Supreme Court allowed state law authorizing only licensed physicians to perform abortions, it struck down most of the state abortion regulations it reviewed. The Court would rule differently, however, in *Webster v. Reproductive Health Services* (1989) and *Planned Parenthood of Southeastern Pennsylvania v. Casey* (1992), cases concerning Missouri and Pennsylvania laws that are widely recognized as authorizing a significant expansion of state abortion regulation.[8] The *Casey* ruling is particularly important for understanding state abortion policy because it articulated a new minimum standard for state abortion policy in place of the *Roe* trimester approach: states could regulate abortion at any point in pregnancy, but those regulations must not place an "undue burden" on the woman seeking abortion.

The limits of states' power to regulate abortion were tested again beginning in the mid-1990s. During this period, one of the policy priorities of the right-to-life movement was criminalization—except when the life of the mother was in danger—of a particular abortion procedure that came to be called partial-birth abortion. While President Bill Clinton's vetoes twice blocked efforts to ban the procedure nationally, many states proved friendlier. In all, thirty-one states enacted partial-birth abortion bans by 2000.[9] When the U.S. Supreme Court heard a challenge to Nebraska's law in *Stenberg v. Carhart* (2000), however, it ruled 5–4 that the states had gone too far in restricting women's access to abortion, citing among other things the absence of a "health" exception to the ban.[10] Following a change in the composition of the Court and some changes to the bill's language, the Court later reversed itself, upholding the federal ban in *Gonzales v. Carhart* (2007).[11]

Contemporary State Abortion Policy

Since *Roe v. Wade,* and especially since *Casey,* state policymaking on abortion has most commonly concerned the use of public resources for abortion and the extent to which abortion can be regulated. Frequently debated regulations touch on parents' role in minors' abortion decisions; building, licensing, safety, and other standards to which abortion providers and facilities must adhere; and the conditions that must be met for a woman to provide her informed consent to abortion. Another category of state legislation has dealt with fetal rights, including fetal homicide, the circumstances under which the unborn are recognized as persons under state law, and the regulation or criminalization of abortion at certain developmental landmarks. Pro-life groups continue to maintain that abortion is wrong because it ends the life of a human being. But in state politics, to some extent, this theme has taken a back seat to arguments about the psychological and physical risks they believe abortion carries for women, especially in the absence of stricter regulation. Meanwhile, pro-choice groups have resisted most of these attempts to regulate and de-fund abortion. They argue that such policies add financial, logistical, and emotional hardship to women seeking abortion; incrementally erode the basic right to abortion; and unnecessarily single out a legal procedure for special and costly scrutiny, ultimately threatening the availability of abortion. While pro-choice forces have pushed some of their own legislation, their advantages under the *Roe v. Wade* status quo have left them mostly in a defensive position.

Unless otherwise stated, all abortion policy data come from NARAL Pro-Choice America,[12] Americans United for Life,[13] or the Guttmacher Institute.[14] Readers should consult the Current Moral Issues Policy box for tips on the interpretation of abortion policy data. Figure 27.1 summarizes the relative rankings of states in their regulation of abortion, based on how many of a possible thirteen representative abortion regulations were in effect.

Use of Public Resources for Abortion

Policy concerning the use of public resources for abortion has taken several different forms. Early legislation, such as the Missouri legislation upheld in the *Webster* decision, concerned whether abortions not deemed medically necessary could be performed by state-employed physicians and in state medical facilities (Missouri said "no"). As of 2011, twenty-one states had laws that prohibited certain public employees or grantees, such as those who administer state family planning programs and others involved in health and social services administration, from providing abortion referrals. States' long-standing practice of contracting with or otherwise accepting Planned Parenthood as a provider of family planning services has also periodically been challenged by pro-life policymakers. These policymakers argue that since Planned Parenthood is the nation's largest abortion provider, funds provided to Planned Parenthood for family planning and other medical services indirectly subsidize abortion. The early 2010s saw a fresh wave of attempts to restrict eligibility for family planning funds to organizations that did not provide abortions, but most enactments faced legal or administrative challenges from the federal government, Planned Parenthood, and others.

The financing of abortions under Medicaid, the federal-state program providing health insurance to low-income people, has also been contentious but the issue has now largely stabilized. While the federal government will pay for Medicaid enrollees' abortions in cases of rape, incest, and danger to the life of the mother, states are allowed to

CURRENT MORAL ISSUES POLICY: OUTDATING THIS BOOK AND CONFOUNDING ITS COUNTERS

The moral issues covered in this chapter are hot agenda items and are associated with many different (and changing) kinds of policy proposals. Newly enacted moral issues policies, especially those concerning abortion, commonly end up in court, where their enforcement may be temporarily or permanently blocked. Specific state morality policy choices, then, are in a constant state of flux. Nonetheless, figures and policy data presented in this chapter can usefully identify the states' relative positions on the underlying moral issue questions. Readers desiring more up-to-the-minute facts on state adoption of the policies discussed in this chapter can consult online sources such as the following:

- The "State Center" at the Guttmacher Institute (research organization supporting abortion rights), www.guttmacher.org/statecenter
- "Map of State Laws and Policies," by the Human Rights Campaign (pro–gay rights advocacy group), www.hrc.org/resources/entry/maps-of-state-laws-policies
- "Assisted Suicide Laws in the United States," by the Patients Rights Council (coalition of groups opposing euthanasia and assisted suicide), www.patientsrightscouncil.org/site/assisted-suicide-state-laws
- "State of the States," by the American Gaming Association (trade association for casino industry), www.americangaming.org/industry-resources/research/state-states

Examining how different organizations from different sides portray policy developments on the same issue can reveal differences of perspective about the scope and significance of a law and the likely trajectory of future policy. It can sometimes also produce what appear to be disagreements over policy facts, such as how many states have enacted a particular law. In moral issues policy, these disagreements result from such matters as whether organizations differentiate policies that have been enacted from policies that are actually in effect, and whether a policy "counts" if amendments watered down a bill before its passage. Groups may also disagree on whether the policy they count is a law, itself, or a court's or administrative agency's interpretation of that law.

FIGURE 27.1 **Extent of State Abortion Regulation**

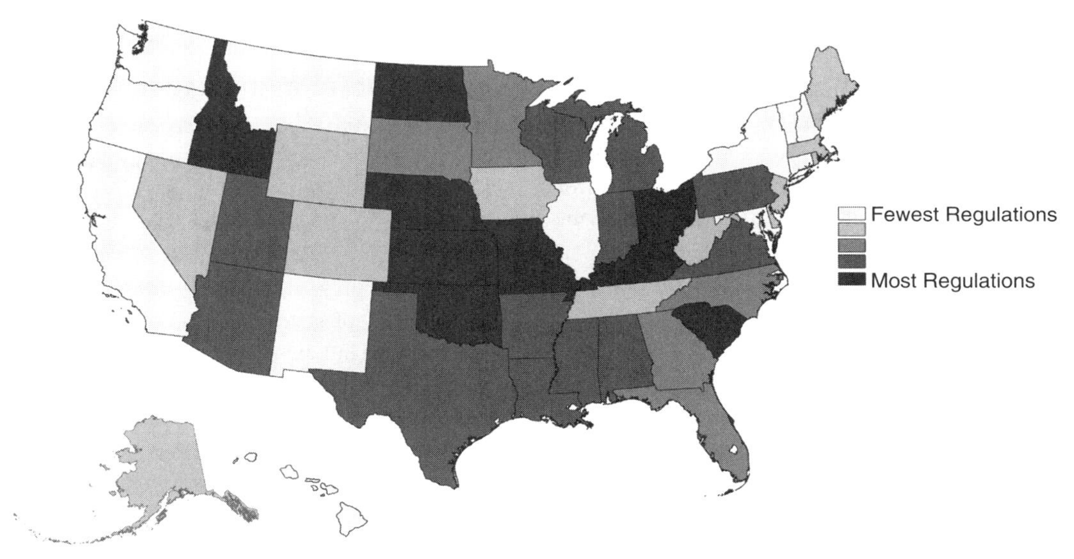

SOURCES: Americans United for Life, 2012; Guttmacher Institute, 2012; NARAL Pro-Choice America, 2012.

decide whether to use their own contributions to Medicaid to pay for other abortions. As of 2011, seventeen states covered abortion fully under Medicaid. A similar issue has arisen as states plan the health insurance exchanges created by the federal Patient Protection and Affordable Care Act of 2010, through which individuals and small businesses receiving health insurance subsidies under the law must purchase their health insurance. While national pro-life groups failed to achieve a federal legislative ban on public dollars for health insurance plans that covered abortion, fourteen states as of 2011 had barred insurance plans that included abortion coverage from their exchanges.

Parental Involvement in Minors' Abortions

In *Casey,* the Supreme Court authorized state laws requiring parental consent for a minor's abortion so long as minors could alternatively request a judicial waiver of parental consent. As of 2011, forty-four states had some type of parental involvement law on the books, though courts had blocked some of these. The nature of parental involvement also varies from state to state. Some states require that parents be notified of the abortion, rather than having to provide their consent, and states differ in whether they require the notification or consent of one or both parents. Some states' laws allow the involvement of other adults in place of the parents, while others allow the physician performing the abortion to waive parental involvement.

Regulation of Abortion Providers and Facilities

As of 2011, forty-five states had enacted policies that NARAL calls Targeted Regulation of Abortion Providers, or TRAP, laws. The contents of TRAP laws vary in their detail and stringency from state to state. The TRAP laws in most of these forty-five states specify that only licensed physicians may perform abortions. TRAP laws that go beyond this minimum commonly mandate statistical reporting, and also regulate the facilities in which abortions can be performed. Half of the states had laws that limited the performance of late-term abortions, and sometimes earlier abortions as well, to hospitals or ambulatory surgical centers, the latter meaning that abortion clinics would have to be licensed as ambulatory surgical centers in order to offer abortion there. TRAP laws in a small number of states regulate abortion providers as hospitals or ambulatory surgical centers, applying to them similar building and safety codes that specify staffing requirements and such detail as the size of hallways and rooms. Some TRAP laws require abortion providers to have admitting privileges at local hospitals to accept their patients in cases of emergency. Due to litigation and other reasons, TRAP laws in as many as sixteen states are at least partially unenforced.

Informed Consent for Abortion

Perhaps the most noticeable change in abortion policymaking between *Casey* and the present time has been the proliferation of state policies about what women's informed consent for abortion must involve. Uncommon before 1992, informed consent statutes existed in thirty-three states by the end of 2011. Informed consent laws typically require that the abortion provider give women a state-approved brochure, website, or other presentation that includes information about the abortion procedure, the risks of abortion, fetal development, and practical support available to the woman should she choose against abortion. Many states also pair this requirement with a waiting period, usually eighteen to twenty-four hours, before the abortion can be performed. Increasingly, states are also requiring ultrasound imaging of the fetus prior to the abortion procedure. While the performance of ultrasound exams is a routine part of current standards of care for abortion, state ultrasound laws add that the woman be offered the opportunity to see the image.

Rights of the Unborn

The right-to-life movement has long sought state laws conferring or implying fetal personhood, though those efforts have picked up steam and met with more success in the 2000s. Thirty-seven states' codes as of 2012 allowed for third parties to be charged with homicide when their crimes against a pregnant woman resulted in the death of the unborn; twenty-eight of these laws were applicable from the moment of conception onward. States have taken several measures that are largely symbolic now, but that pro-choice advocates fear could erode legal and political support for abortion rights over time. These include declarations that life begins at conception and "trigger laws" that would ban abortion in the state if *Roe v. Wade* were overturned. A newer strategy—passage of state law declaring personhood to begin at fertilization—was recently tested and defeated by Mississippi voters. The pro-life movement itself was divided on this matter, with some groups warning that the move could backfire by mobilizing pro-choice supporters and inviting a Supreme Court ruling on the matter that they believed would go against them. Another recent innovation, the Pain-Capable Unborn Child Protection Act, bans abortion at those stages when some studies have demonstrated that the unborn are capable of feeling pain—currently about twenty weeks after conception. This policy had been enacted in five states by the end of 2011, and the National Right to Life Committee has identified its diffusion to more states as a priority for subsequent years.[15]

Pro-Choice Initiatives

Key pro-choice group initiatives pertaining to abortion include measures to protect abortion clinics from violence and harassment and codification of the right to abortion in state statutes and constitutions. As of 2011, sixteen states had clinic protection laws (a federal clinic protection law also applies to all states). These typically criminalize attempts to block access to abortion clinics as well as certain types of harassment of abortion providers and persons entering their clinics. Three states' laws also include buffer zones around clinic property that pro-life demonstrators and other unauthorized persons are prohibited from entering. "Freedom of choice" acts, which legislate a right to abortion, have been enacted in seven states, while sixteen states include language in their constitutions that protects the right to abortion.

Determinants of State Abortion Policy

Studies suggest that state public opinion plays a leading role in the content of states' abortion policy. Furthermore, public opinion may be growing in importance to state abortion policy, such that it is now more closely associated with state abortion policy than different measures of elite abortion attitudes. The presence of a ballot initiative in a state magnifies the effect of state public opinion on abortion policy, even while the initiative campaign is vulnerable to influence by national political forces. While state publics' general ideological direction has historically shown little relationship to abortion policy, this appears to be changing as abortion is transformed from an issue that cuts across existing partisan and ideological lines to one that defines those lines.

State-level interest group activity is another important determinant of state abortion policies. The balance of power between state pro-life and pro-choice political action committees significantly predicts the restrictiveness of state abortion policy. Increasing percentages of Catholics in a state consistently predict more restrictive abortion policy. Meanwhile, studies find mixed evidence for the importance of state NARAL membership and the extent of evangelical or fundamentalist Protestantism.

Research is divided over the role of governing political elites in state abortion policymaking. The failure of many (though not all) studies of state abortion policy to find a relationship with the partisan distribution of legislative seats and other elite political measures may again reflect a time period in which partisanship, ideology, and abortion attitudes were less well correlated than they are now. It may also reflect the responsiveness of representatives to constituent opinion, and the fact that many studies do not explicitly consider control of state government. Partisan control of government indeed appears to have grown more important to state abortion policy over time. State legislatures' ideology, as well as the ideological leanings of citizens and state supreme courts relative to the state legislatures, is associated with abortion policy, suggesting that legislatures craft abortion policy while anticipating how other important actors will react. The share of women in state legislatures has received special attention as a determinant of abortion policy, but studies find conflicting results on its impact. The balance of the research, however, leans toward the conclusion that an increasing share of women in a state's legislature keeps policy more pro-choice. This conclusion is probably less likely to reflect *women's* position on abortion than the abortion position of *women who seek and win elected office,* since there is little gender gap on abortion attitudes in the mass public.

Effects of State Abortion Policies

Many studies have examined the outcomes of abortion policy, often focusing on whether abortion regulations and restrictions on public funding of abortion are associated with decreases in abortion incidence. The preponderance of studies finds that they are, and some of the strongest evidence has come from the most recent studies. While some scholars fear that these abortion reductions mean increases in unintended births, others argue that individuals are more likely to abstain from sex or use contraception more aggressively as abortion becomes more complicated to obtain.

GAY RIGHTS

State legislative, executive, and judicial branches, as well as state electorates themselves, have arguably been still more important arenas for policymaking on the topic of gay, lesbian, bisexual, and transgender (GLBT) rights. Whereas many of the priorities of the gay rights movement and its countermovement have stalemated at the federal level, both sides have scored victories in friendly states. GLBT rights groups most commonly frame their cause as a quest for civil rights for a stigmatized minority, though they are also increasingly trying to portray family formation by same-sex couples as a matter of promoting family values. Opponents of same-sex marriage and related policies have been backing away from older arguments about the morality of homosexual relations. Instead, they emphasize the instrumental benefits of traditional marriage for children and society and concerns about a slippery slope for family life, religious freedom, and other matters that they believe could flow from changing the traditional definition of marriage.

The Federal Role in State Gay Rights Policy

Until the 1990s, the federal government maintained virtually no minimum requirements for states' gay rights policy. The Fourteenth Amendment to the U.S. Constitution, for example, does not include sexual orientation or gender identity as protected categories; nor do federal civil rights statutes. The U.S. Supreme Court, in its 1986 decision in *Bowers v. Hardwick,* had also upheld states' rights to enforce antisodomy laws.[16] Occasionally in the 1970s and 1980s, same-sex couples sued in state court for the right to marry, but these suits, all of which failed, received little attention. Texas in 1973 became the first state to enact an explicit ban on same-sex marriage, but no other state did so until the 1990s. Several states, however, began crafting or expanding their nondiscrimination laws to cover gays and lesbians, beginning with Wisconsin in 1981.

A 1993 Hawaii Supreme Court decision that appeared to pave the way for that state's legalization of same-sex marriage raised same-sex marriage on the national agenda and provoked federal as well as state responses. In 1996 Congress and President Bill Clinton enacted the Defense of Marriage Act (DOMA). DOMA expanded the bounds of state authority in some respects while constraining it in others. It specified that the federal government would only recognize marriages between one man and one woman. States were also allowed to refuse to recognize same-sex marriages performed in other states. This would limit the impact of state decisions to marry same-sex couples, while preserving the one-man, one-woman definition of marriage that other states adopted against a situation in which same-sex couples could wed in other states and then return back home. In a 2013 ruling on *United States v. Windsor*, the Supreme Court would eventually overturn the portion of DOMA denying federal recognition to same-sex marriages, including states' traditional authority over marriage law in its rationale.[17]

Though the Court stopped short of finding a federal right for same-sex couples to wed in *Windsor* and in the ruling it issued on the same day in a California same-sex marriage case, the federal government had earlier begun to articulate some conditions for state policy on gay rights. These came via the Supreme Court's 2003 decision in *Lawrence v. Texas.*[18] Overturning *Bowers v. Hardwick,* the Court invalidated the antisodomy laws that remained on some states' books. While states still could decide whether to recognize same-sex unions, they could no longer criminalize gay sexual relations.

Contemporary State Policy on Select Gay Rights

While same-sex marriage is arguably the most salient contemporary gay rights issue, the GLBT movement agenda has also included policy that would tackle the following problems: employment discrimination, violence based on sexual orientation and gender identity, HIV/AIDS, health care access, the treatment of GLBT issues in sex education, and the treatment of GLBT families under family law. Treatment of all these policies is beyond the scope of this chapter. Instead, this chapter will emphasize facts and findings pertaining to same-sex unions, and to a somewhat lesser extent, a range of nondiscrimination policies. These issues were chosen because of their public salience, the amount of attention they have received from scholars, and many scholars' beliefs that same-sex marriage, relative to other issues, fits a morality policy framework quite well. Unless otherwise noted, data on the status of state public policies comes from the Human Rights Campaign, a prominent GLBT rights advocacy group.[19]

Authorization of Same-Sex Marriage

As of August 2013, thirteen states and the District of Columbia issued marriage licenses to same-sex couples (see Figure 27.2 and the Current Moral Issues Policy box).

Massachusetts, the first state to perform same-sex marriages, did so in 2004 when the legislature responded to a state supreme court decision that barred the denial of marriage rights to same-sex couples. The November 2012 elections marked the first time that same-sex marriage was approved by popular vote, and it happened in three states: Maine, Maryland, and Washington. Same-sex marriage has since been legalized elsewhere, including California, where the U.S. Supreme Court's 2013 ruling in *Hollingsworth v. Perry* ended years of skirmishing among voters and different branches of California government over same-sex marriage.[20] In a ruling that dealt with standing to sue in federal court rather than with same-sex marriage itself, the Court allowed a voter-enacted constitutional amendment defining marriage as between one man and one woman to be reversed when state officials refused to defend it in federal court.

Bans on Same-Sex Marriage

Following the Hawaii Supreme Court decision, a flurry of states passed statutes defining marriage as between one man and one woman. This included Hawaii itself, whose voters enacted a statutory ban on same-sex marriage in 1998 when legislators put the question to public referendum. A subsequent wave of policy-making activity focused on constitutional amendments that limited marriage to one man and one woman. While this activity started earlier in some states, the bulk of state constitutional amendments were enacted in 2004 and later, following the Massachusetts court ruling on marriage. As of August 2013, twenty-nine state constitutions limited marriage to one man and one woman. Another six states banned same-sex marriage by statute only.

Civil Unions, Domestic Partnerships, and Select Benefits

Several states, including some that now allow same-sex marriage, offer legal status to same-sex relationships without actually calling them marriages. Called civil unions or domestic partnerships, these policy instruments provide the same sets of rights enjoyed by spouses to same-sex couples. Vermont, which now allows same-sex marriage, had been the first state to offer this option; that law represented a response to a 1999 state supreme court decision. As of August 2013, six states that did not authorize same-sex marriage extended civil unions or domestic partnerships.

Other states offer select benefits to same-sex partners. One example is that of the six states that extend spousal-equivalent hospital visitation privileges to a patient's same-sex partner while not otherwise offering marriage or some form of civil union. Another is Wisconsin's limited domestic partnership law, versions of which had existed in some other states that have since legalized same-sex marriage.

Adoption of Children by Same-Sex Couples

Another flash point in the debate over same-sex unions concerns whether same-sex couples should be allowed to adopt children. As of June 2013, two states (Mississippi and Utah) enforced laws barring adoption by same-sex couples, while a Michigan court decision about adoption by unmarried couples had the same effect. Eighteen states plus the District of the Columbia allowed same-sex couples to adopt children jointly. The same number of states allowed second-parent adoption, adoption of a same-sex partner's child. In several other states, either or both of these adoption options were available in select local jurisdictions.

FIGURE 27.2 **State Marriage Policy, August 2013**

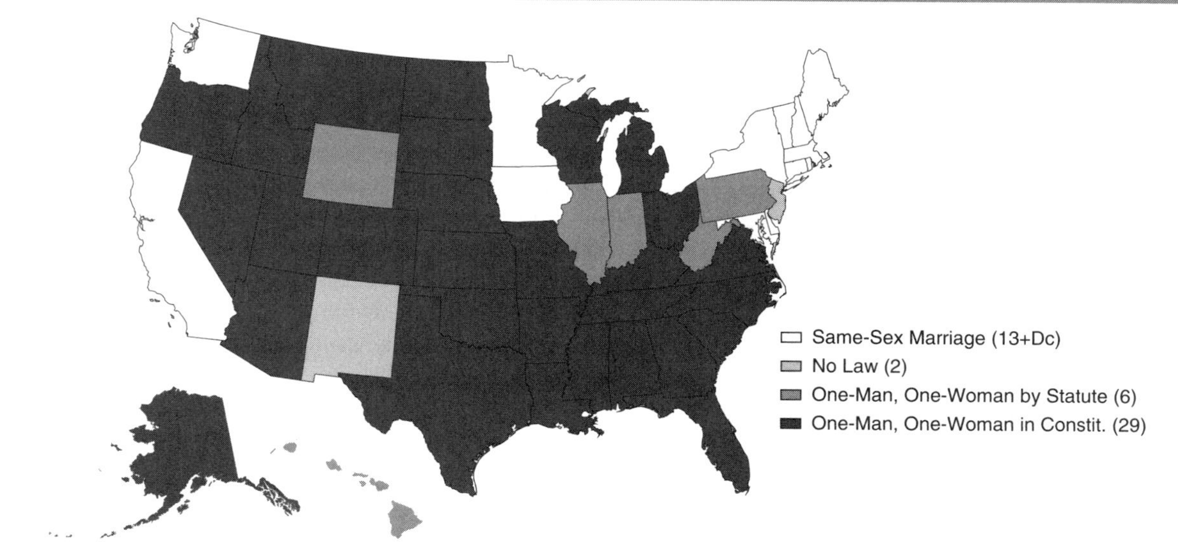

SOURCE: Human Rights Campaign, 2013.

Other Laws

A second prominent area for state policymaking on gay rights issues has concerned whether states should take affirmative action to include sexual orientation and gender identity and expression as protected classes under various statutes, most prominently nondiscrimination laws, hate crimes laws, and increasingly, a largely new series of policies aimed at combating bullying and harassment in schools. As of June 2013, twenty-one states and the District of Columbia had employment nondiscrimination laws that covered sexual orientation; seventeen of those states and the District of Columbia also covered gender identity or expression under those laws. Hate crimes statutes enhance penalties for perpetrators of crimes determined to be motivated by hatred of particular demographic, social, and/or religious groups. Of the forty-five states (plus the District of Columbia) with a hate crimes statute, thirty-one jurisdictions included sexual orientation, and fifteen of those thirty-one also extended hate crimes statutes to gender identity and expression.

Determinants of State Gay Rights Policy

State policy choices on gay rights issues have been somewhat harder to explain consistently than state policies on abortion. The variables associated with state gay rights policymaking also vary with the type of right under consideration (e.g., equal employment, marriage), the scope of law, and the conditions under which policy is enacted.

The balance of research on the correlates of states' gay rights policies concludes that public opinion toward gay rights policies or toward homosexual relations is an important predictor of state gay rights policies, provided those policies' issues are highly salient. As measured by mentions in the *New York Times,* gay marriage and civil unions are by far the most salient gay rights issues, and it is on those issues, along with second-parent adoption, that state policy corresponds most closely with public opinion. As of 2009, for example, state public policy on same-sex marriage, civil unions, and same-sex second-parent adoption was aligned with opinion majorities on these issues for forty-six, thirty-seven, and forty-three states, respectively.[21] Public opinion appears to be growing over time as a predictor of same-sex marriage policy, and it now appears to trump political elites' attitudes. The general ideology of states' citizens also contributes to gay rights policy. For less salient gay rights policies, public opinion is less important, though not irrelevant.

Research also typically links organized interests to states' policy on same-sex marriage and other gay rights matters. State policy tends to be closer to the positions of the GLBT movement where GLBT interest groups have more resources, religious conservative interest groups are less active, and evangelical Protestants make up a smaller share of the population. All these measures seem to be closely related to public opinion, however, which can make it a challenge to discern which factor is more important.

Measures of legislators' partisanship, ideology, and gay rights voting records are sometimes associated with state policymaking on gay rights issues. Legislators' views seem to decrease in importance as the salience of the policy issue increases, and for same-sex marriage, they are generally less important than public opinion. In sum, citizens grow relatively important, and legislator characteristics less so, as issues enter the public arena more fully.

The relatively less important role for elites also makes sense in light of the importance that direct democracy institutions have played in setting state policy on same-sex marriage and other gay rights issues. State constitutional amendments, now the preferred vehicle for same-sex marriage bans, typically require voter approval. Consideration of other gay rights measures via initiative and referenda is common as well. Research is mixed, however, on how much direct democracy facilitates such legislation after public opinion is taken into account and whether direct democracy strengthens the opinion-policy linkage on gay rights policy. (See Chapter 6 for further discussion of this topic.)

Policy Outcomes

Same-sex marriage is too recent a policy to conclusively evaluate its consequences. Limited research on outcomes for same-sex couples after a civil union or civil marriage suggests that many of the individuals involved may come to experience a greater sense of social inclusion and legitimacy. There is also evidence that same-sex couples in legally recognized relationships show better psychological health than same-sex couples in unrecognized committed relationships.

ASSISTED SUICIDE AND A "RIGHT TO DIE"

The legalization of physician-assisted suicide is the most recent policy focus of the right-to-die movement. As currently understood, physician-assisted suicide involves the prescription or provision of a lethal drug by a physician to an individual, who would then use the drug to kill himself or herself. Earlier policies advocated by the right-to-die movement included legalization of voluntary euthanasia, in which a doctor administers a drug or other intervention that will kill a patient, and the recognition of advance directives, legal documents in which a patient specifies the types of medical interventions he or she does not wish to receive in end-of-life situations. Physician-assisted suicide was a particularly hot issue during the 1990s, as advocates sought policy change in state and federal arenas, and when Michigan's Dr. Jack Kevorkian gained public notoriety for assisting dozens of individuals with suicides using his own invented devices.

Right-to-die advocates, who have been led by single-issue groups such as the Hemlock Society (now named Compassion and Choices) and select individual physicians, argue that individuals should be able to end their own lives rather than endure the pain, loss of autonomy, and fear of becoming a burden on their families that may accompany the natural progression of disease. Furthermore, they argue that individuals should receive help in doing so in order to ensure that their death is as peaceful as possible. Prominent opponents have included medical associations, which stress such policy's violation of their ethical codes and orientation toward healing, the Catholic Church, right-to-life groups, and disability rights groups. The latter fear that individuals will feel coerced into assisted suicide, that involuntary euthanasia will follow, and that the disabled will be most at risk.

The Federal Role in State Assisted Suicide Policy

The federal government has set no floor for state policy on assisted suicide. In *Washington v. Glucksberg* (1977) and *Vacco v. Quill* (1997), the Supreme Court denied that there was a constitutional right to assisted suicide.[22] It signaled willingness to revisit that decision, however, should the practice gain acceptance in the states. The federal government does, under the Controlled Substances Act, regulate the drugs that are typically used for assisted suicide. The George W. Bush administration attempted to use that authority to override state policy allowing assisted suicide, present at that time only in Oregon. This was challenged in court, leading to a ruling in *Gonzales v. Oregon* (2006) that this action trespassed on traditional state authority to regulate the practice of medicine.[23]

Contemporary State Assisted Suicide Policies

Though the federal government left decisions about assisted suicide to the states and right-to-die advocates have pushed the issue in state legislatures, courts, and direct democracy campaigns, legalization of assisted suicide has seen little uptake. The first assisted suicide law in the United States was Oregon's Death with Dignity Act, first approved by voters in 1994. The act allowed physicians to prescribe lethal drugs to persons wishing to end their lives, and it set up conditions that patients and physicians would have to meet before the prescription was written. Patients would have to be deemed terminally ill, for example, and sufficiently competent to decide on suicide. In 2008 Washington voters approved a similar initiative. Assisted suicide is also ambiguously legal in Montana, where the state supreme court ruled in 2009 that an existing statute did not prohibit physician assistance with suicides. Meanwhile, as of 2012, thirty-nine states other than these three (whose general anti–assisted suicide statutes remain on the books) have explicitly criminalized assisting a suicide. Five other states and the District of Columbia have common law prohibitions on assisted suicide, while the law is unclear in three states (Nevada, Utah, and Wyoming). In most of these nine jurisdictions, language in other statutes or administrative rules implies prohibition of assisted suicide.[24]

Demonstrators representing the organization Not Dead Yet protest in front of the U.S. Supreme Court in Washington, DC, on October 5, 2005. In Gonzales v. Oregon, *the Supreme Court revisited the emotionally charged issue of physician-assisted suicide in a test of the federal government's power to block doctors from helping terminally ill patients end their lives. In its ruling on January 17, 2006, the Court sided with the states, noting that the regulation of medicine was a power entrusted to states.*

SOURCE: Karen Bleier/AFP/Getty Images.

Determinants of State Assisted Suicide Policies

Scholars have offered negative media coverage of assisted suicide, lukewarm public support, the controversial nature of the policy, and the efforts of opposing interests as reasons why assisted suicide is not legal in more states. To explain why right-to-die advocates focused and succeeded the most in the Northwest, they also cite the region's libertarian leanings on moral issues as well as the smaller percentages of Catholics and other religious people.[25] Surely another reason involves the relative accessibility of the initiative and referendum in these states, since state electorates appear to be the preferred arenas for right-to-die advocates. At the time of this writing, however, physician-assisted suicide was rising on the agendas of states in New England, another region characterized by lower religiosity and liberal attitudes toward moral issues.

Outcomes

Through 2011, Oregon reports that 935 people had received prescriptions for lethal drugs under the Death with Dignity Act and 596 had died from taking those medications.[26] Opponents of assisted suicide point to Oregon's statistical reports, scholarly journal articles, and anecdotal evidence to argue that many of those who died under the law were not actually terminally ill, did not receive adequate mental health screenings, and may have been pressured by others. Some new scholarly research, while acknowledging some problems with the law, argues that outcomes would be worse in the absence of legal physician-assisted suicide with safeguards.

GAMBLING

Gambling in the American states has been criminalized and legalized in waves. The most recent and ongoing wave of gambling legalization and expansion began in earnest in the 1970s, though the first modern lottery adoption, in New Hampshire, occurred in 1964. Lotteries had just begun to diffuse across the states when the legalization of casino gambling became the next important frontier in state gambling policy. In 1976 New Jersey authorized casinos in Atlantic City, joining Nevada (where gambling had been legal for much of the state's history). As of 2012, all but seven states (Alabama, Alaska, Hawaii, Mississippi, Nevada, Utah, and Wyoming) ran lotteries.[27] Only nine states prohibited casino gambling: Arkansas, Georgia, Kentucky, New Hampshire, South Carolina, Tennessee, Utah, Vermont, and Virginia.[28]

The federal government has largely left gambling policy to the states. One important exception, however, concerns gaming on Native American reservations, something scholars have also hypothesized is a factor in the expansion of state gambling policy. The federal Indian Gaming Regulatory Act of 1988 endorsed and set up a regulatory framework for casinos on tribal lands; so long as some form of gambling, such as a lottery, was legal in a state, the state could not block tribal casinos.[29] Christopher Mooney suggests that the expansion of tribal gaming eventually legitimated casinos and shifted the dominant frame of state gambling politics from one about morality to one about economics[30] (also recall Is Morality Policy Really about Morality? box).

Indeed, advocates of liberalized gambling policy have increasingly emphasized its potential to increase state revenues, and polls of state publics show that the vast majority of citizens believe that gambling is acceptable. Some states' lawmakers have also helped to move gambling from the realm of morality policy by earmarking revenue for particular purposes, most significantly, education. This practice disrupts an otherwise well-established link between the size of a state's evangelical Protestant population and its gambling policy.[31] States are more likely to adopt lotteries in election years, implying their popularity, and under divided government, suggesting that lotteries can represent a bipartisan compromise on revenue generation. Lotteries and riverboat (but not land-based) casinos also diffuse regionally, consistent with a scenario in which states compete for revenue. Though fiscal arguments for gambling are prevalent, states' actual budget situations at best only weakly enhance the likelihood of lottery or casino adoption. Last, the determinants of gambling policy may differ with the type of gambling involved and the arena (legislatures versus direct democracy) in which liberalization is attempted. For example, corporate interests are much more important players in debates over casinos than over lotteries; while casino legalization would appear to enhance the profits of some industries, other entertainment and gambling interests fear competition.

A review of research on the consequences of state gambling policy finds mixed or inconclusive evidence about gambling's purported economic benefits and social costs. Casino gambling provides an initial boost to state economies, but this effect dissipates quickly. While lotteries enhance state revenue, casino gambling is actually linked, on average, to a net revenue loss for states. The latter finding requires further research to explain, but it may represent casinos' harm to other revenue-producing industries. Expansion of gambling is not conclusively linked to increases in crime. Attempts to estimate the cost of a broader set of social ills thought to be linked to gambling addiction are fraught with methodological problems, and therefore also inconclusive.[32]

CONCLUSION

The discretion states can exercise on moral issues policy questions improves the likelihood that policy on these salient and polarizing matters reflects the preferences of state publics. While states' policy choices do not entirely reflect ideas and processes internal to a state—national interest groups often work with state affiliates to direct and fund legislative efforts—the opinion of state publics on moral issues is a key factor. States publics' religious identities (or lack thereof) and allegiances to interest groups are also very important and sometimes difficult to disentangle from public opinion. Over the last several years, policy in a large number of states has shifted toward tighter regulation of abortion and fewer controls on gambling. States have been rapidly polarizing over same-sex marriage, while physician-assisted suicide has been slower to catch on in the states. Particularly as national party polarization intensifies, states should be the busiest arenas for moral issues policymaking well into the foreseeable future.

NOTES

1. Jeffrey R. Lax and Justin H. Phillips, "Gay Rights in the States: Public Opinion and Policy Responsiveness," *American Political Science Review* 103 (2009).

2. Donald P. Haider-Markel, "Policy Diffusion as a Geographical Expansion of the Scope of Political Conflict: Same-Sex Marriage Bans in the 1990s," *State Politics and Policy Quarterly* 1 (2001).

3. Christopher Z. Mooney, "The Decline of Federalism and the Rise of Morality Policy Conflict in the United States," *Publius: The Journal of Federalism* 30 (2000).

4. Christopher Z. Mooney, "The Public Clash of Private Values: The Politics of Morality Policy," in *The Public Clash of Private Values: The Politics of Morality Policy,* ed. Christopher Z. Mooney (New York: Chatham House, 2001).

5. Christopher Z. Mooney and Mei-Hsien Lee, "Legislative Morality in the American States: The Case of Pre-*Roe* Abortion Regulation Reform," *American Journal of Political Science* 39 (1995).

6. *Roe v. Wade,* 410 U.S. 113 (1973).

7. *Doe v. Bolton,* 401 U.S. 179 (1973).

8. *Webster v. Reproductive Health Services,* 492 U.S. 490 (1989); *Planned Parenthood of Southeastern Pennsylvania v. Casey,* 505 U.S. 883 (1992).

9. Mahalley D. Allen, Carrie Pettus, and Donald P. Haider-Markel, "Making the National Local: Conditions for National Government Influence on State Policymaking," *State Politics and Policy Quarterly* 4 (2004).

10. *Stenberg v. Carhart,* 530 U.S. 914 (2000).

11. *Gonzales v. Carhart,* 550 U.S. 124 (2007).

12. NARAL Pro-Choice America, "Who Decides? The Status of Women's Reproductive Rights in the States," 21st ed. (Washington, DC: NARAL Pro-Choice America, 2012).

13. Americans United for Life, "Defending Life 2012" (Chicago: Americans United for Life, 2012).

14. Guttmacher Institute, "State Policies in Brief," 2012, www.guttmacher.org/statecenter/spibs/index.html.

15. Dave Andrusko, "In a Year of Important Pro-Life Victories, None Was More Important Than Passage of the Pain-Capable Unborn Child Protection Act," *NRL News* (Winter 2012).

16. *Bowers v. Hardwick,* 478 U.S. 186 (1986).

17. *United States v. Windsor,* 570 U.S. ___ (2013).

18. *Lawrence v. Texas,* 539 U.S. 558 (2003).

19. Human Rights Campaign, "Maps of State Laws and Policies," 2013, www.hrc.org/resources/entry/maps-of-state-laws-policies.

20. *Hollingsworth v. Perry,* 570 U.S. ___ (2013).

21. Lax and Phillips, "Gay Rights in the States."

22. *Washington v. Glucksberg,* 521 U.S. 702 (1997); *Vacco v. Quill,* 521 U.S. 793 (1997).

23. *Gonzales v. Oregon,* 546 U.S. 243 (2006).

24. Patients Rights Council, "Assisted Suicide Laws in the United States," February 6, 2012, www.patientsrightscouncil.org/site/assisted-suicide-state-laws/.

25. Henry R. Glick and Amy Hutchinson, "The Rising Agenda of Physician-Assisted Suicide: Explaining the Growth and Content of Morality Policy," *Policy Studies Journal* 27 (1999).

26. Oregon Public Health Division, "Oregon's Death with Dignity Act: 2011" (Oregon Public Health Division, 2012).

27. Kevin Duncan, Alex Raut, and Joseph Henchman, "Lottery Tax Rates Vary Greatly by State" (Washington, DC: Tax Foundation, 2012).

28. Timothy W. Martin and Cameron McWhirter, "Kentucky Trots toward a Vote on Casinos," *Wall Street Journal,* January 4, 2012.

29. Ronald M. Pavalko, *Risky Business: America's Fascination with Gambling* (Belmont, CA: Wadsworth, 2000).

30. Mooney, "The Decline of Federalism and the Rise of Morality Policy Conflict in the United States."

31. Patrick A. Pierce and Donald E. Miller, "Variations in the Diffusion of State Lottery Adoptions: How Revenue Dedication Changes Morality Politics," *Policy Studies Journal* 27 (1999).

32. Douglas M. Walker, "Overview of the Economic and Social Impacts of Gambling in the United States," in *Oxford Handbook on the Economics of Gambling,* ed. Leighton Vaughan Williams and Donald Siegel (Oxford: Oxford University Press, forthcoming).

SUGGESTED READING

Camobreco, John F., and Michelle A. Barnello. "Democratic Responsiveness and Policy Shock: The Case of State Abortion Policy." *State Politics and Policy Quarterly* 8 (2008): 48–65.

Conger, Kimberly H. *The Christian Right in Republican State Politics.* New York: Palgrave Macmillan, 2009.

Haider-Markel, Donald P. "Policy Diffusion as a Geographical Expansion of the Scope of Political Conflict: Same-Sex Marriage Bans in the 1990s." *State Politics and Policy Quarterly* 1 (2001): 5–24.

Halva-Neubauer, Glen A., and Sara L. Zeigler. "Promoting Fetal Personhood: The Rhetorical and Legal Strategies of the Pro-Life Movement." *Feminist Formations* 22 (2010): 101–123.

Lax, Jeffrey R., and Justin H. Phillips. "Gay Rights in the States: Public Opinion and Policy Responsiveness." *American Political Science Review* 103 (2009): 367–386.

Lewis, Gregory B. "Bypassing the Representational Filter? Minority Rights Policies under Direct Democracy Institutions in the U.S. States." *State Politics and Policy Quarterly* 11 (2012): 198–222.

Lewy, Guenter. *Assisted Death in Europe and America: Four Regimes and Their Lessons.* Oxford: Oxford University Press, 2011.

McFarlane, Deborah R., and Kenneth J. Meier. *The Politics of Fertility Control.* New York: Chatham House, 2001.

Mooney, Christopher Z. "The Decline of Federalism and the Rise of Morality Policy Conflict in the United States." *Publius: The Journal of Federalism* 30 (2000): 171–188.

———, ed. *The Public Clash of Private Values: The Politics of Morality Policy.* New York: Chatham House, 2001.

New, Michael J. "Analyzing the Effect of Anti-Abortion U.S. State Legislation in the Post-*Casey* Era." *State Politics and Policy Quarterly* 11 (2011): 28–47.

Pavalko, Ronald M. *Risky Business: America's Fascination with Gambling.* Belmont, CA: Wadsworth, 2000.

Pierce, Patrick A., and Donald E. Miller. *Gambling Politics: State Governments and the Business of Betting.* Boulder, CO: Lynne Rienner, 2004.

Rimmerman, Craig A., and Clyde Wilcox, eds. *The Politics of Same-Sex Marriage.* Chicago: University of Chicago, 2006.

Wetstein, Matthew E. *Abortion Rates in the United States: The Influence of Opinion and Policy.* Albany, NY: State University of New York, 1996.

Chapter 28

Criminal Justice Policy and Public Safety in the American States

Nicholas P. Lovrich, Faith E. Lutze, and Nichole R. Lovrich

Beginning in the 1980s, sweeping legislation at both federal and state levels increased the number of people sentenced to prison, lengthened prison terms, increased civil penalties for convicted felons, and severely limited the discretion of judges and corrections administrators. These changes resulted in rapid increases in the prison and jail population unparalleled in any other developed nation. On any given day approximately 2.5 million people are held in county jails, federal detention centers, juvenile detention centers, state and federal prisons, or military prisons, with an additional 5.5 million people being supervised in their respective communities through probation or parole. This population equates to an estimated 1 in every 31 people in the United States being under some form of state control. Worldwide, it has been estimated that one-quarter of all incarcerated individuals are imprisoned in the United States.[1]

Although the United States as a whole trended toward being more punitive over the past several decades, the extent to which the individual states followed the federal government's "get tough on crime" position varied widely, with some leading the charge in punitive measures while others were more measured in their approach. As noted in Chapter 20, the states differ greatly in how their courts are organized, what behavior is criminalized, how criminal offenses are adjudicated, and what penalties are assigned to criminal offenses. Given this wide variation, this chapter provides an overview of trends and developments in state-level criminal justice policy and discusses what gave rise to these trends and developments. First, we review the major ideological changes that occurred nationally related to criminal justice, specifically corrections, and the resulting consequences leading to state-level legislation resulting in mass incarceration. Second, we identify state-level conditions that affect the adoption of either punitive or restorative justice policies across the states. Finally, we present evidence of a noteworthy contemporary trend in state governments and criminal justice institutions that moves beyond costly, generally ineffective, overly simplistic punitive measures to innovative alternatives steeped in an understanding of social capital, evidence-based practices, and a more holistic approach to addressing the mass incarceration phenomenon.

FROM REHABILITATION TO RETRIBUTION

In the late 1800s a "new penology" emerged in response to an unsuccessful state prison system steeped in harsh and abusive practices that failed to reform offenders and protect society. Prison experts of the time convened what became known as the Cincinnati Congress of 1870 and developed a set of principles to reform and guide the field of corrections.[2] These principles, which promote the use of prisons for offender reform rather than punishment, were adopted and implemented widely across the states during the Progressive Era (1900–1920). This led to the construction of prison reformatories to promote offender rehabilitation, the use of indeterminate sentences to permit attention to individual differences, the maintenance of separate facilities for women and children, the use of separate juvenile courts to tend to the special needs of children, the use of parole boards to release the reformed offenders from prison, and the use of parole supervision to help ex-offenders reintegrate into the communities to which they returned upon their release.[3] Progressive conceptions of good government and the rehabilitative correctional model guided corrections practice at the state and local level for most of the twentieth century. During the 1970s, however, a confluence of social and political events and scientific research came together to bring the rehabilitative ideal into serious question. The demise of rehabilitation and its displacement by a just deserts or retribution-oriented model of justice was rapid; the adoption of this perspective on crime and punishment laid the foundation for a dramatic increase in the use of the criminal justice system to solve societal problems arising from social unrest, global economic restructuring, and criminal activity. A direct consequence was that the number of persons in prison or on probation or parole increased quickly and significantly (see Figure 28.1).

FIGURE 28.1 **Prison, Probation, and Parole Populations, 1980–2010**

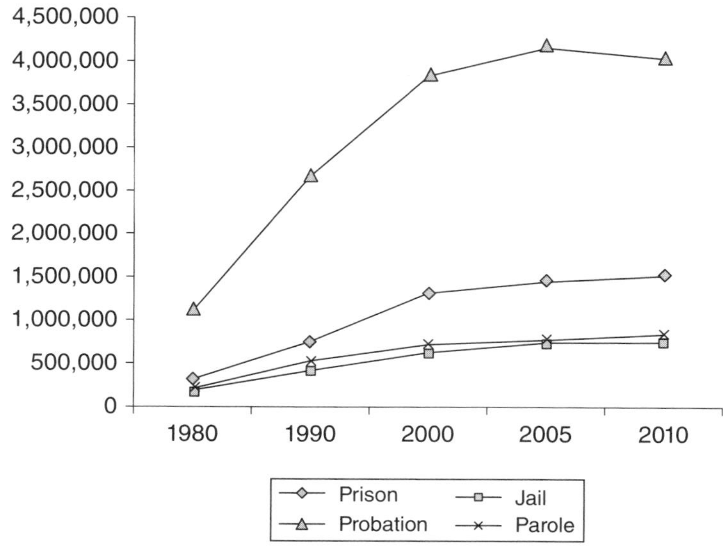

SOURCES: Adults on probation, in jail or prison, and on parole (United States, 1980–2006), *Sourcebook of Criminal Justice Statistics Online*, www.albany.edu/sourcebook/pdf/t612006.pdf; L. E. Glaze and E. Parks, *Correctional Populations in the United States, 2011*, Bureau of Justice Statistics (Washington, DC: U.S. Department of Justice, 2012).

The social and political unrest of the 1960s and 1970s brought about an expansion of civil rights for racial minorities and a major enhancement of women's rights, along with the advent of the Vietnam War and significant expansion of the reach and range of the criminal justice system in American society. Police practices and prison conditions came under close public scrutiny, giving rise to charges of racial bias, abuse of authority, and excessively violent officer response to demonstrations, including highly publicized occurrences on college campuses such as Kent State University, the University of California–Berkeley, and New York University, as well as prison riots such as Attica and Folsom. In addition to social unrest, crime rates began to rise virtually everywhere in the country during the 1960s, not peaking until the 1980s. Although the overall crime rate leveled off with respect to property offenses, violent crime continued to increase until the 1990s. Increases in violent crime were driven principally by young, urban males between the ages of fifteen and twenty-four, and media depictions of "super predators" fueled fears that many American youth were out of control and that the criminal justice system was limited in responding due to the legacy of showing lenience to juvenile offenders. As a result, the criminal justice system was strongly criticized simultaneously by conservatives as being too lenient and permissive, and by liberals as engaging in bias and systematic abuse of state power to control the impoverished and racial/ethnic minorities.

In time both liberals and conservatives would come to focus their attack on the rehabilitative model as constituting a major shortcoming of the criminal justice system in general, and of corrections in particular. In the simplest of terms, liberals argued that the failure to implement effective rehabilitation unnecessarily subjected citizens to longer periods of incarceration, especially minorities and women, and created additional harm by releasing inmates who were ill-prepared to be successful after release. In general, conservatives argued that the failure of rehabilitation put society in danger by releasing offenders from prisons and jails under the guise of being reformed, but who then were allowed to revictimize society virtually unchecked.

The political discontent with rehabilitation was also fueled by scientific research and the publication of several major studies during the 1970s that attacked the credibility of the treatment model. Robert Martinson's report, published in 1974, is most often cited as the scientific evidence fueling the political momentum disfavoring the rehabilitation model and confirming the doubts of critics regarding putatively ineffectual outcomes associated with long-standing rehabilitation programs and practices.[4] Martinson reviewed 231 studies of correctional interventions and concluded that it was not clear what really worked as intended in correctional rehabilitation. His findings were quickly turned into the mantra that "nothing works" in the area of correctional rehabilitation. Rebuttals to Martinson's study quickly appeared, including a reassessment by Martinson himself, published in 1979, showing that many correctional interventions, when theoretically informed and appropriately targeted, did indeed reduce recidivism.[5]

These findings, however well-documented and persuasive to the criminal justice research community, were largely ignored by state-level policymakers determined to make the state criminal justice system writ large, and the individual offenders therein, more accountable for restoring order and achieving safe communities.

The conservative crime control model, firmly grounded in the desire for retribution, became the guiding philosophy of the criminal justice system; federal policy and state-level statutes alike increasingly reflected the "get tough on crime" refrain heard on campaign trails across the country. The shift from offender reform to dispensation of harsh punishment and belief in deterrence associated with expectations of arrest and certain punishment was complete in most states by the 1990s. State-level legislative initiatives to increase the punitiveness of the criminal justice system, both in terms of the criminalization of many behaviors and the harsh punishment of deviance from societal norms, were both plentiful and widespread across the states. The states of the South lead the way in the race to get tough on crime, with Montana joining their ranks; Florida is particularly noteworthy in its punitiveness. On the other end of the spectrum, the New England states stand out as clear holdouts against the tide, with Maine and Massachusetts serving as exemplars.

The "war on crime" and later the "war on drugs" would ultimately have a transformative impact on the use of the criminal justice system to achieve social control and make punishment the primary use of prisons. For example, many states shifted from indeterminate to determinate sentencing and reduced the discretion of judges by implementing sentencing grids and guidelines, establishing mandatory minimums for drug, sex, and gun crimes. Some states enacted "three-strikes" laws requiring life in prison for those convicted of three felonies. Thanks to the efforts of tough-on-crime members of Congress, the federal government would also pass "truth in sentencing laws" featuring monetary incentives for states mandating that serious and violent offenders serve at least 85 percent of their minimum sentence. Mandatory sentences and truth in sentencing laws would limit the discretion of corrections officials and parole boards from releasing inmates early to reward good behavior or as a safety valve tactic when prisons become overcrowded. Most of these state laws shifted power away from the state's judges and corrections officials and instead concentrated power in the police and prosecutors during the arrest and charging phase of the criminal justice process. These laws weakened many of the long-standing checks and balances necessary to moderate the severity of punishment and that are traditionally shared across police, courts, and corrections personnel.

State statutes and administrative policies also came to reflect the exertion of greater control over prisoners released into the community. Community supervision policies (i.e., parole and probation), generally viewed as soft-on-crime approaches to offender management, would become more diligent through increased surveillance, tighter monitoring, and greater enforcement and accountability for violation of conditions of release. Many states implemented intensive supervision programs, shock incarceration, electronic monitoring, sex offender registration, and other related programs geared toward closer tracking and more thorough detection of offender noncompliance. In addition to criminal penalties, the federal government and many state governments instituted civil penalties to be applied to those convicted of specific types of crime, especially drug and sex offenses. For instance, restrictions were placed on felons from receiving public housing, student loans, licensure for state-certified occupations, and the right to vote. Sex offenders were required to register with the police and were prohibited from living near parks, schools, community centers, or any place where children are typically present. These civil penalties place additional burdens on offenders, many of whom are returning to disadvantaged families and communities, making it more difficult to find a place to live, enhance their education, improve their vocational skills, and secure stable employment. Under these circumstances the likelihood of being noncompliant with supervision and being returned to prison increases substantially.[6]

The culmination of mass incarceration, combined with the dire circumstances of many ex-offenders, their families, and the communities to which they return, has created great challenges for policymakers and practitioners. For instance, an estimated 750,000 people are released from prison each year in the United States, and an estimated 67 percent of them fail reintegration into society due to a technical violation (e.g., failure to fully comply with conditions of release) or commission of a new crime within three years of their release. Most of those released from prison are male (93 percent), young (under age thirty-four), undereducated (33 percent less than high school), were unemployed at the time of their arrest (33 percent), and are over-representative of racial and ethnic minorities (38 percent black and 20 percent Latino). Those leaving prison are also more likely than the general population to experience mental illness, poor physical health, addiction to drugs and/or alcohol, infectious diseases, learning disabilities, homelessness, and violent victimization.[7]

Mass incarceration, given its disproportionate impact on the disadvantaged, has resulted in extreme hardship for some local communities. Poverty and incarceration are not equally distributed across the United States; poor, urban communities often suffer the burden of "concentrated incarceration" in which a significant proportion of citizens are displaced through "coerced migration" in and out of jails and prisons. For instance, according to a 2009 publication of the Pew Center on the States, one in forty-five whites, one in twenty-seven Latinos, and one in eleven blacks are under some form of state control.[8] In general, black men have a 29 percent lifetime chance of serving at least one year in prison, compared with 16 percent of Latinos of any race and 5 percent of white males. Young, poor black men are incarcerated at a rate far exceeding that of any other group, and in some disadvantaged urban neighborhoods one in every three are under some form of state control involving jail, prison, probation, or parole. Young black women have also been disproportionately affected by punitive policies, experiencing a dramatic increase in their incarceration rates since the 1990s. Concentrated incarceration causes economic and social instability for the very communities that are least able to absorb offenders returning to the community from their incarceration.[9]

Punitive policies and mass incarceration have placed a significant economic burden on many state and local governments. The "imprisonment binge" resulted in the need to build substantially more state prisons to accommodate the influx of new prisoners. For instance, from 1997 to 2003 spending on corrections increased 1,173 percent, compared with 505 percent for education, 572 percent for hospitals and health care, 577 percent for interest on the debt, and 766 percent for public welfare. Building and sustaining prisons has hampered the ability of state governments to provide many of the social, educational, and health care services known to offset the pains of poverty and ameliorate many of the conditions highly correlated with crime.[10]

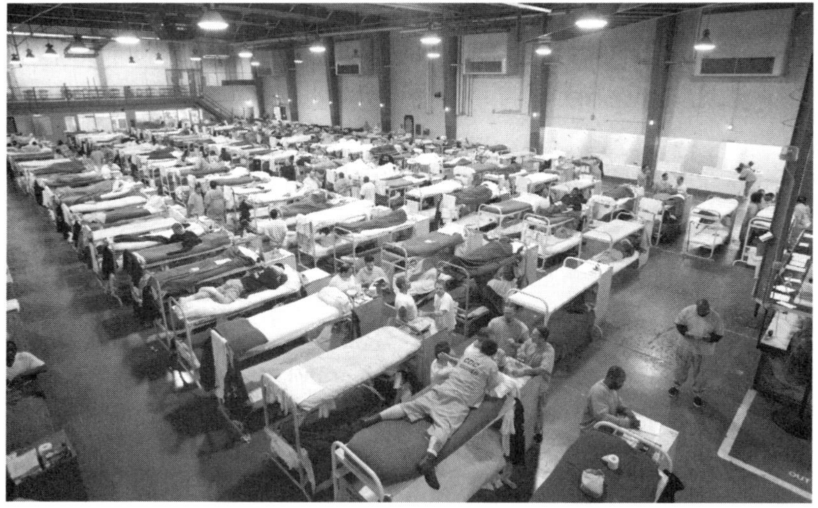

In this May 20, 2009, file photo, several hundred inmates crowd the gymnasium at San Quentin prison in San Quentin, California. The U.S. Supreme Court on May 23, 2011, endorsed a court order requiring California to cut its prison population by tens of thousands of inmates to improve health care for those who remain behind bars. In a 5–4 decision, the Court held that conditions in the prison system violated the Eighth Amendment's ban on cruel and unusual punishment and that the reduction is "required by the Constitution" to correct long-standing violations of inmates' rights. The order mandated a prison population of no more than 110,000 inmates, still far above the system's designed capacity.

SOURCE: Eric Risberg/Associated Press.

DIFFUSION OF CRIMINAL JUSTICE POLICY ACROSS THE STATES

In spite of the considerable variation among states with respect to their adoption and implementation of punitive policies, understanding the criminal justice policy-making context and cross-state policy diffusion process continues to be a rather neglected area of inquiry among criminal justice and political science scholars alike. In fact, more fully understanding the policy diffusion process might provide policymakers, academic criminologists, and political scientists the opportunity to speed the diffusion of evidence-based policies shown to work well in specific state settings. In the past, the replication of ideologically driven policies that tend to sabotage offenders, increase the burdens of disadvantaged communities, and lower the capacity of local governments to reduce crime and increase community safety has too frequently been the norm in policymaking at the state level.[11]

Several factors appear to influence a state's adoption of a particular criminal justice policy, ranging from political ideology to differences in public safety–related contextual factors. As noted in Chapter 25, each type of policy domain, such as health care, education, or environmental protection, tends to have its own set of dynamics and conditioning factors. In the criminal justice domain, studies generally identify the four areas that predict diffusion as ideology; proximity to other states that are innovating; mass-media framing of public safety issues; and contextual factors such as crime rates, racial composition, and existing resources. The findings are generally mixed on which of these various factors are most important for different types of policies (e.g., the criminalization of behaviors, the stiffening of penalties for offenses, the duration of confinement), but there are noteworthy trends that strongly suggest that transmission of punitive policies is somewhat predictable.

Whether states are ideologically more conservative or liberal appears to influence the adoption of criminal justice innovations. States identified as more conservative tend to adopt more punitive crime control measures, regardless of other influences. State policymakers tend to learn of innovations from their counterparts in states with similar political leanings, a practice that simplifies identifying what legislation or justice programs may be most receptive to their own constituents if implemented. States that feature a relatively high level of belief among citizens that effort versus luck accounts for economic well-being tend to support harsher penalties and tend to have higher rates of incarceration.[12] Some researchers have suggested that racial animus dictates American punitiveness over and above beliefs about escalating crime and beliefs about the weakening of the work ethic and moral decline of society. They argue that the American embrace of mass imprisonment and support of the death penalty is due to the fact that these punishments are disproportionately used against people of color, especially African American offenders; for these critics, the legacy of racism that once brought the nation to a civil war has not yet been fully resolved.[13]

In addition to ideology, the geographic proximity to other states and mass-media content featuring sensational crimes have also been studied with the presumption that states that are close in proximity or feature similar media coverage of sensational crimes will be more likely to share policy innovations emphasizing punitiveness. Overall, the research on proximity suggests that there is no direct association between states that share contiguous borders and policy diffusion, but states within geographic regions do tend to share justice policy innovations. Media focus on sensational crimes also appears to matter in the diffusion of criminal justice policy. It appears that sensational cases generally initiated by heinous crime spurs public interest and inspires political actors to respond. Media coverage of crime assists policymakers to take symbolic action by creating new law in response to an immediate issue or to strengthen existing laws promoting an appearance of being tough on crime to gain public support.[14]

While diffusion of innovations does happen, there are also some barriers to policy innovation and diffusion that arise from fragmentation. Several researchers argue convincingly that the fragmentation of the system between police, courts, and corrections exacerbates an already complex criminal justice system. This fragmentation often creates support for conflicting ideologies, leading to innovations in one part of the system that sabotage the success of innovations in another part of the system. For example, the efforts of juvenile courts to keep at-risk youth in school and avoid the "school to prison pipeline" can run headlong against schools and police collaborating on SRO (school resource officers) programs to rid schools of disruptive and poorly performing students. At the state level, the criminal justice policy-making process involves numerous players, being made up of elected officials, unelected administrators, interest groups, community groups, professional groups, and the mass media.

Given the symbolic nature of criminal justice policy, innovations are often adopted within the context of powerful moral, ethical, and cultural concerns about the social order, and as a consequence policy change is often driven not so much by what is effective but rather what is dictated by deeply held principles or opinions about what is morally right at the moment. Anne Schneider and Helen Ingram's insightful work on the negative social construction of offenders is most telling in this regard, and helps explain the strong attraction of punitive public policies for candidates for public office.[15]

CROSS-STATE DIFFERENCES IN PUNITIVE VERSUS RESTORATIVE FRAMING OF CRIMINAL JUSTICE POLICY

One laudatory feature of federal systems of governance is that states very often take rather different approaches to commonly shared problems, and over time those states with the most favorable outcomes in dealing with shared problems become the source of constructive change in other states. Can it be said that such a process is taking place with respect to get-tough-on-crime and corrections policies that have led to the phenomenon of mass incarceration? There is some evidence that precisely such a positive ultimate outcome of comparative cross-state differences is taking place at the present time in the area of state-level corrections.

The first step in addressing this question is that of developing a common metric by which to characterize states with respect to how punitive their criminal justice systems are in their basic operation. For example, some states are quite comprehensive in their prohibitions and their criminalization of behavior, in their sentencing of violations, in their attachment to just deserts in the treatment of offenders, in their harsh punishment of repeat offenders, and in their intolerance of parole/probation violations. In contrast, other states are rather sparing in their prohibitions and criminalization policies, more lenient in the sentencing of offenders, more committed to restorative justice than just deserts in managing offenders, and more tolerant of relapses in the area of parole and probation violations or drug court client relapses. Most fortunately for the analysis presented here, such a comprehensive common metric has been developed with contemporary data, and it is available for use here.

Building on two earlier rigorous attempts to construct multidimensional indices of state-level punitiveness undertaken by Michael Tonry and James Whitman, Besiki Kutateladze developed such an index, which features five dimensions based on forty-four distinct characteristics of state criminal justice systems.[16] We make use of the Kutateladze index given that it is based on near-contemporary data from many sources and features the most comprehensive assessment of state-level criminal justice policies available. The sources upon which Kutateladze drew were the

U.S. Bureau of Justice Statistics, the Uniform Crime Reporting Program, the Office of Juvenile Justice and Delinquency Prevention, the National Corrections Reporting Program, the National Judicial Reporting System, Corrections Yearbook, the Death Penalty Information Center, Human Rights Watch, Amnesty International, state penal codes, and, importantly, research monographs, published journal articles, and occasional popular press pieces based on investigative journalism and professional journalistic fact verification. As described by Kutateladze, "an attempt was made to compile the most recent data and check their reliability with secondary sources. If any numbers were missing, the numbers for the preceding years were used. . . . If an indicator had more than three empty cells, it was deleted from the analysis despite having theoretical significance."[17]

Five Dimensions of Punitiveness and Forty-four Indicators

In drawing upon the literature on state punitiveness, Kutateladze identified five dimensions of state policy that guided his search for multiple indicators of each. Those five dimensions were (1) political and symbolic punishment; (2) incarceration; (3) punishing "immorality"; (4) conditions of confinement; and (5) juvenile justice. Each of these dimensions features multiple indicators, and the ultimate index of state punitiveness represents a grand mean of the dimension means, with each dimension contributing equally to the final result. Drilling down into the specific measures, the following are among the specific indicators included in the forty-four-item index of state punitiveness in criminal justice policy: for *political and symbolic punishment,* policies relating to life imprisonment, death penalties, sex offender registries, disenfranchisement, and three-strikes offenses are coded for punitiveness; for *incarceration,* rates of incarceration and mean sentences meted out for a range of felonies are coded; for *punishing immorality,* arrests for prostitution, commercialized vice, drug abuse, gambling, and public drunkenness, as well as statutory rape and age of consent provisions, are coded; for *conditions of confinement,* prison overcrowding, spending on prisoner services, inmate deaths incurred in confinement, inmate-on-inmate violence, inmate-on-staff violence, and lawsuits filed against correctional facilities and staff are coded; and for *juvenile justice,* the age for juvenile court jurisdiction, policies on treating juveniles as adults, juvenile incarceration rate, juveniles serving life without parole, and overcrowding in juvenile facilities are coded.

Kutateladze's painstakingly thorough research resulted in a score for states that clearly differentiates their punitiveness on the five dimensions of comparison. That score is reported in Table 28.1, in descending order with the least punitive state (Maine) at the top and the most punitive state (Florida) at the bottom, alongside the crime rate of the state.

States at opposite ends of the Kutateladze index have taken very different approaches to deviance and criminal conduct in their respective state criminal justice systems. A simple comparison of the states provides some insight into strong regional differences and powerful social dynamics at play in the process of establishing crime control policies in the American states.

For the states toward the top of the continuum, those aspects of the punitive approach to the wars on crime and drugs have been tempered by policy and program adoption. For example, in these states at-risk youth remain in the jurisdiction of the juvenile courts rather than being transferred to adult courts if more serious offenses are involved. In the states toward the bottom of the continuum at-risk youth are much more likely to be transferred to adult court, and to remain under that jurisdiction until they reach adulthood. Likewise, in the more restorative states sex offender labelling covers a narrow range of offenses for juveniles and adults alike, whereas in the more punitive states many offenses (e.g., indecent exposure, inappropriate touching) gain the label of sex offender and that label stays with the person regardless of subsequent treatment and changed behavior. In similar manner, in the more restorative states the use of "problem-solving" courts—where therapeutic jurisprudence is used to correct problem behavior instead of relying upon incarceration—tends to be commonplace for drug offenders, driving-under-the-influence traffic offenders, parties involved in domestic violence, and mental illness–related offending; in the more punitive states these types of courts, and the treatment programs associated with them, are far less frequently present. The conditions of confinement for juveniles and adults alike are typically adequate to good by most standards in the more restorative states, and poor to downright horrible in the more punitive states. While the variety of policies and programs is considerable even among the more restorative and the more punitive states, there is nonetheless a clear tendency for the former to reflect more charitable views of offenders and the latter to reflect more retributive views toward those who violate state laws.

From the evidence assembled by Kutateladze it is clear that U.S. states differ greatly in the way they have sought to provide for their public safety vis-à-vis the criminal justice institutions and practices they have adopted. The more restorative states have relied far less on incarceration and deterrence than their more punitive counterparts, and they have developed a wide range of policies and programs geared toward alternatives to detention, provision of diagnostic and therapeutic services, and creation of community-based services and public/private partnerships for offenders.

A simple correlation between the Kutateladze index and crime rates offers further insight. There is a strong, statistically significant correlation between the index and the crime rate (r = .48), suggesting that states with more punative

TABLE 28.1 **Ranking of States on the Punitiveness of Their Criminal Justice Systems**

	Punitiveness score[a]	Crime rate[b]		Punitiveness score[a]	Crime rate[b]
Maine	1.137	2,588	Colorado	2.079	3,197
Rhode Island	1.207	2,906	Wyoming	2.089	2,817
Minnesota	1.255	2,984	Arkansas	2.111	4,280
Vermont	1.337	2.414	Massachusetts	2.119	2,798
North Dakota	1.394	2,163	Kansas	2.152	3,080
West Virginia	1.406	2,728	Oklahoma	2.161	3,966
Alaska	1.523	3,782	Nevada	2.164	3,805
New Jersey	1.532	2,479	Nebraska	2.164	3,132
Hawaii	1.585	3,876	Indiana	2.164	3,538
Oregon	1.596	3,455	Pennsylvania	2.181	2,655
Missouri	1.601	3,989	Louisiana	2.193	4,474
New Hampshire	1.653	2,311	California	2.201	3,259
Wisconsin	1.676	3,294	Tennessee	2.265	4,502
South Dakota	1.697	2,033	Ohio	2.285	3,677
Utah	1.75	3,486	Illinois	2.297	3,287
New Mexico	1.793	4,293	Delaware	2.312	4,093
Washington	1.776	4,074	Maryland	2.416	3,778
Michigan	1.821	3,332	Texas	2.46	4,351
New York	1.821	2,353	Montana	2.463	2,898
Iowa	1.916	2,680	Alabama	2.249	4,218
North Carolina	1.943	4,165	Virginia	2.492	2,642
Idaho	1.946	2,324	Georgia	2.528	4,202
Connecticut	2.014	2,627	Mississippi	2.537	3,293
Arizona	2.042	4,300	South Carolina	2.645	4,714
Kentucky	2.069	2,861	Florida	2.719	4,441

NOTES:

a. An index based on five dimensions containing forty-four separate items. See the text for a description of the items. Lower numbers indicate less punitive policies.

b. Crimes per one hundred thousand (mean rate for 2007–2011) from indices of total violent crimes and property crimes.

SOURCES: Besiki Kutateladze, *Is America Really So Punitive? Exploring a Continuum of U.S. State Criminal Justice Policies* (El Paso, TX: LFB Scholarly Publications, 2009); Federal Bureau of Investigation, Uniform Crime Report, www.fbi.gov/about-us/cjis/ucr/ucr.

laws also tend to experience higher crime rates. To be sure, we cannot assess the causal direction here—whether higher crime rates lead a state to address crime with tougher punishments, or whether less punitive policies reduce crime rates. What we can observe, however, is the variation. High crime states are places with more punitive policies, and low crime states are places with more restorative forms of justice. One other possibility here for further research to address is the extent to which this correlation is endogenous; that is, the definition of certain behaviors and active enforcement increases the apparent rate of crime. In this sense, the choice of justice system may be related to observable crime.

Yvonne Estrada, Lacey Copenhaver, DaChelle Black, and Diane Billings (left to right) are the first graduates from ReMerge, Oklahoma County's prison alternative program, in Oklahoma City, Oklahoma, on Monday, March 25, 2013. In Oklahoma, the state that incarcerates more women per capita than any other state, a new program called Women in Recovery provides an alternative to prison for nonviolent women, with priority given to mothers. The first group of women graduated from the program on Monday.

SOURCE: REUTERS/Steve Olafson.

Despite this wide divergence in state approaches and policies toward criminal justice, the investment in criminal justice education and research that began with President Lyndon Johnson's administration upon the formation of the President's Commission on Law Enforcement and Administration of Justice, is bringing more social science–informed content to the criminal justice policy process.[18] The Omnibus Crime Control and Safe Streets Act of 1968 created major programs in the form of the Law Enforcement Assistant Administration (LEAA) and the Law Enforcement Education Program (LEEP), which provided a foundation for building criminal justice programs on U.S. college and university campuses throughout the country. Some of the most important benefits of that early investment and subsequent support for criminal justice teaching, research, and public service in academe have come in the form of increasingly well-informed voices contributing to the public debate on public safety issues.

CHANGING TIMES: REEVALUATING PUNITIVE POLICIES

With the onset of the recession of 2008 and the slow economic recovery being experienced in virtually all areas of the country, states across the land—restorative and punitive alike—have become particularly interested in reducing their expenditures on corrections in the pursuit of fiscal responsibility. In searching out potential economies to be had without sacrificing public safety, programs of long-standing operation in the restorative states have come in for particular attention in states that are revenue-starved. Because the recession of 2008 was brought about in major part by a financial system that was near collapse, the recovery from this type of recession has been long and painfully slow for many states, particularly those in the Rust Belt and where home foreclosures have been widespread. When state legislatures are confronted with persistent, difficult trade-offs between maintaining public health programs, public schools and universities, and jails and prisons, more and more legislators from both political parties have been anxious to hear about new ways of dealing with offenders in less expensive ways. To their credit, criminal justice researchers have been actively engaged in offering suggestions and making policy and program recommendations based on systematic study.

In this regard, columnist Shawn Vestal has noted the following in the context of a cross-state comparison:

> The report *The National Summit on Justice Reinvestment and Public Safety* shines a light on various corrections alternatives being tried around the country. Many of them focus on community-based solutions—less prison and more social-service efforts to connect offenders to community, family and responsibility. Among the solutions showing effectiveness, the report says, are identifying and tracking repeat offenders, strengthening community supervision and concentrating services in areas where offenders live. The report highlights a comparison between the differing approaches in Florida and New York. Between 2000 and 2007, both states changed their incarceration rates. Florida's went up 16 percent; New York's went down 16 percent as it shifted toward community-oriented solutions. Both saw reductions in crime, but New York's was twice that of Florida.[19]

Taking a similar line of argument, John Buntin's article in a recent issue of *Governing* magazine highlights the noteworthy effort of a number of states to implement the ideas expressed in the *National Summit on Justice*

Reinvestment and Public Safety report.[20] The states coming in for specific attention in Buntin's article are the following—listed with their respective ranks on the Kutateladze punitiveness index: Kentucky (25); Colorado (26); Arkansas (28); Louisiana (36); Ohio (39); Texas (43); and South Carolina (49).

The pattern of adoption of new policy initiatives in the area of mass incarceration is clearly that of the initiation of restorative justice–inspired policies and programs on the part of traditionally more punitive states. In large part the result of fiscal constraints and the openness to change often occasioned by financial hardship, the adoption of restorative justice–inspired policies and programs in the more punitive states likely also represents an example of the "institutional isomorphism" phenomenon witnessed in many areas of organizational life. This is a process whereby early adopters of successful programs and/or practices are emulated for various legitimacy-enhancement reasons by other organizations in a particular organizational or institutional field.[21] Such a pattern of adoption was documented in the area of policing practices[22] and is likely taking place in the corrections area along similar lines.

It can be argued that purposeful improvement of public policy outcome does occur from time to time in the American government setting on the basis of cross-state transfers of effective policies and programs. It would appear that such improvement is occurring in the area of state corrections and public safety policy at the present time, with the most progress being made in the states most in need of tempering their punitivity. Even with these changes noted, however, there remains a world of difference between the ways juvenile and adult offenders are treated in "stand your ground" versus "duty to retreat" states; in the New England versus the Confederacy states (see Self-Defense under the Law box); and in the states that have liberalized their marijuana laws versus those that have remained true to the federal policy of criminalizing production, distribution, possession, and use of the banned

SELF-DEFENSE UNDER THE LAW: PUNITIVE STATES MOVE FROM *DUTY TO RETREAT* TO *STAND YOUR GROUND* STANDARDS BY AN EXPANSIVE VIEW OF THE CASTLE DOCTRINE

The common law principle of the right to self-defense has at its core the concept of *reasonableness*. Because people will vary in their definitions of reasonableness, state legislatures have attempted to introduce more specificity into the concept by requiring that a person under serious threat of harm under most circumstances has a "duty to retreat" before resorting to use of force in self-defense. Under this principle a person under duress must seek to defuse a confrontation or retreat to safety if possible; having taken these steps, the use of force—even deadly force—is then permitted as an aspect of self-defense.

Twenty-nine states have such provisions in their laws. The duty to retreat idea is premised on the belief that human lives will be saved if people are motivated to defuse confrontations and/or seek safety if they are being threatened. If this rule is in place and is followed by a person under threat of harm, it is easier for prosecutors to prove that a killing was not in self-defense when it is suspected that an unreasonable use of deadly force has occurred.

There has been a long-standing exception to the duty to retreat known as the Castle Doctrine. In 1914 then-judge Benjamin Cardozo (later justice of the U.S. Supreme Court) articulated the concept this way: "It is not now and never has been the law that a man assailed in his own dwelling is bound to retreat. If assailed there, he may stand his ground and resist the attack. He is under no duty to take to the fields and the highways, a fugitive from his own home."[1]

In recent decades a number of the more punitive states have enacted "stand your ground" laws that extend the Castle Doctrine line of thought beyond the home. In Florida, the law reads that a person who is attacked anywhere he or she is legally present has "no duty to retreat and has the right to stand his or her ground and meet force with force, including deadly force if he or she reasonably believes it is necessary to do so to prevent death or great bodily harm."[2]

Two strong Castle Doctrine states are Florida and Texas. In Florida, as noted, one does not even have to be in one's home. In Texas, citizens are allowed to apply the Castle Doctrine rationale to protecting their homes, cars, or places of business or employment, using force (including deadly force) when an intruder has unlawfully entered or is attempting to enter using force; is attempting to remove someone from the home, car, or workplace by force; or is attempting to commit a crime such as rape, murder, or robbery. No duty to retreat is required.

Texas law changed from duty to retreat to the new stand your ground standard in 2007. According to the *Houston Chronicle,* the number of "justifiable homicide" cases increased significantly in that city as a direct consequence of these changes. With this new understanding of the Castle Doctrine in Texas, it is possible for citizens to legally kill people in many situations in which police are not allowed to take a citizen's life.

In Florida, the stand your ground law came into national prominence in February 2012, when George Zimmerman shot and killed an unarmed seventeen-year-old African American, Trayvon Martin. In July 2013, a jury in Florida acquitted Zimmerman of any crimes associated with Martin's death.

1. *People v. Tomlins,* 107 N.E. 496 (NY Ct. App., 1914).

2. 2012 Florida Statutes, Title XLVI, Chapter 776, Section 013(3).

MARIJUANA LAWS IN FLUX IN MANY STATES: STATE-ORIGINATED CHANGES IN CRIMINAL LAW DESPITE FEDERAL GOVERNMENT OPPOSITION

There are significant variations across states in many areas of criminal law; of particular interest in recent years have been changes in laws dealing with marijuana, a drug that remains on the list of dangerous, illicit drugs maintained by the federal government. As far as federal law enforcement goes, marijuana is a banned substance, and its production, distribution, sale, and possession constitute a violation of federal law. Nonetheless, many state legislatures have liberalized their drug laws with respect to marijuana despite the fact that federal law on the matter has not changed since the original inclusion of marijuana on the banned illicit substances listing decades ago. While conflicts in law exist now and will most certainly increase in this area in the future, for the time being the continued listing of marijuana on the federal illicit drugs list raises reasonable uncertainty about federal law enforcement actions as a myriad of individuals and businesses in the liberalizing states ramp up their efforts to conduct increasing levels of commerce in marijuana.

In some states medical marijuana laws permit their citizens to secure a permit to use marijuana to manage a variety of medical conditions. Along with this provision for permits is a system for establishing and operating medical marijuana dispensaries regulated by the state. The states that have enacted such statutes are Alaska, Arizona, California, Colorado, Delaware, Hawaii, Maine, Maryland, Michigan, Montana, Nevada, New Jersey, New Mexico, Oregon, Rhode Island, Vermont, and Washington.

In other states, the approach has been to decriminalize the possession of small amounts of marijuana on the part of adult residents. The core idea underlying these statutes is that law enforcement and the courts should not expend resources on arresting and prosecuting drug possession by recreational users of marijuana. The states that have enacted such laws are Alaska, California, Colorado, Connecticut, Maine, Minnesota, Mississippi, Nebraska, Nevada, New York, North Carolina, Ohio, and Oregon.

In some states medical marijuana and decriminalization have both taken place; these states are Alaska, California, Colorado, Maine, Nevada, and Oregon.

In 2012, two states with strong initiative traditions—Colorado and Washington—featured ballot propositions calling for the legal sale of marijuana through state-approved dispensaries for recreational use purchase. The states will tax and regulate the growing, distribution, conditions of sale, and places of approved use of the marijuana products in question. In these states the citizens via direct legislation established this policy for their states despite the objections of federal authorities such as U.S. attorneys and the nation's drug czar, Gil Kirlikowske.

Clearly, several states are not waiting for federal guidance on the matter of marijuana. How any particular state will treat a person in possession of a small amount of marijuana will remain unclear for most Americans for some time, given the continuing opposition of the federal government. As *The Weed Blog* advises its readers, "There is no substitute for having a lawyer represent you when you get into trouble."[1]

1. The Weed Blog, www.theweedblog.com.

substance (see Marijuana Laws in Flux in Many States box). In some states the school-to-prison pipeline is in clear operation, while in others the effort to keep at-risk youth strongly connected to schooling constitutes a major goal of collaboration among schools, juvenile courts, and social service agencies.[23] While diversity continues to characterize the landscape of American state-level criminal justice policies and practices, the trend is clearly reflective of a retreat from the most punitive policies long prevailing in many American states.

NOTES

1. Pew Center on the States, *One in 31: The Long Reach of American Corrections* (Washington, DC: Pew Charitable Trusts, 2009).
2. Al Pisciotta, *Benevolent Repression: Social Control and the American Reformatory Prison Movement* (New York: New York University Press, 1994).
3. James Austin and John Irwin, *It's about Time: America's Imprisonment Binge,* 3rd ed. (Belmont, CA: Wadsworth, 2001); David Garland, *The Culture of Control: Crime and Social Order in Contemporary Society* (Chicago: University of Chicago Press, 2001).
4. Robert Martinson, "What Works? Questions and Answers about Prison Reform," *The Public Interest* 35 (1974): 22–54.
5. Ted Palmer, "Martinson Revisited," *Journal of Research in Crime and Delinquency* 12 (1975): 133–152; Robert Martinson, "New Findings, New Views: A Note of Caution Regarding Sentencing Reform," *Hofstra Law Review* 7 (1979): 243–258.
6. Christopher Mele and Teresa A. Miller, *Civil Penalties, Social Consequences* (New York: Routledge, 2005).
7. Joan Petersilia, *When Prisoners Come Home: Parole and Prisoner Reentry* (New York: Oxford University Press, 2003).
8. Pew Center on the States, *One in 31.*
9. William J. Sabol, Heather C. West, and Matthew Cooper, *Prisoners in 2008* (Washington, DC: Bureau of Justice Statistics, 2009); Direct Expenditures for Correctional Activities of State Governments, Sourcebook of Criminal Justice Statistics Online, 2008, www.albany.edu/sourcebook/pdf/t1112006.pdf.

10. Todd R. Clear, "A Private-Sector, Incentives-Based Model for Justice Reinvestment," *Criminology and Public Policy* 10 (2011): 585–608.

11. Karim Ismaili, "Contextualizing the Criminal Justice Policy-Making Process," *Criminal Justice Policy Review* 17 (2006): 255–269.

12. Rafael Di Tella and Juan Dubra, "Free to Punish? The American Dream and the Harsh Treatment of Criminals," *Cato Papers on Public Policy* 1 (2011): 55–107.

13. James D. Unnever and Francis T. Cullen, "The Social Sources of Americans' Punitiveness: A Test of Three Competing Models," *Criminology* 48 (2010): 99–129.

14. Tiffany Bergin, "How and Why Do Criminal Justice Public Policies Spread throughout the U.S. States? A Critical Review of the Diffusion Literature," *Criminal Justice Policy Review* 22 (2011): 403–421; Jackson Williams, "Criminal Justice Policy Innovation in the States," *Criminal Justice Policy Review* 14 (2003): 401–422.

15. Anne Schneider and Helen Ingram, "Social Construction of Target Population: Implications for Politics and Policy," *American Political Science Review* 87 (1993): 334–347.

16. Michael Tonry, ed., *Penal Reform in Overcrowded Times* (New York: Oxford University Press, 2001); James Q. Whitman, *Harsh Justice: Criminal Punishment and the Widening Divide between America and Europe* (New York: Oxford University Press, 2003); Besiki Kutateladze, *Is America Really So Punitive? Exploring a Continuum of U.S. State Criminal Justice Policy* (El Paso, TX: LFB Scholarly Publishing, 2009).

17. Kutateladze, *Is America Really So Punitive?*, 15–16.

18. The commission issued its influential report, *The Challenge of Crime in a Free Society*, in 1967. It can be found at https://ncjrs.gov/.

19. "Career Criminals Plague City," *Spokesman Review* (June 27, 2012): A5, A7. The report can be found at www.justicereinvestment.org.

20. John Buntin, "Game Changers," *Governing* 25 (February 2012): 34–39.

21. Paul J. DiMaggio and Walter Powell, "The Iron Cage Revisited: Institutional Isomorphism and Collective Rationality in Organizational Fields," *American Sociological Review* 48 (1983): 147–160.

22. George W. Burruss and Matthew Giblin, "Modeling Isomorphism on Policing Innovation: The Role of Institutional Pressures in Adopting Community-Oriented Policing," *Crime and Delinquency* (July 14, 2009).

23. National Juvenile Defense Center, National Juvenile Defense Standards (Chicago: MacArthur Foundation, 2012), www.njdc.info.

SUGGESTED READING

Austin, James, and John Irwin. *It's about Time: America's Imprisonment Binge*, 3rd ed. Belmont, CA: Wadsworth, 2001.

Bergin, Tiffany. "How and Why Do Criminal Justice Public Policies Spread throughout the U.S. States? A Critical Review of the Diffusion Literature." *Criminal Justice Policy Review* 22 (2011): 403–421.

Clear, Todd R. *Imprisoning Communities: How Mass Incarceration Makes Disadvantaged Neighborhoods Worse*. New York: Oxford University Press, 2007.

———. "A Private-Sector, Incentives-Based Model for Justice Reinvestment." *Criminology and Public Policy* 10 (2011): 585–608.

Cullen, Francis T., and Cheryl L. Jonson. *Correctional Theory: Context and Consequences*. Thousand Oaks, CA: Sage, 2012.

Garland, David. *The Culture of Control: Crime and Social Order in Contemporary Society*. Chicago: University of Chicago Press, 2001.

Kutateladze, Besiki. *Is America Really So Punitive? Exploring a Continuum of U.S. State Criminal Justice Policy*. El Paso, TX: LFB Scholarly Publishing, 2009.

Lowenkamp, Christopher T., Edward J. Latessa, and Alexander M. Holsinger. "The Risk Principle in Action: What Have We Learned from 13,676 Offenders and 97 Correctional Programs?" *Crime and Delinquency* 52 (2006): 77–93.

Lowenkamp, Christopher T., Edward J. Latessa, and Paula Smith. "Does Correctional Program Quality Really Matter? The Impact of Adhering to the Principles of Effective Interventions." *Criminology and Public Policy* 5 (2006): 575–594.

Lutze, Faith E., Wesley Johnson, Todd R. Clear, Edward J. Latessa, and Risdon Slate. "The Future of Community Corrections Is Now: Stop Dreaming and Take Action." *Journal of Contemporary Criminal Justice* 28 (2012): 42–49.

Petersilia, Joan. *When Prisoners Come Home: Parole and Prisoner Reentry*. New York: Oxford University Press, 2003.

Pew Center on the States. *One in 31: The Long Reach of American Corrections*. Washington, DC: Pew Charitable Trusts, 2009.

Pisciotta, Al. *Benevolent Repression: Social Control and the American Reformatory Prison Movement*. New York: New York University Press, 1994.

Tonry, Michael, ed. *Penal Reform in Overcrowded Times*. New York: Oxford University Press, 2001.

Whitman, James Q. *Harsh Justice: Criminal Punishment and the Widening Divide between America and Europe*. New York: Oxford University Press, 2003.

Chapter 29

Education Policy

J. Celeste Lay

THE MOST SIGNIFICANT FEDERAL EDUCATION policy of the last thirty years was George W. Bush's major domestic accomplishment: No Child Left Behind (NCLB), passed on January 8, 2002. Over the past decade, NCLB has dominated the policy and political streams in the domain of education policy at both the federal and state levels. The policy passed in spite of entrenched interests on both sides: conservative opposition to federal government programs, especially in what is considered a state and local function; and longtime liberal opposition to the standards, accountability, and school choice movements. Not surprisingly, the coalition of these groups has frayed. Today, this bipartisan effort (supported 384–45 in the U.S. House and 87–10 in the U.S. Senate) has become a political hot potato.

Even so, one of the major effects of NCLB has been a significantly larger role for the federal government in setting the direction of education policy within states and local districts. Although it is still the case that the vast majority of school funding comes from state and local governments, the federal share has grown dramatically in the past twenty years—from 5.7 percent in 1990–1991 to 10.8 percent in 2011–2012. Bush's NCLB and Barack Obama's Race to the Top have forced states to make significant changes to their schools in the areas of standardized testing, school accountability, school choice, and management of personnel.

Many Americans believe education to be in a state of crisis. The annual Gallup poll on education demonstrates that since 2000, more Americans have been dissatisfied than satisfied with the quality of education students receive in K–12 schools. In a 2009 CBS poll, only 5 percent of respondents gave U.S. public schools the grade of an A. The crisis rhetoric is not new. The 1983 report that sparked much of the current concern about the education system, "A Nation at Risk," noted that scores on standardized tests had declined throughout the 1960s and 1970s. American students were no longer scoring among the top in comparison to students in other nations. Although the report has been debunked, the idea that American kids are falling behind their peers has proved to have remarkable staying power.[1]

Much evidence suggests the crisis is overblown. Educational attainment has climbed dramatically since the 1960s. In spite of hand-wringing about the achievement gaps between the poor and rich, or between minority and white students, throughout the 1970s and 1980s, when discussion of a "crisis" gained traction, gaps began to close between these groups.[2] Gaps began to open again, many argue, when targeted public funding began to wane. Why, then, do so many people believe public education is in such dire straits? To many, failing schools indicate bleak futures, economic and social decline, and the loss of the American dream.[3] As the economy has changed and average Americans earn less for doing more, public schools have borne the brunt of the blame. Furthermore, many believe there is a sinister element to the crisis rhetoric. Edward Banfield noted in 1974 that applying a crisis label where no crisis really exists is dangerous and can cause governments to adopt policies that are "wasteful and injurious," and when no progress is made, to conclude the policies were an "inevitable failure."[4] Many scholars and advocates believe this is exactly the motivation of some reformers—to destroy public schools by creating a crisis and placing impossible objectives on schools.[5] When schools fail to eliminate achievement gaps or to meet benchmarks, only radical reform is an option.

This chapter examines the literature on many significant education policy issues of the past decade. It focuses on NCLB by summarizing what it was intended to do, how states have responded, and the evidence about how effective the policy has been within the states in achieving its goals. The chapter chronicles the evidence on a variety of other educational issues: school choice and charter schools, the Race to the Top program, and teacher quality. Each section focuses on variations across the states.

NO CHILD LEFT BEHIND

No Child Left Behind (NCLB) was a reauthorization of the Elementary and Secondary Education Act (ESEA) of 1965. Although some scholars argue that NCLB did not radically redefine the education system, most contend it was more of a revolution than an evolution.[6] NCLB built on the Improving America's Schools Act (IASA) of 1994 and the efforts within some states to increase accountability and standards. By the early 2000s, most states had already moved in the direction of establishing content standards in core subjects, but IASA had only encouraged (not mandated) states to implement standards and assessment systems. In 2000 only thirteen states were testing students every year in reading and math.

NCLB was premised on the idea that with high educational standards, regular assessment and attaching high stakes to students' outcomes, states could ensure that no one was falling through the cracks and provide motivation to those at the bottom to improve. It also marked a significant shift in the way the nation looks at equity in education. For decades, equity meant that everyone had access to the same education or the same amount of funding for education (see School Funding box). Today, reform advocates on the side of greater accountability and higher standards contend that an equal education exists only when students achieve the same outcomes.

The law mandated that all states establish educational standards, and that by 2005–2006 public schools begin to administer annual statewide standardized tests in reading and math to all students in grades 3 through 8. Furthermore, a sample of fourth and eighth graders in each state is required to take the National Assessment of Educational Progress (NAEP) test in reading and math every other year so that there can be some comparison across states. In addition to annual testing, the key elements of NCLB included adequate yearly progress (AYP), publication of test scores, and sanctions on failing schools. Individual schools have to meet state targets for AYP in order to achieve the ultimate goal of bringing all students up to the "proficient" level by 2013–2014. Schools would be required to publish their scores, breaking down the data by race, class, disability status, and English ability. Finally, for schools that fail to meet the AYP targets, the law required increasingly harsh sanctions until, at five consecutive years, the school could be subject to closure and takeover by the state.

Opposition from the States

It did not take long for states to rise up in opposition to NCLB. Critics contended the law was an overreach of federal authority into a policy domain generally left to states and localities. The National Conference of State Legislatures opposed the legislation, and in 2003 the National Governors Association released a statement calling for greater flexibility and additional funding. Some states, such as Virginia, opposed the law because they viewed their own programs as superior. In 2004 school officers from fifteen states sent Secretary of Education Rod Paige a letter asking for more flexibility to determine AYP within their states. Several states also passed laws prohibiting districts from implementing NCLB unless there was adequate federal funding. The Bush administration believed it had to take a hardline approach to prevent states from gaming the system, so there was relatively little flexibility in the first several years.

In the first year after the bill's passage, the federal government increased funding substantially for the new requirements; however, the appropriations for NCLB were not sustained, and by 2005 the level of funding did not keep up with inflation. Furthermore, NCLB created new requirements on states in order to maintain Title I funding, leading many critics to declare the law an unfunded mandate. According to plaintiffs in a case against the U.S. Department of Education, Congress failed to fully fund NCLB from 2002–2006, appropriating $30.8 billion less than was authorized by NCLB and thus requiring states and local school districts to pick up the difference or risk losing valuable Title I funds.

In 2006 school districts in Michigan, Texas, and Vermont, as well as the National Education Association (NEA), sued the U.S. Department of Education (*Pontiac v. Spellings*) to have NCLB set aside as an unfunded mandate. After a trial judge rejected the plaintiffs' arguments, a three-judge panel of the Sixth Circuit Court of Appeals granted a rehearing with the full court. In 2008 the appeals court affirmed the trial court's decision (in an 8–8 decision), and in 2010 the U.S. Supreme Court failed to grant a writ of certiorari. Thus NCLB is not considered, at least legally, an unfunded mandate, and the federal government can require the states to meet particular objectives in exchange for education funding—even if this means the states must fund a portion of the costs to meet the federal government's objectives.

Criticism of NCLB grew each year after the law was implemented. According to Gary Orfield, the controversy was "wholly predictable" because of the sweeping nature of the changes required. As of 2006, "The Bush Administration [had] not commissioned independent research on the implementation of the policy and refused to admit rather obvious mistakes until virtual rebellion took hold in the field."[7] Given the outrage within so many states, even those with staunchly conservative governors, the Department of Education began to negotiate individually with states to alter their accountability plans. The results of such negotiations quelled some criticism in the short term, but they also created a great deal of confusion.

SCHOOL FUNDING

Average per-pupil spending varies dramatically across the fifty states and the District of Columbia. In 2008–2009 it ranged from $6,612 in Utah to $19,698 in the District. The five states that spent the most on per-pupil spending were the District, New York, New Jersey, Alaska, and Connecticut, averaging $17,045 per student. The five states that spent the least on each student spent less than half this amount, on average: Utah, Idaho, Oklahoma, Arizona, and Tennessee. Regionally, the Northeast spent the most on each student and the South spent the least, with the Midwest and West in between, respectively.

Per-Pupil Expenditures by State, 2008–2009

Northeast		South		Midwest		West	
Connecticut	$15,353	Alabama	$9,048	Illinois	$11,592	Alaska	$15,353
Delaware	$12,109	Arkansas	$8,854	Indiana	$9,254	Arizona	$7,929
D.C.	$19,698	Florida	$8,867	Iowa	$10,055	California	$9,503
Maine	$12,183	Georgia	$9,649	Kansas	$10,201	Colorado	$8,782
Maryland	$13,737	Kentucky	$9,038	Michigan	$10,373	Hawaii	$12,399
Massachusetts	$14,540	Louisiana	$10,625	Minnesota	$11,088	Idaho	$7,111
New Hampshire	$12,583	Mississippi	$8,064	Missouri	$9,891	Montana	$10,189
New Jersey	$17,076	N. Carolina	$8,518	Nebraska	$10,846	New Mexico	$9,648
New York	$17,746	Oklahoma	$7,878	N. Dakota	$9,802	Nevada	$8,321
Pennsylvania	$12,299	S. Carolina	$9,228	Ohio	$10,902	Oregon	$9,611
Rhode Island	$14,719	Tennessee	$7,992	S. Dakota	$8,543	Utah	$6,612
Vermont	$15,096	Texas	$8,562	Wisconsin	$11,183	Washington	$9,688
		Virginia	$10,928			Wyoming	$14,628
		W. Virginia	$10,821				
Average:	**$14,762**	**Average:**	**$9,156**	**Average:**	**$10,311**	**Average:**	**$9,983**

SOURCE: "Per Pupil Expenditure," Federal Education Budget Project, New America Foundation, http://febp.newamerica.net/k12/rankings/ppexpend.

The federal government also calculates information about the variations in per-pupil spending on K–12 education within states. Each state is assigned an "equity factor" in accordance with the Education Finance Incentive Grant formula. The U.S. Department of Education calculates the equity factor for each state by comparing per-pupil expenditures for each school district with the average per-pupil expenditure for each state, weighted according to district population size and poverty level. On average, spending varies within states by about 13 percent. With only one school district each, the District and Hawaii have no variation in spending. Louisiana has the highest degree of inequity, by far. The state spends an average of $10,625 per student, but with an equity score of 43 percent; this means that within the state, the amount per pupil varies from $6,056 to $15,194. In contrast, West Virginia's range varies only from $10,280 to $11,362.

Changes to Original Law

In 2005 Secretary of Education Margaret Spellings announced a new plan that would give states greater flexibility in meeting the federal mandates. There were several changes that could affect all states, if they applied for them, and states could request specific waivers from particular provisions of the law. For example, in 2005 Texas negotiated with the Department of Education to limit the percentage of special education students who could take alternative assessments to 5 percent instead of the mandated 3 percent for

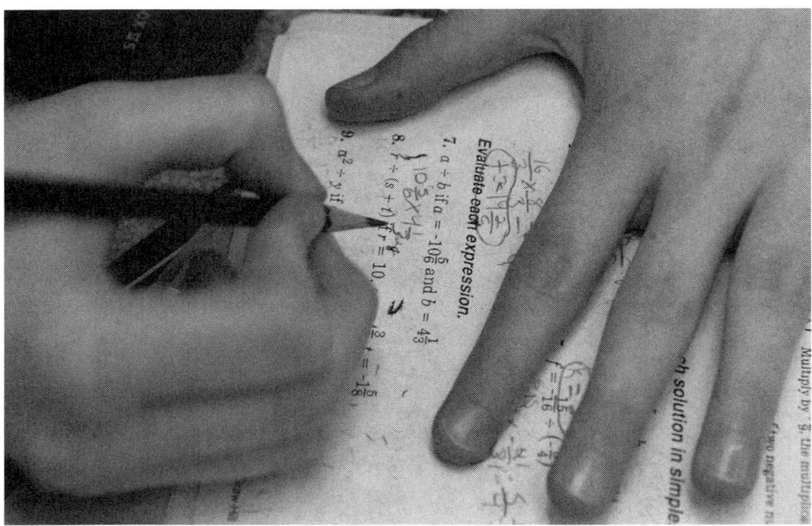

Seventh-grader Staci Daniels completes her math problem in class at the Coquille Valley Middle School Wednesday, April 12, 2006, in Coquille, Oregon. The No Child Left Behind Act required all students above second grade to be tested periodically in math and reading.

SOURCE: AP Photo/Rick Bowmer.

other states. In addition to state-level waivers, individual school districts also began to apply for waivers. In 2005, four Virginia districts were given waivers that allowed them to reverse the order from NCLB and offer students supplemental educational services before offering them transfer options.

By 2006, waivers and policy changes had led to significant diversity in implementing NCLB mandates. Thirty-one states changed the way they counted disabled students for the purposes of calculating AYP. Forty-three states took advantage of the rule changes giving greater flexibility in assessing limited-English-proficient students. Few states had exactly the same requirements, assessment procedures, methods of calculating particular subgroups, or even methods of determining AYP. According to Gail Sunderman, "Since the kinds and number of changes states have adopted are not uniform across states, with each state requesting its own configuration of amendments, it is difficult to unravel the impact these changes are likely to have."[8]

Effects

Given that changes to the law have been accomplished on such an ad-hoc basis, it is unsurprising that sorting out the effects of the law has been a difficult process. As of 2008, all states had statewide assessments in mathematics and language arts, and forty-seven states had assessments in science. Although the grades in which students are tested vary across the states, they typically begin testing students in grade 3 and stop annual testing in grade 8, meeting the minimum mandates of NCLB. Several states (twenty-six) test high school students in one grade only, often in grade 10. Only Iowa requires annual testing for students in all grades (K–12).

The NAEP test remains the primary means to compare student test scores across states. Table 29.1 presents the percentage of students in each state that scored proficient on the NAEP fourth- and eighth-grade math and reading tests in 2011. Compared with 2003 (the first year after NCLB was passed), all but six states had significantly higher scores on the fourth-grade math test in 2011. The results were not as successful in eighth grade, where math scores in twenty states were not significantly different from 2003. Fewer states had significantly higher scores on the reading tests in 2011 compared with 2003: only fourteen states had higher scores on the fourth-grade tests and ten states had higher scores on the eighth-grade tests. In 2011 the District of Columbia had the lowest percentage of proficient students in both grades on both tests. The highest scores were in New Hampshire (fourth-grade math), Massachusetts (eighth-grade math and fourth-grade reading), and South Carolina (eighth-grade reading). Even so, only in South Carolina did a majority of students score proficient, and only on the eighth-grade reading assessment.

Six states had significantly higher scores than in 2003 on all four tests, and four states lacked significantly higher scores on any of them. These results (and many others) suggest that though some states have made progress in raising test scores, gains have been sporadic and varied. Results reveal few patterns in the types of factors that contribute to rising scores. No smoking gun has appeared that demonstrates best or worst practices. For example, there are no differences between the successfully progressing states and those with no progress in terms of averages in teacher salary, experience, or education. Furthermore, though all six successful states have elements of school choice, so do all four of the states that exhibited no progress between 2003 and 2011.

One of the primary goals of NCLB was to eliminate achievement gaps between subgroups, but these gaps were prevalent in 2011 on both the math and the reading NAEP tests. In all states with measurable numbers of African American and Latino students there were significant gaps with white (Anglo) students. The same was true with regard to socioeconomic class. Every state had significant differences between those who were eligible for the federal school lunch program and those who were not.

TABLE 29.1 **Math and Reading Scores by State on the National Assessment of Educational Progress, 2011**

State	Fourth-grade math percent proficient	Eighth-grade math percent proficient	Fourth-grade reading percent proficient	Eighth-grade reading percent proficient
Alabama	25*	17	25*	24
Alaska	31*	28*	20	28*
Arizona	29*	24*	21	26
Arkansas	33*	24*	24	26
California	28*	19	19	21
Colorado	37*	31*	29	36
Connecticut	37	28	30	38*
Delaware	34*	25*	29	29
District of Columbia	17*	14*	13*	14*
Florida	32*	22*	27*	27
Georgia	31*	22*	25*	26
Hawaii	33*	24*	21*	24*
Idaho	34*	28*	26	31
Illinois	31*	25	25	30
Indiana	37*	27	26	30
Iowa	37*	26	27	31
Kansas	42*	32*	28	33
Kentucky	34*	24*	28*	33
Louisiana	24*	19*	19	21
Maine	38*	29*	26	34
Maryland	35*	29*	29*	34*
Massachusetts	45*	36*	35*	40
Michigan	30	25	25	29
Minnesota	41*	34	27	35
Mississippi	23*	16*	18	20
Missouri	36*	25	26	33
Montana	40*	35*	28	38*
Nebraska	34*	26	28*	32
Nevada	31*	23*	21*	24*
New Hampshire	47*	33*	33	36
New Jersey	41*	33*	32*	39*
New Mexico	26*	20*	17	21
New York	30	23	26	31

(Continued)

(Continued)

State	Fourth-grade math percent proficient	Eighth-grade math percent proficient	Fourth-grade reading percent proficient	Eighth-grade reading percent proficient
North Carolina	38	27	26	28
North Dakota	41*	34	30*	32
Ohio	38*	31*	27	33
Oklahoma	31*	23*	22	25
Oregon	30*	25	23	30
Pennsylvania	39*	29*	30*	34
Rhode Island	36*	27*	28*	30*
South Carolina	31	25*	22	25
South Dakota	36*	33*	26	53
Tennessee	26*	19	21	25
Texas	34*	31*	23	25
Utah	36*	28	27	33
Vermont	41*	33*	30	39*
Virginia	37*	29	28	32
Washington	33*	29	26	32
West Virginia	28*	18	22	23
Wisconsin	39*	32*	26	32
Wyoming	38	30	28	35

NOTE: *Significantly different ($p < .05$) from state's results in 2003.

SOURCE: U.S. Department of Education, Institute of Education Sciences, National Center for Education Statistics, National Assessment of Educational Progress, various years, 1998–2011 Reading Assessments.

In 2011 Secretary of Education Arne Duncan told Congress that nearly 80 percent of the nation's public schools could be labeled failing under NCLB due to their inability to meet AYP. Some education policy analysts have contended that Duncan's numbers were overblown. An analysis by the conservative Center on Education Policy at George Washington University indicates that 49 percent of the nation's schools were failing to meet AYP in 2011. The range of scores, however, is dramatic. On the low end is Wisconsin, where only 11 percent of schools failed to meet AYP in the 2010–2011 school year. On the other end is Florida, where 89 percent of schools failed to meet AYP. The trend line is heading up. In 2006, 29 percent of the nation's schools failed to meet AYP; the percentage increased to 35 percent in 2008 and 39 percent in 2010 before jumping to 49 percent in 2011.[9]

The across-time figures belie the fact that scores are the result of many factors. One factor is undoubtedly student learning, but it is far from the only one. States change their testing procedures or proficiency cut points, each having the effect of raising or lowering the number of failing students/schools. For example, from 2008 to 2009 the proportion of South Carolina schools missing AYP targets fell from 81 percent to 41 percent. While this looks like a significant achievement in student learning, the state legislature responded to the 2008 numbers by reducing the level of achievement defined as "proficient." This hardly meets President Bush's purported goal of limiting the "soft bigotry of low expectations." According to the Center on Education Policy, "Differences among states in academic standards, testing systems, accountability policies, and other areas make it impossible to compare AYP results in a meaningful way, either across states or within the same state over multiple years."[10]

Without being able to make meaningful across-time or across-space comparisons about what works, one of the keys to modern reforms—evidence-based learning—is impossible. Even if it were possible to accurately compare states to one another, there are few surprises in the schools that are meeting AYP. In a 2005 study of six states (Arizona, California, Georgia, Illinois, New York, and Virginia) the schools that have been identified as "needing improvement" are those where a majority of the enrollment is black and Latino, while those schools meeting AYP have predominantly white and Asian enrollments.[11]

The assumption of NCLB was that differences in test scores were primarily due to—or at least could be remedied by—schools' (and teachers') effectiveness. Yet education experts have long argued that differences in test scores across subgroups reflect children's background characteristics before they enter school.[12] NCLB does not account for the differences schools encounter when children arrive. The idea is that it is the responsibility of schools to make up any disadvantages students have, and that it is up to federal policy to provide the motivation for schools to do so through high-stakes accountability measures. The evidence is unsurprisingly mixed about how well this program is working.

President Obama supports annual testing and accountability standards, as well as the basic principles of competition and educational choice. His administration does not want a major overhaul of NCLB. It would postpone the 2013–2014 goal of 100 percent proficiency to 2020 and make some modifications in how schools could determine progress. Secretary of Education Duncan has given states increasing flexibility in meeting the law's mandates. States can request flexibility from specific NCLB mandates that they believe are stifling reforms—but they must show they are transitioning students, teachers, and schools to a system aligned with college- and career-ready standards for all students, developing accountability systems, and undertaking effective reforms. The administration's educational philosophy can be seen most clearly in its Race to the Top program.

RACE TO THE TOP

Given that there has been no congressional overhaul of NCLB, the Obama administration has been limited in implementing particular aspects of its educational plans. However, through the American Recovery and Reinvestment Act (ARRA), President Obama could push through some of his educational agenda. The act primarily aimed to stave off job losses: $39.5 billion was made available to local districts and higher education institutions for averting staff reductions and programmatic cutbacks, and $8.8 billion went to modernize facilities. It also, however, provided $4.35 billion for Race to the Top, a competitive grant program designed to encourage and reward states that are creating the conditions for education innovation and reform and seeing significant improvement in student outcomes (primarily test scores).

To be eligible for Race to the Top, seventeen states changed their laws to allow student test scores to be taken into account in evaluating teachers, thirteen removed caps on the number of charter schools that can be established, and forty-eight agreed to consider adopting common academic standards (thirty-four of which formally approved the new standards within a few months of their publication). With this program, the Obama administration became a powerful advocate for high-stakes standardized testing and charter schools.

Only two states—Delaware and Tennessee—were designated to receive funds in the first round of Race to the Top funding. In the two subsequent rounds, an additional sixteen states, plus the District of Columbia, have been awarded funds, including Arizona, Colorado, Florida, Georgia, Hawaii, Illinois, Kentucky, Louisiana, Maryland, Massachusetts, New Jersey, New York, North Carolina, Ohio, Pennsylvania, and Rhode Island. A few states opted not to apply for the program at all, while several others opted out in the second round of funding. According to the first set of state reports released in January 2012, most states used the first year to set the groundwork for reforms they will put in place in the next several years.

SCHOOL CHOICE

With Race to the Top and NCLB, school choice has become a greater reality for more children. In recent years, a plethora of new schooling options have arisen. Voucher programs; small, specialized alternative schools; magnet schools; and charter schools all offer different educational options under the banner of public education. Choice has become more popular as faith in government institutions has receded. Many reformers believe that because government-run schools are a monopoly, they have no incentive to improve, and that they work to serve the interests of the adults in the system (teachers and bureaucrats) rather than the students.

Advocates of greater privatization and more choice contend that the public system has failed generations of students and radical reform is the only option to fix the system. The best options, supporters argue, give consumers (i.e., parents) choices that will prod poorly performing schools to improve. These advocates are not all libertarian-minded reformers who hate big government. They also include several groups who view school choice as a means to promote their interests or values. Opponents counter that privatization merely exacerbates the problems in public schools with large populations of disadvantaged children, diverts resources from public schools, and increases race- and class-based inequalities.

Charter Schools

Charter schools are today widely viewed as the newest savior of a failing public school system. Charter schools are publicly funded schools that are governed by a group or organization that has a contract (or charter) with the state or city. The charter is granted for a fixed period of time, with the idea that the school will be held accountable for its results. If it fails, the charter will not be renewed. In exchange for accountability comes freedom from administrative bureaucracy, giving teachers and administrators flexibility and opportunities for innovation. Furthermore, it is believed that market pressures will raise the quality of schools for all students as parents move their children from poorly performing schools to better ones. Critics of charter schools, like other privatization options, argue that these schools pull away resources and the most motivated families from traditional public schools, leading to even greater gaps between the few who are able to get into a charter school and the majority who are left to underfunded traditional schools.

Minnesota passed the first charter school law in 1991. From 1999 to 2010, the number of students enrolled in public charter schools more than tripled from 340,000 to 1.4 million students (about 3 percent of public school students), including 4,952 schools (5 percent of total). Charter schools operate in forty states and the District of Columbia, and include a significant portion of the "market share" in the District of Columbia (where 42 percent of public schools are charters) and Arizona (where 22 percent of public schools are charters). In the other thirty-nine states with charter schools, they represent less than 11 percent of public schools, but this share is growing rapidly, especially in certain places (see New Orleans School System box). States without any charter schools include Alabama, Kentucky, Maine, Montana, Nebraska, North Dakota, South Dakota, Vermont, Washington, and West Virginia. State laws determine the process for authorizing charter schools and how they can be managed. With one exception, only nonprofit organizations can apply for a charter, but in many states, the governing board can subcontract the school's management to a for-profit company known as an educational management organization (EMO). In Michigan, for example, 80 percent of the state's 294 charter schools are run by for-profit EMOs.

The original charter concept in Minnesota was to allow teachers and parents who shared an educational vision to work within the existing public school system to create schools they believed would help particularly disadvantaged kids. Although some charter schools today continue down this path, others operate primarily with a market rationale. According to Leigh Dingerson, there are three types of charters: free-market charters, mom-and-pop charters, and charter franchises.[13] Mom-and-pop charters resemble the early Minnesota vision; they are usually run by experienced educators, may have a special focus (such as a pedagogical niche), and tend to be single schools. For-profit corporations operate free-market charters, often operating dozens of schools across the country. They promise to use public funds more efficiently to make a profit and improve student performance. Charter franchises, such as Knowledge Is Power Program (KIPP), are usually large, nonprofit operations that bridge some of the elements from the mom-and-pops and the free-market charters.

In 2010 the widely viewed documentary *Waiting for Superman* played on the heartstrings of many by chronicling several children "stuck" in failing public schools and trying desperately to win the lotteries that would give them a spot in a charter school. Along with this film, many media portrayals imply that the country needs more charter schools to fix the broken system. Though there are some highly touted successful charter schools, such as Geoffrey Canada's Harlem Children's Zone, the social

During the fourth annual Georgia School Choice Celebration and Rally on January 31, 2013, in Atlanta, Georgia, students and teachers from Atlanta Heights Charter School join other students in celebrating the passing of the Charter School Amendment. The Charter School Amendment, approved by voters in November 2012, expands educational opportunities for kids by providing for the approval of public charter schools upon the request of the local community.

SOURCE: Associated Press Photo/*Atlanta Journal-Constitution*, Jason Getz.

NEW ORLEANS SCHOOL SYSTEM

New Orleans has the largest percentage of public school students in the country attending charter schools. In the 2011–2012 school year, over 80 percent of public school students attended a charter school. The city's experience provides some illuminating examples that are hardly unique to the charter school movement. In the public sector, the city has a mix of charter schools and noncharter public schools. Most of these schools are operated by the Recovery School District (RSD), which began taking over schools in New Orleans (and other parts of Louisiana) prior to Hurricane Katrina in August 2005. In November 2005 the state legislature voted to take over all of the city's schools that performed at or below state averages and give operational control to the RSD. At that time, only a few schools remained under the control of the Orleans Parish School Board (OPSB)—they were, unsurprisingly, the city's highest performing schools. Today, about 78 percent of the public schools are run by the RSD. Most of the other schools are run by the OPSB.

The noncharter public schools in New Orleans operate in a nontraditional setting. All public schools in the city are open enrollment (i.e., no neighborhood catchment area); charters can place caps on enrollment, leading to lotteries in the highest performing schools. Furthermore, neither the RSD nor the OPSB honor the collective bargaining agreement of the United Teachers of New Orleans.

The evidence about the effectiveness of the city's charter schools is mixed. From 2006–2007 to 2010–2011, as the number of charter schools climbed, New Orleans's scores on the state's fourth- and eighth-grade reading and math tests improved, as did scores on the graduation exit exam. School performance scores were higher in charter schools than in noncharter public schools operated by the RSD. Most argue the comparisons, however, are not apples to apples. Some charter schools' enrollments are filled by lottery or on a first come, first served basis, but few charters serve all comers. Most have selective enrollment policies. According to a 2011 poll of New Orleans parents, 88 percent said their child's public school required an application; 31 percent required a discipline contract; 70 percent required parental participation; and 49 percent required test scores, past report cards, or a writing sample.[1] Unsurprisingly, the schools with the strictest selective admissions are the highest rated public schools in the city.

According to one report, school performance scores were highest in the non-RSD schools, with the most significant gaps in performance between the OPSB charters and the RSD noncharter schools. Although RSD schools' scores have improved slightly since 2006, the gaps between these schools and the others have not closed at all. RSD charters are required to have open enrollment and to provide transportation to all students, and scores in these schools are considerably lower than in other types of public schools without these requirements.[2]

Although most parents (74 percent) believe the direction of New Orleans public schools is getting better, there are still some problems with the system. Charter school advocates, for example, commonly assume that parents will choose schools on the basis of the school's academic achievement or curriculum. This belief is essential for the assumption that school choice will inevitably force the poorly performing schools to improve academically. However, much research indicates that good information is often scarce, and there are a variety of nonacademic reasons that are important to parents, such as access to transportation.[3] It may not be the case that simply giving parents options will automatically lead the "bad" schools to change their behavior in response to market incentives. Clearly, if New Orleans is to be a model for the nation's public schools, there are many issues yet to be worked out.

1. Cowen Institute for Public Education Initiatives, "K–12 Public Education through the Public Eye: Parents' Perceptions of School Choice," research brief, December 2011, www.coweninstitute.com/wp-content/uploads/2011/12/Public-Opinion-Poll-2011-Fina11.pdf.
2. Cowen Institute for Public Education Initiatives, "The 2011 State of Public Education in New Orleans," research brief, July 2011, www.coweninstitute.com/wp-content/uploads/2011/07/2011-SPENO-report.pdf
3. Mark Schneider, Paul Teske, Christine Roch, and Melissa Marschall, "Networks to Nowhere: Segregation and Stratification in Networks of Information about Schools," *American Journal of Political Science* 41 (1997): 1201–1223; Schneider, Teske, Marschall and Roch, "Shopping for Schools: In the Land of the Blind, the One-Eyed Parent May Be Enough," *American Journal of Political Science* 42 (1998): 769–793; Schneider, Marschall, Roch, and Teske, "Heuristics, Low Information Reality, and Choosing Public Goods: Broken Windows as Shortcuts to Information about School Performance," *Urban Affairs Review* 34 (1999): 729–741.

science research tends to indicate that charter schools are not much better at educating children than are traditional public schools. In 2008 Jeffrey Henig examined the state of the literature on charter schools and discovered that though they do not exacerbate racial or economic segregation, they are less likely to accommodate students with special needs and those who are English-language learners. Test scores in charter schools tend to be lower than in traditional public schools.[14] After a thorough evaluation of five major dimensions of charter schools, Jack Buckley and Mark Schneider write,

> We believe the push for charter schools . . . has been characterized by too many promises that are only, at

best, weakly supported by evidence. . . . Wishing that competition and choice will somehow unleash the "magic of the market" that in turn will produce better educational outcomes ignores the extensive infrastructure necessary to make markets work. And the assumption that charter schools are a cure for the ills of urban education flies in the face of the evidence that we (and others) have assembled.[15]

TEACHERS: SOURCE OF PROBLEM OR SCAPEGOAT?

In spite of the evidence that out-of-school factors play the most critical roles in educational success, teachers have recently borne the brunt of the blame among those who believe the nation's school system is in crisis. Since 2010, a few states have led the charge against public school teachers and/or their unions. The fight between the teachers' unions and Gov. Scott Walker (R) in Wisconsin in 2011 was perhaps the most visible, but policies in Florida, Indiana, New Jersey, Ohio, South Carolina, and Tennessee have also pitted politicians against teachers. There are two major complaints about teachers. First, some argue that many teachers are ill-trained and unprepared to teach; second, some believe that teachers' unions protect bad teachers and/or obstruct reform efforts at the expense of students.

In terms of teacher quality, some are concerned that undergraduate students choosing to go into teaching are not the strongest students (even though studies show there are no differences in exam scores or grade-point averages among education majors and nonmajors).[16] Low salaries and prestige are usually blamed for the inability to attract the highest achieving students. Teacher salaries peaked in the early 1970s and now fall considerably behind similarly trained graduates in the private sector. The average salary for a public school teacher in 2009–2010 was $52,361; this is nearly $14,000 less than a registered nurse, $4,500 less than a branch manager at a bank, and nearly $20,000 less than a paralegal with a bachelor's degree. Like everything else, salaries vary considerably across the states, with predominantly rural states paying much less than states dominated by urban areas. South Dakota has the lowest average ($38,837), while New York has the highest ($71,633). Of the ten states with the lowest average salaries, only Missouri and Utah have major urban areas. Conversely, of the highest paying states, all have significant urban populations.[17]

As state houses and governors' offices have become stocked with fiscal conservatives dealing with budget constraints, there has been little support for increasing teacher salaries. Instead, policymakers have focused on improving instruction by increasing the standards for teachers, in spite of evidence that enhanced requirements do little to improve teaching. In 1991 Richard Murnane and colleagues wrote, "Increased training requirements . . . do not improve the teaching skills new entrants bring to the classroom," but they do reduce the number of prospective teachers. Furthermore, "These popular policies aimed at improving teaching will fail to achieve their goal. As this failure becomes evident, public support for teacher salary increases will diminish, and . . . teaching will again be a low status, relatively low paying occupation, perceived to be the occupational choice only of those with no better option."[18] The statement was prescient. As states have moved to codify higher standards for teachers, the rhetoric about the inadequacy of teachers has gotten worse.

There is solid evidence that teacher quality is one of the most important school factors in explaining student performance. However, there is no agreement about how to define "quality." The relationship between teacher education or experience and student outcomes is tenuous. Steven G. Rivkin and colleagues find that there is "no evidence that having a master's degree improves teacher skills," and though "there appear to be important gains in teaching quality in the first year of experience . . . there is little evidence that improvements continue after the first three years."[19] Even so, NCLB requires all states to ensure that students have a "highly qualified" teacher in the classroom. The law defined teacher quality in terms of measurable factors, such as teacher education, even though evidence has suggested this has little tangible effect on student outcomes. Under NCLB, teachers must have a bachelor's degree and full state certification, and they must prove that they know each subject they teach. Teachers demonstrate their competency by majoring in the subject they teach, passing a state-developed test, or obtaining an advanced certification from the state or a graduate degree. Older teachers show their competency through a combination of experience, expertise, and the professional training they have garnered over time.

These requirements have proven most difficult in the poorest schools, especially rural schools. Table 29.2 shows the highest level of education among teachers within each state and the percentage of teachers who have the most and least experience in the classroom. Nationally, the highest level of education for a plurality of teachers is a bachelor's degree (47.4 percent); 44.5 percent have master's degrees. The most highly educated teachers are primarily in the Northeast, while the states with the smallest proportion of teachers with a master's degree are in the South and other predominantly rural states. Although research indicates that teacher experience is more important than education, a third of all public school teachers have three or fewer years of experience. Since the 1980s, policymakers have been concerned about the "graying" of the workforce, but research indicates that many factors are responsible for high rates of teacher turnover: inadequate support from

TABLE 29.2 **Highest Degree Earned and Years of Full-Time Teaching Experience for Teachers in Public Elementary and Secondary Schools by State, 2007–2008**

State	Bachelor's degree	Master's degree	Less than three years in classroom	Twenty or more years in classroom
Alabama	44.3	46.9	31.3	18.2
Alaska	56.3	36.3	27.5	20.7
Arizona	49.1	41.6	34.6	18.4
Arkansas	58.6	34.1	25.7	31.6
California	52.7	34.3	35.9	20.3
Colorado	42.9	48.4	37.9	16.8
Connecticut	19.2	64.3	29.7	27.1
Delaware	38.2	53.0	43.3	18.2
District of Columbia	41.3	45.3	29.9	25.5
Florida	60.9	34.1	35.0	22.8
Georgia	38.8	43.4	32.4	21.4
Hawaii	46.9	32.6	34.3	18.6
Idaho	66.1	29.7	31.0	22.8
Illinois	45.5	49.8	35.6	21.6
Indiana	37.4	57.0	32.3	29.4
Iowa	59.8	37.9	30.5	28.2
Kansas	53.0	41.8	30.2	29.6
Kentucky	20.9	57.5	35.5	24.2
Louisiana	71.9	23.5	33.3	26.3
Maine	54.4	37.9	27.0	29.1
Maryland	42.6	47.0	37.1	24.8
Massachusetts	30.6	62.0	39.9	21.8
Michigan	37.2	57.6	32.5	21.8
Minnesota	41.6	51.4	28.5	23.6
Mississippi	56.6	37.2	31.8	25.1
Missouri	47.2	47.5	34.2	20.8
Montana	62.8	33.4	26.9	33.3
Nebraska	53.1	44.2	24.2	34.2
Nevada	41.5	49.5	37.3	19.4
New Hampshire	49.4	45.4	31.7	26.0
New Jersey	55.8	36.5	40.8	24.1
New Mexico	53.0	39.5	35.6	21.5
New York	11.8	77.6	38.0	20.6

(Continued)

(Continued)

State	Bachelor's degree	Master's degree	Less than three years in classroom	Twenty or more years in classroom
North Carolina	64.6	28.0	37.3	22.0
North Dakota	68.2	28.1	23.3	34.7
Ohio	37.9	62.3	29.9	26.3
Oklahoma	66.5	28.9	31.4	27.0
Oregon	37.0	52.3	31.5	21.0
Pennsylvania	45.3	45.2	33.6	27.2
Rhode Island	44.7	48.7	37.0	23.1
South Carolina	40.9	52.1	31.5	28.5
South Dakota	66.8	30.9	23.7	32.4
Tennessee	44.9	43.0	28.8	26.8
Texas	70.1	26.3	31.2	24.0
Utah	61.1	30.3	32.9	21.2
Vermont	42.6	50.0	30.5	27.3
Virginia	57.4	36.1	32.8	26.5
Washington	31.4	60.7	27.8	25.5
West Virginia	39.5	51.6	26.4	37.4
Wisconsin	44.8	49.3	32.4	26.4
Wyoming	56.0	37.6	27.3	29.9
Total United States	47.4	44.5	33.6	23.7

NOTE: Figures in cells are percentages.

SOURCE: National Center for Education Statistics, "Digest of Education Statistics, 2010," U.S. Department of Education, 2011–2015.

school administration, student discipline problems, limited faculty input into school decision making, and low salaries. Recent attacks on teachers' unions and states' efforts to strip public school teachers of many benefits are likely to decrease the number of experienced teachers.

At the same time that federal policy has pushed states to increase teacher standards, some states have resisted. In 2012 Louisiana governor Bobby Jindal (R) signed legislation that would strip teachers' tenure protections, give superintendents and principals hiring and firing power, tie teacher pay to student performance, use the state's public school financing to pay private school tuition for qualified low- and moderate-income students, and allow charter schools to hire teachers with no state certification. The certification process in Louisiana is fairly minimal, but allowing charter schools to hire noncertified teachers deals with shortages of teachers willing to work with no job protection and for less salary and benefits. The pedagogical arguments for this policy are less clear. These provisions are all part of conservative efforts to privatize public education and to strip power away from teachers' unions. Teachers remain one of the largest unionized workforces in the country. Nationally, nearly 74 percent of public school teachers are members of unions. As seen in Figure 29.1, South Carolina has the lowest percentage of teachers in unions, with 26.9 percent; Connecticut has the highest, with 98.8 percent of its teachers belonging to unions. Some argue that teachers' unions have been the single biggest obstruction to meaningful education reform in the states where they are strongest, and many of the changes to education policy within the states have attempted to reduce the power of unions.[20]

In 2010, eleven states modified some element of their tenure policies, largely to make the process of terminating a teacher's contract easier or more transparent. Some states have eliminated the use of the term *tenure,* opting instead to refer to *continuing contracts.* Several states have

FIGURE 29.1 **Percentage of Public School Teachers Belonging to a Union or Employees' Association, 2007–2008**

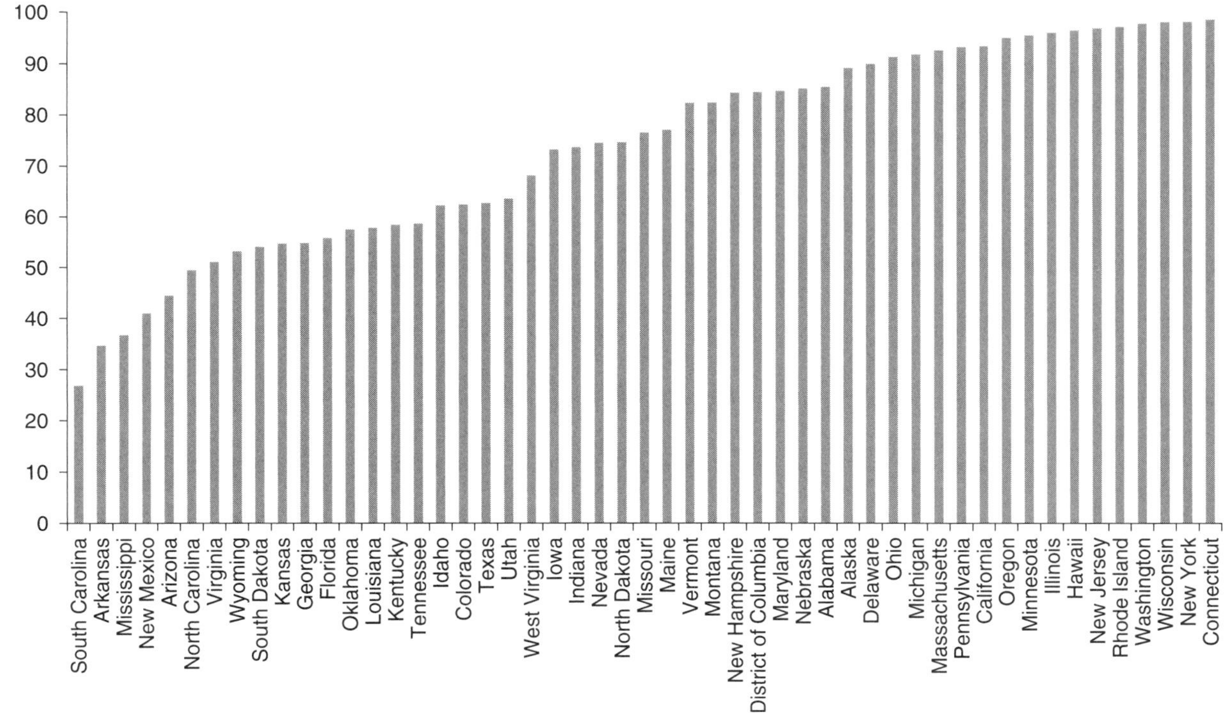

SOURCE: National Center for Education Statistics, Schools and Staffing Survey (SASS), 2007–2008.

eliminated the seniority system completely, including Florida, Michigan, Nevada, and Tennessee. The efforts of the federal and state governments, as well as private foundations, to force schools to tie teachers' performance evaluations to student outcomes has also weakened the influence of unions. In spite of scant evidence on the effectiveness of merit pay to improve students' scores, it is a hallmark of the policies pushed by reform advocates. Union leaders have begun to recognize that if they are to have any influence over the direction of education policy, they have to participate in discussions with anti-union forces and adapt to the new policy regime.

CONCLUSION

In the past ten years, the country has witnessed a sea change in education policy. Until recently, education policy was one of the few domains in which the federal government's reach had not extended very far. This began to change in the 1960s with the Elementary and Secondary Education Act, but only at the margins. Today, however, the federal government is increasingly entangled in nearly all elements of primary and secondary education. Due to federal policy mandates, every state now has its own set of educational standards that are tied to specific benchmarks. Similarly, all states now conduct standardized testing for the vast majority of students in elementary and junior high school. States and individual schools report their students' test scores. Through Race to the Top, the federal government is pushing states to create more charter schools and tie teachers' salaries to students' test scores. The effects of these policies are unclear, largely because of the variations in implementation. States continue to exercise their power in the federal system through the process of requesting waivers from NCLB mandates and choosing how doggedly to compete for Race to the Top funds. Furthermore, states still determine the benchmarks for proficiency, and many states have altered how they define "proficient" performance so that their scores show improvement. States' educational goals, however, are increasingly tied to federal policy goals.

As of 2013—the year in which all states are supposed to have raised test scores to proficiency—it is obvious that NCLB has not succeeded in this goal or in eliminating achievement gaps. There has been some improvement in students' test scores, to be sure, but Americans continue to believe there is a crisis in the nation's public schools. The policy has been successful, however, in bringing education to the top of the nation's political agenda and, in the midst of foreign conflicts and economic crises, keeping it there. Thus far, it has survived a backlash from states and from activists who argue it not only represents a significant overreach of the federal government, but its focus on high-stakes standardized tests has substantial detrimental effects on the evaluation of teachers, the curriculum in schools, and the overall educational experience for students.

The past decade has also brought to the fore a set of critical questions around the definition of public schools. If a school has selective admissions criteria and gets a great deal of its financial support from private foundations, is it a public school? If schools can place caps on enrollment so that they must hold lotteries wherein 10 to 20 percent of applicants gain entry, are they really public schools? Are schools still public if they send the government's money they receive to a for-profit corporation that chooses to deliver educational services in ways that lack transparency? If teachers are accountable only to administrators and private boards rather than to publicly elected school boards, and they have no protection from capricious actions against them, are they still working in public schools? These are some of the important questions with which we must contend as we continue to reshape the public school landscape.

NOTES

1. Gerald W. Bracey, "April Foolishness: The 20th Anniversary of 'A Nation at Risk,'" *Phi Delta Kappan* 84 (2003): 616–621.
2. Linda Darling-Hammond, *The Flat World and Education: How America's Commitment to Equity Will Determine Our Future* (New York: Teachers College Press, 2010), 20.
3. Jennifer L. Hochschild and Nathan Scovronick, *The American Dream and the Public Schools* (New York: Oxford University Press, 2003).
4. Edward Banfield, *The Unheavenly City Revisited,* 2nd ed. (Boston: Little, Brown, 1974), 24.
5. Gerald W. Bracey, *On the Death of Childhood and the Destruction of Public Schools: The Folly of Today's Education Policies and Practices* (Portsmouth, NH: Heinemann, 2003).
6. NCLB was more of an evolution: Lorraine M. McDonnell, "Surprising Momentum: Spurring Education Reform in States and Localities," in *Reaching for a New Deal: Ambitious Governance, Economic Meltdown, and Polarized Politics in Obama's First Two Years,* ed. Theda Skocpol and Lawrence R. Jacobs (New York: Russell Sage Foundation, 2011), 233; Paul Manna, *School's In: Federalism and the National Education Agenda* (Washington, DC: Georgetown University Press, 2006). NCLB was more of a revolution: Patrick J. McGuinn, *No Child Left Behind and the Transformation of Federal Education Policy, 1965–2005* (Lawrence: University Press of Kansas, 2006).
7. Gary Orfield, "Foreword," in Gail L. Sunderman, "The Unraveling of No Child Left Behind: How Negotiated Changes Transform the Law," The Civil Rights Project, Harvard University, February 2006, www.eric.ed.gov/PDFS/ED490859.pdf, 6.
8. Sunderman, "The Unraveling of No Child Left Behind," 39.9. Alexandra Usher, "AYP Results from 2010–11 to May 2012 Update," Center on Education Policy, Graduate School of Education and Human Development, George Washington University, www.cep-dc.org/displayDocument.cfm?DocumentID=403.
10. Wayne Riddle and Nancy Kober, "State Policy Differences Greatly Impact AYP Numbers," Center on Education Policy Graduate School of Education and Human Development, George Washington University, 2011, 6.
11. James S. Kim and Gail L. Sunderman, "Measuring Academic Proficiency under the No Child Left Behind Act: Implications for Educational Equity," *Educational Researcher* 34 (2005): 3–13.
12. James S. Coleman, *Equality of Educational Opportunity,* Washington, DC: U.S. Department of Health, Education, and Welfare, Office of Education (OE-38001 and sup.), 1966; Stephen W. Raudenbush, *Schooling, Statistics, and Poverty: Can We Measure School Improvement?* (Princeton, NJ: Educational Testing Service, 2004).
13. Leigh Dingerson, *Reclaiming the Education Charter: Ohio's Experiment with Charter Schooling* (Washington, DC: Education Voters Institute, The Forum for Democracy and Change, 2008).
14. Jeffrey R. Henig, *Spin Cycle: How Research Is Used in Policy Debates: The Case of Charter Schools* (New York: Russell Sage Foundation, 2008).
15. Jack Buckley and Mark Schneider, *Charter Schools: Hope or Hype?* (Princeton, NJ: Princeton University Press, 2007), 267–268.
16. Gerald Bracey, *Reading Educational Research: How to Avoid Getting Statistically Snookered* (Portsmouth, NH: Heinemann, 2006), 5.
17. National Education Association, "Rankings of the States 2010 and Estimates of School Statistics 2011," December 2010.
18. Richard J. Murnane, Judith D. Singer, John B. Willett, James J. Kemple, and Randall J. Olsen, *Who Will Teach? Policies That Matter* (Cambridge, MA: Harvard University Press, 1991), 3–4.
19. Steven G. Rivkin, Eric A. Hanushek, and John F. Kain, "Teachers, Schools, and Academic Achievement," *Econometrica* 73 (2005): 417–458, 449.
20. Tom Loveless, ed., *Conflicting Missions? Teachers Unions and Educational Reform* (Washington, DC: Brookings, 2000); Terry M. Moe, *Special Interest: Teachers Unions and America's Public Schools* (Washington, DC: Brookings, 2011).

SUGGESTED READING

Berliner, David C., and Bruce J. Biddle. *The Manufactured Crisis: Myths, Fraud, and the Attack on America's Public Schools.* Boston: Addison-Wesley, 1995.

Bracey, Gerald W. *On the Death of Childhood and the Destruction of Public Schools: The Folly of Today's Education Policies and Practices.* Portsmouth, NH: Heinemann, 2003.

———. *The War against America's Public Schools: Privatizing Schools, Commercializing Education.* Boston: Allyn and Bacon, 2002.

Buckley, Jack, and Mark Schneider. *Charter Schools: Hope or Hype?* Princeton, NJ: Princeton University Press, 2007.

Burch, Patricia. *Hidden Markets: The New Education Privatization.* New York: Routledge/Taylor and Francis, 2009.

Chubb, John E., and Terry M. Moe. *Politics, Markets, and America's Schools.* Washington, DC: Brookings, 1990.

Darling-Hammond, Linda. *The Flat World and Education: How America's Commitment to Equity Will Determine Our Future.* New York: Teachers College Press, 2010.

Fabricant, Michael, and Michelle Fine. *Charter Schools and the Corporate Makeover of Public Education: What's at Stake?* New York: Teachers College Press, 2012.

Henig, Jeffrey R. *Rethinking School Choice: Limits of the Market Metaphor.* Princeton, NJ: Princeton University Press, 1994.

———. *Spin Cycle: How Research Is Used in Policy Debates: The Case of Charter Schools.* New York: Russell Sage Foundation, 2008.

Hochschild, Jennifer L., and Nathan Scovronick. *The American Dream and the Public Schools.* New York: Oxford University Press, 2003.

Kosar, Kevin R. *Failing Grades: The Federal Politics of Education Standards.* Boulder, CO: Lynne Reiner, 2005.

Loveless, Tom, ed. *Conflicting Missions? Teachers Unions and Educational Reform.* Washington, DC: Brookings, 2000.

Manna, Paul. *School's In: Federalism and the National Education Agenda.* Washington, DC: Georgetown University Press, 2006.

McDermott, Kathryn A. *High-Stakes Reform: The Politics of Educational Accountability.* Washington, DC: Georgetown University Press, 2011.

McDonnell, Lorraine. "Surprising Momentum: Spurring Education Reform in States and Localities." In *Reaching for a New Deal: Ambitious Governance, Economic Meltdown, and Polarized Politics in Obama's First Two Years,* ed. Theda Skocpol and Lawrence R. Jacobs. New York: Russell Sage Foundation, 2011.

McGuinn, Patrick J. *No Child Left Behind and the Transformation of Federal Education Policy, 1965–2005.* Lawrence: University Press of Kansas, 2006.

Moe, Terry M. *Special Interest: Teachers Unions and America's Public Schools.* Washington, DC: Brookings, 2011.

Raudenbush, Stephen W. *Schooling, Statistics, and Poverty: Can We Measure School Improvement?* Princeton, NJ: Educational Testing Service, 2004.

Ravitch, Diane. *The Death and Life of the Great American School System: How Testing and Choice Are Undermining Education.* New York: Basic Books, 2010.

Sunderman, Gail L., James S. Kim, and Gary Orfield. *NCLB Meets School Realities: Lessons from the Field.* Thousand Oaks, CA: Corwin Press, 2005.

Wong, Kenneth, and Gail Sunderman. "Education Accountability as a Presidential Priority: No Child Left Behind and the Bush Presidency." *Publius* 37 (2007): 333–350.

Chapter 30

Environmental Policy

David M. Konisky

STATES CONFRONT A DIVERSITY OF ENVIRONMENTAL problems. For some states, air pollution is a major concern. California, for example, has long suffered from significant air quality problems. About 95 percent of the state's population currently resides in a county that is not fully meeting national ambient air quality standards for pollutants covered by the federal Clean Air Act (CAA).[1] Elsewhere, water quality is a more significant concern. While residents of Iowa enjoy good air quality (the state is nearly fully compliant with national ambient air quality standards), a large proportion of the state's rivers, streams, and lakes are failing to achieve their designated uses (e.g., being fishable, drinkable, swimmable) under the federal Clean Water Act (CWA). A 2010 state water quality assessment found that 76 percent of the state's rivers and streams and 79 percent of the lakes, reservoirs, and ponds that were assessed were in some fashion impaired. In other states, natural resource challenges dominate the agenda.[2] In Maine, for example, forestland covers about 90 percent of the state. Because most of these forests are owned by private landowners, the state government must find ways, mostly nonregulatory, to promote forest management that not only allows for the development of forest products important to the state economy, but that also encourages land stewardship and protection of wildlife habitat.

Many problems also extend beyond state borders. Air pollution from out-of-state electric utilities and factories, for example, often contributes to air quality problems in downwind neighboring states. Furthermore, some pollutants are emitted into the upper atmosphere, contributing to regional problems such as acid rain and global problems such as climate change. These interstate and global problems are particularly vexing for environmental governance because they create a spatial mismatch between problems and government jurisdictions, and state governments face conflicting incentives on whether they should devote efforts to address them. More generally, this spatial mismatch creates difficult political and policy challenges for state governments, addressing environmental problems on top of the problems that are solely internal to the state. For political scientists interested in understanding how states respond to these challenges, it also creates opportunities to develop and test theoretical frameworks to explain variation in policy performance across the country. The main sections of this chapter discuss current issues and research in addressing intrastate, interstate, and global problems, respectively.

STATE ENVIRONMENTAL POLICY AND INTRASTATE PROBLEMS

In addressing problems that are intrastate in nature, states must balance their environmental protection goals (be they strong or tepid) with other, sometimes competing policy priorities. Owing to diversity in political, economic, and social circumstances, states will balance these priorities differently. Advocates for a strong state role in environmental policy suggest that this is a strength of American federalism. Empowering states with authority and flexibility to manage their own problems, they argue, leads to policy innovation and democratically more legitimate outcomes. In addition, proponents suggest that it can lead to more economically efficient solutions than a one-size-fits-all policy imposed by the federal government. Skeptics counter that allowing states, rather than the federal government, to have a leading role can result in uneven environmental protection across the country. While some states will adopt sufficiently protective measures, they argue, others will not.

These contrasting viewpoints reflect an enduring debate in U.S. environmental policy regarding which level of government should have a lead role in managing problems. Through the 1960s, responsibility for environmental protection and, particularly, pollution control rested primarily with state (and local) governments. By 1970, however, a consensus had emerged that state governments had largely failed to address the most pressing problems. In response to growing citizen demand for more action, the federal government enacted major pieces of legislation such as the CAA and the CWA that significantly shifted the balance of power from the states to the federal government. These and other statutes often included national standards for emissions and pollution abatement technology, permitting requirements, reporting mandates, and other across-the-board obligations for affected industries. The federal programs largely preempted prior state efforts, curtailing a good deal of the autonomy and flexibility that states had previously enjoyed.

This "federalization" of environmental policy in the 1970s was by no means absolute, as the states retained a central role in policy implementation. Most major federal pollution control programs are designed under a model of regulatory federalism, in which responsibility is shared across levels of government through the principle of partial preemption. Under partial preemption, federal officials (usually the U.S. Environmental Protection Agency [EPA]) set national standards and establish the procedures by which these standards are to be enforced. Individual states are then invited or required (depending on the statute) to develop laws and administrative programs that are consistent with these standards as a condition for being authorized to enforce them within their borders. State standards must be at least as stringent as those of the federal government, but in most cases they can also exceed them. For states that fail to get or do not seek authorization, or what is often referred to as primacy, the EPA administers the program itself through one of its ten regional offices. States are free to rescind primacy at any time, and the EPA can also revoke it if the agency determines that a state is not appropriately carrying out federal mandates. According to the most recent estimate from the Environmental Council of the States, the states operate approximately 96 percent of delegable federal programs.[3]

Although the EPA is responsible for ensuring a base level of uniformity in performance across the country, states in practice have enormous discretion to determine how vigorously to enforce federal environmental statutes. One of the main reasons is that the EPA's oversight is extremely inconsistent, and as a result, states often fail to meet national goals and frequently neglect to take necessary enforcement actions. Empirical analysis of state inspections of regulated entities, for example, has shown that inspection rates vary across the states, with some states pursuing aggressive compliance monitoring and others less so.[4]

In addition, states can choose whether to adopt standards that exceed national standards, and whether they want to take on problems not covered by federal laws. Many states choose not to do so, and about half have in place specific restrictions on adopting measures that go beyond national standards.[5] But others do take such actions. Environmental policy scholars often point to California as a leader in this regard, particularly in how the state has addressed its severe air pollution problems. The example they use most often regards its emissions standards for motor vehicles. When Congress mandated new emissions standards for motor vehicles as part of the 1970 CAA, California already had stricter tailpipe emissions standards in place. For this reason, the state received a waiver from federal preemption, and it has been able to continually ratchet up its standards above those required by the federal government. Over the years, many states (and the federal government) have elected to formally adopt California's higher standards. California's efforts to address air pollution do not stop with motor vehicles. The state has also put in place ambient air quality standards for many pollutants that exceed the national standards, and has set standards for additional pollutants not covered by the federal law.

Another example of state policy leadership is Iowa's efforts to reduce nonpoint source water pollution. The federal CWA as written in 1972 primarily addressed water pollution from point sources such as industrial dischargers and municipal wastewater treatment facilities—that is, sources that discharge pollution directly into waterways. Water quality problems, however, are also caused by pollution carried through runoff from agriculture, forestry, mining, and other activities, as well as runoff from urban areas. Managing pollutants (e.g., sediment, fertilizers, pesticides, herbicides, oil, heavy metals) from nonpoint sources is difficult because of its diffuse nature. In Iowa, the problem stems mostly from agricultural activities, and for many decades the state has pursued a set of policies to reduce sedimentation and the use of chemicals through a combination of regulatory actions, voluntary initiatives, and educational efforts with much success, all of which go beyond the modest requirements of the CWA.[6]

While these examples illustrate the exemplary efforts that some states take to address their specific environmental problems, other states display reticence to take on their challenges. The issue of mountain top mining in parts of Appalachia provides a good example. Mountain top mining is a technique in surface mining in which the top layers of mountain rock are removed using explosives in order to expose coal seams from which coal is extracted. The rock and other material blown away in the process is disposed of in valley streams, burying headwaters and causing what many scientists and environmentalists believe is permanent damage to ecosystems. This practice is employed in parts of Kentucky, West Virginia, and Virginia, and despite years of protests from environmental advocates in these states and nationally, the states have maintained that the technique is a safe and efficient way to mine coal. The Hydraulic Fracturing and the States box discusses how states have addressed the environmental concerns associated with development of another major energy input: natural gas through the process of hydraulic fracturing.

HYDRAULIC FRACTURING AND THE STATES

Natural gas production through the process of hydraulic fracturing or "fracking" is one of the most important developments for U.S. energy markets and policy in decades. This technique for extracting natural gas from shale rock involves the injection of high-pressure water, with sand and various chemicals, a mile or more below the ground (hydraulic fracturing can also be used to extract oil). The pressure inside the well causes the shale to fissure, allowing the gas to release up through the well to the surface, where it is captured, stored, and ultimately shipped via pipelines to energy markets. Hydraulic fracturing has been used in some form in the United States for more than a half-century, but its use has expanded in recent years because of advances in technology that enable horizontal drilling. Shale gas is particularly plentiful in the Marcellus Shale, which runs through parts of several eastern states, including Maryland, New York, Ohio, Pennsylvania, and West Virginia. The influx of natural gas from the Marcellus Shale and other locations has had a large effect on energy markets. Over the four-year period from 2006 to 2010, the annual production of shale gas increased almost fivefold, and the low cost of natural gas has led to fuel-switching at many power plants, mostly resulting in the displacement of coal.

This "gas revolution" has been touted by the oil and gas industry and many political leaders (both Republicans and Democrats) for being domestic and "clean." Natural gas burned to generate electricity results in considerably less emissions of both conventional and toxic air pollutants when compared with coal, as well as about half of the carbon dioxide. Despite these benefits, many environmental advocates and local communities have raised concerns about the potential adverse impacts. The drilling process itself consumes enormous amounts of freshwater resources, and wastewater from the process must be treated, recycled, or safely disposed because it carries toxic pollutants such as mercury, arsenic, and cadmium, in addition to radioactive compounds. There are also myriad concerns about the potential pollution impacts, including the contamination of groundwater aquifers and drinking water wells, diminished local air quality, and the migration of gases and chemicals to the surface.

To date, regulation of hydraulic fracturing has mostly fallen to the states. (The U.S. Environmental Protection Agency did propose regulations on some aspects in April 2012.) Not surprisingly, the state response has been varied. In Pennsylvania, the use of hydraulic fracturing to extract shale gas from the Marcellus Shale has been actively promoted by the state. According to data from the Pennsylvania Department of Environmental Protection, in 2006 there were 81 active natural gas wells in the Marcellus Shale; in 2011 the number had grown to 8,176.[1] By contrast, Maryland and New York have each imposed temporary moratoriums, due mostly to concerns about potential adverse environmental impacts. And Vermont enacted a law on May 17, 2012, that banned the use of fracking altogether. (This is largely symbolic, given that there is not much shale gas in the state.)

In addition to these decisions either to allow or disallow the use of hydraulic fracturing, states have also developed rules regulating various aspects of shale gas operations, ranging from construction of well pads and drilling and casing a well to controlling air emissions to storing and disposing of wastewater. Perhaps the most contentious issue in state regulation has been the extent of disclosure required for the chemicals used in the process. Many of the chemicals used in hydraulic fracturing are hazardous, and they could create environmental and health problems if spilled or otherwise released. Many states have adopted rules requiring that shale gas operators disclose the chemicals (or additive components) used in fracking fluid to the relevant government agency (not necessarily to the public), although most do not require them to reveal the specific "recipe," which the oil and gas industry argues is a trade secret.

1. Pennsylvania Department of Environmental Protection, "PA DEP Oil and Gas Reporting Website—Statewide Data Downloads by Reporting Period," 2012, www.paoilandgasreporting.state.pa.us/publicreports/Modules/DataExports/DataExports.aspx.

Distinguishing the states in terms of policy leaders and laggards is part of a long-standing aim of scholars to understand the determinants of state environmental policy effort—that is, why do some states adopt stronger environmental protection measures than others? Among the challenges for scholars interested in answering this question is to develop measures that accurately depict a state's effort at a given moment in time, and in a way that is commensurate across states. Studies typically employ one of four basic empirical strategies for measuring state environmental protection efforts: (1) programmatic indices of environmental policies adopted; (2) the amount of government spending on environmental protection efforts; (3) the amount of private-sector pollution abatement expenditures, which is viewed as a proxy for regulatory stringency; and (4) counts of regulatory enforcement actions. Although these measures are often implicitly treated as interchangeable, they in fact measure different aspects of state environmental policy.[7]

A couple of decades of research on this question have produced several explanations. First, scholars have noted that state effort is often directly correlated with the severity of the problems in the state. This is often referred to in the literature as policy matching, and it was evident in the examples discussed above regarding California and air pollution and Iowa and water pollution. In several broader studies of this phenomenon, scholars have found policy matching in the areas of toxic releases, hazardous waste sites, groundwater contamination, and air and water pollution.[8]

A house at night with the hydraulic fracturing ("fracking") Hawley drill site behind it in Forest Lake, Pennsylvania. The recent expansion of this method of extracting natural gas from shale rock has raised environmental concerns, and much of its regulation has been left up to the states.

SOURCE: © Amy Sussman/Corbis.

Second, research also suggests an important role for state fiscal and administrative capacity. Several studies of state environmental policy have found that states with the financial resources to produce effective policy often have stronger environmental programs. Institutional capacity has also been found to be an important determinant. State legislatures vary significantly in their ability to effectively make and oversee policy, and several studies have found that states with professional legislatures tend to produce stronger environmental policies.[9] Policy implementation in the states rests with administrative agencies, and these too vary in their ability to accomplish environmental protection goals. Past research has shown that organizational effectiveness in environmental policy implementation is associated with greater administrative budgets and personnel resources.[10]

A third important set of determinants are state political conditions. Scholars have argued that an environmentally leaning citizenry will generate pressure (electoral or otherwise) on state governments to put in place strong environmental programs. Environmental ideology in the state is typically measured using either survey data on public attitudes or proxy measures such as general political ideology or congressional voting scores on environmental issues. Several studies have found that states with "pro-environment" citizens tend to have stronger environmental programs.[11] Other research has found that state environmental policy is related to the preferences of organized interests in the states, and specifically that policy responds to the strength of state environmental and manufacturing interests.[12]

Last, scholars have argued that political control of state government tends to be correlated with state policy effort. The typical assumption is that states with state capitals under Democratic control (governor and state legislatures) are more likely to favor strong environmental protection efforts, while those under Republican control prioritize economic growth. There is some empirical evidence supporting this conclusion.[13]

STATE ENVIRONMENTAL POLICY AND INTERSTATE PROBLEMS

Interstate pollution externalities create immense challenges for environmental governance. As a case in point, consider the Mississippi River. The headwaters of the Mississippi River are located in northern Minnesota, and the 2,550-mile river, the longest in North America, winds its way along ten states before entering into the Gulf of Mexico in Louisiana. This single river system drains about 40 percent of the United States, and with it all of the pollution from upstream agriculture, industrial sources, and human sewage. Each year this pollution contributes to a large hypoxic area or "dead zone" in the Gulf of Mexico. This dead zone, which in some years has been as large as 8,000 square miles, results from the depletion of oxygen levels to a point insufficient to support marine life due to the algal blooms created by the overload of nutrients such as nitrogen and phosphorous. The effect of the dead zone on the commercial seafood industry in Louisiana and Texas is substantial.

Who bears responsibility for this problem? And, more important, what policy instruments can be put in place to address it? The fundamental challenge is that upstream states have few incentives to limit pollution from sources within their borders. While state governments in Illinois, Missouri, and other upstream agricultural states could impose requirements that farmers limit their use of fertilizers, for example, this would impose burdens on local farmers, with most of the benefits enjoyed by downstream states (this is another reason why Iowa's efforts are exemplary). Because all states have similar incentives, the causes of the dead zone are left largely unaddressed.

This type of problem reflects a classic "tragedy of the commons,"[14] and is just one of many examples of interstate environmental concerns that exist in the United States.

Another example is interstate air pollution, which has a long history of creating disputes between states. Since at least the beginning of the twentieth century, neighboring states have blamed each other for causing their air quality problems. In one case, Georgia blamed pollution from copper smelters in neighboring Tennessee for despoiling its forests and orchards, and for creating health problems for residents in bordering counties in Georgia. The Supreme Court agreed in the 1907 case, *Georgia v. Tennessee Copper Co.*[15] In recent years, there have been several state-to-state disputes regarding air pollution. In 2006, for example, New Jersey sued the EPA, claiming that the agency had failed to control the emissions from a coal-fired power plant located just across the Delaware River in Pennsylvania. New Jersey argued that the emissions from this coal plant were making it difficult for the state to meet ambient air quality standards required by the CAA. Five years later, the EPA granted a petition from the New Jersey Department of Environmental Protection to require that the Pennsylvania plant significantly reduce these emissions.[16]

Management of these types of problems often requires intervention of the federal government. A recent example is a regulation EPA issued in July 2011 to limit power plant emissions that cross state lines, contributing to air quality problems in other states such as ozone and fine particulate pollution. The new rule, known as the Cross-State Rule, will require (pending the outcome of legal objections from some affected states) that midwestern and eastern states limit power plant emissions of sulfur dioxide (SO_2) and nitrogen oxides (NO_x) to help downwind states achieve compliance with national ambient air quality standards.

Absent federal intervention, states can also coordinate their policies in an effort to achieve a common goal. This type of policy coordination, however, is often challenging to sustain, given differences in state policy preferences, turnover in political leadership, competing economic interests, and variation in administrative capacity. As is discussed later in the chapter, a good example of the challenge in sustaining multistate policy coordination can be seen in recent efforts to reduce greenhouse gas emissions. Another example detailed in the Asian Carp and the Great Lakes States box regards the efforts of several states to address the potential Asian carp problem in the Great Lakes.

One approach to coordinating policy on shared problems is to create formal bistate or multistate compacts (see Chapter 4, Interstate Interactions). Many states have advocated the use of compacts as a strategy for forestalling further centralization of authority at the national level.[17] Compacts have been adopted by states to address various types of environmental and natural resource policy problems, with the most frequent use being to set up rules for the allocation of water from rivers. The Colorado River Compact, for example, has been in place since 1922 and coordinates the allocation of water from the Colorado River among the seven participating states (Arizona, California, Colorado, Nevada, New Mexico, Utah, and Wyoming).

For social scientists, a key question is whether these types of interstate externalities are the result of deliberate actions of state governments. Strategic state governments have incentives to promote these externalities, since they can internalize the benefits of economic activity (i.e., employment, tax revenue) while simultaneously exporting any associated environmental and health costs to other states (or countries for those states bordering Canada or Mexico). This type of behavior is often referred to as "environmental free riding."

Recent empirical work has tested for environmental free riding among the U.S. states in a couple of ways. First, scholars have analyzed patterns of pollution at interstate borders to determine if pollution levels in border areas are higher than in nonborder areas. Higher pollution levels may suggest that states are deliberately exporting pollution to neighboring states. Although some studies have found elevated pollution levels at borders, other work has found little such evidence.[18] A second stream of research has sought to directly investigate the role of government action, particularly regulatory enforcement. Scholars have focused on enforcement because of the enormous discretion that states have in the ways in which they pursue enforcement of major federal pollution controls laws (as discussed in the previous section). Empirical work, however, has found little evidence of states slacking off on their enforcement efforts at regulated facilities located near interstate borders, although it has identified weaker regulatory enforcement directed at facilities located near international borders with Canada and Mexico.[19]

The environmental free riding literature remains unsettled. Although there is good evidence of elevated pollution levels near interstate borders, scholars have yet to pin down the state actions that cause it. While several studies would seem to rule out regulatory enforcement, there are other policy instruments that state regulators could use to promote pollution spillovers, particularly permitting and siting policy. Of course, it also possible that higher pollution at interstate borders is unrelated to state government behavior altogether. Interstate borders are often located along natural features, such as major rivers, which promote population centers, commerce, and industrial agglomeration, and the high pollution levels observed may just be a consequence of these activities.

Environmental free riding is just one of the interstate-related concerns that emerge when responsibility for managing environmental problems rests with the states. Another problem that has received considerable attention from scholars stems from the tendency of some state

ASIAN CARP AND THE GREAT LAKES STATES

Asian carp are nonnative, invasive species of fish that scientists believe may significantly harm the Great Lakes ecosystem. Several species of Asian carp were brought into the United States in the 1970s by the aquaculture industry to help clean up algae-filled ponds on commercial fish farms. Two species—the bighead carp and the silver carp—escaped due to accidental releases and flooding of the Mississippi River, and they have been migrating northward since. Today, Asian carp are prominent in the Mississippi and Illinois River systems, and according to some estimates, they comprise more than 95 percent of the biomass in these rivers.[1] Asian carp species are especially invasive because they are large fish with voracious appetites, they reproduce quickly, they have no natural predators, and they are of little value as either commercial or sports fish. Asian carp have yet to enter the Great Lakes, but because the Chicago Sanitary and Ship Canal connects the Mississippi River to Lake Michigan through the Illinois River and the Des Plaines River, there is a ready-made pathway for the species to enter the Great Lakes ecosystem.

The most important concern about Asian carp entering the Great Lakes is the likely ecological impact. Asian carp would compete with fish native to the Great Lakes, with repercussions up the food chain, ultimately affecting commercial species such as lake trout and walleye. The Great Lakes are also home to many federal and state endangered species, which could be affected by an influx of Asian carp. Last, the silver carp is known for jumping out of the water at the sound of boat motors, which can cause physical harm to people and property, threatening recreation and tourism in Great Lakes states.

Scientists and policymakers have long been aware of the threats posed by Asian carp to the Great Lakes, and several efforts have been made over the past decade to control their migration. In 2002 the U.S. Army Corps of Engineers constructed a multimillion-dollar electric fence system in the Chicago Sanitary and Ship Canal to prevent Asian carp from traveling into Lake Michigan. The fence deters but does not kill the fish. When the electric fence was undergoing maintenance in December 2009, the state of Illinois treated a stretch of the shipping channel near Lockport, Illinois, with a toxic chemical to kill the fish, but later DNA tests indicate that the species made it above the barrier.[2]

Debates persist about whether these types of approaches can keep the Asian carp species out of the Great Lakes in the long term, and relations between the states have deteriorated significantly over the issue. Five states—Michigan, Minnesota, Ohio, Pennsylvania, and Wisconsin—have taken legal action against the Chicago Sanitary District, the entity that manages the shipping channel, as well as the U.S. Army Corps of Engineers. On three occasions, these states have filed a petition with the U.S. Supreme Court for an injunction to force them to take more aggressive action to contain the migration of Asian carp. The Supreme Court has refused each of these petitions, most recently in February 2012. Still pending is a lawsuit from these states that seeks to shut down the locks that allow water to flow between the Mississippi River and the Great Lakes. The city of Chicago and the U.S. Army Corps of Engineers are reluctant to take this step because the lock system is the primary means used to manage flooding. The ultimate goal for Michigan and the other states is to completely separate the Mississippi River and the Great Lakes, which would largely eliminate the Asian carp risk.[3] Doing so, however, would be an immense and very expensive engineering project, and might include re-reversing the flow of the Chicago River. The dispute is unlikely to be settled any time soon, which illustrates the difficulty that states have coming to agreement on a problem threatening a common resource such as the Great Lakes.

1. Asian Carp Regional Coordinating Committee, "AsianCarp—The Problem," 2012, www.asiancarp.us/documents/AsianCarp-TheProblem.pdf.
2. Michigan Department of Natural Resources, "DNR—Asian Carp Fact Sheet," 2012, www.michigan.gov/dnr/0,4570,7-153-10364_52261_54896-232231-,00.html.
3. Codi Yeager, "Third Time's Not a Charm: U.S. Supreme Court again Denies Request to Stop Asian Carp," *Circle of Blue*, February 29, 2012.

governments to trade environmental protection for economic development. The use of lax environmental standards as an instrument to attract mobile capital has long raised concerns about downward regulatory competition, potentially leading to an environmental "race to the bottom." The central idea of the race to the bottom theory is that, confronted with interstate competition for mobile capital, states have incentives to adopt lenient environmental standards in an effort to attract polluting industries. These incentives may lead states to reduce their standards to gain a comparative advantage over other states. If all states behave similarly, the result will be an overall lowering of standards across the country to the level of the least stringent state. The race to the bottom argument is an example of the well-known "prisoner's dilemma" often cited in game theory, where self-interested behavior leads to outcomes inferior to those that are arrived at by cooperation.

There are several alternative notions of state regulatory competition that are important to recognize as well. First, some scholars have argued that regulatory competition is likely to generate stronger (not weaker) environmental standards, often pointing to the case of automobile emissions standards discussed previously, in which both the federal government and many state governments have frequently adopted California's more stringent standards. This phenomenon has been called the "California effect," or more generally, a regulatory "race to the top." An alternative argument for upward regulatory competition is that some states may want to create a climate that deters pollution-intensive industries. With this objective in mind, state regulators may adjust their own environmental regulatory effort to meet or exceed that of other states. Second, it is possible that state policy is driven only by the types of intrastate factors discussed in the last section, and not by economic competition with other states. According to this argument, there is neither downward nor upward regulatory pressure from other states.

Concerns about the impact of interstate economic competition on environmental regulatory stringency reflect a more general concern that many elected officials view economic growth and environmental protection as competing policy objectives. This tension is often apparent in national politics, but also figures prominently in state politics. Just days after taking office in January 2011, the newly elected Republican governor of New Mexico, Susana Martinez, reversed a state regulation that was about to take effect that would have required annual cuts in greenhouse gas emissions of 3 percent through a cap-and-trade regime.[20] In addition to doing away with the regulation, Governor Martinez dismissed the members of the Environmental Improvement Board that had imposed the rule a month prior, arguing,

> New Mexico has recently suffered from an anti-business environment exacerbated by policies which discourage economic development and result in businesses setting up shop across state lines. . . . Unfortunately, the majority of EIB members have made it clear that they are more interested in advancing political ideology than implementing common-sense policies that balance economic growth with responsible stewardship in New Mexico.[21]

In a similar type of decision, the Republican governor of Maine, Paul LePage, announced in his first month in office a plan to cut environmental regulations in the state. In unveiling the plan in January 2011, Governor LePage provided the following justification: "Maine's working families and small businesses are endangered. It is time we start defending the interests of those who want to work and invest in Maine with the same vigor that we defend tree frogs and Canadian lynx."[22]

Scholars have studied states' environmental regulatory behavior for evidence of the type of downward movement of environmental stringency suggested by the race to the bottom theory. The most direct implication of the theory is that states make decisions about their own environmental stringency in light of the decisions of economic competitor states. Two specific, testable propositions directly follow from this implication. First, a state's environmental regulatory behavior should respond to that of competitors; or, in other words, there should be strategic interaction in state regulatory practices. Second, the pattern of strategic interaction should be one in which states respond to competitor states' regulatory behavior only when this behavior puts them at a disadvantage for attracting economic investment. In other words, not only should states respond to each other, but the response should be asymmetric such that states with more stringent regulation than their neighbors should then decrease the stringency of their own regulations.[23]

The most recent research on this subject has come to mixed conclusions. A couple of studies using data on private-sector pollution abatement costs as measures of state regulatory stringency have found that the costs incurred by industry in a given state are positively associated with these costs in economic competitor states. These studies further find that there is an asymmetric pattern to this state responsiveness, but not in a way reflective of a race to the bottom. Rather, states react to changes in abatement costs in competitor states that have initially more stringent environmental policy, but not to states with initially less stringent environmental policy. This pattern of strategic interaction is more in line with a regulatory race to the top.[24]

Additional empirical tests of the race to the bottom argument have examined measures of state regulatory enforcement. One study of surface mining regulation found that states do respond to neighboring states' enforcement behavior, and that the pattern of the responsiveness is consistent with a race to the bottom.[25] In a separate study of state enforcement of the CAA, the CWA, and the Resource Conservation and Recovery Act, there was strong evidence of strategic interaction among the states, but not of the asymmetric pattern suggestive of only downward regulatory pressure. Instead, states were found to respond to other states' enforcement efforts, both when they were more stringent and more lax than their own.[26]

STATE ENVIRONMENTAL POLICY AND INTERNATIONAL PROBLEMS

Environmental problems in the states, of course, also may transcend not just state borders, but international ones. States that border Canada and Mexico, for example, confront additional challenges. Managing shared resources such as the Great Lakes or the Rio Grande River require cooperation, and activities are often coordinated through formal bilateral institutions at the national level, often with state governmental participation. In the case of the Great Lakes, the United States and Canada created the International Joint Commission as part of the Boundary Waters

Treaty of 1909, and collaborative efforts (not always successful) to improve the water quality of the Great Lakes have continued since. In the case of the Rio Grande, there are a variety of treaty- and nontreaty-based institutions in place to organize management of segments of the Rio Grande River that make up the U.S.-Mexico border, as well as segments in each country separately.

In addition to these bilateral problems, states are also engaged with environmental problems that are global in scope. One of the most notable developments in state environmental policy and politics over the past decade has been the adoption of policies to address the quintessential global problem: climate change. Scholars have devoted a lot of attention to states' policy engagement with climate change, particularly in light of what most commentators agree is reluctance by the federal government to seriously take on this issue. The states have been at the forefront in many regards, adopting policies that either directly or indirectly reduce the greenhouse gas emissions that scientists believe are causing climate change.

Why would states choose to take on a problem that is global in scope? It is an intriguing question, given that any effort by a single state, even a large one such as California or Texas, would make only a small dent in worldwide greenhouse gas emissions. Scholars have provided several different explanations. First, many states view such policy as contributing to their economic development goals. This is especially true of renewable energy mandates, which not only shift electricity generation away from fossil fuels, but also may spur investment in "home-grown" businesses. Second, some states believe that they have already begun to experience the adverse effects of climate change, such as sea level rise, severe storms, and prolonged droughts. Third, some states adopt policies to project themselves as policy innovators, often with an objective to advance national policy and/or to encourage other states to join their efforts. Last, in many states, policy has been pushed by organized interest groups and advocacy coalitions and/or citizens through direct democracy or litigation.[27]

State policies to address climate change range considerably. About half the states have established some sort of target for reducing their level of greenhouse gas emissions, and many of them have developed specific climate action plans to coordinate state policy. These action plans vary considerably in their aspirations and consist of different mixes of policies to achieve their goals, including energy efficiency initiatives, renewable energy mandates (more on these below), and promotion of alternative fuel vehicles. Of the states with climate action plans, California is the only one that has set binding limits on future greenhouse gas emissions.

Renewable portfolio standards (RPSs) are a policy tool that has proven to be especially popular. An RPS is a mandate that electricity providers obtain some minimum amount of their power from renewable energy sources (e.g., wind, solar) by a particular date. As of July 2012, thirty-one states had adopted a binding RPS requirement for their state (seven other states have adopted voluntary goals), and about three-fourths have done so in the past decade. In most cases, RPSs have been put in place through legislation, but in Arizona and New York they were put in place administratively, and in Colorado, Missouri, and Washington through ballot initiatives. State RPSs range in the amount of renewable energy they require, as well as in their date of expected achievement. In general, RPSs aim for about 10 to 20 percent of their electricity to come from renewable technologies in about fifteen to twenty years in the future, although some states set more ambitious goals. Hawaii's RPS requires 40 percent of its electricity to come from renewable sources by 2030; California for 33 percent by 2020; Connecticut for 27 percent by 2020; and Illinois, Minnesota, Nevada, Ohio, Oregon, and West Virginia for 25 percent by 2025.[28] In addition, many state RPSs reward in-state generation of renewable energy to encourage development of these technologies in their states, and elected officials often justify RPSs for their economic benefits as much as for their environmental benefits.

Studies of the determinants of policy adoption of RPSs have come to mixed results. Several scholars have identified a strong role for intrastate factors such as renewable energy potential, citizen and elite political ideology, and interest group strength, while others have found policy diffusion to be an influential factor, with states emulating the policies of geographic neighbors.[29]

Mandates for renewable energy serve to address climate change by replacing fossil fuels in electricity generation, thereby reducing greenhouse gas emissions. One approach pursued by some states (and sometimes in partnership with some Canadian provinces) to more directly limit greenhouse gas emissions is to coordinate efforts through regional initiatives. The specifics of each differ, but the Regional Greenhouse Gas Initiative (RGGI), the Western Climate Initiative (WCI), and the Midwestern Greenhouse Gas Reduction Accord (MGGRA) were each originally envisioned as a cap-and-trade regime to reduce regional emissions in an economically efficient way.

The RGGI had ten founding members: Connecticut, Delaware, Maine, Maryland, Massachusetts, New Hampshire, New Jersey, New York, Rhode Island, and Vermont. The program establishes a cap on carbon dioxide emissions from large power plants at 2009 levels through 2014, and then reduces the cap by 2.5 percent annually through 2019. Recent analyses of the first three years of the program have found that average annual carbon dioxide emissions declined by 33 percent overall, and by an average of 23 percent in each participating state, compared with emission levels before the start of the program. Moreover,

Massachusetts governor-elect Deval Patrick, left, reiterated his commitment to the regional greenhouse gas initiative (RGGI), an interstate cooperative effort to reduce greenhouse gas emissions, on Saturday, December 16, 2006, at a Climate Change: Local Solutions to a Global Crisis forum sponsored by U.S. representative Marty Meehan, center, at the University of Massachusetts Lowell. Cooperative initiatives are one way states attempt to address global issues.

SOURCE: AP Photo/Lisa Poole.

the auctions for carbon allowances have generated about $1 billion in revenue for the states, much of which has been reinvested in energy efficiency and other programs to reduce greenhouse gas emissions.[30]

The other two regional climate initiatives are not as far along in development, and each faces considerable threats of not moving forward as designed. Seven states are part of the WCI in some capacity: Arizona, California, Montana, New Mexico, Oregon, Utah, and Washington (as well as four Canadian provinces). The WCI aims for economy-wide emissions reductions, sets a cap of emissions at 15 percent below 2005 levels by the year 2020, and applies to greenhouse gases other than just carbon dioxide. Allowance trading under the WCI was originally scheduled to begin in January 2012, but its start has been delayed significantly. The MGGRA was agreed to by six midwestern states—Illinois, Iowa, Kansas, Michigan, Minnesota, and Wisconsin (and one Canadian province)—but this regional initiative has not advanced very far since its conception.

Each of these regional climate initiatives was established under specific economic and political circumstances, which have changed in important ways since. First, each initiative was envisaged before the fiscal crisis and economic downturn that began in late 2007. Second, the initiatives were put in place under gubernatorial administrations that were more interested in taking action on the climate issue. Third, there has been a softening of public opinion on climate change, suggesting less citizen demand for a strong policy response.

As a result of these, and perhaps other, factors, there has been considerable retrenchment in each of the three regional climate initiatives. In May 2011, for example, Republican governor Chris Christie withdrew his state of New Jersey from the RGGI, arguing that the initiative "does nothing more than tax electricity, tax our citizens, tax our businesses, with no discernible or measurable impact upon our environment."[31] The pullback from the WCI and the MGGRA has been even more substantial. California is the only remaining U.S. state actively participating in the WCI, with the rest either formally withdrawing in the past couple of years or delaying participation. And the six states that created the MGGRA are no longer pursuing coordinated action at all. In general, the states have been lauded by many environmental policy advocates for their coordinated pursuit of policies to address climate change. While much of this credit is well-deserved, the fragility of these arrangements highlights the difficulty of sustaining policy coordination across the states.

CONCLUSION

States are certain to remain a key player in U.S. environmental policy. Whether in adopting strategies to address the particular problems that plague them, working with other states to resolve interstate issues, or contributing to the resolution of international- and global-scale problems, the states have an important role in current environmental protection efforts. But, as has been highlighted throughout this chapter, states' responses to environmental problems vary, and environmental protection is just one policy priority that they may pursue. Competing priorities, particularly job creation and economic development, often result in reluctance to impose new burdens on industry, and can create incentives for states to free ride on neighboring states or to pursue lax environmental policy more generally. These incentives, coupled with other factors such as conservative state political ideology and political cultures that oppose government intervention in the economy, often translate to unwillingness among some states to devote significant attention and resources to environmental problems. As a result, performance in policy adoption and implementation is uneven across the country, and this is unlikely to change any time soon.

NOTES

1. United States Environmental Protection Agency, *Green Book,* 2012, www.epa.gov/oaqps001/greenbk.

2. United States Environmental Protection Agency, *Iowa Water Assessment Data for 2010,* 2012, http://ofmpub.epa.gov/waters10/attains_state.report_control?p_state=IA&p_cycle=2010&p_report_type=A.

3. Environmental Council of the States, August 2010 Green Report, 2010, www.ecos.org/files/4157_file_August_2010_Green_Report.pdf.

4. David M. Konisky and Neal D. Woods, "Measuring State Environmental Policy," *Review of Policy Research* 29 (2012): 544–569.

5. Environmental Law Institute, *Federal Regulations and State Flexibility in Environmental Standard Setting* (Washington, DC: Environmental Law Institute, 1996).

6. DeWitt John, *Civic Environmentalism: Alternatives to Regulation in States and Communities* (Washington, DC: CQ Press, 1994); and William R. Lowry, *The Dimensions of Federalism: State Governments and Pollution Control Policies* (Durham, NC: Duke University Press, 1992).

7. Konisky and Woods, "Measuring State Environmental Policy."

8. Alka Sapat, "Devolution and Innovation: The Adoption of State Environmental Policy Innovations by Administrative Agencies," *Public Administration Review* 64 (2004): 141–151; Dorothy Daley and James C. Garand, "Horizontal Diffusion, Vertical Diffusion, and Internal Pressure in State Environmental Policymaking, 1989–1998," *American Politics Research* 37 (2005): 615–644; Lowry, *The Dimensions of Federalism.*

9. Scott P. Hays, Michael Esler, and Carol F. Hays, "Environmental Commitment among the States: Integrating Alternative Approaches to State Environmental Policy," *Publius: The Journal of Federalism* 26 (1996): 41–58; Neal D. Woods, "The Policy Consequences of Political Corruption: Evidence from State Environmental Programs," *Social Science Quarterly* 89 (2008): 258–271.

10. Sapat, "Devolution and Innovation"; James P. Lester, "Federalism and State Environmental Policy," in *Environmental Politics and Policy: Theories and Evidence,* ed. James P. Lester (Durham, NC: Duke University Press, 1995).

11. Daley and Garand, "Horizontal Diffusion, Vertical Diffusion, and Internal Pressure in State Environmental Policymaking"; Hays et al., "Environmental Commitment among the States"; Woods, "The Policy Consequences of Political Corruption."

12. A. Hunter Bacot and Roy A. Dawes, "State Expenditures and Policy Outcomes in Environmental Program Management," *Policy Studies Journal* 25 (1997): 355–370; Evan J. Ringquist, *Environmental Protection at the State Level* (Armonk, NY: M. E. Sharpe, 1993).

13. David M. Konisky, "Regulatory Competition and Environmental Enforcement: Is There a Race to the Bottom?" *American Journal of Political Science* 51 (2007): 853–872; B. Dan Wood, "Modeling Federal Implementation as a System: The Clean Air Case," *American Journal of Political Science* 36 (1992): 40–67.

14. Garrett Hardin, "The Tragedy of the Commons," *Science* 162 (1968): 1243–1248.

15. *Georgia v. Tennessee Copper Co.,* 206 U.S. 230 (1907).

16. Angela Delli Santi, "State Reveals Plan to Sue EPA over Pollution from Pa. Plant," Associated Press, December 8, 2006; Aliza Applebaum, "EPA to Require Coal Plant to Cut Emissions Affecting Air Quality in Warren, Morris, Hunterdon, Sussex," *Star-Ledger,* March 31, 2011.

17. Ann Bowman and Neal D. Woods, "Strength in Numbers: Why States Join Interstate Compacts," *State Politics and Policy Quarterly* 7 (2007): 347–369.

18. Wayne B. Gray and Ronald J. Shadbegian, "'Optimal' Pollution Abatement—Whose Benefits Matter, and How Much?" *Journal of Environmental Economics and Management* 47 (2004): 510–534; Wayne B. Gray and Ronald J. Shadbegian, "The Environmental Performance of Polluting Plants: A Spatial Analysis," *Journal of Regional Science* 47 (2007): 63–84; Eric Helland and Andrew B. Whitford, "Pollution Incidence and Political Jurisdiction: Evidence from TRI," *Journal of Environmental Economics and Management* 46 (2003): 403–424; Hilary Sigman, "Transboundary Spillovers and Decentralization of Environmental Policies," *Journal of Environmental Economics and Management* 50 (2005): 82–101.

19. Gray and Shadbegian, "'Optimal' Pollution Abatement"; David M. Konisky and Neal D. Woods, "Exporting Air Pollution? Regulatory Enforcement and Environmental Free Riding in the United States," *Political Research Quarterly* 63 (2010): 771–782.

20. Felicity Barringer, "2 Environment Rules Halted in New Mexico," *New York Times,* January 6, 2011.

21. State of New Mexico, Office of Governor, "Governor Martinez Terminates Environmental Improvement Board Members," January 4, 2011.

22. Leslie Kaufman, "G.O.P. Push in States to Deregulate Environment," *New York Times,* April 15, 2011.

23. Konisky, "Regulatory Competition and Environmental Enforcement."

24. Per G. Fredriksson and Daniel L. Millimet, "Strategic Interaction and the Determinants of Environmental Policy across U.S. States," *Journal of Urban Economics* 51 (2002): 101–122; Arik Levinson, "Environmental Regulatory Competition: A Status Report and Some New Evidence," *National Tax Journal* 56 (2003): 91–106.

25. Neal D. Woods, "Interstate Competition and Environmental Regulation: A Test of the Race to the Bottom Thesis," *Social Science Quarterly* 87 (2006): 174–189.

26. Konisky, "Regulatory Competition and Environmental Enforcement."

27. Barry G. Rabe, *Statehouse and Greenhouse: The Emerging Politics of American Climate Change Policy* (Washington, DC: Brookings, 2004); Barry G. Rabe, "States on Steroids: The Intergovernmental Odyssey of American Climate Change Policy," *Review of Policy Research* 25 (2008): 105–128.

28. Center for Climate and Energy Solutions, U.S. Climate Policy Map, 2012, www.c2es.org/what_s_being_done/in_the_states/state_action_maps.cfm.

29. Sanya Carley and Chris J. Miller, "Regulatory Stringency and Policy Drivers: A Reassessment of Renewable Portfolio Standards," *Policy Studies Journal* 40 (2012): 730–756; Thomas P. Lyon and Haitao Yin, "Why Do States Adopt Renewable Portfolio Standards? An Empirical Investigation," *The Energy Journal* 31 (2010): 133–157; Daniel C. Matisoff, "The Adoption of State Climate Change Policies and Renewable Portfolio Standards: Regional Diffusion or Internal Determinants?" *Review of Policy Research* 25 (2008): 527–546; Jess Chandler, "Trendy Solutions: Why Do States Adopt Sustainable Energy Portfolio Standards?" *Energy Policy* 37 (2009): 3274–3281.

30. Regional Greenhouse Gas Initiative, Inc., "Investment of Proceeds from RGGI CO_2 Allowances," February 2012; Regional Greenhouse Gas Initiative, Inc., "97% of RGGI Units Meet First Compliance Report Obligations," June 4, 2012.

31. Mireya Navarro, "Christie Pulls New Jersey from 10-State Climate Initiative," *New York Times,* May 26, 2011.

SUGGESTED READING

Daley, Dorothy, and James C. Garand. "Horizontal Diffusion, Vertical Diffusion, and Internal Pressure in State Environmental Policymaking, 1989–1998." *American Politics Research* 37 (2005): 615–644.

Hays, Scott P., Michael Esler, and Carol F. Hays. "Environmental Commitment among the States: Integrating Alternative Approaches to State Environmental Policy." *Publius: The Journal of Federalism* 26 (1996): 41–58.

Konisky, David M., and Neal D. Woods. "Measuring State Environmental Policy." *Review of Policy Research* 29 (2012): 544–569.

Koontz, Tomas M. *Federalism in the Forest: National versus State Natural Resource Policy* (Washington, DC: Georgetown University Press, 2002).

Lowry, William R. *The Dimensions of Federalism: State Governments and Pollution Control Policies* (Durham, NC: Duke University Press, 1992).

Rabe, Barry G. *Statehouse and Greenhouse: The Emerging Politics of American Climate Change Policy* (Washington, DC: Brookings, 2004).

Rechtschaffen, Clifford, and David L. Markell. *Reinventing Environmental Enforcement and the State/Federal Relationship.* Washington, DC: Environmental Law Institute, 2003.

Ringquist, Evan J. *Environmental Protection at the State Level* (Armonk, NY: M. E. Sharpe, 1993).

Scheberle, Denise. *Federalism and Environmental Policy: Trust and the Politics of Implementation* (Washington, DC: Georgetown University Press, 1997).

Vig, Norman, and Michael Kraft. *Environmental Policy: New Directions for the 21st Century.* Washington, DC: CQ Press, 2013.

Chapter 31

Health Care

Laura Katz Olson

Both public health and individual health-related services are foremost state obligations. Today, health spending averages between 25 percent and 32 percent of total state and local budgets, largely in the realm of personal services. Medicaid and the Children's Health Insurance Program (CHIP) represent the lion's share of the latter, but states also may provide medical coverage for persons who lack health insurance, persons with developmental disabilities or psychiatric disorders, and state and local employees, as well as funds for government-run hospitals, nursing homes, and clinics. The health care sector is simultaneously vital to state economies, representing a significant portion of their business activities, jobs, and tax revenues.

The goal of this chapter is to present the extensive array of state health obligations, and briefly assess how well they are fulfilled. It begins with a broad discussion of public health, next highlighting two specific areas of concern: tobacco and substance abuse policies. The chapter then turns to an examination of Medicaid, delineating its main features, climbing costs, various means of coping with the consequent budgetary pressures, and other dynamics of the program. The last part of the chapter examines the interplay between state concerns and the 2010 federal health care reform bill.

PUBLIC HEALTH

Together with their localities, states have a significant and expansive role in public health but only limited resources with which to carry out this role. At the same time, local entities, along with community-based groups, depend on grants from the state to discharge their share of health-related obligations. Critically, states with the most pervasive health needs tend to have the least ability to pay for them.

In the main, states are expected to maintain or improve the general health of their residents. Among their numerous responsibilities (generally provided through their public health departments) are the development, implementation, and evaluation of specific policies and programs; enforcement of public health laws; and dissemination of information about community health issues. For instance, states serve their residents through special hotlines and link them to available medical and related services (such as legal aid; child, spousal, or elder abuse assistance; organ donations; and crime victim supports).

States may also provide vaccinations directly to residents or make them available to local governments or school systems, screen or test for selected conditions (e.g., tuberculosis, sexually transmitted diseases, breast cancer), offer help for certain disorders (e.g., autism, diabetes, AIDS, cystic fibrosis), and develop best practice guidelines for treatments.

As discussed below, to varying extents states enact antismoking and antidrug policies. Obesity, which has more than doubled in the past fifteen years, also has become a focus of concern: in 2012, slightly more than one-third of the American population (seventy-eight million adults and thirteen million children) were considered obese, a condition that can engender severe and costly maladies, in particular asthma, diabetes, coronary and circulatory disorders, and strokes. Accordingly, many states and localities have initiated anti-obesity campaigns, especially for children, and other types of measures to prevent and combat the problem. These include weight assessment, counseling, nutrition, and educational programs, often through Medicaid or with other federal assistance.

Another essential state health obligation is to collect health data on vital events, problematic situations, and the availability of certain services. These duties consist of recording births, deaths, infant mortality, and the incidence of specific illnesses (e.g., cancer, lead poisoning, diabetes, sexually transmitted diseases) as well as surveying and reporting on the prevalence of risky behaviors.

State officials correspondingly review the number and type of health facilities and providers in their jurisdictions. Through their chief medical examiner's office, states even investigate deaths of a suspicious, unusual, or unnatural nature.

Just as important, public health departments monitor toxic substances and contaminated foods, prepare bioterrorism readiness plans, and are the first lines of defense against the outbreak and spread of infections and contagious diseases. They are responsible for addressing public health emergencies, including conducting laboratory tests, documenting cases, collaborating with national health officials to educate and reach out to the public, and curtailing the extent of destruction. As a recent case in point, in coordination with the U.S. Centers for Disease Control and Prevention (CDC), Colorado's Department of Public Health led the way in dealing with the 2011 multistate outbreak of listeriosis, a bacterial infection, linked to cantaloupes grown within its jurisdiction.

Likewise, states are obliged to license and regulate restaurants, food service operators, other health-related businesses (e.g., body piercing salons, swimming pools, tanning facilities) and enterprises producing hazardous substances (e.g., biomedical waste, radioactive materials). In some states—for instance, Utah and Virginia—manufacturers, suppliers, and importers of bedding, upholstered furniture, and allied firms are licensed and inspected to promote hygienically clean products and protect against allergies. States evaluate other potentially dangerous conditions and mishaps as well, such as accidents in the workplace.

A man receives a flu shot as he sits on his scooter during a drive-thru flu shot clinic October 2, 2009, in Napa, California. The county health department held eight drive-thru shot clinics where seasonal flu shots were given free to anyone who attended in an effort to vaccinate as many people as possible before the start of the flu season.

SOURCE: Photo by Justin Sullivan/Getty Images.

They similarly oversee medical facilities, including hospitals, ambulatory surgical facilities, and psychiatric institutions, as well as certify health professionals such as doctors, physician assistants, nurses, psychologists, and psychiatrists. States establish requirements for training, continuing education, malpractice insurance, and the like; build and support medical schools; and fund research. In a number of states, they scrutinize the health insurance industry, providing rules and guidelines.

In aggregate, states clearly have sizable obligations in the area of public health and accomplish them with varying degrees of resolve, thoroughness, and financial commitment. According to the 2011 American health care rankings, Vermont is the most effective state, followed by New Hampshire, Connecticut, Hawaii, and Massachusetts. Mississippi is at the bottom of the list, followed by Louisiana, Oklahoma, Arkansas, and Alabama.[1] The ratings take into account the degree of problems such as violent crimes, infectious diseases, binge drinking, obesity, smoking, and medically uninsured households; the extent of public health funding, immunizations, usage of early prenatal care, and availability of primary care doctors; and outcome factors that arise from adverse environmental conditions, risky behaviors, and lack of medical care. The data, which have been collected annually for twenty-two years, suggest that overall health in the United States has deteriorated by 69 percent since the 1990s. Although there has been progress in smoking cessation, premature deaths, unnecessary hospitalizations, and preventable mortality from cardiovascular diseases, these advancements have been offset by increases in obesity, diabetes, and the number of children living in poverty.

Tobacco Control

Tobacco is a multifaceted issue that can attract the interest of state policymakers (at least in places that do not rely financially on tobacco crops) because it is simultaneously a revenue source and a public health concern. State actions include a mix of government regulations, reports, informational drives, programs, and excise taxes. Federal mandates, such as requiring states to ban the sale of tobacco products to minors, along with federal grants for antismoking campaigns, also have fostered efforts to curb the use of tobacco products.

Unquestionably, smoking is a leading preventable cause of illness, disability, and death in the United States. It is directly responsible for a significant percentage of lung cancer cases, and is a factor in coronary heart disease, cardiovascular and pulmonary disorders, and other serious health problems, causing nearly 470,000 deaths annually. Even secondhand smoke is now recognized as contributing to these adverse conditions.

Burdened with persistent and often growing gaps in their budgets, in recent years a number of states have instituted new or higher excise taxes on the purchase of cigarettes and other tobacco products. Lawmakers who are reluctant to raise income, sales, or corporate taxes because of political repercussions may argue for cigarette taxes, noting that they are a valuable tool in deterring smoking.[2] These taxes range from seventeen cents per pack in Missouri and thirty cents in Virginia to a high of $4.35 in New York (and $1.50 beyond that in New York City). The federal government collects its share as well—$1.01 in cigarette taxes as of 2012.

Every state also has enacted antismoking measures; roughly two-thirds of them are relatively strong laws, and most are wide-ranging. Smoking bans may include restaurants, bars, private workplaces, and/or government buildings.[3] In some areas, local laws may be even more stringent than state laws. However, pressure from tavern owners, tobacco companies, restaurants, and other lobbyists have prevented tough laws in some states (e.g., Mississippi, Texas) and are weakening laws that are already in place in others (e.g., Nevada, which now allows smoking again in bars and some restaurants).

Antismoking campaigns, especially information about the hazards of tobacco usage, have become *de rigueur* among many state policymakers. Some states offer prevention and cessation programs. These and similar activities are funded mostly through the millions of dollars the states obtain annually through the multistate tobacco master settlement agreement: in 1998 the five largest U.S tobacco companies agreed to pay them a total of $246 billion over twenty-five years, beginning in 2000. Nevertheless, tobacco control projects often get shortchanged because substantial portions of the settlement dollars have been diverted to other health undertakings or even to state general budgets.

The CDC has recommended a minimum amount of money that each state should spend on antitobacco initiatives in order to be effective, but in FY 2011, no state had spent the recommended amount: in fact, more than 80 percent of the states spent less than half of the required resources, and four states (Connecticut, Nevada, New Hampshire, and Ohio) allocated no money for such endeavors.[4] Indeed, on average, states had cut funding by 36 percent over four years, and earmarked roughly only 3 percent of their annual tobacco settlement money and tobacco excise taxes for antismoking programs.[5]

Not surprisingly, although government antismoking efforts have met with measureable success in controlling the use of tobacco products among the U.S. population, it has leveled off in the past several years. Nearly one-fifth (19 percent) of American adults are still dependent on tobacco, totaling over forty-five million people, down from 42 percent in 1965.[6]

Substance Abuse Policies

In the area of substance abuse, states have a much larger policy-making role than the national government and are liable for the bulk of the expenditures, although there is an array of small, supplemental federal grants offered for this purpose. All the same, governors and state legislators generally do not view prevention and rehabilitation services as a particularly high priority in their overall agendas. Instead, they have mainly dealt with drug matters through the criminal justice system, especially in more recent decades, and with alcohol-related issues as a means for generating revenue.

By the end of the twentieth century, fewer than one-third of the approximately ten million Americans with serious alcohol or drug-related disorders had access to rehabilitation services.[7] When they were publicly available, the restricted time frame for assistance, and the quality of the services themselves, prevented many individuals from achieving a long-lasting recovery, especially among low-income families. During the economic downturn from 2002 to 2004, and again since the great recession of 2008, states reduced addiction-related programs.

Only about 20 percent of the limited chemical dependency resources are allocated to deterrence (mostly media campaigns and grants for community, school, and local government prevention projects) and rehabilitation services, with treatment receiving somewhat greater attention than preemptive actions. For the vast majority of states, both of these endeavors together total, on average, under 0.5 percent of their budgets.[8]

In fact, similar to tobacco products, alcohol is mostly viewed as a source of revenue by the states. Assessments on hard liquor, wine, and beer generate substantial income—about $6 billion annually by 2009—but just a fraction of that amount is dedicated to substance abuse programs. During economic downturns, states may increase taxes on alcohol sales because such a tax is a more politically viable source of revenue than personal income, corporate, or sales taxes. Some states, for example Pennsylvania, own and administer the liquor stores themselves, thereby bringing in even more money.

According to the National Center on Addiction and Substance Abuse (CASA), because there has been such slight interest in and few funds allocated to ameliorating drug and alcohol addiction, states are forced to spend billions of dollars to clean up what the organization calls "the wreckage" (crime, illness, and the like). These outlays typically account for 16 percent of state budgets; roughly one-third of the expenditures are devoted to the criminal justice system, with most of the remainder utilized for medical care, typically through Medicaid.[9]

Indeed, beginning in the 1980s, the vast majority of states (along with the federal government) shifted their focus from treating drug abusers to incarcerating them. The war on drugs, especially crack cocaine, engendered new laws, strict enforcement, and harsh punishments. Across the states, officials engaged in determined efforts to arrest drug transgressors, and adopted tougher penalties that generally included mandatory minimum prison sentences or stringent sentencing guidelines. In many cases, even first-time culprits caught with small amounts of illegal drugs were dealt with severely. Consequently, as more people were jailed, and with longer sentences, states confronted a massive expansion of their prison population, escalating incarceration expenses, overcrowded jails, and the pressure to build more prisons. By 2005, slightly over 80 percent of states' justice-related outlays were allocated to drug infractions.[10]

Concerned about these mounting costs, a few states, including Arizona in 1996 and California in 2000, began creating programs specifically aimed at treating low-level offenders in lieu of jailing them. Other states, for instance Washington in 2003, have implemented limited screening, intervention, and short-term rehabilitation services. In a similar vein, in 2009 Kentucky enlarged its in-prison treatment opportunities for inmates, and Louisiana permitted parole for people serving life sentences related to less consequential heroin activities. Beginning in 2009, a number of states altered and reduced mandatory minimum sentences for certain types of drug offenses, and modified or restructured penalties in other ways.[11] Regardless, states have a long way to go in rectifying the imbalance between imprisonment and supportive services for illicit but personal drug activities.

THE MEDICAID PROGRAM[12]

Enacted in 1965 as Title XIX of the Social Security Act, Medicaid is a labyrinth of fifty separate state plans that is jointly financed by the federal and state governments to deliver health services to low-income households. The national share, Federal Medical Assistance Payments (FMAPs), is based on the relative per capita income of each state, ranging from 50 percent to 77 percent. Currently, there are roughly sixty million people, representing nearly 20 percent of the population, participating in the program.

Although there are extensive federal regulations, the states are primarily responsible for setting eligibility requirements, provider fee levels, benefit packages, and other crucial aspects of their individual plans. As a result, Medicaid programs vary notably across the states. Certain benefits are mandated by the federal government, including hospital care, laboratory and X-ray work, skilled nursing homes, family planning, and physician care. But states can choose from among slightly more than thirty optional services to offer (e.g., prescription drugs, dental and vision care, rehabilitation and other therapies, durable medical equipment, and personal care).

To become eligible for Medicaid, households must meet their state's income threshold; these tend to be stringent and, in many states, far below the federal poverty level (FPL). As of January 2011, the median upper limit among the states is 64 percent of the FPL for working parents, and 37 percent for jobless parents; childless adults are ineligible in most jurisdictions.[13] Recipients also must fit specific categorical requirements that tend to disadvantage certain people, such as childless adults. Federally mandated groups have changed over time, mostly through gradual, targeted expansions aimed primarily at the aged, the disabled, pregnant women, and children.

To be sure, income eligibility levels for children tend to be somewhat higher, especially because of CHIP, enacted in 1997. Twenty-five states cover children with family earnings up to 250 percent of the FPL. CHIP is a capped block grant program, with higher federal matching rates than Medicaid; states have much latitude in both eligibility and the use of the funds. Initially limited to ten years, the program was reauthorized in 2008 after two vetoes from President George W. Bush.

In contrast, at times certain adult populations have been cut from the programs, such as when the linkage between Aid to Families with Dependent Children and the adults' automatic entitlement to Medicaid benefits was severed through the Personal Responsibility and Work Opportunity Act of 1996. In addition, in that same year states were precluded from receiving federal matching funds for legal immigrants who had lived in the country for less than five years; undocumented immigrants have always been barred from the program.

The Escalating Medicaid Bill

Medicaid enrollments and funding have climbed steadily over the decades, generating a persistent source of financial strain for states. At an overall cost of roughly $399 billion in 2011, Medicaid is not only the fourth-largest component of the federal budget but also comprises a significant and growing share of total state spending, escalating from 10 percent since the mid-1990s to nearly 24 percent today. In most states it is now the second most costly item paid for through state-generated funds, accounting for an average of 16 percent of general fund outlays. The program is gradually putting fiscal pressure on other state obligations, including public schools and higher education.[14]

Rising expenditures have been engendered by such factors as high inflation in medical charges relative to overall price increases; the HIV/AIDS epidemic; technological advances in health care; an aging population; and the expansion of the categorically eligible, especially those who are disabled. The dually eligible population, the approximately nine million individuals entitled to both Medicare and Medicaid, has been the states' most expensive group, accounting for 15 percent of enrollees but 40 percent of total Medicaid costs.

State budgets are particularly stressed during economic downturns: the number of people who lose their jobs and health insurance tends to rise, thereby promoting a growth in Medicaid participation just when state tax revenues are declining. For every 1 percent increase in the unemployment rate, there are roughly one million more Medicaid recipients, while state revenues drop from 3 to 4 percent.[15] Since the turn of the twenty-first century, states have faced budgetary pressures most of the time, amounting to about $200 billion in deficits between 2002 and 2004.[16] The recession of 2008 has been particularly challenging: from its start to the end of 2009, Medicaid enrollment increased by six million people; in 2010 and 2011 participation rose another 7.2 percent and 5.5 percent, respectively.[17] As Medicaid costs went up, nearly every state faced one of its most severe shortfalls in revenues; from FY 2009 through FY 2011, total budgetary gaps amounted to $430 billion.[18]

To assist the states during the 2001 recession, Congress granted them $20 billion. Again, responding to the states' dire fiscal condition, the federal government provided another $83 billion in enhanced FMAP dollars as part of the American Recovery and Reinvestment Act (AARA) of 2009, an extra $14 billion through an extension of the fiscal stimulus money, and $5 billion more in reduced liability for their Medicare Part D "clawback" obligations. (When the Medicare program took over Medicaid funding of outpatient prescription drugs for dually eligible elderly and disabled individuals, the states had been forced to reimburse the federal government an equivalent amount.) The federal supplements cushioned states' fiscal distress to a limited extent, covering, on average, about 40 percent of the deficits.[19]

States not only react to national inducements, but they also seek to leverage greater amounts of federal money on their own. Indeed, over the decades the two levels of government have engaged in an annual tug-of-war over how much of the escalating Medicaid bill each will pay: the states have persistently devised means for maximizing the federal share through creative financing schemes (provider taxes and donations, the Disproportionate Share Hospital program, intergovernmental transfers), while, in turn, the national government has attempted to shift more of the monetary burden to the states.

Responses to Fiscal Distress

Since the 1990s, states have received increasingly greater authority over their Medicaid plans, mainly through congressional enactments (e.g., the Deficit Reduction Act of 2005) and U.S. Department of Health and Human Services (DHHS) waivers allowing them to disregard certain federal regulations for demonstration projects. In more recent years, particularly through the Social Security Act section 1115 waivers, states have been able to render broader structural changes. Scholars differ on whether and the extent to which such flexibility promotes a circumvention of beneficiary rights as opposed to allowing policymakers to design plans that meet the unique needs of their individual states.

With separate Medicaid programs, histories, tax bases, cultural and ideological attitudes, resources, and political makeups, each of the states has struggled independently—and distinctively—in dealing with increasing Medicaid outlays. Because state officials are generally reluctant to raise income, sales, or corporate taxes when encountering reduced revenues, they have resorted to a patchwork of stopgap measures to meet their expenses, including issuing new bonds, drawing on tobacco settlement money, enacting or enhancing sin taxes on tobacco and alcohol products, and tapping into any available rainy-day reserves.

Concomitantly, to varying extents states reduce Medicaid eligibility, cut provider fees, curtail the type and amount of benefits, and enact other cost-saving policies such as drug formularies. However, they currently face maintenance of effort (MOE) restrictions regarding eligibility: as a condition of receiving AARA funds, states have not been allowed to cut such thresholds or render enrollments more difficult than the standards in place as of July 2008. There is a similar MOE clause under the Patient Protection and Affordable Care Act (ACA) for state eligibility policies in place as of March 23, 2010, through 2014 for adults and through 2019 for children.

Accordingly, state reductions had to be focused elsewhere, especially on provider fees and benefit packages. Since the 2008 recession, every state has cut the Medicaid program through at least one of these approaches. Predictably, the most common strategy has been to freeze or reduce payments to providers because such actions deliver the most immediate budgetary results: in 2009, two-thirds of the states implemented such an action. Still, sixteen states restricted services. The following year, thirty-nine states curbed reimbursements and twenty trimmed benefits.[20] A growing number of them also added or increased beneficiary cost-sharing. Since the short-term infusion of enhanced FMAP percentages ended in mid-2011, despite ongoing revenue shortfalls, state economizing endeavors have become even harsher.

While states were trimming various aspects of their Medicaid plans, many of them were simultaneously enlarging eligibility and easing enrollment and reauthorization procedures, primarily due to new federal mandates, bonus payments, and other financial incentives under the ACA. However, newly eligible populations were likely to receive scaled-back benefit packages, higher cost-sharing, and caps on the number of people allowed to enroll in Medicaid.

From Fee-for-Service to Managed Care

Utilizing the Social Security Act's section 1915(b) waivers to circumvent federal freedom-of-choice provisions, states increasingly have turned to managed care organizations (MCOs) and primary care case management programs as another means for reducing their expenditures. These prepaid insurance plans have grown steadily since the 1990s, along with the percentage of for-profit firms. They are dominated by large insurers as well as Medicaid-only companies (e.g., Amerigroup, Centene, and Molina), the latter serving nearly three-fourths of total MCO users.

At first, states launched voluntary managed-care options, but eventually turned to mandatory enrollment. At the same time, they have expanded such coverage from specific regions within the state to larger geographic areas. Although policymakers initially targeted mothers and children, many of them are now moving more elderly and disabled recipients into these capitated insurance arrangements, including people requiring long-term care, in an attempt to achieve statewide implementation.

Across the states, participation in at least some form of managed care has risen from 48 percent of Medicaid clients in 1997 to 56 percent in 2000, and reached 74 percent by 2011.[21] At present, only Alaska, New Hampshire, and Wyoming have eschewed prepaid plans entirely. For the most part, state officials have claimed that MCOs can deliver high-quality services at a lower price than fee-for-service Medicaid providers, but the evidence is mixed on both of these claims. Indeed, a number of studies have found significant consumer and physician dissatisfaction with managed care in such states as Florida and Kentucky.

Long-Term Care

As is the case with other pieces of their Medicaid plans, there are wide variations among the states in terms of the size of their aged and disabled populations; the qualifying criteria for long-term care; the scope, type, and amount of assistance available; and reimbursement policies. Nonetheless, long-term care—especially nursing homes—comprises one-third of total Medicaid program costs nationwide. Even so, less than one-sixth of the elderly and two-fifths of severely disabled younger people in need of long-term care actually receive assistance through Medicaid.

Mandated under federal law, institutional services have long been a key economic force driving Medicaid's escalating expenditures and of paramount concern to state officials seeking to control them. Yet the majority of states have adopted medically needy options, allowing them to cover nursing home residents whose income exceeds their standard Medicaid eligibility thresholds. In addition to meeting certain conditions related to their physical or cognitive functioning, participants must first deplete nearly all of their assets and relinquish their income toward their care, except for a small personal allowance. Consequently, along with serving the poor, Medicaid can also be viewed as an entitlement of sorts for previously moderate-income elderly and disabled persons.

The number of elderly who require long-term care has increased over the decades. Since the enactment of Medicaid, the population aged sixty-five years and over has doubled, from 20 million (10 percent of the population) to 40 million people (13 percent of the population). The group most needing long-term care—individuals aged eighty-five years and older—have been the fastest growing segment, currently reaching more than 5.8 million. Because of the approximately 78 million baby boomers who began to reach the age of sixty-five in 2011, the demand for long-term care is expected to escalate dramatically in the upcoming years. Such changes portend intensifying pressures on state Medicaid budgets.[22]

An institutional bias in Medicaid policy and practice has precluded significant resources for home- and community-based services (HCBS). However, funding has grown incrementally since the 1990s, and more rapidly in recent years, mainly because states view at-home supports as a means of saving money if substituted for nursing home care. The vast majority of outlays for home- and community-based services have been through the Social Security Act section 1915(c) waivers that allow such services as home health aides, personal care attendants, adult day care, and respite care. Over two-thirds of the states have recently expanded home- and community-based services, which currently accounts for nearly 45 percent of the long-term care expenses, up from 19 percent in 1995.[23]

On the whole, the most costly Medicaid recipients are low-income disabled younger adults and children, especially those with severe mental impairments and developmental disabilities: they are more likely to live in noninstitutional settings (mainly using home- and community-based services) or reside in intermediate care facilities for the mentally impaired. Although most frail elderly persons relying on Medicaid are still placed in nursing homes, the percentage of them receiving home- and community-based services has been rising. In many states, the shift from nursing homes to home care has come at a considerable price to individuals requiring long-term care and their families, including higher eligibility thresholds, enrollment ceilings, per capita spending caps, and waiting lists.

Impact of Health Services on State Economies

The influx of Medicaid, CHIP, and Medicare funds into state economies stimulates economic growth, employment, and tax revenues. Health services and supplies now represent the largest sector within the U.S. economy, representing more than 17 percent of the gross domestic product. In the case of Medicaid/CHIP, much of the local beneficial effects can be attributed to the federal matching dollars, which bring in massive amounts of outside capital. These two programs are now the leading sources of federal grants to states, representing nearly half of the total they receive from the national government.

Health care sector dollars are vital everywhere, but some places rely heavily on them for their fiscal well-being. Hospitals, for example, rank among the top ten businesses in several cities, including Boston, Cleveland, Detroit, and New York. In certain rural areas, where jobs are scarce, nursing homes or hospitals may be major employers. These establishments, in turn, are often dependent on public-sector money. Health-related government funds not only purchase actual medical care and equipment but also have a multiplier effect, generating spending and jobs in other sectors of the economy. Therefore, regardless of their views on the Medicaid program itself, governors and state legislators must weigh any curtailments to their Medicaid plans—which would result in a corresponding drop in federal subsidies—against the potential losses in revenue and employment.

Vested Interests

A large number of health-related businesses and professionals also have significant financial interests in Medicaid.[24] To varying extents, hospitals, nursing homes, home health agencies, MCOs, pharmaceutical companies, durable medical equipment firms, medical laboratories, pharmacists, doctors, dentists, and others not only benefit from Medicaid/CHIP payments, but also are powerful lobbying interests and campaign contributors at the state level, where many of the key decisions affecting them are made. For example, nursing homes, which are dependent on Medicaid for nearly half (45 percent) of their total income, are particularly influential with elected state officials through affiliates of the American Health Care Association (AHCA).

Managed care companies, which garner well over 16 percent of total Medicaid outlays, devote millions of dollars to sway governors and legislators to expand their contracts and enlarge reimbursements, mainly via affiliates of America's Health Insurance Plans (AHIP) and Medicaid Health Plans of America. Because Medicaid accounts for 17 percent of the hospital industry's overall income, affiliates of the American Hospital Association (AHA) attempt to maximize their fees in every state. Many other health-related professionals and industry trade associations also are formidable forces influencing health policies and bolstering even further the growth of Medicaid spending across the states.

Comparing State Medicaid Plans

In 2007 the Public Citizen Health Research Group (PCHRG) ranked all of the state Medicaid programs based on eligibility levels, scope of services, quality of care, and reimbursement policies, using fifty-five indicators. According to the survey data, the preeminent state Medicaid programs, in descending order, were Massachusetts, Nebraska, Vermont, Alaska, Wisconsin, Rhode Island, Minnesota, New York, Washington, and New Hampshire. The states with the most inadequate plans, beginning with the worst one, were Mississippi, Idaho, Texas, Oklahoma, South Dakota, Indiana, South Carolina, Colorado, Alabama, and Missouri. The researchers do warn, however, that even the top plans were sorely lacking in at least some aspects of their coverage, benefit packages, cost-sharing requirements, and quality of care.[25]

NATIONAL HEALTH INSURANCE AND THE STATES

Enacted by Congress in 2010, the ACA aims to insure nearly every U.S. citizen, mostly through an extension of Medicaid to all households with income up to 133 percent of the FPL, tax credits for low- and moderate-income families, and an individual mandate to have insurance coverage. Prior to the legislation, slightly more than 16 percent of Americans were uninsured annually, but wide-ranging variations in programs and policies across the states fostered corresponding disparities in coverage. For example, nearly 25 percent of the population in Texas, and approximately 20 percent in Mississippi, Nevada, and New Mexico, had no health insurance, compared with 10 percent or fewer in Hawaii, Maine, Vermont, and Wisconsin.[26]

With the passage of the ACA, roughly sixteen million previously uninsured people had been expected to gain coverage through the Medicaid expansion, the main beneficiaries being childless adults; parents, especially those with grown offspring; children; and individuals on waiting lists for capped waiver programs. It is projected that another sixteen million individuals will buy policies through state-established health insurance exchanges; families with incomes between 100 percent and 400 percent of the FPL will be eligible for subsidies, based on a sliding scale. Such households will be entitled to an essential benefits package from a "qualified" plan, with tax credits set to the Silver plan, the second-lowest offering available. Small firms, which also can purchase policies in the health insurance exchanges to insure their workforce, will receive financial incentives from the government as well under the provisions of the ACA.

Primary responsibility for implementing the ACA and enforcing its regulations is firmly anchored in the states. Yet the health reform law presents numerous financial, administrative, and tactical challenges for them. For one, enlarging the number of insured residents and sustaining the coverage will not be straightforward. Despite the subsidies, relatively high premiums and other cost-sharing obligations could deter low-income workers and even middle-income households from signing up for a policy or even using health care services. Moreover, premium assistance is designed to rise in conjunction with the growth in personal income, even though the historical record shows that the actual cost of health insurance tends to rise faster than personal income.

Outreach, particularly for Medicaid, will be demanding as well; a significant percentage of households that currently qualify for the program do not participate. Among other difficulties will be the development and implementation of effective exchanges, including creating procedures for navigating the complexities arising from such issues as differing federal matches for distinctive populations and the vicissitude in family earnings. States can apply for federal funds to assist them in setting up the exchanges; for those states that fail to establish exchanges, the DHHS will develop and administer a federally operated exchange.

In this April 16, 2013, photo, the Arkansas House majority leader, Rep. Bruce Westerman, R-Hot Springs, signals his intention to speak against a Medicaid funding bill in the house chamber at the Arkansas state capitol in Little Rock. The funding provision passed, paving the way for the state to expand Medicaid to an estimated 175,000 additional enrollees in 2014 (as calculated by Arkansas Insurance Department consultants).

SOURCE: Associated Press; Danny Johnston, photographer.

Paying for Medicaid expansion is of considerable concern to state policymakers. Significantly, twenty-six states, predominantly those with Republican governors and/or Republican legislative majorities, have reacted vociferously against the ACA and have appealed certain aspects of the measure to the U.S. Supreme Court. In addition to contesting the individual mandate, they questioned whether Congress had exceeded its constitutional authority in requiring states to expand their Medicaid programs, which they argued would be unduly burdensome. In particular, the federal government is fully funding newly mandated enrollees for only three years; beginning in 2016, the states' share will gradually grow from 5 percent to 10 percent by 2020. Conversely, many supporters of the ACA argue that the additional federal dollars are a windfall for states, allowing them to provide health coverage to their residents at minimal cost to their budgets. In June 2012 the Supreme Court upheld the individual mandate but ruled that Congress could not force the states to participate in the Medicaid expansion. As a result, a number of governors are threatening not to join in, thereby significantly reducing the projected sixteen million more uninsured people that the ACA will cover through Medicaid.[27]

Ensuring sufficient and quality providers will be another significant issue confronting state policymakers. The United States already has a dearth of primary care doctors, disproportionately affecting rural areas and low-income inner cities. Even before the enactment of the ACA, the national shortage was projected to grow. The influx of millions of newly insured Medicaid and private-pay patients generated by the health reform legislation is expected to worsen the situation. The paucity in the number of practitioners will have a particularly adverse impact on Medicaid participants, who in many areas currently have difficulty finding doctors, especially specialists, who are willing to treat them. Thus still more Medicaid patients than today may be forced to rely on community health centers and government-run hospitals for their medical care.

CONCLUSION

States clearly have enormous, wide-ranging responsibilities in the area of public health, but they are sorely constrained by limited resources. They also implement these policies, regulations, and programs with divergent levels of interest, intensity, and budgetary commitments. Medicaid, too, varies appreciably among the states, depending on the condition of the economy and the political will of elected officials. In nearly all states, however, an increasing source of fiscal distress is putting considerable pressure on other aspects of state obligations. Now in charge of implementing the recently enacted national health insurance reform measure, states are encountering ongoing administrative and fiscal challenges, not the least of which is the expansion of Medicaid. The success of the ACA's goal of achieving affordable, near-universal coverage will depend on how well each of the states commits itself to the complex and demanding tasks ahead (see Toward Universal Coverage: Massachusetts box and Toward Universal Coverage: Vermont box).

TOWARD UNIVERSAL COVERAGE: MASSACHUSETTS

Through the Patient Protection and Health Care Reform Act of 2006, Massachusetts now covers nearly 98 percent of its 6.5 million residents with some form of health insurance, the highest in the United States. Even prior to the new law, the Bay State had a relatively low rate of uninsured households (under 10 percent), strictly regulated insurance companies, and an ample uncompensated care fund, supported through assessments on insurance companies and hospitals, together with federal and state contributions.

Low-income families continue to receive assistance through Medicaid/Children's Health Insurance Plan (CHIP) programs (MassHealth). Since passage of its reform law, the Bay State has engaged in a concerted outreach effort that has enlarged enrollments in these plans materially. The centerpiece of the Massachusetts experiment is "the Connector," which links uninsured individuals and small firms to private health insurance. Its board of directors is responsible for key decisions regarding policy, regulations, and other aspects of the program. Serving as Massachusetts's health insurance exchange, the Connector is now central to the state's implementation of the Patient Protection and Affordable Care Act.

Households with gross earnings up to three times the federal poverty level (FPL), and not eligible for Medicaid or CHIP, can choose among various Commonwealth Care (CommCare) plans, currently available through five managed care organizations. Families are entitled to subsidies, on a sliding scale, based on their income and the plan in which they enroll. In addition to disallowing deductibles, the Connector restricts the amount of client co-pays and patients' total out-of-pocket outlays. People with incomes below 150 percent of the FPL receive their premium coverage at no charge.

For higher-income adults, and firms with fewer than fifty employees, the Connector offers Commonwealth Choice (CommChoice) options, through eight insurance companies at present. Participating firms must provide four types of plans, all having different premiums, benefits, deductibles, and cost-sharing requirements; however, they are required to meet minimum credible coverage standards that include certain mandated services and benefits. Each plan has a fixed actuarial value that is set by the board of directors. Ranging from the lowest to highest in worth, these include the Bronze, Silver, Gold, and Young Adult plans.

For companies with more than ten employees, the state has implemented a play-or-pay directive: they must either provide insurance that meets a "fair and reasonable" test (at least 25 percent of their workers are enrolled, with firms funding at least 33 percent of premium costs) or they have to pay an assessment, initially set at $295 per worker not participating in any of their plans. Furthermore, businesses incur a free rider surcharge for any of their employees receiving assistance from the Health Safety Net pool (the renamed uncompensated care fund).

Every resident is obliged to buy some type of health insurance or else pay a penalty that depends on his or her income; households with incomes under 150 percent of the FPL are not penalized.

The Connector establishes an affordability schedule that determines the highest percentage of income a household should pay for insurance coverage and exempts families from the individual mandate if their costs are beyond this sum. Just over 40 percent of newly insured residents are in private coverage, primarily through their employers, but also via the Connector and the newly merged individual and small-group markets.[1]

To date, the Massachusetts health care reform act has not only augmented coverage but has achieved other accomplishments as well. For one, more people have been able to seek medically necessary services. There also has been a reduction in unnecessary emergency room visits and an improvement in overall quality of care. However, health insurance enrollees have experienced high and growing premiums and co-payments; at least one-fifth of the state's residents had to forgo at least some care and medications because of the costs.[2]

Adequate access to providers by Medicaid participants and other low-income patients is another ongoing problem, especially in rural and other underserved areas. Families living in such places, alongside low-income households more generally, often rely on community health centers, nurse practitioners, physician assistants, and safety net hospitals. The legislature, through the newly established Massachusetts Center for Primary Care Recruitment and Replacement, is now attempting to strengthen the state's primary care workforce.

Both MassHealth and CommCare are heavily financed through federal Medicaid matching funds. Nevertheless, the success of Massachusetts's health care reform has come at a steep price, generating a mounting share of its budget. By 2011, health spending represented 37 percent of the total, up from 21 percent in 2000. Indeed, the number of subsidized families participating in the CommCare plan has grown considerably from the original estimate, accompanied by a greater than expected subsidy schedule, leading to larger outlays than anticipated. Hospital costs also are conspicuously higher than in other parts of the nation, mostly because of the extreme concentration of hospitals (especially academic medical centers) and insurance companies (Blue Cross/Blue Shield accounts for over half of insured households).[3] At the same time, similar to other states, the 2008 recession has increased eligibility for Medicaid/CHIP while reducing state revenues. In response, officials have increased the state's cigarette tax, dropped thirty thousand legal immigrants from coverage, delayed some scheduled increases in provider fees, and cut back on adult dental services for certain households.

Despite the fiscal challenges, policymakers are attempting to maintain eligibility thresholds and benefits, improve the coordination of care, enhance the quality of services, add new programs, and expand its Safety Net Care Pool, which has served to finance much of the reform effort. They intend to further these objectives with enhanced federal dollars: as part of its three-year extended Medicaid waiver, in 2012 the state received $26.7 billion from the national government, $5.7 billion more than its previous allocation.

1. "Massachusetts Health Care Reform: Three Years Later" (Menlo Park, CA: The Henry J. Kaiser Family Foundation, Kaiser Commission on Medicaid and the Uninsured, September 2009), www.kff.org.

2. Ibid.

3. Ibid.

TOWARD UNIVERSAL COVERAGE: VERMONT

Vermont is the first state to have enacted legislation implementing a single-payer health care system. Signed into law in May 2011 by Gov. Peter Shumlin (D), Act 48 seeks to replace other health insurance plans, excluding those already in place by employers who are self-insured. Intending to begin the process of putting "Green Mountain Care" into effect by 2014, if early federal waivers from the Affordable Care Act and Medicaid are attained, policymakers are now laying the groundwork for what they envision as universal access to quality, affordable health coverage in the state.

The plan features an independent Green Mountain Care Board: among its several responsibilities are to oversee cost-control initiatives, review and set provider fees, and design the health benefits package. Providers will be paid through a single claims procedure and payment system, along with standardized rates. Importantly, the state aims to devise a means for enlarging the pool of providers to meet the expected growth in demand for services. Although the scheme will be state run and financed, officials will outsource some administrative tasks (e.g., claims processing) to private-sector insurance companies, using a competitive bidding process.

In addition to enhanced federal resources, the state anticipates that it will meet the expenses for expanded coverage and relatively generous benefits through lower administrative costs (derived from the various single-payer features), eventual elimination of fee-for-service payments, a reduction in fraud, delivery system integration, and malpractice reform. Although Act 48 contains alternative financing possibilities, it left the actual method undecided; as of May 2013 it still has not been resolved.[1]

1. For detailed background about the act, see William C. Hsiao, Anna Gosline Knight, Steven Kappel, and Nicolae Done, "What States Can Learn from Vermont's Bold Experiment: Embracing a Single-Payer Health Care Financing System," *Health Affairs* 30 (July 2011): 1232–1241.

NOTES

1. American Public Health Association, the United Health Foundation, and the Partnership for Prevention, "America's Health Rankings: A Call to Action for Individuals and Their Communities" (Minnetonka, MN: United Health Foundation, December 2011).

2. For example, see Richard J. Bonnie, Kathleen Stratton, and Robert B. Wallace, *Ending the Tobacco Problem: A Blueprint for the Nation* (Washington, DC: The National Academies Press, 2007).

3. American Lung Association, "State Legislated Actions on Tobacco Issues: State Tobacco Cessation," 23rd ed. (Washington, DC: American Lung Association, 2011), www.lungusa2.org/slati.

4. Ibid.

5. National Center on Addiction and Substance Abuse (CASA), "Shoveling Up 11: The Impact of Substance Abuse on Federal, State, and Local Budgets" (New York: Columbia University, May 2009).

6. U.S. Department of Health and Human Services, "Ending the Tobacco Epidemic: Progress toward a Healthier Nation" (Washington, DC: U.S. Department of Health and Human Services, Office of the Assistant Secretary for Health, August 2012), www.hhs.gov/ash/initiatives/tobacco/.

7. Drug Strategies, "Critical Choices: Making Drug Policy at the State Level" (Washington, DC: Drug Strategies, 2001), www.drugstrategies.org.

8. Ibid.

9. CASA, "Shoveling Up 11."

10. Ibid.

11. For detailed discussions of these altered drug policies, see ibid.; Drug Strategies, "Critical Choices"; Nicole D. Porter, "The State of Sentencing: 2009 Developments in Policy and Practice" (Washington, DC: The Sentencing Project, 2010), www.sentencingproject.org; Nicole D. Porter, "The State of Sentencing: 2010 Developments in Policy and Practice" (Washington, DC: The Sentencing Project, February 2011), www.sentencingproject.org; Marc Mauer, "Sentencing Reform: Amid Mass Incarcerations—Guarded Optimism," *Criminal Justice* 26 (Spring 2011): 27–36.

12. More detailed information about the Medicaid program can be found in Laura Katz Olson, *The Politics of Medicaid* (New York: Columbia University Press, 2010).

13. Martha Heberlein, Tricia Brooks, Jocelyn Guyer, Samantha Guyer, Samantha Artigo, and Jessica Stephens, "Holding Steady, Looking Ahead: Annual Findings of a 50-State Survey of Eligibility Rules, Enrollment and Renewal Procedures, and Cost Sharing Practices in Medicaid and CHIP, 2010–2011" (Menlo Park, CA: The Henry J. Kaiser Family Foundation, Kaiser Commission on Medicaid and the Uninsured, January 2011), www.kff.org.

14. The National Association of State Budget Officers, "State Expenditure Report" (fiscal 2010–2012 data) (Washington, DC: NASBO, 2012), www.nasbo.org.

15. Vic Miller, Andy Schneider, Laura Snyder, and Robin Rudowitz, "Impact of the Medicaid Fiscal Relief Provisions in the American Recovery and Reinvestment Act (ARRA)" (Menlo Park, CA: The Henry J. Kaiser Family Foundation, Kaiser Commission on Medicaid and the Uninsured, October 2011), www.kff.org.

16. Henry A. Coleman, "State Government Finances: A Review of Current Conditions and Outlook," in *State Health Policy,* 4th ed., Joel C. Canter, ed. (Washington, DC: CQ Press, 2006).

17. Chris Lee, "States Face New Budget and Workforce Challenges as Temporary Federal Aid Nears End and Health Reform Planning Heats Up" (Menlo Park, CA: The Henry J. Kaiser Family Foundation, Kaiser Commission on Medicaid and the Uninsured, September 30, 2010), www.kff.org; Miller, Schneider, Snyder, and Rudowitz, "Impact of the Medicaid Fiscal Relief Provisions"; Vernon K. Smith, Kathleen Gifford, Eileen Ellis, Robin Rudowitz, and Lauren Snyder, "Moving Ahead Amid Fiscal Challenges: A Look at Medicaid Spending, Coverage and Policy Trends, Results from a 50-State Medicaid Budget Survey for State Fiscal Years 2011 and 2012" (Menlo Park, CA: The Henry J. Kaiser Family Foundation, Kaiser Commission on Medicaid and the Uninsured, October 2011), www.kff.org.

18. Vernon Smith, Kathy Gifford, Eileen Ellis, Robin Rudowitz, and Laura Snyder, "Waiting for Economic Recovery, Poised for Health Care Reform: A Mid-Year Update for FY 2011—Looking Forward to FY 2012" (Menlo Park, CA: The Henry J. Kaiser Family Foundation, Kaiser Commission on Medicaid and the Uninsured, January 2011), www.kff.org.

19. Tracy Gordon, "Update: State Budgets in Recession and Recovery," policy brief (Menlo Park, CA: The Henry J. Kaiser Family Foundation, Kaiser Commission on Medicaid and the Uninsured, October 2011), www.kff.org.

20. Lee, "States Face New Budget and Workforce Challenges"; Vernon Smith, Kathleen Gifford, Eileen Ellis, Robin Rudowitz, and Laura Snyder, "Hoping for Economic Recovery, Preparing for Health Reform: A Look at Medicaid Spending, Coverage and Policy Trends, Results from a 50-State Medicaid Budget Survey for States, Fiscal Years 2010 and 2011" (Menlo Park, CA: The Henry J. Kaiser Family Foundation, Kaiser Commission on Medicaid and the Uninsured, September 2010), www.kff.org.

21. "Medicaid Managed Care Enrollees as a Percent of State Medicaid Enrollees" (Menlo Park, CA: The Henry J. Kaiser Family Foundation, Kaiser Commission on Medicaid and the Uninsured, July 1, 2011), www.statehealthfacts.org.

22. National Institute on Aging, "Aging in the United States: Past, Present, and Future" (Washington, DC: U.S. Department of Commerce, Economics and Statistics Administration, Bureau of the Census, 2010).

23. "Medicaid Home and Community-Based Services Program: Data Update" (Menlo Park, CA: The Henry J. Kaiser Family Foundation, Kaiser Commission on Medicaid and the Uninsured, December 2012), www.kff.org.

24. More information about the data in this section can be found in Laura Katz Olson, *The Politics of Medicaid* (New York: Columbia University Press, 2010).

25. Annette B. Ramirez and Sidney M. Wolfe, "Unsettling Scores: A Ranking of State Medicaid Programs," Public Citizen Health Research Group (PCHRG), publication no. 1807 (Washington, DC: PCHRG, April 2007).

26. "Health Insurance Coverage of the Total Population," states (2010–2011), U.S. (2011) (Menlo Park, CA: The Henry J. Kaiser Family Foundation, Kaiser Commission on Medicaid and the Uninsured, July 1, 2011), www.statehealthfacts.org.

27. *United Federation of Independent Businesses et al. v. Sebelius, Secretary of Health and Human Services, et al., 567* U.S. ___ (2012).

SUGGESTED READING

American Lung Association. "State Legislated Actions on Tobacco Issues: State Tobacco Cessation," 23rd ed. Washington, DC: ALA, 2011, www.lungusa2.org/slati.

American Public Health Association, the United Health Foundation, and the Partnership for Prevention. "America's Health Rankings: A Call to Action for Individuals and Their Communities." Minnetonka, MN: United Health Foundation, December 2011.

Bonnie, Richard J., Kathleen Stratton, and Robert B. Wallace. *Ending the Tobacco Problem: A Blueprint for the Nation.* Washington, DC: The National Academies Press, 2007.

Coleman, Henry A. "State Government Finances: A Review of Current Conditions and Outlook." In *State Health Policy,* 4th ed., Joel C. Canter, ed. Washington, DC: CQ Press, 2006.

Drug Strategies. "Critical Choices: Making Drug Policy at the State Level." Washington, DC: Drug Strategies, 2001, www.drugstrategies.org/.

Gordon, Tracy. "Update: State Budgets in Recession and Recovery." Policy brief. Menlo Park, CA: The Henry J. Kaiser Family Foundation, Kaiser Commission on Medicaid and the Uninsured, October 2011, www.kff.org.

Halahan, John, and Linda Blumberg. "Massachusetts Health Reform: Solving the Long-Run Cost Problem." Washington, DC: The Urban Institute, January 2009.

Heberlein, Martha, Tricia Brooks, Jocelyn Guyer, Samantha Guyer, Samantha Artigo, and Jessica Stephens. "Holding Steady, Looking Ahead: Annual Findings of a 50-State Survey of Eligibility Rules, Enrollment and Renewal Procedures, and Cost Sharing Practices in Medicaid and CHIP, 2010–2011." Menlo Park, CA: The Henry J. Kaiser Family Foundation, Kaiser Commission on Medicaid and the Uninsured, January 2011, www.kff.org.

The Henry J. Kaiser Family Foundation, Kaiser Commission on Medicaid and the Uninsured. "Massachusetts Health Care Reform: Three Years Later." Menlo Park, CA: The Henry J. Kaiser Family Foundation, Kaiser Commission on Medicaid and the Uninsured, September 2009, www.kff.org.

Hsiao, William C., Anna Gosline Knight, Steven Kappel, and Nicolae Done. "What States Can Learn from Vermont's Bold Experiment: Embracing a Single-Payer Health Care Financing System." *Health Affairs* 30 (2011): 1232–1241.

Lee, Chris. "States Face New Budget and Workforce Challenges as Temporary Federal Aid Nears End and Health Reform Planning Heats Up." Menlo Park, CA: The Henry J. Kaiser Family Foundation, Kaiser Commission on Medicaid and the Uninsured, September 30, 2010, www.kff.org.

Mauer, Marc. "Sentencing Reform amid Mass Incarcerations—Guarded Optimism." *Criminal Justice* 26 (2011): 27–36.

Miller, Vic, Andy Schneider, Laura Snyder, and Robin Rudowitz. "Impact of the Medicaid Fiscal Relief Provisions in the American Recovery and Reinvestment Act (ARRA)." Menlo Park, CA: The Henry J. Kaiser Family Foundation, Kaiser Commission on Medicaid and the Uninsured, October 2011, www.kff.org.

National Center on Addiction and Substance Abuse (CASA). "Shoveling Up 11: The Impact of Substance Abuse on Federal, State, and Local Budgets." New York: Columbia University, May 2009.

Olson, Laura Katz. *The Politics of Medicaid.* New York: Columbia University Press, 2010.

Porter, Nicole D. "The State of Sentencing: 2009 Developments in Policy and Practice." Washington, DC: The Sentencing Project, 2010, www.sentencingproject.org.

———. "The State of Sentencing: 2010 Developments in Policy and Practice." Washington, DC: The Sentencing Project, February 2011, www.sentencingproject.org.

Ramirez, Annette B., and Sidney M. Wolfe. "Unsettling Scores: A Ranking of State Medicaid Programs." Public Citizen Health Research Group (PCHRG). Publication no. 1807. Washington, DC: PCHRG, April 2007.

Smith, Vernon K., Kathleen Gifford, Eileen Ellis, Robin Rudowitz, and Lauren Snyder. "Hoping for Economic Recovery, Preparing for Health Reform: A Look at Medicaid Spending, Coverage and Policy Trends, Results from a 50-State Medicaid Budget Survey for States, Fiscal Years 2010 and 2011." Menlo Park, CA: The Henry J. Kaiser Family Foundation, Kaiser Commission on Medicaid and the Uninsured, September 2010, www.kff.org.

———. "Moving Ahead Amid Fiscal Challenges: A Look at Medicaid Spending, Coverage and Policy Trends, Results from a 50-State Medicaid Budget Survey for State Fiscal Years 2011 and 2012." Menlo Park, CA: The Henry J. Kaiser Family Foundation, Kaiser Commission on Medicaid and the Uninsured, October 2011, www.kff.org.

———. "Waiting for Economic Recovery, Poised for Health Care Reform: A Mid-Year Update for FY 2011—Looking Forward to FY 2012." Menlo Park, CA: The Henry J. Kaiser Family Foundation, Kaiser Commission on Medicaid and the Uninsured, January 2011, www.kff.org.

Chapter 32

Immigration

Tristany Leikem and Shanna Pearson-Merkowitz

WHAT ROLE DO STATE GOVERNMENTS play in the regulation of noncitizens within their borders? This question has been debated in several recent Supreme Court cases and has been at the heart of immigration policy since the early years of the union. The federal government has consistently asserted the right to maintain immigration policy; however, state lawmakers have consistently inserted themselves into the immigration policy arena. For the past two hundred years, when federal immigration policy failed to address new immigration issues or became ineffective, states have taken matters into their own hands. Following a time-honored pattern, when this situation has occurred, state governments (usually those facing a large increase in immigrants) pass legislation aimed at addressing the inadequacies of federal immigration policy, tilting the immigration power scale. The federal government then reacts by asserting its dominance in the area of immigration law via immigration reform. This chapter examines how state actions in the area of immigration often thrust immigration into the national limelight, focusing attention on the inadequacies of current federal law. The historical account provided here examines the push-pull relationship between federal and state governments, and how immigration policy is continually caught in the middle.

HISTORY OF STATE ACTIONS ON IMMIGRATION

Contrary to popular immigration lore, the United States did not have completely open borders prior to the passage of the first federal immigration laws in the late 1800s. Although there were no restrictive quotas on immigration, states were free to restrict immigration through local regulations. At the same time that states competed for immigrant labor and advertised immigration through promoters in various European countries, they also enforced public policies to ensure they were only receiving the types of immigrants they desired. Among other forms of immigrant regulation, states conferred and removed rights of residence, forbade the entrance of classes of immigrants, and adopted entry taxes.

The Foundation of Federal Jurisdiction

A series of Supreme Court cases in the 1870s established the exclusive legal authority (also known as plenary power) of the federal government to regulate immigrant admissions. In *Henderson v. the Mayor of the City of New York* (1875) the Supreme Court declared that states violate the commerce clause of the Constitution by imposing head taxes.[1] In *Chy Lung v. Freeman* (1875) the Court ruled that "the passage of laws which concern the admission of citizens . . . of foreign nations to our shores belongs to Congress, and not to the states."[2]

In the anti-Asian and anti-immigrant climate of the late-nineteenth and early twentieth centuries, the federal government used its exclusive authority to determine immigration negatively. That is, the federal government did not set up rules on who should be admitted to the country, but instead specified who should be excluded. In a series of laws spanning from 1875 to 1929, the federal government excluded contract laborers, prostitutes, paupers, convicts, "morons and idiots," the disabled, those suffering from contagious diseases, those likely to become "a public charge," those who were illiterate, the Chinese, the Japanese, and all other Asians. Between 1921 and 1929, Congress also passed a series of quota laws limiting the admission of immigrants from most European countries. The most important among them, the National Origins Act of 1924, established an annual quota of 150,000 for Europeans and formally banned Japanese immigration. The federal government supplemented the new admissions restrictions with the creation of a bureaucratic system to regulate entry and patrol the physical borders of the country.

Nativism and Language Laws

After the Supreme Court set up the plenary power of the federal government, states could no longer explicitly regulate immigrant admissions. Rather, they used their police and other powers to regulate the lives of immigrants. States could not outright force people to leave the country, but they could make it hard for some of them to stay.

A strong nativist movement arose during the first two decades of the twentieth century, fueled by World War I, scientific racism, the anxieties produced by the end of the frontier, and the growing complexity of American society that many Americans were not ready to navigate. One key concern for states during the early part of the twentieth century was how to achieve the assimilation of various European immigrant groups into American society. To that effect, some states created "Americanization programs" that required immigrants to learn the language, habits, and values of the United States. Additionally, states elevated English as the "official" language of the state. At the heart of the English-only movement was the idea that to be unified and patriotic, everyone living in America should speak English.

The first official language laws were passed in Nebraska and Illinois in the 1920s nativism wave following World War I, and the movement was the antecedent to the enactment of federal quotas on immigration. Nebraska's Siman Language Law made English the state's official language and stipulated that every person in any capacity or at any school would teach all subjects in English only, and that foreign languages would be taught only after a pupil passed the eighth grade. The state of Illinois followed Nebraska's example, and several other states considered similar legislation.[3]

The Problem of the "Back Door"

At the same time that nativists and other groups were campaigning against immigrants, seasonal migrants from Mexico were meeting local demands by performing low-skilled agricultural work. Restrictions on European and Asian immigration left an employment gap that Mexican migrants were quick to fill. Texas and other southwestern states that relied on these migrant workers vigorously petitioned the federal government to exclude Mexican immigrants from the quota laws and even ease other requirements such as the literacy tests, the $8 visa fee (imposed in 1917), and public health tests and checks. Farmers and their supporters in Congress used biology and scientific racism to argue that Mexicans would never seek to move north in search of better jobs. Texas farmers fought vigorously against U.S. Border Patrol investigations on Mexican farm workers and encouraged the unauthorized entry of Mexican labor across the Rio Grande.[4]

The Great Depression reversed the tide of Mexican migration, as the public grew concerned about the economic and social effects of Mexican immigrants on the country. Economic conditions greatly affect public opinion toward immigrants, and Mexican laborers were vulnerable to public wrath, especially in areas outside of Texas. Between 1928 and 1932, local and state government in collaboration with the Immigration and Naturalization Service (INS) (now the U.S. Citizenship and Immigration Services [USCIS]) and the Border Patrol "repatriated" to Mexico more than five hundred thousand people of Mexican origin, many of whom were American citizens.

The "back door" became operational again in 1942 as Americans left for the war and many southern black families moved out of agriculture and into industrial jobs in the North. Once again, Mexican seasonal workers became the answer to American agriculture's need for seasonal manual

The Bracero Program, a U.S. immigration policy that allowed Mexican migrant workers to enter the United States legally to labor in U.S. fields, was in existence from the early 1940s until the mid-1960s. In this photo, a Great Western Sugar Company employee checks a bracero's name against the trip roster as others load their belongings on the top of a bus in Colorado. Similar guest worker programs have been debated during recent discussions on immigration reform.

SOURCE: Photo by Ira Gay Sealy/*The Denver Post* via Getty Images.

labor. The Bracero Program legally brought 4.6 million Mexican migrant workers to the United States over twenty-four years. Over the quarter-century that the Bracero Program was in place, there existed a push-pull relationship between immigration policy and conflicting public and private interests. At the same time that the INS was issuing bracero visas to meet growers' labor demands, the Korean War and the McCarthy era sparked more public demands to control immigration. Border Patrol began to carry out a mass apprehension campaign that detained and deported over one million Mexican immigrants. However, during this campaign the INS more than doubled the number of bracero visas. In this manner, the INS successfully mitigated public fear while simultaneously processing and sending the apprehended immigrants back to the places where they had been arrested; in the words of Douglas Massey and his colleagues, the United States government was able to "have its cake and eat it too" when it came to immigration policy.[5]

The Bracero Program eventually met its match in 1964 as the Civil Rights Movement led to the 1965 Immigration and Nationality Act Amendments, which abolished the national origins quota system and allocated visas according to a seven-category preference system. Despite the adjustments in visa allotment, the reallocation did little to deter immigration. The reduction in visas only shifted immigration from the legal to illegal realm because the demand for labor was still strong. It was no surprise that immigration made its way back to the top of the political agenda soon after a decade of U.S. economic hardship in the 1970s.

THE GROWTH OF UNDOCUMENTED IMMIGRATION AND STATE RESPONSES

As a product of changes to national immigration policy made by Congress in 1965, the demography of the immigrant population changed drastically. In 1960 immigrants to the United States still predominantly hailed from European nations. However, shortly after the passage of the Immigration and Nationality Act of 1965, immigration from Latin America and Asia began to outpace European immigration. Today, over 75 percent of the immigrant population comes from either Latin America or Asia (see Figure 32.1).

Immigrant populations have historically been concentrated in several states. In the post–World War II era, Mexican and other Latino migrants in particular have located in states that border Mexico. However, Illinois, New Jersey, and New York have also been traditional immigrant destinations. As the main receivers of immigrants, these states

FIGURE 32. 1 **Percentage of Total Immigrant Population, by Region of Birth, 1960–2010**

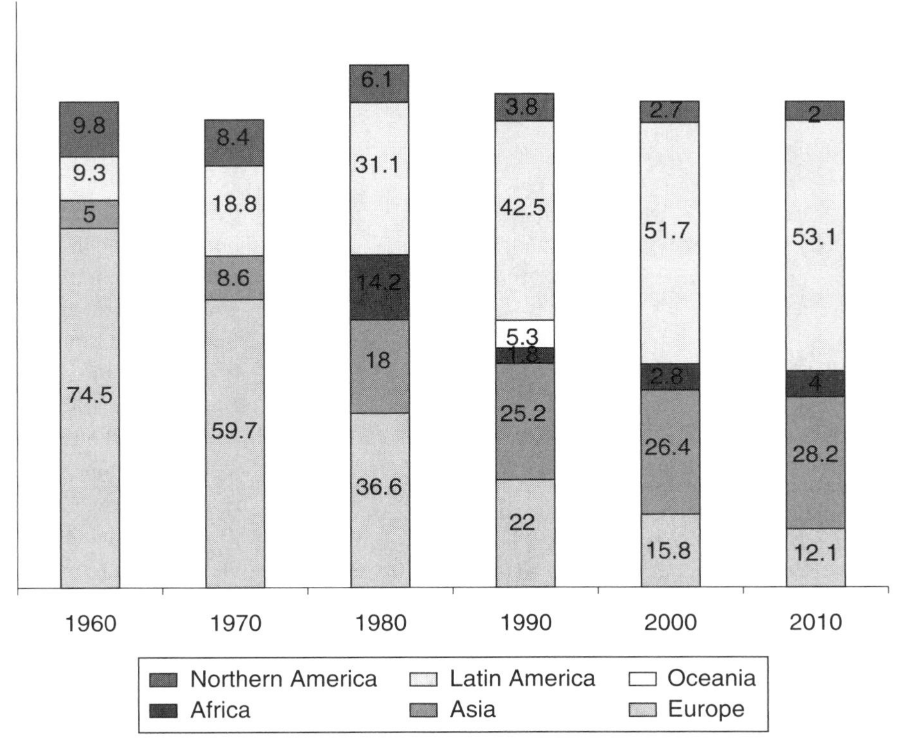

SOURCE: Migration Policy Institute.

implemented laws and policies to help integrate immigrants but also to penalize and exclude them.

Following the recession of the 1970s states sought to regulate both legal and undocumented immigrants. Alien land laws made a comeback in the 1970s, when fears emerged that Middle Eastern oilmen would buy up American farm and industrial lands. The 1980s witnessed a renewal of English-only legislation that continued through the 1990s and 2000s, fueled by perceived economic and cultural threats, economic insecurity, racism, and ethnocentrism.

At the same time, states started devising ways to combat undocumented immigration more directly. The first state efforts in this area targeted employers of undocumented immigrants. Although popular, employer sanctions were difficult to implement and replete with political problems, as industry groups strenuously objected to this type of regulation.[6] As a result, states sought to innovate by targeting the services available to immigrants.

The first such attempt was enacted in Texas and sought to exclude undocumented immigrant children from receiving a public primary and secondary education; however, the law was invalidated in *Plyler v. Doe* (1982) when the Supreme Court extended the equal protection clause of the U.S. Constitution's Fourteenth Amendment to all residents subject to state laws.[7] This Court decision has since invalidated several subsequent state attempts to exclude immigrants from educational services.

The Reappearance of Federal Restrictions and Penalties

Following the national attention paid to Texas's and other states' attempts to exclude immigrants, in 1986 Congress passed the Immigration Reform and Control Act (IRCA). Lawmakers hoped that IRCA would deter illegal immigration, since the law was modeled on several state initiatives and was comprehensive in nature. However, IRCA did little to slow immigration, and through the 1980s well over one million undocumented immigrants entered the United States.

Since it was clear that IRCA was not stemming undocumented immigration, Congress passed another Immigration Act in 1990. Again, however, the efforts of Congress failed to address the underlying reasons for undocumented immigration: economic inequality between sending countries and the United States. During the 1990s, 5.1 million undocumented immigrants entered the United States. In effect, by 2000, about 3 percent of the U.S. population was residing in the country without legal documents.[8]

This crowd attending the march and rally in support of immigration rights on the National Mall on March 21, 2010, holds a photograph of President Ronald Reagan, who signed the Immigration Reform and Control Act (IRCA) on November 6, 1986. The IRCA, which was based on several state initiatives, reformed U.S. immigration law. The act made it illegal to knowingly hire or recruit undocumented workers; required employers to attest to their employees' immigration status; and granted amnesty to certain immigrants who entered the United States illegally before January 1, 1982, and had resided here continuously. The act also granted a path toward legalization to certain agricultural seasonal workers and immigrants who had been continuously though illegally present in the United States since January 1, 1982.

SOURCE: Photo by Marvin Joseph/*The Washington Post* via Getty Images.

California's Proposition 187 and Congressional Response

The massive growth in the undocumented population was primarily concentrated to just a few states, which prompted several state initiatives. In 1994 voters in California passed Proposition 187. The measure, which intended to deny illegal immigrants welfare benefits, nonemergency health care, and access to public education passed by a wide margin: 59 percent to 41 percent. Although much of Proposition 187 was eventually invalidated in a 1995 case, *League of United Latin American Citizens (LULAC) v. Wilson*,[9] the anti-immigration movement in California and the media attention garnered during the campaign propelled the issue of undocumented immigration to the national agenda.

The debate in California over immigration made the national news, and images of flocks of undocumented immigrants swarming border checkpoints became an image that almost no politician in the country could ignore. In response, Congress passed the Illegal

Immigration Reform and Immigrant Responsibility Act (IIRIRA) in 1996. IIRIRA greatly enhanced the U.S. Border Patrol, tightened the procedures for foreigners seeking asylum, limited judicial discretion in immigration cases, added new financial requirements for sponsors, and established stringent provisions for criminal and undocumented aliens. In regard to limiting public benefits, IIRIRA took a few specific cues from the states. It made undocumented immigrants ineligible to receive Social Security benefits and some educational benefits; additionally, states were given authority to limit assistance to all immigrants. In the same year, the Personal Responsibility and Work Opportunity Reconciliation Act (PRWORA) famously ended "welfare as we know it" and devolved the decisions about whether or not immigrants could access most public benefits to the states.

However, contained within the IIRIRA was a provision that would further affect immigrants and perpetuate the state-federal policy battle. IIRIRA added section 287(g) to the Immigration and Nationality Act, and thereby created a window of opportunity for state and local involvement in immigration enforcement. The section allows the federal government and states to enter into a Memorandum of Agreement (MOA) that authorizes local law enforcement officials "to perform a function of an immigration officer in relation to the investigation, apprehension, or detention of aliens in the United States."[10]

The Evolution of Section 287(g)

Despite its creation in the mid-1990s, the first section 287(g) agreement was not signed until 2002. The events of September 11, 2001, in which commercial airliners were hijacked and flown into the World Trade Center in New York, the Pentagon in Washington, DC, and a field in Pennsylvania, played a major role in motivating states to seek enforcement authority under section 287(g).[11] Florida signed the first section 287(g) MOA with the federal government after state officials learned that several of the 9/11 hijackers who had overstayed their visas once lived in the state.[12] To some, section 287(g) was seen as a convenient way to increase security by using local officials to create a "force multiplier" effect: as of 2012, over 1,300 officers were trained and certified nationwide under section 287(g).[13] Originally, the program was implemented as a targeted agreement, focused on apprehension of immigrants accused or convicted of crimes. However, by 2006 some localities changed the program's goal to apprehending as many undocumented immigrants as possible regardless of their criminal records. Today, many jurisdictions have instituted dual goals for the program: a focus on criminals and a second focus on undocumented immigrants who have no criminal record.

The section 287(g) program has been very controversial because it makes subnational governments responsible for immigration law enforcement, which some legal scholars view as a violation of the plenary power doctrine. It is also questionable how effective section 287(g) has actually been and whether it has done more harm than good by moving police from a focus on enforcement of issues like domestic violence, gangs, and drugs to immigration.

Maricopa County, Arizona, exemplifies many of the problems associated with subnational enforcement of national immigration laws. In 2007 Maricopa County entered into an agreement with ICE, and the local sheriff, Joe Arpaio, zealously implemented the MOA. Within three months from program initiation, the sheriff's office showed a $1.3 million deficit and a decline in emergency response as deputies were pulled off patrol to staff immigration units.[14]

In December 2011 the U.S. Department of Justice (USDOJ) released a twenty-two-page report accusing Maricopa's sheriff of "unconstitutional policing" and egregious civil rights violations. It also noted that the Maricopa Sheriff's Office failed to adequately investigate over four hundred sexual abuse cases.[15]

THE STATE OF THE STATES: IMMIGRATION AND STATE LEGISLATIVE RESPONSE

The Growth in the Immigrant and Undocumented Populations since 2000

Between 2000 and 2011 the immigrant population grew from 9.3 million to 11 million.[16] This growth was primarily driven by a thriving U.S. economy that required the skills and labor provided by undocumented immigrants. Demand for labor was high, and the U.S. population could not produce the number of construction and service-industry workers needed to keep up with the pace of growth. Since the economic boom did not affect all places equally, some cities felt the effects of the growing undocumented population more than others. Indeed, most of the cities with the largest undocumented and documented immigrant populations are those that benefited most from the economic boom.

In 2008 about two-thirds of the nation's undocumented population resided in eight states: Arizona, California, Florida, Georgia, Illinois, New Jersey, New York, and Texas. Importantly, much of this growth was in locations within these states that have not historically seen many immigrants. Particularly in new gateway cities and states, the vast majority of the growth in immigration occurred in the suburbs.[17] And unlike previous waves of immigrants whose skin tone was similar to that of the native population, the ethnic and racial makeup of immigrants in the modern era is more diverse. Thus the last decade has ushered in a more racially and ethnically diverse group of immigrants to places not used to receiving them.

Although these states host the majority of immigrants in the nation, other areas in the country struggle to respond to rapid increases in their immigrant population, regardless of documentation status. As Table 32.1 shows, between the years 2000 and 2010, foreign-born populations began moving to states that had never had a significant immigrant population.

States that have historically little exposure to immigrants experienced a relatively large influx (see The Immigrant Influx in Maine box). Thus, while the overall number of immigrants in these states may appear very low, the rate of change is dramatic. In these circumstances immigration may be particularly disconcerting to a state's residents and its elected officials due to the newness of outsiders to the community, especially given that these immigrants are not only linguistically but also racially and ethnically different. Research suggests that there is a strong correlation between the growth of immigration and the likelihood of a nativist or anti-immigrant response by the citizens. Localities that experience a sudden increase in their immigrant population are more likely to introduce anti-immigrant policies.[18]

As a result of the uneven population distribution, some of the states with the largest numbers of immigrants, and other states with rapidly large increases in immigrant populations, have begun to voice their concerns over the increasing presence of (particularly undocumented) immigrants in their states through policy initiatives. Primarily, these complaints have focused on the perceived economic strain on public services. Whether or not immigration provides an economic stimulus or a financial drain is a topic of much debate both in the public sphere and in the academy.

Evidence suggests that immigrants have many positive effects on the U.S. economy. In 2010 households headed by

TABLE 32.1 **States Ranked by Percentage Change in the Foreign-Born Population, 2000–2010**

	2000	2010	
State	**Estimate**	**Estimate**	**Percent change**
Alabama	87,772	168,596	92.1
South Carolina	115,978	218,494	88.4
Tennessee	159,004	288,993	81.8
Arkansas	73,690	131,667	78.7
Kentucky	80,271	140,583	75.1
North Carolina	430,000	719,137	67.2
South Dakota	13,495	22,238	64.8
Georgia	577,273	942,959	63.3
Indiana	186,534	300,789	61.3
Nevada	316,593	508,458	60.6

SOURCE: Migration Policy Institute.

undocumented immigrants paid $11.2 billion in state and local taxes. Another 2008 report estimates that the removal of all illegal immigrants from the country would result in a $551.6 billion loss in economic activity and a $245 billion loss in gross domestic product (GDP).[19] Certainly, though, the popular image is that immigrants use more services than they pay for. Undocumented immigrants in particular are accused of using state and local services but not paying taxes. This argument is only partially true—undocumented immigrants pay property, sales, and other non-income taxes even if their wages are paid in cash. Additionally, undocumented immigrants who are paid using falsified documents also pay income tax and pay into Social Security and Medicare. Furthermore, after paying into these national programs, undocumented immigrants have no ability to access the benefits if and when they become age-eligible; nor do they have the ability to get back any money from the federal government that they paid in income tax but did not actually owe.

Despite the failure of federal law to address immigration issues adequately, Congress has been unable to pass comprehensive immigration reform and, as a result, the amount of state-sponsored immigration legislation has made a dramatic increase. In 2005, 300 bills pertaining to immigration were introduced and 39 laws were enacted. In 2006 the number of immigration bills introduced and passed almost doubled, and by 2011, 1,607 bills were introduced and 197 laws were enacted.[20]

The nature of state-sponsored policies is varied and broad. Topics like immigrant access to public services, ability to vote, and right to an education have all been addressed by one state law or another; however, the intent of the law is what defines the state's attitude toward immigrants. Some states have chosen to legislate in a manner exclusive of immigrants, while others have striven to include and incorporate them.

Exclusionary Policies

Restrictive laws can be divided into those that directly target undocumented immigrants and those that target employers who hire them. The stated intent of this type of legislation is to raise the cost of staying in the United States so high that undocumented immigrants will voluntarily leave. These laws are also expected to act as deterrents for future undocumented migration. Indeed, Alabama's House Bill 56 (HB56), the Beason-Hammon Alabama Taxpayer and Citizen Protection Act, is justified in the state code as aiming to make everyday life so difficult for undocumented immigrants that they choose to "self-deport."

The most popular and widespread legislation targeting employers involves the requirement to use E-Verify. The Basic Pilot-Employment Eligibility Verification Program (promptly renamed E-Verify) was created as part of IIRIRA in 1996. E-Verify is an Internet-based program designed to help employers verify the work authorization of all potential

THE IMMIGRANT INFLUX IN MAINE

Although most discussions of immigration focus primarily on the Latino population, migrants to the United States come from a number of countries. Maine has seen an increase in its immigrant population, particularly in its refugee population. The state experienced a 24.5 percent increase in its immigrant population between 2000 and 2010, an increase of 8,975 persons. In the previous decade, from 1990 to 2000, Maine's foreign-born population grew by only 395 persons. Unlike most other states, Maine's foreign-born population is primarily made up of Asian and African immigrants. By 2010, 26.8 percent of the foreign born in Maine were from Asia, 23.0 percent were from Europe, and 14.3 percent were from Africa.

A refugee is defined as a person who is unable or unwilling to return to his or her home country due to well-founded fear of persecution as a result of race, particular social group membership, political opinion, religion, or national origin. Each year, the United States sets a numerical ceiling for refugee admittance. In 2011 the cap was set at eighty thousand and broken down into limits by world regions; the limit for Africa was set at fifteen thousand. African refugees have flocked to Maine in hopes of finding relief from persecution in their native countries. The towns of Lewiston and Portland in particular have become beacons of hope for immigrants seeking asylum. Although tension still exists at times between African populations and other residents of the Pine Tree State, the general response to the influx of immigrants has been positive.

CASE STUDY: LEWISTON

Since a family of Somali refugees settled in Lewiston in 2001 and began encouraging their fellow countrymen to do the same, this town has been transformed. In downtown Lewiston, Somali retailers sell goods from Africa, operate restaurants, and provide other services to the community. Between 2001 and 2007, about 3,500 Somalis settled in the town of Lewiston. Sudanese, Congolese, and other African migrants soon joined the Somalis. At first, townspeople worried about the growing immigrant population taking jobs and overloading social services; however, the African migrants are generally credited with reviving the town's commerce and boosting university enrollment in the area. Overall, foreign-born students contributed $37 million to the state's economy during school year 2009–2010 through tuition, fees, and living expenses. Although enrollment at the University of Maine dropped statewide between 2002 and 2007, enrollment at its Lewiston campus jumped 16 percent.

Somalis and other African immigrants have been quick to become active community members. In 2011 several Somali refugees ran for public office through a write-in campaign for a spot on the Lewiston School Committee. However, although one candidate received 41 percent of the vote, none were elected.

CASE STUDY: PORTLAND

Portland has become a hub for refugees and immigrants from Burundi, the Democratic Republic of the Congo, Djibouti, Rwanda, and Somalia, and Portland's nonprofit Immigrant Legal Advocacy Project (ILAP) provides legal assistance to low-income residents. However, in 2010 ILAP stopped accepting new cases after applicants for political asylum increased from one hundred to four hundred applicants. The city has also welcomed Sudanese immigrants, who first arrived in Maine as refugees fleeing civil war. As locals have begun to incorporate the refugees, tensions have arisen between Sudanese immigrants and police. In 2009 police fatally shot twenty-six-year-old Sudanese refugee David Okot. Police said Okot refused to show them his hands and subsequently pointed a gun at them. Additionally, the unsolved shooting of Sudanese hospital security guard James Angelo in 2008 has left many Sudanese refugees feeling uneasy about relations with local police.

The community began to heal after the shootings. Residents and refugees planted bulbs in memory of Angelo and Okot, and the Department of Justice sent a federal mediator to resolve tensions between the Sudanese community and local police. Officials and community members continue to search for ways to incorporate immigrants in a positive way. In 2010 eighteen refugees from the Congo, Somalia, and Sudan graduated from a state-sponsored Refugee Leaders Capacity Building program. The program taught its students leadership and organizational skills in the hopes that they would lead their refugee communities in the integration process. In 2011 city officials discussed making one out of three days of farmers' markets an international farmers' market, featuring local farmers from Burundi, the Congo, Mali, Rwanda, Somalia, and South Sudan, who have grown both local and foreign crops.

SOURCES: J. Batalova and A. Lee, "Frequently Requested Statistics on Immigrants and Immigration in the United States," Migration Policy Institute, 2012, www.migrationinformation.org/USfocus/display.cfm?ID=886; T. Bell, "Sudanese Community Has Diverse Makeup," *Maine Sunday Telegram*, March 15, 2010, www.pressherald.com/archive/sudanese-community-has-diverse-makeup_2008-09-13.html?searchterm=lewiston+somali; A. Cullen, "Struggle and Progress: 10 years of Somalis in Lewiston," *Lewiston Sun Journal*, December 18, 2011, www.sunjournal.com/news/city/2011/12/18/struggle-and-progess-10-years-somalis-lewiston/1127846; J. Ellison, "The Refugees Who Saved Lewiston," *Newsweek*, January 16, 2009, www.thedailybeast.com/newsweek/2009/01/16/the-refugees-who-saved-lewiston.html; D. Hench, "Mediator Helping Police, Sudanese Resolve Tensions," *Portland Press Herald*, March 4, 2010, www.pressherald.com/archive/mediator-helping-police-sudanese-resolve-tensions_2009-10-26.html?searchterm=david+okot.

employees by comparing information from employers with information from the Social Security Administration (SSA) and the Department of Homeland Security's (DHS) immigration databases. Many states now have an E-Verify requirement despite the fact that E-Verify has been shown to encourage more employers to hire people off the books. The system is also known for erroneously rejecting legal Latino and African American workers far more often than white workers, which increases discrimination in the hiring process.[21]

States have also sought to make undocumented presence more costly by empowering local and state police to enforce federal immigration law. In addition to signing up for section 287(g) agreements, states have argued that they have the authority to enforce federal immigration law under their own police authority. Arizona's Senate Bill 1070 (SB1070), officially titled the Support Our Law Enforcement and Safe Neighborhoods Act, passed in the spring of 2010 and declared that undocumented entry was equivalent to criminal trespass punishable with prison terms. SB1070 prohibited undocumented immigrants from soliciting work and also required all noncitizens to carry their passports, visa documentation, or green cards at all times and increased penalties for harboring or transporting undocumented immigrants and for hiring undocumented labor.

However, after Arizona passed its immigration bill, the USDOJ filed a lawsuit claiming the law was unconstitutional. In June 2012 the Supreme Court overturned most of the law.[22] The one provision left standing by the Court requires local law enforcement to check the immigration status of anyone they suspect might be in the country illegally. Opponents of the law noted that this part of the law could lead to racial and ethnic profiling by police and other state officials required to enforce the legislation.

Alabama passed its own omnibus immigration legislation, the previously mentioned HB56, but Alabama went a step further, requiring that all schools check the immigration status of students. Although Arizona's law gained far more media attention, HB56 was the most sweeping state anti-immigration law in the country at the time. It requires that an individual's immigration status be checked any time a person comes into any contact with a government institution, whether that be enrolling children in school, reporting a crime to the police, or paying bills or taxes. The law also makes it illegal to help any undocumented person in any way, even if the entity is a church or another nonprofit institution.

Alabama's law has been widely criticized for creating chaos within the state. After the passage of HB56, farmers complained about their crops rotting in the fields after workers disappeared; members of the military who could not prove citizenship in the state said they could not register to vote; and scores of people claimed to have almost been kicked out of their homes after the Alabama Department of Revenue could not verify their immigration status. Most striking to many observers was the number of Latino children (even those who were legal residents or citizens) kept out of school because their parents feared arrest or police harassment as a result of the law.[23]

The law also had significant consequences for the state's economy. Among the first arrested under the law were a German Mercedes-Benz executive and a Japanese Honda executive who were pulled over (separately) in routine traffic stops. Both executives were arrested on immigration violations because they were not carrying the documents mandated by the state law. Both executives were in the state legally and on business with factories located within the state.

The unintended consequences of the Alabama immigration law are so widespread that even Republican legislators who originally voted for the bill began to consider how to rewrite it. However, anti-immigrant feelings run so high in Alabama that the political capital needed to reverse such a law may be insurmountable.[24] These laws and similar legislation (mostly in the South) have invited significant controversy. Along with the Arizona ruling and other injunctions against the Alabama law by state and federal courts, lawsuits were filed in several other states that passed similar anti-immigrant legislation.

Inclusionary Policies

Vast attention has been paid to restrictive state legislation. However, some states have responded to their immigrant populations in positive ways. Many local governments have inclusionary policies that promote immigrant well-being and acculturation. Policies concerning the declaration of a city as a "sanctuary," immigrant access to health care and public services, access and affordability of higher education, English-language instruction, and translation and interpretation laws serve as a counter to exclusionary policies.

Beginning in the 1980s, some religious institutions declared themselves sanctuaries for Central American refugees not granted asylum under the Refugee Act of 1980. These sanctuary institutions welcomed immigrants and attempted to shield them from anti-immigrant resentment. Opposition to the passage of IRCA also fueled the sanctuary movement. By 1986, twenty cities and the states of New Mexico and New York had passed resolutions designating the locations as sanctuaries for immigrants.[25]

In direct contrast to recent omnibus immigration enforcement laws enacted in states like Alabama and Arizona, sixty-five counties, cities, and local governments explicitly prohibit their police and officials from enforcing federal civil immigration law. Additionally, four cities and one county prohibit the collection and/or disclosure of information about citizens' immigration status even though 1996's IIRIRA outlawed such city bans from sharing information with the federal government. Immigrant-friendly state actions from 2011 included inclusive immigration legislation in the areas of health and public benefits. California supplemented its Fostering Connections Act with guidance for Child Protective Services (CPS) on caring for immigrant children, and also allows legal immigrants to be eligible for Medicaid Coverage Expansion and the Health Care Coverage Initiative. Indiana now provides childcare to migrants who are victims of domestic violence, and Nevada and Connecticut now allow legal immigrants to participate in their state health insurance exchanges.[26] In general, there are four institutional policies that local governments utilize to support immigrants: (1) establishing a multipurpose agency to serve immigrant residents; (2) accepting *matrículas consulares* (an identification card from the government of Mexico) as a valid form of identification; (3) offering municipal identification cards to undocumented residents; and (4) allowing noncitizen residents to vote in local elections.[27] Additional state assimilation efforts include English-language courses, naturalization test preparation, translation and interpretation laws that require official documents be published in multiple languages, and other programs that promote citizenship.

The DREAM Act

The DREAM Act was first introduced in Congress in 2001 by Sens. Orrin Hatch, R-Utah, and Richard Durbin, D-Ill., in the Senate, and Reps. Howard Berman, D-Calif., and Chris Cannon, R-Utah, in the House. The DREAM Act provides a pathway for undocumented high school graduates to obtain permanent residency and potentially U.S. citizenship via college enrollment or military service. In most states, students who are not citizens or permanent residents must pay out-of-state tuition to attend higher education institutions and are not eligible for in-state tuition rates. The act is intended to address the challenges that U.S.-raised and educated immigrant students face when trying to gain a postsecondary degree or when searching for work as adults.

The DREAM Act would remedy these issues by providing conditional legal status to undocumented residents younger than thirty-two years of age who (1) were under age fifteen upon entrance; (2) have lived in the United States for at least five years; (3) have graduated from a U.S. high school; (4) show "good moral character"; and (5) are not inadmissible or deportable under criminal or security grounds of the Immigration and Nationality Act. Consequently, students could obtain permanent residence after two years of college or military service. Like other immigrant legislation, the DREAM Act has been deadlocked in Congress; however, state efforts to provide access to higher education to undocumented immigrants reflect its popularity.

Although states do not have the ability to grant citizenship, which is a critical component of the DREAM Act, increasing immigrant access to higher education has been addressed by a few states. IIRIRA effectively restricted state residency requirements and in-state college tuition benefits. In response, some states enacted legislation that allowed undocumented immigrants to receive in-state tuition under specified conditions (see The Politics of In-State Tuition for Undocumented Immigrants in Maryland box). States were able to circumvent the condition in IIRIRA that commands states to provide the same benefits to all U.S. citizens as offered to undocumented immigrants by basing in-state tuition requirements on educational requirements, rather than residency. California even offers financial aid.

Although eighteen states have rejected similar legislation, in 2004 Kansas became the eighth state to allow undocumented children to qualify for in-state tuition. An unlikely candidate (Kansas is generally thought to be anti-immigrant), the legislature passed the bill after proponents framed it as a way to encourage higher education for all Kansan children. Gary Reich and Alvar A. Mendoza credit the bill's passage to the advocates' skillful framing, in which they successfully reframed the issue to focus on the positives of educating the workforce rather than "rewarding aliens."[28] The popularity of the DREAM Act and its state equivalents is attributed to its focus on rewarding good behavior, patriotism, and higher education for those who did not make the choice themselves to migrate to the United States but instead are here as a consequence of their parents' actions. Although several states have increased access to higher education, DREAMERS, as these children have come to be known, still find themselves in a catch-22 because the federal government is still the sole issuer of immigration documents and work permits. DREAMERS may graduate from college with marketable—even needed—skills for the economy, but they do not possess or have access to work permits. Therefore, they often find themselves unable to qualify for work even after they have attained a college or graduate degree.

FEDERAL RESPONSE TO STATE IMMIGRATION LAWS

On the federal level, the possibility of immigration reform remains doubtful. Immigration is a politically risky issue for both parties. Ever since the 1986 reforms failed to deliver the changes they promised, immigration has become one of the most contentious issues in Congress. The threat of terrorism has also made meaningful immigration reform much more difficult in the post-9/11 world. Other national issues, such as health care, the war on terror, and the economy, have also overshadowed immigration. Although many recent presidents have campaigned on immigration reform, holding a coalition together in Congress has been difficult for even the strongest presidents.

President George W. Bush campaigned on immigration reform and proposed a bipartisan bill that would (1) increase border security; (2) create a guest worker program to help farmers and others who rely on migrant workers; and (3) create a pathway to citizenship for long-term residents. The bill was scheduled for a vote on September 11, 2001, but as America underwent the most deadly terrorist attack in its history, the vote was tabled. In the aftermath of 9/11, the conversation about immigration was changed: Republicans and Democrats who had supported

THE POLITICS OF IN-STATE TUITION FOR UNDOCUMENTED IMMIGRANTS IN MARYLAND

The Illegal Immigration and Immigrant Responsibility Act (IIRIRA) of 1996 prohibits states from offering resident tuition rates to undocumented students unless the rate applies to all U.S. citizens regardless of state residency; however, states have found a loophole in this stipulation.[1] By basing in-state tuition on high school attendance and graduation requirements rather than residency, states have circumvented federal law to offer in-state tuition to undocumented students. Twelve states currently offer in-state tuition to undocumented immigrants, and Maryland is set to be the thirteenth. Sen. Victor R. Ramirez, a Democrat of Prince George's County, introduced Maryland's own version of the DREAM Act via Senate Bill 167 (SB 167). The bill was passed in 2011 by the Democrat-controlled Maryland General Assembly and signed by the Democratic governor, Martin O'Malley.[2] The law extends in-state tuition benefits at community colleges to undocumented immigrants who attend at least three years of a high school in the state of Maryland and subsequently graduate, as long as the graduates' parents can prove they pay Maryland taxes. After two years at community college, undocumented students would have the option of transferring to a state university at the in-state tuition rate.

The controversial bill had both supporters and opponents, and although SB 167 was passed by the state legislature, it did not immediately go into effect. Opponents, who said SB 167 was unfair to taxpayers, successfully petitioned to stop the bill from being implemented until the question was decided by the voters via referendum.[3] On November 12, 2012, Maryland became the first state in the nation to approve a law extending in-state tuition to undocumented immigrants through popular vote. The referendum was supported by 58 percent of voters.

1. Kyla C. Grant, "Maryland Dream Act Expected to Pass," ABC News, March 11, 2011, http://abcnews.go.com/Politics/maryland-dream-act-expected-pass/story?id=13095720#.T3pH0RyxSls; Warren Richey, "In-State Tuition for Illegal Immigrants Survives, Supreme Court Declines Case," *CS Monitor,* June 6, 2011, www.csmonitor.com/USA/Justice/2011/0606/In-state-tuition-for-illegal-immigrants-survives-Supreme-Court-declines-case.
2. Annie Linskey, "National Group to Aid In-State Tuition Repeal," *Baltimore Sun,* September 22, 2011, www.baltimoresun.com/news/maryland/politics/bs-md-judicial-watch-in-state-tuition-20110922,0,7672063.story.
3. Ibid.

the legislation now had to deal with the fact that the hijackers had come to the United States on temporary visas and had overstayed without detection. One had also run amok with local police, but his immigration status had not been unearthed. Since then, Congress has largely been deadlocked on the immigration issue, particularly on the subject of comprehensive immigration reform.

A major challenge to immigration reform at the national level is the political capital that is required to create a bipartisan alliance. Like his predecessor, President Barack Obama campaigned on comprehensive immigration reform; but while trying to pass a health care reform bill, he publicly commented that immigration was too large an issue to take on at the same time. Subsequently, the financial crisis largely kept immigration reform off the table. However, there has been a renewed focus on the subject by some core members of the Republican Party, particularly in the Senate, who see the future of the GOP tied to the electoral proclivities of the Latino population. However, like their predecessors, members of Congress who wish to pass immigration reform have to navigate treacherous waters by satisfying anti-immigrant constituencies who wish for a total focus on border enforcement, immigration advocates who want a path to citizenship for the undocumented, and the business community who wants an increase in the number of visas for high-tech immigrants.

Lessons from the states also inform the parties about what is at stake. Immigration policy changes have the potential to rapidly produce partisan change. In the wake of Proposition 187 in California, Latinos flocked to the Democratic Party and California changed from a red to a blue state. Prior to the passage of these propositions Latinos had about a one in three chance of identifying as a Democrat. But after the passage of three anti-immigrant propositions the likelihood that a Latino voter would register as a Democrat was well over 50 percent.[29] Additionally, the Latino population grew rapidly during this time and was very young; this fact, coupled with the frequent use of anti-immigrant ballot initiatives, has contributed to partisan change in the state as well.[30] The political-wedge issues in California led Latinos to seek naturalization, and those who were naturalized during the 1990s continued to register and vote at higher rates than fellow Latinos in Florida and Texas.[31]

Indeed, since immigration policy is frequently ethnically charged, the policy positions of the political parties have tended to alienate not just the group targeted, but the white majority as well. Republican state initiatives passed between 1994 and 1998 that targeted immigrants and Latinos actually shifted partisan attachment among whites in California to the Democratic Party due to the initiatives' partisan nature.

Today, Republicans stand to lose significant numbers at the ballot box if they turn off Latino voters. The struggle between recruiting Latino voters into the Republican fold and satisfying an anti-immigrant base has put the Republican Party in a difficult place. Politically, it has been better for the Republican Party in the short term to take a hard anti-immigrant stance. However, many political advisers have pointed out that this may not be to their long-term political advantage, as the Latino and Asian populations in the United States are growing steadily, particularly in some battleground states.

Of course, some academics and policymakers now question whether a comprehensive immigration package is actually necessary. The rate of undocumented immigration from Mexico, the largest of the undocumented immigrant-sending countries and the country most singled-out by immigration reformers, today is nearing zero. At its peak in 1999, 55 out of every 1,000 Mexican men entering the United States were entering illegally. Today, it is only 9 in 1,000, and dropping. Additionally, fewer immigrants with documents are staying permanently. Instead, immigrants are using their visas to travel for work to the United States and then returning to their country of origin. Comprehensive immigration reform has historically consisted of four goals: (1) reducing illegal immigration; (2) increasing temporary work visas; (3) granting more permanent resident visas; and (4) legalizing existing undocumented migrants. Given that few undocumented immigrants are entering the country and that many legal immigrants are coming to work and then returning home, "the first two goals have effectively been reached, and mass legal immigration by relatives of citizens satisfies the third."[32] This leaves the question of whether comprehensive immigration reform is necessary or if Congress can now turn its attention to how to deal with the millions of undocumented immigrants who have made the United States their home and who are not going to go anywhere, particularly youth raised in the United States and parents with citizen children.

The continued failure of the federal government to address the limitations of current immigration law has led many states to continue their search for their own solutions. There is no doubt that state legislatures will continue to create local solutions to immigration problems. Nonetheless, immigration policy requires federal reform to effectively address the complex issues behind the inadequacies of the immigration system.

NOTES

1. *Henderson v. the Mayor of the City of New York,* 92 U.S. 259 (1875).
2. Gerald L. Neuman, "The Lost Century of American Immigration Law (1776–1875)," *Columbia Law Review* 93 (1993): 1833–1901; *Chy Lung v. Freeman,* 92 U.S. 275 (1875).
3. Raymond Tatalovich, *Nativism Reborn? The Official English Language Movement of the United States* (Lexington: University Press of Kentucky, 1995).
4. Alexandra Filindra and Jane Junn, "Aliens of Color: The Multidimensional Relationship between Immigration Policy and Racial Classifications in the U.S.," in *The Oxford Handbook of the Politics of International Migration,* ed. Marc R. Rosenblum and Daniel J. Tichenor (Oxford, UK: Oxford University Press, 2012).
5. Douglas S. Massey, Jorge Durand, and Nolan J. Malone, *Beyond Smoke and Mirrors: Mexican Immigration in an Era of Economic Integration* (New York: Russell Sage Foundation, 2002).
6. Alexandra Filindra, "E Pluribus Unum? Federalism, Immigration, and the Role of the American States" (PhD diss., Rutgers, 2009).
7. *Plyler v. Doe,* 457 U.S. 202 (1982).
8. Jeffrey S. Passel, "Estimates of Size and Characteristics of the Undocumented Population" (Washington, DC: Pew Research Center, 2005).
9. *League of United Latin American Citizens (LULAC) v. Wilson,* 908 F. Supp. 755, 786–87 (C.D. Cal. 1995).
10. Illegal Immigration Reform and Immigrant Responsibility Act (IIRIRA) of 1996, Public Law 104–208, 110 Stat. 3009, 1996.
11. Michele Waslin, "Immigration Enforcement by State and Local Police: The Impact on the Enforcers and Their Communities," in *Taking Local Control: Immigration Policy Activism in U.S. Cities and States,* ed. Monica Varsanyi (Stanford, CA: Stanford University, 2010).
12. Amada Armenta, "From Sheriff's Deputies to Immigration Officers: Screening Immigrant Status in a Tennessee Jail," *Law and Policy* 34 (2012): 191–210.
13. U.S. Immigration and Customs Enforcement (ICE), "Fact Sheet: ICE Agreements of Cooperation in Communities to Enhance Safety and Security (ACCESS)," 2012.
14. Afton Branche, "The Cost of Failure: The Burden of Immigration Enforcement on America's Cities" (Washington, DC: The Drum Major Institute for Public Policy, 2011).
15. Marc Lacy, "U.S. Finds Pervasive Bias against Latinos by Arizona Sheriff," *New York Times,* December 15, 2011.
16. Jeffrey S. Passel and D'Vera Cohn, "Unauthorized Immigrant Population: National and State Trends, 2010" (Washington, DC: Pew Research Center, 2011).
17. Audrey Singer, "The Rise of New Immigrant Gateways" (Washington, DC: Brookings, 2004).
18. Shanna Pearson-Merkowitz, "Punitive Immigration Reform in the States: A Test of Four Models" (presentation at the annual State Politics and Policy Conference, Hanover, NH, June, 2011).
19. Immigration Policy Center (IPC), "Strength in Diversity: The Economic and Political Clout of Immigrants, Latinos, and Asians in the United States," 2012.
20. National Conference of State Legislatures (NCSL), "State Laws Related to Immigration and Immigrants," 2012.
21. Immigration Policy Center (IPC), "How Expanding E-Verify Would Hurt American Workers and Business," 2010.
22. *Arizona v. United States,* 567 U.S. __ (2012).

23. Jeremy B. White, "Alabama Immigration Law Prompts Immigrants to Flee School, Jobs, Homes," *International Business Times,* October 4, 2011.

24. Jack Hitt and Jonathan Menjivar, Reap What You Sow—This American Life Radio Series Episode 456, 2012, www.thisamericanlife.org/radio-archives/episode/456/reap-what-you-sow.

25. Miriam J. Wells, "The Grassroots Reconfiguration of U.S. Immigration Policy," *International Migration Review* 38 (2004): 1308–1347.

26. Brooke Meyer and Ann Morse, "Immigration Policy Report," National Conference of State Legislatures, 2011.

27. Pablo A. Mitnik and Jessica Halpern-Finnerty, "Immigration and Local Governments: Inclusionary Local Policies in the Era of State Rescaling," in *Taking Local Control: Immigration Policy Activism in U.S. Cities and States,* ed. Monica Varsanyi (Stanford, CA: Stanford University Press, 2010).

28. Gary Reich and Alvar A. Mendoza, "'Educating Kids' versus 'Coddling Criminals': Framing the Debate over In-State Tuition for Undocumented Students in Kansas," *State Politics and Policy Quarterly* 8 (2008): 177–197.

29. Shaun Bowler, Stephen P. Nicholson, and Gary M. Segura, "Earthquakes and Aftershocks: Race, Direct Democracy, and Partisan Change," *American Journal of Political Science* 50 (2006), 146–159.

30. Joshua J. Dyck, Gregg B. Johnson, and Jesse T. Wasson, "A Blue Tide in the Golden State: Ballot Propositions, Population Change, and Party Identification in California," *American Politics Research* 40 (2012), 450–475.

31. Adrian D. Pantoja, Ricardo Ramirez, and Gary M. Segura, "Citizens by Choice, Voters by Necessity: Patterns in Political Mobilization by Naturalized Latinos," *Political Research Quarterly* 54 (2001): 729–750.

32. Jorge G. Castañeda and Douglas S. Massey, "Do-It-Yourself Immigration Reform," *New York Times,* June 1, 2012, www.nytimes.com/2012/06/02/opinion/do-it-yourself-immigration-reform.html?src=recg.

SUGGESTED READING

Baron, Dennis. *The English-Only Question.* New Haven, CT: Yale University Press, 1990.

Bowler, Shaun, Stephen P. Nicholson, and Gary M. Segura. "Earthquakes and Aftershocks: Race, Direct Democracy, and Partisan Change." *American Journal of Political Science* 50 (2006): 146–159.

Chavez, Jorge M., and Doris Marie Provine. "Race and the Response of State Legislatures to Unauthorized Immigrants." *The Annals of the American Academy of Political and Social Science* 623 (2009): 78–92.

Chavez, Leo R. *The Latino Threat: Constructing Immigrants, Citizens, and the Nation.* Stanford, CA: Stanford University Press, 2008.

Coleman, Matthew. "The 'Local' Migration State: The Site-Specific Devolution of Immigration Enforcement in the U.S. South." *Law and Policy* 34 (2012): 159–190.

Dyck, Joshua J., Gregg B. Johnson, and Jesse T. Wasson. "A Blue Tide in the Golden State: Ballot Propositions, Population Change, and Party Identification in California." *American Politics Research* 40 (2012): 450–475.

Espenshade, Thomas. "Unauthorized Immigration to the United States." *Annual Review of Sociology* 21 (1995): 195–216.

Filindra, Alexandra. "E Pluribus Unum? Federalism, Immigration, and the Role of the American States." PhD diss., Rutgers, 2009.

Filindra, Alexandra, and Jane Junn. "Aliens of Color: The Multidimensional Relationship between Immigration Policy and Racial Classifications in the U.S." In *The Oxford Handbook of the Politics of International Migration,* ed. Marc R. Rosenblum and Daniel J. Tichenor. Oxford, UK: Oxford University Press, 2012.

Grieco, Elizabeth M., Yesenia D. Acosta, Patricia de la Cruz, Christine Gambino, Thomas Gryn, Luke J. Larsen, Edward N. Trevelyan, and Nathan P. Walters. "The Foreign-Born Population in the United States: 2010." Washington, DC: U.S. Census Bureau, 2012.

Hernandez, Kelly L. *Migra! A History of the U.S. Border Patrol.* Berkeley: University of California Press, 2010.

Jones-Correa, Michael. "All Immigration Is Local: Receiving Communities and Their Role in Successful Immigrant Integration." Washington, DC: Center for American Progress, 2011.

Law and Policy 34 (April 2012): 105–236. Special issue on state and local creation and enforcement of immigration law.

Lewis, Daniel C. "Bypassing the Representational Filter? Minority Rights Policies under Direct Democracy Institutions in the U.S. States." *State Politics and Policy Quarterly* 11 (2011): 198–222.

Massey, Douglas S., Jorge Durand, and Nolan J. Malone. *Beyond Smoke and Mirrors: Mexican Immigration in an Era of Economic Integration.* New York: Russell Sage Foundation, 2002.

Meyer, Brooke, and Ann Morse. "Immigration Policy Report." National Conference of State Legislatures, 2011.

National Conference of State Legislatures (NCSL). "State Laws Related to Immigration and Immigrants," 2012.

Newton, Lina, and Brian E. Adams. "State Immigration Policies: Innovation, Cooperation, or Conflict?" *Publius: The Journal of Federalism* 39 (2009): 408–431.

Pantoja, Adrian D., Ricardo Ramirez, and Gary M. Segura. "Citizens by Choice, Voters by Necessity: Patterns in Political Mobilization by Naturalized Latinos." *Political Research Quarterly* 54 (2001): 729–750.

Passel, Jeffrey S., and D'Vera Cohn. "Unauthorized Immigrant Population: National and State Trends, 2010" (Washington, DC: Pew Research Center, 2011).

Reich, Gary, and Alvar A. Mendoza. "'Educating Kids' versus 'Coddling Criminals': Framing the Debate over In-State Tuition for Undocumented Students in Kansas." *State Politics and Policy Quarterly* 8 (2008): 177–197.

Schildkraut, Deborah J. *Press One for English: Language Policy, Public Opinion, and American Identity.* Princeton, NJ: Princeton University Press, 2005.

Singer, Audrey. "The Rise of New Immigrant Gateways." Washington, DC: Brookings, 2004.

Tatalovich, Raymond. *Nativism Reborn? The Official English Language Movement of the United States.* Lexington: University Press of Kentucky, 1995.

Tichenor, Daniel J. *Dividing Lines: The Politics of Immigration Control in America.* Princeton, NJ: Princeton University Press, 2002.

Varsanyi, Monica, ed. *Taking Local Control: Immigration Policy Activism in U.S. Cities and States.* Stanford, CA: Stanford University Press, 2009.

Waslin, Michele. "Discrediting 'Self-Deportation' as Immigration Policy: Why an Attrition through Enforcement Strategy Makes Life Difficult for Everyone." Immigration Policy Center, 2012, www.ilw.com/articles/2012,0329-waslin.pdf.

Wells, Miriam J. "The Grassroots Reconfiguration of U.S. Immigration Policy." *International Migration Review* 38 (2004): 1308–1347.

Wong, Carolyn. *Lobbying for Inclusion: Rights Politics and the Making of Immigration Policy.* Stanford, CA: Stanford University Press, 2006.

Chapter 33

Welfare

Richard C. Fording

COMPARED WITH MOST WESTERN NATIONS, the financing and administration of U.S. social welfare programs is relatively decentralized. State and local governments have traditionally been responsible for a sizable share of social welfare spending and have enjoyed even greater discretion in setting benefit levels and eligibility requirements for many programs. This is especially true for programs targeted for the poor. For this reason, state politics scholars have devoted much attention to studying state welfare policy, exploiting the variation in state policies to better understand the role of the political environment in the formulation of state policy and the effectiveness of social welfare programs in achieving their goals.

This chapter summarizes this literature on state welfare policies. The chapter begins with a brief history and descriptive overview of the social welfare system in the United States, focusing most heavily on the programs that are most important to state and local governments. The next section summarizes studies that seek to explain variation across states and over time in welfare policies, where scholars have debated the relative importance of political and economic factors, racial cleavages, and the impact of decentralization on welfare policy outcomes. The chapter then turns to the literature on the effectiveness of welfare programs, focusing on the programs for which states have displayed the most variation in program design.

SOCIAL WELFARE PROGRAMS IN THE UNITED STATES: A HISTORICAL AND DESCRIPTIVE OVERVIEW

The social welfare system that we know today is largely the product of two significant bursts of policy-making activity. The first and most important historical period occurred during the Great Depression, when the foundation for the current system was first laid in the form of the Social Security Act of 1935 (SSA) (see Welfare Programs and the Great Recession box). The SSA is credited with designing a social welfare system social policy experts often characterize as two-tiered. The upper tier consists of social insurance programs, which are funded by contributions from program beneficiaries and generally cover broad segments of the population, regardless of income. The SSA created two major social insurance programs that are still in existence today—Social Security, which provides cash benefits to retired workers, their survivors, and the disabled; and Unemployment Insurance (UI), which provides cash benefits to unemployed workers.

The lower tier consists of what are termed public assistance programs. These are programs that are purely redistributive in the sense that they are funded mostly by nonparticipants through taxes, and participants pay a relatively small share, if any, of the program costs. These are also the programs that most Americans have in mind when they use the term *welfare.* Two of the largest contemporary public assistance programs today—Temporary Assistance for Needy Families (TANF) and Supplemental Security Income (SSI)—can be traced back to the SSA. This lower tier also consists of state and local General Assistance (GA) programs, which provide cash assistance to a wide range of poor persons who are ineligible for federally funded (or subsidized) public assistance programs. In contrast to social insurance, public assistance programs tend to be highly targeted and limited to the poor. They also tend to be either partly or completely (e.g., GA) decentralized, meaning that state and local governments are responsible for funding a sizable portion of program costs, as well making important decisions regarding eligibility rules and benefit generosity.

The second important period of policy innovation occurred during the 1960s, amidst a wave of protest movements and President Lyndon Johnson's War on Poverty. This era saw the passage of legislation that created two of the largest public assistance programs in the country today. The food stamp program was passed in 1964 to provide food

WELFARE PROGRAMS AND THE GREAT RECESSION

One of the most significant expansions of public assistance programs in recent decades occurred during the early months of the Obama administration in the form of the American Recovery and Reinvestment Act of 2009 (ARRA), known more generally as the "stimulus." ARRA was signed into law by President Barack Obama less than one month after he had officially assumed the presidency; however, he began working on the legislation almost immediately after being elected in November 2008. The primary goals of ARRA were to reduce unemployment; invest in infrastructure, education, health, and "green" energy; and provide relief to those most impacted by the recession through an expansion of several social welfare programs. The Congressional Budget Office estimated that the total cost of ARRA would be nearly $800 billion by 2019; however, the majority of the spending was front-loaded, and approximately $500 billion had been spent by the end of fiscal year 2011.[1] The key poverty-reducing provisions of ARRA included measures to expand federal spending for several important public assistance programs, in addition to changes to the tax code that would benefit the working poor. Some of the most important specific provisions include the following:[2]

- an expanded Child Tax Credit for lower-income, working families with children;
- an expanded Earned Income Tax Credit (EITC);
- additional weeks of emergency unemployment compensation benefits;
- an additional $25 per week for unemployed workers to supplement their unemployment benefits;
- a $250 one-time payment to elderly people and people with disabilities who receive Social Security, Supplemental Security Income, or veterans' benefits;
- an increase in food stamp benefit levels; and
- supplemental "emergency" funding for states to use for the Temporary Assistance to Needy Families (TANF) program.

The literature on welfare caseloads finds that welfare participation is generally responsive to the economy. That is, caseloads increase during economic downturns and decrease during recoveries. In the figure we see how three of the most important safety net programs fared during the most recent recession. As can be seen, participation

Participation in Unemployment Insurance, Food Stamps/SNAP, and AFDC/TANF, 1990–2011

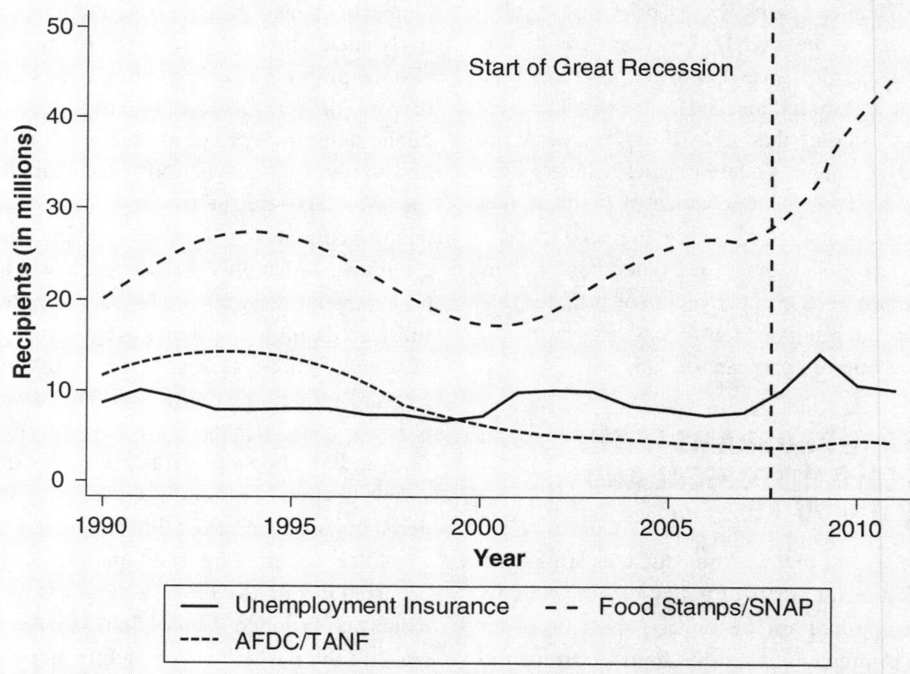

SOURCE: Congressional Budget Office, "Estimated Impact of the American Recovery and Reinvestment Act on Employment and Economic Output from October 2011 through December 2011," February 2012.

in Unemployment Insurance (UI) and Supplemental Nutritional Assistance Program (SNAP) increased significantly during the recession. However, TANF caseloads failed to do so and have remained rather flat throughout one of the most severe economic crises in U.S. history.

Like other features of state TANF programs there was considerable variation in TANF caseload change across the states during this period. Indeed, about a quarter of the states saw no increase or a further decrease in welfare caseloads during this two-year period, while the other states saw minor increases in caseloads. One reason for this variation, it seems, is that the emergency funding for TANF offered by the federal stimulus was optional and states had the discretion to apply or not to apply for federal assistance. Many states turned down the money, or failed to apply for the full amount they were entitled to apply for under ARRA. It is therefore not surprising that there has been such variation across the states in caseload responsiveness, and that this variation has followed the same pattern as that found for TANF benefit and eligibility levels. According to a recently published study, caseload increases were most likely to be seen in states that (1) experienced relatively higher growth in unemployment during the recession, (2) were under Democratic Party control of state government, and (3) had a lower percentage of the welfare caseload that was black.[3]

1. Congressional Budget Office, "Estimated Impact of the American Recovery and Reinvestment Act on Employment and Economic Output from October 2011 through December 2011," February 2012.
2. Arloc Sherman, "Poverty and Financial Distress Would Have Been Substantially Worse in 2010 without Government Action, New Census Data Show," Center for Budget and Policy Priorities, November 7, 2011, www.cbpp.org/cms/index.cfm?fa=view&id=3610.
3. Joe Soss, Richard C. Fording, and Sanford F. Schram, *Disciplining the Poor: Neoliberal Paternalism and the Persistent Power of Race* (Chicago: University of Chicago Press, 2011).

vouchers to poor people across the country. Today, this program is known as the Supplemental Nutritional Assistance Program (SNAP). The Medicaid program was created in 1965 to provide access to health care for a large segment of the nation's poor. Its passage was coupled with the passage of the Medicare program, which provides health care for the population covered by Social Security. Like Social Security, Medicare was designed in a nearly identical fashion as a social insurance program. This era also witnessed a significant expansion of many existing public assistance programs. One of the most controversial expansions was the increase in benefit generosity and the broadening of eligibility rules within the Aid to Families with Dependent Children (AFDC) program. As a result of this expansion, between 1960 and 1970 the number of AFDC recipients more than doubled and the average benefit level for an AFDC family increased by 65 percent. This program eventually evolved into the TANF program in 1996.

The significance of these two historical periods can be seen in Figure 33.1, which plots the total amount of government spending (combined federal, state, and local) on social welfare programs as a percentage of gross domestic product.[1] Spending on "pension" programs largely consists of spending on Social Security, but it also includes other government pension programs for retired government workers and veterans. "Health" spending is dominated by spending on Medicaid and Medicare, but also includes smaller government-funded health care programs. Finally, spending on "welfare" programs reflects government spending on programs targeted for the poor. Collectively, these programs comprised only .8 percent of gross domestic product (GDP) at the onset of the Great Depression in 1929. Spending within each category has significantly increased over time, and total social welfare spending now comprises nearly 20 percent of GDP.

The history of U.S. welfare investment since the War on Poverty–era expansion has followed two distinct paths. Most analysts agree that the direction of these paths has been strongly determined by the attitudes Americans have toward different subgroups within the poverty population, and judgments of their "deservingness" of public aid. For programs serving the so-called deserving poor—the elderly, disabled, and "deserving" unemployed—the years since the 1970s have been characterized by centralization, stability, or even growth in benefit generosity. Programs serving the so-called undeserving poor (i.e., single-parents and nondisabled, nonelderly adults with less stable work histories) have followed a much different trajectory. This is partly evident in Figure 33.1, where we see that in contrast to government investment in health and pension programs, public spending on welfare—which includes most of the programs that serve the undeserving poor—peaked in the 1970s and declined slightly with each economic recovery through the mid-2000s. Yet the trend in aggregate spending does not tell the full story, as some programs suffered more than others. One of the most significant developments during this period was the steady decline in the generosity of the AFDC program, which until its termination in 1996 was the largest cash assistance program available to poor families. The decline in AFDC benefits coincided with a long-term reduction in the generosity of state GA programs. As late as the mid-1970s, every U.S. state had some type of GA program in place to provide assistance for poor individuals and families who were ineligible under AFDC and SSI standards. But

FIGURE 33.1 **U.S. Social Welfare Spending as a Percentage of Gross Domestic Product, by Expenditure Category, 1913–2010**

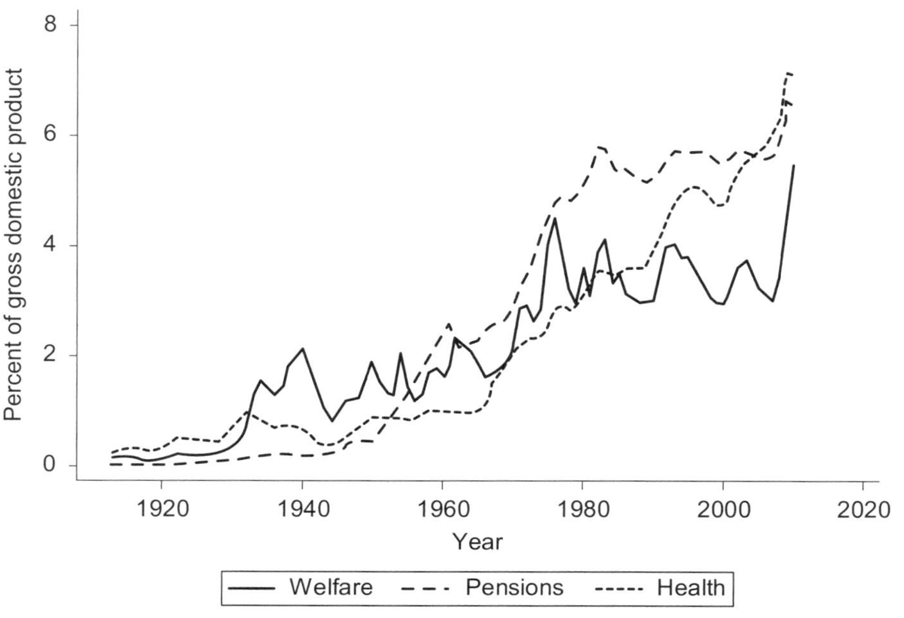

SOURCES: Executive Office of the President, Office of Management and Budget, *Fiscal Year 2012: Historical Tables, Budget of the U.S. Government* (Washington, DC: U.S. Government Printing Office). State and local spending data were obtained from United States Census Bureau, *State and Local Government Finances.*

by 1996, as many as eighteen states had abolished GA entirely and GA benefits in many other states had been severely restricted.[2]

While states were slowly reducing benefits, by the 1980s they were also working to tighten eligibility requirements through state policy innovations known as "demonstration projects," which allowed the states to experiment with changes to the AFDC program. In 1996 national legislation was finally passed in the form of the Personal Responsibility and Work Reconciliation Act of 1996 (PRWORA). Although PRWORA affected most of the major, federally funded public assistance programs, its biggest impact was on AFDC, which was abolished and replaced by TANF. Many of the reforms adopted as state demonstration projects—including work requirements, time limits, and various other behavioral conditions for receiving aid—were included as mandatory requirements (or in some cases state options). And importantly, if TANF recipients failed to comply with any of these new conditions, they were subject to tough sanctions, which in many states meant immediate cessation of TANF benefits, as well as food stamp benefits.

PRWORA had a major impact on several other programs in addition to TANF. One of the most important and controversial reforms was a ban on the receipt of federal aid—including TANF, food stamps (now SNAP), SSI, and Medicaid—to most legal immigrants during the first five years of their residency in the United States. States may use their own funds to provide benefits for immigrants during their first five years in the country, but as of 2010 only a handful had chosen to do so. The food stamp program was targeted for major cuts in funding, and work requirements were to be enforced, with strict penalties for noncompliance. And within SSI, eligibility was effectively tightened through changes in the disability determination process for children. Yet, although access to Medicaid was affected by the immigrant restrictions, the Medicaid program emerged largely intact. In fact, the 1990s is generally regarded as a period of significant expansion of health care access for low-income Americans through the expansion of Medicaid eligibility and the adoption of the Children's Health Insurance Program (CHIP), which provides matching funds for states to provide health care for children from low-income families.

SOCIAL WELFARE PROGRAMS TODAY

The two-tiered design of the U.S. social welfare system remains largely intact today. Table 33.1 helps to illustrate this fact by providing a descriptive summary of some of the most important social insurance and public assistance programs in the United States today. The table reveals several key differences between the two sets of programs that are important in understanding the politics that surrounds them. First, eligibility for the three social insurance programs—Social Security, Medicare, and Unemployment

Insurance (UI)—is much broader. Each of these programs now covers over 90 percent of the labor force. In contrast, eligibility for public assistance is much more restrictive, as all applicants must pass an income test. Public assistance programs are also much more likely than social insurance programs to be targeted to specific demographic groups. In particular, households with children, the elderly, and the disabled are most likely to be eligible for assistance.

A second characteristic that distinguishes social insurance from public assistance programs is that state and local governments tend to have significantly more policy-making discretion and financial responsibility for public assistance. The two most significant examples of decentralization can be seen within the Medicaid and TANF programs, and this has resulted in a great deal of variation in eligibility and benefit levels across the states. For example, as can be seen in Table 33.1, there is notable variation in Medicaid payments. A significant portion of this variation can be explained by the discretion that states have in deciding what types of medical services to cover. The federal government reimburses states for about two-thirds of program costs as long as the states cover certain services. However, state governments have

TABLE 33.1 **Characteristics of Major U.S. Social Welfare Programs, 2010**

	Social insurance programs			Public assistance programs			
	Social Security	Medicare	UI	SNAP	SSI	Medicaid	TANF
Historical origin	1935	1965	1935	1964	1935	1965	1935
Eligibility	Retired workers, their survivors, and disabled	Retired workers, their survivors, and disabled	Unemployed workers	Individuals and families living below the poverty threshold	Elderly and disabled people living below the poverty threshold	Limited-income families with children, SSI recipients	Low-income families with children
Recipient rate (percent of U.S. population)	17.5	15.0	4.6	13.0	2.6	20.2	1.4
Average monthly benefit	$1,074 per person (cash)	$410 per person (medical services)	$1,268 per person (cash)	$133 per person (food voucher)	$570 per person (cash)	$461 per person (medical services)	$232 per person (cash + services)
Funding source	Payroll tax	Payroll tax	Employer tax	General revenue (federal)	General revenue (federal and optional state)	General revenue (federal and state)	General revenue (federal and state)
Total cost	$713 billion	$248 billion	$79.5 billion	$68.3 billion	$43.3 billion	$389 billion	$35.8 billion
Total cost (percent GDP)	4.9	1.8	.6	.5	.3	2.7	.3
Administration	Federal	Federal	Federal and state	Federal and state and local	Federal	Federal and state	Federal and state or local
State variation: monthly benefit level (minimum-maximum)	None	None	MS: $784 HI: $1,692	None	ND: $423 HI: $989	CA: $294 CT: $798	Cash benefit for 3-person family: MS: $170 AK: $923
Eligibility	None	None	Significant	None	None	Significant	Significant

SOURCES: Social Security, Medicare, SSI (Social Security Bulletin, Annual Statistical Supplement 2011: www.ssa.gov/policy/docs/statcomps/supplement/2011/index.html); SNAP (U.S. Department of Agriculture, Food and Nutrition Service: www.fns.usda.gov/pd/snapmain.htm); UI (U.S. Department of Labor, Employment and Training Administration: http://ows.doleta.gov/unemploy); TANF (Department of Health and Human Services, Administration for Children and Families: www.acf.hhs.gov/programs/ofa/data/2010fin/table_a2.pdf); Medicaid (2009 data obtained from the Kaiser Foundation: www.statehealthfacts.org/comparecat.jsp?cat=4&rgn=6&rgn=1).

many options to cover additional services with the same level of federal reimbursement, or with state funds. The states also have a significant amount of discretion in deciding who is eligible for Medicaid. As a result, we see a significant amount of variation in Medicaid coverage across the states that cannot be explained by variation in poverty rates. For example, in the state of Maine approximately 21 percent of the population participated in Medicaid in 2010, despite the fact that the poverty rate in the state was only 11 percent. In contrast, the poverty rate in New Hampshire (13 percent) significantly exceeded the Medicaid participation rate of 8 percent.

Although the degree of variation is already quite substantial, state health care spending under Medicaid is destined to display even greater variability due to the implementation of the Affordable Care Act. As of 2013, states have a strong incentive to expand eligibility to poor, non-elderly, nondisabled adults without children due to the requirement that the federal government pay for a large majority of the costs. Yet some states have already declared that they will not choose to expand eligibility, thus leading to even greater inequality in Medicaid access and services. State health care programs are discussed in more detail in Chapter 31.

There is even greater variation in the benefits and eligibility requirements within the TANF program. As Table 33.1 indicates, the state with the lowest monthly benefit level in 2010 (for a family of three with no other income) was a mere $170 a month. Alaska had the highest benefit level for an equivalent family, at $923 a month. The average benefit level across all the states was $436. The states also vary a great deal in their TANF eligibility policies. The federal government requires that all states enforce a number of different rules, yet they are free to set their own standards for these rules as long as the state's standard is stricter than that of the federal government.

Finally, a third difference between social insurance programs and public assistance programs is that social insurance programs tend to be more generous than public assistance programs. The one exception to this in Table 33.1 concerns health care, where Medicaid and Medicare benefits appear to be relatively similar when spending is calculated on a per recipient basis. However, for cash (or, in the case of SNAP, near-cash) programs, the benefits paid by public assistance programs are much smaller than the cash payments provided by social insurance programs.

EXPLAINING VARIATION IN STATE WELFARE POLICIES

Over the past fifty years, political scientists have devoted a great deal of attention to state welfare policies in an effort to better understand the variation across states in welfare programs. Although this has led scholars to examine a number of different programs, researchers have devoted a considerable amount of attention to AFDC and TANF.

Rep. Keith Kempenich (R-Bowman) testifies in favor of HB 1385, a bill relating to drug testing people in the Temporary Assistance for Needy Families (TANF) program and Supplemental Nutrition Assistance Program (SNAP), on February 5, 2013, in Bismarck, North Dakota. Kempenich said the drug testing would be similar to that involved with most places of employment. Due to the decentralization of social welfare programs, states are able to establish their own eligibility and benefits requirements, as long as such requirements are stricter than federal requirements.

SOURCE: AP Photo/*The Bismarck Tribune*, Tom Stromme.

Economic Conditions and Welfare Policy

According to the oldest and simplest view of the history of welfare, expansion of welfare can be traced to changes in economic conditions. Perhaps the most influential of the theories rooted in economic conditions is modernization theory, most associated with the sociologist Harold Wilensky.[3] Writing from this perspective, a number of historians and social scientists have linked expansion of welfare programs to periods of rapid social and economic change brought on by increasing industrialization and urbanization. A second reason for welfare expansion from this perspective is that economic modernization (i.e., industrialization) is expected to bring with it greater economic resources, and thus an increased capacity to finance a welfare state. The majority of studies of state welfare policies over the last five decades have found at least some support for the importance of economic conditions, as these theories would suggest. Perhaps the most frequently supported hypothesis is the correlation between state per capita income and welfare spending.

State Political Environments

In 1966 political scientist Thomas Dye published a book that would ultimately have a significant impact on the direction of state politics research.[4] Dye found that state policy measures were rarely related to indicators of the state political system. Rather, state policies (including welfare policies) were most strongly determined by state economic variables. What followed was a steady stream of research by political scientists who sought to challenge these early findings. The features of the political environment that have received the most attention in this research include the following: electoral incentives generated by interparty competition, partisan control of important state policy-making institutions, the political ideology of the electorate, and lower-class mobilization and insurgency.

Although electoral incentives might originate from a number of environmental factors, state politics scholars have devoted the most attention to interparty competition (IPC), based on the seminal work of V. O. Key, and later his student Duane Lockard. Basically, the IPC hypothesis predicts that in one-party or noncompetitive states, the incumbent government is not likely to pursue policies that are in the mass interest, such as social welfare programs. This is because "it is easier for a few powerful interests to manage the government of the state without party interference since the parties are not representative of the particular elements that might pose opposition to the dominant interest groups."[5] Despite the plausibility of this thesis, empirical support over the years has been mixed.

Fewer studies have addressed the influence of party control of state government on state welfare policy, and much like the former case, the evidence does not consistently demonstrate that party labels matter in the way that we would expect (i.e., that Democratic states have more liberal welfare policies). The few early studies that addressed this found little support for a direct and significant effect of Democratic control. Subsequent endeavors, employing theoretical and methodological improvements, have provided somewhat stronger results, with some studies finding the effect to exist only under certain (often rare) conditions.

Many studies have examined the impact of public attitudes, and in particular the effect of the general ideological orientation of the electorate on state welfare policies. For many years, this hypothesis could not easily be tested due to the lack of reliable, state-level measures of public preferences. This problem was solved to some extent by the pioneering work of Robert Erikson, Gerald Wright, and John McIver, who used survey data to construct a direct measure of mass ideology for each state during the mid-1980s. Their research clearly demonstrated the importance of public opinion on what they termed state "policy liberalism."[6] This relationship between state citizen ideology and state policy has since been found to exist for the more specific area of state AFDC and TANF benefits, as well as state Medicaid policy, where states with a higher proportion of "liberal" citizens have been found to offer more generous benefits.

In addition to the effects of these institutional variables, researchers have also linked welfare generosity and expansion to the political mobilization of the lower class and collective protest. This research is inspired by the influential work of Frances Fox Piven and Richard Cloward, who argued in a series of books and papers that political elites are most likely to increase welfare generosity when they are threatened by the political mobilization of the poor, either through electoral mobilization or insurgent collective action.[7] Studies that have tested these claims have generally found support for them.

EXPLAINING STATE WELFARE RETRENCHMENT

The primary motivation of the studies reviewed thus far has been to better understand why some states have invested more heavily in public assistance programs than other states. As the decades of the 1970s and 1980s passed, scholars began to take notice of the steady decline in public assistance generosity, especially within the AFDC program. To account for these trends in state welfare policy, two alternative perspectives on welfare policymaking have been offered in recent years.

Federalism and Welfare Benefit Competition

Many scholars have alleged that the decline in AFDC/TANF benefits has been due to a "race to the bottom" in welfare policymaking since 1970. Inspired by economic theories of location decisions, the race to the bottom hypothesis consists of two assumptions. First, it suggests that welfare benefit levels play a significant role in the residential choices of the poor, and that poor persons will migrate from states with low welfare benefits to those with more generous assistance.[8] Second, the race to the bottom thesis predicts that states compete with surrounding states to offer the least generous welfare assistance so as to discourage poor people from moving to their state. Policymakers, it is assumed, engage in this benefit competition because they recognize that the poor are costly to maintain and think that the presence of a large poor population in a state hinders efforts to attract firms and investors.

Many studies have tested for the possibility of benefit competition by examining the relationship between benefit levels in a state and benefit levels in neighboring states, assuming that the two should be positively correlated if states do actually compete. Of the studies that rely on this approach, all find some evidence of strategic interaction among states in the determination of welfare benefits, but the findings vary concerning the strength of this relationship. Some studies conclude that states match reductions in neighboring states' benefits on a dollar-for-dollar basis, while others find a moderate relationship. In one of the most recent and innovative studies on this question, Michael Bailey and Mark Rom compared the correlation between a state's benefit level and its neighbors' benefits across three different programs—AFDC, SSI, and Medicare.[9] The correlation is significantly stronger within the AFDC program, which is what should be expected if the race to the bottom thesis is correct due to the greater level of decentralization within AFDC. Given the balance of the empirical evidence, it would seem that benefit competition has played at least some role in the decline of AFDC benefit generosity over time. Yet this explanation, at least on its own, is unable to account for the termination of AFDC and its replacement with TANF.

Racial Attitudes and Welfare Policy

The second of these alternative explanations for the decline of state welfare generosity cites the importance of racial stereotypes in the design of welfare policy. Historical accounts of welfare policymaking clearly indicate that race was one of the primary influences in the construction of the U.S. welfare state during the passage of the New Deal.[10] Yet there is considerable evidence that racial prejudice continues to affect state policy choices. The link between racial attitudes and welfare, it has been argued, is rooted in contemporary stereotypes about blacks, and in particular the belief that blacks are "lazy" compared with other racial and ethnic groups.[11] Consequently, as blacks have become synonymous with welfare policy and poverty, the impact of white racial stereotypes on welfare issues has presumably increased over the years, leading to a steady decline in welfare generosity.

Studies of state welfare policy have consistently found support for this theory. Using data for the fifty states, several studies have found that AFDC benefit generosity is negatively related to the share of the state's poor population that is black. This relationship continues to hold today under TANF. Fewer studies have examined the effect of racial context on state Medicaid policies, but among those that have the findings have been similar. The share of the state welfare caseload that is black has been found to be negatively related to Medicaid benefit coverage and eligibility.[12]

There is equally strong evidence that race has had a significant role in state welfare reform efforts. The black share of the AFDC caseload has been found to have been a strong predictor of state initiatives to implement restrictive reforms within AFDC using federal waivers in the 1990s.[13] More recently, several studies have documented a strong relationship between the black share of the TANF caseload and several important policy choices under TANF. This research has found that states with relatively larger shares of black TANF families are more likely to have adopted stricter sanctions, tougher work requirements, stricter time limits, and a family cap.[14] Given the uniform downward pressure of benefit competition, and the inequity in welfare generosity created by racial diversity in the poor population across the states, it would seem that decentralization of welfare programs has had significant consequences for the poor, and especially poor persons of color.

THE IMPACT OF WELFARE POLICIES ON POVERTY AND WELL-BEING

In addition to research on the formulation of state welfare policies, scholars have utilized the variation in state welfare policies as a "natural experiment" to evaluate the impact that welfare programs have on poverty and other indicators of well-being. The final section of this chapter reviews this literature. The section begins with a summary of the research on the impact of welfare programs on poverty. The section then discusses the literature on the impact of welfare on various behaviors of the poor, including indicators of family structure, reproductive behavior, and work effort. The section concludes with a review of the impact of welfare reform, and especially the many new rules reflected within the TANF program.

Welfare and Poverty

One of the most enduring debates in American social policy has been whether welfare programs are a cure or a cause of poverty. This debate reappeared on the national political scene in the wake of Johnson's War on Poverty and the dramatic expansion of public assistance generosity. Combined with unprecedented growth in welfare caseloads, this expansion of public assistance led to expectations of a significant reduction in the U.S. poverty rate. Yet while poverty did decrease significantly during the 1960s, the poverty rate stabilized by the 1970s and has remained in double digits ever since. As progress against poverty slowed, the criticism began to mount, particularly among conservatives. Much of the criticism was directed at the AFDC program, which until 1996 was the largest cash assistance program for the able-bodied poor. Critics of AFDC claimed that in combination with in-kind benefits provided by the food stamp and Medicaid programs, AFDC had come to undermine work incentives. Consequently, it was argued, AFDC not only failed to reduce poverty, it may even have served to increase poverty by encouraging the poor to choose welfare over work.

Others offered an alternative perspective, however, maintaining that welfare expansion significantly improved the lives of the poor, and that work disincentive effects were relatively small, if they existed at all. Acknowledging the fact that poverty did not decline as much as the architects of the War on Poverty had hoped, they argued that this was due to a combination of factors, including the decline of the manufacturing sector in the economy, the failure of wages and public assistance benefits to keep pace with inflation, and demographic changes promoting the growth of economically vulnerable female-headed families. According to this perspective, public assistance reduced poverty, although the magnitude of this reduction has been masked by other forces.

In this picture, Sara Garcia searches a Minnesota state employment site for a job as a nursing assistant with her one-and-a-half-year-old son, Donovan, on her lap. Her daily routine consists of being with her children and constantly searching for jobs on the Web. It's the tenth anniversary of Minnesota's most significant—and controversial—welfare overhaul, designed to "end welfare as we know it." In 1988 every state in the country was required to abolish its old system and create a new one that rewarded work and had a five-year time limit.

SOURCE: Richard Sennott/*Minneapolis Star Tribune*/ZUMAPRESS.com.

A large body of research attempts to examine the net impact of public assistance on poverty by examining the aggregate-level relationship between welfare benefits and poverty rates. Several studies have assessed this relationship using national-level data. Perhaps the most well-known of these is by Charles Murray, who argued that increases in welfare generosity associated with the War on Poverty led to an increase in the poverty rate.[15] This conclusion sparked a series of rebuttals that claimed that the trends in national-level poverty observed by Murray were driven by economic stagnation and demographic changes.[16]

Recognizing the small number of observations available when analyzing national poverty rates, several scholars have examined the relationship between welfare and poverty at the state level. Unlike the national-level studies, which have typically combined expenditures on all welfare programs into a single variable, these studies have generally focused on the effects of a single program—AFDC. Yet, similar to the national-level studies, the findings are decidedly mixed, with some studies finding that AFDC benefits are positively and significantly related to state poverty rates, while others have found a negative relationship. In the most recent and comprehensive study to address this question, Richard Fording and William Berry examined the effect of state welfare generosity (AFDC, food stamps, and Medicaid) during the 1960–1990 period. They found that the size of state AFDC payments were negatively related to state poverty rates prior to the 1970s, but that reductions in state benefit levels rendered AFDC ineffective in lifting poor families above the federal poverty line in the years afterward.[17]

The Impact of Welfare on Behavior

Numerous studies have attempted to estimate the effect of welfare programs on a variety of behaviors among the poor. The largest of these literatures exists for the study of work incentives, where scholars (largely economists and sociologists) have examined the relationship between the benefit level in a state and a range of outcome variables including work effort, welfare entry, welfare exit, and the duration of welfare spells. These studies have been extensively reviewed, and the findings are relatively consistent. As Robert Moffitt concludes, AFDC benefit levels have generally been found to "generate nontrivial work disincentives" and to be significantly related to welfare participation and turnover. The magnitude of this effect, however, has been a matter of dispute.[18]

Fewer studies have examined the effect of benefit generosity on the growth of female-headed families, which accelerated at a rapid pace beginning in the 1960s. Yet there is still a substantial literature on this question. The two most important paths through which female-headed families are formed is through divorce or the decision not to marry. Social scientists have studied both of these outcomes, and like the literature on work incentive effects, this literature has also been extensively reviewed. The earliest studies, conducted with data from the 1960s, found no evidence of any effects of state benefit levels on female headship, divorce, or marriage. Studies that have relied on more recent data have found some evidence of a possible effect, but the magnitude of the effect has been consistently small and not nearly large enough to account for the dramatic increase in female-headed households seen since the 1960s. Indeed, as Moffitt concludes in his review of this literature, "The failure to find strong benefit effects is the most notable characteristic of this literature."[19]

One of the most controversial debates in the recent literature on welfare policy concerns the validity of the welfare migration thesis. Patterned after economic theories of residential choice, the welfare migration thesis suggests that welfare benefit levels play a significant role in the residential choices of the poor. Specifically, the migration hypothesis predicts that poor persons will migrate from states with low welfare benefits to those with more generous assistance. In their influential book advancing their race to the bottom theory of welfare benefit competition, Paul Peterson and Mark Rom claimed support for the welfare migration hypothesis based on the finding that when a state's benefit levels are high, the size of its poverty population increases. An alternate approach to research on the race to the bottom thesis has been to test the migration hypothesis with individual-level data. A number of such studies have been conducted, and as Jan Brueckner concludes in his review of this literature, the evidence is decidedly mixed.[20]

The Impact of Welfare Reform

Over the past two decades, a large literature has examined the effectiveness of welfare reform in achieving its goals. Today, there is broad agreement among scholars that welfare reform has succeeded in reducing program caseloads. Although studies have reached different conclusions regarding the precise impact of TANF compared with other factors such as the economy or the expansion of the Earned Income Tax Credit (EITC), a comprehensive review finds that TANF is responsible for about a 20 percent decline in welfare caseloads since 1996.[21] Although welfare caseloads have declined in every state since the introduction of TANF, this research finds that the magnitude of the decline was largest in the states that adopted the strictest bundle of TANF rules, and in the fourteen states where the administration of TANF has been significantly devolved down to local governments through a process known as second-order devolution.[22]

There is far less consensus, however, regarding the mechanisms through which TANF has reduced welfare caseloads, and thus whether TANF has been successful in achieving the goal of promoting economic self-sufficiency among the poor. The first wave of studies examining the short-term effects of TANF generally concluded that TANF had a positive effect on the employment and earnings of single mothers, yet the earnings effects were much more inconsistent and modest in comparison to the employment effects.[23] More recent studies that examine the long-term effects of TANF, as well as its impact across the income distribution, are less optimistic and suggest that the most disadvantaged poor women are actually worse off.[24] Concerns over the possible negative effects of TANF on the well-being of the poor are also heightened by several alarming trends. Between 1994 and 2005, the percentage of TANF-eligible families receiving TANF decreased from 84 percent to only 40 percent according to statistics published by the U.S. Department of Health and Human Services. This figure is undoubtedly lower in the aftermath of the 2009 recession due to the combination of increasing poverty rates and a lack of growth (and even a continued decline in many states) in the TANF rolls. The number of families living in extreme poverty (less than $2 per person per day in a given month) increased sharply from 1.46 million in 1996 to 2.4 million in 2011, with most of the increase concentrated in families affected by welfare reform.[25] Finally, there has been increasing concern over the growing population of "disconnected women," defined as the percentage of low-income women who report themselves as neither working nor on welfare. According to some estimates, the size of this population doubled between the mid-1990s and mid-2000s, and now stands at 20 to 25 percent (depending on the precise definition) of all low-income women.[26]

CONCLUSION

This chapter has reviewed the research on state welfare policies, focusing most closely on public assistance programs for which state and local governments enjoy the most discretion in setting benefit levels and eligibility rules. Due to the decentralized tendency of public assistance programs, the policies governing them have historically displayed a great deal of variation across states. Scholars have utilized this variation to study the causes, as well as the consequences, of state welfare policies. Studies of the causes of welfare policy have found that a number of factors may contribute to explaining variation in benefit levels across states and over time. Although economic prosperity has long been thought to contribute to expansion of social welfare programs, over the last few decades scholars have increasingly come to understand how welfare policies are shaped by state politics, public opinion, racial diversity, and competition induced by decentralized administration. If proposals for further decentralization of social welfare programs are successful, this body of research suggests that this may result in patterns of variation that are similarly rooted in state economic, political, and demographic characteristics.

Studies of the impact of welfare programs on the poor have been more numerous, yet far less decisive. A handful of studies have examined the impact of welfare benefit generosity on state poverty rates, but the findings have been inconclusive. This may be due to the complexity of the many causal mechanisms involved, or simply due to the inherent limitations of the poverty rate (which excludes many types of noncash welfare benefits) as a measure of well-being. A much larger body of research exists that has examined the effect of welfare generosity on various behaviors, including work effort, welfare participation, marriage and reproductive decisions, and residential choices. This research has produced mixed results for each one of these questions, with the exception of the research on work effort, where welfare benefit levels have been found to be positively related to welfare participation and duration, and negatively related to work effort. However, it should be noted that the magnitude of these effects is far from clear. In addition, many of these studies also find strong effects for local labor market conditions, including wage levels.

NOTES

1. Federal government spending data reported in this chapter were obtained from Executive Office of the President, Office of Management and Budget, *Fiscal Year 2012: Historical Tables, Budget of the U.S. Government* (Washington, DC: U.S. Government Printing Office, 2012). State and local spending data were obtained from United States Census Bureau, *State and Local Government Finances.*
2. Cori E. Uccello, Heather R. McCallum, and L. Jerome Gallagher, *State General Assistance Programs: 1996; Assessing the New Federalism* (Washington, DC: Urban Institute, 1996).
3. Harold Wilensky and Charles Lebeaux, *Industrial Society and Social Welfare* (New York: Free Press, 1965).
4. Thomas R. Dye, *Politics, Economics, and the Public* (Chicago: Rand McNally, 1966).
5. Duane Lockard, *New England State Politics* (Princeton, NJ: Princeton University Press, 1959), 337.
6. Robert S. Erikson, Gerald C. Wright Jr., and John McIver, *Statehouse Democracy* (Cambridge: Cambridge University Press, 1993).
7. Frances Fox Piven and Richard A. Cloward, *Regulating the Poor: The Functions of Public Welfare* (New York: Vintage, 1971).
8. Paul E. Peterson and Mark C. Rom, *Welfare Magnets: A New Case for a National Standard* (Washington, DC: Brookings, 1990).
9. Michael A. Bailey and Mark Rom, "A Wider Race? Interstate Competition across Health and Welfare Programs," *Journal of Politics* 66 (2004): 326–347.
10. Jill Quadagno, *The Color of Welfare: How Racism Undermined the War on Poverty* (New York: Oxford University Press, 1994).
11. Martin Gilens, *Why Americans Hate Welfare: Race, Media, and the Politics of Antipoverty Policy* (Chicago: University of Chicago Press, 1999).
12. Colleen M. Grogan, "Political-Economic Factors Influencing State Medicaid Policy," *Political Research Quarterly* 47 (1994): 565–588.
13. Richard C. Fording, "'Laboratories of Democracy' or Symbolic Politics? The Racial Origins of Welfare Reform," in *Race and the Politics of Welfare Reform,* ed. S. F. Schram, J. Soss, and R. C. Fording (Ann Arbor: University of Michigan Press, 2003).
14. Joe Soss, Sanford F. Schram, Thomas Vartanian, and Erin O'Brien, "Setting the Terms of Relief: Explaining State Policy Choices in the Devolution Revolution," *American Journal of Political Science* 45 (2001): 378–395.
15. Charles Murray, *Losing Ground* (New York: Basic Books, 1984).
16. William Julius Wilson, *The Truly Disadvantaged* (Chicago: University of Chicago Press, 1987).
17. Richard C. Fording and William D. Berry, "The Historical Impact of Welfare Programs on Poverty in the American States," *Policy Studies Journal* 35 (2007): 37–60.
18. Robert Moffitt, "Incentive Effects of the U.S. Welfare System: A Review," *Journal of Economic Literature* 30 (1992): 1–61, at 16.
19. Ibid., 31.
20. Jan F. Brueckner, "Welfare Reform and the Race to the Bottom: Theory and Evidence," *Southern Economic Journal* 66 (2000): 505–525.
21. Jeffrey Grogger and Lynn A. Karoly, *Welfare Reform: Effects of a Decade of Change* (Cambridge, MA: Harvard University Press, 2005).
22. Byungkyu Kim and Richard C. Fording, "Second-Order Devolution and the Implementation of TANF," *State Politics and Policy Quarterly* 10 (2010): 341–367.
23. Rebecca Blank, "Evaluating Welfare Reform in the United States," *Journal of Econometric Literature* 40 (2002): 1105–1166.
24. James P. Ziliak, "Introduction," in *Welfare Reform and Its Long-Term Consequences for America's Poor,* ed. James P. Ziliak (New York: Cambridge University Press, 2009).
25. H. Luke Shaefer and Kathryn Edin, "Extreme Poverty in the United States, 1996 to 2011," policy brief no. 28 (Ann Arbor: National Poverty Center, University of Michigan, 2012).
26. Rebecca Blank and Brian Kovak, "The Growing Problem of Disconnected Single Mothers" (Ann Arbor: National Poverty Center, Working Paper Series #07–28, 2008).

SUGGESTED READING

Abramovitz, Mimi. *Regulating the Lives of Women: Welfare Policy from Colonial Times to the Present.* Boston: South End Press, 1988.

Blank, Rebecca. "Evaluating Welfare Reform in the United States." *Journal of Econometric Literature 40* (2002): 1105–1166.

Dawson, Richard, and James Robinson. "Interparty Competition, Economic Variables, and Welfare Policies in the American States." *Journal of Politics* 25 (1963): 265–289.

Dye, Thomas, R. *Politics, Economics, and the Public.* Chicago: Rand McNally, 1966.

Erikson, Robert S., Gerald C. Wright Jr., and John McIver. *Statehouse Democracy.* Cambridge: Cambridge University Press, 1993.

Gilens, Martin. *Why Americans Hate Welfare.* Chicago: University of Chicago Press, 1999.

Grogger, Jeffrey, and Lynn A. Karoly. *Welfare Reform: Effects of a Decade of Change.* Cambridge, MA: Harvard University Press, 2005.

Handler, Joel F. *The Poverty of Welfare Reform.* New Haven: Yale University Press, 1995.

Key, V.O., Jr. *Southern Politics in State and Nation.* New York: Random House, 1949.

Lieberman, Robert. *Shifting the Color Line: Race and the American Welfare State.* Cambridge, MA: Harvard University Press, 1998.

Lockard, Duane. *New England State Politics.* Princeton, NJ: Princeton University Press, 1959.

Mead, Lawrence M. *Beyond Entitlement: The Social Obligations of Citizenship.* New York: Free Press, 1986.

Peterson, Paul E., and Mark C. Rom. *Welfare Magnets: A New Case for a National Standard.* Washington, DC: Brookings, 1990.

Pierson, Paul. *Dismantling the Welfare State? Reagan, Thatcher, and the Politics of Retrenchment.* New York: Cambridge University Press, 1994.

Piven, Frances Fox, and Richard A. Cloward. *Regulating the Poor: The Functions of Public Welfare.* New York: Vintage, 1971.

Plotnick, Robert, and Richard F. Winters. "A Politico-Economic Theory of Income Redistribution." *American Political Science Review* 79 (1985): 458–473.

Soss, Joe, Richard C. Fording, and Sanford F. Schram. *Disciplining the Poor: Neoliberal Paternalism and the Persistent Power of Race.* Chicago: University of Chicago Press, 2011.

Trattner, Walter I. *From Poor Law to Welfare State: A History of Social Welfare in America,* 6th ed. New York: Simon and Schuster, 1999.

Wilson, William Julius. *The Truly Disadvantaged.* Chicago: University of Chicago Press, 1987.

Ziliak, James P., ed. *Welfare Reform and Its Long-Term Consequences for America's Poor.* New York: Cambridge University Press, 2009.

★ GUIDE TO INFORMATION AND DATA ABOUT THE STATES

The Internet has been a boon to the production of data about the states and, especially, to making it widely available. As a result, the past dozen years or so have seen an explosion in collections of information about the states. Moreover, whereas studies prior to around 2000 often had to content themselves with examination of some subset of states about which data could be found, fifty-state analyses have rapidly become closer to the norm.

In this guide, we document sources—often, but not exclusively Web sources—of all manner of state-level data. Our focus is on sources that provide systematic coverage of all states, especially ones that include data over time. In keeping with the scope of this volume, we include information on state politics, broadly conceived, but also on a wide variety of policy matters.

It would be impossible, of course, to include every relevant website about every conceivable aspect of state politics and policy. Nonetheless, we believe that sources listed here provide the interested reader with an entrée into a wide swath of political and policy arenas. Even the relative expert may find a few sources that have escaped his or her attention in the past.

A note on our citation of websites: We typically provide "upper-level" sites, as a listing of highly specific sites would increase the number of citations to the point of making the compilation far less accessible. Thus, for example, we list the URL of the National Center for Education Statistics (NCES), http://nces.ed.gov, rather than the URLs of the many datasets NCES provides. Occasionally this means that it will take some "digging" to uncover the specific information that a reader is seeking. Besides making the compilation more compact, however, one often finds that such rooting around uncovers unexpected treasures in the form of data that one had no idea existed at all, much less in the form of easily accessible, systematic coverage.

We hope readers will make use of many of the collections listed here and will have the thrill of coming across unexpected treasures on more than a few occasions.

General Sources

Congressional Information Service. *American Statistics Index: A Comprehensive Guide and Index to the Statistical Publications of the U.S. Government.* Washington, DC: Congressional Information Service, 1973–. Annual, with monthly supplements. Available online at LexisNexis Statistical DataSets (http://academic.lexisnexis.com).

Definitive guide, multiply indexed, to statistics "of probable research significance" in government publications; 1974 "Annual and Retrospective Edition" includes not only items in print but also significant items published over the preceding decade.

Congressional Information Service. *Statistical Reference Index: A Selective Guide to American Statistical Publications from Sources Other Than the U.S. Government.* Washington, DC: Congressional Information Service, 1980–. Annual, with bimonthly supplements. Available online at LexisNexis Statistical DataSets (http://academic.lexisnexis.com).

Index of statistics from private and public sources other than the U.S. government; complements the American Statistics Index.

Council of State Governments, www.csg.org

Publisher of biannual and annual The Book of the States, *which has been published since 1935 and available online since 2000 and contains hundreds of detailed tables and graphics covering the organization and operation of state governments; provides collection of state-level databases on topics like business incentives, state performance.*

National Conference of State Legislatures, www.ncsl.org

Wide-ranging information on contemporary issues along with data about redistricting, term limits, early and absentee voting, and voter identification requirements; current information about party composition of state legislatures, state legislative leaders, legislative staffs, and more.

State Politics and Policy Quarterly (Data Resource) http://academic.udayton.edu/sppq-TPR

An eclectic collection of datasets submitted by contributors to State Politics and Policy Quarterly *and others engaged in state politics research; lists sources for state-level data covering a variety of social, economic, and political topics.*

U.S. Census Bureau, www.census.gov

Provides a large collection of national, state, and city data as well as links to state data centers through the State Data Center Program.

Campaign Finance and Political Action Committees (PACs)

The Campaign Disclosure Project, www.campaigndisclosure.org

Database of campaign finance disclosure laws covering the fifty states, the District of Columbia, and the Federal Election Commission; includes a graded assessment of each state's disclosure programs.

Campaign Finance Information Center, www.campaignfinance.org

Summarizes and links to campaign finance data made available online by each state; describes the format of the available data, and the races, years, and transaction types covered.

The Gubernatorial Campaign Finance Database, www.unc.edu/~beyle/guber.html

A unified database of campaign expenditures for all gubernatorial candidates from 1977 until the present.

Influence Explorer, www.influenceexplorer.com

Tracks political contributions at the federal and state level as well as earmarks, grants, and contracts by state.

Justice at Stake, www.justiceatstake.org

Provides links to data on candidate fund-raising and advertising expenditures in state judicial campaigns.

National Institute on Money in State Politics, www.followthemoney.org

Database of campaign contributions for all state-level candidates in primary and general elections; includes information about candidates, political party committees, and ballot committees.

Courts Data

NOTE: Many states maintain online searchable databases containing information about cases originating within the state. These databases are typically searchable by keyword, index number, and names of involved parties.

Bureau of Justice Statistics' Courts Data Collections, www.bjs.gov

Collection of datasets relevant to the U.S. and state courts, which includes (among other topics) data on caseloads, court system organization and structure, numbers of and disposition of criminal and civil cases, and governance of court systems; jury qualifications and verdict rules; and processing and sentencing procedures for criminal cases.

Civil Justice Survey of State Courts, www.ncsc.org/Services-and-Experts/Areas-of-expertise/Civil-justice/Civil-Justice-Survey.aspx

A series of surveys conducted in 1992, 1996, 2001, and 2005 examining civil litigation trends across states; includes information on the nature of cases filed, the disposition of cases heard, and damages awarded.

State Court Caseload Statistics: Annual Report. Williamsburg, VA: Conference of State Court Administrators and the National Center for State Courts, 1976–. Annual.

Data on judicial workloads in the state courts.

State Supreme Court Data Project, www.ruf.rice.edu/~pbrace/statecourt

Information on state supreme court decisions in all fifty states during their 1995 through 1998 sessions; includes information on some twenty-one thousand decisions and biographical data for all justices during this period.

Economic Data (*see also* Taxes)

Bureau of Economic Analysis, http://bea.gov

Extensive data on gross domestic product (GDP), income, and employment at the state and local level.

Bureau of Labor Statistics, www.bls.gov

Data on employment, wages, and prices at the national, state, and local level.

Census Bureau, Federal, State, and Local Governments, www.census.gov/gov

Information on revenue, expenditures, numbers of public employees, etc., for state and local governments, and numbers of various levels of local governments.

County and City Data Books, www2.1ib.virginia.edu/ccdb/

Extensive data from 1944 through 2000 on a variety of socioeconomic indicators and demographics at the city, county, and state level.

Economic Policy Institute's State Economy Track Data, www.epi.org/resources/research_data

State-level data on employment and unemployment covering the years 1981, 1990, 2001, and 2007.

Inforum's EconData, http://inforumweb.umd.edu/econdata

A collection of time-series state-level datasets including information on earnings and income, employment by industry, wages and salaries, and state economic profiles.

Election Administration and Voter Turnout (*see also* General Sources: National Conference of State Legislatures)

ElectionLine, www.electionline.org

Nonpartisan clearinghouse with frequent, nationwide updates about election reform, along with analytic reports on selected topics.

Pew Center on the States, www.pewstates.org/issues/election-administration-328132

Reports, analyses, and interactive databases concerning election administration by the states. One project, Being Online Is Still Not Enough, rates states on the accessibility of state election websites, while the recently introduced Elections Performance Index (EPI) offers a comprehensive evaluation of election administration in the fifty states and the District of Columbia.

United States Election Assistance Commission, www.eac.gov

Research, reports, and data on election administration issues. The Election Administration and Voting Survey collects information from state and county election officials about ballots cast, voter registration, military and overseas voting, and voting technology; the National Voter Registration Act Survey collects information on voter registration trends; the Uniformed and Overseas Citizens Absentee Voter Act (UOCAVA) Survey tracks at the county level the number of UOCAVA ballots sent and received, and their disposition.

Voter turnout, http://elections.gmu.edu

National and state turnout rates for voting age population (VAP) and voting eligible population (VEP), which corrects voter turnout figures by accounting for voting-age persons who are ineligible to vote due to felony convictions or noncitizenship and for overseas eligible voters, from 1980 to the present; provides data for 2012 on early voting.

Governors; Gubernatorial Elections, Job Approval Ratings (*see also* Election Administration and Voter Turnout; Legislative Election Data)

Congressional Quarterly's Guide to U.S. Elections. 6th ed. Washington, DC: CQ Press, 2009.

Superb collection of vote returns for presidential, gubernatorial, and House elections since 1824, Electoral College votes since 1789, senatorial elections since 1913, presidential primaries since 1912, and primaries for governor and senator since 1956 (in southern states since 1919); biographies of presidential and vice-presidential candidates; lists of governors and senators since 1789; discussions of and data on political parties and presidential nominating conventions throughout the nation's history.

Dubin, Michael J. *United States Gubernatorial Elections, 1776–1860: The Official Results by State and County.* Jefferson, NC: McFarland, 2003.

Detailed compilation of early gubernatorial elections.

Glashan, Roy R. *American Governors and Gubernatorial Elections, 1775–1978.* Westport, CT: Meckler, 1979.

Details about state governors (such as birthdays, party affiliations, principal occupations, terms of office) and election data; continued in Mullaney (see below).

Job approval ratings (JARs), www.unc.edu/~beyle/jars.html

Approval ratings collected at the state level for governors, U.S. senators, and presidents from the mid-1900s through 2009; survey questions cover both general job performance assessments and evaluations of officials' handling of specific policy issues.

Kallenbach, Joseph E., and Jessamine S. Kallenbach. *American State Governors, 1776–1976.* Dobbs Ferry, NY: Oceana Publications, 1977–1982.

Election results and biographical data on governors.

Klarner, Carl. Governors Dataset, www.indstate.edu/polisci/klarnerpolitics.htm

Dataset at the state–year level covering 1961 to 2010 (with limited coverage of earlier years for some variables) including demographic data about governors in office and data about terms and term limits.

Mullaney, Marie. *American Governors and Gubernatorial Elections, 1979–1987.* Westport, CT: Meckler, 1988.

Continues the volume by Glashan (see above).

———. *Biographical Directory of the Governors of the United States, 1988–1994.* Westport, CT: Greenwood Press, 1994.

Details about state governors (such as birthdates, party affiliations, principal occupations, terms of office); continues earlier volume.

Politico (elections), www.politico.com

Maps and tables of state- and county-level results for gubernatorial (and national) elections from 2002 to the present; state polls about presidential primary and general elections, U.S. Senate, and some congressional district races.

Scammon, Richard M., Alice McGillivray, and Rhodes Cook, eds. *America Votes* (series); *America at the Poll* (series). Washington, DC: CQ Press, 1956–.

Convenient compilation of vote totals and statistics by state for general elections and primaries for president, governor, and senator, principally since 1945 (comparable district-level data for members of Congress); county-level totals and statistics for most recent general election for president, governor, and senator; state maps with county and congressional district boundaries.

Initiative and Referendum Data

Ballotpedia, http://ballotpedia.org

Provides links to state ballot measures and state-by-state information on ballot qualifications and processes; petition drive deadlines; and descriptions, analysis, and results for ballot measures.

Initiative and Referendum Institute, www.iandrinstitute.org

State-by-state information about initiative and referendum processes and provisions and reports on all current propositions, including a database of the number and approval rate of initiatives on the ballot in each state since 1904 and a database of the availability of initiatives in 2005 in the thousand largest U.S. cities and ten largest cities in each state.

National Conference of State Legislatures' Initiative and Referendum Resources, www.ncsl.org

Reports and data about initiative and referendum availability and provisions across the United States; includes a state-by-state database of initiative and referendum legislation since 1993 and a state-by-state database of ballot measures since 1892, with summaries and analyses of provisions in recent years.

University of California Hastings Law Library, http://library.uchastings.edu/research/online-research/ca-research.php

Limited to California, but gives pdf images of all propositions and initiatives, 1911–2012.

Legislative Election Data (*see also* Election Administration and Voter Turnout)

CQ Press Voting and Elections Collection, www.cqpress.com/product/928.html

Online, searchable database with information about individual races as well as summary information related to open seat races, party switches, race competitiveness, and so on; fee based.

Lilley, William III, Laurence J. DeFranco, Mark F. Bernstein, and Kari L. Ramsby. *The Almanac of State Legislative Elections.* 3rd ed. Washington, DC: CQ Press, 2007.

Maps and statistical profiles of the geographic, economic, and political composition of state legislative districts.

Party control of state legislatures, www.governing.com/gov-data/politics/2012-state-legislature-elections-map.html

Interactive map showing changes in party control in state legislatures as a result of the 2012 elections.

State legislative election returns, ICPSR Study No. 34297 www.icpsr.umich.edu

Comprehensive data on state legislative election returns from 1967 through 2010; includes information on district and candidate attributes.

U.S. Census Bureau, www.census.gov

Starting in 2005, demographic data on state legislative districts (above and beyond the racial/ethnic composition used for redistricting).

Legislatures and Legislative Roll Call Data

NOTE: Most if not all state legislatures now provide online bill tracking and have also archived that data. Many go back to the mid-1990s. One can use these archives to gather information regarding sponsors, final dispositions, content, committee assignments, etc. Many provide full text of all versions (e.g., introduced, amended, final) of every bill. Typically these are searchable by bill number and/or sponsor(s).

Dubin, Michael J. *Party Affiliations in the State Legislatures: A Year by Year Summary, 1796–2006.* Jefferson, NC: McFarland, 2007.

Extensive data on states' electoral processes, term lengths, legislature size, and membership by party, election dates, and more.

National Conference of State Legislatures, www.ncsl.org

Compilations of laws and data on elections, redistricting, term limits, and other topics, as well as links to websites of individual state legislatures.

The Open States Project, www.openstates.org

Beta site includes database, for many but not all states, of detailed information on state legislative bills and the activities of legislators and committees.

Silbey, Joel, ed. *Encyclopedia of the American Legislative System: Studies of the Principal Structures, Processes, and Policies of Congress and State Legislatures since the Colonial Era.* 3 vols. New York: Scribner's, 1994–1996.

A thorough treatment of the national and state legislatures.

State Legislative Sourcebook. Topeka, KS: Government Research Service, 1986–. Annual.

A guide to finding detailed information on state legislative material, including offices, addresses, phone numbers, and price lists; a list of state statistical abstracts (or near equivalents), of widely varying quality, can be found in recent editions of the Statistical Abstract of the United States.

State partisan balance, www.indstate.edu/polisci/klarnerpolitics.htm

Dataset spanning 1937 to 2011 including information on partisan control of state legislatures, governors' offices, and state institutions.

Personnel, Structures, and Rules

The Center for American Women and Politics (CAWP), www.cawp.rutgers.edu

A wealth of data about women in and running for elective office in the United States, particularly at the national, state, and state-legislative levels.

Joint Center for Political and Economic Studies' National Roster of Black Elected Officials, www.jointcenter.org

Lists black elected officials by office with summary tabulations on historical trends and comparative state figures; the Roster of Black Elected Officials is available for a fee.

National Association of Latino Elected and Appointed Officials, www.naleo.org

Includes a directory of Latino elected officials, and profiles and electoral projections for Latino candidates for state legislature; although rosters/directories (especially noncurrent ones) are for sale and are not easily available or accessible for free, they may be available through interlibrary loan.

National Governors Association, www.nga.org

Searchable database of biographical information on current and former governors; includes staff directories and contact information for each governor's office, election returns data from 2009 to the present, and a collection of reports and publications concerning the functions and powers of each governor's office.

Numbers and types of governments (U.S. Census Bureau), www.census.gov/govs/go/index.html

A collection of reports and data including numbers and types of local governments within a state, descriptions of local governments within each state, comparisons of governments' authority between and within states, and key statistics on state and local governments.

State and local government on the net, www.statelocalgov.net

A complete directory of state and local government websites.

State Yellow Book, New York: Leadership Directories, 1973

Some statistics, but emphasizes contact information for executive and legislative branches, including departments, commissions, agencies, and legislative leadership and legislative committees; continues State Information Book *(www.leadershipdirectories.com).*

Public Opinion Data

Note: Many universities and local news sources collect public opinion data within the state in which they are located. See the website for Cornell Institute for Social and Economic Research (www.ciser.cornell.edu/info/polls.shtml) for a list of sources of polling data with a state or regional emphasis.

Citizen and state ideology, http://rcfording.wordpress.com/state-ideology-data

A measure of state citizen ideology and two measures of government ideology.

Gallup Poll, www.gallup.com

Large, historically rich collection of survey data concerning politics, the state of the economy, personal well-being, and many social issues—most extensive coverage is at the national level.

Odum Institute, University of North Carolina, www.irss.unc.edu/odum

A searchable archive of public opinion survey data at the national and state level dating from 1958 to the present, covering a range of social, economic, and political topics; includes the National Network of State Polls.

PollingReport.com, www.pollingreport.com

Aggregates polls on numerous contemporary issues; subscriber pages contain state-by-state data from election and issue polling: campaign polls, media polls, academic polls, and polls by political, business, and public-interest groups.

Roper Center for Public Opinion Research, www.ropercenter.uconn.edu

An extensive collection of datasets produced from surveys conducted at the national, state, or regional level pertaining to a wide variety of social, economic, political, and current topics.

Public Policies

Note: There are vast amounts of data on the Web covering all manner of social issues. Many of these are government-sponsored; some are sponsored by independent, nonpartisan groups; others are maintained by advocacy groups but may still contain good descriptive information. Many sites are well-maintained, including not only up-to-date information but, increasingly, historical data as well. The following data sources are just a sampling of the many resources available.

Abortion and Reproductive Health

Guttmacher Institute, www.guttmacher.org/statecenter

Information and data on state reproductive health laws and statistics; includes data on pregnancy, abortion, availability of contraceptives, and funding and availability of family planning services and facilities; provides interactive tools that allow for comparisons of reproductive health policies across states.

Agriculture

National Agricultural Statistics Service (Department of Agriculture), www.nass.usda.gov

Agriculture-related data and statistics for every U.S. state and county; includes state-level agricultural profiles with essential statistics, as well as data on production and prices of key commodities.

Crime Data

Bureau of Justice Statistics, www.bjs.gov

Corrections, employment and expenditure, law enforcement, and victim data collections; extensive data—often available at the state and city level—about crime and the justice system.

Federal Bureau of Investigation, www.fbi.gov

Uniform Crime Reports from the FBI provide data from 1995 to the present on all types of crime, including crime rates by state and cities with a population over one hundred thousand.

Criminal Justice

Death Penalty Information Center, www.deathpenaltyinfo.org

State-level database of statistics related to capital punishment, searchable database of executions since 1977, state-by-state historical and current information about death penalty laws, and links to external reports and datasets on the topic of capital punishment.

The Sentencing Project, http://sentencingproject.org

Pro-reform advocacy website with state-by-state criminal justice data; includes information on incarceration, racial disparity, drug policies, juvenile sentencing, felony disenfranchisement, and other topics.

Education

National Center for Education Statistics, http://nces.ed.gov

Datasets about all levels of education at the state and school district level, including statistics about a district's schools, financials, higher education institutions, student demographics, library resources; extensive information about the National Assessment of Educational Progress and other (mostly national) programs.

Energy

U.S. Energy Information Administration, www.eia.gov

Extensive information about state energy reserves, supply, production, prices, distribution, consumption, and environmental footprint.

Gaming

American Gaming Association's State of the States Survey, www.americangaming.org

Data on the national and state-level economic impact of the casino and gaming equipment manufacturing industries; includes public opinion data and data on trends in casino patronage. See also, for state gambling laws, www.gambling-law-us.com.

Health Care

Centers for Disease Control and Prevention, www.cdc.gov

A wealth of health care data at the national and subnational levels, although some searching may be required to find the data one is looking for; one point of access for online data is http://wonder.cdc.gov.

Kaiser Family Foundation, www.kff.org, StateHealthFacts.org, www.statehealthfacts.org

Information and data on hundreds of health care topics, including health care reform, costs, public opinion, insurance, and more.

Medicaid, www.medicaid.gov

State-level information on health care systems, requirements, and management, including data on Medicaid enrollment nationwide and by state; managed care enrollment; Children's Health Insurance Program (CHIP) design by state and enrollment figures.

U.S. National Library of Medicine (National Institutes of Health), www.nlm.nih.gov/hsrinfo/datasites.html

Vast source of data, statistics, and survey results at the national, regional, and state level covering a range of health- and health care–related topics; see also State Resources for additional data and information exclusively at the state level.

Lesbian, Gay, Bisexual, and Transgender

Human Rights Campaign, www.hrc.org/resources

Database of state laws and state court decisions searchable by fourteen issue categories and by state; includes maps that visually classify states based on the degree to which their policies and laws are LGBT-friendly, and a city-level "Municipal Equality Index," which rates 147 major U.S. cities on forty-seven criteria relevant to LGBT legal protections.

Social Security

Social Security, www.ssa.gov/policy

Links to the Annual Statistical Supplement and other data sources for information at the federal and state levels about Social Security, Medicare, Supplemental Security Income, and other social insurance programs.

Taxes

Tax Foundation, http://taxfoundation.org

Data—much of it up to date and available for a decade or more—on taxes at the state and local level including income, sales, corporate, excise, and property taxes, as well as data on business tax climates, tax burden, etc.

★ INDEX

Page numbers referring to figures, photos, and tables are followed by (fig.), (photo), and (table).